EXPECT NO HELP

THE LIFE AND TIMES OF JUMPIN JACK FLASH

Common Sense from
an uncommon Source

CESSPOOL JONES

ARPress LLC
45 Dan Road Suite 5
Canton MA 02021
Hotline: 1(888) 821-0229
Fax: 1(508) 545-7580

Ordering Information:
Quantity sales. Special discounts are available on quantity purchases by corporations, associations, and others. For details, contact the publisher at the address above.

Printed in the United States of America.

ISBN-13: Softcover 979-8-89330-502-9
Hardcover 979-8-89330-503-6
eBook 979-8-89330-504-3

Library of Congress Control Number: 2024900516

EXPECT NO HELP

The Life and Times of Jumpin' Jack Flash...
Common sense from an uncommon Source

Common Sense: A 360 degree complete conception of situation or environment around you either short or long term --versus-- 3-Dimensional perception and rational used in decisions to produce most favorable results.

This phrase is not 'collective' by no means. This phrase is about complete 'individuality' because after all...no one even has the same fingerprints. However, how this phrase is deciphered by all individuals is part of what this non-fiction novel details from the 1960's to the present. This novel is backed up by actual facts and history, good and bad. Much of our recent history is discussed in "Expect No Help" as to the how and why these things happened...but none of it is erased in this novel. Because, when you erase history, good or bad...then you really haven't learned anything at all. But by reading this book, I think it can help you see 360 degrees regardless of the topic being discussed. It may sound like sides are being taken but facts are facts and the author is only laying out what actually happened. If anything gets erased, then how are they going to know well into the future what not to do! "Expect No Help" starts out when the author was in grade school back in the early 60's and how he got caught up in the new revolution in the 70's. Pretty sure getting married and having kids is what saved him. You wouldn't believe how many friends he had who never saw the 80's including 2 brothers. It is mentioned that if you are looking at the Poppy field...you also need to be looking in the mirror because there...you are looking at reality. Nothing is real in a Poppy field and the author echos this in this novel. That's only a drop in the bucket of what's in this novel of things that have effected or will effect our lives. It is also mentioned how the year 1967 threw this country into a gradual loss of personal and family responsibility throughout the recent generations which is the main reason why we don't come home anymore when the streetlights turn on. "Expect No Help" is written by someone who really never was a writer. An incident that happened to him sometime ago made him look at the past and afraid of the future, so he decided to pen it down so others can learn...360 degrees. This novel is actually a nuclear cookbook for the future because 360 degrees is not a problem to this author and how a regular Joe can see the future the way he does makes it hard to put the book down. Every angle of every topic is dissected to the bone and sometimes he lets the reader decide. Sometimes turning a page is difficult simply for the fact...it might be mind-reading you while you are trying to figure out how many times you gotta read that page. But that's for you to decide. This book is written the very same way we all talk with words that we all say but not in any dictionary so that anyone from a stoner to a P.H.D can understand it. Lastly, if you have tunnel-vision...you might wanna wear a helmet when reading this and if that don't work...put the book down and find something else to do. Capeichio!!

Cesspool Jones...kin to Ellis Dee

NUCLEAR COOKBOOK WARNING

When someone who really is not a writer writes a novel, it's usually because he wants to get something off his chest whether fiction or not. Here's a pretty good one. A non-fiction novel detailing the recent history of this country from the 60's on to the present from an average working man who was there, containing the good with the bad with facts only. Philosophy is also inserted but only when it makes sense so that both the Left and the Right can understand this...even though one is much more 'collective' than the other. Other than that, philosophy is left by the wayside at your local juvenile college where it belongs...not even sure about that anymore. Fantasy don't work in the real world or in this novel. Reason being...philosophy has been recently distorted by many tunnel-vision-sheeplepeeple-clones and it really doesn't make any sense anymore like it used to when philosophy was written by people way back in the past whose names will carry on forever. "Expect No Help: the life and times of Jumpin` Jack Flash... common sense from an uncommon source" is a novel that will not only open your eyes, but will also open your mind...or slightly tilt it in a way you probably ain't seen before. But that all depends on who you are. This novel has also appeared in "Publishers Weekly" because it does have the ability to open many minds. It also has the ability to question your open or closed mind and if you don't like the question or the intent...then close the book and find something else to do...or get out of your mindfield. I am fully aware of all the fantasy-philosophy that is polluting many young uns` fragile eggshell minds nowadaze...so here iz another warning! To the sect of society that likes to spend all day at Starbucks...this is for you. Eggshells break very easily so if I were any of you, I would wear an over-sized pink Spartan helmet when reading this as to not get any boo-boo's

when the pages up and slap you in the face and only read ten pages atta time so you can walk it off to git right. 580 pages so put on dem` dancin` shoes!! No one, including myself has anything against any of you at all. We just wonder how you can stare at a computer and drink coffee all day long and not move a muscle for the entire afternoon. What's in that coffee!!
Capeichio!!
Cesspool Jones
reach me: johnnywarts@gmail.com

DEDICATION

To all the working stiffs—white, black, or blue—who see the light at the end of a lifelong tunnel who make it all worth it. Thank you, Rusty and Esther . . . who made this book possible.

America; before, after, and beyond. *A cookbook for the future.*

Expect No Help: "The life and times of Jumpin Jack Flash" Common Sense from an Uncommon Source as seen by C. Jones.

AUTHOR'S NOTE

Our subject about whom this book is written about is one whose life could have been anybody's anywhere in the world, who's had to work for a living while realizing his or her place in modern society. This pertains to the most of us. Not taking anything away from anyone who has lead a charmed life, he realizes that America is the land where timing is of the utmost essence where fate and luck, along with a little brains, can combine to enhance one's individual being. He's smart enough to know that out of 300 million people in the United States, that is not possible for everyone and he congratulates all of those throughout the races and classes to whom lady luck has bequeathed her riches to. He has no animosity or ax to grind toward anyone whose had the chance to take the American dream to its fullest, knowing we all, being American . . . have, for the most part, had the same chance. That is what America is all about. Except for small minority of spoon-fed, tuck-me-in trust fund babies, which don't really sound all that bad, we all know this. Most of us appreciate our successes, especially when our goals were shattered with unimaginable results. However, even with the keenest insight on many aspects of life, he has by bad timing, strange circumstances, and with not the kindest of luck . . . realizes that at his age time is running out, and wonders after all these years, is the goal of easy living going to elude him? Not Rockefeller rich, but taking it easier later in life because after all of your toils . . . it is now affordable.

In this story, I will start from the beginning in the 'Wild West' Sixties all the way to the present time and examine his life, psychology, and attitude toward modern present day society. Some of the language used in doing so, where appropriated only by myself along with the subject of this novel every now and then, is deemed somewhat necessary, which only extends the passion of the situation or philosophical view, depending on the whatabouts or whereabouts we are in this novel and could be viewed as offensive to certain people with certain views, but as we all know, you must get over it . .. otherwise you will just get consumed. Getting consumed, just even for the littlest of issues, doesn't seem to bother too many folks anymore. If that's a problem for some, then some outta stay away from the rest of this book since it is based primarily on contemporary issues that are tearing apart the fabric of all aspects of life from the atom out and this writer feels it's high time to speak his mind just like all the rest of us. Beware! . . . a bad heart! The truth is where we start! I believe that once you hit a certain age . . . certain could be debatable, and turn around and look back, then turn back around and look forward, you'll see what I'm talkin' about. I'm talking about trying to know what's goin' on even though mine is only one perspective. More is better, but less for some strange reason seems to be more acceptable nowadays. That's why I wrote this mess. I want more in everything I see all around me. 'Cause that way, I can give some back. If I make some friends along the way, then that's good. If not, but I don't think so, then that's the way it goes. But no one tries like me. Aside from that, what instigated the energy needed to write a novel about this guy was not the fact that I've known him since early grade school but how in the recent past everything in his life seemed to have turned somewhat brown. The way in which he deals with all this is what I find inspiring and admirable. Except for a couple of stumbles and some occasional faceplants that we all like to avoid, he sees that there is no other choice but to get up, brush the dust off, and carry on at all costs. But recently, just after cleaning up the last mess, once again, something else tells him to open up the wrong door for the umpteenth time. Most of the time he said no. Anyhow, this is my essay of failing to keep a good man (for the most part) down.

INTRODUCTION

By now we should all know what went right and what went wrong with ourselves. Some of you probably aren't really old enough to cipher' something as profound as that, but believe me, as time rolls on, you'll probably see what I'm talking about. Life is like your Christmas stocking on the fireplace mantle every year, you never know what you're gunna get. Year to year . . . then day to day. Heard something like that alittle while back some time ago. Think we all did. We think about all the factors involved so far. Timing, decisions, fate, a little brains, and Lady Luck . . . usually in that order. Sometimes Lady Luck rides shotgun for some of us which is good. This story is about someone who really can't quite figure out to this day what happened or even how, even into midlife. If there ever was a Jumpin' Jack Flash, I couldn't think of anyone other than the subject of this novel. He seems to fit in with most, if not all folks, and even has a common name. He could be anyone of us. He could be your cousin, your co-worker, your husband, your next door neighbor. He could be you. He could be me. Some of you will side with him and some of you won't. But he don't care either way. *But he cares when you don't.* But he also knows that things don't always change for the better just because he gets older and wiser. Sometimes the older one gets, the more routine sets in and the looser one gets. Sometimes the expected becomes the unexpected, which could make visa versa become versa visa. This to me sounds like a problem lookin' for a place to breed. Maybe alittle deep, but what ain't anymore? Problems will always arise, just like the tidal waves, and are to be dealt with no matter how failsafe your boat may seem to be at that time, but it seems to me there are lots of problems that I've seen that could have been dealt with rationally . . . one man's point of view, that seem to be coming apart at the seams. Sometimes that's your or our owns' fault, sometimes it's not. No blame game here, but actual real life. Believe me, he knows that all too well. Change is constant, always in motion. Some is good, some not. Change makes the world go around. There's nothing you can do about it *except to expect it.*

Even though he's not the most religious person I know, he knows that as life goes on, so does human suffering. No one really escapes that, even though you think you might. It could be said that the Son of God was sent here to save mankind but instead got nailed to a cross and we've been paying for it ever since. It could also be said that that's nothing but a fairy tale. It also could be said that just because you can't see something, that doesn't mean it don't exist. I don't remember the last time I saw a molecule. But I do remember the first time. Had a little help with that. I think it was a molecule. That was some time ago. I'll probably discuss alittle absurdity as I get into these rantings of a lunatic, all the way from the beginning to the end. One man's lunacy is another man's sanity. Another man's junk is another man's treasure. Someone's philosophy is another man's nightmare. Sorry about the old-time clichés, but those are some of the truest ones. Within this novel are perceptions of ideological, philosophical, religious, and social avenues traveling from all directions trying to merge into one lane. Some aren't going to make it, as logic and *common sense* weed out the insane from the sane. But what is sanity? I hope I can help figure that all out as I jump into the fire page by page. I'm not afraid of fire. It exists the same as I do, it lives off air. We both have a lot in common besides that. It seems to burn anything, good or bad. But that's my little problem that seems to keep on smoulderin,' no matter what we do!

But as we all know, we are nothing more than products of our own decisions and ambitions. To make a decision, facts and emotion are usually the main ingredients. Sometimes your decision was really thought out and it still ran through your fingers and made a mess. Our subject is having this problem as we speak. Decisions alone do not chart the course of one's life. Lady luck can look like Scherry Pop-Tart on a Kentucky derby stallion with long blonde hair, or she could look like the southend of a northbound moose. Untimely or timely . . . timing toys with us also as we take on another day. But aside from luck and timing, fate seems to toy with us the most. This is an unforeseen force that rears its untimely head anytime, anywhere. It cannot be controlled. Your decision, good or bad, had been made for you without your consent. Now, wadda ya do? Human nature contends that when something unexpected happens to you adversely, it simply cannot be your fault because you had no control over it. You had no warning. Maybe sometime in your past, you inadvertently put all the pieces together by being in certain situations, did what you thought was right or even wrong for that matter, rewrote your own philosophy to accommodate a problem at that time, or any other factor that made the unexpected happen. To me, that is fate. With certain exceptions, I think we are all masters of our own fate. Sometimes things happened unexpectantly no matter what but as in quite a few instances, sometimes they don't. Sometimes it's overwhelming with no end in sight. Right now, our subject is being barraged with multiple situations that are now taking their toll on his life and quite possible going to change it. Another step down. He takes the blame. No one else will. He knows he has gambled on decisions that didn't work out. Sometimes being the master of your own fate should be left to random, but usually your past overrides anything random and you must accept it or try to change what caused it. Even though the subject of this novel is older than he wants to think, he also knows that it's never too late. He has found that by looking at the situation or multiple situations, as in his case . . . to offset the onslaught, he views his problems as challenges, not barriers. When you see things as obstacles and roadblocks, you have a tendency to falter and stumble alittle bit easier. That makes defeat alittle bit closer. That makes you alittle bit weaker. To view the difficult as a challenge instead of a barrier, gives you more of a chance. You have some kind of chance. It might be slim, but I'll take slim over none at all. That's *hope* and hope is good. Hope things get better. But if not? That's okay. I still need the practice. So doesn't our subject. When he falls down and breaks, he picks up all the pieces, and puts them back together even though some might be missing, and then moves on. But alittle bit smarter. This would be construed as maturity as the learning process never stops. That's how we acquire wisdom as we age. It is called experience, pure and simple. It is something we try to pass down to newer generations as rules and guidelines to follow to make life easier. But as history has showed, experience must be learned to be actually retained. But to me, new and newer generations must simply learn on their own. This is how *passive change* is brought upon society. Take another day; inject a little change. That's what this book is about. It's also about *forced change* in which I got some kinda problem with. In this novel, we'll see how our subject feels about both kinds of change, and his philosophy, ideology, and folklores he possesses. Seems like quite a few folks forgot about American folklore. The word *folklore* even has the word *folk* in it. Depends on how you spell it or define or re-define it, as is commonly done nowadays. America at its worst or maybe at its best according to some, at least by what I see and hear almost daily, but if that's the best for some, then all of some has a lot in common with everyone 'cause everyone has something to say and we shouldn't ever forget that. Seems like some are forgetting themselves as strange as that sounds. Some are inviting Frankenstein into our midst. *Is it a crime to fall in love with Frankenstein?*

Some of the things I learned from Jumpin Jack have almost an eerie glow like the pale glow of a torch burning on a wall somewhere in the catacombs somewhere under Rome. He can scare you. He can hold you captive while doing so. He can change your mind. You can change his. He can look at your nightmare and show you his dreams. He thinks he can help. What he told me years ago seemed to have all come true. His thoughts have never changed even as a child to now. Does that make him some kind of seer?, or when he was sixteen, was he really forty-five? . . . or at forty-five, was he just turning twelve? That's something I'm still trying to figure out. Ever get a break when you so desperately need one? It could appear as a favor from someone or just appear out of nowhere. Fate? Who really knows but our subject will take fate over a favor. With his lack of proper schooling, he's very lucky he knows the definition of common sense. He knows the good and he knows the evil. He also knows the closer the evil, the easier it is to see where all the poison is coming from. He's confident. Confident enough to know that *if you can't do it on your own, then it simply cannot be done at all.* Expect no help. But what he's not is stupid. But he's done a lot of stupid things. Does that make one stupid regardless? Everyone's done some stupid shit sometimes in our lives. When you do something stupid, you are no longer ignorant. Now you know. If you do it again, then you have been reduced to stupid again and now you hafta prove yourself to others in the future. Even for the simplest of things and that's not really not good at all. Life's hard enough. Why make it harder? We will all endure trials and tribulations throughout our lives. It's all the problems encountered in which we deal with that molds to what we become.

Some problems are big . . . some aren't. Conquering them once again molds us into what we are. But sometimes they become so overwhelming some of us begin to question our own character. Cracking under pressure is only normal for some people. Not for the subject of this novel. The day he cracks is the day he gave up. He doesn't have much love for the *oppressors* of modern man. He'll stand by the weak. He views problems as ants. You see one crawlin' all on you. You simply brush it off. Next day you see ten or so crawling on the same spot, and as before, you brush them off. But it takes a little longer this time. Time is money, you know. The next day, you're all ate up with ants crawling all over the place . . . all on you, inside and out. Only thing missing is the queen. That's a whole lotta little problems combined to make one big one. It is how you react to a situation like this that either sends you on a mission of redemption, no matter what, to defeat this . . . or sends you to the doctor's couch. It did none of that for our subject. It sent him to jail. He's still smarter than the average politician, but because of some sound decisions and some not, some bad timing, and some southend luck, he is probably destined to remain a piece of construction trash on the jobsite probably until the day he dies. But here's a story about someone who *refuses to give up* even when outnumbered a hundred to one. So twist the fate, then twist the wick, 'cause Johnny took another lick.

Sincerely,

Cesspool Jones

A. Common Sense
   1. A 360 degree complete conception of situation or environment around you, either short or long term, versus the amount of three-dimensional perception and rationale used in decisions to produce most favorable results.
   2. An ability to be able to use the brain at fullest potential even under adverse conditions and to tell the eyes and hands exactly what to do.
   3. To be able to see and feel around you, and to tell the brain how much rationale to be expended for best results.
   4. To be able to repeat this process daily without breaking the circle.

B. Nonsense—Any other method of decision making not prescribed in part A.

C. First Amendment—Freedom of speech, freedom from speech impediments.

D. Speech Impediments
   1. To take part C and use it to promote social and moral inept situations,
   2. Ability to redefine part C so as to maintain legality of part C.
   3. To promote a social and moral pseudo-society.
   4. To be able to speak without regard; for personal agenda only.
   5. To take national fabric and tye-dye it thus dilution of red, white, and blue in the name of part C.
   6. To stutter, stammer, or experiance other obstacles in speaking.
   7. To speak and not listen.
   8. To listen and do nothing.
   9. To do nothing.

E. When you run out of dollars . . . use your sense.

CONTENTS

PART ONE

THE BEGINNING

In everyone's life . . . exceptions noted, being a kid was probably the most carefree and stress-free times of our lives. Senseless stress on childhood is why exceptions are noted. Couldn't wait to get off the school bus and begin your search for your place in social circles kids always seem to form. Your very young social circle starts out small and close-knit and other kids three or four blocks away seem like endless miles. As you slowly or quickly grew, depending on how old you are depending on who's reading this right now, your existence seemed to expand with each passing day as you explored all the forests and woods surrounding your horizon. With all those vacant lots, condemned homes, other neighborhoods, sewer systems, and other normal childhood interests you explored; day by day, bit by bit, your horizons were expanding. Johnny crawled around with his buddies in sewers under parts of town because they thought it was as straight as the crow flies. There are also other reasons for me to pen Johnny's existence. What you and me see as black and white, he sees it in color and seems to look at things with some kind of twist on most things. But anyways, there was that little cutie in the first grade for whom you did anything but ridiculous to impress her and win her heart. Remember when out on the schoolyard on recess, you saw the object of your affection hanging off of the monkey bars and then you became a gymnast extrordinaire and almost got killed trying to do something even a professional gymnast wouldn't attempt? Got up and blushed a little while all the other kids had a good laugh. That's what made childhood so much fun. Johnny, at his age, still enjoys being a kid, a little too much I will add, but he probably wouldn't have made it this far if it weren't for his forts, frogs, and firecrackers to fall back on. There was a time just before I met Johnny, he told me something that I couldn't believe that a little kid could do, but when Johnny looked me in the eye and smiled like a punk, I knew this *be-um* no bullshit. This story kind of sets the tone of this essay, all the way to the end. Even though he was very young when this happened, what happens all through his life, one will have to decide that he either grew up too early, or never grew up at all. Johnny's got something to say.

Halloween afternoon, 1962. Police tape taping off a small piece of land. Johnny was five or six. In the Deerfield section of town, where he first lived, across the street from his house was this wooded area with open fields, dense woods, creeks and lots of paths and trails where all the kids hung out and cut through from one block to another thus saving lots of time. It was quite popular with all kids in Deerfield at that time Johnny and his buddies built lots of forts in there. While climbing up to a tree fort, someone dropped a hammer from the fort. It caught Johnny right on the top of the head and he dropped to the ground like a used sex-aid and required medical care. Stitches. Johnny hated doctors 'cause he often had to see them. And before that, at the creek across the street, while seeing who could make the biggest splash with the biggest rock, he went down the bank to retrieve his rock 'cause his made the biggest splash. Someone dropped his rock and hit him right on the top of the head creating the biggest gash. Medical care, immediately. He got hurt a lot early in life and it was right about then . . . he realized being stupid hurts. Anyways, that Halloween afternoon he was hanging out with his friends in the woods. He was always the youngest in the crowd and was privileged to be allowed to hang out with second and third graders. Thought he was a Tomcat. It turned out they needed Johnny to accomplish what they had in mind because Johnny was the smallest one there. Keep this in your mind: just because this happened generations ago, that doesn't change the fact that no matter what generation past, present, and future, mankind will always, as with the good will also have its bad moments of bad decision making . . . requiring moments of character soul searching with your own conscience. Sometimes alls we have for some type of salvation is hope. Hope that doesn't happen again. Hope this never happens again.

Since Johnny was there that Halloween afternoon back in 1962, he at the ripe old age of five accepted responsibility for his actions and turned himself in with his dream team of legal viper vultures and walked. Not really, but got into a lot of trouble with his parents. Didn't look good for his father who at the time was a hometown cop and having to have to rope off those woods because of his own son. What these kids had done was booby trapped these woods with the vengeance of Viet Cong. Halloween night would have been tragic had they not been caught especially with all the kids cutting through those woods at night. What they did was dig holes a couple of feet down in the middle of a path, threw broken glass in it and covered it up, making it look like nothing was wrong. However, that's not how they got caught. They also would take soda bottles, break them in half so you could hold the neck and have a weapon if you wanted to but they had different plans than that. Then they tied a string around the neck and suspended all of them over the trail. This was done by picking out trees next to the path that had small trunks and putting Johnny on someone's shoulders directly under a branch above the trail that came out from the tree. He would hold the broken glass bottle in place by putting the string tied to the neck over the small branch and then balance a brick on the string going over the branch, thus making a terrifying booby trap. Some poor unsuspecting soul would brush against the movable tree trunk, disturb the balance of the brick and someone else standing under the trap would first get hit by razor sharp glass and then clobbered by the brick for the *coup de gras*. One of the traps that was already set let go and landed on Johnny. As you see, he's been bandaged up quite a bit and he's only in kindergarten. The brick missed him but he got hit in the hand by the broken bottle. The cut was very small and required only one stitch; however, it cut the big vein on top of his hand creating an arterial gusher. He never had seen, only felt the whacks he took on his head and this was the first time he's seen blood spurt out. He was terrified and freaked out running all around and screaming his lungs out. His buddies try to calm him down and downplay everything so they wouldn't get in trouble. I think that's the first time Johnny said 'fuck you' and ran home. He got home covered in blood and once everything got sorted out, the police went to everyone's house who was involved. Johnny had to snitch and we all know how we all feel about snitches. He should have known right then and there that life was going to be alittle bit of hell. Same as a lot of us, so ya'll know what I'm talkin' about as we are about to hit that super-steep downhill run on the rollercoaster ride of life hopefully outta hell, but sometimes without really knowing what hell is, thus really combobulating things real bad even if only for an instant . . . while at the same time we're all working on trying to solve all the world issues. Real bad timing!

But all in all being a kid was about the most carefree and adventuroustimes of our lives. But I see a difference in childhood, then and now. When I was a kid, the future meant watching *Star Trek* or *Lost in Space*. Now the future means watching out for yourself and watching out for your own ass . . . figuratively and *disgustingly* . . . literally. That's supposed to be society's job not yours. You're still a kid for God's sake! Parenting to me has become a nine-to-five job instead of coming naturally like it's supposed to be. When I turn on the TV and see some commercial on how, when, and why to talk to your children or other parenting skills that *no one should really have to be told*, it makes me wonder what the < socially inappropriate word > happened to our sense of priorities and moral values. Moral values seems to piss some people off nowadays. But that's okay. Because for every action there is a reaction and to force change rather than to accept change naturally usually results in history being made. And when you force change, as in a lot of past cases in the history books . . . it resulted in major milestones in time of ***how wrong forced change is***. Maybe sometimes not quite that rough but you know what all that meant to civilized peoples. Sometimes not that much. That would only be natural. Problem being, "We the people" doesn't seem to carry the clout like it once had, so now I'm not quite too sure of *the Force* like I once knew has any force at all anymore. I can't believe some of the crap I hear nowadays. Anyways, something seems to be wrong with childhood nowadays. It seems to me our modern culture is out to undermine childhood innocence by injecting, almost bombarding, our youngest of generations who will soon be our future that it is nothing but a waste of time. You must get off the playground and get on the ball. Plan your future; every minute wasted on playing hide and seek could be used on the internet computing your net worth after inflation has eroded money you haven't even earned yet. You mustn't get left behind. Don't worry your parents will see to that. Remember the "super-baby" phase America went through in the kinder and gentler Eighties? It's good to see parents wanting successful children, but super-babys? What in God's green earth are those? Babies who kill? Babies with huge heads? Babies with tattoos? Crazy babies? Baby freaks? Babies with perfect hair? Maybe babies? I don't know but I'll take a set of parents who overextend for their children rather than those who don't extend at all. Adulthood is the land of the responsible, like it or not, and by injecting adult matters and/or behavior into children's lives intentionally, that causes unnecessary duress is doing America's future no good. This pertains to all children, not just yours. The internet is another story. Sure, all the information in the universe is at your disposal. All's you have to know is what you're doing and sit there and do it all day long. I just can't see needing information or playing games for ten hours straight. That's not life; *that's the death of life*. I've always had a more active and adventurous childhood by talking to, not typing to other kids. But things change with the times, and state-of-the-art computer science is a result of a natural change since we are always, and will always, be learning something new almost every day. Mentally evolving. Sometimes making life alittle too easy.

I don't like to sound like the doctor of doom 'cause I'm really a happy drunk, but I should get through this little toranado tirade shortly, but there are other issues to which does no one's childhood any good. How can some adults look at children . . . young children as sexual objects? It's so damn common, one just flips the page after reading about it on page fourteen of your local newsrag. Some say it's a disease. *NOT ME!!!* I say it's a crime of complete desecration of childhood innocence by preying on someone alot smaller than you. This is a crime of never being able to come back even if you have done it only once. No second shot except for the one that goes right through the forehead! Makes no difference. May as well have done it a hundred times! The defense says that the perpetrator was mentally unstable at the time of the crime. No shit!!! Who in their right mind would even think about something like that? The victim looked older or dressed provocatively. Makes no difference if the victim is only seven or eight. It's a crime against humanity and with some civil liberties aside, some crimes **deserve no second chance whatsoever.** I believe that society has some rights, not some asshole who just screwed some preteen girl. Johnny's sitting here with me muttering something about vigilantly justice or something like that. There are some things you just have to do yourself. Otherwise, it probably won't get done at all. Or at least not the way it should. ITCOB . . . just don't get caught.

I might talk about that later but now back to Johnny's beginning where he first realized where he was. That was the Sixties. What calm. Came in from the innocent, orderly Fifties like a lamb and went out to the Seventies like a lion. The calm doesn't last long, what with the onslaught that was to become one of the most socially and morally innovative decades since the roaring Twenties. Change is imminent and change is in the air. Pollution was making front pages in the news. When a river just ups and ignites in flames all by itself, that should garner some attention. NASA was experimenting with space travel with the Mercury, Gemini, and eventually Apollo missions that ultimately put man on the moon. Johnny was really into science during these times with biology sets, chemistry sets, an insect collection, microscopes, and telescopes. All those NASA missions captivated him and astronomy became his major at the time. He knew anything about anything nowhere near him. Sometimes he put alittle too much attention into that and while researching something about Mars, sometimes he'd daydream about walking on Mars. Some people to this day say he's still on Mars. Suits him fine with all the who gives a shit, wasn't my fault, you talkin'to me? bullshit we're knee deep in every now and then. Civil rights; the Russians are coming; nuclear age and tests; wild music; real cars; the Cold War, and oh yeah . . . that who-gives-a-shit attitude that ruled the times were the norms of society. Some things never change or maybe that was the beginning of change. Vietnam moved a president. Iraq shook another. If anyone says they don't care about politics they are lying. They like everybody else . . . including myself has something to say. I'll might say something alittle stupid, but not to me, maybe not about that a little later on down the road. No one likes war, just as no one wants to be threatened.

It's not too often I sit down and decide to write a book as a matter of fact, this is the first and last time 'cause once you lay it all out . . . what else is left? But as you can probably tell, I've got some views that to me go back generations mixed with views that were just hatched. Mix those with *common sense*, which is much easier shouted, not doubted as I've seen too many times with some past and recent trails and tribulations that really shouldn't have been tribul'ed or trial'ed at all, and you should be just okay. But anyway Vietnam was barely mentioned in the early Sixties to complete daily coverage into the late Sixties. The Russians scared the crap out of us. Soviet presence was in North Vietnam. Johnny knew all about the war either by TV or by his friend's older brothers who went and came back . . . the ones who did a little different then when they left, sometimes physically. He decided to join the Air Force later on, and joined just before Vietnam officially ended in April of 1975. He's considered a Vietnam-era vet because of that. That has nothing to do with being an actual Vietnam vet. Johnny never saw action and would never make up any bullcrap to the contrary in conversation about past military experiences *out of respect for an actual combat veteran.* He regrets not going and he's glad he didn't. I do have other things I could get off my chest about Vietnam, but there were other issues out there. Social change so dramatic it turned every aspect of life, from religion, music, civil rights, science, and civil disobedience like you wouldn't believe, and everything else upside down. Also, there was the specter of nuclear Armageddon. That was then this is now. There still is. Different players but with a little less honor. He remembers all the fire drills, or what he thought were fire drills back around the days of Halloween massacring. Ducking and covering, hiding under our desks . . . no one told us about no bomb, just a big fire. When we asked where it came from, the answer was from anywhere. People were scared shitless of the bomb.

Every now and then, Johnny and his buddies would venture down into bomb shelters built in a lot of the neighborhood's backyards. Scared shitless is putting it mildly. When they entered those cozy little holes in the ground that emptied into good size rooms, all of a sudden they would be entering a spaceship on Flash Gordon or going after *mole people* they seen on some sci-fi B-movie on feature four-thirty the previous day after school. Scary muthas. Imaginations ran wild down there. We vividly recall *1,000,000 BC* with Raquel Welsh and *Barberella* starring Jane Fonda. We'd think about that too. Something about pretty women, even as little kids. That's way before we even knew what jerking off was. Something also about celebrities *then and now*, either repentant or unrepentant about past political forays instigating much public notice . . . could or would retrace those steps if had the power to do so.

NASCAR was still runnin' moonshine. Unless you ate catfish, cornbread, grits and polk salad (all good stuff), no one heard of it because it was regional, nothing like nowadays. Sports were sports, nothing more nothing less. No reporting athlete's private lives. Never having to have to either. Going to school was your social scene. Friends came from different neighborhoods and other distant areas of town. Your horizons have expanded. Ride your bicycle cross-town to lands you've never seen before!! Constantly moving and expanding. Even when messin' out in the woods, we'd pretend were on patrol after watching *Combat* on TV and build the coolest forts around. Underground or tree forts. We would build forts that could sell for homes nowadays. Do kids build forts anymore? Oh yeah, I forgot, they can build them on the internet. Childhood was your explorer's years. Always wondering. Screw wondering, let's go look for ourselves. As you progressed through school all the way from your infantile beginning all through school, you learned how to handle yourself, what you were, and where you were headed. That's something that's never going to change. We should keep it that way; but I see a little adult interaction through the system of juvenile change that raises an eyebrow or four with me that I'll probably get into later that possibly could get me arrested, but only if I wasn't really thinkin' about the right thing . . . even if that means getting in trouble, then make sure the cuffs not too tight 'cause then . . . I really don't care. None of the aforementioned will make most anyone care about the sometimes-questionable-morally anemic **judicial** *(they could come from the bottom, or could be way the way up, pay as you go for broke)* **system** as we've all grown to know and sometimes bow to . . . where lots of us just cave in to. Alls that said was that there's sometimes you gotta do alittle bad to do alot of good. Sometimes . . . *if you wanna get to heaven, you gotta raise alittle hell.* But it's always too expensive to fight the system even if you're right! If that's what it takes! You know how fricking bad that is!!

One thing I hear about some schools . . . mostly public, is the unacceptable rates of failure some of these schools. This is distressing because of the importance of knowing why things happened and learning from that, and using your knowledge to change the world for the better, is why history is just as important as math. But first you must learn. What's the problem? We could attack the weakest link in the system, the teachers; the ones who make the educational world go 'round. Not the principals or Board of Education Appointees, they're managers and we all know some managers have to be told how things work. You'd think he'd know that already. Also not to mention that teachers now need to be foster parents or mentors and have to know martial arts and wear body armor. No, I don't think teachers are to blame. But there's some that *DO NOT* belong *anywhere near a classroom.* Part of the problem is what they are allowed to teach or not teach. But first, another more important part of the problem is the parents or lack of them. Parenting seems to have become burdensome to some for a host of different reasons' all of which are unacceptable. It was extremely so, every now and then for myself and Johnny, but it comes with the territory. It's not an excuse for something not going right and blaming your situation because you have to take care of a kid. Some of the crap I read in the news is already twenty or so years old in the media.

As mentioned previously, what they are allowed or not allowed to teach. History is something that doesn't mean a damn thing anymore. Some of what's being taught nowadays, to me, *is despicable.* It's every now and then pretty much all about some teacher's misguided, *don't belong in the classroom* agenda. Not really too much factual matter like what we had when we came up. *How dare you try to politicize my kids!!!* That's not your job!!! That kinda stuff usually agitates lots of folks, ***especially this writer.*** Try teaching history for a change! How can the next generation change anything or repeat it for that matter, if they don't know what the hell's goin' on? Did Hitler learn from Napoleon's mistake? What's that? What mistake? Hitler's mistake! And it's all because he heard *a voice.* Check out some of our public schools, that wisdom could sound pretty much the lame! *Pretty dame* lame if you ask this writer. The voice of "Colonel Klink". Education, not quite what it used to be . . . you know, when America sat alittle more on solid ground.

Beware of a stoopid future, Amarika

The diversity of students attending a lot of American schools now is a myriad of different cultures and races. Nothing like the past. Back then, black and white with a little Latino along with some Asians who have been here since great-great-great railroad-worker Grandpa was here. The next time you're on Amtrak, thank a Chinaman for that. Even though they got screwed in the process, they are the ones who built our infrastructure back in the day. I wonder if that's still taught in schools nowadays. Now we are an explosion of different cultures living with and learning from each other. Scores of generations ago, whites were further subdivided by nature of their national origin. That's because they were mostly Europeans, and most Europeans have somewhat similar features. But they still harbored racist attitudes towards each other, but as time went on, things seemed to have smoothed out and now most of America is a land of mutts as generation after generation mixed it up together. Mutts are the best of both worlds and as generations come and go . . . the best of a lot of worlds. That makes anyone stronger. You don't have a choice. Ma and Pa came from different part of the world, and then came you. But now immigrants are so diverse in race, they stand out as foreigners. America it seems . . . seems to accommodate certain parts of the world at certain times, sorta like a cycle. To see such diversity in our schools is the true sign of the American democratic experiment with the oppressed living and learning together. Immigration founded America, but as a professional journalist recently put it "*America has open arms, but now needs to have open eyes.*" Is America supposed to change like this? But I remember one thing: America always changes, almost daily. Because of our acceptance of other cultures and philosophies, we have become a just leader on this rock. But in the back of my mind, will we soon change so many colors that old traditional twentyith century America will soon be all but blotted out? Everyone thinks about the future and that's a mysterious question. Will the continents soon shift? Will the moon change shape? Will the cat soon look like the dog? Two of those can be answered. The third has me wondering. Does that matter? It is how we got here in the first place.

Why does everyone want to come here even when in some countries people have less-than-favorable attitudes towards Americans? I believe that a lot of Third World occupants of Third World countries who have absolutely no say in most important matters within their country believe that they have a chance in America no matter what their political agenda are. A part of that is extremely disturbing because of some of the atmosphere in which we now live in. Oppression, no-hope economies, poverty, civil wars, and demeaning caste-systems are all major factors with immigration. As previously mentioned, past immigration finally lead to complete fraternization with one another, with exceptions of certain peoples who remain to this day as old-world as the day they got here. Johnny's grandparents and all his aunts and uncles on his ma's side still spoke Italian since the day they arrived in America during the great immigration. Most also spoke English also, but not to each other. Chinatown also comes to mind. In metro Atlanta, Asians and Mexicans have their own sub-communities and the culture remains the same. Their children are as American-ized as it gets, which recently has become a problem, and hopefully they realize the importance of their parents' old ways. At the same time, they must not forget about their future role in America. The future in general is the best way to put it. For some . . . the present is the future and the future is science-fiction . . . actually, that could pertain to a lot of us. But nowadays our new explosion of immigration is defined by race. As usual, race is too much of a factor in moving in, getting set in, and living in a new land . . . be it anywhere. I guess people will always wonder why we all being human beings, are so different in physical attributes. That to me is just human nature. All the bullshit since laying eyes upon each other just goes to show how different we really are. America accepts all of everyone's differences and similarities alike. But I believe that to come here, past and especially present, one should bless the land of chance, be glad you got that chance and work together for the common goal. I could go on with this but instead of that, I do have a question: *Is the melting pot hot enough anymore?* Are present-day immigrants going to step up to the common goal? Mix it up? A lot of my friends are willing to do so, but not just that kind of stuff, but with all of American ideology, folklore, traditions, and values with the same respect toward them. Tradition seems to piss some people off also . . . a lot for secular reasons. What is tradition? What is traditional America? It is a country that was created with nothing but blood, sweat, and tears . . . harbored refugees and gave them a home, gave them a chance, and created one of the most humanitarian of empires in the history of empires. Superpower or empire, six or a half-dozen to me. America is a world leader, looked upon that way even after the Civil War with our industrial might. A world leader, not a world bully. That seems to be in question nowadays. American doctrine is to help all those who can't. I just can't see what's wrong with that? Many empires or superpowers throughout history chose to use their might for barbaric reasons with mercy for no one. A small fraction used their might for intellectual and deeper meaning toward their fellow man which goes to show "Who says power doesn't corrupt?" All the countries that dot the earth that practice open societies with malice toward none might be smaller or much smaller than America, but their existence is just as noble as the USA since *goodwill toward man* is a common goal. They're just too far away to learn all that. Newspapers and the media seem to be a bit cloudy and somewhat slimy-alittle-widdy-bit to only learn "just the facts ma'am," not just the no-mind emotions. That's what most of the media means to me . . . no-mind jibberish. Just as cloudy as the early Seventies, but that's just from one lucky man's perspective. One would actually have to travel abroad to find out for sure. Third World populations need some kind of help in participating in decision making within its borders to chart their own course without the sanctuary of immigrating. We all know that a lot of Third World countries are run by *third rate governments* with *third rate people* who choose themselves to govern with all that power. Power doesn't corrupt? In some countries, the majority vote doesn't mean a thing. The loser has more guns and the winner now goes in exile to guess where? Once this changes, then and only then will the burden of immigration be lifted from America and other open societies. Probably never gunna happen. Too many horses drinking from the same pond and guess what? *Screwed all that up, let's go find another pond.* Granted, it might take a civil dispute or two to get there. More and more people are coming here. How many people can you fit on the *Enterprise*? Comfortably, not stacked. What we now have because of this is what's called a *cut-throat economy.* Cut-throat economies make everyone uncomfortable. Especially those who work with their hands. Can't get the job because you're overqualified? What in the hell is that? Can't work your trade because some newly arrived immigrant will do it for half price? What the < word with many meaning > is that!? None of this is new by no means. Our predecessor's way back endured the very same thing with the very same somewhat volatile atmosphere in which this creates. I'm glad that they did endure it all . . . otherwise I might not even be here. I cooda been a disease. That's what I thought while airing out my thumb on the road again as everyone just blew right by me. All past generation Americans aren't really willing to work for less because we know the cost of life from groceries all the way to rent, is always going up for whatever reason. I don't know that one. No one does. What about the six peanuts I make a week? But here's where daily American change remolds itself. Past and present *passive change* comes from great minds from other countries who came, and are still coming to the U.S.A to make a significant impact 'cause for some kinda reason, they have to run too many rapids back from where they came from to be able to do that back from where all of us came from. Both sides of immigration . . . there are two sides: the good and the desperate are something America has handled in the past and must always continue to handle from now to well into the future. It's really hard to blame desperate immigration. I've always said that if I were Mexican and making five dollars a week in Mexico and alls I got to do is put myself north of the Rio Grande tomake five dollars an hour, then guess what? *You won't be able to stop me.* People will always go where it's easier. I know a whole slew of illegal Latinos down here in Dixie who I'll never rat on. That's because they're my friends who've I gotten to know, and friends don't do friends like that!

With all of this being said, I believe in some form of immigration reforms from within our own boundaries to even outside of our boundaries. Especially since 9-11. This hasn't changed everyone's mind though. Some people say it's not proper to condemn an entire race or religion because of the actions of a few. No, it is not. However, in this case, it is trying to define the actions of a few of an entire race or religion to make sure something of this magnitude doesn't happen again. History repeats itself. Maybe some good will come out of all this and after ten or so years pass, we will still retain what we were so tragically taught. Some people say the good will outweigh the evil. Probably will. Some people say I see things the way they're supposed to be, not the way they are. I say get real. Mankind isn't anywhere near that kind of utopian philosophy yet. I say, I see things the way they are and work off of that.

Well enough of all that. I'm gunna lighten up a bit, light up a smoke, crack a bud or two and probably spin one up and get back to the story. Don't tell anyone. Especially ma and my X. Who the hell is Johnny Warts? What kind of name is that anyways? That's his real name. He was that before I met him. He is a very good friend of mine going back to kindergarten back in 1962. You know, that don't seem like a long time ago. Years ago, when we were sittin' in some bar listening to some old timer talking some old time stuff, we would say "How can someone be reminiscing about something so old, it's been rewritten a few times in the history books?" Fact is, when you hit middle age, you'll see how it just seems like yesterday. He was born to a middle class family on Valentine's Day in 1957. Born in the Fifties, now that seems like a long time ago. Seems to remember the massacre. Says when Bogey went out, he came in. The Fifties: radio, black-n-white TV, Hollywood, better food at home than dining out, women doin' what they were told. What's wrong with that? Women don't like that anymore. This is good because I've always put women on a pedestal for the role they play in life. Plus it's easier to look up their skirts. As he progressed into school, it was found in the first grade, didn't get too far, that he had a speech impediment that lets him know he's more human than a human. He went to speech classes all through school to no avail. Nowadays sometime you can tell sometimes you can't. When he was a lot younger, people would think that he was either stoned, stupid or simple. He's talked to women at bars and screwed that all up because they thought he was hammered or something. Probably was. He tells me that whenever he is in a conversation and knows that the upcoming word is going to make him puke out the alphabet backwards, he knows how to rearrange and quickly pick out other words that mean the same thing and use those instead. He says they can make a freakin' dog talk before they can help me. Linoleum gives him hell. Too many same-sounding syllables I guess. Happens to be what he does for a living. After awhile you'd think people would lighten up, but after all these years, it doesn't seem to bother him anymore. One girl even found it sexy. He don't care, he's still looking for a cure. Illegal aliens speak better English than he does.

Coming up in the Northeast as kids, we were limited as to how we could earn a little money. During the winter, two or three of us would knock on someone's door and ask if we could shovel the snow off the driveway and sidewalks for some loot. We'd split up twenty or twenty-five bucks and head to the center of town. Sometimes we would shovel three or four driveways and make CEO pay, but we were too tired to move for a day. When we turned fourteen, we were allowed to pick harvest tobacco on any of the many tobacco farms that existed back then. We made a dollar twenty-five an hour back then, which added up quite well after the week was over. Believe it or not, that wasn't bad for a summer job. Johnny even became pretty good friends with the owner of the farm we worked for, 'cause the owner thought he was alittle offbeat, not quite in step, and saw Johnny do some stupid things and couldn't believe some of the things Johnny would say. This is before dope. It's not just the dope. It also takes the person (any kind) involved to create catastrophe. All the big tobacco leaves we pick were used only for the wrappers on cigars. Almost all of southern New England farmland was tobacco from way back till maybe its demise starting in the 1970's. There still is but nothing like the past. It was a dirty, mud and muddier job that required about fifty or so of us sitting on our asses going along the row picking the first four leaves from the plants on both your right and left. We'd rotated fields until when the summer's gone, alls that's left of the eight foot tobacco plants are their thick stalks. The girls worked in the huge barns where the tobacco was hung upside down to cure. Smelled great. Just like iced tea or sweet tea as we say it in the South. One day out in the field, Johnny had a headache and washed down some aspirins with a Coke. Funny thing about that was back then there was an ingredient in Coca Cola, long since removed, that when mixed with aspirin, the buzz was the same as a Xanax or Quaalude. He passed out on the bus to the next field and his day was over. He learned how to get a buzz by accident. A couple days later, him and a few of his friends washed down aspirins with coke and consequently missed the bus to the next field. Problem was, the field that they were in was in the middle of nowhere. Only thing there was the river. It was the fastest way as the crow flies to town. No boat. They didn't need one. They all floated around four miles or so which took most of the afternoon with nothing but the river swinging under them. This river is a tributary off the Connecticut River and runs adjacent to town and is popular with thousands of shad fish that migrate up the Connecticut River from the sound to spawn. It is every May of every year. The town celebrates the annual shad run with a parade, festivities all over the town green, a Shad queen . . . that's shad, and a center of town party that closes town for an afternoon. The local VFW located across the street is where Johnny and his buddies would hang with endless kegs of beer available. It was an anything kinda goes day: shit-faced by noon, second wind at night. With all the massive, well-planned out parties scattered all over the town after the festivities were over, almost every year we'd hear about some road fatality involving someone we knew or a friend of a friend. One year on *shad derby* night, Johnny was at a huge party down by the Connecticut River with his wife. She was eight months pregnant with their second child. On his way out on the dirt road that ran in and out of this area of the river, he lost control of his van. She was in the front seat. Just as the van was about to flip over, it was stopped perfect by a tree. Could have been tragic had it not been for that tree. His wife and other people fell into the river when they opened up the doors. Eight months pregnant and in the drink at four in the morning! Good work, Charlie Brown. She got fished out and took all night to get the van out. We usually partied there quite often. Nothing like hanging out by the river bank.

Getting back to our tobacco picking years. It has since all but vanished. During the tobacco cashcrop heyday, even Hollywood got involved. They made a movie circa 1960 starring Troy Donahue called *Parrish* about competition amongst all the tobacco farmers. My buddies' house was in that movie. Big 'ole house. I could say a few things about Hollywood and I think I will. Groovin' to the left, never lookin' right, Hollywood candy tastes like . . . . wait . . . that don't rhyme. What rhymes with *make-believe world?* If there ever was an out of touch segment of society, tinsletown puts the word *fantasy* in capital letters, even when not in front of a camera . . . then Hollywooddlyville with a *capitol kyeu* would be it. Anyhow, the tobacco industry up north is all but gone except for a few farmers left. I guess it's from all these ultra anti-tobacco assholes who seem to know how to take care of other people's health 'cause they're too fucking stupid to care for themselves. Maybe so. But look at what they did to a pack of smokes. Last I knew, tobacco was legal. Maybe not the best thing for ya, but I'll be the judge of that. Smoking really isn't that good for you, or in another way of natural reasoning, really isn't a good thing to do, but if anything good can come from smoking would be this and this only. Time flows like water . . . gone like that. If you're a smoker and wanna grow old slowly instead of the other way around (time flies as you get older) like what you always hear, then try making twenty cigarettes in a pack last the entire day with five or so left over when there's twenty-four hours in a day.

In his hometown, his father and grandfather were very well known. His dad's father was known by everyone as "Babe." He played semi-pro ball back when Babe Ruth ruled the diamonds. He's met and played with Babe Ruth and was called "Babe" from then all the way to his death in 1978. He also had a speed skating record in New England back in 1919. Johnny still has his skates. He even has his gun. His father's name was "Rusty" because he's got red hair. As is also with Johnny. Johnny's grandfather on his ma's side was pure Italian who also had red hair. A lot of red hair. Both Babe and Rusty worked in law enforcement with Babe becoming Chief of Police in Johnny's hometown and Rusty working in Hartford as a detective for the police force for some time. But for most of the time, he was uniformed. Both these men had achieved huge recognition from all facets of law enforcement with an occasional news clipping or two, about how they did their jobs. Babe went out on detail with the FBI back in the Forties and Fifties and was partly responsible for the eight o'clock pm deadline to buy any alcohol in Connecticut after eight. Back in the Fifties, in northern Connecticut, there was a string of package store robberies wherein the robber would then execute everyone caught in the robbery gangland style. Back of the head. A mean m#thaf$cka. Babe was involved in the capture, even staking out inside package stores ready if the robber/ killer entered. Not before all the package store merchants decided to close at eight instead of eleven, rather risk a late night massacre. Been that way ever since. As a matter of fact, that person who committed these crimes was the last person ever executed in Connecticut. That was in the early Sixties. There was one other whose execution was recent, but he had to petition the governor for his payment to society. Actually had to beg to die. There's two more in the Nutmeg state (look this up) whose crimes deserve nothing but **Taliban torture**, nothing less! I'm pretty sure other crimes of such cruel and heinous behavior has been committed in Connecticut since then deserving the same fate. But no capital punishment! Connecticut must be a kinder and gentler state with little regard for the victim and more for the perpetrator. We used to live in Connecticut. We've seen terrible crimes on the news and in the papers that met the requirements of *an eye for an eye*. Who do ya gotta kill? How many? I could care less about no cold blooded killer who killed his defenseless wife . . . or a rapist, child molester or worse . . . what's worse than that?, on death row if that's where they need to be. A crime of passion . . . caught your wife red-handed with SpongeBlob McGoo doin' the wooga-booga is probably the only leeway I'll allow for some kinda mercy. What would you do?, besides laugh. As a matter of fact, someone messin' with one of the kids, adultery, and breaking and entering all should be crimes where anything goes. Do what you have to do. No consequences to worry about. Muslim law deals with rapists with absolutely, positively no mercy whatsoever. Ouch!! Lemme see ya do it again, asshole! I really got no problem with that even though for whatever reason, the Muslim women victim was somehow at fault. Come again??

Anyhow, Rusty started out in law enforcement about the same time Johnny was caught trying to kill people on Halloween. He eventually left the hometown for Hartford to pursue his own career. I'm pretty sure he wanted to get out from Babe's shadow and forge his own path. He was respected by his peers on the force in part for his commitment to remain on the streets, leaving the desk job for some manager. He paid more attention to the threat to society, rather than to fleece society as with the system we presently have. He was someone . . . some . . . not all present day officers could learn from. Some already know. Cops back then pretty much left the 4th Amendment intact with *sufficient probable cause* being the only way to pursue an arrest. Seems like some cops out there right now, can't even spell the phrase anymore. I'm pretty sure they could only if America could re-learn how to spell responsibility. But that's a whole 'nuther story.

Back in the early days, doctors used to make house calls. "Incomprehensible!" one might say. That's before they were tamed by the lawyer's leash. What were they thinking? Trying to accommodate their patients without them having to leave their homes! No lawyer is gunna allow that! Won't be able to figure out who can sue who. Why are doctors always being sued all the time? 'Cause they're rich, that's why. Eat the rich. Easy money and yeah . . . medical mistakes are made, but don't prey on it! I'd like to see what doctor malicious-malpractice would do to lawyer litigate-some-insurance-company while all knocked out on the operating table when no one's watching. But anyhow, the doc would show up and make everything all right . . . or as in Johnny's case, make everything all wrong. When he got sick, he'd know that the doc was on his way over because of the crowd that would show up. His uncle, grandfather, neighbors, and Rusty's friends would all of sudden show up. That's because that's how many people it took to hold him down for his shot. While screaming at the top of his lungs, he would kick or try to bite anyone, pull hair, or do anything to make the doctor stop. I can honestly say that my best friend was a stark raving lunatic.

With Babe on one side showing Johnny sports, on the other side was his grandfather on his ma's side, a bull of a man instilling how important physical fitness was to him and how important it was going be to Johnny. He did this by showing Johnny the importance of the most basic but brutal exercise, the push-up. To this very day, he never forgot that and still pounds out hundreds at a clip. He elevates his feet on a bar stool to get that burn to make a work-out a work-out. His Italian grandfather's name was Raffaele and was a short, stocky bull of a man who looked like he did more push-ups than Johnny. That's what makes being a mutt great. You get the best of both worlds. Both worlds made Johnny a pretty good athlete, and he had the stamina to go the extra mile. That's what separates the good from best. He never got to be the best, but no one tried like him.

Early life was all sports, no dope. That came later like a tidal wave. But anyhow, he went from baseball to football to basketball year after year. In the northeast, organized winter sports were hockey and basketball. Johnny loved hockey. There's nothing like playing hockey. Kids favoring hockey who can skate better at age seven than most people can walk. But there was something about shooting hoop that captivated him and he chose basketball over hockey and the rest is history. He actually never made the NBA. He messed around with long distance running even holding the high school two-mile record for a stretch. Myself and Johnny played on every team playing every game except soccer. We tried tennis but there is no such thing as full contact tennis. Until then, we choose not to play, unless of course women were playing also. With my southend luck, I'd be going against the ones who are also on the women's Jell-o wrestling team. They'd have me in the pretzel hold in no time flat. After a week of being tied up in a most unusual way, it's time to tap out. Probably gunna have to use one my toenails. Useless information of which I'm full of. We had soccer in school back then but you played it if you didn't make the football team. And I like the game of soccer as long as I'm not watching it or playing it. It's the same as golf. It's too boring to watch and it's too hard to play. Running around non-stop all day and heading someone else's head who's also trying to head the ball sounds like it hurts too much to me. Five shots to put the ball in a little tiny hole six hundred yards away is just not going to happen. Seems impossible to me. Tiger Woods is a golf genius simply for the fact that he reminds me of my childhood hockey buddies who could skate better than most of us could walk before we even learned how to talk.

But back in my day, there was no such thing as a *soccer mom.* Our ma's were content watching us play on the baseball field, gridiron, or basketball court while tending to the concession stands. We all played sports as kids. I've always believed that introducing your children to sports is one of the smartest things a parent can do. What's a sound mind without a sound body? But there's something I want to get off my chest; I just want to know, what is a soccer mom? Is it something that's politically correct, or someone who's just scared of reality? I don't like reality either . . . too expensive, but I deal with it. Someday, one of my kids might get hurt. Maybe sports, or maybe something else, but that's life. Is a soccer mom someone who will go the extra mile to ensure that her son or daughter will never get hurt playing sports? Sorry, but that's not sports. Sports means getting bruised . . . even when playing soccer. Would she deny his right to play football, especially if he really wanted to play? What if he wanted to join the service? The big bad world is out to get my kids!! Mine too, but to shield them from an actual real life actual environment, be it rural or urban, is to impede on their social evolution, sorta speak. I don't like broken kids either, but sooner or later, it's bound to happen. Johnny's oldest son snapped his arm like a toothpick when he was only five. Should have seen that mess. But it got fixed. I'm aware that much worse could happen also, but to live in fear because of fear itself and ignore things that will never go away is the same as living in a utopian, all-by-myself-bubble-boy world, will never get hurt fantasyland . . . that to me, makes me laugh. Read the papers, if that don't burst your bubble, then nothing will. *See no evil, hear no evil, speak no evil.* Stay in your stupid bubble, you don't got what it takes to recognize the evil. That, also to me, is an insult to basic *common sense.* Also to the origins of common sense. That would be before man had any usable language skills and used mostly gestures to communicate with each other. But the gestures made sense. Can't even do that anymore! Common sense seems to have taken a back seat in a lot of issues recently.

I believe that the soccer mom has some part in that. But not the whole problem. Some are just too damn pretty to do any wrong. Got MILF? Get yer' mind out of the gutter; that means, "Maybe I Like Fantasy." Maybe it means something else to someone else, but they're married. That's what it means to me. That means "off limits" as strange as that sounds to an unsound mind. Don't do it! I wouldn't want it done to me. Bear in mind, I see things the way they are, not back asswards. Utopian philosophy sounds great and one could say, "Let's start now." Good idea, but I say let's deal with the platefull of shit we have in front of us first. To hear someone profess nothing but fantasy from behind a gated subdivision, complete with someone in some association telling you how to live, is comical and sometimes breaks me out in hysterics. *What scares the shit out of you cracks me up.* And there's nothing wrong with me, 'cept maybe, the spider nest in my hair. Probably gotta do something about that. I think I'm gunna work on my profile, like maybe change it. Gotta get the Orkin man in here first. But aside from that, to get to the top of the ladder, one must touch every wrung . . . even if one or two mean war, or some other problem that will never go away. Bear in mind . . . everything could always get better. *All the players* involved in a mess need to see the common goal. That seems to be the problem and I don't see how hiding from it or anything else is gunna help. And remember this. Soccer moms have some kinda political force, all levels of government and mostly with the Left. I could be wrong, but it seems they are pushing a futuristic ideology that we haven't evolved into yet. All the players need to be interested for that to work. Some need to be forced to play. So the next time you hear some lamebrain, well thought out intellectual scrabble-word jibberish in response to a serious issue, think about what they should be saying and why they aren't. When you see your state capitol or county-seat courthouses' parking lots filled up with nothing but mini-vans and Range Rovers, don't say I didn't say so.

But asides from all that, I am going to try to portray Johnny's life the best I can so I, and anyone else can see where he went wrong, if he went wrong, if everything was wrong and he was always right, or going back to the future, how he got it back after being wrong. Starting out young, he was mesmerized by science and sports. Now that's not bad, beats flowers and ballet. As a matter of fact he liked sports so much . . . not watching but playing, his final year playing baseball was in 1994 when he was almost forty. There's something about being on a baseball diamond. He loved his position . . . behind the plate. Always in the game. There's something about getting in the batter's box that can't be explained. It's pure eye-to-hand reaction. The brain's not even involved in the hit. Too fast. He had to sit out the last half of the season that year because of an on field injury that made him see a bright, brilliant orange flash. Took six months for the pain to go away. The last time he saw an orange flash like that playing sports was on a kick-off return during football practice. He wasn't even the kick-off returner but the ball was kicked real low and he snagged it out of the air, ran up the middle and got pasted. Helmut to helmet . . . he thinks. Not on purpose, he's alittle crazy, but not stupid, but that's what happened. During practice the A-team would play the B-team which Johnny was on and being on the B-team made them play that much better. Not just with sports, but in everything you do in life. But you learn it faster and better with sports. But he never lost the ball, but not only did he sit out a couple of plays, he could have used a couple of days. The best thing about playing football is being able to get up after the play is over. That would be a soccer mom's nightmare. But it's no big deal, they wear helmets equipped now with radar and small-arms defenses with razor wire and everythang.

Being the competitors we once were, we at our age could still do it. Johnny, with a few months intense training could probably still do it and compete and win. I know I used to live across the street from him and gave him all the competition he could handle. There can be only one. Yeah, there can be more than one, but you'll never know unless you try. Not to try to finish, but to *finish first.* Not just sports, but in anything you do. Competition breeds the best and all open societies rely on it. Lack of competition provides only the mediocre. That's not progress. That's stagnant . . . starts to smell after a while. I hope I'm wrong but I do believe sometime back, some high schools were planning to eliminate their valedictorian race because competition was not politically correct. Valedictorian competitors are looking for the highest GPA to win. In essence, it's a race. Wouldn't a move like that infect the mind with mediocrity 'cause that's all it takes now to pass? Karl Marx comes to mind. Who came after him? Let's see, there was Lenin, then went to Stalin . . . *good kid*, then to Kroushnov, Brezhnev, and then finally to someone with a brain . . . Gorbashev. Aside from the latter, they all competed, but just forgot to tell the rest of Russia about it. They put Russia behind almost a century. We don't want that. They never had elections. That could be construed as a landslide. Didn't Saddam Hussein just recently win the polls by a hundred percent just before his world collapsed? Absolutely amazing! It's amazing that some people actually believed that. What's wrong with some good old-fashioned competition? America was built on it and relies on it. Seems to bother some people nowadays. It seems to have been in the line of fire of America's newest and most embarrassing chapter in her life. Political Correctless. Children shouldn't compete anymore. *Might make them good at something.* Who the hell came up with this crap? Political correctless is turning this country from the *USS Enterprise* into the Good Ship Lollipop. Not my ship! This ain't whatcha call rock the boat; this is worse. It's called sink the boat! What kind of people are responsible for this? Old school tradition? No, more like *new school newborns* who are the same size as adults who seem to know how to communicate. Very well, at that. Since when is it okay not to be offended? Can't take it? Then stay in bed 'cause it's a very offensive world out there. Intentionally or not, someone is going to put a dent in your day. Pass a law to make what dented your armor illegal or get real and realize that not everyone really cares about you and no magic wand is going to make all the wrongs right. Pass another fucking law, and ***I'm gunna start makin' up my own.*** Seems like lots of folks are offended by some old folklore, or some other traditional written in stone philosophy that's been sewn into our past and just can take it anymore. I feel your pain. Two words: To hell with your almighty presence; if you can't see the importance of maintaining our foundation, for it is what we are all about, and not question its doctrines, reword it, redefine it, and look at it as the land that *let you get what you got*, then you need to leave. Well, that was alittle more than two words but it all means the same. Lots of crap I see and hear really gets me going and I really hate to get started. Especially working like a dog and going nowhere, but nothing like the mood of America at real time. Right now, as you read. But that's my problem; going nowhere while trying to get somewhere, but I deal with it, but sometimes not too seriously. I really don't expect the radical change that some people are calling for to take root with much of America in the foreseeable future because when push comes to shove, some people aren't going to budge. The only changing I see are the diapers on all these offended babies out there. Shit really stinks too . . . smells kinda like baby shit. But competition. Why do you think our stock market is so tricky? Not CEO tricky, but its own internal components which make it work. That's because you have no choice but to use your own head, with or without professional help, to figure out which company or corporation in which to fly with while knowing that there are fifty or so other companies competing for the same product. There's only room for three. Hope you did your homework or that your stockbroker went to bible study, 'cause all the rest of those companies become chum in the portfolio. Those companies who won the contract competed with each other just as the investor chose one stock or fund over another. Competition made Rusty the cop he was and Babe the pillar he was in town. So much so that Babe's funeral in nineteen seventy-eight, it was attended by all facets of law enforcement, even the FBI. Johnny can also tell you about the FBI but on a different stroke. He did not pursue any of the interests of his predecessors, and chose to test the waters of those times, and his is an entirely different story.

Since both of us were sportsmen in our day but now sit out the thrill of victory and the agony of defeat, we both express many interests in sports. Baseball, football, NASCAR, women's tennis, basketball, women's beach volleyball, women's anything, etc., are all sports that grab your attention especially while watching the excitement of a rivalry. Bears-Packers, nineteen-eighties Celtics-Lakers, American League East, and Billy Jean King versus Bobby Riggs are the mortar between the bricks that keeps sports as solid as the year they were conceived. As kids we played sandlot and organized, and just about everyone we knew could play the hell out of any sport. Kids favoring hockey and skating at age six or seven better than most people could walk. No baseball was safe. They were hit all over the place eventually getting fouled into the woods, where some still remain to this day. We'd both reminisce about the glory years every now and then. One night while slugging down some cold ones at Applebee's in Gainesville, Johnny reminisced a little too much and thought he still owned his two-mile record. He walks there because of legal problems and it takes about fifteen minutes one way. He decided to run home 'cause he said he felt good, and for a week after that, it took him fifteen minutes just to get out of bed. Then fifteen minutes just to get to the bathroom. Then fifteen minutes for whatever.

We both watch sports. But sometimes what I'm watching makes me question why I'm watching. Sports, that's it! No off-field news, salaries, private news, or anything else that has nothing to do with nothing but *on the field*. I think a comparison of sports of yesteryear to the present is in order. No question about it, bigger is better. A lineman on a pro team back in the Sixties wouldn't even be big enough to be a safety nowadays. Not that the sport wasn't as good as the present. In fact, many people would probably argue the opposite. That's the allure. Records from the ghostly past that still stand! Some records have been surpassed, even shattered . . . but others seem to have been made by a superman or something. Cy Young's five-hundred and eleven wins, Pete Rose's five-thousand or so career hits, Wilt Chamberlain's hundred points in one game, Tom Dempsey's sixty-something yard field goal that was recently tied after thirty years are historical gems that modern athletes use to rate themselves. But we do get better as we progress with time. Look at McGuire and Sosa back in ninety-eight. They both broke Roger Maris thirty-seven year old record. Barry Bonds will soon own both the single season and career home run record. With all the stuff I hear about steroids, even back in the Seventies, I do know they don't do anything for eye to hand reaction reflexes. Yeah, the ball goes farther but putting the bat on the ball is the single most hardest feat to accomplish in all sports. Mark Spitz . . . back in the 1972 Olympics in Munich where the very first televised Arab attack on Jewish athletes was seen worldwide in horror, won seven gold medals in swimming setting world records at the same time. Those records wouldn't constitute a third or fourth place nowadays. But by reading back into time to compare yourself to a famous athlete, even modern day athletes, is the catalyst to compete and just get better. Can't do the job? Someone else will. Mark Spitz was someone who could and I'm sure when someone on some swim team ties or breaks one of his records he screams out about it. Michael Phelps sure did. But sports is sports. That's not really true anymore. Now I watch about salaries, endorsements, politics, lawyers, lawsuits, who's fucking who this week, and all kinds of other crap that has nothing to do with *on the field*. Modern society isn't just confined to the common man anymore . . . you can be famous and rich now to participate. I guess I just don't possess an inquiring mind. I just like statistics. But I do get a little irritated by some of the salaries I hear about. Nothing against supply and demand but what's going on here? A quarter of a billion dollars to A-Rod to play a kids' game before he went to the Yankees? Hope the Rangers never win again. I can't blame A-Rod, I would have done the same. Lee Trevino made eight thousand dollars when he won the 72 PGA. Wow!! Last-place caddies make more than that nowadays. I just can't seem to make the sting in my face go away every time a famous athlete gets paid. This is stuff that the media eats up. Athletes not respecting where they are in society compounded by others, including the media, doing whatever to bring that athlete down is not good for the cause either. If I was John Rocker and some punk reporter secretly taped my conversation and then ran it . . . I'd be getting out of jail right about now. Alls he said was what this country has become which a lot of people already know. So whad day doo? They get offended. Somebody get me a tissue, please! Yeah, he could have been a little more dignified in doing so while using language everybody else uses too. Everybody else. That's the part that gets me. But Rocker paid the price. Cost him a career. Yesteryear, no reporter would have considered a *punk move* like that but back then reporters never had to interview athletes about a double murder or a missing wife. You know, I've done some pretty stupid shit in my time but if opportunity knocked and gave me a Red Sox uniform complete with a contract and ballfield to play on, I would clean up my act or at least try to. Some people should smarten up because whether they like it or not, they are role models. Anyone know what kids are? One last note . . . Barry Bonds breaks Hank Aarons career home run record . . . Barry Bonds gets divorced, is seen around town with some hunch-backed, pot-bellied, buck-toothed, bald-headed, monobrow, one-legged, onetime fly-girl midget. Which makes the papers? Come on now, try again. We don't care about sports! We're in trouble.

Johnny's father was Irish. His ma was pure Italian. Needless to say, he's a hothead. Absolutely no patience whatsoever. Most of what he owns he has had to replace, sometimes more than once, 'cause something went wrong and he smashed it all up. One time he couldn't get a tire off a car. One of those late Seventies Cougars where the rim somehow fuses itself to the studs even when the lug nuts are removed and even King fucking Kong couldn't even get it off! That really pissed him off! The car looked like it got hit by a train times ten after that. Another time he couldn't pull in a major radio station at his house. The whole damn stereo got slammed into a wall. He says he can't control himself. I say try to . . . do anything, whatever it takes. That kind of behavior is very upsetting. Sometimes stuttering lights his fuse. Other times, it just makes him just shut-up. Sometimes, he lives in a *social distortion*.

His mom was reared in the north end of Harford back around World War II. The north end of Hartford back in those days up to the Fifties or so was predominantly of Italian heritage. All of Johnny's aunts married Italian and all his cousins are Italian Americans. Johnny and his sisters are the only half breeds in the lot. Back in those days there was no Interstate 91 or 84 that take up much of the north end today. There was a street called Front street that no longer exists, where his great-grandmother owned tenement houses that she rented out. Wonder what rent cost back then? Don't care at the moment 'cause the "Munsters" just came on. Back in half hour. We could all learn alittle from Herman. But anyway, Johnny is lucky he has got his mom. By *the hand of fate*, she survived the great circus tent fire in Hartford in 1944 because she wasn't there. Johnny's aunt's and his ma got stood up for ride to the circus that day. Funny how things work. Apparently to waterproof the big tents they used paraffin to coat the canvas. It's flammable and musta a got a cigarette tossed on it. A hundred and forty-four people died that day. Many were never identified including a little girl who was buried in Hartford with a grave marker that only read "Little Miss 1565." Fifteen sixty-five was the number of the grave plot. She was finally identified in 1990 by a Hartford firefighter who just couldn't let her go down as just a number. Turns out she was from upstate Massachusetts and was returned there. Alls she ever got in her short life was her name and that took forty-six years to do. At least I didn't forget her. Johnny's family would spend Christmas and Easter in Hartford with all the cousins, uncles, and aunts and the feast was anything but short of magnificent. Johnny does not remember anything about the Italian heritage in the north end. He wasn't around then. Since those times Hartford has changed. Where all the Italians once lived is now major freeways occupying a lot of land. It is a part of Hartford erased. Never existed. Only in photos. After a certain amount of generations pass on, *don't lose those photos.* Since that happened all the Italians migrated to the south and that is where they remain to this day. Johnny only remembers Rosalyn street next to the Newington-West Hartford line . . . right in the corner. This area is where there once was a massive southend party during the summer that just got too big to contain. You want Italian food? You shoulda came here. Even the restaurants in the southend served food just like Johnny's grandma made. Everyone a Paisano. Not really but you know how that goes. Now, the north end of Hartford has been predominately black since the Sixties and is a much different landscape of what it was back in the Fifties. It has since deteriorated into a watch your white ass part of town. Johnny can tell you about Stowe village. He can also tell you about a football team years ago from Stowe village. Way before dope. They were called the "Stowe Village Firefighters." That's when Johnny was playing football for the town league. His team was the Vikings. Naturally, the Firefighters were all black and Stowe village is a city project apartment complex. One tough fucking complex!! Or at least back when Johnny was buying dope there. To this day he recalls that team when a conversation about football. People would ask. What are you talking about? The Firefighters? He would say "Yeah, you should have seen them." May as well talk about them, especially when we always came in second to them. Anyway the southend has been Italian for all of Johnny's life. All holidays except Thanksgiving were Italian. Thanksgiving was at his dad's folks in his hometown. Inlaws have a way to regulate such functions so as not to not piss off future relations with people who soon may be legal fodder for child support and/or alimony. He listened to either family and learned about how everything once was and how it got to be the way it is now. There can be nothing more important than the foundation of long roots in an old family. Nowadays, that's almost a lullaby. Everybody moves out then moves on. But to me, it is very important. Times are a-changin.'You'd be amazed at the stuff grandpa would tell you if ma wasn't there.

When during a holiday, Johnny tells me he can't find anyfood anywhere like what his great aunts and grandma used to make. Thanksgiving has never been the same since childhood. Neither has Christmas or Easter with all of Johnny's grown-up relatives speaking nothing but Italian, his great aunts wearing tents for dresses, his grandpa listening to Italian opera, and all his cousins asking him what was all the grown-ups saying. But I always say *ain't no time like the present* and probably most other people like myself just get hammered on holidays. Reverse evolution; can't always go forward. Sometimes too much work. Especially Thanksgiving football. Can't even wipe my own ass sometimes during the second game. Wherezzz the kids when you need them? When in the southend, this is where he really learned the power of the push-up. Sometimes holidays were hell. With the discipline he learned in boot camp and the lessons of being fit he learned from his grandpa, he always found jail time to be the right time to pound out a stupid amount of push-ups a day. Just do it. Even on the outside he feels not whole unless he punishes himself with a solid workout. For a quite few years straight, out of the three hundred and sixty-five days we got in our year to come, he'll manage at least a few days behind bars. Like one little stretch for passing around counterfeit three-hundred dollar bills with a picture of Slapshot MaGoo . . . one of the MaGoo brothers in the middle. It's pretty good how things you learn to keep it goin' just never goes away. Especially physical stuff like that. Johnny cries a little bit about all this 'cause his kids will never have what he once had: grandfathers. He knows what grandparents did for him. Rusty passed on early in Johnny's life, and Johnny's wife's father, God bless his soul, lived in Nevada when the kids were coming up. His kids never got the extended values. That puts more pressure on the parent. You now have two jobs. We all know that's impossible, and that's a crying shame. Only a grandfather can be a grandfather. His kids' grandmothers love them all to death, but the geographical problems allows for virtually no time together. His family's dilemma is parallel to most others: nomadic. Family bondness is not extinct by no means, but just stretched out a little bit. America is a big country. Johnny never thought he would become a nomad. Last thing on his mind. Now, he's not sure what's coming around the next turn. Funny how things change. Sometimes that's not so funny. Finally landing in Georgia, he still moves here and there but with one time here, he thought he finally landed, and gets a chance to plants some roots. It's what's he landed in is *what's this novel's all about.*

Johnny thought the world of Rusty and as he got older and became a sorta like "don't answer to no one kinda person," their relationship became a little strained. This jumps up a few years but with Johnny being Johnny and the whole damn town knowing about it, things did get a little tense. But there are stories like this that can only be told and understood by another family member. This happened around 1980 before Johnny met his wife. He had just got a job working for the postal service and was working at a rural town twenty or so miles away from his own town called Granby. A friend of his from town moved up there sometime before and lived within walking distance from the post office. That was good since Johnny screwed up his driver's license and did a lot of walking at that time. As I progress, we'll see how not much has changed. Every now and then Johnny would walk on over to his buddy's house to spend his lunch hour. This guy who lived there with his girlfriend sold all kinds of dope. Anything, any weight. Johnny was pretty much looked at as just a cool piss ant just looking for a buzz. Never got involved with much of anything. Too much weight scared him. Anyway, this guy also had this big Belgian shepherd. German shepherd with longer fur. One big ass hundred and forty pound dog. No fat, just one dog you want on your side. The dog's name was Demon Dog and he was a big huge friendly baby who liked Johnny and was a really great dog. Whenever something went wrong, like a bad dope deal or the such, Demon Dog would take the brunt of the frustration boiling over. This pissed Johnny off. He asked for and got Demon Dog one day. He hit the road with his thumb out in the air trying to get a ride and stood there for a long time with this mule just trying to get a ride. No one is gunna pick up someone who's got a dog that weighs the same as the person who's trying to get a ride. He then tells Demon Dog to stay in the woods while Johnny continues to air out his thumb. Demon dog just sits in the woods not letting Johnny out of his sit. A very keen and obedient dog. A car finally stops. Johnny whistles to Demon Dog and they both hop in the car. The driver freaks out and Johnny assures him the dog is okay and begs for the ride. It worked. The driver was a little irked when demons body straddled the front seat with his rear legs on the rear seat and his front legs on the front seat all the while licking the hell out of Johnny for saving him. He finally made it to his folks house because at that time he was staying there a little while to regroup. He puts Demon Dog in the two-car garage, gave him food and water and blasts off to the local tavern on a real pretty Sportster he just bought.

Some people call Sportsters bitch bikes. Not this one. It's got a six inch over rake on the neck of the frame so that even though it looks like a chopper, the gas tank sits right on top of the motor like it's supposed to. Chevy orange exhaust pipes with a motor with alittle over a hundred horses. He once made it to Marconi beach in Cape Cod from Hartford, Connecticut in a little less than a hour and a half. I wouldn't recommend that. He knocked off an hour if you obey the laws. Not too many people asked Johnny to ride it 'cause of the short drag handlebars that he preferred. Sorta a crazy bike, but that's the way he liked it. He bought this bike while his drivers license was under suspension by law. No license over a nasty car wreck that he caused previously. But he drove it anyway. Who cannot drive a gorgeous bike just because you're not legal? You really shouldn't but he just didn't care and rode that bike to hell and back twice. Good for him. Now I don't condone illegal driving by no means because the consequences cost too much, and you can lose your driving privileges. But what did you do to lose your license? Sometimes not much. That's a scary reality, but anyhow, he rode his Sportster to the bar that day. He closes up the place and rides home. The motor made Demon Dog bark like hell when he pulled into the driveway. He runs into the house and quiets the dog down real quick so as to not wake up Ma. No one knew Demon Dog was in the garage except Johnny. All night long at the bar he was wondering how he was going to tell his folks about an animal that looked like it ate the same amount per day as a tiger. He parks the bike in the garage and goes upstairs to the kitchen. At this time Rusty pulls in from the Windsor House, a popular bar and restaurant also in town, pretty close to the place where Johnny was at. Rusty bought Johnny his first very beer at the Windsor House. It is now gone. I hear it's now a CVS. Very nostalgic. Every town should have one. Just make sure it occupies sacred ground. They both closed up the saloons they were in and drove home after consuming alcohol. They sound like criminals. They just left the bar after closing. Rusty is a cop, he's not a criminal by no means. Some people . . . Rusty, more than Johnny know the consequences of car wrecks. Not pretty. Some people know when to leave when the gettin' is good, some people just know better. Took Johnny alittle more time than it should to understand all this. But if drinking three beers at the bar makes you a criminal?, then we may as well close them all down. Make sense? A closed society would do just that because logically . . . no bars, no criminals. Yeah, you can drink at home, but it's not been publicly served because that would go against all logic.

Where'zz Spock? I could really use someone like that right about now. Looks like I'm condoning drunk driving. Not really, I'm just trying to figure out why the responsible are lumped together with the irresponsible, that's all. One of the reasons would be that's *there's no real fine line between the both.* We've been here before for many years, and I think it's time for America to realize that there really is such a thing as a responsible person, even sittin at the local tavern for a couple of hours. I know cops who do the same thing and I don't see them gettin' screwed by the system, and believe me, I would never drop a dime. No one likes a stinkin' snitch, no matter what. But there are exceptions of other crimes that will hit you in the face like an atom bomb. Drop a C-note or the bomb (just jokin') if you got any idea what I'm talking about! Sittin' in a bar for a couple of days don't even compare to some od'a crap I see and hear in the news nowadays! But where's the logic of getting put in the system after drinkin' only three beers at some club or tavern? Do you realize that at any givin time in America or anywhere else in the world, most everyone sitten' at a bar and/or restaurant for more than two hours or so, and enjoying themselves with a laugh and a drink at a power lunch is a criminal? That is actual fact according to law. Sorry about the lack of public safety, but I think I safety is more on most folks minds than you might think. Impaired is impaired, plain and simple. Three beers isn't gunna do me in, plain and simple! Maybe four; after that, I'll just puke up a couple of empty beer cans and maybe blow a couple more out the ass end out all over the floor. I'm sorry but what I'm talking about is no joke but I just can't help it, I'm on my twenty-ith beer. *But I'm not driving.* It just seems like that alls' the people are to the law (local lawmakers) nowadays are nothing but sources of rolling revenue to keep the county in the black. We have some very stiff fines for all infractions, no matter how miniscule. Maybe that would be a deterrent to not do it again. It would make anyone think twice about doing it again, especially DUI. I believe that it's a combination of the both but with so much money to be gotten from the roadways, what comes first? Of course it's the dollar bill. But it's almost neck-n-neck with road safety, otherwise, why are there police in the first place? Alcohol impairs? Then do what happened back in 1920: Contain the problem, and piss almost everyone off. Make it illegal. With all that tax revenue from alcohol sales, that's never going to happen. If it does, triple the cost of what you normally buy at the grocery store. Three beers nowadays costs could balloon from a couple of hundred into the thousands. Three little beers. Three beers maybe gets my left do-dad a little buzz! But that's only me. Three beers could seriously impair someone else. That's why we got what we got. Thanks to DUI laws, most of us know when the getting is good or if some of us missed the boat, it's time to call a taxi. But if I can pass a field sobriety test once, then make me do it again two or more times. Make it harder if you want. Tell me to float. If I can do all that and I'm not floatin' already, then *whatz the problem?* Three beers, maybe a couple more, isn't gunna Quaalude me out into the ozone. But what if I hadn't eatin' a thing all day? That's why you gotta watch your ass and those around you, even miles away, and that's why things are the way they are. All of this is dangerous talk because of some of our rather cavalier and somewhat irresponsible modern society would turn three beers into thirty. That's too bad for the millions of criminals sitten' in some gin mill at any given time in the country who are trying to impress some chick over a few drinks. DUI laws save lives, plain and simple. Not good enough. Let's just go into the bars and assume everyone there is going to drive anyway and arrest anyone caught sittin at the bar. That already happened in America alittle while back. Good idea, Adolph, but can't we just tase' em' in the face instead? That'll put a jolt in their sorry little drunken lives. Sounds like a blast to me! Anyways, they are both up in the kitchen and decide to fry up some BLTs. Those are good. As all this progressed and the bacon cooked and the bread toasted, it became time to get the lettuce and tomatoes. Johnny looks in the fridge and finds only the tomatoes. He says to Rusty," I'll watch the bacon and you go downstairs to the other fridge and grab a head of lettuce. Totally brain-dead by this time, he completely forgets about Demon Dog in the garage where the other fridge was. Rusty enters the garage and is met with a bark that knocked tiles off the wall. It woke up the entire household. Now bear in mind, Rusty had a buzz . . . who knows about Johnny. Rusty flies up the stairs with the finesse of Michael Vick faster than Superman and tells Johnny, "There's a huge, hairy Tyrannosaurus in the garage!!" Where'd he come from?" Johnny says, "Oh yeah dad, I forgot to tell ya, I got a dog. A real big one." Johnny explains and all is well because of the family's love of animals. They're eating BLTs and now Demon is upstairs and he knew he was "in like Flynn." *That's very important for an animal.* It was right then that very night Johnny sensed a problem. He was right. When he moved out later, Rusty said the dog stays. If it made Rusty happy, then it made Johnny happy. Demon was now Rusty's dog. Nothing like a couple of good dogs in the house. No tarantulas . . . what kind of pet is that? Good name for a sports car or a motorcycle. Pretty good name for a big-ass spider too!

As Johnny came up over the years, he was Rusty's firstborn and only son. They did a lot of stuff together in the early years, and who wouldn't be proud of his son? Johnny's high-school attitude was taking its toll on their relationship, especially when he just about stopped coming home or came really late at night by sneaking in his window. This is awhile before he drove. And knowing the whole town the way he did, he would decide to run from point A to point B every now and then no matter what the distance. A lot of that was done on railroad tracks all by himself. He'd be at some throwdown and knew he had to be home. He'd be at a party and knew he had to be home. Wait till really late, then run across town to his parents' house and sneak in. Being fit and on the track team has its complements. One time he called a friend's house miles away to see what's up. He says to Johnny that he's got some dope and to come on over. Johnny knocks on the door not too much later than if a car had stopped at a convenience store on the way and his buddy looks out and asks, "How did you get here?" seeing no car in the driveway. "I ran." "Are you out of your blaze-glazed-half-burnt mind? How far was that?" "I don't know but I'm here!" "Come on in, hit this, then drink that." Far out. But finally he just moved out for a while every now and then when he was a junior and senior. Move back for awhile to re-group and do it again. It was always at the same place, in someone's huge-ass attic with rafters. Not trusses, so they had their own entire room. Even slept on hammocks hanging from adjacent rafters. A couple of high school idiots living like phantoms of the Opera just about answering to no one. They would talk about the next day. School might fit in, but if it didn't, there's always the next day. If Rusty could see Johnny now he'd see that Johnny would chose to live, especially with all the chaos in which he lives now, with the morals and family values he learned from all of his family during the wonder years. He can't take back the past and knows that Rusty knew that during the attic years, he knew Johnny would never really lose grip. But Johnny did make him wonder. Not too much has changed and Johnny's grip seems to have gotten stronger even though there were periods of losing alittle space in time, but he always maintained some kind of grip throughout all of that. Rusty's gone, but Johnny thinks about him everyday. He was just too cool to die, but it happened. *Rusty's passing forever changed his family.* Johnny's ma, Esther, never remarried. She's content living with his memories and knows there really isn't anyone else out there who could ever fill the shoes of someone you just had to know. A strange thing. Rusty died on Patty's, Johnny youngest sister's birthday on January twenty-third, and as he died she had this dream of him walking away and waving bye to her as he disappeared. We all know this is true because she was absolutely content that knowing he was going to be all right and we believed her. If that doesn't make one think. God works in mysterious ways. Some I care not to know. Rusty's been dead about twenty years now. But even now, if you visit his grave today during a blizzard you'll see how the snow melts away from his grave no matter how deep it is everywhere else. That's because he was so shit-hot his grave is still warm. Goodbye Rusty; your son is doing what he can to carry on the tradition. Thank God you and Esther brought him up. I don't think anyone else could. He's now walking and talking on his own.

I just had discussed a little religion. Atheists take notice: Skip this next essay, or better yet, check this out. This little discussion just might prove you right. When someone discusses religion, it can be wrapped up in a nice neat package or it can't be contained in any package and just makes a mess. I could see some atheist believing his view since we all know faith and religion are centered around the unseen. Some have to see with their own two eyes. "You got to have Faith" doesn't really make too much sense to them since the word faith was included. Faith cannot be seen. Maybe I can see though some kind of translucent meaning of what it's all about, but for mankind being here for the first place, I see a reason. When nothing changes, but in fact gets worse, I really can see how someone can blame a lack of God, whose supposed to make things better, for making things worser than one would like. I just believe that there is a reason for all the human pain but I just don't know why. Neither does an atheist. Please excuse the atheist bashing, but I'm just politically erect. Not 'cause I'm a pig or anything like that, but because the human mind is a terrible thing . . . to waste. But I believe that religion is an advanced form of mythology of man all throughout the ages in trying to understand his origin and meaning on earth. To start off here, Johnny would go to church every Sunday with his sisters and his ma. Being catholic, he would also attend catechism and received his first Communion and his Confirmation, two of the seven Holy Sacraments of the catholic religion. He chose *Dominick* as his Confirmation name in honor of an uncle who died in 1966. Matrimony was the last sacrament he received. That was in 1982. Johnny did not like church at all. Not for what it stood for, but for that one hour that seemed like a week. When his mom said let's go he tried everything to get out of it. But Esther would have none of that and if she had to drag him by his lips then that's what got done. Sundays used to piss him off. Sit, stand, kneel, stand, sit, float, and all that done over again and again used to drive him and his sisters nuts. Getting stoned would have help but he didn't even know what that was back then. When he brought his own children to church many years later, he would often get stoned and relax and begin to think about why he's there in the first place. He thought about current events and tried to connect them to the sermon being preached. He found it gratifying. *Why are we here? Anybody else out there? How big is the universe? When did time begin? Where's Jimmy Hoffa?* Except the latter, religion tries to put this all in perspective. Religion. What a mess that word or concept has become. It now causes internal strife in many countries, most recently . . . the U.S.A. Other countries seem to have trouble with other denominations of religions within their borders. But now it's under fierce attack, most notably the Christian faith . . . not by other religions, but by others of no religion. Do you let a small contingent of loudmouths dictate the spiritual fate of America? I would hope not, but I believe in religion, all faiths. But I also do believe in science. Now I'm no Jesuit Monk or anything like that, that would distort science to enhance beliefs, but science has proven a lot of things. One of them is some type of adaptation which could be construed as evolution to the changing conditions, namely climate to continue the future of the inhabitants of our planet's biosphere. That means the big bad world is out to get you. I believe in my faith as well as everybody else believes in theirs, but as previously mentioned, I also believe in science. It was Johnny's favorite subject. I believe that Moses split the Red Sea. I believe in natural disasters. I believe in quantum physics even though I got no idea how anyone could even begin to figure that science out. I believe that water was actually turned to wine. As a catholic myself, I believe all of what I learned about the Bible. The Bible is vague on specific dates as to when major biblical events happened. That's called the unseen. Your faith, no matter what denomination, is based on mostly ancient writings written eons ago, written by the founders and the foundation of all religions to which we all still strictly adhere to. How would science fit into all this?

Creationism versus evolution. Islam versus the rest of the universe. One just as volatile as the other. I do believe Moses did it one way or the other. In trying to explain our existence from mythology to now, mankind has been warring for centuries over religion and maybe some ideology, but not as much . . . because many centuries ago, ideology really didn't mean too much, whereas the Christian religion was the law. Check out what happened to you if you were deemed a witch. When I say law, that be no joke. Mental evolution took care of that little problem. But the debate between the Cross and the monkey has both the scientific and spiritual world in trench warfare to which is now making news with much public input with some public schools now including creationism in its curriculum. This is what I believe . . . I believe *one cannot exist without the other.* First of all, as one believes in faith, one cannot discount science and all of that it has shown us. Science has proved many things . . . the age and evolution of the planet earth itself, its geological past and future, space physics, medicine, chemistry, alchemy, and other things that can't be seen with the human eye. The big-bang theory is scientific. The edge of the universe as seen with Edwin Hubble's telescope is said to be *the Face of God.* That could be construed as religious. I see them both as intertwined. Let me explain in detail as to what I think. As to the million-year-old fossils showing a close resemblance to modern humans, monkeys and gorillas also mimic our structures. They are present, not ancient past. But like ourselves, they also have a past. Bear in mind that they also have opposing thumbs. They are the same as all the evolution of ancient species. There's much evidence of mankind going back eons ago. But that doesn't mean anything to anyone in regards to creationism. And it shouldn't. But just as science doesn't exist nowadays with some religious philosophies, it was the opposite, with religion not existing with very ancient man back when clubbing meant someone got really hurt. Imagine clubbing back then. Crush her skull and drag her home before she got rigor mortis. Seems like women have always been taking a lot of shit. Not the ones Johnny meets. They all want payback. He seems to talk to the ones whose grandmas told that story for the ages all the way to the present where he now resides. Even crap in which he had no say stings his face. Adaptation was and still is the way evolution progressed through the ages. *Miller's experiment* back in the Fifties showed that with certain elements of the periodic table, when mixed with some of the conditions back in ancient earth, mainly carbon, also mixed with the conditions of the planet at that time . . . somehow those conditions created a virus. Just like the way it is now; right time at the right place. Not a damn things changed! A virus is the simplest form of life. DNA with a jacket on, as simple as that. How could a virus mutate into a human? This kinda sounds like hallucinated sci-fi on something off the streets. This is way before religion. It would probably have a few stops on the way before that happened, but *why* is what the theme of this essay is all about. It's all about adapting to your environment to ensure survival.

Viruses go to all the kingdoms; plants, animals, and two-legged animals with brains like plants. The very first virus didn't have the word *human* written on it somewhere. This is gettin' pretty deep, but bear with me. Help me out if you can, I'm just makin' all this stuff up as I try to figure it all out. It had the word *survival* written on it. How it did that is beyond me, but it happened. Get the flu lately? A virus has remained a virus to this day, but maybe in certain parts of the planet back then, where other certain conditions were met, maybe they combined to form . . . maybe a sponge. One of the proven first forms of life on earth had a fingerprint. Check out human DNA and take a look at what's on the bottom of the pile. Sure looks like the makings of a sponge to the scientific community involved in such matters. You can discover things on the Discovery Channel. I don't have a clue what DNA looks like . . . a sponge or Sponge Bob. But I did stay at a Holiday Inn express last night! I'm trying to hook all this into my take on religion, but I need to go on with a little more of this satanic jibber-jab to get my point across. Evolution does not mean we are total descendents of monkeys and apes. It means that some species either adapted or went extinct or were in bed with the wrong species and this is what happened. Something new and just as mutts do, they get the best of both worlds thus making it stronger. I think that's a pretty good way of looking at it. It becomes as always, survival of the fittest, which then turns into survival of the smartest. Modern man did in no way come from neanderthal man as some people still believe. They are two entirely different species and as one advanced, the other went extinct. This was modern man's last conquest and *homo-sapiens* have ruled the planet since. To become *homo-sapiens* as the end result would be by a series of changes throughout the millions of years which pales to the earths' age in which the two-legged stagger walking human-wannabe has what it takes throughout the endless eons of time to keep the human brain alive to let it evolve to what we have now. Other similar species also existed throughout all of this. They just didn't have what it took and died off. Monkeys and apes exist to this day because back then, their brains just weren't big enough to get past instinct and this is what they got. Nothing like the original *Planet of the Apes*. Their brains were as big as Johnny's. We all came from somewhere and after leaving there, we, as did all other species, relied on basically instinct still without cognitive skills to guide us to chart our days, months, and years. All that changed when modern man became a thinker. Learned how to make stones sharp enough as to use them as tools. Also to look to the sky and begin to wonder, especially at night. Ancient mythology interprets many aspects of life, with one God to one aspect. Thus many false idols as we all know now. But back then, they didn't comprehend any God as the only God. I think ancient mythology was an embryonic ideology to explain our existence at the time, while always realizing all those questions . . . . the *whens, hows, and whys* we are here? How did this happen? Many aspects of life thus many gods . . . earth, wind, and fire, and many more. I can't really say that mythology endured to see religion as we know it presently, but that can be argued. My religion forbids it. Last I knew there were no false gods as widely believed back in ancient Europe in the Middle East. My Middle East studies are severely lacking. I only started watching after parts of New York City, parts of the Pentagon, and part of rural Pennsylvania were all blown to hell. Empires like Mesopotamia, the Assyrians, the Sumatrans, the Babylonians, and the Persians and all the way to the Ottomans are cultures that shaped this planet to this very day. But before the inception of the Islam religion, I'm pretty sure that ancient Middle Eastern man had some kind of interpretation of the same questions European ancients were trying to decipher.

Much can be said about our ancient predecessors, about our mental evolution over theirs. But bear in mind, some of the sharpest minds ever to appear on earth are thousands of years old. *Some of the greatest feats of man happened eons ago.* These people realized how the motion of the stars and the sun ran in cycles that took hundreds and thousands of years to complete, how all that had a profound effect on mankind throughout the endless ages. This remains true to this day. They invented a chart to measure time in seconds, minutes, and hours, and then looked up to chart all of the constellations that make up the zodiac, which affects us to this day. This took numerous generations requiring state-of-the-line communication at those times to make our presently known time tables. They still remain authors to this day. This all was written, if not before all the Bible is being constructed. But I believe that when man became able to think about a "higher and unseen" force and comprehend on his own, that's when God interjected spirituality into man. This would be my interpretation of Adam and Eve. The very first ones to feel it. However, after sin, I think that's when all the mythology erupted to cloud mankind's view so that he might falter. Does that mean that our ancient pagan predecessors who were not able to believe in *the Christ* are forbidden to share the fruits of his labor? Good question whiz-bang. I believe our good Lord looks after all of His, even those who didn't even know. Ignorant, not stupid, then and now . . . hopefully. When God saw that man was ready, we felt religion. Religion isn't based on instinct. Neither is mythology. Paganism and early religion existed basically around the same time. It's very easy to get alittle lost in a discussion such as this. So we had to wait for a religious transformation. So we waited. Stir that up with a little science, and this is the very gist of what I'm trying to convey to all of the football cheerleaders all over the land. Everyone else too. I don't think anything happened out of thin air, except biblical miracles and I do not discount anyone's opinions to believe otherwise. Just don't make it law. Likewise I'll do the same. We all must remain true to our faith, if there's going to be any hope at all. We all rely on our own faith of the unseen and practically unknown powers of the "higher level," of whatever religious denomination. Some people, then and now, aren't even allowed to chose a religious denomination of their free will. Some nowhere-in-the-middle of nowhere politics also behaved in the same way, resulting in massive chaos on a grand scale. World War II comes to mind, and Adolph only brought ruin to his vision. To try to make others do your evil-bidding and think that only you can do their thinking, even for millions . . . is nothing but an illusion. Nothing more. There are more people out there who think for themselves than not. "Higher level" means one thing to someone, something else to another. To me, it means passing the test of life . . . to pass or fail to a damnation of eternal problems. Big ones . . . crimes such as murder, even in the name of faith makes your eternal future seem nothing but catastrophic. It just doesn't seem to me that murder in the name of Islam justifies the very well-planned carnage besieged upon its victims or enemy simply for the fact they are different or think different. All the bullshit since laying eyes upon each other . . . but this is much different. The entire world is different in many vast ways . . . cultures, even jungle people, races, and religions, rituals, folklore, national origins, tribal origins, and so on and for one faction of the world biosphere to wreak fire and pain to others simply for the fact that they are nonbelievers rocks the *Enterprise* from port to starboard and I don't like it. While all denominations of religions are rejoicing for the same fate for mankind preparing for the next level, I just cannot see any "higher level" condoning the maiming, murder, and malice of anyone for the advancement of that particular religion. *Parts* of Islam comes to mind. Their book says nonbelievers are nothing but cockroaches. Last I knew, cockroaches got stepped on and exterminated. If that don't raise the hair on the back of your ass, then you're a tougher target than I am! To all you nonbelievers out there, this a real problem and it's not going to go away. At least not by shaking hands. Get me another Harvey Wall banger, I don't want to hear that all that crap! All the Harvey Wall bangers in the world aren't going to make all of this go away! If you never believed in anything your whole life, at least let your grandkids be allowed to believe in something. Always think about the future . . . if not yours . . . then everyone else's. Sounds like some 1960s propaganda. USA style. Shoulda been there, wild. But if not, like I said before, ain't no time like the present. So I say, "Let's deal with it." I feel that most inhabitants of the earth are good people . . . the problem most are still persecuted. Religion is the spiritual and mental evolution leading us from then paganism and mythology, to now, goodwill to all mankind no matter what suffering is besieged upon us, natural, divine, or ourselves. I just believe that science is one of the major tools for trying to dissect much of our past, including religion. I see some connection. However, I see no light at the end of the tunnel in regards to the theory of Darwinism, even with sufficient evidence, and the fierce flames of the Scopes trial, which was debated scores of generations ago, still burns as bright now as it did then.

But I wasn't there, Scopes or Noah. I was somewhere else. I only have faith. With that being said, even with my very strict faith, I don't know what came first, the chicken or the egg. As mentioned, the whereabouts and whenabouts of historical biblical sites and dates are forever left to vague scriptures. Some are obviously known . . . many you simply must believe. I believe that science hasn't properly deciphered the shroud of Turin, or in fact, the shroud of Turin hasn't properly deciphered science. A lot more needs to come to light, science or not, to pass judgment on this. It looks very real to me. Carbon date or not, there is nothing else in the world like it. This is all Christian historical past. This is only for believers. To most others, it sounds like science fiction, especially the Red

Sea. Most people look at other people's faith with some kind of alienating outlook that *their* outlook or belief is wrong. That's okay because civilized people can live with people with different beliefs and still live each day with respect towards each other, and live and let live. The world's way too big for everyone to believe the same way. Race shows us that we even look different, so why not believe different. Maybe we can learn a little this, a little that from each other, and we will all know how that works and how sometimes it don't. But back to the theory. Science and God, the birth of the universe, the wonders of the cosmos, crazy-intense extraterrestrial forces that stretch the imagination of man . . . even creating new sciences, like quantum physics are frontiers that help in deciphering our existence. What if it does mean more than that? Think were the only ones out there? The physical properties of the universe are debatable to even members of the scientific community involved in the same studies. So is religion. It is also debatable to members of all the rest of us who believe in the Divine. To me, God is the greatest scientist, producing the most complex terrestrial and extraterrestrial environments that science hasn't even come close to understanding . . . and probably never will. Already in nature exists conditions that no scientist can even begin to understand. In the ocean deep exists species of fish and other organisms that produce their own light and electricity to survive. Their DNA makes human DNA look like child's play and these creatures can't even think! What about fireflys? It would take a human ten tons of LSD to light up like that! However, I do believe that in death, many of these mysteries are answered, provided you passed the test of life that was given to you. Mankind has used religion to try to decipher some of these mysteries while still in flesh and blood. This leads to problems. Some are rational, some are not. We now have in America religion being brought to the public by certain grammar and high schools, stating that evolution is nothing but a theory. Evolution is nothing more than adaptation to the environment. That's what it really is. Look at all the species, especially sub-species that live in crap no one else would. They have no choice because of their size and environment so they adapt. It has been proven that this process takes a ridiculous amount of years, about the time of dinosaurs. What's next, dinosaurs didn't exist? I own one. He's purple and his name is Dino and keeps on throwing me outside all the time. Science has proven that there was no man or mammals around at that time. Back to the beginning. When did man first appear on earth? I have my own opinions, but religious problems persist elsewhere besides the U.S. In the Middle East, where the mother of all clusters now resides, the Islamic faith states that only in Jihad, is murder and mayhem is condoned. Other than that, it is a religion where people are faithful like in no other religion and just like other religions, there are fanatical beliefs that upsets the rest of the *Enterprise.* People worship snakes in parts of America. Snakes? Not Johnny, they scare the crap out of him. He worships the "great Mali Wali." Very holy. Very scary too! Sounds like a false god to me. He told me that Zeus was nuthin' but a religious pessimist that pretty much sounds like some futuristic D.C. creature-feature sorta like in T.V. land including parts of underground Washington and wasn't gettin' him nowhere, so he switched. Parts of underground where?

Some people believe that murder and chaos in the name of religion leads to all the things in the afterlife that one could not obtain in flesh and blood including a whole bunch of virgins. I like all that, but I think in reality after committing heinous acts of martyrdom, killing your unsuspecting enemies who are only enemies because they are different, one would wake up to the afterlife only to find that your virgins are a bunch of peace loving honeys who abhor violence and all that goes with it, like most, if not all, virgins. If me or Johnny ever did something like that!, we'd wake up on the afterlife slab only to see a bunch of something that I would never want to see. *Too late now. Bend over, got something for ya, open up and say ahh.* Soundz likes hell to me. I can go on and on about all of this and nothing will change the minds of the so-called persecuted, except a bullet. That's not what we want to do, but it seems that's what we have to do. We didn't fly the planes into the temples of Islam nor would we. But with all the unanswered questions regarding religion and science, I cannot help but see some equilibrium between the both. But as previously mentioned, some schools in the South, and some in Idaho and Kansas are making creationism their main theory about the origins of man, thus relegating Darwinism to elective course. I believe this is dangerous and sets a precedent for fanaticism of religion here in the U S. The schools involved have a host of different religions and beliefs amongst them, and to be forced to learn something that should be taught only in religious sectors will soon splinter closeknit communities that disagree with religious teachings in school. I'm not against religion in public schools by no means. I believe in the "Pledge of Allegiance," "Under God," and a moment of silence to pray on their own accord. Those who can't even agree with that are not looking at the past or the future, only the very very selfish present and have an axe to grind, using children as the grinding wheel. Countries whose foundations and governments are based solely on religion are confrontational and somewhat unstable. Anyone in Kansas been watching the wonderful world of Middle East living? Expect this to further fester on down the road as with any mention of the word *religion*, free people will not tolerate to believe in something in which they don't. Say what you want about unseen faith, but I'll say this. Without faith, then it becomes every man for himself. Anyhow, the sundial in Topeka says it's time to move on.

One last note on Roman Catholics is the stoutness, strictness, and direct implication of sin just by thinking about it. May as well have done it. Johnny has a rough time with this. According to him he can't even think. Or just don't look at women anymore. Muslims can have all kinds of wives. He can't even get one. He thinks that if he changes his name to Mustafa or Abdullah Reems, all that will change. But I want to state my view of the strictness. Very strict. It's the only religion where the heads of the church, cardinals, bishops, and priests must remain celibate. That means no hunka-chunka or bunga-punga with the opposite sex. I don't want to get into catholic doctrine or history, but everyone is human and has sexual needs. One must really believe to take a vow of celibacy. But as we all know by now, that's not entirely true anymore and that's too bad for the religion. I think the Catholic faith needs to regroup in the twenty-first century and come up with some kind of leeway for members of its clergy because I'm sick and fucking tired of hearing about all this child molestation amongst its members. However, as one cannot judge an entire group by the actions of a few, the same goes here. But I am very disturbed by some of the gay crap I hear involving priests and children. Male or female, it is a disgusting crime and the priest who got beaten to death in prison was long overdue on what he deserved. *Betcha he won't do it again.* This very hard to write about because all Catholics look up to our priests in times of good and bad. They are always there, even when you need them. That's very reassuring to me. I wish this shit never happened, but it did. I could never live a celibate life. That is, of course, if I'm doing ten to twenty. I love women . . . some more than others. I think that sex is a gift from God to allow us to procreate ourselves in the name of the survival of the species . . . the horny male. I like to bunga whenever I can and to say "Nope, can't do that," would be more than I could bear. I would look down at my balls, and I may as well just chop 'em off and sew 'em on a ballerina. That way, they would be just as useless as those found on a male ballerina. What's the sense? But priests do it for the faith and one must respect that. Okay enough of that. What'd ya think? Either you love me or hate me or love to hate me or vice versa, which is okay because it's been like this for forty something years. I get challenged so in return I spit out my venom, which smells like perfume to the wise, and smells like shit to the rest. Got no major problem with that. Man, I need to get off my high horse and get back on my jackass like I'm used to. I'm really not one to let it all hang out 'cause my business is my business, but now, it's everyone's business because I got something to get off my chest and it's about time to unload some baggage. One more thing about life, death, and religion. It's called abortion. What can we say about that? Not much, because a million dollars to someone is a million problems to another. Taking five-hundred thousand bucks to fix five-hundred thousand problems is not going to work. It's either one way or another, and I care not to open up this carton of crap. You either go to McDonald's or Burger King. You can't do both at the same time if that makes any sense, but I will say this. With our *anything goes* society that now says that if I make a mistake . . . like an unexpected baby, then I have to take care of myself . . . for only myself, 'cause that's alls I have room for. Mistakes of passion that winds up in murder tells me that if we can't even make a distinction between ourselves and ourselves when conceived? . . . then some of us really ain't that human at all. What about the hit-n-run father? Then he needs to be locked up for as long as it takes for society to raise his kid. This ain't about child support, but more about *don't do the fathern' if you can't be the father.* Don't put this all on the ma . . . she's left with an agonizing decision . . . most of the time where there's nowhere to go. If it's 'cause of rape? . . . then I'll do the abortion myself. But I will say that partial-birth abortion just for abortion, the mother's life isn't in any danger? . . . is pure hardcore murder, plain and simple. Jesus will make the doctors who do it pay. Picking on someone a lot smaller than you!! I believe I was also a fetaloid sometime ago. Glad mom didn't go see Doctor Death.

As Johnny is progressing through his early life, he learns that he has some kind of control problem. This really pisses his ma off. This happens quite often. When something goes wrong, he smashes up everything all around him and then he gets smashed up by his ma. Doesn't really learn anything from the lesson his ma is trying to tell him. This process repeats itself at least twice a week. He put his parents through hell and now really regrets it. Talking to your problem child as we are now instructed to do, simply wouldn't work with Johnny. He would spit in your face and then ask for some ice cream. His ma would oblige by making him wear it instead of eating it. Ritalin, anybody? I don't know too much about child dope except I think it should be the absolute last resort with all other means been done twice. He really got into school, and by the fourth or fifth grade, his interest in history and science started to shine but also at that young age, he even taught himself flatulence as a second language. It is also around this time he realizes that the human brain isn't such a terrible thing and is capable or could be capable of magnificent things, good and bad. As tightly wound as he was, I still consider him a normal person who can exist in modern society and adapt to all or most present-day norms. The human mind is just as mysterious and haunting as deep space. We barely know it. Johnny has a brother-in-law who is autistic, and who also adheres to all present-day norms like most of us. Being with mental illness doesn't diminish one's ability to properly adapt to social environments, it just makes it harder. Some of it just makes me wonder in total awe. For instance, the blind and substantially retarded person who can play any classical vercietto and other styles of classical music on the piano just by hearing it once and only once. Close your eyes and you would think it's Mozart. Another person who can tell you what day of the week it was about anything that happened in the past. For instance, in about two seconds if you asked him what day it was when Alexander the Great took the throne, he would tell you what day of the week it was. And if he said Friday, reverse calendars proved him right every time. I don't know if anything was said about if he could tell the future days of the weeks or if that were even possible. I know about the calendars that go a couple years into the future, but what about twenty thousand years ahead? And then there's someone else who could take a knife and a bar of soap and carve it into a museum quality masterpiece in less than five minutes. He could carve the Taj Mahal out of a bar of Irish spring. They all had one thing in common. They were autistic, but what makes me really question this mushy blob of matter under my dome are all the parts involved, or lack of them to make it all work. It even has a memory. By lack of parts, this be no joke. One night, I saw on TV a educational show that showed a perfectly normal teenage girl with no physical or mental problems whatsoever. Then they showed a CAT scan of the cranium of someone else who was also without any problems, mental or physical. You know how they look, the active brain . . . keyword active, appears all lit up with a yellow and red a shape resembling the brain as we know occupying the entire skull. Then they showed hers. The only part of her brain that was lit up was only a small portion the size of an egg on one side of her head. The rest was dead, just like parts of *some people's* brains that keep on gettin' flushed down the crapper every morning. Those are your damn brains for christssakes! Her mind required only one fraction the brain matter for acceptable life. Explain that! As I said before, we barelyknow it, but some people think that they got a real good handle on it. These would be our psychologists and psychiatrists, who seem to have all the answers nowadays. The local bartender seems to help out in time of need and after one hour, you tip him a few pieces. You save around two-hundred and ninety-five bucks. It is called a civilized man's way to deal with trials and tribulations. To deal with problems, shortcomings, frustrations, anger, wide-eyed wonderment, closed-eyed decision making, and so on and so on, mankind has evolved into what we have now. It is a reason for something not going right, either short-term or long-term and blaming it on the big bad world. There are other reasons . . . that's why there is psychology. That much is true, but fighting back, not caving in, seems to work a hell of a lot better. I call psychology a mixture of theoretical science mixed with alittle bullshit to hold all the bricks together. A lot of bricks, a lot of bullshit. Johnny's a little nuts, but he knew what he was doing crazy or not. Some people don't know or do they? That's the $64,000 question was some answers I wouldn't pay sixty-four cents for. Some people pay three hundred duckets an hour for the same answer.

Psychiatrist, neurologist, voodoo, medicine men, brain surgeons, doctors, shamans, Druid priests, psychologists, psychics, mind readers, zombie dolls, and oracles. In this discussion sometimes I can't tell one from the other. Even Sigmund Freud from the middle 1800s seems a little flim-flam to me. In Johnny's family, as with my own people, all of us were brought up old school mixed with some new school. Ain't no time like the present. That's called being well rounded. All of us grew up to be fine respectable people. We all know what type of behavior is to be expected, no matter where you are at. How you act in accordance to your immediate environment is equal to the respect you have for other people. We all started out as children; then, against our will, we grew into adults. Wasn't such a smooth ride for some of us, now was it? Boy to man, girl to woman . . . ready or not here I come. Now, I do realize I should have at least an associates degree to talk about something like this, but alls I did was high school which I'm sure this has been detected by some of you by now. A little military life also which can't be traded for anything, combat or not. I wish I did a little college start out plan ahead and reached a masters or Ph.D. Depending on your major or specialty, that would determine whether it's just *piled higher and deeper* as I hear sometimes. Pay no mind to that. The more you know is where it's at. College is where the secondary education needed to propel the country forward is obtained, and as some religiously biased countries in certain parts of the world frown upon it, I endorse all the benefits and results one receives from college and everything else about it . . . except the professors. But as we came up, a lot of factors good and bad, play throughout your metamorphosis into adulthood. I do see how people can be manipulated sort of speak by a combination of bad elements, mainly fear and deprivation. Somehow this happens to kids. That's devastating to a kid, and equally devastating to think it's always going to be that way. But most parents aren't as demented as that, so I think other factors make me ask how whatever it is I'm trying to figure out. I do value the progress that modern psychiatry and psychology has made over the years and how it benefits millions of people. Not all people are gunna find any kind of transition from bad to worse a good thing, but I do know of a transition that if it happened all the time, would put a scare like none other. What if I experienced nightmares all the time? I could see how that could torment a soul, especially being afraid to go to sleep.

Especially when they're ghost nightmares. Something like that would really put a psychiatrist to the test.

But anyhow, is it me?, or does it seem like there's an enormous increase of ratio of the mentally ill nowadays as opposed to the past, taking new a newer generations into consideration? Are things really that bad? One place you'll never find me is sittin' on Dr. Psycho's couch all confused up on the seventeenth floor downtown somewhere. Well, someone could say that's because I'm not mentally tortured it would be foolish for me to be on Dr. Psycho's couch wasting his time. No, not really. I got the same story. I came up a little rough. Had some of the same problems. Still got some of them. Even got new ones. It's overwhelming at sometimes, but I don't need no witch doctor trying to pass it off as if falling apart about it is okay. And it now even has a modernized medical name. I got a name for it. I call it "get back on the horse" or "jackass," whichever you prefer. But as some of us know, even myself, is that sometimes the bartender's words of advise just don't go far enough for the safe sanctuary that makes us feel better or somewhat understand the situation in question. Feeling safe, as far as I'm concerned . . . is feeling secure about whatever you're thinking about . . . even security. I slew my demons . . . but I knew what they were before I knew what they could be. As previously mentioned, some of them even know how to take care of our kids 'cause we're too fucking stupid to do it right anymore. Johnny ain't the only kid out there who needed an attitude adjustment every now and then. Now it's frowned upon and basically illegal. Yeah, I know about all the child abuse in the past that led to all this, but as I mentioned, most of us are not that demented. Zero-tolerance, a k a zero-intelligence, quelled that problem but in doing so punishes all the rest of us who are sane. It took Johnny a long-ass time to learn the simplest things. And I was beginning to wonder if he actually liked all the beatings. He was beyond spankings, and sometimes it might spill into that. Suppose on of my kids comes home after a nasty felony, no matter what age, then he's gunna get beat not spanked. Niney-nine percent of children with behavioral malfunctions, require only a spanking. It's the other one percent that's got the shrinko werld all confused on any floor. Throughout history, raising children is probably one of the hardest jobs one will undertake. Showing them right from wrong. When they hit four or five . . . maybe alittle older, if they haven't learned right from wrong by then, soon you will be in trouble. When other people look at your kids with disgust and contempt cause they're beating the hell out of theirs, or anything else in which young children will not understand because they're *TOO YOUNG* to listen like an adult or acting up like normal kids do, that and that only is when a real good spanking is in order. Otherwise, by the time they're eight or nine, they'll be telling you what to do. The shrinko world seems to think otherwise. Bartering and reasoning with little children who've yet to develop any usable cognitive skills will solve the problem of little Junior beating the piss out of little sister Lisa. You should talk to him and expect in return, "Yes, Mommy dearest, due to the stress of a little Lisa's inability to recognize my right to exist as a fluid entity and to my basic needs to pummel the crap out of her, I realized I have crossed the line, and in the foreseeable future, I will circumvent my frustrations by jerking off instead. Thanks Ma." Problem solved. I hope no one has to spank their kids, but since they still come from the womb and not the test tube . . . children will be children.

To try to untangle the web of wires inside our domes is a daunting task at that and I can just imagine how hard that must be. It would be easier to count the grains of sand in Florida's coasts. I know progress because I've seen progress . . . mostly with drugs but also with dedicated people who truely believe they can help. But they can help you after diagnoses with certain drugs. I can do that on my own . . . laffing, smoking but . . . only joking. But also, that's not what I'm talking about. It's the "shot in the dark" theories that raise my eyebrow. No drugs involved, only with the people who come up with this shit. Like this, back in the Seventies the psychiatric community had what they thought was the Holy Grail of mental madness. They had discovered a woman named "Cybill" who seem to possess a host of different personalities, around twenty or so. Each personality wasn't just contained to the female gender. She was also Buffalo Bill I think. I could see where this could be a problem. You talkin' to me? I'm not sure, who are we today? All the top shrinks at the time gathered like the cure for cancer was found. It was big and on the news. Hollywood even made a movie about it. Now I know a con-job from a blow-job and I believe this chick was blowing smoke right up their brainstems, laughing all the way to whatever she was trying to accomplish. Me and Johnny got a kick out of this. Flash forward to 2001. On the news one night, what was once thought to be the holy grail of shrinkdom turns out to be a hoax. We knew that thirty something years ago. Good for her. I knew that something like that could never happen back in the Seventies, because something like that can only happen after watching too much Barney or those other kids shows that pretty much turn them into mush, and those character crushing shows didn't exist back then.

I've seen mental illness. You have too. I have seen people who I can definitely tell that I'm talking to someone who has some kind of connection problem with some of the neuro-stem cells upstairs. Whether or not drugs can help is not what I'm talking about here. It's the ones whose psycho-cells upstairs seem to be the same as mine, who seem to make up a lot of the mentally tortured nowadays that make me ask the question, "Is there something wrong with me too?" I don't think so. We all have crazy thoughts every now and then, but most of us don't act on them. Mentally retarded people make up some of our population and if that's not being punished, then I don't know what is. Why did God do that? What did someone do to deserve that? Does it happen and subspecies? What would a retarded elephant do? Same as all the rest of them . . . dodge bullets. *Something really needs to be done about that and don't get me started.* Someone needs to form an elephant army, one that protects all the elephants and all their buddies that they don't stomp on. But anyhow, that's mental illness and one can plainly see it. I don't question that or lesser illnesses that can be helped with drugs. What I want to know is, what was the beginning of a mental problem that I question in this essay, and while still children, and why wasn't it nipped in the bud? Kind of a stupid question, but I've been told before that I'm not the sharpest knife in the drawer. Like I said before, I had so many things go south, it almost became ritual. I guess I got lucky and slew the demons before they got me. I know that the psychiatric community is doing everything it possibly can to untangle the mind to make sense of it all, but I just got a problem with Dr. Psycho listening to your bullshit for an hour, tell you how to deal with it, maybe dope you up so you can make sense of it all for an hour or so, and send you on your way for three-hundred pieces. I can sling it all over the place just as good as they can . . . or maybe they can make it look like the bartender can't . . . maybe that's why they can make you what you need to be at that time. Ain't no time like the present! *Is it him or me? What's it gunna be?* It's not the loot, it's the simplicity. We all need someone we can lean on sometime in our lives. The seriousness of life I guess. I can fall down, need some help in getting up and say something that really needs saying or listen to something that really needs hearing and receive some pretty intelligible advice from friends and family. Alot of these people who occupy these couches already know what's going on or going wrong and just need a little help or a kick in the ass. The fucking rat race. Everything costs so much. Johnny just got his psycho diploma in the mail for two-hundred bucks and the doc is in starting tomorrow. Wanna go from bad to worse? He don't care either way, sounds like easy money to him.

As Johnny was coming up in his hometown, his parents moved within the town three times. He got to attend almost every school in town. They went from a small house to a larger house to the house ma now resides in nowadays. It seemed like every time one of his sisters was born, they moved. This moving around had some kind of effect on him 'cause every time he became part of the gang, he moved. This is back in early childhood and going crosstown to see your old buddies just didn't exist. Your horizons back then stretch maybe three blocks. No matter where he lived, he was always the runt of the pack. Nowadays he's one of the eldest in the pack. It's amazing what aging can do. But be careful what you do with it . . . it can kill you. He didn't get to see past friends until he entered middle school to where all the different neighborhoods were bussed. There were so many kids in his town they had to build another middle school. After not seeing them for years at a stretch, things just seemed different. He got close to people but only at arm's reach. Nowadays he does better with acquaintances more than with friends. He's got some down-home people . . . just not like one should at his age. Roots are a thing of the past. Only roots he's got are in the refrigerator. He'd rather travel alone and meet new people than to travel with other people. He don't know it, but there's a crowd everywhere he goes. That's 'cause his head is like a condo, with people coming and going at all times of the day. He just changes his mood to let someone in or out. Didn't we just discuss something like that alittle while back? He'll check out the town on his own. That's how he met his wife. He cares about people, but doesn't. If he can, then they can. He expects nothing less. If you can't, he'd probably help you then push you off the ledge. Fly or die. If you die, he blames your wings, not his push.

He's got a soft spot for kids and animals. They are all his friends. He's very polite toward women, often calling them ma'am. He isn't bothered by what anyone thinks of him as long as no one thinks he's some social misfit or livin' off a tangent somewhere. While his sisters were chic and en vogue, he was silhouetted somewhere in the background. He was at the party but in someone's car going down the highway. He could live on a mountain. He could live in metro. He could do solitary for however long the man says so. Doing what he has to do is one of his creeds. Doing what he wants to do is one of his fantasies.

During the Sixties, he came up grammar school and turned thirteen in 1970. The sixties were all frogs and forts. Plus the Sixties saw him do some dumb things as a kid that when he thinks back on, he usually cracks a cold one and smiles while shaking his head. Swimming in flood zones, BB gun fights, playing with trains . . . not toy trains like normal kids . . . and this fixation with fire that even around eight or nine years old caught the police's attention. Playing with trains. A combination of sheer luck and being frozen in fear got him through this day. One day all of his buddies were having a contest to see who could stand the closest to a moving train. He just had to win this one. While watching the trains roll on by, he noticed how much wider they were in than the actual tracks. They hung over each side of the tracks by at least two feet or so. Then he noticed how high it was from the bottom of the train cars to the ground where all the rocks were. Enough room to squeeze a person into. When the next train approached, everyone got to their place by the tracks and to everyone's astonishment, Johnny runs to the tracks and lays down about a foot or so away from the rail on the track, and the train goes right over him. The sound made him instantly terrified and when he saw the wheels that close to him, he started crying. All his friends started crying too, because they thought Johnny was no more. When it passed, he got up and ran around in hysterics and cried for the rest of the day. Hey Rusty, check out your kid. He's fricking crazy. Rusty would've had a heart attack had he seen that.

He vividly recalls the rebellious atmosphere of the country at these times. Kinda like now except as we are experiencing a rift between both parties. Back then the rift was between old America and radical change. Damn, not a damn thing's changed! *Even the players are the same.* Everything was being questioned. Authority was the devil. Still is sometimes. He watched a lot of his friends' older brothers go from Wally Cleaver to Jimi Hendrix in a relatively short period of time. He had many opportunities to change along with them, with all the psycho pills and dope flowing like water all around him. I can't begin to count how many times the pipe came to him and he just passed it on. Athletes just didn't do that. Well, back then. Not too sure about now. Right next door to Johnny's house were friends of Rusty's and Esther's. There was also a son and a daughter . . . a little bit older than Johnny, three or four grades above him. Their daughter was real hip and would throw these wild ass parties right next door. Johnny liked this. She was also very pretty. That's when he realized that as you get older, things just get better with the opposite sex. He knew girls being that pretty were for something, but still just couldn't quite figure out what for. Looking at playboy magazines blew his mind. He was goin' in the right direction. He didn't know too much, but he knew that. These were some wild parties. We were good friends with her brother and we would always be at these parties. Naked chicks losing at strip poker and dope is all we saw. This was the place to be, but no dope. We just didn't do that but loved the scenery. This is about when Grand Funk, Three Dog Night, and the Beatles were hittin' it. We saw a lot of Wally's walk in and a lot of Jimi's walk out during these times. We came real close to going to Woodstock with these people but Rusty got wind of that and put the brakes on that right quick.

When dinner and the homework was done, Johnny would watch TV with his family and would also watch the number one sports attraction, the Boston Red Sox. Conigliaro, Yazz, Petrucelli, Longborg . . . and oh yeah, that 1967 World Series. We all watched that. Couldn't even talk to Rusty for a week after that. They finally did it in 2004. Won the big dance. Should have won the previous year too. Did it again in 2007. Nothing like the American league East to spice up a rivalry battle. Even though the Yankees always made the cut at the end of the year, the Red Sox are better. Even though they weren't, that's the stuff you heard all over. Team loyalty over standings in the papers! Only in the northeast can you find at the end of a cul-de-sac three houses with three different baseball local favorites. One is for the Mets, another for the Red Sox, and the other for the Yankees. Find three houses anywhere else in the country that close to each other with such diversity amongst fans because all three teams are relatively local.

Much diversity in pro ball in the northeast with three different professional baseball teams living pretty much right next to each other.

We watched regular TV also. By regular, that meant no cable. It wasn't around back then. But there was something called pay TV. We didn't have it. The Sixties was very tame TV as compared to our present standards. I can take it or leave it nowadays. Not because I disagree with its primetime choices, but because I just can't sit around and watch a sitcom anymore. I have no attention span unless it's for sports, educational ie: Discovery, History Channel, "the Mangled Life", or a real good flick like "Beatledude." But I am a little irked by some of the crap I see on TV, all through the day and well into prime time. First of all,we need more commercials. Three hundred and eleventy-twelve just isn't enough for one hour. Even the History Channel sold out. By the time I finish watching the battle for Guadalcanal, it could have happened all over again by the time the show is over. Thirty-three percent of one hour is nothing but repetitive, piss me off commercials. But that has always irked people throughout TVs brief lifespan. No, there's something else. I'm not going to say we weren't influenced at all by the TV we had back then. Sitcoms back then were situated in all different settings, depicting all different times and environments. *The Munsters, Get Smart, Lost in Space, Gilligan's Island, Sky King, Voyage to the Bottom of the Sea* were just a piece of different TV shows with a bunch of different ideas floating around in Hollywood back then. Ya think there's still something floating around in Hollywood nowadays? Doesn't seem like the Yankee Doodle Dandy image it once possessed anymore. In fact, some "famous" remarks raise an eyebrow or two and sometimes the hair on the back of my neck. What happened? That's a mystical question with comical answers. Also, in fact, that's a good thing because all Americans can speak and assemble, and how does one learn from the other if the other isn't allowed to speak or assemble? We have a good system, but far-left hatred and ***near-sight-a-ness*** is putting the fire out in America's furnace. Enough jibber—jabber. Anyways while watching all these TV shows, Johnny would notice how the pretty leading actress would be situated by either some fast-paced scene or appearance to insinuate sex. That's as close as it got. You had to use your filthy imagination for the rest. Imagine being marooned in the middle of nowhere with Maryann and Ginger! *Imagine some idiot trying to get them* *rescued!* We thought that Batman was nuts for not wantin to bat-bunga with Batwoman upside down. Rub an ancient genie bottle and out pops a pretty superfine genie! Waking up to "Oliva, Oliva" on *Greenacres* in the morning are all things we all thought about and all the ingredients to think about women were there for us to watch . . . except one. You can touch mine if I can touch yours. Whoa! Get back! Leave mine alone. You broke yours off! Hodga do that? Sexual barriers have been broken, and I'm not sure if that's good or bad. Sure it's good to know certain things early in life, but it is equally important to let things fall into your life naturally the way it's supposed to be, not because alls the directors and producers in TV know that sex sells . . . and nothing else. XXX and insinuations of, are more common shots in TV than say . . . all the commercials combined. When I was a kid, we didn't have all the tits and ass, as close to penetration is possible, why stop at that?, no vulgarity, or show the whole world how fucked up you are on "the Jerry Springer show." TV gave me something to work on as a kid. Just as it is doing so at the present. I'm just concerned about the output after ingesting the input. Hey!, did you see how Captain Jigalo scored that luscious babe? Doesn't make any difference if the kid who saw that at seven o'clock at night is only seven or eight. He'll grow into it in about a week. To me, it's playing around with the future. A possible future of moral lawlessness. I just cannot see too much good come out of adulterized kids.

I'm pretty sure by now you've might have read a gay this or fag that along the way. I've got some gay friends down here in Atlanta and had some back north. They're all cool and I got their backs . . . not what you're thinking either, anytime and likewise, but it is something I will never understand. I'll just as soon understand the sub-atomic structure of the center of Pluto before I ever understand that. It's what I do understand that I think I'll comment on. First of all, most of these people are normal in appearance with regards to present-day norms as with most of us. You know the unwritten code . . . **your behavior versus others' respect.** No one even knows your sexual orientation unless you tell them. The way any morally responsible person conducts themselves, gay or not. Not to some people. These are the ones who only care about themselves. It's the *in your face* gay-is-the-only-way-to-go-won't-be-happy-until-even-my-dog-is-gay people who are professing all this while walking around looking like some sideshow-freakathon-lookin'-for-some-lovin'-manboy-in-spandex that's got my temperature. Change is natural, but it must go at its own pace. I see too much change in too little time. *Five minutes is five minutes, not five years.* Not that I can ever see such a change become a reality in my lifetime and beyond. We all saw the impact of traditional values at the 2004 presidential election. I will say this and I don't give a damn about any backlash from anyone, but all this innovative gay crap on TV, as innovative as it is, is a perversion of social values making damn near anything socially acceptable. Europe did that years ago. I give that continent about another fifty or so years. Pretty hard to keep it goin' when your buddy's hairy ass is more appealing than the queen's. You wanna watch that on TV? Then get a pay-for-it channel on cable so my seven year old don't have that crap *accessible* to him when I'm not home. I don't like that at all! After World War II, all the soldiers came home and saw their girls, and that's how we got our fabled baby boomer generation. Wouldn't have been any generation after that, if they had just saw each other. Remember the foxhole back in Normandy? How could I forget it? That just shows me that it's *not quite as mainstream* as some people are so desperately trying to force us to believe. And these marriages . . . what marriages? Last I knew, all five major religions scattered all over this planet for centuries have not significantly changed that much, if at all. Why start now? Playing with fire if you ask me. *Gays are people too,* with the *same rights* as everyone else, religious and all that but when you're messin' around with one of the seven Holy Sacraments, I just see a problem that is going to snowball well into the future and make one huge mess. Other than religiously sanctioned marriage, gays shouldn't be persecuted for doing what they do, they deserve all the bureaucratic procedures that everyone else gets while cruising through the course of life . . . from insurance all the way to probate. But the day I go to a wedding to see two dudes get hitched is the day I just stopped caring about the world in which my son's son's sons will have to live in. That means that the future will have to deal with God in the same way that the distant past was dealt with during the *partying years* of Sodom and Gomorrah. Well, let me step out of this just as gracefully as I stepped in: "Queer eye for the weird guy" just came on. In this episode, Poodles tells Puddles that he was mugged by a reverse-knob-job and wonders if he would like the udder end instead, 'cause mercy mercy me, life ain't what it used to be. Don't give me no shit over this . . . nuthin's what it's sposed' to be anymore!!

While on the subject of TV, I'll ask,whatever happened to the old-fashioned good ol' fun-for-the-whole family variety shows? *Dean Martin, Ed Sullivan, Glenn Campbell, the Smothers Brothers, Carroll Burnett, Sonny and Cher, Red Skelton, Flip Wilson, and Jackie Gleason* to this day, even as dated as they are, are some of the funniest clips made from scratch and gave birth to many stars, some of whom are still in front of the camera. *Rowan and Martin's Laugh-In* was the birth of the modern era as we know it now. Turn on and tune out was the call of the wild. Sitcoms followed suit. *The Monkeys, Mary Tyler Moore*, the young pretty divorcee unheard of on TV a few years prior. *The Brady Bunch*, the new and improved stepfamily all mirrored the modern day at that time. I remember *The Rat Patrol* and I remember *The Rat Pack.* Could the Rat Pack survive today? Smoking and getting drunk on stage with a rolling bar at a Las Vegas show. Alls I would see would be all those politically correct *clones* crashing the party 'cause it's hurtful to do those awful things to yourself. Apparently being an adult doesn't qualify one to make safe or not decisions. Yeah, some people think there's nothing wrong with that and your version of safe has nothing to do with mine. Well anyway, I really can't comment too much on present TV, 'cause I don't watch much mainstream TV or have anything to do with kapooters or electronics and think the internet is 2000 light years away. Johnny's worse. He can't even sit in the movie-house and watch a movie. He says they take too long. He loses interest and starts making noises while throwing popcorn all around. Not too bad for middle age.

Well, all is cool with the Sixties. Kind of like no rules anywhere, but there were. No one really cared. If things were that open nowadays, there wouldn't be enough paper for all the mugshots and prints. But there seems to lots of rules nowadays. If you're going to get caught, you'd better not be poor. That's the earthly version of hell. Starts out in limbo and seems to never go away. This entire novel was conceived while Johnny was doing a little summer-long stretch in Gwinnett County lockup in Georgia back in 2002. He got caught. He says the only things they didn't have in there were tennis and golf. Much better than jails up north. You don't even know if you'll be alive the next day at the Meadows in Hartford. On one fine day while standing in front of the judge in Connecticut, he was given the choice of fines, community service, or forty-eight hours in a drunk jail that used to be some army camp. He said, "Lock me up." Well, the drunk bus was full, and there was no more room so he went to the Meadows instead. As you can see, this was for a DUI. He was in an open dorm during the winter of 1993. The place is overcrowded like you wouldn't believe 'cause the jail is warm and it only makes sense to stay warm rather than die in the blistering cold. Sometimes you do what you have to do, not what you want to do. He got put in a two-man holding cell with eight other people, some not too friendly. Plus it's full of different street gangs. On the local news at six o'clock on TV, someone is shot dead on the streets. Half the dorm knows the victim; the other half know the shooter. On another fine day, the first day to be exact, Johnny's in line getting his lunch. He's got his tray with all of this food is looking for a table. He takes two steps and his tray and himself get sent to the floor. Never saw it coming. Comes to find out, gang-bangers eat first and he cut in line by accident. They stomped on all of his food and as he just sat back and watched rather than get shanked at around three in the morning. A lot of good brothers seen this and hook him up with some food later on. He says the black-eyed peas he got in there with the best he'd had north or south. But by a series of bad decisions versus tough choices, more often than not, most of his recent character-building situations he's been getting into left him with only a few, limited choices to chose from: bad or worse.

But that's ancient history. In this case in Georgia, he's in for forty-five days during the summer of 2002 for driving without a license for the sixth time in five years. Forty-five days isn't really enough time to lose it all, or as in his case again, but when you're living day-to-day on a wing and a prayer, being a father at that and failure is all you see, it's more than enough time. He even manages six days in the hole . . . real jail, for refusing to cut his hair. Hard-timers are laughing at all this but six days in the hole sucks. Never lost his sight through all of this and didn't need no pills to kill the pain. Withstand the shot. You really got no choice and just come out of it a "little bit smarter" is what he says. However, this was a nasty shot, and he came out of it with practically nothing. One dog and homeless for nine months or so. Some of his friends helped him out during these times staying here and staying there like a piece of old furniture, but as the old saying goes, "No place like home." All his stuff was packed up in a blowed-up van parked out in the woods and remained that way for over a year. He was truly lost. He takes it like nothing happened . . . just another challenge, no piss and vinegar but as it is. Start over, you got no choice. Standing back and looking at all this, I can say that I see it a little differently. This was a bad one. Everything he had all up in smoke and I can honestly say *that if it could rain pussy, he'd probably get hit on the head with a dick.* Not too much is sliding his way around these times but I'll get to that rainstorm later on during a gully-washer. But I got a few things on my mind to say about getting caught. It rearranges everything. Nine times out of ten, the judge already knows you're guilty. It's your job to lessen the blow. Even that one time when you think you're right, you'd better have a fat wallet . . . otherwise you lose. Humble yourself like Johnny did in front of the judge. He had some charges; probation violations, leaving the scene of an accident, and engaging the police a high-speed chase, which was dropped. Actually, the cop who caught him let that go. Never made it to the judge. That was the biggest break he ever got from the system in his entire life. Do yourself a favor and attend next years policemen's ball. Just be cool and respect their job and leave all the shit at the house. He's never seen that cop ever again.

But anyhow, he's now in jail trying to make bail. He can't do it because of his Massachusetts Department of Welfare ID. He has to have kinfolk in Georgia for help. He's got none, he only has his kids who were only in their teens back then. He's on the phone instructing some of his friends to be his ma, uncle, or nephew, anything that means kinfolk. The booking deputies are overhearing all this and laughing their asses off. He gets a hold of one of his carpetlaying buddies who tells Johnny that after he sells all his dope to come up with the money, he'll bail him out. Whatever it takes, I guess. Johnny gets out around one o'clock a.m. He was on probation in another county and stupidly tells his probation officer about the previous day on the phone. His PO (probation officer) tells him that if anything happens, he'll see to it that another sentence would be run concurrently with the one he's already on. Stinkin' lying sack of lawyer shit!! Johnny drives to his probation officer, senses something is not right and parks in the parking lot next door to the probation office and hides the keys somewhere in the pickup bed. Then he enters the spider web. He's arrested right on the spot and is sent to Gwinnett County lock and love shack. Lock the doors, love the food. He's the only person I know who's been booked and processed in two different counties in less than twenty-four hours. It was his insight that kept his truck from being towed, probably never to be seen again. He had someone come and get it. After two weeks of no bail, he is now allowed to stand in front of the magistrate judge for a set bail. However, his PO now tells Johnny that he's going to speak first, and requests that Johnny do a hundred and eighty days. Johnny wants to rip his head off and shit down his neck! He's got Johnny right by the gustanzos. His PO has three cases that day, and Johnny's is last. He lost the first two and Johnny's nervous because surely he can't lose all three. His PO speaks and Johnny's devastated. One hundred and eighty days are inevitable. Then the judge asks Johnny if there's anything he'd like to say before sentencing. Johnny says, "Yes, Your Honor." He stands up in his oversized green jailhouse jumpsuit and first states that he knows he's guilty. There is no dispute; I know why I'm here your honor. However, if I had a regular job or my destination were the same day after day, I would not be standing here today. Being a local contractor, I travel all over. I have people who drive for me come and go. Not enough work, too much work, and work's too hard, too many hours, money disputes, and other things, and sometimes I'm left hung out to dry. I have a family so I must work. He goes on for about five or six minutes and is finally told to be quiet by the judge. The judge is apparently moved by all this and knocks off a hundred and fifty days off the sentence. Johnny looks over and smiles at his PO with that *up your ass* expression on his face. Dickhead lost all three, and his job I heard. Moral of the story; don't do anything stupid, but if you do . . . pretend you're rich. They'll never know. You have the right to remain silent. Everything you say will be misquoted and used against you. In this case, that usual scenario didn't work.

Well, anyhow, he hits the Seventies. It's all sports and physical fitness. He remembers Arnold when he won his first Mr. Olympia. One big mutha@#$a! Sorry about that Arnold, but apparently you impressed him, because that's when he first started working out with weights. However, he was not allowed to play football at all in high school due to an accident he had back in junior high. This here was a life-changing experiance, and he still must cope with this problem to this day. He almost couldn't get into the military once they seen his x-rays. "What the hell happened to you?" he was asked. He explained. It was April 12, 1972, ten o'clock in the morning and Johnny was in gym class. They were doing gymnastics and Johnny was almost a damn wizard on the trampoline. No harness lines, just doing stuff that would sometimes draw the audience. All of his buddies were pretty good too. If he can do that, what else can he do? Not much after this. Now bear in mind, this was a professional trampoline, not one of those round ones you see in some people's backyards. This one was rectangular and was folded in half, stood up on its wheels and stored somewhere as to not take up too much space. To accomplish this, the entire gym class at the end of class would all line up along one half of the trampoline and push it up so it was perpendicular to the floor, give it a push, and then gravity does the rest is as it slammed down on the other half. The other half now had the first half on top of it and it was now folded in half. It was then stood up on its wheels and rolled away in the corner of the gymnasium. One half must weigh around for five-hundred pounds or so. Now what he did reminds me of an acid freak who thinks he can fly . . . *but really can't.* He was the only one on the wrong side of the trampoline with his arm resting perpendicular to the floor as if in an arm wrestling position on top of the blue padding all around the perimeter of the trampoline. This was before dope, so no one can explain why. Well, this huge mass with lots of momentum comes crashing down his arm, not even hesitating a split second when it hit, but slammed shut like his arm wasn't even there. When they all ran to the other side to lift it off his arm, it kinda wasn't there. It snapped his forearm like a twig and his hand was hanging out of the trampoline jammed into his armpit turned a hundred and eighty degrees from the way it was supposed to be. When they lifted it off, both forearm bones popped out and were drivin into the blue padding. He took his right arm and grabbed his mangled arm and pulled the bones out of the padding and then exclaimed "I need a doctor." I guess when something that traumatic happens, your brain overrides the incident and somehow you pull through. He pulled out around three inches of bone from the padding and knows what his bone marrow looks like. It took three operations to fix, and to this day, he's only got around seventy-five percent full use of it. His x-rays tell of a nasty accident. He was only thirteen years old when this happened. What a way to start out . . . deformed. Years prior, he learned being stupid hurts. See what happens when you drop your guard?! Not to be outdone by anyone, his firstborn son Justin breaks the same arm in the same place with the same severity when he was only five. The exact same break . . . like having two elbows on the same arm. They had better luck with him and now in his twenties, you really can't tell. Johnny wore a cast for so long, the red hairs on that arm all turned jet black. He looked like a freak for awhile with one skinny scrawny deformed arm with black hair and a normal one. He wore long-sleeved shirts for over a half a year while working that arm back to normal.

Because of that, high school football was out of the question. However, he was allowed to play football on the town league. He wore a special pad. He did a lot of sports with the town, including CYO basketball, playing all the other church teams. Plus playing town basketball also, the gyms were always open. Grab your ball and play all day and night. One time a buddy and myself walked into a gym with jai alai cestas made of wicker strapped to our hands and then slammed the ball into the wall, thus clearing out the people shooting hoops. "What the <rough word for bad word> you assholes doin'? You're gunna kill someone!" We apologized and left. Jai alai was big for awhile up in Hartford and Milford back in the Eighties.

But about now he's going from middle school to high school and now sees his own buddies succumb to the psychedelics and psychotics that go along with it when you first dive in. A brave new blow-your-mind world. Not too sure about brave . . . more like uncharted waters. After he took that first step, he still kept sports in his life. But that didn't last long with the new lifestyle colliding with the old one. What didn't help was all great music being made back then and prior, that lured us all away to all the great concerts we saw. Actually, it did help. Wouldn't change a thing. I look back on all the killer shows we have seen and now how it seems so mysterious. It was a real loose lifestyle, and some people don't survive it. Some people do, but you can tell that they either had too much, or they shouda thought twice. Johnny survived it quite well, but even though the door got slammed shut recently, you have to see how lucky he is to be alive. Not for the joy of life or happy for the hell of it, but because just by being there a second sooner or later a few different times, he should have been squished, squashed, run over, paralyzed, broken in half, or should have free-fallin' into huge rocks, and other incidents that should make anyone think twice. He would do lots of things without thinking first. *Want that rush? Then don't think about it . . . just do it.* Please don't listen to any of this unless you're well insured or crazy. He's got one the strongest guardian angels in heaven. Only angel up there that rides a H D. But anyhow, while watching everybody turning on, he threw the bong into the ring. He held out for quite some time, but now it was all about the buzz and the music. He had the privilege of coming up when all the great rock was so good, it was stigmatized as being evil, not embraced the way it is now with corporate sponsors now using rock for marketing. He remembers the *Ed Sullivan Show* bringing on acts like the Beatles, The Rolling Stones, The Doors, Sly and the Family Stone, and others and saw that rock 'n roll was the way of life and became mesmerized. Rock 'n roll was everywhere. The Standells were on the *Munsters* on one episode. Herman was a beatnik, predecessor the hippy. Boyce and Hart were on *I Dream of Jeannie.* I believe they along with Neil Diamond wrote some songs for the Monkees. A little song called "Psychotic Reaction" came out when he was only about ten or so and he couldn't believe what he was listening to. He really liked it.

When "In-A-Godda-Da-Vidda" came out in 1967, all of AM radio freaked out. There was no FM back in those days. Suddenly, all kinds of great bands, which most of us know today were formed and the rest is history. Rock music was the shout of the day, same as rap is nowadays. When rock got into the late Sixties, that's when if it wasn't all about drugs, peace, and women . . . it just wasn't livin.' Johnny got through all this and made it to the early Seventies. Not bad for those days. The Beatles left their "yeah, yeah, yeah" chorus for Helter-Skelter. The Stones got satanic. Early Pink Floyd was audio acid. Twenty-five or six to four? *Who put the garlic in the glue? Who called the Irishman a Jew?* Betcha ten bucks I heard that before. Johnny loved all of this, and by the early seventies, he was hooked. As he was sliding in head first into a drug-induced haze, he also listened to music that helped him stay sane and stable. This came in the form of black blues bands and Motown. In contrast to modern rap, old-school soul had sounds and lyrics that mirrored all the social dilemmas that were plaguing the country back then, especially with black folks, and unlike rap, was spreading the word largely by its blues background, which keeps it timeless from the day they were recorded to the present. The Temptations did more with their music to address social ills at the time, than say 'Iggy Pop and the Stooges' were doing with their music. That's okay 'cause one was for this and the other was for that that and *Funhouse* is still to this day the greatest good time eat-the-worm album ever done. If you like some real good, hardcore rock-n-roll, then *Funhouse* is what you want to hear. That's an album, about thirty-five years young from when this was writtin' that will still be hard to top. To me, there's none better. Johnny finally got to see *the Stooges* at Midtown Music Festival in Atlanta in 2001. But anyhow, rap and hip-hop as its predecessor, also mirror contemporary society . . . only in a different way. *Speak what's on your mind or forever hold your peace.* Rap has shown all of America and most of the world how some of the inner city lifers have to live right now and throughout all the past generations of city-project living. Yeah, some could do better but choose the easy way out. Same as the most of us, but not so scary. He listened to and had most of the stuff that was out, even P. Funk. Everybody remembers P. Funk? All of his stuff was on 45s 'cause those were cheap. When I was a lot younger, I often wondered how some bands would sound like in the future. Especially Jimi Hendrix. Can only imagine on that. I did predict back in those days rock would take a dive, which it did in my opinion. Remember the 80s? There were some bright spots back then, but they were far and few in between. And no one could have predicted the metamorphosis from soul to rap . . . not even black folks then. You won't find too many older whiteface crackers like me who like it all from A to Z with some favorites. Favorites come in all styles of music. From old school to "Deez Nuts" and beyond, music no matter what kind, even classical, has got to have two main ingredients, otherwise its chum. Who cares. It's gotta have beat and it's gotta have style even if it's copycatted. One without the other is like sugar, but no spice. I don't know about you, but sugar and spice and everything nice make the world go 'round. No beat no spice no matter what kind of music.

Rock, like rap, has the same thing in common, either the song's got it or it don't. Try again. *The Chronic* isn't just one of the best rap albums around . . . it's one of the best ever, all the way back to old school. I can hear all you moms out there, but never overlooked talent, especially when it's trying to tell you something. Rap uses violence for conveying its message, and violence gets attention. Just check out the rest of the world. Problem is nowadays, some of it is being brought to the same low level that TV does with its prime time porno for all the kiddies to see and now hear. I know that the radio bleeps out words of wisdom so that our adulterized juveniles won't know what's goin' on. How adulterized do we want out kids? But I don't care, 'cause if anyone or any group gots something to say or sing that sounds like it needs to be said or sung, then lay it out there along with the sugar and spice. Even gansta sounds good with a woman in the background. Long ago, I was watching the *Arsenio Hall Show* and while in a monologue he had mentioned the Ohio Players and asked, "Remember them?" You could almost hear a pin drop. Seemed like no one knew. I thought that that was strange. I'm just a dumb-ass white boy and I knew. "Fire" and "Love Rollercoaster." Yeah, it's dated. So ain't Wheaties but they're still good. How do you forget stuff like that? I'd like to see Outkast hang it out for as long as the Stones have. I'd like to hear some Stones songs rapped out but I'm pretty sure I got no say in that. Outkast got the talent to outlast. But back in those days, not only were rock and Motown moving at light speed, so was easy listening music. Stuff his parents listened to. Johnny thought all this music just sucked. That was then and this is now, and he's glad his parents injected some sanity into his musical persona. Herb Alpert, Brazil 66, Nat King Cole, and others from those carefree days produced music that will also forever become timeless. As time marches on, some later styles of music will soon be forgotten with each passing day. Later styles of rock forgot how to roll. Easy listening has always remained true to itself. Boy bands are just that . . . boys. Not really, but c'mon! But that's just my perspective. Don't mean *shee'at*. I wonder if someone could sound like Tull? Tony Snow sure did! Diane Warwick and Bert Bacharach? Bring your date to that one. Patsy Cline or the Yardbirds? Either way. But back in those days he couldn't care less about all this while listening to "Temptation Eyes" or the Beatles, and now appreciates what he heard from his parents' stereo to this day, 'cause "Walk On By" and "Chances Are" are just as good as whatever kind of tunes you like.

One thing I do notice about contemporary music is how high-tech it seems to have got. I don't need a cassette tape or even a CD anymore. I can store eleven billion songs somewhere my laptop. Someday when I learn how to download, I would like to retrieve any song I want and burn it onto a disk. I understand that's very taboo nowadays. What's the difference between the bootleg cassette tapes of yesteryear and copying and the swapping of files nowadays? Well, I'm not too technologically challenged to realize that that would be like comparing the abacus to the computer. In the past, I've heard of, and seen about enough bootleg tapes in the market to catch the attention of record execs. Enough to irritate but not really enough to break the bank. You know what kind of money they make. Enter the computer and information highway. That's not necessarily true anymore. Virtually all music can be downloaded for nothing the same way we recorded our tapes. It's the volume of music for sale that is just there for the taking by the public that's got all the record execs on the warpath. You can see the recording industry's dilemma. Profit over progress. Computer sciences are advancing everyday to even think that enforcing copyright laws for profit is going to stop the progress is like taking the 100 mile per gallon carburetor and shelving it forever. How the record business, whose pattern of existence hasn't changed since Elvis deals with this without enforcing laws without completely conceding to progress is the dilemma that I see. No one can stop progress, no matter how big you are. As far as the carburetor, I think it's all but impossible to coax the same amount of power from the big V-8 on one tenth the fuel. But as I said a while back, there was no FM. Now we got FM. I get to hear the same song by Fleetwood Mac three to four hundred times a week. I haven't heard "White Punks on Dope" once.

By now, he's in high school. Freshman year in 1971 was all sports. By his junior year he went from sports fanatic to basically a part time junkie. What used to be was exactly that. I remember the first time me and Johnny smoked a joint. It was insomeone's van going down the road. He thought the road was going to come through the windshield. Johnny, after that started hitten' all the psycho pills that were going around back then. Then came some of the stupid stuff. Like one day his buddy and himself were driving down to Virginia Beach after blowing off school. Drop the car off to someone in the Navy stationed at Newport News and hitchhike back. They immediately went broke when they got there. They would raid gardens, and do an occasional dine and dash, and had dope that kept them from being hungry. They stopped by a friend's place, who lived in Elizabeth, New Jersey and stayed there for a few days. First-time Johnny's done MDA. Don't even ask. It will make you like him. He thought those three letters meant something about some disease. Not much difference between the both. They were supposed to be in school, but they had a blast anyways. Some other time while taking all four lunches at school, I saw him over out in the field with some other people. I walked up and ask him if he's ready for the trackmeet after school. He's got a beer and is messin' around with some mescaline he ate earlier. He tosses the beer and is wondering if he should attend the meet in such a state. He thought the trackmeet was the next day. His event requires eight laps around the track and he managed a fourth place finish. After that, he threw in the towel and his junior and senior years included no sports whatsoever. He had been consumed. It seemed all downhill from now on. Problem being, he couldn't see it. It took many years and some self-abuse for him to see the light.

While enjoying those days, he also got a job at Bradley Field International Airport, just north of Hartford in Windsor Locks. Complete with an air museum. There was a real, just-like-a-midwest tornado that ripped the shit out of the north part of town and parts of Windsor Locks back in 1979. It got the museum, but that's all been healed by now. There's no damage like the damage from a tornado that can explain the nightmare. But he works at the employee cafeteria and the coffee shop upstairs that's open to the public. He is a short-order cook and dishwasher when needed. He loved his job 'cause he got to know everyone from towns all around them. Coulda made a TV show about this job. Got to know all kinds of places to go besides his home town. One of those jobs where anything goes. Even dumb stuff like this. He made a customer a milkshake and he put some chopped onions in it. He told a buddy, "Watch this." When the customer inquired as to what was the solid stuff in the shake, he replied, "chopped onions." The customer threw the shake at Johnny but he kinda knew that might happen, and dodged the flying shake. Somehow he didn't get fired. That's because everyone, even the supervisors were just like him. He drove a 1969 droptop Camaro that was all sterioded up from the 327 Chevy mouse motor up front all the way to the 4:11 see-ya-laters in the back. He would drive it to school . . . any school, any school except his. He would go to one of his co-workers' school in some other town, hang out all day in the parking lot, then go to his own school for last period. Johnny and one of his buddies once got caught walking around some other school barefoot. The inquiring teacher they came across in a hallway asked them who they were. They said they were new. The teacher then inquired about the lack of shoes and one thing led to another and they got caught up in their own web. You guys don't look like you know too much, but you should at least know what school you're supposed to be in. Come to my office. No doubt about it, his academics took a hit. Didn't even know what sports were by then. But this novel isn't only about flameout. It's also about knowing how to stay on the surfboard no matter what, even if it's just your first time. *Sharks love flameouts.*

By the time he got to his later years in school, the word *Vietnam* wasn't causing as much a threat as it was a few years earlier. He remembers the Easter Offensive in 1972, and even with the peace talks, everything escalated again, and for while he figured that it would happen again, when it's about time to graduate. But as we all know, that didn't happen and in 1973, a lot of POWs were released and the draft was rescinded. Anyone remember POW bracelets? You can't begin to imagine the draft. That's because it made no sense for a bullshit war only because it was commanded by civilians and Army brass thousands of miles away, and the draftees knew that they were nothing but pawns on the chessboard. I want my team leader to be part of my own army, not some protected politician who doesn't even own a gun. At least with a draft nowadays, it would be something for which worth fighting for. Need to take a poll on that. But back then, we would see the older brothers of our friends look at page two of the local newspaper and match the lottery numbers to the ones on their draft card, and more often than not, we'd see the look of doom on some faces. We saw lots of people burning their draft cards and all the draft protests. I'm told that the draft protests during the Civil War were the biggest America's experienced, but for some reason, I don't recall those. I only go back as far as the massacre. We saw people come back messed up and it scared the living bejezus out of us. What if by some twist of fate, we had to go? To run and hide? Thus making it hard to even look at yourself in the mirror? Or to go and put your life in fate's hand? Fate is all you got left. No one decides to step on a landmine. Johnny joined the Air Force. Family tradition. A lot of people got out of it by attending college. That was for rich kids, plus they furthered their education at the same time. Rich kids couldn't care less about education, just as long as they remain stateside. Going to school for proctology kept you out. That's a tough call, not for the implications of that decision, but *how many more assholes do we need?*

If my kid ever comes up to me and tells me he's gunna be a proctologist, then I'm gunna look at him a little differently. I know that we need them but that's still a tough call. Anyway, we all know that everything ended in April of 1975 and all the stress was gone. A war in which we got the upper hand, but still lost. Guerrilla warfare on their own soil, and we only left because Joe Six-Pack's kids were all getting all shot up and Congress saw that soon they would have to send in their own. When Washington first sent us in, we couldn't shoot first. We had to wait until fired upon. What the hell is that? Do not blame the U.S. military for the defeat, but put the blame squarely where it belongs . . . on Congress and the likes. Not quite as vile as the present, but politicians need to work with the military more than as I often hear, rather than against the military!! Anyone can call a war, ten thousand miles away. We handed the enemy pretty much everything except their asses and those got shoved down their throats and Congress still screwed that all up.

Just so some *newcomers* who might want to know before a possible public deviation from the truth, the American military showed why the American military is what it was and will always be, despite fighting in nothing but suicidal, guerrilla, "win at any cost" enemy mindset . . . same as now, but the threat of internal (their own people) retaliation was too much for the democratic free world to win the hearts and minds of the Vietnamese people for anything to take root. And that is the only way for anything to take root, you gain someone's confidence through "for the common cause and the common man, that means all of us", whatever it takes to get to that understanding to another or others. The enemy represented everything we are not . . . same as present conditions, a totalitarian state, who knew our misconceived doctrines like breaking off after they crossed over into Cambodia and Laos, even when we had both hands around their <you know what> necks. We had LRRP (lerps) and recondo but there's nothing like a good 'ole down-home B-52 to grab your attention. *Crawl in those holes maggots, time for a little landscaping.* Ahh, the smell of homemade napalm . . . the best kind. Remember, napalm sticks very well to bad guys and little kids. That was then and now is now. Pretty much the same problem only for very different reasons. One thing that hasn't changed though . . . we're only trying to help. Whoa, everybody quiet down, sit down and let me try to make some kinda sense of it all.

Well, that didn't work. *I shouldn't have to say anything . . . we should all know this by now.* We now have to deal with Islamic covert fundamentalists all over the Middle East, while dealing with a low world opinion against us. How nice. But it was us who got attacked. Iraq is now a haven for terrorists. What was it before? Club Med? We are hated by a lot of Third-World cesspools that stink up this planet. Maybe by cleaning up what makes up these cesspools . . . the Mickey Mouse governments, maybe all of the inhabitants of these countries will have a chance to see what we're all about. Is that our job? some say. By our, that means all the free world. I can only comment on this later. But when I do comment later, I really don't see it any way else since the entity that's in place for such actions doesn't or hasn't the ways and means to help out. This would be the United Nations, conceived to help out the world. Yeah, they mean well, but when living with that decision scares the living shit out of them, I don't see much leadership. It wouldn't bother me at all if they were moved four hundred miles east. They'd be just as effective.

I've never been on campus before, but I shouldn't let that stop me from commenting on extended secondary education. Alls I gots is four degrees in alcoholism . . . workin' on me fifth. This is what you want: a chance to excel. I've seen so many people take that chance and screw it all up. Johnny's youngest, Amanda, graduates high school in 2005, and he wants her to go. Who wouldn't? But lately a lot of universities are about as American as camel-shit pie. Back in Vietnam, it was the students. Now it's the professors. What a contrast. What happened? Maybe our hypercritical baby boomer generation never left college. They simply went from student to professor. Dropped the anti-establishment attitude in the Sixties, and took the all about me- me-me Eighties to new heights. A complete turnaround of beliefs. When JFK's famous words *Ask not what your country can do for you, ask what you can do for your country* were still reverberating around the country, their faces were still buried in the bong. When they saw that that didn't pay the bills, pad the portfolio, or buy the shoreline cottage, they became what they despised so much in the beginning. Talk about coming full circle!! How convenient! I can't sit here and write negatively about colleges because I know that not all colleges are as anti-tradition as I'm led to believe, and a college education is coveted and can open doors that otherwise will remain locked to anyone else. But what's up with all of this philosophical tidal waves of forced change that seem to go against the grain of some of our two-hundred forty year old wood? Some things are as solid as the "Charter Oak" tree in Hartford. Connecticut was founded there. Some people want to chop it down. My question is "Why?" *Chop it down* is a metaphor . . . not logging. Some college lecturers degrades marriage, and pisses on the military for using the atom bomb in Japan. Tell that to Joe grunt who lost half his buddies on Okinawa. Some know how to run the country better than the president, or they think. From now on, everybody gets paid the same and you are all entitled to all that even though you only did half the work as your co-worker standing next to you. That's been tried before. Don't work. Socialism does exist in some countries, most notably our northern neighbor, and does work . . . but only to an extent. When competition is diminished, so is everything else. *Capitalism breeds imagination and innovation.*

Students are told Christopher Columbus was a barbaric savage. So were white men headed west years later. Don't hear too much about them except the romanticism of the era in which they lived. That doesn't change the fact that Columbus was the second European to arrive in North America in 1492. The Vikings were first and have now settled down in Minnesota. Most of them now play football. So why do they now piss on a piece of American history? Say what you want about Columbus, but I'll say this. Considering what modern day Navies have to endure with mother nature nowadays, these people did the very same thing six hundred years ago in wooden dingies with sails and planks. *Planks for whiners* just like what I hear all over the *trenchcoat media* day after day. I like Columbus Day even though I work it for straight time. Some professor at Columbia University even went as far as telling his class why for the sake of political science, the United States needs to lose everything in Iraq. That's his right, I guess. It's anyone else's right to see that his right is beaten to the point, he'd wish he'd never had said that. Are we on the same page here? Other professors are also making news by taking the First Amendment to new heights. In the name of the First Amendment protection, they can demonize anything or whatever America represents or what it stood for in the past. Do they have that right? Some might not like this, but yes they do. I'm part of the some who don't, but that's not my call. That's America, good or bad, for better or worse, till debt do us part. So, you fight back. This is not the first time America has been attacked from within. You do not let a vocal majority or minority, depending on whose reading this, contaminate college minds. One way or the other, some people who have not yet settled into the American dream, or even the chase for it by now and can't cope for some reason or another, need to literally change countries in their own minds while changing their own diapers. Not Depends . . . those are for adults. Neil Diamond wrote a pretty good song called *Forever in Diapers*. Please don't sue me . . . just tryin' to make a point. But I hope to hell that's not true.

America is supposed to change. That's the basis of our national ideology. Change could be for the better, or from what I hear sometimes on campus, for the worse. Either way, it should remain natural. Throughout history, most forced change did nothing but invite disaster. I'm not going into specific instances 'cause we already learned about that back in school, because I know that if you force me or anyone else to change drastically practically overnight . . . I'm really not gunna like it and it's gunna give me incentive to do whatever I need or want to get my point across also . . . civily of course. This country is crawlin' with too many diaper-wipers and I wish I was talkin' about babies!! Please keep all this shit up so that I can finally see the sleeping giant in America wake up again. Been asleep for many-something-moons or longer years now . . . or later. You wanna try and change my country like that? David's not gunna have it that easy this time. David might not be the good guy this time. And that's really a hell of way to put it from my perspective. Conservative professors? I'm sure, but for some reason, they are the minorities in the classroom. It's like they have leprosy. Liberal professors? As sure as the sun appears every day. It's like they have ecstasy. Why are all the conservatives and liberals on the verge of civil war? I see that coming, but why? Is it because that one stands for one thing, and the other for something else, and now or soon after, our national ideology is just going to be brushed aside so one can dominate the other? Countries are borne by government. The same countries also die by it. As you can plainly see, I'm alot of old school. But sometimes there's nothing like new school. Best new school that comes to mind happened in 1776. It took liberal people to make that happen. You want change? How about we just overtake your colonies and call them America? So you see, it goes both ways . . . which seems to be the *in* phrase in Congress nowadays. But nowadays it's going in reverse. You want change? Then change for the better, not for some of this I'll-do-your-thinking-for-ya-futuristic-utopian -garbage-that-I'm-not-sure-if-I-would-want-to-live-in-even-if-it-existed-today. Everything now becomes the way most liberals envision. Now what? Depends on the liberal. Just like everyone else, everyone thinks just alittle bit different no matter what the label. There's two kinds of liberal people out there; the one's who remember history, and the one's who never learned from it. One of the two was responsible for that infamous half-wit saying from the courthouse many years ago; *not-guilty by reason of insanity*. Only the sane can't kill. The insane are supposed to kill. But anyhow, everybody is now friends. That's pretty good. No problem with that. Wine pours from every spout. Children are innocent until age twenty-one. If not, that's okay . . . they're supposed to do that. We see things the way they're supposed to be. The way things really are, are really really bad so we'll just ignore it and it should go away if everybody is real nice to one another. I like your philosophy . . . really do, but we're probably centuries away from "Star Trek." Weren't they still fighting something on that show every week? Natural *change* is where it's at. Five minutes will always be five minutes. Natural change is going to take forever, the impatient will say. No it won't, it'll only take as long as how long something natural takes. Not a second sooner, not a second later. When something is right, we'll all know about it. When only half of us know, it needs to go back in the pot, not in my face.

Just about everyone I know thinks like this, but strength in numbers doesn't seem to matter anymore. I wanna know why. Liberalism is like a small tree growing in the forest amongst all the big redwoods (conservatism) that have been there many years before. Liberalism means change, so in order to change something, something else has to previously exist . . . good or bad. Either it grows out of the shadows, or it dies. The two will never mix and at this point in time, won't even find a common denominator. That's what gets me alittle agitated. Everyone is worried about a *Brave New World* in which we now live and others are worried 'cause gays can't get married to each other. *That became a main topic within the democratic section of Congress* ***not too much later*** *than when 9-11 happened.* **priorities, Priorities, PRIORITIES!!** Liberalism is what brought us here. Ask any Revolutionary war vet. Conservatism is what's going to keep us here. Ask any 9-11 survivor. Liberalism is supposed to mean change for the better. Changing for the unnatural *world of wondering without reasoning* with no seasoning is one of the reasons this book has been written. Some more stupid crap I wrote throughout this mess . . . this time it don't get erased. I even season my beer. But Johnny is nothing but some two-bit—drop-shot-screw-the-government-junkie, but he still die for this country. It's the best thing earth has got. Not because of the almighty America. But because we can help. The December '04" tsunami comes to mind. So don't generous humanitarian aid to under-privalaged countries in Africa by President I-can't-even-say-his-name. I'd like to see some of these professors debate Washington, Adams, and Jefferson on just what their interpretations and strangulations of the First Amendment means to them, as opposed to what it was originally meant to be. I'm just going to leave this at that. Can't fight anymore. I'm on my tenth beer, and I concede. Everything I just said is wrong and stupid. What am I? Joe nobody trying to screw up the world? Or someone who's heard enough. Let your parakeet decide. Why not? May as well. They're birdbrains and that's pretty much what I'm used to nowadays. You know how piss poor that is? Define the First Amendment. It only takes up a few paragraphs, but nowadays it could take up to Ken Starr's vanload of anti-Bill Clinton rantings. He sure didn't like Clinton. Political hatred? That guy looks like he can't even spell the word *work*. Sure worked on that vanload. Hate the SOB that bad? To hell with the vanload!! Back of the head. The sword is mightier than the pen if you're that friggen pissed! Clinton messed up by getting caught on something that I think he shouldn't have done, why get married? But I don't think that in the process he messed up the country. Define shit. Brown and disgusting, just like this debate. This dialogue is starting to smell, so it-soon-time to move on. But not before this. Did Charles Manson's opinion matter? Used to . . . but life, liberty, and the pursuit of happiness were in peril. Did Jim Jones opinion matter? Ask the survivors of nine hundred ghosts. I believe they thought of themselves as some kind of professor. What kind? This is what I'm trying to figure out at the present with our trusted scholars teaching our young, impressionable college students something that I think really *needs to be looked into*. Call it what you want. I call it future insurance. College life is supposed to be the springboard of your career. If it's marred by some biased professor, then I believe that he or she should be held accountable for conspiracy to retard your full potential by using cult-like tactics. Lay out all sides, that's how one solves a problem. When Amanda comes home from college doing the goose-step, Johnny will be on the six o'clock news that night. Take that to the bank! My kid comes home from college on break with the thousand yard scare because some biased asshole college professor is trying to indoctrinate her? Then I'll also make the front page of the *New Ya'rk Times*. Then it's off to prison with the biggest ear-to-ear smile you ever saw on a condemned man. Why can't they just leave America the wicked alone? Bye, bye, Miss Sorority pie, 'cause your sons and your daughters are questioning why, why the veterans and military are willing to die . . . freedom for your college that's why. We preserve freedom of speech by dying for it so that it can be used to attack ourselves. I'm lost. Musta zagged when I shoulda zigged. Touch a nerve? Good. Got any nerve? Hope so. Never nervous? Who cares.

Well, anyhow, Johnny is still a schoolboy. He's at the threshold of his adolescence, and he is about to test the water of those times by diving without looking first. He looks back now at high school and smiles about it with no remorse. He looks back at those years for justification for what he does at the present. He knows the ramifications had he not run that course back then and chose to open up that lifestyle years later. He learned early in life the consequences of his actions. For every action, there always will be a reaction. That's basic. He's in a bit of a situation as I pen this sentence and knows why and even if he could change it, views it as just character building. How much more character building does someone of almost fifty years of age need? He should be an apostle by now and could use some relief but I guess his character still needs shoring up. Had he walked the straight and narrow way back and deviated from that much later, I don't think he would've learned anything worthy enough to save his ass at the present. In other words, learn it all as soon as possible, the good and bad, so that you'll have enough smarts to know what to do when you fall and no one is there to catch you. Sometimes we break laws. Sometimes you only need to bend them. Hard Knock State says: *It's not what you know that's going to help you, it's what you don't know that's going to hurt you.* Just like the tuition college, Hard Knock is just as helpful. If not more when the shit hits the fan.

When Johnny was ten or so, his parents and uncle Jimmy bought a real nice A-frame cabin in southern Vermont. It is somewhere along the West river up Highway 30 near a small little town called Newfane. Biggest town anywhere near is Brattleboro. If you like mountains and wilderness, you'll fall in love up here. Creeks that you can drink out of to this day. Spear fishing in a two feet of water. Like frog legs? We speared those too. This was Rusty's hideaway. You want to see a bunch of cops cut loose and have a good time? They were off duty . . . which we know they never really are . . . but up there they were off duty. When you're that isolated, you are off duty. Johnny and his buddies loved hanging around these guys. They were all armed, relegating Johnny and his friends to BB guns and slingshots. As the generations pass, he would take his own two sons up to the cabin for the same reason Rusty went. Just the three of them. Not being stupid, he was also always armed with a rifle and a .38 for close calls. You never know out of the woods. Wild beast or worse, wild human. Either way, firearms tame the wild. This may sound a little weird, but Johnny would hate to take down a wild beast for doing what only comes natural. Wild humans can think.

One night in the late Eighties, he brought both Nick and Justin up to the cabin. Amanda was still a baby at that time. Womenfolk stayed at home while the men folk went out in the wild. Sounds pretty nineteenth century or so. Sounds like a good time also. He brought all his shit; beer, alittle weed, and a bunch of cassette tapes he recorded or stole depending on how you look at it. He also brought some food he got at the local general store at the bottom of the mountain. When he got out of the car after he arrived at the cabin, he turned to Nick, who was asleep in his car seat in the front seat and was horriflyed by what he saw. Nuclear Nick, before he went to sleep, had unraveled every cassette tape with which he brought up to rock out with. Alls he saw was cassette-tape spaghetti and the top of Nick's head. That's all you could see of him 'cause unraveled cassette spaghetti was everywhere. Johnny almost left him on the side of the road. Little Nick put a crimp in the night he had planned. While he was driving up there, he didn't catch what Nick was doing 'cause it is so dark on the dirt roads with no street lights and the tunes were wide open.

Night-vision goggles wouldn't even work up there. Dark side of the Moon. Well, there is a local radio station out of Brattleboro that was pretty good, so they just gathered wood and enjoyed a nice bonfire. Johnny practiced his marksmanship, and when a shitty song came over the radio, looked over at Nick. Justin said, "Don't do it dad, he's my brother." Johnny and the boys ate what they cooked on the fire and when that was over, he showed them how he could light off firecrackers in his mouth. Shoulda seen Justin and Nick's eyes when they saw that. How does one learn how to do something like that? Years later, while doing the same thing, he blew his bottom lip apart and knew something went alittle wrong. When you get alittle loose, pay alittle attention to the absurd. Especially when you're alittle lit. Whatz a big lit? The next day, they were out in the woods looking for quail or anything else to eat. Justin wanted to carry the rifle and wouldn't shut up about it, so Johnny disarmed it and gave it to him. As they transversed the woods, they came across a local woman who lived nearby where they were. She sees this little kid carrying a rifle and looked at Johnny like he's crazy or something. Plus Johnny was telling Justin and Nick some stupid, mindless stuff about aliens hiding in the woods spying on them, which she overheard. He got embarrassed because of how real he made it sound. She looked at Justin with the rifle. She turned to Johnny and shouted "What kind of father are you?" That pissed him off and he replied, "The kind who teaches his kids how to kill at an early age," at this point just wantin' to piss her off hard. They depart and he now scopes the area real good before talking any dumb shit and everything is good. As good as it's going to get with her.

During the winter, unless you have a snowmobile, you'll have to park on the bottom of the mountain and walk up. Naturally, we had snowmobiles. Beautiful, pristine, pearl white winter wonderland in the middle of nowhere with nothing but dense forest all around you. Rusty taught Johnny how to ski when he was skiing for the ski patrol way back in the sixties. He learned how to ski when he was ten or so. Both his sisters skied in the beginning but moved on to much more tamer activities after enough wipeouts. He still knows how to ski, but it's been ten years or so since he skied. Being in Metro Atlanta and all. The snow down here, you really can't ski on. If you ever do ski down a mountain of that, don't get caught, they'll give ya a million years. We would all gear up for the winter and head up to the cabin for a weekend of skiing. The cabin was situated next to a lot of big ski resorts like Stratton, Killington, Mount Snow, and others. We put on small backpacks to carry all our stuff like dope and brandy . . . *blackberry* to be exact. Plus rolling papers, lighters, and maybe a beer or two. Beers were always in cans and the brandy in the goatskin or a plastic container. No glass. Wiping out could be catastrophic. Not only does a half pint keep you warm, but you have a tendency to turn your skiing up a notch or two. At least with Johnny, not much fear on the slopes. One time when skiing with Rusty, he saw Johnny do some pretty good stuff on some pretty steep jumps and sternly reminded Johnny that he had two kids. Amanda wasn't born yet. Another time while skiing with his buddies, he sold about an ounce of hashiesh broken down into grams going up the chair lift all day long. They like to have fun on the slopes and hang out at the ski lodge at night. I do remember this one time he got impatient with a kid who had wiped out on landing after being launched off this killer jump. It was Johnny's turn next and this kid kept on slipping trying to get off the icy landing zone. Johnny waited long enough and gave that jump everything he had. He was close to two stories in the air and landed about two to five feet away from the kid. Lots of two's but even two inches can make or break it forever gone. Lots of people turned their heads 'cause it was that close. He caught a lot of shit for that. Almost had to leave the mountian for the rest of the day 'cause some of the ski-lodge personel that saw that and talked to him the same way you or anyone else would talk to a two-legged, hammered-toed, no-headed, smart-ass Sloth. He told me, "You should have seen his eyes on my way down."

But it wasn't all just skiing in the winter. They would leave the cabin at night and often go to Brattleboro or anywhere to hit the clubs. His sister Patty, and her boyfriend, Johnny, and his wife were in some club and Brattleboro and heard about some pretty good band playing at a ski lodge on Route 30 going back toward the cabin, so they went. They stayed there till closing and noticed how the snow fell throughout the night and accumulated to over a foot it and it was still snowing. They didn't have a snowmobile so they had to walk up the mountain when they got back. The snow was about up to your upper thighs, right around where they are attached to the lower ass. Johnny's wife is a little more dressed for clubbing, not hiking 'cause no one anticipated the sudden snowfall. Johnny tried to piggyback her but the snow was too deep. Patty had boots in the car, his wife didn't. So he told her to just walk in his steps and she'll be okay. He's took these giant steps, which she can't navigate thus pissing her off hard. She's cussing the shit out of him and throwing anything she can find at him. He got a kick out of it and almost got his shit bit off later on that night. And he wonders why he's divorced.

He would also take the whole family plus sisters, cousins, brother-in-law, and anyone in the family, and friends up there for weeks at a time during the summer. The upstairs was one big ole' giant loft so everyone was comfortable. They would take to the army corps dam up in Townsend or find all the high cliffs from which you can dive from at all the creeks all over the place. After swimming, it was time to whip out the fishing rod and catch dinner. On vacation during some summer, he's up there with his brother-in-law Sal, who has his family, and Johnny told him he knows where there is a nudist part of the creek way up the creek. Sal says let's go. They tell everyone they'll be right back. While traversing the path to get there, what Johnny fails to tell Sal is that a couple of hundred yards past the nudist beach there is also a fagalo beach and takes him there first for a joke. They get there and alls you see are all these naked fa'galos . . . that's Italian, just a wockin' and a wollin'. *You had to see this.* Johnny is trying to keep from bustin' out laughing. Then these twodudes walk on by with one leading the other by a chain. Guess where it was attached to? Sal sees that and that's when he realizes what's going on. He looks over at Johnny with the look of utter confusion coming across his face and says to Johnny, "What the hell is wrong with you?" Johnny says, "See that one over there? He like-a-you mo' than he like-a-me. I never be da same." "Fu*k you!, they all like dickbrains like you and you should be beat . . . asshole!! Lets get the fug otta here!" Johnny can't contain himself anymore and bursts out laffing real loud, thus pissing off a lot of fa'galos. Itz not nice to laugh at people, but blatant pretty weird, strange-o behavior like that is something that I find kinda amusing. Why? Only God knows. Only the gay. Men that is. Gay women seem to have alittle bit and alot more morals than that. I don't know about you but I can't think of too many things worser than getting beat up by a queer . . . especially a naked one, so they left while dodging a few rocks. They wound up at the nudist beach and spent the whole day partying with naked chicks. Not really partying, just a lot of standing around for the hell of it.

But aside from that, way back around 1967 or so, Johnny seen a bear walking around the cabin grounds like it owned the place. When it saw Rusty, it scooted away. Johnny's running around inside the cabin screaming, "bear! bear! bear!" coming out of him at the top of his lungs. At about the same time, he was up there with a friend whose parents let him come up with Johnny's family. One day they walked up the next mountain which took all day. Way out in the deep woods . . . . messin' wid Sascrotch! They got lost and Rusty sent a posse out to look for them. When they realized how lost they really were, they decided to build a lean-to out of twigs, branches, and leaves. While doing so, they hear this loud, piercing scream directly behind them which scared the hell out of them. They turn to see this little tiny fawn about a foot and a half tall just standing there by itself. The doe musta got shot. They abandoned the lean-to and the fawn followed them everywhere they went even screaming when it can't keep up. They got back to the cabin after the searchers got back from them looking for them and now Rusty's got the game warden there to help find Johnny and his buddy. They came walking up with a baby deer trailing right behind them. The game warden took the fawn and Johnny wondered about its fate after seeing all the dressed deer hanging everywhere. He just recently seen five bears up behind a nightclub in Helen, Georgia in the mountains in the northeast part of Georgia. The mama and the papa and the three cubs. They were raiding the dumpster and we all stayed away. Bears need to live to, so let's just turn all the woods into subdivisions and screw all the wildlife. Check out metro Atlanta expansion. No planning. Just bulldoze everything in the way, no matter what. County planning seems to be pretty much nonexistent down here, which I'm sure is the same anywhere money can be made. Makes me wonder sometimes if we all live in Kickback County. Another thing that pisses him off are poachers. Kill a bear only for its gallbladder? He would just love to give poachers the *same chance* they give their prey. Out of nowhere. Go home and have a beer or two afterwards. But anyhow, the cabin becomes a part of life and is still in the family. His sister Patty now owns it.

Well, Johnny is still growing up. While coming up, as previously mentioned, he was always the runt of the pack, always the youngest. He learned a lot of things from these guys and when he was around in the third grade, someone showed him how to make a Molotov cocktail. What a thing for a third-grader to learn. Enter the fire gods. He was mesmerized and sometimes starting a fire put him in a trance. This went on for a couple of years with each new fire, a new experience. They would make their molotov cocktails and blow them off under a huge culvert under Ford road underneath where Deckers brook ran. This amplified the explosion and at nighttime the huge fireball would light up the whole area while they ran like hell. This caught the attention of some of the neighbors and an occasional visit by the police. Somehow most of the neighbors had an idea of who was behind all of this but we said nothing 'cause that's a whole lotta trouble. We believe that one night Rusty psycho-analyzed Johnny and tricked him into spilling his guts, but not before this happened thus getting them all caught. One day, Johnny had an accident with his Molotov thingamadood-a-ler. He lit the rag soaking with gasoline and when he went to throw the bottle the lit rag fell out of the bottle and all of the gas inside ignited and blew out of the bottle like it had jet thrust. It got all over his hand and burnt him up pretty good. When Rusty seen that, it was all over with the underground war zone and everyone was in trouble. Once again, Johnny causes some wrath. During the same years, right next to the culvert was a town park complete with a pond and an island in the middle, and also a huge public swimming pool with both a one-meter and a three-meter diving boards. On weekends, the town would sponsor 'splash parties' that started at around five or six in the afternoon and lasted into the night. The pool was surrounded by a very tall chain link fence that kept us out because we were too young. This was about the time of the first Super Bowl; the Beatles were on top and Gilligan was king of TV. We would stand there all night watching our buddies smoking cigarettes and talking to girls in bikinis.

But those days are long gone. So are the diving boards. Go to a town pool and see if you can find a three-meter board. Any town, any pool. Johnny learned all the acrobatics he used in the future off of this board. He became very competitive in high diving and learned very intricate dives, going straight into the water just like you see in the competitions. In doing so, the learning experience requires trial by error. That means belly flops in trying to perfect a dive. He, along with others, would walk around the pool, beat red on the stomach just trying to walk off the sting for a few laps. That's how you learn. There is no other way. Now you can't learn, that's 'cause there are no big boards. What happened? They seem to have gone the way of the dinosaurs. What I suspect is the emergence of a syndrome that has thoroughly and completely enveloped our modern society. It's called "Everything Is Now Insured." Everything is now guaranteed . . . even our safety. I feel safe, but now a little bored. Enter the insurance lawyer, a nitty-gritty-roll-your-sleeves-up-get-your-hands-dirty-work-in-the-trenches *fallacy*, 'cause all of that is nothing but pure bullshee'at. Insurance companies must have these lawyers to determine cause, prevention, and solution of an insurance case. In doing so, they now control the entire country. The U S government, as mighty as it is, now takes its orders from all the major insurance companies. Government wants something, insurance sees high risks, and government changes its mind. By government, I mean from the feds all the way down to the Mayberry RFD. Diving boards at local public pools run under the level of local government at the moment. Now, we're talking lawyers. Say what you want. *The real watchers of the American dream are true lawyers.* True lawyers are a rare breed nowadays. True lawyers are lawyers who to this day haven't gotten their P's mixed up. They stand for principle, not power. Most lawyers I hear about or see on TV seem to have their P's mixed around, probably because of easy money. Principle takes a backseat with them and easy money rides shotgun. I got more respect for a street thug entering a bank with ill intent, fully knowing the consequences of his actions, than some piece-of-shit lawyer, who is playing golf and charging his client three hundred duckets an hour at the same time. How do you be a lawyer while working a golf course simultaneously? Easily, when you get caught and alls you get is your balls rubbed by the judge, there are no consequences worthy enough to make you think twice. Us common folk get locked up hard when we steal. It's not just the lawyers but all the sheeple out there are also to blame. A lot of sheeple are common folks also, just like you and me. Maybe you, but definitely not me. I think the town got sick and tired of little junior's parents asking if the town had liability insurance 'cause little junior did a three meter belly flop and made his parents cry. They didn't so little juniors parents called a lawyer and the town somehow was forced to by *lamebrain insurance.*

Lamebrain insurance is what I call our safety insurance. We are all liable for our own actions and sometimes someone else's actions also affect us in some adverse way, but for some insurance lawyer to make sure that Adam sues Eve because of the serpent just shows the rest of the world of how damn lazy some of the average Americans has become. Why work when I just pound it up your ass, even when it was my own fault! Since we don't know how to be safe, some frigging insurance company is going to make sure we are so they don't have to pay out another dime, 'cause after all, it wasn't little juniors fault. You're on a three meter board, way up high! Of course it was little junior's fault! Last I knew, three meter belly flops killed no one, as long as you land in the water. Little junior's parents didn't like what they saw . . . poor juniors beet red stomach . . . and sued. Screwed it all up for people who like high diving, but hey!, they got theirs. Let me set some people straight. Not a goddamn thing I can think of is guaranteed! Nothing. Maybe death, taxes, and all that shit, but that's about it. Insurance, no matter what kind, will help you out when in need, but you are basically starting over. It won't get your health, car, or house back, but eases the pain of going through something like that. Different house, different car, and a new lease on life with new health . . . and that's a good thing. That should be the only reason insurance exists. Not to govern my life. I can do that on my own. For a town to guarantee that little junior won't get hurt on a competition diving board is absurd, and to be forced to obtain liability insurance to make sure that if he does everything is okay, is not okay, because we all suffer. Even people who weren't at the pool that day. The big board that Johnny learned off had a big sign stating its hazards and the pool even had lifeguards, but sheeple see right through that all the way to the money they can extort from the town. The fucked up part is it's all legal. If there's no water in the pool, okay, then the town now has a legitimate problem. That would be about the onlyest, and I really mean that, way all of the signs and lifeguards would be ineffective as I see it.

We used to ski just across the Massachussetts-Connecticut state line. Like at a small mountain called Mt. Tom in a town in Massachusetts called Holyoke. During the summer back in the early Eighties, the owners of Mt. Tom decided to spice up the summer months with what they called the 'alpine slide.' It was a one-man bobsled with a manmade track that snapped together that ran from the top of the mountain to the bottom.

It's just like you see in the winter Olympics with the same hairy sideways turns that looks like a lot of fun. We took the chairlift up and got in line for our turn to fly down the track. The sleds had hand brakes, but we didn't use them and instead relied completely on lean. On one of Johnny's trips down the track, he made it to the bottom like a rocket. You're supposed to hit the brakes and stop 'cause the end of the track is about three feet off the ground at the very end. Not him. He came around the last turn sideways with his hands in the air, not on the brakes and came off the end of the track at about sixty miles per hour. He became airborne and just like a bowling ball, took out all the stacked sleds from all the other previous riders. He was told to leave and not to come back. As mentioned, this was quite some time ago but now, it has also disappeared. It's gone because of insurance or more accurately, the lack of it. I think we are all accountable for our decisions and actions and when something goes wrong with that, we should learn from that, not blame someone else. People kill people, not guns. The day I see a gun walk up and shoot someone all by itself, somebody pinch me so I don't think I'm back in 1973 working that acid. Anyways, somebody fell off the slide. I fell off a few times. Rounded up my sled and got back on. Not them. They sued. Don't go down the fucking track if you live in a guaranteed world!! Of course yer gunna wipe out eventually! Asshole!, you screwed it up for us real people who know that nothing is guaranteed, even staying on the track, but hey . . . you got yours. I hope you fall off your horse and wagon. Thanks a lot! What are we gunna do? Insure the fact that we can't have no more fun anymore 'cause some fukwad (I believe that's a word) lawyer says I might get hurt? Think about that the next time you leave your bed in the morning and stand up 'cause there's not too much safety in the course of life. If there is, it's up to you, not some slob-job insurance company. I could comment some more on all this but not before I get back to Johnny Torch.

He had just gone through the firestorm and was forced to put the gasoline and bombs away for many years, but as I progress, the voice of stupidity will come calling again a couple of times, one of which was quite strange. But the voice sees that the firestorm is one the back burner so let's try something different. Howabout a gunfight! No they were only nine or ten so they had BB guns and pellet guns. But nevertheless, people got hurt, some of them pretty bad. We formed teams. One neighborhood against the other. We had four or five kids on our team, including two brothers. The other neighborhood had about the same. We were out in the woods on patrol and were careful 'cause those things hurt, BB's and pellets, real bad. Johnny heard a noise and went off to inspect it. Little did he know, he walked into an ambush. He got peppered and started screaming while running out of there. He blocked his eyes and ran blind through the brush, into trees and ran right through a creek. He dropped his gun but managed to retrieve it while taking a few more hits. When I seen him, he was all welted up and real pissed. Time for revenge. So we set up our own ambush. While waiting for the enemy, Johnny was gathering and stockpiling a bunch of rocks. I look over and soon we all had a bunch of rocks. The enemy soon entered our kill zone and we pretended that they caught us by surprise, and they ran right into our trap with big smiles on their faces. Johnny turned someone's smile upside down when he clobbered him with a rock the size of a baseball right in the head. We overpowered them with superior firepower. "Rocks! rocks! they got rocks!," is all we heard as they ran like hell with some even dropping their guns in the process. Some needed stitches. Later that day, all of their parents were going door to door with their dinged up kids and we all got into trouble. He got his revenge all right, and we should have never listened to him. We even knocked one kid senseless and he freaked out, thus scaring the crap out of all of us. We thought we damn near killed him. The two brothers in our posse had a taste for trouble, but mostly with each other. While digging out a hill out in the woods for an underground fort, they got into an argument with each other. When one turned his back, the other took his shovel and slammed his brother in the back of the head. A homerun swing. His head splits wide open and he tumbled all the way down to the creek. "What'd ya do that for?," Johnny screams. "You killed him!" Not really, but it was a bloodbath. The assailant drops his shovel realizing that he screwed up majorly and scoots off into the woods. He wouldn't come out with his ma screaming at the top of her lungs how she's gunna rip his arms off and pull out parts of his rib cage. Shoulda heard her, she was pissed. Johnny screamed back, "What about his thingys? Ain't cha gunna rip those off too?" Everyone else who was there that day finished the fort and they all just kicked back in it and laughed about the day. We weren't even teenagers yet when all this happened and every now and then we'd drive out into the woods.

Yeah, we would find a car every now and then. We would buy an old boat for around twenty bucks or so and drive it all through the woods. We'd smash it into trees, roll it over on some steep hill on purpose then smash it into some more trees and big rocks. Shoulda seen what these cars looked liked after we got through with them. We'd get a hold of a Galaxy 500 and when we got done with it, it was about the size of a Volkswagen. One of the cars we got was pretty nice and we decided not to smash it all up. It was time to hit the streets instead of the woods. Problem was, when we decided to take to the open road, it broke down. Being pre-teens at the time, we didn't know how to wrench a car and couldn't fix it. Johnny said no problem, my father is asleep right now, 'cause at the time Rusty was working the graveyard shift, and we'll just take his car. He won't mind. Johnny was so embroiled in driving on the street instead of the woods, he talked us all into stealing Rusty's old Ford Falcon. This would be the first car he boosted. May as well start at home. He only stole two more in his life to this very day . . . one for fun, the other for necessity. We hit the highway and now we were really broadening our horizons. However, we got stopped by the police at a stop light 'cause the cop who pulled up next to us looked over at us and when he saw that none of the occupants, especially the driver hadn't started to grow hairs yet, the lights came on. That didn't make Rusty look good and Johnny's ma took care of that. He wouldn't even look at a car after that.

If you hadn't already guessed by now, Johnny started to mess around with dope. I shouldn't and I'm not gunna get into some of his dope stupor days so I can try to tell you all what not to do and how much it costs if you do. And I'm not talking about no money. If you wanna?, he can tell you what to watch out for, like your future or lack of it. Meth. Death. Once again, it takes two to tango but if there ever was a drug that is nothing but pure poison, meth would be it. The worst of the worst! Damn near the same as dogs licking up anti-freeze by accident. But this ain't anti-freeze and this ain't no accident. But just as his life was or is, so goes this novel. Nothing in order. One day he's in his forties, the next day he's sixteen. So this novel is going to parallel his life. There's no other way to explain his existence than to look in his eyes and see where he's at, at the moment. To start out let's check out the early Seventies. Johnny doesn't really want to. Living in the past taught him that the past will *always* haunt you for life, and no matter what good you do about it, will not undo any past undoings, so fuck it . . . crack another beer. But make sure you open up the top of the bottle . . . any other way?, then you'll need a la'yer to do it for you. Anyhow, those years got him real good, especially all the LSD. He got into the dope game as a youngster and as I progress on his lack of progress, he will tell you now what a mistake one can make by letting your world revolve around fantasy, which is what the dope game is all about. One thing could lead to another and soon you will find yourself in a confusing maze, dependent on others for a way out. I can explain a little more in detail later on, but dependency to me is nothing but a four-letter word. He never got that low because of dope. It was other factors that knocked him off his horse, but stuff like I'm gunna explain should show most people how dangerous drugs can really get. Don't laugh and sneer 'cause you think you seen it all 'cause somehow in some kind of altered state of mind which just might be just what it takes to see what's in the mirror in front of anybody butt booty but you, maybe you really seen nuthin' at all cept'what you wanna see because that's what drugs can do to you. It can even make you understand geometrical manafrustrations such as that last line of shit. I'm not too sure if that made any sense at all. All that friggen dope! Wish I could do it all over again, not the dope part, and rearrange a few things. I can't but maybe I can help. As previously mentioned, it takes two to create catastrophe, but somehow he managed to always stay one step ahead of the demon until one day he got caught up in his own trap. You wanna play around with hard dope?, then read on so you know what not to do, but anyhow, he knows like you wouldn't believe. These were about the loosest days he's ever lived. LSD. Something smaller than a speck of dust on the *window pane* with the power of LSD could have the power to enable Mickey Mouse to take down King Kong. That sounds kinda strange. Sometimes on an acid trip, you don't even know that you're gettin' beat in any kind of game and you just don't stop. It could make an ant beat a bull. There is no pain, no second guess, no second best; you are it, no thinking twice, sometimes no thinking at all, and most of all, let's do it again. And again and again. However, this comes back to haunt him later in life. No flashbacks or anything like that but something that scared him so bad, he wondered if he had done himself some irreversible damage. I'll get to that later. Wish I didn't have to but he did it to himself.

During these daze, he was at a New Year's Eve party from 74 to 75. This was a little weird. Imagine being at your friend's house with his parents also being there on new years. The parents are downstairs sipping wine and champagne all by themselves while upstairs in their son's twelve by twelve bedroom there's twenty or so people just going apeshit off the walls and ceiling. Cars parked all over the place. No one downstairs except ma and pa watching the ball drop at Times Square . . ."200 Motels" upstairs. To open the door to let someone else in the room, people had to climb on top of each other so the door had clearance to open at all. Johnny's ma would have come up the stairs like a heavyweight prize fighter if that happened at his house. He says to this day that was a very cool party. Very Seventies. Electric kool-aid everywhere. Same as the previous week at the Christmas party up at Bradley International airport where he was working at. That party is etched upon his mind forever. Sounds like get a life, that's so long ago. You just had to be there. Remember, the laws up in the northeast only had baby teeth back then and if a party at an international airport in real time went on like this one, it would be on CNN, FOX . . . and probably on BBC. They would probably condone it. Big Bad Continent. That would be us. We can't just do anything right anymore. How about Bring Back Churchill. They got that with Tony Blair but they just can't realize that 'cause they're too busy bringing back Neville Chamberlain. Get in step and diplomatic negotiations with Adolph just did not work. Check your history the next time you go on the air. Man, I just can't seem to keep myself from flying out to left field all the time. As strange as this sounds, let's get back to LSD. Well, not really like what that just sounded like but the consequences thereof.

LSD became a way of life for a while and it had its pro's and con's. We just never saw the cons. The only pro's we saw was the fact that it was a lot of fun at the time. Timothy Leary saw lots of pro's. I'm told that when he was locked up for awhile, he was allowed to glow for two hours after lights out. Acid did open up something in Johnny's mind that he never knew he had prior. They say that the average human being only uses ten to fifteen percent of the brain in all daily activities. We haven't evolved into the rest yet. You don't wanna either, you'll need a set of wheely bars just to hold your head up. Maybe acid could help as very strange as that sounds. For instance, Johnny had some trouble with advanced mathematics in high school, such as algebra and beyond, and more often than not, got a C grade at the best. Not so when tripping so hard, his brains ran out his ears. He would ace every test to the point where he was getting A's in math. Somehow, he could see through the intimidation of E=MC squared and understood it with nary a problem. This is no lie. I was there and could not believe how fast he did his homework and ace it the next day at school. I thought this was amazing and he did too. While looking through the window pane doing his homework, he would know that the next day, all would be forgotten so while all tripped out, he would write down how he accomplished the feat in terms he would be able to understand once he landed, and that's how he learned math in high school. I wouldn't believe it either 'cept for the fact I was there to see it happen. Acid was fun just as long as you don't think you can fly from the twenty-ith floor. That became a problem with some people back then. What good are you if you became Albert Einstein on Mr. Natural as you are doing 100 m.p.h on your way to the street below? Not much. As a matter of fact, we both have witnessed some friends of ours who once they landed back on solid ground from a trip to Pluto and back, not quite the same before they left . . . and some remain that way to this very day. A very scary drug. Makes crackrock look like Gerber's baby food and that's no shit. The only pro's I can see is that it's not around anymore. Well, not the way it was at least. But as usual, it took Johnny a real long time to realize that living in wonderland was doing him no good. It's not a narcotic or habit forming by no means, but when you see hallucinations like the ones I saw, you seem to come back for more. This happened to all who messed around with this shit. I can attest to the quasar power of this drug in which when I took it I dropped one little drop in my eye with an eyedropper and saw shit that will stay with me until the day I croak.

We were all on top of this huge cliff located in Connecticut. To be exact, it was at a place called Spoonville Mountain in a town called Tarrifville near Hartford. It is pure country, or at least itwas the last time I was there. It was nighttime and we all did some Mr. Natural, which is very potent. Now I certainly don't want anyone out there to try any of this 'cause you might think what you've been reading sounds pretty cool because it really ain't and because in reality, it *scares the living shit* out of most people, including myself because my fantasy/reality DMZ means that sometimes losing your mind 'cause of your own hand is the same as walking through a minefield you wandered into because you're so fucked-up and trying to make it out alive. Actually, I should cease and desist right here and now but here goes for all the inquiring minds out there. While getting off real hard on this stuff, I looked up at the deep, dark night sky only that's not what I saw. What I saw was a blood red sky, with all the stars all different colors just bouncing around at warp speed like they were in some pinball machine from hell. That was something, but it pales in comparison to when I turned and looked at the moon. It was so big I could reach out and pick up my own moon rocks, or at least that's what I thought at the time. No Apollo mission needed, just one little tiny piece of plastic the size of a flea. The moon was bright purple, then it changed to colors I still have never seen since, then back to purple then it started to drip into space and I damn near had to slap myself to smartin up alittle bit. That shore didn't work. This went on for 'bout a half a day, but we didn't know what time was, not what time it was, but completely lost in space and time. The next day when I landed, I assimilated all that happened the previous night and wondered how something that small could affect the mind to the point you are traveling through outer space. Sounds stupid but that's the closest to the moon I've ever been. I have an eight inch Schmidt & Cassergrain professional telescope that moves with the rotation of the earth to take space pictures that's so powerful, I can stick it up your grown up baby butt and see your soul, and that don't even come close to what I saw that night. If you ever forget about something like that, that means you're dead. That was just one of many.

Looking at moving cars was pretty cool. They stretched back and forth sort like an accordion. Kinda like a super SUV. Don't know if it's a city bus or a Volkswagen beetle. There was also an episode when we decided to climb this very high cliff that was damn near straight up in Granby, Connecticut where Johnny eventually begin his postal career. This is many years before that. Professional rock climbers have died here. Picture an almost ninety degree cliff, about so high that if you fell from not even halfway up, you're dead. It had nooks and crannies onyo which to grab that made it look enticing. Naturally, everyone was tripping. Johnny gets half way up, then looks down and freaks. Tripping that hard didn't change the fact that one wrong move, dude, you're dead. He froze for about forty-five minutes and became scared motionless. Talk about freaking out? And your life is on the line! All of us screamed not to look down again, take your time, make every move correct and he finally made it. Talk about a rough trip! He kissed the ground, then "kissed the sky" when he finally got to the top. He had a buddy who went to a very well established and renowned prep school in his hometown, and he got dope from there that would eventually filter out into town that was some of the best around, especially the acid. Johnny would skip school and his buddy would blow off super school also and together they would round up about five or six more stoners and set off somewhere, usually some other town school where Johnny knew someone and all of them would set off into the woods and drop some acid. Kinda like gettin' in tune with nature, 'cept much of the nature they would see was from other planets back in those days. They once built a bonfire. Should have seen it. Half the doggone woods. Thank God there was a creek nearby.

But back in those days, it was anything goes. Didn't care about no consequences; no remorse, no one to answer to, no second guess on what was going on that day, and consequently, no future. That happened to some of us. Some people saw the latter, some didn't. A very haunting concept to think about. But all this was incomprehensible to Jethro Warts back then and each and every party became more and more extravagant than the previous one, and was held wide open in some open field, or some gang house, or somewhere with no regard to the law, and even when they showed up, things didn't always go their way like nowadays. One party comes to mind to show an example of the baby teeth laws that we had at the time. This was the 1974 graduation party held out on the outskirts of the north part of town called Rainbow where he would eventually live sometime in the future of this novel. It was at a place called the pits because the sand needed for construction or sand for the roads during the winter was obtained here, and eventually a huge sand crater was created. This area of town was off limits to other parts of town 'cause if anyone showed up who wasn't on the guest list, they usually had a bad day. Had to be part of the posse or don't show up. But for the graduation party, rules were lifted for that weekend and hundreds of people showed up. We had around eighty kegs of beer and a flatbed for rock bands to play on, and this went on from Friday all the way to the beginning of the next week and consequently, the law showed up. This area was located next to a tobacco field, and there was only one way in and one way out 'cause the other dirt roads leading to the pits were intentionally blocked with cars everywhere so as to keep the police out. Here comes only one police car and as he's heading up the narrow dirt road leading in, he started taking some hits with everyone throwing anything they could get their hands on including big rocks which made him slam it into reverse to get the hell out. By the time he got out, his squad car looked like a bowl of hammered fuck. No cop ever came back. For a party like that, I was amazed at the lack of proper policing at the time in accordance to what would happen at a party like that in real time. But bear in mind, this is way before America became a police state. First of all, the party was at the outskirts of town but it was huge with cars and bikes coming and going all night long. Cars everywhere, even in the cornfields running wide open. That's a very bad idea. Me and Johnny were sitten' in the back of some old boat plowing through the ten feet high corn stalks when all of a sudden someone going the other way missed us by ten feet or so and scared the shit out of us. We got out of the field and told all the other crazies that if you go in the field, you ain't the only ones out there. If we hit head on, no one would have even known, 'cept us. But it was just a party, not hurtin' anyone. An occasional fight or two, excessive good times, and a whole lot of noise in the middle of nowhere. Whether or not it was on public or private land, I'm not sure, but the law still showed up. If it was private property, then the owners didn't care 'cause even though this was a big party, this happened all the time at the pits. Plus, I think it was owned by some large tobacco conglomerate. It really wasn't nice what happened to the squad car, but back then some people did not like the law.

America was going through a generation gap back then which fueled these rebellious feelings. In real time like now, more often than not, I hear the same thing. But not just by a bunch of dope-smokin' punks, but by some people who don't even look the part. No one likes a police state, especially me and my southern fried homies! Nowadays, when I have contact with the police and he gets out of his cruiser and walks up to my window, I don't know anymore if I'm gettin approached by a public servant who wants to know what my problem is, or if I'm gettin approached by someone who is going to give me a problem. Too late now, you're stopped.

To me, that's very scary. Givin' me a problem with fifty thousand volts. That's even more scary. May as well kill me 'cause someday, somehow, I'm gunna see how you like it too if that's the last thing I do. Hope that's never necessary but I'm not to sure anymore nowadays. Some police seem to abuse their job alittle too much. If I get tased and I really do deserve it for being a total asshole and the cop has no other recourse . . . that's my fault now isn't it? It's the other times that I often hear about that reminds me of an M-16 in a child's hands. Lots of the public are now conceived as the enemy nowadays, not all of us, just some of the ones who drive. How could policing change that much to where some of us simply refuse to exercise our God given rights of life, liberty, and happiness along with justice for all because the only justice is for you 'cause you made the mistake of walking home from Moe's instead of driving because you're crib is close by. I thought that's what we're supposed to do when safety comes first. You're on your way home from Moe's and some county mounty pulls up and wants to get to know you, where you are going, where you just came from, what's the capital of Borneo, and he figures out that you just left Moe's. Obviously, Moe's is a gin mill and now he gets out of his squad car for further investigation. The phrase "county mounty" is in no ways derogatory. It just sounds pretty cool. During the investigation, you come clean and tell the officer that Moe's is really a bar and that while in that bar, you drank a few beers or drinks. Who cares what you drank, you still chose to walk. Calling a cab would have been my method of transportation but I also believe that you have the right to walk down the road while observing the acceptable norms of society. That means no staggering or stumbling, fuckin' wid people on the way home, or such so that you might become profiled by the police as a public drunk. This story gets real worse, but it's real, so ain't fifty years for fifty times . . . . what?? Something not quite like that almost happened to these guys. But they did the right thing and walked instead of drive 'cause they knew that they really couldn't. So what does this punk-ass judge do? He says he'll suspend their driver's licence *anyways* even though they did the right thing. Society now works against us couldn't be more truer than that. I'd like to meet that judge in Moe's parking lot one dark stormy night, bring him inside, watch him knock down a few cold one's, then watch him drive home like most of them do. Screw up your own life, not someone else's!!

Sometimes nowadays being profiled means that you're 98.6 and breathing. Sometimes, not all the time. Not all view the public as such. Being black or having long hair helps them figure you out. Being black and having long hair. Damn, we got ourselves a black Charles Manson. How did all this come about? I might have a problem with some police but I'm not stupid. We only have ourselves to blame. The police presence we have now is merely nothing but a reflection of present day society. Damn near everyone now has something to hide. Now I'm also not as opinionated enough to know that no one likes a public drunk. Annoying and smelly. Three hundred beers and you're gunna have a problem, and rightfully so, but three beers cost the same as three hundred in court. I got some kind of a problem withthat, especially when you're walking instead of driving. But none of that matters 'cause Robocop administers a field sobriety test and you pass with flying colors. Not good enough for Wyatt Earp and now you must blow into the cash register and you fail. You are now public drunk and the county wins again. Back to the question, why? The seeds of aggressive policing were sowed generations ago, more specifically by the baby boomer generation. Best thing about boomers is that they came from the greatest generation ever. I'm a baby boomer, and so is Johnny, but we don't walk the beaten path. We usually wind up being beaten on the path. The end of docile policing was just around the bend and sometimes we are now guilty till proven innocent. Lack of responsibility has metamorphisized into lack of guarrenteenment of some of our basic rights. I have no disrespect for the institution of policing or soldering for one's country and both those jobs are the noblest professions anyone can undertake for either one's country or locality. There is nothing more anyone can ask from a job. You are now a guardian and we all know the responsibility that comes with that. As with our local police, name any other law enforcement agency that is there first when the shit hits the fan. There is no one. Our locals are the first on the scene, and bear in mind the scene can become federal, but the locals showed up first. They deserve the utmost respect. But to me, some of the *cowboy in us* seems to have spread across the thin blue line. That leads to problems 'cause they all dress the same and now I can't tell John Wayne from Bonnie and Clyde. How come a lot of the Bonnies behind a badge look like linebackers or bulldozers? Pretty hard to go out with a female cop nowadays, unless you're in intensive training. Let me see if I can air all this out and pin down some of the variables and circumstances involved here for me to comment so much on law enforcement, from Barney Fife all the way to the Supreme Court.

I need to go back a few, back to the beat cop. The beat cop was a daily fixture to all the people on his beat, merchants and regular folks alike. He was one-on-one with the public because he was in your restaurant, butcher shop, shoe shop, chop shop, laundry mat, and tenement houses. Everyone had the utmost respect for him because he was a guardian and became a part of your life as he protected your presence while on his beat. Beat cops were friendly and formed a bond with most folks on their daily beats. That was just basic survival while watching out for the blocks he walked. Certainly can't piss off regular folks you walk by everyday and expect smooth sailing, now can you? Of course not. People would trust the beat cop with their first born. Beat cops are pretty much a thing of the past, with some metro areas using bicycles and horseback to keep a human face on the force. That's not bad. Beat cops never really viewed anyone as the enemy unless you screwed up on his patrol and earned your fate by committing some crime worthy of being collared and cuffed. They had their eyes open and enforced basic laws. Other than that, no one really feared the beat cop. Some police nowadays thrive off public fear. We now fear the police, mostly for monetary reasons and not really for jail time even though you now get sent to jail for farting sideways, because it now costs so much just for average traffic violations.

Running red lights or stop signs, stupid speeding, and getting flagrant DUI's are not average. Those are serious. Ever get in a car wreck? Those violations require the same 'don't care about no one else but me, even my own safety' mindset as those found in predatory crimes such as rape, murder, and child crimes, or anything else where no one else's considerations are considered except their own. They need to pay for that, and as with most stupid traffic violations as those just mentioned, the courthouse sees that these people pay hard. That's a good thing. Running a stop sign somewhere in rural America is much different from running a stop sign in metro anywhere. Both equally against the law, but with a noticeable difference. *Country Joe* can see for miles around and knows he's no rolling menace. City boy can't see anything but a limited city view as we all know it from his windshield. Running metro traffic signals is as dangerous as it gets.

Like trying to never get hit running figure eights. Years ago, in the rural areas around southern Massachusetts, playing chicken or something like that with your lights off blowing through stop signs in the night became the thing to do. Everyone!, get in, we're goin' for a cruise! Health insurance paid up? To make a stupid story short, in one accident, multiple people died. The asshole who did this, of course lived. I really don't remember how hard the law came down on him. But I do know how hard the law nowadays could come down on country Joe for running a stop sign even while being the only car on an open road along with the traffic cop, of course who got him. He could be in the same amount of trouble as city boy who took out an entire family while running stupid down Peachtree street in downtownAtlanta. If country Joe gets profiled . . . that means an enormous amount of questions from the officers or half the police force show up, and usually something happens. Half the time, after quite some time on the road, you get cut loose and off you go. It's the other half that got you 'cause you had something to hide no matter how miniscule, and bound and determined officers don't care or you never had a chance right from the get go.

With the erosion of our 4th Amendment throughout the ages, the police really ain't tramping on your rights as one would think. They are only doing what they are allowed to do. The police really aren't really the problem at all. You gotta cut deeper to find the cancer. It's what some of our fascist lawmakers are coming up with to ensure that law and order will go hand-in-hand with zero-intelligence to make sure that the public will financially support the county's fiscal year no matter how miniscule the traffic violation may be. This leads to quotas. Adolph Hitler was one of the first to support quotas. Not like what I'm talking about though . . . his quotas lead to death. Don't think that you're being picked on during a traffic stop though, even though you might feel that way . . . a lot of police stops have done exactly what they're supposed to do, *to provide law and order.* But anyways, the argument is that the roadways are public property and therefore you give up part of the 4th Amendment when you are on a public road, driving or walking. Somehow, the roads have been turned into a 'no mans' land. Police state?? Has it always been that way? If not, then I gotta major malfunction with this and I do see both sides of the issue, but mostly my side. I also know what The Bill of Rights says about that. It pretty much says I only got the right to try to stop the bleeding nowadays. If there's any bleeding goin' on, check out the open wound on the 4th. Let it bleed. If a cop for even an instant thinks that his life is in danger for whatever reason, then I would hope that he would take that amendment along with the gaping open wound and shove it so far up the perpetrator's rear bumper that when he opens up his mouth for the dentist, there's another copy of one of our founding documents. Anyone can have a problem with anyone especially nowadays but if you gotta problem with the police, which to some is easier *said than dumb*, 'cause if you do something like that?, then you are no better than the problem you think is wrong in the first place, which might make you an idiot. It's pretty easy to fool a fool of an idiot nowadays. No foolin'? Calling any cop you see a pig is exactly the same as calling any black person you see a nigger. ***How do you know?*** Fuck yer *race car*!!! I'm pretty sure that most of some of us got that one . . . . 'cept brother Warts. His soul is white, but his Savior sees way before and beyond that, but nowadays he can barely even save himself. I got a solution; Paint it black. If yer gunna judge a book by its cover . . . *black and blue*, then you need to judge the cover of the comic book from which you or anyone who thinks like that came from first. As you can see by now, some of my problem with the police pertains mostly to some traffic stops. How important is the traffic cop? Compare his squad car on the road to an antibody in your bloodstream. Both working for the good of mankind by transversing an immense tributary-like system, one all of the roadways, and the other, our bloodstream. That important! We need both. Before that, it was the beat cop. But the beat cop smiled. Not too much to smile about sometimes, but treat me like some kind of human, but if I'm wrong?, then you can spit in my face if you want 'cause after all, I'm wrong. As previously mentioned, this is a very noble job. With all the garbage out there . . . forensics, detective work, undercover, homicide and vice, cold cases, shootouts and car chases shows you just how important it is to have law and order. From the traffic cop all the way to the chief of police, they all deserve our utmost respect. Some just make that hard to do. In most cases with our law enforcement, the job is big enough for the officer, in other cases . . . the officer is too big for the job. Some beat on paraplegics and kick the living shit out of handcuffed women while denying them their basic rights. Do that to my daughter, and I will put it on you so hard, you'll need a enemassuse just to fart out your ears ***and I don't care what you are***! Think about your own daughter the next time you slap anothers!!

I just have a problem with cowboys on the force. Get off the horse dickhead, and put down the repeater. Believe it or not, I'm on your side so get the gun off my head. And *NEVER* smack my daughter around. Rusty started out in Hartford by walking a beat. That was the early to the middle Sixties just after he left from being a hometown cop to become a city cop. Any difference? Yeah, one's got bigger fish to fry, the other sometimes is looking for a fish fry. But when Rusty was pounding the bricks on the street, some beat cops sometimes had days when there were incidents as with this story. Walking one end of a beat to another seems kind of boring, but incidents like this goes to show how dangerous being a cop really is. Johnny remembers one day back in the late Sixties when Rusty came home from work really pissed. One of his friends who also walked a beat was killed one day by his own gun at the Charter Oaks housing projects in Hartford. The assailant apparently overwhelmed the cop, who Johnny knew, took his gun, and unloaded all six rounds in the revolver. No sixteen in the clip, one in the chamber back in those days. Most of the bullets hit him and he died instantly. Here's the part where things get somewhat murky. During the trial of this piece of shit for killing a cop, faculty and/or students but mostly faculty at Trinity College in Hartford petitioned that somehow it wasn't really the assailant's fault and somehow society was more at fault. Say what??? As mentioned before, girl to woman or boy to man, you are now an adult and if you can't conduct yourself without creating havoc, then the only person I see at blame would be yourself, not society. Society is guilty of a lot of things; *reading your mind is not one of them.* But anyhow, justice was only half- served because of overeducated-imbeciles with apparent power who fought tooth and nail for the assailant. This really pissed Rusty off. What about the cop and his family? Funny how with a superior education, some people can't see past their noses. Some people receive much too much education than their intellect can digest and sometimes shit up part of their brains, *verbally*, and say things that make other people look at each other and say, "Did you hear what I just heard?" I just have one question regarding all this and I know it's not all necessarily true, but I ask, "Do you have to sacrifice raw common sense and real time reality for crackshot education?" *No one makes it out alive without common sense.* I know how to calculate time and space, thus making them both mathematically intertwined, and I also know which shoe goes on what foot, and I hope that's not as rare as I often hear. I don't really know all that but it sounded pretty good. But bear in mind, you're dealing with two feet with each one holding on to five toes! I don't care what anyone says, that's pretty damn tough! And no, c'mon now, they're not two feet long!

But anyhow, the beat cop worked that way for over a hundred years up until around the Sixties and Seventies when most of all city police chose to be more mobile than in the past to adapt to a changing society. A changing society like you wouldn't believe. Myself and Johnny were in our early teens when change was the mood of the country, just like it seems nowadays. Only difference was the anti-establishment of the Sixties has now become the anti-American of the twenty-first century. No, wait a minute, that's all the same. Back then, it was tear apart tradition; nowadays it's piss on tradition then stomp all over it. But it involved pretty much the same players . . . *baby boomers who once called cops pigs back then, and now, the same people who completely espouse everything about the police they once despised.* Not to piss on boomers, but nowadays, generation X and Y have seem to have also been infected by new-age philosophies and the such. I thought that older age and experience had the bulk of the wisdom. Hope no one ever forgets that, 'cause that's the way it's been since day one and no over-educated asshole will ever tell me otherwise. Can never really be over-educated . . . just don't ask me to tie your shoes. Seems like some tiny tots out there have somehow been there before.

But society changed drastically back then with blue laws and taboos being lifted on just about anything, making almost nothing sacred no more. Even religion got involved. The Hindu religion entered America at all points, especially airports, with their disciples roaming and preaching their agenda, but what really made the point was when the Beatles adopted the Hindu faith as their own. As I knew back then when this happened, this was only a fad. But they made some real good tunes with it. But what really interested the anti-establishment community was the Hindu love bible that shows seventeen thousand different positions in which to bunga-punga by. Sexual intercourse while standing on your head? Almost broke my friggin neck! This love bible was called the 'the Kahma Sutra' and was a must read for those defiant times. If you didn't have a copy on your coffee table, you were on the other side. I like all that and some night I would love to do Hindu for a change. But a lot of all this radical change produced anarchy in the streets from Watts in 1965 to the Chicago Seven and Kent State plus many assorted fire damaged riots scattered all over America's cities and burbs. The right to assemble was taken to its fullest value with people either rioting or protesting something, most notably Vietnam, thus becoming to what can be construed as a mob, and consequently, the police were called in. This was looked at *us against them* by all the players. The police were members of the hated establishment and now with most of old school traditional American values at peril, such as mom and apple pie . . . a century old recipe, and entrenched regimented mid-twenty-ith century living routines, day in and day out, patriotic honor, and the notion that the husband works while the women keeps a home, children doin' what they're told . . . even teens, not an evil thought in the house, and most of all . . . family values to show the future generations. Then came the Sixties and put a halt to all that *tom foolery*, and that's how we got here. I might have blew past a couple of things but you should be able to get the jist of all that. The right to assemble now has become the right to disassemble with all the chaos in the streets and in the news. Sometimes Rusty would come home just beat clean plum slap up trying to quell a riot in the north end of Hartford with about a hundred or so cops alongside of him.

Johnny recalls one night back in 1966 when Rusty came home from work just beat all up. In uniform. However, that night he was providing security for a Rolling Stones concert at the outdoor Dillion stadium, which is now long gone and all the women who wanted to get to Mick Jagger had to go through him and they did. Good to be Mick Jagger . . . this is pretty cool. When the Stones came back to Hartford in 1981 on the 'Tatto You' tour, they inquired about Rusty providing security for the rest of their tour, but he couldn't do that. Job and all that said no. Johnny's first rock concert was at Dillion stadium. He saw the Grateful Dead way back in the early Seventies. People walking around with big cardboard signs stating any kind of drug you wanted to prescribe yourself just like the beer man at a Braves' game way down yonder in Georgia where we all live now. Try something like that now at a concert. Don't listen to me. The police were called to a lot of rock concerts back then for many reasons, band left too early, politically orientated tunes, and sold out which was usually the main reason. The late Sixties protesters were mainly for alittle looser and casual lifestyle which meant that along with your Harvey Wallbanger, maybe you smoked a joint or two that was accompanied with some kind of chemical. Keep your shit together and what's wrong with that? Even Gunga Din did it. So did Kahma Sutra. Can't seem to let that go. Problem was and still is keeping your shit together seemed to have taken a back seat to getting' your groove on. Here comes *the man* because present time society at the time said enough's enough. We want our neighborhoods and blocks back. Now, to quell all this chaos, the police now had to deal with the *us-against-them* situation and resort to crowd control tactics to handle civil disobedience. To anyone younger than thirty, the police were the devil; to anyone older than fifteen nowadays, some of them really don't look like angels . . . or is that a crack in the windshield? The southern police at the same time were dealing with the civil rights movement that found leadership with Martin Luther King in ways that bordered the criminal. To police all over the country, much of America's cities and universities had now become domestic battlefields. Enough was enough, then Kent State happened. That had more to do with the National Guard but the message was the same. Kent State brought up many emotions when it happened, many of which I see today. Even though that was the first time in America's history that an American militia (the National Guard) fired upon its own citizens with deadly results, not much of mainstream America really cared for these rioting college students and thought that more shoulda died. Blatant anarchy, even when you think you're right, will get anybody's attention, especially the law. But that's some pretty tough law if you ask me! But don't get in the way and . . . never mind . . . don't get me started.

Not only were the police fighting ideological and political civil disobedience, but at the same time they were also fighting for old- school America, and nothing was going to change if they could do something about it. But as we all know, once change is in the air, it's hard to make it go away. That's a scary concept to think about nowadays, but I'm sure it musta been just as scary all through our past when changing times were a comin'. New age culture and philosophy pushed their way into most aspects of society, modern movies, new age entertainers, wild stuff on TV, our church puttin' up its organ for a guitar instead . . . and somewhat reluctantly, was finally accepted by mainstream society. The battle was over and as usual, change won with the police no longer manhandling overwhelming mobs, going back to old-fashioned police work to make a living. The people responsible for this forced change upon society were five to ten years older than us, and they are the ones who sowed the seed. We didn't sow anything, by the time we came up, the seed was a full blown tree with all the goodies hanging off for us to pick and enjoy. Alls we did was gather the fruits of their labor. We didn't have to fight, and consequently neither did the police anymore.

Except for an early Seventies protest on Vietnam every now and then, things were much calmer as time progressed throughout the Seventies. The police seemed to adapt to a wait-and-see mindset rather than a shoot first and ask questions later attitude toward the public. A lot even looked hip so as to blend into modern culture when off duty. Rusty grew a mustache and had pork-chop sideburns. But getting caught with dope could mess up your immediate future back then because some laws were changing so as to keep up with the blatant drug use. When I say blatant, I mean blatant. Sometimes more blow on the bar than alcohol. Chopping up lines on your dessert plate you didn't use after dinner at some restaurant to relax with after eating. Getting stopped by the police and the person riding shotgun continuing to drink his beer and hit the joint. Cop looks in and says, "Just go, get out of here." We all looked at Johnny and said, "Are you out of your goddamn mind? We could have been arrested!" He said, "Did we?, then shut the <don't say this to your parents> up!" Sorry about the scientific word, there's even a town in Pennsylvania called that. That means that I can say it with no regards but just as long as I clean it up. Sounds like a pretty cool town to me. During the disco days, you had to be a real idiot to get arrested for dope during a routine traffic stop. You actually had to show it to him. Sometimes not quite as cut and dry as that, but close, and now people pretty much did whatever they wanted with little regard towards responsibility and that was the embryonic stage of our present day situation. If you chose not to be responsible, then the courts will see to it that you are and pay for the mischief you brought upon yourself or others. A lot of us had entered the big bad world, and after beating it week by week, we celebrated on weekends with not much regard for others as we tore up the weekend. We put the party on wheels and that did not mix too well with an irresponsible mind at the wheel. Now something had to be done with all the carnage caused by all the party goers going nowhere on the highways causing much grief and sadness to themselves and others. Especially others who were not at fault. Coalition groups such as MADD popped up all over the country and rightfully so, but like everything else, adopted a zero-tolerance mindset, just throwing away the merits of each case and instead choosing to just pull the lever for the trap door. Next! Close up all the bars. They only cater to criminals. I don't like beating this dead horse over and over again but I'm sick and tired of being asked, "Sir, have you been drinking?" before he asks for my license, registration, and insurance at ten thirty in the morning. But I would feel a lot better with all the drunks off the road, but that's never gunna happen. I earlier explained what I think is happening but that makes no difference 'cause the law is the law and our present day traffic laws including DUI gives the police *carte blanche* to do and say whatever they want in their relentless pursuit of public safety. Who says they can stop your car? You show them all your papers and documents to drive, get them back, then are asked, "Sir, may I search your vehicle?" No you cannot! Sheeple would say, "Well, if you got nuthin' to hide." They just don't get the point. Wrong answer, 'cause they'll hold you there until some *probable cause* is fabricated out of thin air and now you at the mercy of "4th Amendment specialists" who will get you for something. Not good. Now I certainly know that this scenario is not learned in the police academy, unless warranted, and I have a lot of cop friends who give the benefit of the doubt instead of viewing the driver of the vehicle with nothing but disdain. Used to be the police only dealt with the driver, now they go through all the passengers just looking for more money for the county. With our ramshackle society at the present, someone in that car is probably hiding something, usually a benchwarrant, and some time in the future I'm just afraid that our homes where we all live will get treated the same as we're treated on the road. *NOT IN MY LIFE TIME!* What will they be able to do next? Coughing up rights for security might work for sheeples, but for people who know their history, that just seems to snowball into socialism or fascism. Not in the name of democracy, and I question that.

Our national roadways are merely the veins that carry all the cars (cells) throughout America to keep it going. We now have very aggressive safety laws because some of us are too stupid to be safe anymore that screws it up for all the rest of us that the police rigorously enforce. And I know I'm getting off on a tangent here but I'm pretty good at being safe all by myself and I'm also aware that we do need safety laws 'cause out of three-hundred million people, someone is bound to screw up. What if some of us get hurt on the road? Here's where I fall off the tangent. "What if?," is a 64,000 dollar question. "What if?" could be another term for *probable cause* nowadays. I know that motorcycle helmets and seat belts help immensely, but if I choose to not wear them, then that should be my choice, not the government. Both those laws were passed by pressure from insurance companies as preventive measures so they wouldn't have to pay out as much because seat belts and bike helmets help prevent more traumatic injuries. That's a given. I didn't forget about the 'what ifs.' But collecting insurance from every registered vehicle every month since the late Seventies didn't generate enough revenue, only like a hundred trillion a year . . . multiply fifty million cars and trucks by an average one hundred pecsos a month, work that out to years and I think I'm close. My calculator don't go up that high, but anyhow, government and insurance had a baby and named it *You Pay Us, We Might Pay You*. Tough ass sentence! Seat belt laws were meant to be an optional law, meaning that if you got stopped for already existing laws and you weren't wearing it, you got fined for that also Now it's a main reason for traffic stops. Once again, the police didn't come up with this, it came from above . . . the Upper Po-leese. No one's ever heard of 'em . . . 'cept me. Once stopped, the police now have the right to go all the way back to your past, even when you were a delinquent fetus. As mentioned before, we brought all this upon ourselves. We are sometimes presumed guilty of something until they figure out that we're not. I don't know about you, but I didn't do it, leave me the <pretty rough word> alone. I don't like police states. Back to the *what ifs*. How much of all this hides behind the shadow of our Fourth Amendment? Aren't the police supposed be there when something happens? Certainly, prevention is always a good thing for everything, but when does prevention and intrusion start butting heads? As for hassling passengers, we are a less-than-moral nation in real time and if some kind of probable cause is there, not no *what if*, then I can see when that would be justified. But that's not gunna happen so when everyone's ID comes back clean, leave us alone and no, you can't search my car or anything else. Law says get a warrant, so do so or meet my lawyer. Something about the last part of that last sentence that makes me thinks of vultures, lookin' for a hit without working, for some reason. Maybe it's all those ambulance chasing commercials splattered all over TV. What's worse? Ambulance chasers? . . . or the super-rich insurance companies who won't pay up when something bad happens?

Many arguments can be argued over *prevention versus intrusion* with each providing more pro's than con's, and that is a problem. As mentioned, the 'what ifs' are the instigation for intrusion. We cannot base laws simply on 'what ifs' for the fact that the law was framed as a guideline for civilized culture to live by and what if all of a sudden the law says for your own good, you shouldn't be here or there, or look at that, or anything else that I can figure out on my own, 'cause this might happen to you. Maybe it will or maybe it won't, but I'll be the one who decides that 'cause I'm a rational adult . . . every now and then. But if I do go there or look at that and have done nothing wrong, it makes no difference . . . I am now under the scrutiny of the police. This is what we live in now. Another term for this would be *profiling*, whether racial or not. Instead of working off of made up 'what if's', maybe by working on 'what happened' would suit society alittle better. Basing your law enforcement on an assumption that something could happen is preventive, and to keep a presence around that is smart, and that's why a lot of people think twice before doing something stupid. That's a good thing. Passing laws based on assumption that guilty is guilty, thus throwing away all the merits of each docket of the same law that was broken and lumping all the defendants of those cases as one, takes the blindfold off Lady Liberty and puts it squarely on all the defendants. I like to see what's goin' on in court. Assuming that something is going to go wrong and to "judge" the laws around all the 'what ifs' instead of 'what happened' is intrusion. That's not a good thing. A lot of this just pertains to traffic stops 'cause that's where you are assumed guilty until you show you're not. For the most part, once the officer sees that everything is in order, you are cut loose with a warning or a citation. It's the times that with some traffic stops which leads to the raping of the 4th amendment is what this little tirade was all about.

What do you think of roadblocks? On holidays, I got no problem with that 'cause of all the joyous partygoers who really should just stay where they are, but don't do that. On any other day, it just reminds me of the county wanting to make more money and using the police to collect it. But we all need to be proper on the road, legal and all, and some people like to make their own laws regarding all that and I can't think of any other way the police can determine who's who and who ain't. Are roadblocks the only answer? Probably not, but they are the most effective. It just seems to go against one of the main reasons why America was conceived in the first place. Last I knew, that was a lesser type of government than what America was supposed to be. Howabout this. Ever see a motorcycle cop? Picture this, you're getting paid to ride a Harley and tote a 9mm all day long. What more do you want? Howabout a get out of jail card. Orange or yellow. Either way, they both don't work. Johnny's Monopoly card simply pisses off the arresting officer. Once and probably the only time, it or something like that actually worked for Johnny. Just as the cuffs came out while standing behind his car, Johnny said, "I got an official legal status from the city of Worchester," which was the size of a credit card and Johnny didn't take another lick this time. As a matter of fact, he and the almost arresting officer talked to each other like the way one likes to be talked to and he wound up laying all the carpet in that cop's house shortly thereafter. But still I need to turn a few more nuts and bolts, maybe alittle light welding on him too, but he needs to stay out of trouble. We all need to stay out of trouble.

Caution, you are now entering a trouble free zone. That's never gunna happen, but if some of the sheeple out there had their way, you would probably see trouble free zones posted all over the place. How would they do that? Simple, by going against everything I had just petitioned. Security over rights. They believe guilty till innocent. They base their agenda solely on fear. Every stranger is a potential threat. Yea, that could be all true, but to always assume something like that puts your life always on the defensive, which kills life, and I believe that, that is some of the foundation of our aggressive policing and life smothering liability insurance. I refuse to believe that the dark side of mankind has overpowered the good side. Yeah, many of us have a lot more to hide than anytime in the past but I know lots of people with skeletons in their closet, and they are good people. Sometimes good people make bad decisions. They might bend the law and likewise, they'll bend over backwards to help someone out.

What's wrong with that? Some, not all police believe otherwise. The bad has overpowered the good. If that public persona gets worse as time goes on, what will it be like in the future? *A Clockwork Orange*?? Fight back if that happens! If it's not too late!

Routine traffic stops should be handled as such with the officer being a representative of his county or town; that is, until it stops being routine and the officer is only doing his job. Problem being, some officers seem to abuse their job along with the public which leads to public-relations problems. You could be squeaky clean but that don't mean much. Some of the cowboy in us is now seated in the driver's seat of some squad car. I call that crossing up your P's. Principle being the reason to serve, but power being the driving force for some to serve nowadays. I believe this is on a far more personal level. As a kid, I've seen a lot of other kids taking more shit than anyone should. Picked last for the sandlot ball game, bullied around, the brunt of jokes a few times too many, and other things that really shouldn't, but does happen. Ready or not, boy to man, girl to woman, put it all together, but that was hard to do. With the heavy childhood baggage which will always stay in the back of the mind, and now along with a badge, power, and most of all, revenge or redemption becomes the driving force to serve. Instead of "To serve and Protect," it's now to pay back and get even for some. Problem being, most cops are uniformed and I can't tell one from the other. You know, I never really had any problem with black cops. Seems like the cowboy stops there. I'm not pulling no race card; just telling you what I've seen, that's all. This might be because of their differences in childhood upbringing. Most of the childhood demons I previously mentioned just did not affect many black kids, and I've seen that. Many did not take that kind of shit, but gave it right back. If you do not agree, then please explain all those tragic school shootings that happened all too frequently in the past. I don't recall any black kids participating in all that carnage. They seem to not keep all that childhood grief all pented up, 'cause they've already taken care of that problem right then and there. Not those white little shit stains. They just couldn't take it anymore and just like a terrorist, they unloaded in any direction with no regard for no one. A crime like that deserves no mercy whatsoever! I care not about the age of any perpetrator. From eleven to eleventy-twelve you do something like that and your life is now over. No second chance!! . . . .

maybe a second shot when you turn seventy-five or eighty. That should teach ya that no one really cares for that kind of juvenile "acting up."

Enough of my criminal knowhow or knownot . . . it's time to get back to the story. Johnny's pretty much the same as most of us, which means he is nowhere near perfect. This lead to two DUIs up north. Those were the only ones he's had. One was in Connecticut and the other was in Massachusetts. It was damn near impossible to not get the first one. No it wasn't . . . don't drive hammered. He wasn't hammered but he had been in the club most of the night, and he felt it. Little did he know, half the police force was parked across the street from the club where he was at. The preachers ma would have gotten one that night had she left the club. Incidentally, some time before that at the same club, he lost his brakes on his Monte Carlo in the parking lot. He was on a hill and had nowhere to go except into about four or five parked cars. What a mess. He cut his lights and screwed, even with no brakes and got away. Sounds like a total lack of responsibility, but the thought of not being able to afford to drive anymore overwhelmed him and he only did what comes natural. Get the hell out. But anyhow, when he got stopped upon leaving the bar, the officer finds a couple of joints on him. He goes through the court system and is left with a ten thousand dollar lawyer bill. Pretty expensive night. Sound familiar to anyone out there? He should have paid it 'cause the lawyer was a family friend. Rusty had already passed on when this happened. He had a wife, three toddlers, and a mortgage from hell. He just couldn't afford it and the lawyer knew that and pretty much gave Johnny a break. He knew Johnny's financial situation and didn't expect much from him right from the get go but still helped him. What if he got a lawyer from the yellow pages? Myself, I'll tell the judge to lock me up for as long as he wants, 'cause I'm not paying ten grand to anyone for two stinkin' joints along with what in my mind was a DUI trap. Sounds like I got some kind of attitude problem. DUI is serious shit. You lose control of your car and it becomes a moving manned missile, only without the warhead. Couple that with no-mind responsibility and someone is gunna have a problem . . . usually someone who is nothing but a victim of someone else's bad decision. The other DUI is an episode in which he shouldn't have even looked at a car that night. He turned three into thirty that night. We have tough ass laws for stupid things like that 'cause some of us just don't care. He cares now. But with all the fuck-ups and misfits out there, I don't expect any change in the DUI laws 'cept that they might get worse, but alls I want to see is that the pastor's wife who had two glasses of wine with her lunch doesn't get rammed as hard as Joe-Who-Gives-A-Shit-Lets-Down-A-Case-And-Ride-Blow.

Well, it's back to childhood. Right about now he's in middle school and he had a paper route. He delivered the morning paper, *the Hartford Courant* and his buddy delivered *the Hartford Times* which went under back in 1976. In the winter time he used Rusty's snowmobile when that was the only way to get around real early in the morning so that he would make school on time. Back then, we had paper route collections, which meant the paperboy would go house to house each week to collect seventy-two cents a customer for a seven-day delivery. As little as that was, it was good enough for us. One of his customers would make him wait a month or two to get paid all at once. This pissed him off. During the winter months, he would take that customer's paper, soak it in some slush water, let it freeze into a cinder block, then deliver it. He would deny the complaint all the time, and finally that customer had to get his paper elsewhere. Johnny refused to deliver it and when he rode by the customer's house, he would flip him off just like some street punk. Bad lattitude from day one.

But it was about this time the voice of stupidity arose from a long sleep and said, "Remember me? Where's your Zippo lighter?" Johnny said, "Right here." Brought back fond memories of everything up in flames back in the day. On Sundays, both *the Courant* and *the Times* were delivered in the morning, and by the time their routes were finished, they had quite a few big, fat Sunday papers left over. That's when it hit him; why don't we just burn them? Then they saw a huge tobacco barn that was vacant of cured tobacco because of the season. So they decided to light up all the newspapers in it so that they both could watch a real big fire. They piled up all the newspapers next to some dried up timber of which the barn was constructed of, lit them and that didn't take the barn down. What's it gunna take to take down a barn twice the size of a basketball court? That question was on top of Johnny's mind. It bugged him real bad. For practice, they started brush fires and burnt up anything that they could. Then one day they overstepped their limit for not getting caught. They got caught all right. One day they went out to a tobacco field and cut off a huge piece of cheesecloth. Cheesecloth is a very thin but strong netting, sorta like a spider web that completely enveloped a tobacco field no matter how many acres it was 'cause tobacco plants like heat and cheesecloth kept all the summertime heat in the field. Sorta like the biggest tent you ever saw. Put a match to cheesecloth and it goes up just like flash paper. I'm sure by now, cheesecloth has been improved so that it don't explode anymore like it used to. Johnny once rolled a blooter out of flash paper for someone. Shoulda seen that. But cheesecloth was just what the doctor ordered. They went to someone's house and scoped out the two car unattached garage with a car in it and decided this was it. This was in broad daylight . . . which was stupid mistake. They got in the garage, attached all the cheesecloth to the interior of the garage covering all the walls and the ceiling and lit it. They were seen running from the scene, and realized that they were spotted and bolted into the woods. The garage along with the car took a pretty good hit, but it still stood and the car had most of the paint burnt off of it. You wanna talk about trouble? Johnny's parents realized that they had a problem who was around twelve or thirteen years old and Johnny paid pretty hard for that one. After all the dust had settled, Johnny was on his own. His buddy had hung up his Zippo. Not Johnny, his was still half full, not half empty. Waste not, want not. He possied up with some other friends, firebugs like himself who had their eyes set on tobacco barns.

About this time, there was a rash of tobacco barn fires that really pissed off the farmers, but Johnny had to get his. This fervor was about the same as drug addiction but this fire came from earth, not from hell. Johnny's never been to rehab, but he had to go to firebug school. That was his ma and if you know what *spare the rod, spoil the child* means, then you know what I mean. Nowadays, that's a bad phrase but only for stupid people. One night he finally got his. It was at night and at a town a couple of towns east of his hometown. You could see the fire for miles around. Firetrucks were everywhere. He and his buddies were in the woods watching the whole thing. To this day, he never got caught. As I talk to him in present time, he says, "Can you believe that? I used to be a torch." A pre-teen arsonist. However, this also comes back to haunt him also. He sounds like he needs a friggen exorcism for christssakes. Enough hauntings! He can't take it anymore! I got a new idea for Exorcisms. I would chant this only once and real real loud. "Everybody!! Get the hell out of this house immediately . . . and leave everything behind!!! . . . NOW!!" But nowadays, he knows how to make almost anything obtainable anywhere into something lethal. He knows how to make homemade landmines, napalm, and very crude cannons and guns . . . not that he would ever unleash any of that to anyone unless you mess with his daughter or his daughter's cousins, *'cuz d'airz a dozen on me couzin, can't cha' hear dem' fuckas buzzin'* but someone like him needs to be in Iraq. He agrees with that. He says he can't make it here or anywhere else. The military says he's too old to make his mark in the world, but he sez he could smoke just about anyone half his age in boot camp and he says, "Why does age matter as long as you still got it?"

Anybody know who Roger Clemens is or Randy Johnson? Howabout Ricky Henderson? They still can, so can Johnny. Ricky's been retired for quite some time but when he was still playing professional ball at age forty he could steal second base better than most people half his age could. As long as you treat your body and soul like the temple it is, the only thing you can do as you move on in years is to just get better with age. Just like wine, we get better as we get older. That could go both ways. It all depends on how you treated your temple when you were younger. Treat it like shit and alls you're gunna wind up with is half a bottle of MD 20 20 that's half empty, not half full. What I'm talking about is young, sound bodies and minds evolving into the same bodies and minds as they get older . . . but that requires something that takes lots of guts. The guts I'm talking about is something that you must reach way down to find then grasp with a death grip. This is called discipline, plain and simple. A four letter word to a lot and that's a big problem in our country right now. If you start out cheap and easy, chances are, you might wind up cheap and easy. What a sorry way to treat your temple, the only one you got. Bear in mind, America is the land of decisions, timing, and fate and I've seen cheap and easy fly all the way to the top. Also bear in mind, there are almost three-hundred million of us and when cheap and easy makes it to the top, the main ingredient involved to make that happen is usually luck. I don't know about you but I feel rain again 'cause my luck comes down *in the strangest ways.* Roger, Randy, and Ricky know what discipline means, so doesn't Johnny even though no one knows who the hell he is, except me. Cheap wine will always remain cheap wine, treat yourself better than that. If you don't, pretty much no one else will and that's lesson numero uno in life. Lesson numero dos is that if you look in the mirror and see cheap and easy, bear in mind it's never too late to start all over again. Change is always imminent, make it so if need be. If you need some help, never be afraid to ask someone. We all need someone we can lean on and if you wanna little baby, you can lean on me. You also need to watch what you put in your body, whether eating or anything else. Johnny told his ex-wife one time, he said, "If we are what we eat, then I'll be you by tomorrow." Enough of all this morality bullstuff 'cause I'm pretty sure we all knew that but I feel alittle bit better. Time to get back to methamphetamines, hungry children, *stupid politicians*, obesity, farm animals on the force, lack of discipline, and crackwhores. Where do we start? Howabout heterosexual marriage? Nah, no one is interested in that anymore. Howabout psychopathic extraterrestrial humans? Nah, they run America now. When dat happen? Howabout atheists? Nah, they run America too. Howabout mom and apple pie? Nah, ma's not home and camelshit pie tastes much better. What about chicks? Only under one condition. Does whatever I say. Well, while sitten' here all by myself . . . howabout Johnny? Now we got something so we all can learn whatever it is he knows. As I pen this part of his life, he's still going downhill, about ready to flameout. He always knew the consequences of his actions but still walked to the edge of the cliff blindfolded and somehow managed to not take that last step. He always valued intelligence, common sense, and textbook schooling, and became a mixture of all three. But at these times, he valued much more the thrill of the moment. Screw the cliff, if it happens it happens. He would probably do an olympic type dive . . . in his dreams, on the way down. If yer gunna flameout, do it in style. He cared not about the reaction to his actions and cared not about who cared about his actions. He tells me in real time that he can't believe some of the things that he said yes to. Very little regard to what he did back then. He knew that eventually that maybe there would be some consequence, but he said he'd cross that bridge when he got there. Sometimes there was no bridge in sight when he needed one, so he just waded through the pond, just stepping on crappies along with alittle crap all the way across.

For instance, one day he decided to ride his ten speed bike to school. A clear, concise mode of thinking wasn't in the cards right from the very second he woke up in the morning. He lived about four or five miles from school and decided for the trip to fill the water bottle attached to the bike. Only thing was is that he filt it with whiskey instead of water and by the time he made it to school, it was bout' empty. Everyone hung out in the parking lot and when they saw Johnny pull in on his bike, his buddies knew he was in trouble. He had already fallen off the bike once and he was a bit bloodied up. He tells me that he remembers absolutely nothing of that day to this very day. His buddies dragged him over to the pole vaulting cushion out at the track and he passes clean plum slap out. The football field and track were shared by both the middle school and the high school. During the day, the middle school girls' gym class is out on the track. Anyways, he wakes up and wound up scaring the shit out of all the girls and the police were called. He wound up waking up around eleven o'clock that night with all his family standing all around him 'cause they thought that this was it. All over for him. Carelessness can't go on forever. He got suspended from school for two weeks and he hasn't seen that ten speed to this very day. Getting drunk is getting drunk . . . getting stupid is just plain flat out sheer insanity. You got no guard and other people could do your thinking for you, and that's no good. He has done some moving before thinking as you can see and to write about him and his philosophy is about the hardest thing I've ever done. Some of the things he tells me most of us could care less about and other things he says can only come from someone who's been there and learned the hard way. It's not the best way some times, but sometimes learning hard is the only way for some people. But to hear all this from Joe Citizen Warts, according to him, who probably never had a chance right from the very beginning sorta reminds me of all of us. Most of us at best. Probably has got a lot in common; go to work, play by the rules all the way up, likes to play alittle, raise up a family, work some more, and lo and behold, poverty after all these years. Well, maybe not quite that rough but paycheck to paycheck when you're almost fifty just plain flat out stinks. Use your head and that's not gunna happen. We'll see about that as we progress into his adolescence and beyond. *Timing, decisions, fate, and luck* . . . all in that order. Plus alittle brains. Timing requires no brains, just being at right place at the right time. I don't care that you are the best outfielder around or the second Jimi Hendrix reincarnated 'cause I know that outfielders and guitar players are a dime a dozen. Whoever is there when an opening pops up gets the job just as long as the centerfielder isn't playing *purple haze* when there's a man on first and third. It's how real life situations are dealt with that molds us into what we become as we take on misery and adversity which is a part of life. Booker T. Washington is quoted as saying, "It's not how successful a man becomes. It's what he had to overcome to become successful" and that's the most real piece of philosophy I've ever heard.

PART TWO

THE END OF THE BEGINNING

It's over. No more school. Graduation day has come and gone. It's now the real world. We are now on our own. We thought about college. Back then there were these easy-to-obtain, very forgiving government loans for advanced schooling, forgiving for the fact that most were defaulted on and Uncle Sam took another one on the chin. But college bound? Nah, not us, we blew high school . . . why do it again? Johnny went to the military, joining in December of 1974 with boot camp starting in the summer of 1975. I headed west to scope out the rest of the country. Motorcycle or when I got a wild hair, I aired out my thumb for a while. Gotta have lots of time for the latter.

It's at this time we part ways for many years, finally reuniting back in 2002. I will now pen the rest of this from what he tells me since I wasn't around but to see him again in such turmoil is somewhat upsetting to me. To see one of my best old school friends who now looks like he's been dragged through a field of broken dreams doesn't correlate with the image of him when we first parted. Bullets used to bounce off him. Now I see the dings in his armor have long since rusted. He's been taking hits for quite some time. He used to feel no pain. Now he feels every mosquito bite, even on other people. How did this happen to one of the most (probably wrong) coolest, somewhat calmier, and "one man show" confident peopleoids I've ever met? When we hooked back up in 2002, I was relieved to still see that punkish smile for which he was noted for. He's still got more confidence in himself than a lot people doing a lot better than him. By a lot, I mean anyone else out there living in a state of uncertainty like himself no matter how good you're doing. Can barely plan week-to-week, never mind two weeks on the Carolina coast. But one thing hasn't changed after all these years; *we might catch him down but he can't be caught, and he might not sell but he won't be bought.* Live like that, then you got nuthin' to worry or care about. Even his own children are alittle scattered about but cared about. They are his driving wheel, even though they are all grown up now. Wonder how far he would have made it, had he no children? Seems like he was forced to shape up or ship out. I believe they were his saving grace and he agrees. But as we reminisce, he does admit to feeling like somewhat of a failure. Bear in mind, we've just graduated high school and have thirty-five or so years before anyone, including himself, can make that determination. Even though he played hard, he did play by the rules, that's the upsetting part. Lots of piss poor timing, not piss poor ideas. Ideas make the world spin. His keep the American dream alive. I'll discuss other ideological issues in which he believes and other tales in his rollercoaster life that seems to coast in and out of hell more often than not. Same as a lot of us so you'll know what I'm talkin' about.

We have entered the Seventies and joined the real world in 1975. As I had mentioned previously, the Seventies had settled down into a calmer, more laidback era than the previous decade, and early in the Seventies came the power of the mind. The power of the flower had advanced us into first and second warriors of change. Some of us had this notion that we were on the wrong path to happiness and bliss and adopted methods and rituals and such that righted all those wrongs through things such as yoga, natural living, TM (don't ask), severe religious change over night, super-liberal politics, and women's liberation in which I got a kick out of. Women's liberation claimed that all women at those times were deemed second class citizens basing their case on all aspects of life in which they were compared to men at the time. Maybe some of that was true, but they forgot the number one reason why they are superior to any man. They have something that took us all nine months to crawl out of and makes men spend the rest of their lives trying to get back into. Imagine if they all went on strike? Then whatever they want, they get no matter what! No matter whad day doo, whatever they want. But anyhow, aside from those *pretty cool cheesy words* of *sleazy wisdom*, what they did after graduation really wasn't any different from what they did during school. One thing Johnny did do though, was some years before graduation, took his grandfather's advice on physical fitness and push-ups. As he progressed through school, he saw what he was doing to himself and it was then that he decided that for every pleasure, there must be pain, and visa versa. He knew that for the amount of pleasure already begotten, it was time for the pain. He lifted weights until he liked what he saw in the mirror and didn't stop there. Because sports went by the wayside, this made him feel good about himself. When we met again, I did notice how all that sweat and pain really kept up with him and physically, he's pretty much the same as yesteryear except for that long-ass red hair halfway down his back. I told him to cut the bitch hair off but he won't do it. He's got this thing about growing up and not looking like it. His teenage daughter says she'll do it, but he won't let her. To this day, he still pounds out a few hundred push-ups every now and then. He still puts his feet up on a barstool to make it alittle tougher. We're all gunna get old and gray someday. That's okay, just do it in shape and then you can smoke all the cigarettes you want. Should be some wisdom in there somewhere. If you're like Johnny and your light colored hair is hiding that "touch of gray" look for which you're looking for, do what he does. Two little pieces of gray duct tape, one above each ear. In dark bars, no one will ever know. By closing, no one will even care.

As he shapes up, out comes some of this crazy daredevil shit in which he was almost killed that I'll get to later which always made me wonder if he was some kinda part feline. But the summer of 1975 was the last one before Air Force boot camp coming around the bend. They hit every rock concert from the Orphium Theater in Boston to Avery Fisher Music Hall in New York City. They had been doing that for years, but since this was Johnny's last summer home, they put everything in overdrive. Johnny drove his 1969 Camaro and they cruised all over New England. They would go down to Soundview Beach on the Connecticut coast which rocked, or go up to the cabin in Vermont and were always on the road during the night. It wasn't all fun and games without incident however. While sitting in the back seat of his buddies' old AMC Rambler, they were headed towards Manhattan to a rock show. Unnaturally, they were tripping on some acid. They were on their way to see Queen's 'Sheer Heart Attack' tour and when on Fifth Avenue, the muffler fell off. The car sounded like a friggen' tank thus messin' up all the tunes they were listening to. They stop and Johnny gets out and says he'll go and get the muffler and not really realizing that they had been on the road all night and that the muffler was damn near red hot. He got it all right. Tripping the way he was, he just reached down and picked it up with his bare hands. All of a sudden, he's screaming at the top of his lungs and the muffler stuck to his hands as he's trying to drop it. It stuck to his hands like superglue and ripped the skin off as he dropped it back on the road. Even when tripping, pain is pain, and there were no more smiles on his face that night.

All these times of doin' things like this brings me back to another case, just like in court, like one time up at the cabin in Vermont some time ago when they decided to drive up to the cabin, to all go up to party hard with all kinds of stereo equipment including a reel-to-reel tape recorder that was state-of-the-art back in those days. Dino, who several years later would teach Johnny the flooring trade drove up there. Dino didn't know about flooring at the time, we were too busy being junkies at the time. Once again, that *goddang* acid. By the time we got there, we flew in. No one could hook up anything with an electrical plug attached to it. No tunes for hours until someone pulled in a radio station in Brattleboro that was pretty good back then. After their fun in the mountains of southern Vermont, they blasted back off to the beach. They went to Misquamicut beach down in Westerly, Rhode Island, where you can ride the huge waves crashing in on the shore. Johnny caught a good one once and rode it into someone's knee standing on the shore and looked like he lost all twelve rounds from the impact. But it's around these times that he realizes that after all these years of competition diving and trampoline acrobatics, he can now spin flips on dry ground and daring to do this and daring to do that was too tempting, and now him and his more athletic buddies were doing crazy stuff everywhere they went. Lots of times, they would draw a crowd. A good place to learn how to spin a front flip would be on the shoreline. That way when you mess up, you're cushioned by a small layer of water. Do not do any of this if you have even just one uncoordinated bone in your body. If you don't spin fast enough, you break your neck.

There was something he gave back to the community back in the summer of 75 that makes him smile when he thinks about it. Those daze weren't just for fun and games, there was some work also. He got a job as a summer school recreation instructor or the adult in charge of a bunch of little kids at one of the local schools in town. Actually, it was Babe who got him the job. The other councilors knew Johnny and shook their heads when he reported for work the first day. Turns out all the little kids liked Johnny more than the rest of the councilors 'cause he showed them all sports and sports only. Any arts and crafts or guitar hootenannies went to the other councilors. Some of his friends would show up to help out doing sports, playing guitar, or building a toy house out of popsicle sticks. It's when he started to show them how to spin flips, that's when his supervisor stepped in and mentioned liability insurance. At the time he had no idea what that meant, *'cept turn one more flip and you're fired.* Now him and his buddies are diving off cliffs at all the riverside creeks, flooded out quarries, swimming holes with cliffs higher than telephone poles scattered all over

New England. There was a huge creek in Southwick, Massachusetts where to get the desired height to dive at to get the same feeling as standing in a batter's box, one must climb this very tall tree. Once you come to the branch that extends out over the deep water, you must walk it out. You got to go out about fifteen feet or so cause the first ten feet is over land. There's nothing to hold on to so don't shimmy or shake on the ten-or-so-inch diameter branch, or your day is going to be terrible. Johnny's daredevil buddies and running around buddies were Aldor and George. Absolutely no fear whatsoever. It is with these guys a lot of this book is owed to. There was a time all three of them, along with the rest of us along with our girlfriends, were down by Misquamicut Beach but inland a few miles at an abandoned quarry 'cause it flooded. They say all the mining machinery and trucks are still on the bottom way down 'cause of how fast it flooded. Johnny's girlfriend didn't like him diving like that, and she and all the other girls wanted to go to the beach instead. Johnny asked, "Any cliffs like these down at the shore?" She said, "I hope you break your neck." Now the highest cliff at this quarry is way higher than a telephone pole and all three of them had conquered it with very cool dives. Everybody who was there that day had a pretty good show to watch that day. Aldor then sees a small tree growing right on the edge of the cliff and climbs it. Johnny looks up and says to himself, *He's not gunna do what I think he's gunna do?* This small tree puts you up another twenty feet or so and now we got some serious height. The trunk was so small, Aldor had to rock it back and forth and lets go on the way out, thus clearing the cliff by at least twenty feet or so for a perfect dive. In case you're wondering how to survive a really high dive, it goes like this. Don't keep your hands with all your fingers pointed towards the water. Instead, clasp your hands together by interlocking your fingers to make a club to puncture the surface of the water. Keep your neck bent back alittle so that your head hits the water on the hairline, 'cause that's the strongest part of your head. Keep your eyes on the target and if there's any wind that throws you around in the air, turn a flip to get you back on target. Do all that and you can dive off a suspension bridge and you'll be just fine. Don't do any of that! You might screw up and do a 100 m.p.h. bellyflop and I'll be responsible for the explosion. Anyway, if Aldor can do it, so can Johnny. For some reason, he does not rock this small tree that is required to get any forward distance to clear the top of the cliff. Instead, he just pushes off with his feet, thus pushing the trunk backwards, and clears the cliff by less than three feet. Gets absolutely no distance whatsoever. He got real lucky that day because even though he could almost touch the cliff on the way down, it was practically ninety degrees from the surface of the water and even straight down once underwater. If it were like most cliffs where the bottom juts out a few feet, he would have plowed into the bottom of the cliff, and Johnny would be no more. He keeps his eyes open upon entry into the water and told me how he could see the underwater cliff practically right in front of him when he came to a stop. He was lucky because on the way down, the cliff was less than three feet away from his body, and less than two once he got into the water. On the way down, he plowed through some shrubbery growing outward on the side of the cliff and got sliced up pretty damn good for the, "You really just fucked up. Howabout some more of that stupidity pain for the ride down?" When he came to a stop in the quarry, he couldn't believe that he was still alive. He knew that everyone was watching and figured that they all thought the worst. He's got a full breath of air and swims underwater all the way to the other side of the quarry and surfaces to see everyone just freaking out. But just like the Texas Ranger, he came walking up behind them and told them that he went into some spacetime gravitational A-field wormhole nexus and all of a sudden he was standing behind them all and "Why is everyone so upset?"

All in all, the summer of 75 was his first year out of school and now let's get serious about reality 'cause alls you got now are your own two hands and a finally honed brainstem cell. Time to do something. Nah, let's stay in a drug crazed romper room all the way till the day he leaves for boot camp. They hit every keg party, pig roast, river party, every bar and rock concert they could drive to. When the movie *Tommy* came out in 1975, they decided to drive to Boston to go see it for some reason. It was sold out so they just hung out. Next night they decide to drive down to New York City to see it and it was also sold out. They went to Greenwich Village to hang out. Lots of hanging out. It was at these times he was living full time at his buddies attic mainly just for showers and it's time to go.

They also spent lots of time in the woods. There was one time they were way out in northwestern Connecticut when someone told them about these two huge sinkholes in the middle of nowhere. On the bottom of these sinkholes are these tunnels that go way down into the earth. Some of these tunnels are so thin, only one person can go at a time. It's wet down there so you do get muddy on the way down. Both these tunnels end up in this huge cavern in which you could have a party in with lots of room to walk around completely upright. There's even a deep stream going through it on one side of the cave. This is a real cave with stalagmites and stalactites, but the thing that caught Johnny's eye were all the real old initials and dates carved all over the place. So naturally, it now has J.W. '75' in there somewhere. He has never gone back and thinks about that now like it was a dream or something. But the summer is coming to an end and now it's the end of September and time to get real about boot camp. Two weeks away and it's T-minus time. Two weeks is two weeks, so he put the party in overdrive and he felt it all the way down to San Antonio on the flight. But not before one sandlot football game which coulda been televised. Tackle football with no pads to loosen up before military life beckons. Johnny and his buddies went down to one of the local ballparks in town to loosen up with a few beers and some chronic to smoke when they came upon a whole bunch of people at the park. A lot of his party people plus a bunch of jocks who Johnny knew when he was doing sports. Most of the jocks were cool towards Johnny but some others practically despised him for his more cavalier lifestyle he had adopted. Everyone was out of high school along with some underclassmen scattered about on both sides. Some of the jocks walk up to Johnny and his clan and say, "Let's have a football game right now." He says back, "Let's go. Better go and get yer playbook and all the cheerleaders in town 'cause you won't beat us." So many people wanted to play, we actually had a real game with offensive teams, defensive teams, and even special teams. Everyone became Emmit Smith that day. On our side, no one was on the old high school team. They were a bunch of long hair, dope smokin' party people. On the other side was a lot of the old school team both varsity and JV. Johnny was a wide receiver and did all the kickoffs and field goals. He caught one for a touchdown and someone in that play picked up a pretty good and serious whack on the head. He was on our side and had to be carried off the field. On another play, somebody caught Johnny by the hood on his sweatshirt and he slapped the ground so hard, he saw those bright orange stars he was so accustomed to seeing when he screws up. Needless to say, our team beat up the other team pretty damn good and we all decided that we all screwed up by not playing on the old high school team. What cooda been. Johnny's contract had expired during the fourth quarter, so it was time for all that beer and spinach. However, he was called back in the game 'cause there's nothin' like tackle football without all those wimpy padz you are supposed to wear.

Now comes reality. Off to boot camp. He flew the old Braniff airlines from Bradley Field to Lackland Air Force base in San Antonio. I also went through boot camp and I must say it is an experience. I liked it a lot. I think just about everyone should try it to see if you got what it takes. Not just for the military, but for yourself. You don't know until you try. As a matter of fact, in March of 2004, Johnny sent his oldest son into the Army. Johnny's ma wasn't too happy about that, but it made both Johnny and Justin happy. Any of our vocal, "higher up elites" sons or daughters doing the same? Oh, I forgot, they are above all that. They sent in human shields. More like moving targets . . . only when they move. Don't like change for the better? Especially forced change? *Forced* is the obvious problem here. I don't like being attacked the way we were by a sincere-like-you-wouldn't-believe prevalent religious fundamental movement that knows no boundary, not just where the hijackers came from. ***I don't care where they came from!*** We now have a serious problem that *we did not start!!* Not that I'd like to see friendly-fire casualties, 'cause I wouldn't no matter anyone thinks about current affairs the way they are but this is a very touchy subject so I'm gunna touch on it *with alittle fire* alittle later on.

But now, Washington has finally gotten the message and now realizes the value of the enlisted man. No more orders from stupid politicians and now the Army runs the Army and that's a lot better. No more walking around with blanks in your magazine or shooting only when shot at. Iraq was nothing more than part of a world problem, similar to a world cancer that really needed to be looked at. Whether or not you agree with that is up to you but I could add alittle to that, but back to boot camp. I think a mandatory two-year hitch should be in everyone's portfolio. *If it means a draft, then it means a draft.* Females would be excluded. That would be strictly voluntary. I really can't envision my honey in combat. That is also debatable. Look what females did for the French resistance and Yugoslavia's underground fighters under General Tito during World War Two. They schmooved their adversaries, then slew them. Not bad. After doing two years in the service, you'd be amazed on how many people would re-up. The service was a lot of fun and what you learn and how you learn it lets one see just what you are made of. Sorta like a physical IQ test. I think it's high time we listen to past American heroes and heed their advice. JFK comes to mind. *Ask not what your country can do for you*, you know the rest, rings louder and louder with each passing day. I still can't believe that we were attacked in such a way. Some people seem to take almost anything for granted . . . even that it won't happen again. Some people seem to not care to even comprehend on how our freedom was obtained. Some of these people are major players in Washington. Say what? As long as we're born free, then what's to worry about? That's dangerous thinking and I'm beginning to doubt the American resolve, especially amongst some of our well-known elite and certain masses all around us. On Johnny's right arm are tattooed the words, *Never To Be Taken For Granted* done in Latin. Taking anything for granted, especially what you always thought was failsafe for years past and you would have always thought that everything would remain the same is a guaranteed false security. This is very foolish and now time is no time to hide your head in the sand. That makes your ass vulnerable to anything. Harvey Wallbangers are useless here. Not too good in there either. They go up in smoke just like everything else. Young Americans must realize that a lot of the outside world is still a jungle and we always had and will have enemies with extreme resolve. I can see how all that came about but that's another story, but to watch our people holding hands on the way down after jumping out of one of the twin towers just pisses me right the <don't really like this word too much myself either> off.

Nobody ever forget that and pass it on throughout the ages so everyone in the future knows what's out there. I don't think there were too many blue collar jobs lost that day. The twin towers were total corporate, with most of the rings around the white collar. And granted, some of us blue-collars got stepped on by some of these people to get what they got, but you know what? They were my people and that's the bottom line. Our people had to choose to burn or fly. If that don't piss you off, you need to keep that to yourself. I ran into someone who believed otherwise at some gin mill and he shoulda kept it to himself. No free-for-all, but close. Guess what religion he was? I am amazed and disgusted at the international and even national community, who for some reason or another, refuse to acknowledge that the world is changing and not for the better.

Chicken-shit or candy ass. I don't know except that free and open societies are now fair game for ideology that can only be explained as robotic. I know that most God-fearing Muslims all over the world are good people and I really don't know how the 'Ten Commandments' fits into their beliefs, but I shore know how it fits into America's. How could something so behaviorally correct be so wrong? I'm very aware of the separation of church and state in our constitution, but there is no God? God has some bearing on any government, free or not. Let me go back again, way past the beat cop. Back around Jamestown and Plymouth Rock. Columbus showed all of Europe that there was indeed a New World just for the taking. I feel for all the native Americans, both North and South, who took the brunt of that taking . . . but I wasn't there 'cause if I were, it would have been done much more humanely or you would have read about it in People magazine . . . nothing has changed. The "New World" remained so for some centuries, with lots of different European countries sailing over here and setting up shop in both North and South America. At the same time, Europe was emerging from the Renaissance and once again, change was in the air. Absolutism, the Inquisition, Martin Luther's Reformation, the French Revolution by which French democracy was born, and most importantly, the Anglican religion in England are all major factors of our emergence. Especially Henry the VIII Anglican religion. All of this challenged the Catholic Christian empire, which by now had stood for centuries. Hard to make change go away . . . in fact, impossible. But the Pope at that time still had a firm grip on Europe. The Crusades was a disaster but that's another chapter. But just as now, there was much persecution of other people's beliefs. That was especially true in England, whereas the very fundamental and deeply religious Puritans and Shakers were looked at as sinners by the more extravagant Anglican followers, and were jailed . . . or worse, for their beliefs. So they sailed to the new world on the *Mayflower* to be religiously free of any oppression.

George Washington decreed in our constitution that never again will any government have the right to favor one religion over another. We separated ourself from any religion. Somehow, when religion gets mixed up with politics, someone's screwed up opinion usually becomes law.

What about the Taliban constitution? *Howabout alittle fire, scarecrow? Ha, ha, ha!!* America is now embroiled in the same situation from which it was created. However, there is a major difference. No one is persecuted or looked down upon just for believing in a different deity. Now the 'Ten Commandments' and other Anglo-Saxon symbols of religion are very offensive to a small contingent of Americans for a reason that is written into our constitution. Just with that being said, they are somewhat correct on their stance. But I ask, "Is there any country out there who have absolutely no religion in their doctrine?" Let me see. The only one that comes to mind would be the Soviet Union. Whatever became of them? I'm no political major player but I'm pretty certain that of almost all of the countries out there, within their boundaries, race plays a big role in determining the prominent religion. Even among countries that lie thousands of miles apart but on the same longitude, people somewhat look alike. I'm no racist, that's just what I see. One country is one religion . . . another thousands of miles away is another. So maybe race isn't such a major factor. I think it's more tribal than national. The Middle East shows us that national boundaries play a miniscule role in determining countries' prominent religion. Europe was conceived of settlers and nomads just as the U.S. was but that was thousands of years earlier. But at that time, it was still primarily tribal way before countries were carved up on the map. Over the years and moving past mythology, tribes adopted their version of their existence and that's how I think their religion was conceived. Why do you think that we now have billions of different formal last names; ie: Smith, Jones, Warts, Kadiddlehopper and many others. That's why we now have Christian, Muslim, Jewish, Buddhist, Hindu, and others that I can't put my mind on. Either don't mind or no mind to talk about shit like this!

But all countries have some religion in their doctrine whether they're separated or not. The belief in God is what keeps people chuggin.' So why is it attacked? America was founded on the belief in God. Nowhere in our charter does it say God does not exist. It only says that no religion is any better than another and we are free to worship as we please and see fit. That's all. Also if you believe in no God, that is also your right. But the prominent belief in God, no matter what religion, is all over the U.S. "In God we trust," "Under God," "God Bless," are part of apple pies recipe and its been that way since day one. The 'Ten Commandments' exemplifies what we are all about and how we go about it. Nothing more, nothing less. To attack it because it is cast upon public space for all of us to see and by which to live just doesn't make any sense at all. Sure, it's religious but it's also behaviorally correct. What's wrong with that? Someone wrote in some major newsrag that all of the commandments could be construed differently by different peoples. *Thou shall not kill.* **Give me another meaning for that.** It is a part of Christianity under attack. Happy Holidays, no more Merry Christmas anymore. It offends newly arrived immigrants and God knows, we can't have that! It is not politically correct. Who invented that wambly-pambly pussyfart bullshit anyway? I am not offended at all by any religious symbol occupying public land during religious holidays, no matter what. Crosses, Jewish symbols, Santa, nativity scenes, or whatever you believe are part of our religious rejoicing during these times, so why are they pissed on? As mentioned earlier on, religious fanaticism is on the rise in the U.S. and will cause problems in the future. Likewise, secular fanaticism is also on the rise, but only by a few, and will also cause problems in the future. I do believe in separation of church and state and likewise, I believe in the value of living 'Under God,' just as our forefathers thought. If I ever hear about some dumb ass public school banning the Declaration of Independence again because God is mentioned in it, then maybe I'll get my fifteen minutes of infamy in fifteen seconds. ***Get your act on one stage America, our future depends on it.***

Lackland Air Force base. Air Force boot camp was nine weeks. Johnny turned that into fourteen weeks. Get to that later. He arrived in the middle of the night and was military by morning complete with haircut, fatigues, and a squadron with whom to live. A squadron is further separated into flights of forty-five men who live and train together under one roof. A squadron is best described as a company just as a flight is described as a platoon. Air force is alittle bit different as you can see. But this is the discipline he needed at the time. Out of school and directionless wasn't working and he needed this to work all the bugs out. It did but it took many more years for the seed to sprout. *Military discipline* stays with you for life. About this time, he was just starting to shave. He was going through an acne phase and that made shaving quite difficult with him cutting up his face thus pissing off his drill sergeant. No problem. The military has products for anything that you can only get in the military. He was issued a sulfur-based ointment in a small container such as a noxema or vasoline container which had a generic military label on it identifying what it was along with its military identification number on it. It's made to dry out the skin and if done correctly, the acne is virtually gone the next day. Done correctly is the reason for telling you this. On the instructions in big letters, it says wash the face with this ointment and in bigger bright red letters it says rinse immediately. Johnny says to himself, "What the hell is that going to do?", and left it on all night. When he woke up for chow the next morning, his face hurt and felt real tight. Everyone in his flight freaked when they saw him the next morning and some other recruit told him to go look in the mirror. He looked like a four thousand year old Egyptian mummy and he thought that he would never ever look the same again. Dried his face out like a desert lake. Took a few weeks to not get looked at funny. He had a chapped face from hell. It made boot camp just alittle bit tougher. Once embedded in boot camp routine and training, everyone gets into one finely tuned machine. Marching in parade in dress blues gave you a sense of worth even with the hostile attitude expressed by the public around these times. He pounded out week after week until he got involved in a fierce altercation with another recruit that resulted in forty something stitches on his head. Got whacked in the head with another head . . . ouch! His lost. He was set back and put into another flight and that's how he tacked on five more weeks of basic training.

After he completed basics, it was then time to go to his technical school for whatever your MOS . . . the job in which you agreed to do when you first joined the service, which are located at various Air Force bases all over the country. Johnny's tech school was located in lower central Illinois at Chanute AFB in a real small town called Rantoul in 1976. While there, he decided to take some leave time to go back to Connecticut to get his Camaro he told everyone about. He readies for the trip back to base, throws his stuff in back seat, and off he goes. It was winter time on the way back to Illinois and convertibles are tough driving, always fighting the defroster. He made it to Bloomington, Pennsylvania, when the motor let go right on the highway. He secured the car at some car shop, arranged a tow back to Connecticut and decided to hitchhike the rest of the trip. A sign that he made for passing cars to know where he's going was right to the point. It said "west" in big letters and he took his place on Interstate 80 looking for a ride. He got to see a lot of Amish culture out in that part of Pennsylvania which he thought was pretty cool. He got a ride from some dude in a hot rod and after warming up for a while, asked the driver if he wanted to smoke alittle bit of temptation . . . whatever the hell that means? It mean't this. This dude got so fucked up, he damn nearly forgot that he was driving a hot-rod and was way all over the road, even goin' sideways down the snowy road. This scared the crap out of Johnny and decided to part ways and got back on the highway, airing out his thumb once again. It was around one or two in the morning and he froze his ass off until he got another ride. When he saw a sign that said, Chicago 623 miles, he damn near cried. America's a big country. He finally made it to Chicago but the trip was not over and he was in a vicious snowstorm with nowhere to go. In a vacant parking lot, he spots a salvation army clothing box, climbed in it and warmed up for quite some time; most of the night before he hit route 59 heading south and he made it back to base one day late. As usual.

Back on base, he begins to learn the nuts and bolts of air-frame structural repair and also learned that he's gunna like his new career. He met someone at Chanute who many years later, he would meet again in his hometown. With the country as big as it is, that's almost a mathematicaly impossibility. The training he received at tech school was about the best anyone could receive anywhere, with him learning more about an airplane than you could possibly imagine. He learned how to fabricate anything you had to, to keep the plane as structurally sound and aerodynamic as it was the day it was made. The Air Force has the best equipment to make that possible and Johnny really liked what he was doing. The only thing he had a problem with, was how far his squadron was from where he was learning his trade. It was winter in the Great Plains and it was extremely cold and raw. Raw for the fact that when it snows there's no landscape to block the wind and the snow comes down sideways and the cold goes right through you. Being from the northeast didn't prepare him for that. His squadron was the 800 Squadron and it was the farthest away from the center of base. It took thirty minutes to march to school each morning in the numbing cold. It was worth it though. After school, him and his buddies would go to the center of base and find all kinds of things to do . . . legal, because the base was like a small town. Sometimes himself and some buddies would venture off base to Decatur and Champagne, the two largest cities in that area. One of his buddies was from a real small town called Hammon which was relatively close to the base. I don't know about now, but back then it was the only town I can recall where you can stand right smack dab in the middle and see the end of town in all directions. It ended at a fence and after that, nothing but wide open flat land as far as the eye can see. I thought it was pretty cool. I could imagine herds of buffalo.

Anyhow, back on base, Johnny's doin' quite well in school and his whole class formed a click and hung around together after school. Most of them even got transferred to the next base when school was completed. There was an airman's club called the Pit and the Ping where he seen Bob Seger when he formed the Silver Bullet band. He knew that this was gunna be a real good band. He saw them again at the next Air Force base he got sent to and this time when he seen them, they were warming up for Kiss. One night he got so loaded at that place, he went outside and passed out in a snow bank and slept there comfortable until one of his buddies went outside and found him. He was kinda ready for the military but still needed to work out a few more bugs. There was something else that happened on that Air Force base that he occasionally thinks about to this day; in fact, every day especially during a ghost flick. When you get scared shitless in one part of your life, you tend to not forget about it. The barracks that house the 800 Squadron are the oldest on base and once housed Korean war vets. The rest of the base was modernized and made of brick. The 800 Squadron were old wooden structures. They musta run out of money during the modernization of the base 'cause the 800 Squadron stuck out as very old and looked like old barracks you see in an old John Wayne movie. Anyways, upon entering his squadron, word has it that strange things occasionally happen at that squadron and just to pay it no mind if it happens to you. Spooks! And you're supposed to just blow that off? What if they don't like you? Never paid it no mind anyways cause he thought it was bunch of bullshit anyways . . . until one night. He got back from the airman's club late one night and his duty was to wash all the mirrors in the lower south latrine. The bathroom had three sinks and three mirrors that took up around ten feet of the wall. Upon entering the latrine, the light switch was immediately on the left hand side of the wall just like in any room you enter and as you walked about five or six steps in towards the shitters and urinals on the right of the latrine, the sinks were directly in front of the stalls to the left. Directly in front of you on the wall next to the first sink was the light switch within hand's reach for the shower rooms. Now, with these barracks of WWII and Korean War vintage, the walls were much more of a solid construction than any wooden structures built nowadays. The walls are made of lat and plaster and are very solid. Punch one of these walls and you had better be one bad dude, 'cause if not, you just broke your hand. The light switches were those old kind you see in an old church or school . . . you know, the ones that make a loud click when you turn one on or off. He was the only one in this latrine when this happened 'cause it was pitch black when he entered and he was in there for a second or two and checked it out like a paranoid crackhead does when they enter somewhere new. While standing at the first sink washing down the mirror, both of the light switches slammed off at the exact same time by themselves followed by a loud thud in the last stall. All at the exact same time, with a real loud click. Johnny reached over and turned the shower-stall switch back on. He watched himself turn white as a sheet in the mirror, went over to the switch by the door, turned that one on too, and left like a funny car coming off the line. He never went back in there again. Caused quite a commotion when it happened 'cause he screamed, ran up and down the hall, and everyone came out of their rooms to see what was going on. Lots of people, who once they believed him went in the latrine and determined that there was no way that could have logically happened, even taking apart the light switches to see if there was something wrong with them. Similar stories like this were mentioned more often than not throughout his tech school training. He knows that he didn't turn them off and make some loud noise. But aside from that, he completes his training and gets orders to report to Barksdale Air Force base located in Shreveport, Louisiana, along with most of his graduating class.

Shreveport was very cool city back in 1976. Johnny remembers this huge mansion in Shreveport on this hill fashioned into the hippest bar downtown. Shreveport is part of Texarkana, in the Arkansas and Texas area, right in the northwest part of the state where the scenery there was almost haunting. A lot of bayous which were eerie and remote. Armadillos were everywhere, especially on the bayous. If anyone has never been out on the bayous, the best way to explain it to you is endless swamps with roads and trails that cut right through them not more than an inch higher than the swamps themselves. Better not swerve or daydream on these dirt roads 'cause you'll be underwater right quick. Another way to explain them is that they are extremely captivating or romantic when parked there with your date . . . or extremely dark and scary, the kind of setting for an unsolvable crime. You would never get caught. Only a very small portion of Barksdale AFB is used by the Air Force, the rest is bayous. It was the headquarters of the 8th Air Force and it was a SAC base. SAC (Strategic Air Command) doesn't exist anymore because of the break up of the former Soviet Union. The Cold War was over and SAC was decommissioned in the early Nineties. Barksdale was one of the biggest SAC bases in the country with a flight line that was made up of over 160 B-52 bombers and KC-135 tankers. Add to that all the runways, huge hangers, and the logistical area that includes barracks, mess halls, command centers, parking lots, and a whole bunch of endless buildings and that took up the land and there were still more bayous that made up Barksdale than the occupied part of the base. Bigger than a medium size town. The flight line was always busy with all kinds of activity with very loud jet motors always running at all times of the day. This is what Johnny wanted: to be part of the real Air Force. His squadron was the CAM (Consolidated Airframe Maintenance) squadron as the whole base came to know. They made some waves. They were ground support and in their hanger, they had anything available to fix anything on those airplanes for which they were trained for. His posse, many who came from Chanute, got to be pretty well known around the base as people who liked to have a lot of fun, even on the job. Lots of people in the CAM squadron weren't bad people . . . just people who should have been split up after tech school but weren't. I think that was an experiment by the Air Force and I believe it was the last time it was done. This made Johnny really cocky. When told to go clean the officer's latrine, he took one look at what they had done to it and told the officer in charge to "go and get your mother to clean this shit up" and left with the four guys he walked in with. He caught some flak for that but he thought he was invincible back then.

Every day working on B-52's. He liked the responsibility and it was an important job at which he was good at. When other technicians couldn't patch up a crack in a jet fuel tank located in the port wing after a week with the wing jacked up off the ground, he snuck in there and did it himself. Once fixed, he put somewhere around two-hundred pounds of air in it, and after some time went on, it still had all the air in it. But he did have a spotter to make sure no one closed up the hatch while he was still in there and filled the huge tank up with jet fuel. A story they all heard made it illegal to enter any tank without a spotter. While on a mission over Vietnam, a B-52 lost all fuel pressure in one of the wing tanks. Upon inspection, comes to find out, an airman who was in the wing tank got locked up in it, the tank was fueled up, and his bones clogged up all the fuel inlets leading to the jet motors. Pretty rough way to go. Whether that's true or not, I'm not sure but I'd much rather get done in by Piranhas than to go like that. One story he told me was the damage done to a wing by a single bird. He seen the damage. It had hit the leading edge of the port wing right at the fuselage while the plane was cruising around 500 m.p.h. It destroyed the leading edge and even bent a two inch fuel line about a foot and a half behind the leading edge and the wing had to be jacked up for about a week to fix it. Johnny thought a frozen butterball turkey had hit it. They repaired the damage in the most professional manner, even replacing most of the components behind the leading edge, then it was back on the bayous. But bear in mind 'cause lots of this novel is based on curious spontaneity, which usually leads to trouble, he had just gotten out of high school and so didn't most of his buddies and they liked to have a good time.

Somebody told all these guys that right after it rains, especially in the morning, these psycho mushrooms grow right next to or on top of cow shit in all the pastures all over Texarkana. So naturally, they would ride out to a cow pasture close by after it rained to check it out. They would pick a whole bunch after learning which ones to look for, go back to base or somewhere off base, boil them up with sweet tea, drink it, and couldn't believe what these mushrooms could do to you. If you over did it, like they always did, it was pretty close to acid. The scientific term for these mushrooms was *phylosybin* or something that sounds like that. On one occasion, they rode their motorcycles out to a pasture, washed down a bunch of them with a few beers, and stayed alittle too long. Johnny had a 1967 Triumph hardtail that was chopped out pretty far and as he's going back to base, he noticed his handlebars moving all over the place, even criss-crossing themselves although his hands were firmly on the grips. He ignored all that 'cause he knew that wasn't real and had to concentrate real hard to make it back in one piece. When he made it back, he got off the bike and kissed the ground. I'd be lyin' to ya if I told you he wasn't scared. These mushrooms were nothing at which to sneeze at. After that, they went to see Leon Russell on his 'Wedding' tour in Shreveport and were still sitting there when the show was long over. The stage was completely disassembled and they were the only ones left in the coliseum and had to be escorted outside. That's piss poor 'cause the band was probably at their next show by the time these idiots left that one. All from a lowly mushroom.

As I progress through his military life, as you can see he liked to have fun, but on the job, it was all professionalism, as strange as that sounds. He knew his job and vowed not to screw this up too. On the job, the sheer immenseness of a B-52 gave him a self anointed job of its owner sorta speak. He took that job with all the respect a job like that deserves and was good at it, but it was the off duty hours that got him. Yeah, he got kicked out of the service and regrets that especially after 9-11 when he got turned down to re-up. That had mostly to do with his age as previously mentioned. But as he got around with his buddies, he started taking things for granted. Would never get caught. Some of that attitude came from hanging out at the bayous. Why do ya think Credence Clearwater always sang about the bayous? It does something to you.

He stayed a lot off base when after a shakedown inspection with the dope dogs around three in the morning, he almost got caught. The barracks were ringed with military police to watch from what window what was getting thrown out, inspect it, then make an arrest. Lots of people got arrested that night. Not Johnny and his bunkmate. He threw out two ounces of weed from the third floor and heaved that shit a country mile and no one seen it. Not only that, but at random nights before hitting the rack, they would mix up some very ground up pot with some black pepper and sprinkle it all over the carpet. It's ironic that they did that that night. When the M.P.'s entered the rooms with the dogs, the dogs started sniffing the hell out of the carpet and started sneezing like holy hell, one sneeze after another. They were amused enough to start laughing while trying to not to. The pot was eventually found and they tried to pin it on Johnny but he said, you can't arrest me for something you found five hours after the shakedown. That crap coulda come from anywhere. And they didn't. Try that nowadays. No, as a matter of fact, don't try any of that. Use some illusion . . . that's no delusion. He got scared after that and stayed off base at some friends place quite often to relax. He would stay in Bossier City right next to Shreveport with something always going on there. A houseful. He shoulda never moved there with the squadron commander always up his ass wondering where the hell he was all the time. He'd ride his bike back and forth, to base to work, then back to the party at night. They went on a rock concert binge for a while to all the shows that came to Shreveport. One show comes to mind. It was the *Frampton Comes Alive* weekend show that was in Austin, Texas. There were a whole bunch of other nationally known bands there also. Santana, Gary Wright, America, and a bunch of others. Johnny was there in body, but his mind was somewhere else. Too many mushrooms. He passed out in a huge field for over a day, a day that changed his life for the next two months. He was barefoot and wasn't wearing a shirt. Lucky he was wearing long pants. In the burning one- hundred degree Texas heat, he became a rump roast, medium well to well done. He got burned on every exposed part of his body. Massive and hundreds of blisters on his face, feet, back of his hands, and you wouldn't believe his entire upper body. Every exposed part was covered with massive and ugly blisters. He looked like some sci-fi B movie monster. Fries his face all to hell back in boot camp and now this. What's wrong with the dude? It looked like some snake shed its skin when he arose from bed every morning for months. He had to shake out his bedroll every morning 'cause it was just plain disgusting with all the puss and skin everywhere. His beltline was always soaked with puss for over a month. He was allowed to, with reluctance, to put his one stripe on his arm with a magic marker when on duty because he couldn't wear a shirt. He lived in the shade for the entire summer of 76. He was truly a sight. This pissed off the squadron commander and he started to lean on Johnny. This is about the time he refused to clean up officer shit. After that, he seemed to be in trouble all the time and the commander ordered him to move back on base, and then he got sent to the brig for a week or so. But he still loved the Air Force.

Not too many people get to see this, but he got to see a SR-71 Blackbird reconnaissance spy plane land and then take off hours later. He'll never forget that. No airplane leaves the ground like that one. He also got to meet the base commander at the gym where Johnny worked out at. The general was trying to get his last rep up on the bench press and was having alittle trouble with it, and Johnny went over to spot for him. This comes back to help him out during his court-marshal. Things really start to unravel around these times. Even getting on the base baseball team didn't help him out at the end. His bike was having some work done to it so he had to walk a lot. Because of the sheer size of the base, he had a long way to walk from squadron to squadron to see all his buddies. On of his buddies who had a car, got a military DWI and those laws were strict *way before they became civilian*. So he walked a lot. Walk into a mess hall with all kinds of food. What a beautiful sight! Walking got old real fast and at one of his buddy's squadron, he noticed a vacant room that was vacant for months. He had his eye on it and one day decided to move in for a second room to crash in. That's against the rules. You can only have the room you're assigned unless your move is sanctioned by the Air Force. You can't just move anywhere you want like he did. He brought half his shit to that room including a killer stereo. Unbeknownst to him, the previous airman who occupied that room had been kicked out of the service for drug dealing and the MP's also suspected Johnny of doing the same thing. Shouldn't have moved there either. He sold alittle here, alittle there, but nothing like the previous tenant. This guy made a living by moving a whole lot of weight. Johnny just made what he wanted to keep for himself, just a little. Incidentally, on the door to this room, were the words *House of Baghdad*. He thought that this was strange but left it on anyways. Having this other room was real convenient and he was right at home with his tunes blasting all over the place. That room musta been watched cause there was some talk about some ongoing investigation still pending regarding the previous tenant. He now has his bike back from the shop. As he's riding back to his new room, he notices a fire at the squadron he had just moved to. He was a mile or so away and could see smoke everywhere. He rode over to get a closer look and was panic stricken when he seen where it was coming from. Almost dumped his bike. Firetrucks were everywhere. He looks up to see flames just pouring out his new room. Everything was lost, including most of his uniforms. His stereo was melted into a one piece unit, and he knew he was in trouble. Someone firebombed his room. This is the beginning of the end. The squadron commander where the fire took place inquires as to whose stuff was in that room knowing that it's supposed to be vacant. Johnny fesses up and all kinds of things start to happen. That squadron commander lumped Johnny into drug dealing because of the previous tenant and he don't have a leg to stand on. His own squadron commander felt the same way and he's got no alibi. He's never met the previous tenant, even to this very day! It was his reputation he couldn't he couldn't hide from. Buried himself with his cocky-ass attitude and now he's fighting a drug charge he had nothing to do with. The next day while on duty on his plane he was working on, he is summoned by his squadron commander. Remember the FBI that Babe used to work with? Now they're working on Johnny. Just like the X-Files . . . two dudes in white shirts wearing ties, sitting in a chair with the oversized, overhead bright white light and he was now being charged with arson by the FBI. Imagine that! A past firebug now being charged with a fire he did not set! Johnny got immediately pissed and showed it. They kept knocking him off his chair. He stood his ground but still lost. When the F.B.I. informed him that they would make the arson and dope charge stick, he called them everything but the kitchen sink. But he seen the writing on the wall and knew he was in deep shit. That's what this book is all about: *bad fucking decisions and attitudes that always seem to burn us all.* Anyhow, he goes to work each day, but he has been knocked down a couple of notches. I'd be lyin' to ya again if I told that this time he wasn't really scared.

But anyways, something took his mind off of all that for a long time and I'm beginning to think that Johnny is feeding me a line of crap cause this little story makes the one I just made up sound like some kind of fairy tale. To some people out there, that's all this story is gunna amount to. But he don't lie to me or anyone else. He lives by the golden rule, a man's word is either *golden or garbage* and his is not the latter. Go get yourself a couple of beers for this one. If you don't drink, then just keep an open mind. We just had a ghost story but now he wants to talk about something that's just as eerie. He swears on the Bible that all of this happened. Yeah, there's a lot of these stories that are just blowing right off the table just like all my blow on a windy day but stuff like this you just can't make up. If you did? . . . then why? Life's crazy enough. Why make it crazier? One night, Johnny and a buddy of his from Baltimore were riding their motorcycles just off base in Bossier City when they noticed that everything they were looking at had a bright green glow about it. Everything was illuminated by a bright green light no matter where you looked. They both looked up and saw this flattened egg shaped object that seemed like it had a million volts going through it. Go ahead, take five minutes to laugh and let it all hang out . . . done yet? Good, 'cause they couldn't take their eyes off it, and almost locked handlebars, forgetting for a second or two that they were on bikes. They immediately road back to base because this thing was hovering directly above the flight line. It lacked perception meaning that they really couldn't tell how high in the sky it was. But you couldn't miss it and it drew a crowd. Everyone was on the roofs of a lot of the barracks all over base looking at it and after a couple of hours or so, it got kinda boring and Johnny just went to sleep. But he missed the grand finali when the next day lots of people who stayed on the roof said that it just shot straight up like nuthin' they ever saw before. Next day, the Air Force never said anything about it. Johnny's been meaning to go back to Shreveport to see if he could look up some old news clips, if there are any on this subject during the summer of 76. He knows airplanes, from vintage WWII airplanes all the way to the F-22 Raptor, and knows that this was no airplane. He did some investigative research on this matter and found that most UFO sightings occur over or near military installations. Secret projects? Who knows, but this looked like the real deal.

But anyhow, we're talking UFOs. At least I am. That's what Johnny and everyone else who was there concluded. This area of this novel is for believers in anything, especially anything not found on earth. Do you believe in the age and the size of the universe? If so, one must imagine that the earth isn't even a blip on the screen in respective to its environment in all of space. If you take a pound of salt like you buy at the supermarket, dump it out in a paved area the size of a small state. I'll tell you why. Each grain of salt represents a star. Now place every grain of salt seven miles apart away from each other. Try to keep it circular and that would be a viable comparison to the distance of all the stars from each other just in our own Milky Way. To those of you in high school, that's a galaxy and yeah, it's also a candy bar. Our own galaxy, and now you can eat it. There's more space than matter in a galaxy than one would believe. It's a real big universe 'cause that's only one galaxy amongst billions. I don't think that we are the only tenants. Who really knows how many other galaxies are really out there. To me, the earth is nothing more than a spaceship traveling through space on a predetermined course on its way to *who knows.* It's moving at warp speed but not at the speed of light. Einstein proved all that and it's backed up by modern science. Nothing moves faster than light. That is a basic law of physics. Even going at six trillion m.p.h, light crawls at a snail's pace in relation to the immense size of the universe. Now, that pretty much makes interstellar space travel virtually impossible since even when traveling at the speed of light, you've pretty much covered a small portion . . . if any of the universe. Hell, just to get from one end to the other of the Milky Way at the speed of light would take one-hundred thousand years. You gotta have that crazy speed like in the movie *Spaceballs.* Even Marco alien probably has a life span I would presume and they also would either die en route or expend a portion of their lives during space travel. So how do they do it? Here's something that makes sense that I did alittle research on. I also had a lot of help. I barely made it out of high school . . . you know I had some kinda help!

Physicists have theorized the big bang creation of the universe into acceptance by the scientific community. Most of the matter and the elements in the universe were expended from this explosion. Who's to say that all these elements weren't distributed evenly or fused together to form some *aleo-element* just after this explosion. As we all know, we have all the elements known to man listed on the *periodic table of elements.* In present day high school, that means that the element is made by Honda. And yes, it's a SUV. But anyway, all these elements are listed from the lightest element . . . helium, to the heaviest, some unstable radioactive metal. They are listed by atomic number . . . how many neutrons and protons make up the nucleus of the atom, and by their atomic weight, whatever the hell that means. How do you weigh an atom? All of our elements from every kind of metal to every kind of gas and liquid that we know are on this list. The higher the atomic weight, the more unstable the element is such as uranium or plutonium. The higher the number, the more you have to know to work with that element. Plutonium has one of the highest atomic weights, somewhere around 110 or so. Don't hold me to that. That's a very large nucleus. All the force and anti-force is leaking out of the nucleus of these elements, thus making them radioactive. There's too much going on in these massive elements for the nucleus to be able to contain all the action going on in the center of the atom. Some of these elements are man made through physics, but only for a brief instant since we do not have the technology to contain them in an environment in which they can exist. Since they exist at all, they are also listed on the *periodic table of elements.* It's these heavy man made elements in which I'm gunna concentrate on to justify my theory. Imagine unknown to us, elements with atomic numbers up around 150 or so. If physicists tried to mess with something like that, they'd wind up probably blowing up the planet and half the moon. Wouldn't bother me though, I'd be wearing a helmet. But why do all these heavy man made elements blow apart at the seams when they are conceived in laboratories? It's because all those neutrons and protons are fighting each other for space to exist in, sorta like two countries trying to occupy the same space. I'm bigger or badder, so you got to go, something like that. *Something has got to give and if we both can't be here, then none of us can exist is how these elements behave.* There is an intense gravity force within the nucleus trying to hold all this together. It is called a nucleus gravity, somewhat alittle different than gravity as we know it. As you can see by now, I have a P.H.D. in "pollywog crap" and I took it all the way in for another missed opportunity. You don't have to be no space cowboy to make up stuff like this, but it does help, but it is theorized by God-knows-who that the faster you approach the speed of light, the more time is stretched out so that seconds are really years even though it don't appear that way to you while you're haulin' ass through space and time. The faster you go, the really really older you get even though your physical being has not changed one hour. Look at it like this. Take two mirrors. Place them opposing each other with a beam of light bouncing off them at one second intervals while not in motion. Then move them at twenty miles per hour. The straight beam of light bouncing off both mirrors now are not straight anymore . . . because of motion. They are now, in fact, diagonal. Now do it at the speed of light. It'll take ninety years for that beam of light to hit the other mirror whereas if not in fast motion . . . only ninety seconds. Yeah, you gotta at least know some space cowboy out there to run a line of shit like that, but an interesting line of jibber-jab shit that some people are probably already laughing at me about it so I'll just cease and desist. "Laugh at me, not with me," says the cowboy from time.

Anyways, nothing can escape from within itself with an atomically heavy nuclear gravity, whereas we can escape regular non atomic gravity, but only for a brief instant. Just jump up and down. You just broke the earth's gravity by jumping up but the earth's gravitational force, being larger than yours, brought you back down. We do not have the technology to access this nuclear gravity which I believe is crucial for timely interstellar space travel. I believe Marco Alien does. How does it all work? Sit down, start workin that second twelve-pack, light up a smoke, and listin to this. Like I really know, but here goes. First of all, how do black holes exist? Like I know that too. Johnny says they're black. But as we know, the more matter, the more gravity and black holes eat matter in the best possible terms. Black holes are collapsed stars that have used up all the elements within themselves, their fuel, and now has no centrifugal force. I'd try to explain what that is but I'm 'bout over this. For every action there's a reaction. With no more centrifugal force from its mass, it now implodes and if big enough, doesn't stop there. Anything near it gets caught in its gravity?, then it too, becomes part of the monster. Once big enough, not even light escapes its gravity thus the term black. On a high school note, that's why they call them black . . . no light. Need to leave the kiddies alone, not their fault . . . of course not. It's this scenario Marco alien uses for space travel only without using a black hole. I'm pretty sure Marco's got more sense than to go anywhere near a black hole. You see, I probably lost most of you all by now along with myself . . . I gotta read from a book to try to explain all this anyways, but who carez how lost anyone iz, but all that intense gravity warps the fabric of space and time . . . this gets alittle heavy, to the point where stellar objects are a lot closer to each other than they normally would had that super-intense gravity not been there at all. Chug five beers . . . just about the same thing.

What's so hard about that? Marco has figured out how to access the intense nuclear gravity from super heavy unstable elements that we don't know about to mimic the same environment that's found around a black hole. Alls they do is fire up their space hemi and bend space along with time . . . they might be from the future, in whatever direction they want to go to to make objects closer than they really are in passive time, then turn it off, and voila! . . . instant alien. Just add water. What's so hard about that? Johnny does that everyday, just by using what's left of his case of brew. Okay . . . in simpler terms: take a sheet of paper and draw a star on both the opposing corners. Consider that sheet of paper to be one million light years of the universe and now bend the sheet of paper to make the stars you drew touch each other. That's what I'm talkin' about, bending space along with time.

Any of this if true?, would shake up our concept of ideology and question religion as to why. All of this opens up explanation and some kind of adaptation to other life other than our own. After all, God created the whole universe. Johnny says all of this is nothing but pure bullshit. He's got his own theory. He says Marco Alien is out there for a reason. One alien Saturday night, Marco and his buddies went to an alien titty bar and were shocked by what they saw. Nothing but scales, tentacles, antennas, slime, eight mouths, no breasts, suction cups, nine eyes, slithery ooze . . . and did I mention, no breasts. They freaked. Need a new friggen bar! Then, coming in for a landing is Marco's cool cousin, Fluffy, and he bears real good news. I just found this real cool planet and I got these to show ya. He whips out a couple of *Playboy* magazines, opens up the centerfolds and proclaims, "I know where there's whole herds of these," and off they went. Been here ever since. Now I know that some of these little four foot freaks of nature have been noted during some abductions, to seem to like our females more than us. You wanna get rid of these little alien perverts for good? I know some little green hoes who need to be abducted and once these little green fucks get ahold of them, they'll spit out a bunch of these twenty-first century modernized Millie's right quick and we'll never see a UFO ever again. You see, I'm used to Millie, even her mama, 'cause I'm some kind of Martian, so I'm told, but not your favorite Martian. See if anyone gets that.

Around this time, something also happened that made him feel pretty damn good. And this happened on earth. Johnny and all of his buddies were at some creek that had a real good Tarzan swing. One of his buddies who always went to Dallas with them when they went was black and couldn't swim at all. No one knew that and when prodded to hit the swing, he mentioned that he wasn't that good in the water. Johnny's buddy from Baltimore, who was there on that extraterrestrial night, assured him that he would fish him out if needed. Well, after he went off the swing, it was quite apparent that he could not swim at all. Johnny's buddy, whose name was Bill dove in after him. Terror set in with Johnny's black buddy whose name was Mike, and now Bill was in trouble, now in a fight with Mike 'cause Mike had nothing onto which to grab on to and Bill was the closest thing and Mike was only thinking about something to grab so he don't sink. It was nothing personal, only survival. Now Bill is freaking out and screams, Johnny at the top of his lungs. Johnny dives in and by now both Bill and Mike are separated by a few feet. Johnny grabs Mike in a headlock and pulls him back to the bank of the creek and told him to never ever do something you do not know how to do ever again because Johnny also told him it would be a day of infamy when he was there when somebody died and he couldn't do anything about it. It's pretty hard to see anything in those bayous and I don't care if you got X-ray vision. If Mike went under, it would have been all over. But aside from that little episode in life, they all would go to Dallas quite often. One of Johnny's buddies was from Dallas. Johnny loved that town. Why do you think they made a TV show about it back in the Eighties? He couldn't believe how rich his buddy's parents were when they got to that house their first time there. A beautiful mansion. He also couldn't believe the crazy ass parties they would have there with a lot of locals showing up there also. Dallas was cool and I'm sure it still is. Even the gas station attendants were pretty cowgirls. Someone should name a candy bar "Cowgirls." That's a pretty good idea.

But while chillen' in Dallas, he's also thinking about all the shit he's gotta face when he gets back to base. He's still freaking out about being roughed up by the FBI. If he ever told his family about that, he probably would have been told to just stay down south forever. But he also had help in his military demise, no one other than himself. Lunacy, like this. This story is called 'Not Thinking.' Some of the repairs done on B-52s were done by the use of fiberglass as most of us know it . . . fiberglass batting or cloth with a two part resin mix. But for more precise fiberglass repairs that involved a certain tensile strength, they adopted a different method that really had to be learned. This was done with a four part resin mix. A sheet of plastic would be laid over the resin cloth repair, then secured to the damaged area by use of a special clay that was used to stick the plastic down around the perimeter of the plastic. A suction pump removed the air between the resin repair and the plastic. Then a squeegee was used to make it perfect while carefully letting the suction pump do most of the work. When it was hardened, it looked like glass. To make it work, the four part resin must be mixed in order. That means 1,2,3,4, not 1,3,4,2 or any other combination except only 1,2,3, and 4. Any other combination other the way it's supposed to be results in a violent chemical explosion. They shoulda never told this to Airman Johnny. He wanted to see how big an explosion. So one day he rigs up a real long rod that he straps on a plastic container and has in it the last resin to be dumped in which he mixed wrong into another container containing the other three. When he dumped it in, it produced the most terrifying, bright, and loud flash with the most noxious, toxic gas that filled up half a hanger the size of a few basketball courts and had to be evacuated. You wanna talk about trouble? That would be construed as terrorism today and would probably get some pretty rough time over. I'm pretty sure that was the last nail in the coffin.

He has dug a pretty big hole for the military to accept and is told by the squadron commander that they don't need his help anymore. He is threatened with a BCD (bad conduct discharge) and is sent to the base commander for finalization for signature of the discharge and out he goes. Johnny recognized him from the gym and he recognized Johnny. He asked Johnny how much he liked working on airplanes and Johnny replied, "A lot." He also told the General that he was innocent of both those charges and that there was no way he could prove it. The general picked up the file off his desk on Johnny that he got from Johnny's squadron commander and told Johnny, that because of it, alls he could do was "lessen the blow but you still gotta go." He also told him that because a BCD, you'll never get a job in the aircraft industry ever again and switched his discharge to an Honorable discharge. He left the General's office and went back to CAM squadron one last time to say good-bye, grab his stuff and went back to his barracks, the correct barracks. Reality hit him and he just couldn't believe that he was getting thrown out of the military. His buddies didn't want him to leave so he hung out in Shreveport for about a month just trying to find himself. When you get the boot in the military like he did, they're only obliged to get you to the front gate, getting back to where you're from is up to you.

He's bumming around Shreveport for a while and decides to pack up his bike and head north. This is his first interstate motorcycle trip and he got excited over that. He got on interstate 20 and decided to check out the south and got off the highway in Jackson, Mississippi to check it out. That was pretty cool and got a room at some motel, bought some beer and readied for the next day. He got back on the highway for a while, then got off again which turned out to be a mistake. While on a double yellow lane secondary road, he spots a semi tractor-trailer coming at him about a half a mile away, just flying towards him. Paid that no mind 'cause the truck was in his own lane. Johnny rides alittle to the left of the center of the lane, more closer to the double yellow lines than the white line on the right, and when this truck blew by him, the suction or backdraft created by the truck sucked him completely over into the opposing lane. Lucky that there wasn't a car behind the truck or it would have been a perfect centerpunch. He never hit anything but caught the white line on the other side of the road, ran into alittle sand and because of the long forks couldn't hold the bike up and laid it down. This is on some remote road and no one is around. The bike wasn't really damaged at all except that the forks got tweeked 'cause they were so chopped out but still, it was unridable. He's in Mississippi with a broken bike, little money and now a decision must be made. To try to fix the bike and go broke in the process, or say bye-bye and carry on, on foot. He gave the bike to someone he met after knocking on this dude's door saying he'd be back, but never did and hit the road with his thumb. He really wanted to show everyone back home the bike but that's impossible now. While hitch hiking on interstate 20, he's wondering if anything is ever gunna work out or if this is it, yer always gunna be a fuck-up. Little does he know, he hasn't really seen nuthin'yet. He got to Atlanta, which unknowingly to him, would become his home some twenty years later. He recalls Atlanta back in the Seventies and thought that was a pretty cool town and thought about staying there. He was kinda afraid to tell his folks back up north about what happened with the Air Force, but he decided against that and made it to the airport. After paying his airfare, he was left with only three dollars and all of his weed. He got frisked down by this cool dude security dude while just entering the plane on the gangplank and got caught. He just let Johnny move on.

Johnny's back in town, alittle disgraced to himself and had to explain why he never fulfilled his full hitch. Makes up this, makes up that but everyone back home knows him and he can't hide it. But that's the way it goes and he just tells everyone that if you join the service, I'll tell ya exactly what not to do. He gets right back to where he left off from before he joined the service and apparently hasn't learned a damn thing. Rusty wasn't too happy but let Johnny move back home to regroup. He moved in the basement and went to work as a gas station attendant, now a defunct job, for one of Rusty's best friends. All of Rusty's friends hung out there, a lot of cops, and these guys were the coolest bunch of guys in town. Kick back and knock down a beer or two. They liked to make fun of Johnny's lifestyle and occasionally would hear from one of them, "What else you gunna screw up?" A lot of Johnny's friends also worked there and this was a job, but it was also more of a place to hang out once the clock was punched. After punch out, he'd go and get some beer, go back and hang out all night long with Rusty and his buddies. They also did all kinds of towing including police calls. One night while on call, Johnny was sitten' at some bar with one of his co-workers when the beeper went off. They left the club, got the tow truck and went to the accident scene. It was a fatal on Interstate 91 and the car was Monte Carlo that flew off the highway decapitating the driver. It was way down an embankment and had to be winched back up to the road so that it could be towed. The car was demolished. Before being towed back to the garage, it had to be washed down to get rid of all the gore once the body was removed. They did all that and towed it back. The next morning when Johnny and his buddy got to the garage to open up, they took only one step in the building to realize that something was dead wrong in there. It stunk like death in there. Upon re-checking the wrecked car, it was found that they missed some body parts the previous night. They found a part of the driver's head and Johnny will never forget that. Black dude. Afro on one side . . . brains on the other. Pretty damn rough, even with no brains. One thing that he liked about working there was the owner's daughter. He knew her way back from kindergarten when he gave her seven Valentine's day cards on the holiday. She grew up to be one of the prettiest girls in school and he knew that was going to happen even way back around the first grade. He knows women, but back in the first grade? She wouldn't give him the time of day and that's when he realized, *you can't always get what want, but if you try sometime, you get what you need.* Actually . . . you get what you get. What you need comes only after you get it . . . good or bad. More bad timing . . . for the some of us. Not Johnny. He gets nothing. He just don't get it, or maybe he got it. He damn sure thought he got it. Good or bad . . . makes no difference. But now he knows it don't make no difference anymore noways . . . 'cause now he knows. Deep or what!

It is around this time he bought his Sportster. Back on two wheels. If you own a bike, just remember, it don't come with bumpers or airbags and once again, it's time to learn the hard way. He shoulda been killed or seriously injured twice on this bike, but just got lucky. While working for the postal service years after he bought it, he was traveling down an employee parking lot when some woman just backed out her parking place without looking. He was directly behind her and had no choice but to crack the throttle and hope he makes it. He almost did but her bumper just caught the rubber on the very rear of the tire. Just like bouncing a basketball, the bike went flying out from underneath him, flipping once in the air and coming down right next to Johnny. She jumps all over Johnny like it was his fault and he tells her to shut the <that lawless word again> up or he was gunna stuff her in her trunk. She kinda freaked and didn't say anything after that. He did apologize for the lude comments and kinda got embarrassed 'cause of his language. Even an asshole like him has some kind of scruples. Checks out the bike and to his astonishment, it still fired up and was road worthy. He rides away without incident. No police involved. When they say that they didn't see you, usually that's not a lie. That's why I say, the louder the bike, the safer you are. Some people say that's annoying, I say then look where the < dogs do it > you're going. Sorry about the bad word again, but you're not the only ones on the road. The road wasn't just made for you, believe it or not. But about these times, it happens again. This was alittle bit worse. This time he was riding on Interstate 91 during a rainstorm and the rain drops felt like bee stings on his face and he could barely see. A ferocious storm that made him just wanna get home just as fast as he could. He wasn't wearing a helmet which made the rain all that worse. There's no helmet law in Connecticut which I think is good. *Let the rider decide.* I don't need no bureaucracy, insurance or no one else telling me how to run my life because I couldn't care less how anybody else runs theirs. If I get hurt in the process . . . God forbid, that never happens, and you don't wanna help me out 'cause I won't conform to our life smothering rules?, then let me die, if you wanna drive a point home. But I'll be back. If I gotta come back and haunt your shirt-and-tie punk ass till the day you die, I'll make sure that you'll need to wear a helmet for the rest of your life because my spirit will be super pissed that I could have been saved but because it cost too much 'cause some *bureaucratic nematode* said I was breaking the law and just let me slip away. My spirit is a female boxer. Name's Super-Freak she *superfreakyyy*! I know about safety and I know about risks. I can balance out between the both on which is more important at the time. Money, or a lack of, isn't gunna dictate any of my decisions. Healthcare crisis or not, I'm not hurtin' anyone 'cept some lawmaker who probably has some stock in some insurance company. Sounds pretty one-sided, but I'll probably air some more of this out alittle bit more as I pen more of these rantings of a lunatic as I blindly scribble and Babylon. Finger-painting. But anyhow, he gets off the highway to a main drag in town just wantin' to get the hell out of the pouring rain. He comes up on a red light, and not seeing any cars anywhere, decides to run the light. The rain just hurt too much. He didn't see a Camaro coming down a hill into the intersection, and it was now too late. Upon seeing the car about twenty-five feet directly in front of him, at the last second he lays the bike down as to not be involved with the impact. He wound up sliding behind the car by a few feet. The bike slams into the passenger side of the Camaro, wedging itself under the car along and severely damaging the car also as Johnny sails on by the car, sliding on his back and coming to a stop without a scratch on him. Lucky that he was wearing a leather. Once the bike is pulled out from underneath the car, it still fires up. Only a Harley. Surprisingly enough, he doesn't receive any citation from the police and rides away. Never heard from the car owner either.

After a few months at Ma's and Pa's, he rents a big ol' house in the southend of town on New Year's day in 1977 for two-hundred and fifty bucks a month. Lots of things start to happen. It's around these times he got a job as an apprentice plumber which comes in handy many years later with his own houses. During the late Seventies, there was a construction boom and new homes grew like mushrooms. Not those kind. Johnny worked for Joe who owned the plumbing outfit and who was a childhood friend of Rusty. Rusty got Johnny a lot of work around town. They worked through the winter time, roughing in all the plumbing on all the new construction and could barely keep up. He learned the trade fairly well, well enough to change his own boilers in the two different homes that he owned. He was kind of dumbfounded upon learning that the local plumbing codes which pertained mostly to drainage capacity, vary from town to town. What's done right in one town is wrong in the next. Had to be on your toes or all your work gets ripped out, and then redone. That happened a few times. Even for the minorist of things. While working the plumbing trade, Johnny met one of his running around-all-over-creation buddies. He worked with his father in the bricklaying trade. Johnny and George did everything together, even the same women. Most of the dumb-ass shit Johnny does throughout the rest of this book was done with George. One thing that they both had was a penchant for gorgeous, fine ass women. That's what they lived for, which to me, is a very good thing. Girlfriends here, girlfriends there, with periods of no girlfriends just to relax alittle and get home from the bar any time I want without it sounding like a real bad marriage that the neighbors can hear three houses away. While speaking about women, one thing about these two was how shallow they both were. Didn't care what race, creed, or national origin, come from Mars, or anything else just as long as they were real pretty. Deal with the mind later. Didn't care if she belonged to MENSA or was slightly slow either. That's one heavy chauvinistic attitude and I must say that deep down, that is the attitude of most people just as long as they don't mention it to their wives. Johnny's taste in women hasn't faltered to this day, but don't think that he just views women just as life size Barbie dolls to play with. His perception of women has already been stated. He's not gunna lie, he views women as superior to men because they are much prettier. Why do you think that the actual king of an ant or bee colony is really a queen? No man will ever go through life without the support of a good solid woman who will stand by him even when he's wrong. No murder or rape or anything like that. What woman in her right mind would stand for anything like that? The respect that a man has for his woman equals the respect he has for himself. Women bear the most challenging and painful, but life essential role in mankind. They bear our future. With that being said, every woman on the face of the earth deserves the most utmost respect any man can offer. Crimes against the fairer and weaker sex makes Johnny sick. Doesn't do much for me either. When a woman says no, it takes a much inferior mind to continue on. This type of inferiority complex isn't something that can be fixed with rehabilitation, *but with only brutal punishment.*

Johnny holds this philosophy close to his heart, but he's still the shallowest, blinded-by-beauty vulture I know. There are many ways to get in touch with the love of your life. Old fashioned boy meets girl, or modern times rock-n-roll, just type it in. Or you can just stalk 'em then rape'em. Don't kill'em though, they'll live through it and somehow get through this. Don't put the frosting on the cake of the crime, might get in trouble. What is rape? An actual crime?, or a vendetta against my male co-worker 'cause he smiled at me in private, like passing each other going the other way down the corridor. Define rape. Something wrong in Sodom and Gomorrah when shit needs to be defined or told what color it is. Some people who practice politics on the side, from usually out west, define shit as anything but being brown. I think I heard a while back, and if true, then I got a major problem with this, that some politician has mandated that date rape punishment shouldn't be as harsh 'cause if she were awake, she might consent. I like everything that starts out on the west coast 'cause it's new and innovative, but this gets me so pissed, that I begin to shake. Because she can't consent, you can fuck her any which way but loose, but just as long as she remains asleep. If she wakes up?, then you are hardcore rapist, awake or not. Last I knew, women called all of all of the XXX-plicit shots with who they like or liked at the time, who knows?, maybe all of the time. But what will we say if something like the (someone really needs to pay) humiliating, un-thinkable intrusion that happens to women happens to me? Rape is rape just as wine is red. Some politicians spend too much time on the beach and not enough on the bench. Women are human beings, not some piece of prime meat to be sampled at your wish whether she likes it or not and some politicians need to go through the twelve step 'ape to human' course, all eighty million years of it before they ever come up with some bullshit like this ever again. What rhymes with rape? Howabout ape. Apes live on instinct. They don't know. Humans live on thinking and memory. They do know. In this case, the ape is much smarter. Hate to say this but if I ever catch ya fuckin' a human mannequin?, then I'm sorry, you might not see your next birthday. Sorry bout' yer luck, pal.

But aside from my hairy-ass, professionally braided arm pits, and lightly bearded mermaid side . . . probably not gunna mention that again 'cause it ain't true noways, things happen right about now that are meaningless at the present but play into Johnny's future some time down the road a ways.

One day while walking down the road, an old high school friend pulls up and says get in. He was on his way to take the civil service entrance exam for postal jobs opening up. Johnny says he ain't doin' nuthin' anyway and goes along with him down to Hartford to take the test also. He took the test and passed. He really didn't give this any thought but was impressed with himself for passing it. But he's not really interested in working for the postal service. Unbeknownst to him, he would be in the postal service many years later for thirteen years. He is now presently working at an auto junkyard rebuilding starters, alternators, and generators. Some of the people who moved in the house also worked there. I could write another book about the things that happened here, but I'm not. 'Cause it would take many volumes of what you wouldn't believe anyways, and the only volume that I pretty much care about nowadays is that do-dad volume thingamadooder on the wide-open stereo. No writing at all, wide-open tunes says it all. All of us would wind up in a small room somewhere. Why? Who the <leave this blank> knows! Happens to some of us sometimes, but a very cool friend from school moved in 'cause Johnny couldn't afford the rent by himself. Dino was learning the carpet trade and would eventually show Johnny the trade some time later.

Incidentally, just upon release from the Air Force, while still staying at his folks house, Dino came by to pick Johnny up for a stone ride. Dino had a big 'ol Dodge Coronet 500 and they were way out in a remote part of Connecticut called Warehouse Point. Actually, it's located in the Connecticut valley, but it was pretty damn rural, or least the last time I was there. They only had one mary jane cigarette that needed to be rolled up. Since Dino was driving, Johnny did the honors. The stereo was wide open cause they were listening to "Starship Troopers" by Yes which was and still is very cool. Good ass jam. Since Johnny wasn't the best joint roller at that time, Dino had his hand cupped under Johnny's to catch any weed that Johnny dropped. They were on a dirt road with no one around so Dino had his foot off the gas as to ease up on the bumps so Johnny could roll the bone alittle easier. They were puttin' along around two or so m.p.h. goin' really slow when they came up on some railroad tracks that they knew were there. You know how some railroad tracks are raised up sorta like a plateau? Well that's the way these were. They had been there a hundred times before so they weren't surprised by them. As they felt the car going up the incline, Dino had his eyes on the only joint they had and was still making sure that he would catch any weed that Johnny might drop as he was still rolling the mistake. While still twisting the *wick*, with the tunes still wide open and both still oblivious to anything around them, they feel the car level off, then proceed down the decline on the other side of the tracks when they heard what they both thought was a tornado or some kinda instant earthquake. Johnny thought he got nailed by another dinosaur bite. Dino cuts the tunes immediately and they both look behind them only to see an Amtrak train just sailing on right past them one passenger car after another and another. Their car was still on the decline and the train just missed the trunk of the car by about a foot or so. That's how close this was!! They heard the whistle as it cruised on by but because of the tunes, they had no idea that they were giving the train engineer a frickin'heart attack as he was trying to warn the car. The engineer musta blocked his eyes as he came up on the car and probably still talks about that close call at Thanksgiving year after year. Johnny and Dino smoked the badly rolled temptation (bands named after that < only one comes to mind >), then went to some bar and both were shaking so bad, they could barely hold on to their beers. Dino practically had to use all of his feet also! That was just downright close! As this novel is being penned, both Johnny and some other train would meet again. But it also missed.

Working at the junkyard and living at *the house* was pretty cool. Now, this part of this novel should be a lesson on what not to do when you got nothing else to do 'cause this yahoo is lucky to be alive and still know his name. But anyways, this was a house that he lived at that some people still talk about to this very day. First impressions count, but when they last thirty something years? . . . nice work. When Dino moved in, he was a carpet helper, good, but not quite good enough to make it on his own. He would take home all his larger carpet scraps, seam them all up together, different colors and all and then install the carpet in the house. Looked pretty cool, like a collage of colors. Made the place look real lively. People came and went in this place and the kitchen walls where the phone was became a phone directory with hundreds of phone numbers written all over the place. Want a pizza? Look on the wall. There're a few numbers for that. There was one thing that Johnny didn't tell Dino when he moved in. Rats. Not field mice, but Biggy Rat and all his buddies. And all of his rat-ass bitches too. When Johnny was there alone for the first month or so, one night after closing up the Polish home across the street, he woke up in the middle of the night and went downstairs to get something to drink. When he entered the kitchen to pull the pull cord in the middle of the kitchen to turn the light on, alls he saw was about ten or so huge rats just scurry out of sight in less than a second. You'd be amazed at the smallest of places through which a large rat can run through. He went back upstairs and stayed up all night for the rest of the night. He freaked. Together, him and Dino decided to eradicate them with rat poison. This turned out to be a foolish decision because you don't just pick up the carcass, then dispose of it. First you gotta find it. You won't find any of them when they all die in the wall. Rats are all gone and everything is cool for a while. Well, a couple of days go by and Johnny wakes up and hears in the next room that Dino is already up. Johnny's door is closed and he hears Dino open up his door. Next thing he hears is a puking sound, then the front door opens then closes. That was amazing because Dino made it from the second floor and out the door in around two seconds. Being curious himself, Johnny opens his door to investigate. I don't know what's worse, the smell of dead flesh or a dead rat . . . especially a whole bunch of them. I've smelled both. Unexpected circumstances and all that which sucked but anyways Johnny joins Dino outside and they have a real problem on their hands. With towels wrapped around their faces and soaked in aftershave, they go in and go back inside and kick in all the walls until they find them all. After being in the wall for a few days, they ballooned into the size of footballs. Would have made a maggot puke!! If you can make a living, moving piece of rice puke?, you can make bout' anything happen. They repair all the damage and the old black pipe plumbing that they broke in the process.

But they had a good time throughout the summer of 1977. Then came the summer of 1978. I might have skipped some time there, but you can pretty much tell what he was doing throughout all that time. Nothing really noteworthy. Johnny went to the Rolling Stones "Some Girls" concert at the same stadium where the Buffalo Bills play in the summer of 1978 with *some girl* in her car. The show was in Buffalo, New York, obviously and they rode the New York thruway all the way there which is a long ass drive. Took around five hours. After the show, they got stuck in a massive stadium traffic jam for about four or five hours just trying to get out of the stadium parking lot, and finally got free. They left for the thruway around eleven o'clock that night and Johnny had the remains of a pretty good buzz. He was driving. He didn't plan on leaving that late and just wanted to get home, but only made it halfway when he fell asleep at the wheel. She was already asleep. It was lucky that she owned a big Ford LTD. A trucker who stopped after the accident told Johnny and the police that hejust came up on me in the lefthand lane, passed me, then got back in the righthand lane and just kept on going right, never made no attempt to stay in the righthand lane, left the lane into the emergency lane and went into the woods. Johnny woke up when he thought that someone was knocking on the window to wake him up, but it was really all the branches and brush hitting on the window as he was plowing through the woods. He tried to regain control of the car just before it hit a tree, thus sending it back out on to the highway into the median separating both the east and west lanes where it came to rest. He told me that if he didn't wake up when he did, he would have hit that tree head on. The car was hammered but still roadworthy, and they both refused ambulatory service and the police let them proceed on. I told ya that the laws back then had baby teeth. Thank God for big ole' LTD's, but this caused lots of problems between him and her.

But aside from Johnny's brush with death, this house was now becoming Grand Central Station, with people popping in and out at all times of the night. The only rooms that were kept were the four bedrooms upstairs, the rest of the house was trashed all the time. Someone didn't like the radio station that was playing so it got shot up. Wood was being split in the kitchen and thousands of beer cans were strewn all over the place. Motorcycles and parts were all in the dining room, which became the motorcycle garage. Some girl painted the Stones *hot lick* . . . big tongue, on one of the walls that took up the whole wall and she did a real good job. Rusty would stop in every now and then with his buddies, all of Johnny's friends thought that Rusty was pretty cool. They'd take look around and say, "You guys gunna be alive tomorrow?" Billy, who also lived there, did work on Rusty's car. By this time all the rooms upstairs were full and rent was real cheap now. They would tap a keg and if it lasted an hour, that was good. This was a balls-to-the-wall place to live and there wasn't enough room for all the people who wanted to move in. There was actually a waiting list but you had to be part of the posse. Johnny ran the show but everything was done by democratic vote. This was about the time disco music was ravaging the nation. They had girls staying around to help keep the place up in return for a place to stay. The first summer in 1977 was too much too soon, a non-stop monsoon with one party after another after an another. Johnny and Billy had some pretty nice bikes along with just about everyone who stayed there and decided to build a ramp in the dirt driveway to keep out all the cars that clogged the place up all the time. It was about two feet high and they would hit that and almost fly to the front porch when they landed. I'm told that some cars made that jump also. It was around this time Johnny decided to boost a car just for the hell of it. He hid it over someone's house. When asked why it was parked in the backyard and whose car it was, he was cornered and told to get it the hell out. He brought it to the house and asked the same thing. Once he tells everyone what's up, everyone got in it, drove it up to the sand pits up in Rainbow, stopped at the package store, then ran it to death, then torched it. Poor car. Don't get stolen next time!

At these sand pits, there was a very long reservoir that had a hydroelectric power plant dam that produced a lot of electricity for a lot of the town. This is something you don't want to do, unless you like raw, uncontrolled power at your disposal. The power lines that ran out of these generators ran right over the pits. They did not ride the contour of the landscape, but instead ran straight across the pits, even over the hills. When on top of a large hill, these power lines were only twenty-five to thirty feet over your head. We would only do this at night, especially when an airliner was coming in for a landing at Bradley Field. Give the passengers something to marvel about. We would go to a nearby tobacco field, cut off some of the *bent wire* used to hold up all the cheesecloth, get up on one of the hills directly under one of the power lines and heave it up until it short circuited two of the power lines. The first time Johnny was there with some other people and did it, he thought something went terribly wrong. It started fires all over the grass on the hills with fireballs spewing all over the place. Not even the Sun was that bright, and the sound was nothing but pure, raw electrical power. Couldn't hear nothing but what sounded like all the airplanes on the flight line at Barksdale on full throttle all at the same time. Johnny freaked in panic and thought that he blew up the world!

After the first time, you get used to it. The passengers on the incoming flights could easily tell how many people were out there with the thousand foot long shadows that they were casting. Imagine coming in for a landing and seeing that! When hanging out at the local package store in Rainbow at night and you see all the street lights start to flicker about, you know that someone is doin' the power lines. Something like that would also be considered terrorism nowadays.

As one day got more extravagant than the previous, so didn't both of the New Year's Eve parties while he was staying at this house. Just like the one previously mentioned, these were just downright weird. As a matter of fact, nothing like these have ever happened since. I know that some of this is starting to sound like weird science mixed with alittle bullcrap, but I know some people who are still alive and some who ain't who can vouch for everything I think I know or seen. *Babes in Toyland* is more believable than some of what's been said already, but take it from someone like Johnny to tell it like it was, and take it from someone like me to tell the world how it's pretty much gunna be, 'cause we all read the papers and watch the news and what's more weirder than that? Everybody out there knows the sameas me. Just watch the news. Makes ya cry. Makes me blush.

During the winter of 77 to 78, some people that Johnny was hanging around with while working back at the airport while back in school, decided to go to this New Years eve party way out in Tolland, Connecticut. That's a cruise from his hometown especially during the blizzard that was happening that night. To this day, he still don't know any of the people who owned this beautiful, immense house at which they arrived at. One of those kind of parties. There was practically no furniture, just tons of people sitting all over on the wall to wall carpet. The driveway was a very long hill with steep ravines on both sides. On the bottom of these ravines were many, many cars that tried to get up this driveway during this blizzard but apparently couldn't. He thought that was strange. Sorta like a conveyor belt where something went wrong so turn it off, but didn't. While enjoying himself after he got settled, he decided to scope out the upstairs of this place. He's walking around and opens this door to this huge room and walked into some kind of swinger party. Alls he saw was tits and ass, doggy style, three on two, homos, missionary style, and any kind of style and went back down to the kitchen that was green with empty Heineken bottles and told his buddies, "You're not gunna believe this." They all say, "What?" He told them that there was all the free dope you could have . . . alittle white lie, and told them all what room to go to. He pulled out his own dope, which was the first time he whipped it out to show them that night and told them all he got it upstairs just now. They all fly upstairs while Johnny stayed in the kitchen and just waited for the reaction. They all came back down into the kitchen with ear-to-ear smiles and asked Johnny what his version of dope was. This party was; party downstairs and if you wanted some, just go upstairs no matter who or what you were. I don't know about you, but to me, that was strange. Not as strange as the next New Year's eve party.

This time they're at the top floor at the Sheraton in Hartford. Once again, he knows no one there except a few that he ran into. "Been along time, how ya been? Whose party is this?" "I don't know, I just heard about it somewhere." Someone rented out the entire top floor of the Sheraton and had bowls of blow in damn near every room. Didn't have to pay for no booze or dope. Johnny and his buddy were in this room around five in the morning with a mirror and a bunch of lines in it when all of a sudden here comes Five-0 bustin' in all the rooms, arresting damn near everyone. The room that they were in gets raided and guess who's looking at who. There's Rusty just staring at Johnny. He tells him and his buddy to get the hell out of here . . . we'll talk later. Next day, Johnny fesses up. Rusty' been at the house quite a few times and knows what's up, but it was never as blatant as that. Respect. The next night both Rusty and Johnny are at Johnny's folks house in the garage and Johnny was disgraced with himself over this. He tells Rusty that he knows what he's doin and how to go about it without gettin' stupid or hurt. Rusty then says, "What about that stupid little episode last night? That's gotta be the stupiest thing you've ever done!" He tells Rusty that he didn't expect no police raid 'cause it was New Years and that he never gets that loose like at that party. He tells Rusty that believe or not dad, I know what's more important than just a good time. I wanna be something someday. Rusty says that you really got a funny way of showin' it. But he knew Johnny and gave him some advise that Johnny passed down to his own kids which works. Goes like this; *You can do whatever you want, apparently I can't stop you, but when both feet come off the ground, it is no longer up to you.* ***"Better know who the hell your***

friends are!" That's a piece of philosophy that seems to have been long forgotten in this day in age and that my friends, is piss poor! If Johnny can smartin up, then what's wrong with the rest of us?

Something to think about, but at these times Johnny's got about the same smarts as a clam. Like this. One day while down by the Connecticut River shooting river rats to pass the day away with all his buddies, they got bored. There was about ten or so of them all armed with shotguns and other assorted rifles plus some handguns. They were also having some problems with a few of their neighbors. Imagine that! So they get an idea. They decided to split up into two groups. One group puts up their guns in the trunk of Charley's car, gets on their bikes, and flies back to the house screaming that they're coming at the top of their lungs. They all hit the jump in the driveway along with Charley in his beat up Cadillac boat, then get the guns out in plain sight of some of the neighbors, and run inside the house. This was in broad daylight. Then here comes Johnny's group five minutes later and they enter the same way just screaming and cussing about some bad shit that just happened to them that they were just making up to get the attention of the now astonished neighbors. They do the same, get out all their guns and scream, "They're in the house!" and enter brandishing all their weapons like a it were vicious gang fight. Once they were all in the house, it sounded like the Battle of the Bulge in there. The neighbors are now taking cover and running back into their homes. In reality, alls they all did was go upstairs, open up all the back windows and unloaded about a hundred rounds into the backyard ground. The neighbors by now had called the police thinking that there were bodies piled up to the ceiling by now with what sounded like automatic fire with all the guns going off damn near the same time. Damn near the whole entire police force show up with guns drawn. The neighbors are plainly excited while telling the police what they saw and at the same time Johnny comes walking out of the house like nothing happened and ask what's goin' on. When asked about all the gunfire, Johnny says, "Oh that? We want to plant a garden out back and we don't got no garden tools so we loosened up all the soil with our shotguns. What's the problem?" The neighbors were incensed and now the police put together what these guys had done, even making one officer laugh and discount anything else Johnny said or has to say after that. Rusty knows Johnny's landlord and they both show up and they are pissed. The landlord threatens to tell Babe about his grandson and what he's become. Johnny's family had been keeping Johnny's crazy lifestyle a secret from Babe. Babe was ill at this time and died a few months later. Rusty tells the police on the scene to do whatever they want with them. They all got charged with discharging a firearm in an urban area. Johnny, being the last in line of two prominent law officers, got out of serious trouble that time. He now looks back on all this and wishes it could all be different. But he can't. Whether or not he was aware or cared about the strain and embarrassment he caused on his father and grandfather, I don't know, but he shakes his head when he thinks about it. He understands some of the animosity directed towards him from some of the more established citizens of his town and they all knew that he would never follow in the footsteps of his predecessors. That's why he moved away, *never to be seen again.* He also knew himself, and to embark on a career of law enforcement and live the way he did would be to create a conflict of interest. However, some of his friends didn't. Once they became cops, he lost all respect for them. Not because they became cops, but because they desecrated the blue uniform by trying to be something that they weren't. But getting back to the haunted house, he looks back with mixed feelings. It took him many years to learn. But back then, it was all fun. He regrets all of this, but sometimes I catch him smiling about something and I know what he's thinking about.

During the summer of 1978, things got alittle crazier than that. M-80s became the fashion of the day. You remember those? Firecrackers that sounded like shotguns and weren't like any firecracker at all. They packed a serious wallop. They blew up anything they could get their hands on, especially captured rats. Very messy! Johnny's future brother-in-law from the next town over lost two of his fingers to one of these. Somebody he knew threw one out a window of a car, and it hit the top of the window frame and bounced back in on to his lap, and Dee-Dee reached back from the front seat, grabbed it and tried to get rid of it, but it went off in his hand. Ouch!! One night, Johnny left the Polish home and went up to his room to go to sleep. He was walking around in his socks and the light didn't work in his room so he just felt his way to bed. He felt something under his foot, took another step and felt it again. He was pissed 'cause he thought it was dried up puke. He went and got a light bulb and once there was light in the room, he saw that someone had thrown in around ten M-80s in his room and blew his carpet all to shreds. Being in the carpet business nowadays, that doesn't sound like a bad way to remove glued down carpet for a re-lay. No one fesses up and now Johnny must take matters into his own hands. Billy comes home from the junkyard one day just covered with grease and jumps in the bathtub on the first floor. The bathtub was one of those cast iron ones with the claw-like legs. It was an antique one probably worth a few bucks. There wasn't a showerhead so you could only take a bath. On a hot summer day, Billy just wants to clean up. Johnny had a different idea. He waits until Billy was in the bathroom for a while getting comfortable in the tub, then blows open the door and sees that Billy is in the tub full to the top with water and says, "Someone wants to say hello" and tosses a lit M-80 into the tub. Billy, not being stupid, knows that M-80s have underwater fuses and immediately jumps out of the tub just as it went off. Johnny tells me that he had no idea what happened would happen and couldn't believed what he saw. It blew every drop of water out of the tub all the way up to the ceiling and when it came down, it just drained right out on to the floor. The concussion from the blast had blown out the entire bottom of the tub leaving a hole about two feet by one foot, and all the water had run out of the bathroom and down the hall into the kitchen where there was a few people. Their good buddy who was in the kitchen choppin' up some blow was a Vietnam vet and looked at Johnny like he was *charley* or something. They wound up framing out the bottom of the tub with two-by-eights and filt it up with cement. Felt pretty rough on the ass. See what happens when you don't think? Billy would have gotten his balls blown through his butt if he hadn't gotten out of that tub when he did! You're supposed to learn when something like that happens by your own hand but not after Johnny threw a lit M-80 under the drivers seat of his buddy who was driving a Volkswagen Beetle while he was in the back seat some time later. When it went off, the car looked like no one was driving it, 'cause it scared the driver so bad with all the smoke filling the car, it almost looked like one of those suicide car bombs, and by the time he regained control of it, we had crossed all the lanes while out of control. The driver stopped and said to get out. Johnny said that it was only a muscle spasm that made him do it and that it wouldn't happen again.

By this time, *the thrill is gone* and they are all though playing with miniature pipe bombs. He had a friend who lived at an apartment above this bar in town where he saw Kiss when they were still playing in northeast bars. About the same time Aerosmith was doin' the same thing. It's now called the Tobacco Shed but back then it was called the Curb Exchange. There was a period that it was closed . . . for about four years because of a murder that happened in 1973 which is still unsolved to this day before it was reopened into the Tobacco Shed. Rusty's buddy Joe, who Johnny worked for as a plumber's apprentice, bought and refurbished the place and Johnny did a lot of plumbing in there. Anyhow, this dude who lived upstairs dealt blow like you just would not believe, so much so, that the clientele came to him, he never left the apartment during the whole summer of 78. While everyone else had healthy summer tans, Mark looked like Casper the friendly ghost. Mark had this beautiful Italian girlfriend who was a ballerina at the Hartford Stage Theatrical Company. Johnny gets the hots for her also Italian friend but keeps low 'cause of her boyfriend. Johnny grew up with him as a kid, and has known him since childhood and nobody wanted a piece of that. Had better be armed or as bad as bad gets. But since Johnny likes taking chances, and she was so damn pretty, he didn't care one night and Mark's girlfriend wanted to go down to Hartford to party with her friends who also danced with her as ballerinas. So all four of them take off and wind up at a place called the Warehouse, which is a gay bar. Like I said way before, testicles are useless on some of these guys who dance like that. Not to be as closed-minded as that, but I just make the same mistake as society does, *judging a book by its cover.* Not my fault. But Johnny told me that if straight people were as open with their sexuality as these people were and still are, the vice squad wouldn't have enough time or people to handle all the complaints. What if straight people carried on like that? Then you are now considered a sexual deviate and will pay the price. Not these people. Double standard? Dry hump yer girlfriend in a public bar and see what happens! Even though some of these people knew that Johnny walked in with a couple of chicks and knew he was not gay, that didn't stop some people. One dude even had the audacity to tell him that he could make him gay in one night. Johnny replied as he pulled out a knife, "I can make you bleed like a river on the very same night." That was end of that. That's not quite the way he said it, but the message was the same. But most of the queers in there were pretty cool and they respected Johnny for what he was and Johnny, as he got to know them . . . respected them. Plus these people had the best dope around, and for him to hang around a place like that was anything but short of spectacular.

While at this house, they had to endure the Blizzard of 78. It had a major impact on them all as it did with the entire northeast. No one can imagine a storm like this one. It snowed like you would not believe, almost to the point where that if it wasn't snowing all the time, then something was wrong. The bikes were in the house. The cars out in the driveway looked like little humps in the five foot snow . . . then by the next day, were completely covered and the driveway looked like there were no cars in it at all. That's how much snow there was. The cars were completely gone for about a month or so. This house was heated by an old antique oil fired boiler, forcing steam into all the old fashioned cast iron radiators in every room in the house that are common in older homes in the northeast. Naturally, they never had any oil for heat so Billy would bring home around fifteen or twenty gallons of diesel fuel home from the junkyard every now and then to keep the place going. Diesel burns alittle faster than regular fuel oil, so he would always make sure everyone was cumphy-cozy and during the blizzard, he was always bringing it back to the house. The house had no insulation and the wind sometimes would go right through it, making things just alittle bit tougher. This was a real disaster blizzard and everyone at the house thought it was really cool to sit out a regional disaster, which it was according to then President Carter. No one was allowed to be on the roads except those who drove emergency vehicles and the governor of Connecticut enacted penalties for anyone not complying with these rules. That's how bad it was. During the day, they would keep the heat around fifty degrees while everyone who was working was at work. Billy didn't care about no penalties, and neither did Dino. The lack of constant heat made no one care about no nuthin.' But when everyone was home at night, the heat got cranked up. But there was something wrong with the heating system at this place. The firing mechanism was screwed up and it wouldn't fire up just by turning the thermostat up to what temperature you desired. A funny story . . . or at least Johnny thought so. Just before the blizzard, the weather wasn't really that bad so they turned the thermostat off completely during the day. Some girl was staying at the house at the time all day long. But it started to cool off one day and she went to the thermostat and kicked it up a few notches. Of course, nuthin' was gunna happen, so she kept it up all day long. The diesel fuel kept on going in the firing chamber in the boiler but wasn't igniting 'cause of the problem with the system. It had to be lit manually and to be safe and effective, and it took two people to make it work. One person manned the thermostat while the other person went down to the basement to actually light the fuel. The person down in the basement rolled up some newspaper real tight, lit it with a match, stuck it in the little hole above the firing chamber, then screamed GO at the top of his lungs so whoever was upstairs could hear him. The person on the thermostat simply turned it up, thus making the fuel enter the chamber and once it hit the lit newspaper, the heat was on. Problem solved. Well, on that day this girl poured all this unlit fuel into the chamber, it was Dino's turn to light the fuel that night. Johnny was down in the basement with Dino 'cause they were talking about some carpet stuff, 'cause at that time, Dino was showin' Johnny the carpet trade and they were talking about something about it. No one knew that the firing chamber was packed with diesel fuel and when Dino screamed GO to Billy who was on the thermostat, and stuck the lit newspaper in the hole, that's when the whole friggen thing blew up. Johnny was standing on the stairs on the other side of the basement when this happened. The boiler which was about half the size of a small car moved about six inches and pure, thick, black, acrid smoke blew out the real small hole above the firing chamber and turned Dino black in the face just like you see in a cartoon. That's not the funny part. Glad Dino's not here right now because he didn't think this was funny at all and he's lucky that he didn't rearrange the shape of his head. The basement was only about five feet high so to walk around down there, you gotta scrunch down alittle bit so that you can walk around. If you play for the NBA, you gotta crawl. Anyway, when this thing let go, Dino instinctively runs like hell and got knocked completely back where he came from when his forehead from the eyes up slammed into the first joist he ran into. He damn near knocked himself unconscious. He walked around looking like Lieutenant Worf on Star Trek, the Next Generation, same as the first, for around a couple of weeks or so. Johnny got the biggest kick out of that and couldn't stop laughing for a week. Is it just him?, or does everyone else out there get a jolt out of someone else's misfortune the way he does?

But aside from stuff like that, these times are about the same as before. Ain't no time like the present. It's not until he marries in 1982 that things start to smooth out and now he sees that he has now a responsibility to attend to. Maybe marriage is the slap in the face to get in step. He seemed to understand all that and really wanted to make something of himself and he though by marrying probably one of the prettiest women that ever walked the earth would help, well, he seemed to have screwed that all up too. Only in the twilight zone can one try to do something right like that and have it turn out so wrong. But it took twenty years to screw it all up, that's the onlyest good thing about that. To this day, he's still not sure if he could of made it on his own. One important fact that he understood was that he fathered his first child with her while still dating her. A lot of shit goes through a man's mind, or should, when faced with something like that. To run and hide . . . or stand up and shut up and take responsibility by the horns. He thought about a fatherless child. He thought about running. He got friends all over the country and that would have been no problem. Then he thought about how that would have made him more of a mouse than more of a man. No, he knew what he had to do. What was the most important factor involved was that he really loved her and wanted to stay with her wherever she went. But he wasn't ready for this. He was now expecting a child. He always said, "How can anyone duck this?" Even a scatterbrain like him has morals and feelings. And there's always guilt. That's if you screw up and do the wrong thing. He couldn't live like that. It only took him about five seconds to take her hand and make two hearts one. *How could someone do anything else?* But all of this is in his future and don't mean anything back at the house. Back then, he didn't even know her. All of that philosophy I just mentioned is neanderthal to him while staying at the house. He wouldn't understand. If you weren't pounding down the dope and washing it down with a case of beer, you just weren't living. His landlord nearly shit his britches when he showed up unannounced one day and saw the house converted into a garage surrounded by a bunch of who-gives-a-shit-people hanging out. Not to mention the bathtub. Johnny said that it just fell apart on its own. If I were that landlord, I'd be gettin' out of prison right about now.

While at the house during the blizzard, the whole town was practically a ghost town with everybody holed up in their homes. Not only was the heat sporadic, but there was little or no food either. Not a problem. The only place open in the whole southside of town was the Polish home, which was directly across the street from them. The wind was ferocious. If it weighed fifty pounds or less, it got blown away. It was now time to go to the Polish home to pump up their tabs so that they wouldn't starve. Everyone has tabs there. Johnny didn't have any boots so he wrapped his feet in heavy plastic, tied it up on his calves, and put on his green army trench coat and off they went. While on the slick, icy road, he opened up his trench coat and caught the howling wind and sailed right past the Polish home probably doin around twenty-five or thirty m.p.h until he wiped just like one of those ice sailboats I used to see on TV but don't see anymore. When they got into the Polish home, the whole damn town was in there. Something about a nor'easter that brings it all out. Anyhow, all this passes just like everything else and now comes spring. Disco was the craze of the land. *Studio 54*, and all the other less famous dance clubs around the northeast rolled till bout' four or five in the morning almost every night. His sisters were the queens of cool back then, but he just could not adapt. All these clubs were overflowing with blow, and not to mention the women. He just had a problem trying to dance like that but he did adapt to that and got used to it. Nowadays, he thinks back on all that music that all his buddies just could not stand, and I'm not sure if it's age or wisdom, maturity or whatever, but now he thinks that it really wasn't all that bad. Very lively . . . sorta like Mexican mariachi music if that makes any sense.

But there was one place at these times that was everything but disco. This was the hippest bar in Connecticut back then. All the top bands in the area played there, even nationally known bands. This place was called 'the Shaboo' and it was immensely large, with about three or four bars inside it to accommodate the crowds that filled it to capacity every weekend. Only problem was that it was located in Willimantic, which was about an hour drive from the house. Every now and then we'd hear about so-and-so who didn't make it home on the way back and wound up in the morgue. After closing, it was a long, tough drive back home. But they were always there. One night while messin' around with a bunch of valiums, some of them weren't allowed to get in. They all went back to the car, which was parked in the back, and noticed how it used to be some kind of barn or something like that. They also noticed how the whole back of the place was wide open, with the bars being overhead as you entered the back of the place. They all looked around for a way in when someone found a set of stairs that went to this door that seemed to go nowhere. *May as well check it out before hitten' the road back to town.* Turns out that the door was unlocked and when they opened it, there was another door about three feet from that one. They also heard voices. Not caring about that, they just open it, and five or six dudes came walking out of the closet of the dressing room for whatever band was playing that night. The band freaked alittle seeing all these people just pour in their dressing room from the closet. Johnny explained what happened at the door and begged them not to rat on them and the band said no problem. They didn't care if that band sucked. They were very cool. One band that comes to mind was a band whose guitar player/singer came from the same town as Johnny and went to his high school also. They had national hits and had their very own sound. They don't exist anymore, but if you ever want to check out a very good band, check out NRBQ. They even have a following down here in Atlanta to this very day. There was another band that Johnny will never forget, and that's because of their name. The band was called Root Boy Slim and the Sex Change Band, and they were damn good. None of what you heard back then in this place had anything to do with disco . . . just real good rock-n-roll. The Shaboo is long gone. They say it was hit by Jewish lightning back in 1983. So goes another era.

It seems like I've been shoving a lot of dope down Johnny's throat throughout of what you've read of this novel. That's not really true. He did it all by himself with no help from anyone. These are decisions that you should really think about before you ever want to do something like that. Just as there will always be alcohol abuse, the same will always be the same with drug abuse. But I think I can distinguish between messin' with drugs and how they mess with you. As we all know, drugs are bad for you. Not according to all these TV commercials I see all the time. Now I know that doesn't make any sense. Those are prescribed; the ones I'm talking about aren't. All of this hinges on who you are when you decide to do something like dope. As we continually hear in our present day society, drugs kill. That much is true, but again, that still depends on who you are and what you're looking for. I believe . . . and this might come across as alittle murky to some of you . . . that addiction *is a symptom of not really knowing what you're looking for or for that fact, who you really are.* In the process of looking for these answers while dabbling with dope, that's when you give the demon time to wrap both its claws around your neck. And I really can't comment on pins and needles 'cause I only have limited experience on dope delivered with a needle. To me, that's like Satan pulling on your puppet strings, stealing your soul piece by piece, and I pretty much checked out the same day I checked in. This also might come across alittle murky, but I see drug abuse in two entirely different ways. I think this a good thing to hear 'cause if you really want to understand something like this, it's usually more effective to hear it from someone's who's been there, done walked that walk, survived it all, and can better describe to you how all this unfolds . . . rather than hearing it from some of those no-mind zero-intelligence TV commercials that depict anyone out there who has experimented with drugs in the past as some kinda Virginia sniper. Remember, I used to party with Johnny. I also know what's good and what ain't. Not too many angels were in his clan. The first way on how I see it would be called *drug use.* We all use something daily . . . not just drugs to exist and sustain ourselves, whether for work or for play. We use food because we have to use it. We use cars to go and get the food. We use computers and TV for information. Nothing really wrong with any of that. Some of us use drugs Some of us use drugs cause the doctor says so. Sometimes says so alittle too much. The second way I see it, is what we all call *drug abuse.* Some might not agree with this, but like I said before, drugs and everything associated with them are not going to go away any time soon 'cause alls you gotta do is just say no, which ain't bad, but if you really want to tackle a problem, the first thing you must do is to accept reality and all that goes with it. But anyhow, now we abuse food to the point where we all walk around looking like blimps. We abuse our cars to the point where we lose our driver's license or worse . . . kill someone. We abuse our information outlets to where that's all we do twenty-four seven. That makes us fat and lazy, so we eat more food. I know that all these metaphors could be just about anything, but you should be able to grasp what I'm trying to get at here. Moderation is the key to staying sane.

Getting back to who you are and what you want equals to what you get and how you get it. Not everyone gets what they want, no matter what's involved or not involved. Getting addicted to drugs, no matter even if it's just weed doesn't make you any less of a person . . . it just makes that person alittle bit more confused as to where ones' priorities are supposed to be. And I'm very aware of how hard it is to get unaddicted to dope, but what I'm trying to do here is to get to you people out there way before this happens. Don't get me wrong, once the day is over, no matter what time of day . . . usually late afternoon . . . maybe I'm gunna have me a beer and a bone 'cause I think I deserve it. Now if that's all I wanna do all day, well, that's a problem. Just because you don't mess with dope means that people who do are wicked and stupid. This has been going on since man figured out what they were, even the ancients. But I will say it helps to not to judge. But I'm talking about reality and people will be people and alls I'm trying to do is help. It's not so cut and dry as I just made it, but if you follow the golden rule, one can step in, then step out of the opium den or crackhouse for that matter, and carry on with all the responsibilities that life has in store for you. There is only one golden rule in the dope game. It goes like this: ***Know Thyself.*** Knowing when to step out is what I'm talking about; not knowing is what I'm not talking about. You can get addicted if you want, and maybe that's because you can't help it, but I'm alittle more addicted to what I have to do to make my mark in the world, not the other way around. That means "Smartin' up! Know Thyself." Myself, I like whatever I'm messin' with at the time for either relaxation or stimulation, but when the clock tolls reality, it's time to check out whether you like it or not. Like I said before, it's not so cut-and-dry as that, but it's up to you, what you wanna be. I used to mess around with crack cocaine, but my way of fighting off the demon was to not smoke that shit on consecutive days. Never two days in a row, and this went on for almost a couple of decades. Kept me sane. I heard that if you hit a glass dick even just once, then you are hooked. Maybe that's true, but I was more hooked on reality than fantasy 'cause I always thought that it felt better. I like pain 'cause it's real. It's good to know what hell is going on around you. I could have smoked that crap twenty-four seven but I'm talking about crack rock, and it was just my own way of staying real. Getting high is getting high if that's what you wanna do. Staying high is the abuse I'm trying to show all you people out there that is gunna get you in trouble in all of the aspects of life no matter which way you turn. It is the sloppiest of two evils, and those evils will always be with us. Hate to be the bearer of bad news, but that's the way it is. Fight back. Know Thyself. Smartin' up if you need to, to make that work.

After a little lesson like that, I hate to move on to the next episode in Johnny's life. But just like me, he's not perfect, and now it's time to mess with barbiturates or 'beaners' as they were called way back when. This lasted for about three years or so and when it was all over, it made him think about what's really more important. Downers became the drug of choice for everyone at the house, and many kinds were available to them. Quaaludes were the ones everybody wanted. Those could be somewhat compared to a Zanex, or maybe two of them. Quaaludes kicked your ass. But if those weren't available, then there were valium, Canadian blues, tuenols, Grateful Dead reds, and others. Any one of these would put you out a day later and a dollar short right quick. Especially the way these guys did them. What made him think about what's more important was how lucky he was with all the carnage he caused behind the wheel while messin with this shit. That's when he said to himself, *this crap cannot go on any more.*

Between the years from 78 to 81 or so, even while moving out of the house to down to the coast of Connecticut for a while, it was beaners for breakfast, lunch, and dinner. To maintain some kind of acceptable social presence, be it anywhere, while under the influence of these things, and all the things that happened to Johnny because of them is to me, is something I'd rather not do. Being social is hard enough being sober, why amplify it? They would all go the Shaboo after eating ten or so blue valiums all at once and maintain. That's a serious tolerance. More like serious problem. Yeah, he might drop a drink or two and forget his change after getting another one, but he could maintain his presence with no problem. Myself, I'd rather just stay at home and enjoy the buzz and fall asleep during a movie than to go out and become a movie. Too many of these things and it's off to rehab. Johnny's never been to a rehab but I can't imagine why not. Sounds like a one man drug store to me! But he confided to me on how he kept his sanity from crossing the horizon which kept him in the right direction. Rehab. His concept on this matter is somewhat unusual, sometimes cruel, sometimes scary, but to me, it's as real as real gets. First of all, what is rehab? That's Johnny's first question. To him, it's somewhere between his head and his feet. Somewhere within himself. Something invisible slapping him in the face when screwing up. Actually, putting mind over matter making sure the ball don't hit the batter. Looking at the big What If? *What if I can't control myself?* That should scare the shit out of anyone! He believes that if he can't do it on his own, then it simply can't be done at all. I'm alittle more warmer toward help for oneself if a rehab is chosen for overhaul. But still, it must come from within yourself if you want results from a rehab. One must hit rock bottom, or see it coming to choose a rehab. For that to happen, something else has got to happen first, like what happened to your priorities? I now care more about that than anything else, but I was once young and dumb and fulla' dumb, so now I know. Shit happens, so don't life. I know that we all stumble and fall throughout life. Many situations, incidents, tests of faith, and even milestones plus other factors will plague all or most of us. Lost love. Lost loved ones. Lost health. Lost wealth. Lost all the time, and so on. Very hard shit to accept, but suck in your gut, stick out your chest, tighten up your ass, and do the best you can. Very hard shit to accept, and I don't really know how to give any advice to anyone who's gone through any of this, but alls I got to say about that is that I'm very sorry 'cause I seem to feel all human pain, even thousands of miles away. *All people are the same, no matter where they were born or where you come from.* But it's not my pain. That's the problem with the world. We just don't feel it. But a rehab is not the only answer to me, even though you might think it's the last resort, unless you have absolutely have no one else to turn to and that's not a bad thing. What is a bad thing is that there is a big, bad world out there and if you wanna put that all on your shoulders, or you just wanna get f#cked up for the hell of it, then I think I can help. Even though I think of going to a rehab as a form of giving up, which will never change with me, I say look into the mirror and look beyond what's looking back at you and look into its soul. That would be you. Look at what happened to you to make you this way. Don't cry or anything like that. This would only be normal when we all come to a crossroad that works our minds. See it as a release valve for letting you get back to earth. No one is laughing at you, well, at least not me because I shoulda been there, but I took my own advise and pulled through. I did it all by myself; no one else was involved. If I can, then you can, and I've had more shit happen to me that would take Johnny three lifetimes to decipher. And I'm only twelve . . . just kidding, but to succumb to narcotics or anything else to make it all go away is only a *short term method of taking on something that really needs to be looked at as long term.* So frigging what! Look back into that evil mirror and smile back at it and do the right thing or at least . . . try. Now I know that lost forever childen would make me go off, maybe for a lifetime, and that's very understandable and I can see that as a life changing situation. Sorry, I can't help you on that one. And I feel that pain, whatever salvation that may bring. I'm human too, but I've been everywhere . . . 'cept there. I just think that there is no one out there who doesn't have the tools to take care of themselves for whatever life changing they need to do. If you can't figure out how to use them or don't want to, I'll hold yer hand all the way to rehab. If the law says you got to go to rehab and even admit to something that you are not, then I feel sorry for ya and I don't think that anyone has the right to judge that hard no matter who or what they are. Howabout that! Now come and get me. I just had two glasses of wine with my pasta and got stopped on the way home 'cause a tail light was out that I didn't know about. Get me out of jail, but don't put me in AA over two glasses of wine.

But anyhow, if you lose your tools, never get out of bed. You ain't got a clue what a big, bad world it is. Nighty night, dumb ass! Now it's time for Johnny's second question. Why is rehab so stinkin expensive? I didn't know that words cost so much. I know how to say words, even to the point where I could even help out a junkie. Alls I get is alittle dope in return. Go figure! Johnny used to know some people who used to go to rehab. One in particular, like one dude who was a plumber back up north. In and out. Here's the difference between him and Johnny. They both did the same shit. Johnny, even as strange as this sounds, *NEVER* went anywhere near rock bottom as obtuse as that sounds cause it really scared him, but this other dude did . . . 'bout ten times a week. He went to rehab. It worked for him, about fifteen times. He tells Johnny about all his vices and problems while Johnny's still maintaining. "Have another drink dickhead and don't go if you don't mean it." Can't do it on your own? *Then it simply can't be done at all.* Of course, there are exceptions, as with everything else, but not with Johnny. He'll start then stop on his own. But he's not invincible. He thought that it couldn't happen here, *but it can happen anywhere.* It can happen yesterday or it can happen tomorrow and it did . . . and it could be real bad. Please Lord . . . take good care of *Loni* and show her all Your mercy and tell her we all miss her . . . *it was an accident.*

Enough about all our vices, bringing back real bad memories. Johnny was getting to the point where he was spiraling out of control with all these beaners, and it came to a head. The shit hit the fan back in 1980 when he got back from the coast and moved in with Dino up in Rainbow who was staying with a family in a big 'ol house. The father of this family was a professional carpetlayer and showed Dino and Johnny the trade. On one night, Johnny, George, and Dino went up to the pits for a huge party. Firecracker fights and everything. Someone put a firecracker in Johnny's pocket and almost turned him into a woman. Not to be outdone, he stuck one in his mouth and lit it off. How he learned that? is beyond me. But anyhow, they are all eating these Grateful Dead Reds which knock your ass clean plum slap up. Plus there were a few kegs of beer. They decide to leave the party to who knows where in Johnny's van that he used to haul carpet. After being on the road for less than one mile, Johnny crossed the double yellow line and centerpunched the oncoming car. Lucky that the girl in this car was sitting right next to her boyfriend 'cause her side of the car was gone. No one was killed, but what a mess! George went through the windshield and landed behind the car that got hammered and broke his arms. The windshield was found on the side of the road, all smashed up but still in one piece, all rolled up. Dino was halfway through the windshield laying almost on the other car. He was sitting in the middle and somehow, the radio missed him when it shot out of the dashboard and went right through the back window. Johnny was entangled all up in the dashboard and steering wheel with his head on the grass 'cause the van flipped over. Guess where the van came to a rest? Right in the front yard where they were both staying! The family who let them both live there came running out after hearing the loud crash. Johnny says as he's laying there all mangled up, "We're home. What's for dinner?" If yer gunna screw up?, may as well be at home. This the beginning of his driving problems which persist to this very day.

Not even a month goes by when it happened again. This time him and his girlfriend were at a huge pig roast party way out in the woods in Ellington when here comes one of his buddies on his motorcycle and Johnny wanted ride it. He had eaten a whole bunch of valiums and was in no shape to even get on a skateboard never mind a bike. Who's smarter? The guy all trashed wantin' to ride a bike, or the guy who gave the keys to him? Actually, the guy who gave up the keys had no idea that Johnny was that trashed, otherwise he would have never givin them to Johnny. Johnny's pretty damn good at concealing his vices. Anyway, the bike comes back in a pick-up truck with the forks broke clean off. Apparently, when he came up on a gradual turn, he never turned the bike and it left the road and hit a bunch of trees and got demolished. He was about one foot above the road, just flipping and flopping still in motion at around fifty m.p.h. when he cleaned out a rural mailbox with his back and left only about one foot of the four by four wooden post standing. He's lucky that it wasn't a steel one or a crankshaft like some people have. There were some people at this house standing outside when this happened and he heard some girl screaming as she was watching both Johnny and the bike flying through the frontyard. He wasn't wearing a helmet and smashed his head all to hell, but with a head like his, it really didn't bother him that much. He went to the hospital when the party was over after he got back. Anyhow, these people load the bike in the pick-up and drove around for a long time while Johnny was trying to figure out where the hell he was. The *coup da gras* that told him that enough was enough was something that I had to ask other people if it really happened. They said that he shouldn't be alive. This time it's Quaaludes, the mother of all beaners. Three of them. He was at another party . . . lots of parties, when they all piled in someone's car to go down to Hartford to another party and he was riding shotgun and apparently, he never closed the door properly. As they were goin' down the road, the door opened and out he went. While in the hospital, his buddy who was driving told him, "I looked over when I heard the wind and alls I saw were your feet, then the door closes." When Rusty came to see him he said, "Your head isn't even round anymore!" He still has scars on his face because of that. He even got road burns on his gums. His buddy was afraid to go and see what happened after looking out the back windshield and seeing Johnny just flipping ass-over-bandwagon on the asphalt like a downhill skier wiping out. But Johnny realizes that he was three times lucky and laid off the beaners for good.

After hearing my view on rehab, do you think that maybe he should have gone? He still says no. It wasn't the fact that I couldn't stop going balls-to-the-wall, it was the fact that I kept on hitting the wall that made me stop, he says. Johnny got high. He never stayed high. It's just the fact that when he got high, things seemed to always happen. Even though he was the loose cannon of the bunch, he still knew about reality and how it was just around the corner no matter what happened to him. He even kept crackrock in check in the years to come. Even after spending fifteen-hundred bucks one night on it. He wishes he could take back those days and do it all differently, but he can't. We all can't. That's why I say it's never too late to start all over again. Alls he did was learn, maybe the hard way, but he still learned. Alittle too late? Not really, just go back to that quirky little saying that was prevalent back in the Sixties, *"Today is the first day of the rest of your life.* Don't mean shit. It does now. Let me ask another question. Should marijuana be legalized? Johnny's got a pretty stiff opinion about that. ***Absolutely not!!*** Think about this. There's too many yahoos and misfits out there to give a free reign of the marijuana patch to a society that cares *more about the play and less about the work.* Someone couldn't even drive a super oil tanker up in Alaska along time ago without running it into the ground 'cause he was playing at the same time as he was supposed to be working. Being an American myself, I will say this is pretty most the most careless, carefree, and incompetent state I've ever seen this country in my entire life. Seems like no one cares too much about the fellow man, and more about themselves. Not the entire whole masses of the world, but enough to make a difference. Johnny brought to my attention that maybe if the working man were treated more like an asset and less like an expense while busting his stones and sometimes going backwards, maybe all that would change. Something's gotta give soon 'cause with everyone out there talking and no one listening, something that really needs to be heard won't be heard at all with all this mindless chitter-chatter clogging up all the airways.

One last note before I move this tirade on. Expect another airline hijack suicide attack, 'cause some of us just don't learn. Not to be so hard on some of us, but I just don't see any real advancements on anything that pertains to the kind of future we are all going to be living in soon. I know a lot people, past and present, with only a small percentage of clueless or somewhat clueless. This means that for the most part, everyone is pretty much on top of their game. So why is it that these small minority of people seem to be calling the shots? The democratic experiment doesn't operate like that so here's what I think is going on. People in upper governmental jobs who want to keep those jobs at any cost will sacrifice damn near anything . . . maybe even our future while at the same time ensuring that their future is all guaranteed while running this country into the ground. You can take that any way you want and I should comment further on that but Jumpin' Johnny Jizzstain is about to make a move.

It's coming to an end of an era. He was now moving back and forth into the house. Just can't stay in one place. He wants to get a job where he can really support himself. There's got to be more to life than all of this. It's time to step up and look for a career. Now, he can't move back to the house 'cause there was a fire and the place got gutted. This time all his stuff was out. Dino had just moved up to Rainbow where he was learning the carpet trade and where Johnny was learning how to park his van. It was right next to a package store where years before, Babe was staking out when that maniac was running hellfire damnation, killing anyone who happened to be caught in the hold-up, thus making the closing time in Connecticut eight o'clock in the evening. Lots of stuff going on in Rainbow and it was just a bigger version of the house. Also at this time, he gets a call from the postal service from when he passed the civil service test years prior. At the same time, he applied for and got a job at Electric Boat Shipyard on the coast of Connecticut as a pipe fitter when he was hanging out down there. A decision needs to be made. Most people would probably just join the postal service. Most people. He chose to be a pipe fitter because he wanted to expand on his plumbing skills. He wanted to know it all. He briefly thought about the postal service but quickly dismissed it and left town. Who knew that a couple of years later he'd be back up in Rainbow beginning his postal career. He was also still having problems with the girl whose car he wrecked at the Stones. He moved to the coast. She found him. You can run but you can't hide. He kinda worked it out. Anyway, he's now working on nuclear submarines at Electric Boat right on the Thames River in Groton, Connecticut. Right across the river was New London, which was a pretty cool town back then. Right on Long Island Sound, and the scenery was beautiful. He got a room at some boarding house for thirty-five dollars a week. Throws his stuff down and time for a walk. His bike was in the shop getting an engine makeover cause it didn't go fast enough. Actually, it was fast as hell but he wanted a rocket. While walking around getting to know the town, he comes up on a historical part of town called Noank and was impressed on how well preserved it was as a whaling port from the middle 1800s. Reminded him of *Moby Dick*. It was a throwback to the olden ways, with everyone who lived there dressing the way they dressed in 1840, doing the same kind of work, and living the way they did back then. Like going into a time machine. A must see if you're in that area. He likes being alone in a new area just like back in the service. But he's not alone for long. He discovers that a childhood friend from way back is also staying at this boarding house in the basement. Before Jimmy knew that Johnny was there, Johnny knew first. Johnny and one of his pipe fitter buddies were sitten' in the kitchen pounding a couple of beers and Jimmy's door was wide open, leading to the basement. He had no idea that Johnny was in this house. He decided to let Jimmy know that there was a new kid on the block. Something about the last part of that last sentence that makes me alittle queasy. Johnny and his buddy roll up a bunch of newspaper into balls around the size of softballs, lit them then toss them down in the basement. They toss around four or five of these meteorites down the stairs when here comes Jimmy just flying up the stairs only to see Johnny just sitten' there just smiling. He can't believe that Johnny is staying at the same place and asks Johnny if the fire gods had returned. Johnny said that it was just an isolated incident. Jimmy didn't have any wheels either, so they would both walk all over the place, to all the hot spots in town. Occasionally, they would wind up in Mystic which was just another small, beautiful town just east of Groton. Julia Roberts made a movie there sometime later and if you can picture a beautiful New England coastal town, this is probably what you're thinking of.

But now he's workin on nuclear submarines. He liked that. Electric Boat is like a small town within a town. All different trades; pipe fitters, welders, riggers, grinders, and others all working together for a year and a half to produce a working submarine five stories tall and really really long. Just the propeller shaft was around three feet in diameter. He worked on the very first Trident nuclear missile sub. It's called the *USS Ohio* and his initials are welded somewhere in the bilge. His shift is from five to one thirty in the morning and stays up all night when the whistle blows. Not 'cause he wants to, but because it's the same as you or me getting out at five in the afternoon. Sometimes they would get out of work and go to the Mystic River and dig clams all night long. Real good stuff, especially raw, right there on the spot. But it's the size of the Trident that blows his mind. Hugely immense, with all the compartments from the engine room all the way to the bow just packed with stuff. He was proud to be a part of it. Nowadays, a weapon such as that could be viewed as overkill. I'm not so sure. It's not quite as precise as a sniper, foot soldier, or aircraft, and it could be viewed as more like an old WWII battleship with its seventeen-inch guns sending its message over twenty miles away. Don't have to be precise, just close. Artillery or cruise missile, it makes no difference. Get close enough and it's over. I do believe there to be a need for all weapons America had prior to the break up of the former Soviet Union. No, I don't see cruise missiles slamming all over the Middle East into populated cities just to kill a certain few. I can picture better days after our intelligence evolves from breaking old fashioned cryptonic air waves to dealing with an enemy amongst innocent civilians. Even working the internet won't work; everyone now involved is much too smart for that. We are blazing new trails in warfare and still not quite sure which one to take. America doesn't shoot first then ask questions later, and I can already hear some of you all saying *stupid shit* like war is not the answer. Got some bad news. There are no answers including war . . . at least not at the present and the fact that this subject needs explaining at all is **very disturbing** but maybe this little expose might help.

I'm think I'm gunna get alittle abstract to put this all somewhat together. This will be the first and last time. Throughout this novel I've been comparing the U.S. to the *Enterprise.* This I think is good analogy because we had an aircraft carrier that came to life during WWII with the same name. But in this dialogue I am referring to the starship that most of us pretty much know. Kirk or Picard, either way. Now, to put a spin on this, let's compare the entire planet to the *Enterprise.* Not much difference . . . they are both spaceships. This is a pretty good way to help explain why America is now global and why anything global needs our attention. Needs anybody's attention. *The USS Enterprise* is a futuristic space ship that within itself is basically a colony of people working together to sustain survival for their future. Their lives are sustained by means of artificial life support systems. Similar to the same systems used by astronauts and cosmonauts. Think we all knew that, but there are some of us still in school. Picture the earth as the same way . . . a spaceship, only except is that it cannot change course and is much larger and has a natural life support system combined with mass and gravity to allow its inhabitants to live outside of it, on the surface. To maintain this natural life support system, nature creates equilibrium to supply all the species for what is needed for survival. The plant kingdom's waste becomes the animals' kingdoms source of survival and visa versa. Both vessels need the cooperation of all its inhabitants to keep everything functioning properly. Any act of sabotage would be catastrophic especially for the *Enterprise* but that only being fictional would also be devastating to the earth. Look what Saddam Hussein did to the oil wells in the Gulf War. If he would do something like that, then what would somebody else do, if he or she had the capacity? I hear some Islamic extremists would like to destroy huge oil tankers in their own waters. Some people don't care about what's catastrophic 'cause it's not in their backyard. Barbarianism is not extinct by no means . . . it just rolled along with the times, and it got better. Now we have to deal with a group of people bound together by a fundamentalist form of religion and willing to mess with any one's natural equilibrium by use of manmade or natural weapons of extremely destructive power . . . because of their biased views of how life should be. They hate anything western, especially America, and refuse to adapt to anything as time rolls on. Your 900AD lifestyle don't bother me just as my twenty-first century lifestyle shouldn't bother you. But it does. In the future, I see many calamities because of all this and piece by piece the earth or parts of it will become affected to the point that it will not be able to keep itself in check. We cleaned up pollution. Sure about that? Only time will tell. How about all the frogs and other land-slithering species who have no choice but to live in all this man-made chemical slop strewn all over the planet for scores of decades who might perish because of it? They live in our filth. Just because we stand above them and can't smell and see what they have to live in don't mean that we won't be affected by this . . . they are part of the food chain. Break the circle, even of the lowest of species, could very well mean that our future heirs future might have no food chain like we once knew. Progress, science, and technology could . . . if not checked, could very well make our future heirs existence as bleak as all these species who have to live in all of our cleaned-up pollution. And the earth's micro-organism world could probably clean up some biological calamity besieged on one culture by another only after it wiped out its target culture. But we might need to go through another phase of evolution to adapt to our brave new world. Well, maybe not an entire culture, just a city or two. Whew! just a city or two, and not my backyard and my pretty flower bed. This not just environmental; it's also about conflicting cultures into which I shouldn't get into later. How about I tone it down and talk about random genocide and car bombings. Much better. That could never affect my subdivision. Safe within my walls. What about people you don't know who have to endure all this crap who don't have any walls? Howabout the Muslims out there with no walls who have gasoline injected in their veins because they won't conform to radicalism? You had better *get off of that cloud* and come back to solid ground 'cause the future is coming and you had better be prepared. By no means am I an expert on politics, social differences, religion, or anything else, and I have very limited schooling and sometimes I don't know exactly what I'm talking about . . . *so that's why you should listen to me.* America is flexing its muscles and for a very good reason, WE GOT ATTACKED!!! And since no one really knows the murky waters of the Middle East, no ones security is failsafe anywhere on this planet. No one knew Iraq until we went in there. We really really had to know what was next. Someone declared war on us and that someone's ideology is rampant throughout the Middle East for scores of decades and with no end in sight. We probably haven't seen nuthin' but the whites of their eyes yet!

Stopping any religious fundamentalists for any reason is wrong; that is until they resort to genocide and all the other bright and cheery news we hear all about that some people just want to blow off because it's overseas. What about the people who would like to see a safer, more secure world? In America, all religious denominations of all worldwide faiths live for the most part peacefully with each other. Not just America, but also in most parts of the world. What's wrong with that? Apparently a lot. The Islamic fundamentalist is the minority of their faith but the most vocal with their demands that the whole spaceship either convert or die. Let me say this: If you think that all of this is either going to smooth out, go away or perhaps they might come to their senses, you are mortally mistaken. That's why history should be one of the courses on the front burner along with math . . . to chart history, so that you count how many times we have screwed up, so that everyone learns that all throughout history, all the way back to the ancients . . . civilizations and cultures have always tried to dominate each other in the name of ideology, politics, or religion, with ruthless and barbaric ways. Just because we are in the present and are modern doesn't mean that anything's been learned. Don't believe that because we embrace democracy and free trade, that we, and all free societies are above all that Third World ideology because some of that Third World ideologycould very easily come back and take some of our democracy and shove it right back up our asses. Sorry about that . . . alittle rough but not as rough as another 9-11. Alls I want is for people to wake up and realize that the starplanet *Enterprise* is in serious trouble. And no! You don't got all the answers. Neither do I. It takes all of us to come up with that. But leave me out this time . . . my way will just get us all arrested.

Back to the shipyard, where good things happen. The veteran's administration is paying for pipe-fitter school and he's getting real good on the job training. The water systems that deliver sea water to all aspects of the boat on these subs are amazing and staggering in design. Some pipes such as the reactor pipes are used for incredible steam that Johnny wasn't qualified for and other pipes that were used to blow the air out of the ballast tanks on the bow and stern. These let the boat both submerge and ascend to the surface. Other pipes let water in the boat to get desalinated for fresh water. All the water used in the boat comes from holes all over the boat and is controlled the same as plumbing is in a house, only on an immense scale. Working this job was anything but clean and the air inside the sub was sometimes overwhelming with all the welding and brazing going on. While working on two pipes, and trying to get them together, some welder comes up right next to where Johnny and the crew with whom he was working and started to braze a twenty-four inch pipe creating the most acrid, rancid smoke around. Johnny and his crew pack up and leave and spend the rest of the night throwing rocks at jellyfish at the mouth of the Thames River. When you got ahead of the system on which you were working, that gave you some down time, like this. While working in the Trident, he learns of a party going on in the fourth missile tube from aft on the port side, and you either needed to know someone or get in with a special knock. Like I said, it was like a little town.

Some other time and this has no bearing on building submarines (it really has no bearing on anything at all) but one time he got the crabs. Not the ones you eat, 'cause if you do?, you need to stay the hell away from me. It's not that I like to mention anything like this, but it's the way he got rid of them that, let's say . . . was unique. He got them on Bank street in New London and if anyone knew Bank street back then, then you know what I'm talking about. Nothing spells love like venereal disease. Hello, meet sweet Polly . . . Miss Rot'cher Krotchoff. He tried everything from special shampoos, and shaving, to Quell . . . which is made for that, and even gasoline . . . but nothing worked. While on the job, one of his co-workers notices Johnny squirming and scratching all about, very uncomfortably and asks why. After telling Johnny to stay away from him after he tells him why, he tells Johnny what to do about it. Desperate and willing to do anything, Johnny goes out and buys a can of Raid, and while making sure it's not sprayed on some delicate areas, he does it. A can of Raid. Kills 'em dead . . . even a case of the crabs. He forgot to cover one part that almost sent him through the ceiling, but like I said, it was over. Useless information.

Working the second shift was taxing, but he liked the atmosphere. Instead of working on B-52s he now worked on a nuclear submarine. At nine o'clock at night, the whistle would blow for dinner. Everyone would line up at gate and wait for the second whistle; then it was a mad rush to all the vendors lined up on the street and the four bars that were also there. After that, back to the job. After a few months at the boarding house, he rents a nice house with a few people he worked with in Niantic, which is about five or so miles west of Groton down Interstate 95. They have a house right on the beach. In April of 79, the weather was so nice that it was in the nineties for a few weeks. They had all of Rocky Neck beach to themselves day and night. Nighttime on the beach. A good place to be with your honey. Also a good place to throw ice water on some babe's bare back as she's sunning herself with the top undone. Johnny was only forty-one when he did that . . . not his fault. One of Johnny's buddy who lived there had a van. During the winter of 79, he mentioned to his buddies that there was an A-frame cabin up in Vermont that belonged to the family way up in the mountains. Being from Delaware, these guys had never been up there, and it's off to the mountains they went. The snow was its usual, pretty and abundant and he shows these guys all the night spots in southern Vermont. They wound up at a ski lodge at Mt. Snow and the drinks were flowing. Johnny meets some girl there but he doesn't impress her parents, who were also there and was told to leave her alone. He was pretty trashed, so he complied. They decide to go back to the cabin but not before they decide to steal a bunch of liquor at some closed bar they found. They hid the van and off they go into this place to do the evil deed. To make a long story short, they got caught. Made too much noise. Clanking bottles all around or just being stupid doing something stupid. What they didn't know was that whoever ran or owned the bar was around and caught them and they don't know if he was armed or not but this guy was pissed.

Now they have all kinds of bottles in their hands and Johnny's got two bottles of one gallon Gallo bottles of wine in each hand. He had his index finger going through the glass loop on the top of the bottles and couldn't get them out in all the confusion. All hell breaks loose and they're running all over the place trying to get the hell out of there, with bottles hitting the floor while Johnny is running with these two bottles stuck to his hands, and they all heard some loud booms kinda like gunshots as they are ran through the snow back to the van. They made it, and are hootin' and a hoolerin' as they are driving away. They do not get too far when during the celebration when Johnny starts dumping wine all over the driver and consequently, the driver rolled the van over down a hill. After knocking on doors for help, some people who opened their doors looked at them like they had two heads or something. They finally got the van back on its wheels and made it back to the cabin after being stuck all night. Saying to hell with lighting a fire for heat, they just tough it out in the freezing cabin and bundle up and go to sleep. When they woke up because of the cold, Johnny felt an excruciating pain in his lower left leg. As he tried to lift it to see what's up, he saw it was stuck to the bed, and while he attempted to move it, the pain shot right through his entire body. While sleeping, it bled all night long and the blood froze, thus freezing his leg to the mattress. He tried everything to move his leg but the pain was too much and wound up having to cut the mattress around his leg so he could get off the bed. Apparently, this was a nasty gash. Anyway, they get it all together the next morning and drive out of Vermont back to Niantic and while on the road, the heat from the heater warms up the cut up piece of mattress and it fell off. This was a good one, blood everywhere. Back in Niantic, they see how much the van got messed up. Didn't give a shit up back in Vermont, they just wanted this nightmare to end. Someone tells Johnny that if he did get shot, the bullet is probably lead and it might poison him. Could a bullet poison someone? I don't think so but he was told to go see a doctor but he never does. To this day, he wonders that if he got cut up by a bunch of broken glass, got hurt in the wreck, or if he got winged by the bar owner. He goes back to work but deems the job too dirty and finally quits.

Makes his way back to town and moves back to Rainbow. He's got his bike that he got back some time ago which is alls he's got. He rode it throughout all seasons of the year, even through all the snow, but very carefully. He's staying with the family where Dino lives at and now he's a full-fledged carpetlayer and they got tons of work. The father at this house had three daughters and he's running about three or four carpet laying crews and everything is lookin' good. Around this time, he gets another call from the postal service and this time he accepts. Working at the postal service and laying carpet. Doin' pretty good for a change. When he first got into the postal service, he had to work nights at the bulk-mail center in Hartford, standing there all night sorting mail by the first three digits of the zip code. The mail was getting sorted but it wasn't finely tuned yet. That's why they call it a bulk-mail center. In the trade, it's called a BMC. The place was so huge, you couldn't even see the far wall. That's how big it was. He seen all the people sitting at those LST machines in which you got three seconds to punch in the first three digits of the zip code on the letters that fly in front of you nonstop. He vowed he would never do that. They got paid more, but he didn't care. He would quit first. Those machines are probably dinosaurs by now. This was in 1980 and when he left thirteen years later, the postal service was well into automation that made those machines look like model T's. This wasn't looked upon that well by the postal clerk union. But now he's been at the bulk mail center for about a week and he's not too sure. Boring, lonely, and it just sucked. One night there, he was standing with a bunch of other people knocking down this huge carriage with hundreds of trays of letters on it. Hours went by and they all just about got it done when he turned around only to see another one that needed to get sorted. This blows the wind out of his sails. He drops what he's doing, says, "screw this" and as just as he's about to leave the building for good, he hears, "Where do you think you're going Johnny?" He says to himself, *Who knows me here?* and turns around to see his parents neighbor from across the street standing there. He explains to Johnny that he runs the whole show at the bulk mail center during the second shift and still wants to know where Johnny is going. He tells him that this job is not for him and that it is driving him crazy. His neighbor laughs about that and offers Johnny a job at Bradley field loading and unloading mail on and off airliners and cargo planes. Back on the flight line. Funny how a spur of the moment decision and fate combine to change the future. He's back at the airport in the postal service instead of the restaurant. And the airport is right next to Rainbow. Things are looking up. He continuous to work both jobs but he doesn't have to ride to Hartford anymore. He rides his bike to work and on slow days, he just polishes it all night long. This where he got clipped by that woman on his bike in the employee parking lot as she was carefully backing out of her parking place. A lot of people who die out of state are shipped back to Connecticut via air and go through the airport to their final destination. They are in a rectangular cardboard box that are marked head on one end and obviously feet on the other. They made good seats to stretch out and enjoy your lunch on. He viewed it as their last time to help out. While working here, that's when Mount St. Helens blew all to hell. That was a doosey! I'm pretty sure most of us know about what's underneath Yellowstone National Park. It's a volcano but unlike anything else on the planet. It's not a mountain, nor is it a mountain range; in fact, it's basically flat with minor elevations. There are only six or seven of these kind of active volcanoes on the planet. They are called in the geological trade *super volcanoes.* I don't even like the sound of that. Super means bigger and badder. The biggest of the baddest is five miles beneath Yellowstone. Biggest of them all! Why do you think there's "Old Faithful" at Yellowstone? These type of volcanoes makes Krakatoa and Mt. Voluptuous look like anthills. What it is, is a chamber of magma somewhere around ten miles thick, sixty miles long, and twenty miles wide and it's under pressure. Pretty soon five miles of rock isn't gunna be enough to contain it. When it goes, the eruption is gunna last for over a month and is going to change the world like you wouldn't believe! America is going to be covered in shit up to your eyeballs from coast to coast. When Teddy Roosevelt implemented all the national parks in 1903, he had topographical maps for each park, with elevations above sea level pointed out over every gully, hill, mountain, ravine, and so on. Recently, they compared this to new topographical maps using the same pinpoints from 1903 by use of satellites and got some bad news. They found that all these points had risen by about two feet in the past one hundred years and five miles of solid rock may as well be five feet 'cause someday, it won't be strong enough. Life will never be the same. I'm told that this thing erupts around every six-hundred thousand years give or take a month or two, and I don't want put out any more bad news so I'll just leave this at that.

Hey, let's talk about girls! Girls at the post office. I'll get to that in a few and will probably get fired in doing so but since I gots lots of experience in that already, I already know what to expect. You lose your friggen job . . . what else you gunna expect?, dumb ass!! His job is only a ninety day probationary period. After that, he must go to some other postal facility to continue his postal career 'cause there is no opening at the airport. How stupid! He's already there. But that's how the government operates. *From the bottom down.* He wound up at an associate post office out in the country in Granby, a few towns away from hometown. Granby was one of those towns where Johnny met some people who he partied with when he was working at the restaurant at the airport back in high school, so he had places to go. He sometimes needed places to go because he either rode a moped or a ten-speed on the twenty mile trip back and forth to Granby. Flipping your van into the front yard isn't the way you're supposed to park your vehicle according to the law, so they pulled his driver's license. The ride to Granby was hell because most of the long ride was uphill, but the scenery was gorgeous and he had plenty of time to enjoy it 'cause of how long it took. The ride back took less than half the time. Lots of times, he would just say to hell with this and just hitch hike. That's when he tried to get a ride with the biggest dog you ever saw. He did whatever he had to so that he could retain a job with the postal service. He knew Granby very well. It was up here that him, Aldor, and George would do their areo-acrobatics on some of the cliffs that they dived off. It was also here that he was cliff climbing while tripping his brains out. He now looks at rock-climbers as lunatics.

There was a good place to swim at which was called Two Brooks where . . . yer' not gunna believe this . . . two brooks merged into one and attracted many people from many towns. There were salmon which was against the law to catch and they had many a bonfire there. Johnny would bring Demon dog there and everyone else who was there freaked when he cut him off his leash so that he could jump in the water just like everyone else. Once they found out that Demon was just a big baby, they would even let their toddlers ride him around. That's how big he was. One thing that was strange was the fact that Johnny's good buddy who's his daughter's godfather, *Vaj*, lived in the big house just as you entered the dirt road leading into Two Brooks way before Johnny knew him. But he worked at that post office for three years until reassignment. But before that, he would pull split shifts, which just plain flat out sucked. That's when you work from six o'clock a.m. till noon, punch out, then go to someone's house for the afternoon, come back to work all hammered up, then close up. That does have a ring of lacking in work ethic, but once he got the repetition down, from not even having to read the address on the letter to know exactly where it was supposed to go 'cause he's seen the same letter numerous times, to knowing the markings on whatever truck was pulling in by the way it sounded as it backed to the loading dock . . . he pretty much could have done the entire operation by himself. Being a postal clerk depends on how much you can retain in your head without any help. It is a mentally admirable job, especially if you had it down the way Johnny did. Not only could he sort postal routes with ninety-nine percent accuracy in very little time, he could also put one or two in walking sequence so that the mail carrier didn't have to do that. He very rarely did that, that's the mail carrier's job.

Sometimes to piss off a targeted mail carrier, he would sort all the missorts . . . wrong towns, states, and sometimes countries and fill up a pigeon hole cubicle corresponding to the route. The mail carrier would walk up to the supervisor with the handful of mail and say "Look, not one right." Supervisor would look over at Johnny and say, "Good work." "No problem, anything I can do to help." That could be construed as a problem on the work floor, job site, computer cubicle, head case, or even a drug issue, if the employer really wants to be a prick. Work is work, a lot more but nothing less. There are some exceptions, low-paying job comes to mind . . . but for the most of us, not only does it keep all the wolves away from the door, but it gives you a sense of worth. Makes the world go 'round. Keeps the roof shingled and the water hot. In return, we cough up eight hours a day to make that so. Just like in the military, we take orders. We have to, so as to operate as a team to make work easier, or as easy as it's gunna get. If you wanna be a loner on the work floor, get a job at the North Pole, but as for the rest of us, we know what we have to do to keep the torch lit on the front porch. No employer, public or private wants a *yahoo* on the job for many reasons. Safety and productivity comes to mind. But at what cost? You will maintain a positive image on the job for the company at all times. Really got no problem with that. Especially if I'm the employer. I'll stand for nothing less. But what about off the job? Johnny says, "I do whatever I want within reason. It's my time. When I punch in, it's now their time." Provided that you are a rational, sensible, and competent person, what's wrong with that? That's not good enough anymore. Your word don't mean shit no more. You will be randomly drug tested whether that bothers you or not. Here we go again, talking stuff that I shouldn't be talking about! Even if society didn't bring all this upon us, it was still bound to happen. Big brother or some crazy crap like that. Doesn't mean anything that your work record, productivity, and image is meticulous. You are no longer an asset but some kinda liability. It is politically (insurance) correct to induce zero-tolerance upon everyone. That way we are all safer from ourselves. In a way, I could agree with alot of that. Yeah, there are some jobs out there where I couldn't agree more, where lots of people's safety is at stake. Only a fool wouldn't make sure. But when I go to some average, medium or low paying braindead job that even a democrat could do and they want to implement a drug test, that makes me wonder . . . who or what gives them the right to become a mini-government? Whether or not you mess with anything off the job, you should agree that nobody has the right to reach out to me off hours and tell me how to live, that is of course, *if my inadequacy off the job rolls into my performance on the job and I can put other people in harms way.* I'm splittin' hairs here, but let me finish. I can hear all the sheeple from here, but that's illegal. It's for your own good. So ain't child molestation, but

I betcha one of those fine respectable citizens could get a braindead job before some smoke-a-bone the night before menace-to-society maniac. I'm walkin' a fine line here, but for a valid reason. We have users and we have abusers. Common sense should be good enough to weed them out. They usually just don't show up. But by subjecting the entire work force to intrusion to catch a few is an invasion of my privacy. I didn't do anything. Leave me alone! If by some chance something does happen on the job and I don't come out clean, what if it wasn't even my fault? . . . ***what about that?*** Then the employer has all the right to check you out, and if it was my fault? Then I don't have leg to stand on. I'm on my own, no matter what happened to me. What if I lost a limb? Then I'm really on my own but I would hope that some kind of human compassion would come myway. What if I hurt someone else? Now we're really splittin' hairs, herezz where I go over the falls. I don't know.

Do you think that mini-governments act this way because they want to, or because they have to? They are told what to do, not by no government, but by your local insurance company down on Main Street. You might think that government really runs the show, but it's really insurance that shows them the better way to do it. It's cheaper. No longer just by looking at and talking to your employee good enough to know whether or not he's running on all eight, employers are now told that *common sense don't work any more* and now he has to piss in your mouth. Swish it all around. If your teeth get numb, your employee is now busted. If an employee gets hurt on the job, God knows, that never happens, the first thing they do is to implement a drug test. We'll fix that leg later. Come up positive? Then fix it yourself. This a very touchy subject with pros for both sides making sense, but it's still intrusion, because drugs and alcohol impair the body and soul. That's what they're supposed to do, but how you view what you're supposed to do is what I'm talking about. *Know thyself.* Remember, reality comes around six in the morning. I may sound like I'm blowing the drug trumpet but I'm really not. I'm saying that there are many more responsible people out there who value their jobs more than you think and I don't need anybody holding my hand when I punch off the clock. 'Cause I'm on my own time. I don't know about anyone else, but once on the job, you get my best and if that's questioned, then you can kiss my goddamn ass 'cause if it's a urine test you want, then open up your mouth and say ahh. This has nothing to do about common sense but more about money. Employers are told by insurance companies, no drug tests?, then stupid high monthly premiums. Drug tests? Then we'll cut ya a break. What would you do? Not everyone lives like this, but some people like to live it up, light one up, suck one up, then tighten up, and go back to work on Monday and puts in one hundred percent or as much as they wanna give. Unless I'm stone-cold hammered or walk on the jobsite with the thousand-yard stare, leave me alone. But anyhow, what's in my body belongs to me and me only and like I say, if you want some including DNA, which those m#thaf*cke$s already got against my will, then that's the ultimate intrusion and someday I'm gunna get mine back. ***Ask, don't take.***

Got worked up there for alittle bit. Sorry. Someone stole something of mine. There's one thing about the springtime in New England that happens every spring and only in New England. This would be the making of maple syrup, not the factorized stuff that you buy at the supermarket, but real maple syrup, right from the maple tree. Up in Granby, in the springtime, the smell of maple syrup cooking off in large vats at the farms is something that you just gotta experience. They go out to all the maple trees and punch drain spigots in all of them and hang buckets off the spigots and the rest is magic. If you have never had real maple syrup, you're missing out. Caution; it not be cheap, but iz worth it. Since the ride out to Granby was so long, he couldn't help but get back on his Sportster to speed things up. This was wrong with no driver's license and all but with his left arm being impaired from the trampoline accident, it couldn't stop the right arm from putting the keys in the ignition. He didn't care anyways. Also, back around these times the economy was in the cesspool. That's when gold hit up to eight-hundred bucks an ounce. This to Johnny and his buddies was a good thing. When gold goes up, all metals also go up in respect to their base value. Aluminum was the cash crop at the time. Nothing was safe. Johnny and Dino would drive around in the middle of the night and scope out factories and tobacco fields, looking for loot. Most of what they got was scrap, but the irrigation pipes at all the tobacco fields were too tempting. They would go to some tobacco field real late at night, undo the real long pipes from the overhead straps, line them all up, then run them over so that they could bend them in thirds so that they wouldn't hang thirty feet out of the van. Next day, it's off to the scrap yard up in Massachusetts and *cha-ching*! Big ol'check. Not bad for thieving. Everybody got in on that. Sometimes they get to a field only to find it empty of all the irrigation pipes, but lots of tire tracks. On one particular night, Johnny was driving home from the club and drove by a closed machine shop. Please, don't do any of this. He turned around and got in the place. He loaded up all the round metal stock that was around four inches in diameter and ten to twelve feet long and loaded up what he could. He worked up a serious sweat and was there for hours. The next day at the scrap yard, the people there were suspicious of the metal and put a die grinder to it to see what kind of metal it was. The sparks were blue and comes to find out, he took all their titanium, and they ask him about it. Instead of freakin,' he blurts out, "My family just bought all this land and this defunct machine shop is on it and they gave me everything that was left inside it and I'll be back with the tin roof when it comes down." They say, "Okay" and give him a check for seventeen-hundred bucks. Quick thinking works real good.

Now things really start to change. While hanging out in his buddies' apartment above the local tavern in town, he was also always in the club. This is where he met his future wife. Actually, he's seen her before. She was going out with Aldor's younger brother and Johnny always said to himself how absolutely beautiful she was. She got everyone's attention wherever she went, and one night she got Johnny's. At this time, she was seventeen and he was twenty-four. Her boyfriend wound up doing four years at the local prison a few towns over, and that's when they started looking at each other alittle differently than before. He thought about the age difference and actually liked it that way, and along with her beauty, he knew that this was the one. Rusty shook his hand when he first met her. "Maybe this will help calm you down," he said. Since Johnny wasn't really driving at the time, both of them would just pile in the back seat in someone's old boat and go anywhere, anytime, to God knows where. They did everything together and were always together for months at a clip, always in each other's sight. Some men can't live like that, but it didn't bother him at all. He would take her to the Shaboo and learned that they had a lot in common. But just like all couples, it isn't all just wine and bliss. Ya gotta take the good with the bad, the bad being alittle fight they got into one time. At this time they were staying at her ma's house in the basement when they got into alittle tiff. Johnny really don't want me to get into all this, but it happened, and this should be a lesson on what not to do. They slept on a plain mattress on the floor. That's all they had at the time. But anyways, while during this argument, he went to slap her in the face with an open hand . . . not a Mike Tyson slap, but just a wake-me-up slap. Well, that's not what really happened. While she tried to back up to avoid the impact, she tripped over the mattress as she backed up and instead of him catching her on the face, the very tip of his middle finger caught the very tip of her nose and guess what?, he broke it. That certainly was not the intention, but that's the way it worked out. He freaked! Johnny's ma found out and she's the one who called the police, and she was pissed. He tried to tell her that it was an accident but she wasn't buying that at all. But you know what? It would have never happened if he never raised his hand to her. Yeah gents, even though you wanna kill 'em sometimes, don't do it. Something like that could happen.

As some time goes on, they decide to move to East Hartford and move in at some apartment where a couple that they knew was living at. It was right on the Glastonbury line, kinda a long way without a car. Johnny's buddy who occupied the apartment dealt a lot of blow . . . no *scarface* shit but enough to get into a lot of trouble if you got caught. All four of them would go out every night and tear up the nightclubs with Johnny's girlfriend using a fake ID, getting into any club they all went to. Next day, the girls wouldn't get up until four or five in the afternoon. By that time Johnny and his buddy were half lit. It was fast lane living, that's for sure. There was an incident where Johnny's buddy had to go out and make a sale in Hartford. Think it was something like a quarter ounce. Johnny takes off with him and both of them were lucky that the deal fell through 'cause they couldn't find the guy. Remember, no cell phones back in those days. The girls decided that they wanted the blow instead, and while no one was looking, they took it and replaced it with duff that looked like the real thing. Had they made the deal?, they mighta got shot. Didn't bother anyone though, 'cause that shit was flowin' like water in that apartment. There was a big Super Bowl party going on at some club during the day up the road a ways and Johnny's buddy and his girl were gone that day so they both decided to hitch hike to the place. As I said before, they did everything together, especially going to clubs. This was when Montana won his first Super Bowl ring back in 81. But it was time to make a move closer to Granby, because the commute to the post office was hell and he damn near lost his job cause of it. They both move into this big ol' country house out in Tariffville that was a whole lot closer to Granby. Now he could hitch hike to work which was a whole lot easier. The heat from the law because of Johnny's driving problems made riding the bike too dangerous 'cause if he got caught again, Rusty was gunna be real pissed. It was parked over at his folks' garage. This house was a real old house with a huge barn in the backyard with the river running right next to it. It was pure country. Across the river was Tariffville with its only bar because it was a very small town. They would naturally cross the bridge to the bar occasionally and wound up in a little trouble one night while there. After spending their only ten dollars, they were now broke . . . but didn't want to leave just yet. The pool room was in the back room way away from the bar. As Johnny's shootin' pool, his girlfriend is up front hustling drinks. This went on for awhile until while lining up a shot while looking at the pool table, he felt an impact on back of his head and sees brown glass shoot by both sides of his head, and land all over the table. He turned around and got jumped by all these people who've been buying her drinks while she's just giving them to Johnny. He took a couple more shots from some of the bar but grabbed her and they ran like hell back to the house while hiding in the shadows in the nighttime for protection. Lucky for dark nights.

There was once an episode that also happened at this bar way back when Johnny was in high school that showed him that he had what it takes. Himself and two of his buddies walked in and were picked out as city slickers right quick. Nobody did anything but they could hear a few comments being made here and there. It was Johnny's turn to go and get the next round so he walks up to the bar and orders three more beers. There's these three big dudes sitten' at the bar and they start laughing at Johnny 'cause he was walking around looking like Jimi Hendrix, just not fitten' in with the crowd. As he's standing next to these guys, one of them slaps Johnny in the arm and asks, "How's your mother?" Johnny says good. He gets slapped again and now he's really concerned and the same dude says, "How's your sister?" Again, he says good. He now thinks that the world is gunna end. Just as the beers get served to him, he gets slapped by two of the dudes and he's now looking for someone to administer Last

Rites and again, "How's your brother?" Now these guys are laughing their asses off. Johnny ain't got no brother . . . never had and turns to the dude and says, "Dead, Vietnam." Well, these guys just freak out and apologize over and over again and bought the rounds. Good to know how to use your head for something other than just someplace just for all the alcohol to go to. But anyhow they both made it back home in one piece.

It is now that Dino decides to move to Boston in 1982. He decided to do it during a real nasty snowstorm, so Johnny, his girlfriend, and Dino drive up the Mass pike really carefully and while up there, lay some carpet in these huge corridors about a hundred and eighty-five feet long by eight feet wide by using a method known as *planking* for a stretch that was impossible to shrivel and curl up, thus making the carpet flat forever. Any carpetlayer wants know what that means?, and I'm not gunna tell ya. Learn the way I did; the hard way. Actually, call me, I'll tell ya everything . . . wrong. Dino went up there for work reasons to work for a friend of both Dino and Johnny who ran a commercial carpet shop. Dino's been up there ever since. Funny how things change. They were like brothers, now Johnny hasn't seen him in over twenty years. After the job was done, Johnny and his girl went back to Tariffville and weathered out the rest of the winter with many more blizzards to come, but they had their own cozy little room. But with sex, drugs, and rock-n-roll, who cared? Disregard that, Ma.

Also in 1982, Johnny gets an offer to transfer to the post office in his hometown in which he accepts. Just about everyone who worked at this post office either knows Johnny or was a friend of the family and knew him as a toddler. It's like he's working with Rusty's friends whom he thought were all cool. One thing Johnny will never forget were Rusty's friends. Every damn one of them. He moved back to Deerfield, right where he started from. Only this time he moves into his grandma's vacant house with his now pregnant girlfriend. After Babe died, Johnny's grandma stayed there for a while but it got too lonely, so she moved in with his great aunt down the road a piece. Johnny's great-uncle died that year as with his real cool Italian grandfather on his ma's side, who pretty much gave Johnny the fit body that he still has to this day. Bad year for Johnny's family. His great uncle was a WWI vet who knew what combat was. He went *over the top* and got nailed and laid in no man's-land for three days before being captured bythe Germans and spent the rest of the war as a POW. Any of you anti-American anti-military assholes out there get a jolt out of that?, then what happened to him *should happen to you*, and there's no one who can stop or should stop anyone like me or anyone else who values how we are able to protect our values and were instrumental in letting you get what you got. **You need to shut your goddamn mouths!** I saw this back during Vietnam. I'll be goddamn if I see it again!!! Like those magnanimous spaced-out morons out in beautiful downtown Berkley. I'm talkin' about the town council with their tratorious anti-military rhetoric!! *I hope some vet out there has heard enough!!* Yer givin California a bad name, same as some of those Merlin-the-Magician politicians! You know something? I think it's high time that some heads start knockin' the floor! Think before you spew 'cause any anti-military talk gets around real fast. You wouldn't be here as I spew if it wasn't for the U.S. military right now in real time or whatever time and place in space that you are in. What the military is doing now is the same as they have been doing since Tripoli. Don't no one ever forget that!! Don't mean to get that rough, but use your head. Listen to your heart also, but hearts are sometimes meant to be broken. Maybe you don't agree with current affairs and all that and don't like violence, but you need to know where to draw the line!!

But the stories he would tell, along with what Grandpa Ralph would tell, when he wasn't speaking Italian, strengthens the proverb, "Wisdom through age." Anyhow, they now got their own house in his hometown and between the post office and laying carpet, everything is running on all eight. Ma, don't read this part, but he's selling alittle dope on the side, and with all the extra money coming in, it's making them both happy and jovial. When Johnny was a kid, he spent from kindergarten to the second grade in Deerfield so when he moved back there, he knew practically everybody there. Incidentally, most of the houses built in that area were built by Babe before he entered law enforcement. This was back in the Twenties and Thirties. Johnny always ponders another "What if." What if Babe stayed a builder and chose to not enter law enforcement? How would Johnny's life along with the rest of his family's had panned out had he stayed a builder as the foundation of the family as they are always noted to be? Sons and relatives of that don't have to do anything to make their mark in society. That's already been done for them by Daddy. Anything wrong with that? Absolutely not. It coulda been me or it coulda been you, but it wasn't. But you know what? It's gotta be somebody 'cause after all, then what's the American dream all about? It's not just a dream when you wake up in the middle of the night screaming 'cause your fake Bentley just got all smashed up, nor is it an American nightmare 'cause nothing is going your way in life and I know those are tough pills to swallow but like I said before, we all had the same chance. What's a tougher pill to swallow is that most of us are born not quite as equal as others. What you hear about that in our documents of inception are somewhat the same is the same as "objects may appear to be farther than they really are," is the Gods honest truth because we all come from somewhere different. Some of us are born alittle bit closer to achieving the American dream alittle bit quicker than the person born alittle bit farther; i.e. poverty, health problems, social problems (that could mean just about anything), no start up money, stupid bad timing, twists of fate, and anything else that weighs alot that for some reason you just can't shed. That's not quite what it says, but that's the way I see it. That makes us different. Some of us have a better chance than others, and everyone knows that. But being Americans, you bury that somewhere and show 'em where it's at. I got what it takes, so don't you. Just 'cause you're livin' like Johnny, don't mean that you can't find a way out in a dinosaur-eat-dinosaur world that we all live in and to figure out how you can be the best anyone can be . . . even coming from a dirt poor, living in a gut-rot living condition . . . because I know that most people I know don't wanna feel that, and most people will find a way out. Most people . . . not all. Sorry, not all of us try, and I feel bad for that . . . not you, but for the ones who try. You don't care? . . . then I don't care. That's basic life, even before humans could think. But back to the story and the question I asked previously before I was talking to some people who think that they might be trying but really ain't, how would have life had been had Babe stayed a builder? Most likely, his family would have been barons of square miles of lands by now, because after all, we're goin' back eighty years or so and they probably might have been royalty by now as most of us know how working massive expansion of land development from the bottom up which leads to the bottom line. Especially over a period of lots of time. I've never known relatives of builders who live in a state of uncertainty unless they chose to do so. But this what Babe saw back then. Back then, just as now, crime was violent, and he thought that he could make a difference. Or a least try. He knew what he was doing, especially throwing away a builder's status to follow his aspirations. Sure the money's not quite as good, but how many people out there do you know who would put their aspirations over money to try to help out? Not too many. This is what made Babe and Rusty people to look up to and folks, that's as good as it gets. That's why Johnny's hometown belonged to them and with Johnny being Johnny, he felt that it was time to move on when he could.

But way before he did that, he now resides in Babe's house which he also built. He now has a place, a special place to raise up a family. His sons were born while living here. Justin was born February 16th 1983. He had married his girlfriend a few months earlier by *justice of the peace* and now knows what he has to do. First on the agenda, he decides to forgo selling any more dope. He doesn't want to put his family in harms way by either the police or anything else. Easy money, but he lets it go for family reasons. But before that happened, the seed of not really blending in was already planted. Everyone in town knew Johnny's family and some tried to forget about Johnny . . . pretend that he don't exist. He's guilty of coming up during the age of Aquarius. He tells me that he will probably never go back to town because of this, even in a box. He doesn't want anyone enjoying their lunch on his behalf. One cannot change their past, so his nomadic lifestyle suits him just fine. A little rough on his own family but that's another chapter. Besides, he's the first one in his family to up and bolt the way he did and live totally, completely on his own. His thinking is alittle different but once he makes up his mind, only a bullet can change it. That's good and bad. He will cut off his nose to spite his face. He will create the mess, sort the mess out from one to ten, and live that mess better than anyone else I know.

Living in his grandparents house brought back some fond memories of when he was a kid growing up there. When he was a kid, he would see all the neighbors living and working together somewhat like family. Everyone kept no secrets, unless of course they were living John List or something as abstract as that. Barbecues and house parties usually involved more neighbors than family within earshot. Doors were kept unlocked. Problem solving meant going across the street or next door. Whoever was around at the time. All of that is not gone, but pretty damn close. Johnny has laid floors all over the metro-Atlanta area, usually in some subdivision which seems to be the only alternative to owning your own place nowadays. That's not bad because it's your own place, but it does to seem to come at a cost. It just seems that some people who live in these subdivisions . . . many for years . . . don't even know who their next door neighbor is or what he does for a living. That, to me, just means that lots of people are just preoccupied with only themselves . . . not for selfish reasons, but probably more for occupational reasons. Can't be at two places at the same time. I just see an eroding sense of neighborly cohesion with everyone, just going through life wearing blinders while ignoring everything past their backyards or across the street. Some people just refuse to expand past their walls. Neighborly cohesion sometimes means going to the homeowners' meeting held once a month. Not to me, but sometimes just the way it used to be in the Sixties and Seventies seemed to make America more of a grass-roots land to live in with just about everyone on the same page. People felt other people's pain and it hurt. Many people now just seem to feel themselves. *Do that at home, no one can see ya*. We use'sta . . . back in school, write our names and addresses on postcards, tie them to helium filled balloons and let them go. On the other side of the postcard we asked the person who found it after it landed to write on it where it landed at and what their name was plus whatever else they wanted to say. That's still a pretty cool wayto expand beyond your walls but I guess takes too much time. I think that the rat race is responsible for that. The dysfunctional *family dude* couldn't have said it any better: It ain't nuthin' but a human race, running away from hell, but in the same ol' place. After all, how can one family get to know the family next door when both families work both day and night just to keep the shelter safe and sound. Importance takes precedence. People still struggle to make ends meet even with two incomes. I think that too many people overextend themselves, sacrificing valuable time for a piece of American pie. Too much work, not enough play is gunna make America a dull place. I think that this all started back in the me, me, me Eighties when personal gain mean't about how much my net gain was worth than how much my social gain was worth within the community. You might not get rich in the community but everybody knew that and it really didn't matter to anyone how many fifty-two inch TV's you got in your house. *Everyone wants to be a star*. You're better off staying right where you are. Like, buy a starter home first. That's why they're called what they are, and crawl before you walk, walk before you run. Problem in America is everyone thinks that they are natural—born sprinters, which they're not and now paying the price by living on the thirty cents left on the dollar 'cause the other seventy cents pays the mortgage. Not saying that these problems didn't exist back then, but it seemed like time was a commodity that was more abundant in those days. Plus, Ma made dinner in the proper amount of time to prepare Sunday dinner, not in twenty-seven seconds, which is too much time nowadays. But that's what living back at that old house represented to him; all that once was. Speaking of time, with all the overtime at the post office and laying one floor after another, he was finding time in short supply. But he kept all the wolves away from the front door.

Overtime. That's how the working man can enjoy himself alittle easier after paying off all the monthly bills. Johnny found overtime money making the paycheck to paycheck life bearable. Some people don't like overtime, the ones who could care less about their job and the ones who gotta pay it. If we define the word, the first part is *over.* That means above and beyond. The second part is *time.* That means occupying space at a given time. Put the two together and you have been occupying that space for a longer than usual amount of time. Now if we go back in time, like back around the early twenty-ith century we see the working man was looked at as way to make the rich man richer. Damn, not a damn thing's changed. Oh yeah, I'm almost positive it did. Don't get me wrong, I don't like being on the bottom either but there's gunna be a few of us where that's the way it's gunna be, so look at life for what it is and do the best you can. Problem is, seems like we're the only ones who care. A lot of us are doing a job that when back in school, you'd never thought you'd be doing this. *Life goes on while you are making plans.* But what makes life alittle more bearable for us working stiffs is what our early twenty-ith century predecessors had to endure and overcome so that we didn't have to work in the same conditions that they had to. If you look at the birth and history of unions, you'll see that back then, the upper echelon of society, the rich man, were people who took the social caste system to its fullest value. Some thought that their crap tastes just like ice cream and the working man was nothing more than neanderthal. This is what the working man was to them. Making them richer while at the same time, paying them basically crap. Look at what the coalminers had to endure back then in West Virginia. It took a small war and rightfully so to make the mineowners realize that without them, no coal. But without the mines, no pay. So an equilibrium was set, and violently. If that's what it takes, hopefully not . . . but because it takes alittle while to see the asset, not the liability in what helps you maintain a profitable income. But anyhow, any owner of any entity that employs people can do whatever they want. They own the company! Corporate management of human resources has come a long way since then with employers and employees, because the employees have had enough, and coming to equilibrium, realized that this was the best way to keep the company running on all eight. However, being an employee doesn't give us the same rights as them since they run the place by owning it. You can become a shareholder with the company if traded publicly if you wanna get alittle closer to where you work at. If not, you're takin' what their givin' 'cause you're workin' for a livin.' But we owe our eight-hour day and other benefits such as weekends off to our forefathers who had to endure these brutal work conditions. As previously mentioned, brutal workshops have come a long way, to now the work environment we all now enjoy. If something like that existed today and you still liked your job?, you can work for me any time you want and I would then explain to you why getting paid is really a stupid thing. We can thank our local unions for what we got. Unions seem to not have that luster they once had. Are they helping price our jobs oversees? Can America live off just ten dollars an hour and still achieve the American dream? Unions say no as I do also. With *corporate cannibalism* as it is nowadays, without *some* unions, ten dollars an hour could become a very scary reality. But most of us still work paycheck-to-paycheck no matter what perks we're offered. That's what makes overtime so important. It gave Johnny some extra money when he needed it the most, with young children.

I now hear that overtime has become a four letter word with some of our lawmakers. Congress some time ago took that issue up in session and wanted to severely limit to what we could make by occupying a space for an unusual amount of time. Congress, for the most part past and present, no matter what party can't even spell the word *work,* never mind perform it. Some probably have never even heard of what overtime is. Overtime? That means that my clock is twenty-five feet in the air. It's time to fly off the grid once again, but I have never ever been impressed with Congress for obvious reasons, or at least to me. A personal opinion here, but here's what I think of Congress. I never really cared for their head scratching policies in Vietnam, their head in the sand attitudes with volatile socialistic governments just south of the border in the Eighties, their refusal to appoint federal judges who like Norman Rockwell, the fifty-one percent pay hike they gave themselves back in 1990 . . . and the fact that it's just another branch of governmental bureaucratically inept procedure that would rather *dance around the problem* and hope that it just goes away 'cause that would take work to actually make it go away. Just like right now, as we speak. They just seem to flow with the current, go where the wind blows. Post 9-11 national security is now a political football, not a national guaranteed right to every American who demands that anymore. Nothing's guaranteed anymore 'cept random massive explosions in urban areas in which I hope to hell never happens but because of sheer political hatred by the people's party, who really knows anymore. While they are in session playing instead of actually workin' on the problem like they're supposed to do, we soon could be facing the same uncontrollable problems that the rest of the world is experiencing daily. They almost got it right though. They refuse to cough up rights for security. I am definitely down with that. They might be construed as the anti-sheeple . . . . the super-dooper people!! Its funny how things change, even to go against something you always stood for by an event or series of events. To give the police force . . . not your locals . . . but the federal bad boys the right to do anything they can to counter terrorism here in the U.S. is as frightening a concept as one can conjure up. I absolutely refuse to do that, that is, of course until 9-11 happened. I know that everything now because of that is scrutinized, even large monetary transactions. That's too bad 'cause I didn't do anything wrong and now it's harder to get rich than it ever was before. Whereja get all this loot? *None of your goddamn business.* Those days are over because of the world we all live in now. When 9-11 happened, serious global intelligence was born . . . or at least put in overdrive. If it means going to where some of the bad guys go to escape and blend in . . . in open societies such as our own, then that's what exactly needs to be done. So now that means coughing up parts of your world; unwanted intrusion by Big Brother. That goes against my limited ideology, not what I stand for. But I'm not a terrorist, as with ninety-nine percent of all the rest of us so I really shouldn't be fearful of intrusion by Big Brother or is this just another political football being punted all over the halls of Congress? Nothing but fumbles and a lot of missed opportunities is all I see. Very useful information needs to be gotten right then and there when the winds of terrorism blow our way, not after you gotta wake up the judge or wait for him to wake up so he can sign the legal papers so now no one gets in trouble considering what we got to lose. We already learned once . . . or least most of us did. Congress seems to have forgotten all that or maybe because maybe the other party is more evil than the evil out in the rest of the world. I'm sorry, but the rules have changed and I don't like it either, but common sense sez . . . take 'nuther look. Partisan politics is really starting to stink. What we need is a strong-arm dictatorship to shape us up. Whatdaya think about that? Seems to work everywhere else. Maybe so, but not here. But anyways, Johnny looks real good in his old military dress blues. Especially with an AK slung over his shoulder. Even got some pretty cool laws he'd like to lay down. He ain't no fortunate son, just a fifty year old bum. He high-fives me when he hears that. It happens when it happens. He really gots no idea what that means.

We'll go underground and talk about changing the government later, but not only do we have numerous members of Congress who are past flirting with, aiding and abetting the other side and should pay for it . . . which is probably a first, we also have major media along with a whole gaggle of lawyers representing the ACLU giving aid and comfort to a very global anti-American environment all over the planet. *Garden needs weeding.* But by what I seen from Congress in the past, not quite as severe as this but pretty close, like blossoming socialism in Latin America left damn near unintended during the Eighties, this is not a first. Congress seems to be the last at bat. They're supposed to be the first. That's what they were in the past. Be alert . . . we needs more lerts. Partisan politics with love for no one but oneself is a very selfish and power monging mindset, just punting away the principle that shows me that America is entering its renaissance and not for the better. Putting your agenda above all the good of America? Talk about crossing up your P's!! We're way past weeds, they're now wildweeds. Now we all know what party is responsible for our united nation . . . *not nations* . . . they be ignorant . . . don't know no betta.' Let 'dem play, they still be on recess. The party I'm talkin' about would depend on your perception of the matter. For me! . . . to live in a bubble boy world means that you can't have any sharp objects. The world is full of them. Your supersoaker could pop your world. To me, the bubble is alittle bit larger and occupies the third space from the Sun. I see it all, no matter how ugly, *not just what I wanna see.* I see dead people. I see dumb people. Holy Mother of God!!, I see sheeple-peeple! I see people who seem to think they know an awful lot but without proper credentials such as this author. Do we all think that just 'cause what we believe in what we think, that it's all correct? What if we never learned right from the get go? What if we never learned 'cause we have never been there? I try to come off from all angles so as to not confuse the issues at hand, then pick my own road, no matter who or what I vote for. I'm free at the moment. I'm allowed to do that. American freedom, nothing like it, except other countries who live like I do. Go out on the streets and ask all the younger folk how or why they got to be free. Tape it and record it, then send it to *America's Funniest Videos.* Talk about tongue and cheek comedy! Much of the "idiot vote" comes from this sector of America, all throughout America's history. Why stop now? A real idiot is someone who doesn't vote at all. Mickey Moose could be running for president and that's okay with some people cause he's all cute and cuddly . . . alittle big, and has absolutly no bearing on real issues or how to deal with them. Some people vote with the heart even though what's being voted on really needs damn near all of the mind, not just what's on the top of your mind at the moment. Bring your camcorder to Washington DC for the first prize. While prominent democratic senators are punting our national security all over the halls of Congress, beware, Osama or a wannabe, could pick it up and take it in for another touchdown. I'm strictly here for power and even though my embryonic common sense tells me that the world is a dangerous place, no matter what reason one may believe, the other party is more dangerous, and when they pull out that wrench, I'm just gunna throw in another one even though some of my own people out on the battlefield might get hurt. Propose your agenda, but leave the hatred and philosophy of your rants by your fireplace 'cause what you say severely puts all of ours brothers and sisters out there fighting a war that was eventually going to be fought over sooner or later in really bad harms way!!! Some prominent politicians who actually made it this far makes me wonder, how many more times can these dirty ol' jeans be washed before you finally wash out all the genes. *Brave New World* was a book written by Alduos Huxley I believe some generations ago. It kinda mirrors our situation presently. To a few prominent, outspoken democratic senators, it just means finding a new planet at some observatory on some mountain somewhere far away. Aww cool!, look at this one, it's gots rings! What kind of cheese is on the moon? Uhhmm. Yummey yummey. I don't care. I got some in my tummy. There's a message in there somewhere! Need to be around ninety years old to get it though. But didn't they go and get some on all those Apollo missions launched by Stargate SF-1?

Okay, enough of the stupid talk. To the point. To all the people who want to strangle and limit NSA wiretap conversations on suspected terror activity need to back away from the tree a couple of hundred yards and see the rest of the world. It's not too pretty. Neither is another 9-11. I'm sorry that law-biding Middle Eastern people in the U S calling their homeland are being checked out by the NSA. But since their similarities far outweigh their differences to Osama, only a fool in the Oval Office wouldn't do so. Brave new world my friend; you don't like it?, go find another one. Hint, acid works pretty good, it makes everything look fake, the same as you see things on this planet. I feel bad for caught-in-the-crossfire people wanting to talk to their people back home but if there was ever a time for America to look to the devil, this is not a drill. *My darker side whispers, maybe some of the president's political enemies, maybe with ACLU help secretly espouse a war-breeds-terrorism act of terrorism right here in the U.S. and blame the White House for it.* Or probably maybe sometime somewhere far away after George Bush is no longer the president and something real catastrophically bad *once again* happens to the U.S. 'cause for some most-likely-gunn a-happen-forgot-what-happened-reason, we *once again* dropped our guard, because *once again*, everyone forgot or tried to and "A Ship of Fools" hit the top of the charts *once again*. There's nothing more foolish than far-left ideology with **absolutely no back-up** on how to deal with real reasons why things are the way they are and no nearsighted American leader needs to be in D.C. during these times or any times. They could be willing to sacrifice part of America to advance their twisted nonsense into law . . . excuse me, power into law. What if all this leads to optimistic pessimism? What in the < bit too much of this word > does that mean? Power doesn't corrupt???

Can't corrupt *the man* without a plan, now can you? Parts of our people's party is crawlin'with cranaloid cancer . . . and they like it! Mushier said that the president broke the law by looking to the devil for help. What's he got? The dems once had FDR, Harry Truman, and JFK. Now alls they got are *Kuckla, Fran, and Ollie* and that doesn't seem bother any of them! Where have all the little people gone? God help us all. Sorry about that, had to get that off my chest. If I were in Congress, national security, no matter what! . . . and procedure to implement national security rapidly would be on the top of the list of my agenda. But that's just me, alls I am is some out of work carpetlayer with; get this . . . no work. National security will soon become America's top *numero uno sport* and no future leader should ever forget that. Sorry about the blast of reality. Sure beats a blast of hardcore reality . . . if you get my drift.

But now overtime has been thrown into the pit. But I can't really put all that on Congress. Cept'for the *heavy corporate taxes* just making our employers existence less existing, but I think that corporate America itself probably had inadvertently had some hand in that. I'm just speculating, but if I don't wanna pay time and a half, then I'll just send my jobs overseas where there's no such thing as any time . . . never mind overtime. The exploitation of cheap labor. Some one should go to these countries and set up all kinds of unions. I could get shot for bringing that up. Then alls these cheap labor people overseas could become stockholders with 401Ks just like their American counterparts. Always seen as lean, shareholders seem to have gotten fat and obese and some of the trimmings that come with being a shareholder seem like those are also being trimmed. These ain't your fathers' companies. All of this is economically comprehensible since it fits in with the law of *supply* and demand, which is our open society. The supply, being cheap labor, and the *demand* being high priced America. How can we pay for all this when we all have reduced to nothing but commodities? Overtime helps. Overall, the economy is looking better. But for who? If I can manage a company with predicted profits by using only one third of the original work force, I'm gunna do it. Problem being, what about the other two thirds? What are they gunna do, besides lose everything they've worked for all their lives. I got a major problem with that. On my side of the fence, the economy looks like shit because I have now become too expensive. Something's gotta give, and soon, 'cause I'm sick and tired of seeing a lot of my buddies who can work with their hands better than most people can walk tough it out and live in social limbo because no one wants to pay them what they're worth anymore. If we have to resort to what unions had to resort to what they had to do back in the day, then I really got no problem with that. If that's what it takes, but hopefully not. If you got nuthin' to give 'cause everything has already been used up, then that's the way it goes. Leave the American worker alone, it's not his fault. We're not the ones who jack up all of the prices of damn near everything we need to live a normal life. You did! Whoever the < we're not foolin' anyone here > you are!

But anyhow, the postal service. Rain, sleet, and snow. Nothing has been so demanding on Johnny like this. The job itself was probably one of the easiest he's done, nothing like laying carpet. What was so demanding was the shift that he had to work. He had to punch the clock at four in the morning . . . not wake up at four but actually be there at four. Timely delivery of the local mail required that ungodly hour. To Johnny, this was not an easy task. It destroyed any night-life after seven at night. Being in his hometown now, all his buddies would come over or he would take his wife to some house party or some bar, and all of a sudden . . . a crisis. It's now seven at night, and half the people he knows haven't even showed up yet. A good night's rest begins at seven. In the height of the summertime, it don't even get dark till alittle past nine. One might say grow up and take the job for what it is. He just couldn't do that. That part of growing up wasn't passed on to him by his parents. For some of his co-workers, this wasn't a problem. For Johnny, this shift almost killed him. But there were some of his co-workers who had the same problem: one tough ass shift, but survival takes precedence and you do what you have to do. Sometimes he'd be at someone's house and gets off the couch at three in the morning. "Where ya goin?", he'd hear. "To work, gotta be there in less than an hour." "You're kidding?" This be no joke, see ya, and off he went. He's been living at his grandma's house for alittle over a year and now his wife delivers another son. Nicholas was born on July 18th 1984 and now he's got something he always wanted as a kid: brothers. He wished that he had a brother to beat on, alls he had was two younger sisters. They beat too easily, in fact, he always won. But at least in the next generation, there were two of them to carry on the Warts' name. Rusty and Esther were ecstatic.

The insurance from the postal service provided all the ways and means to help Johnny and his wife raise up a family. Funny how the medical bills when Justin was born, somewhere around a thousand dollars exploded to over five thousand dollars three years later when Johnny's daughter was born. Real funny. They now have two babies to care for and believe me, that's not easy. His wife was probably the best mother anyone could be, with nothing but utmost dedication for the care of her children. She did not work for the first decade of their marriage, but instead made sure that all the children were cared for only the way a mother could do. I feel a sense of sorrow for all the single moms out there who now have to be two parents in one. I can't think of anything harder than that. Johnny woulda hung himself. His wife always knew what to do.

When she was out and Johnny was home alone with the boys, it wasn't quite that easy. He knew that when one cried, that made the other one cry. They'd be in their separate cribs in the same room when he would hear one of them start to fuss. He'd run upstairs immediately to try to quiet him down. "Be quiet! Here's your bottle, please! Be quiet!" That didn't work. Now it gets worse. "Shut up, please shut up! You're gunna wake . . . doggone it, now look what ya did!!" They are now both screaming at the top of their lungs and Ma's not home. Johnny's running all over the place trying to figure out what to do. But this is what he didn't do. He never got pissed off. Lots of shit pissed him off but definitely not his children. He got alittle agitated . . . that's only normal, but he never took it out on a human being, not even a foot and a half tall and give it a lesson it would never forget like some of our wonderful parents out there whose own parents should have. Can't take a baby crying? Hell!! Just beat the shit out of it. That will definitely shut em' up! But if you want a normal child, or any child at all, just do what Johnny did. Babies crying will get on anybody's nerves but some of the shit I hear in the media about what some people do to their helpless babies makes me want to puke. Since the perpetrator was only a foot and a half tall, some of these people only get minimal punishment in the system 'cause some how, they were also traumatized. Somehow, this happens. Just remember, *Jesus Christ says you hafta pay, if you don't He'll getcha anyway*. Johnny would love to make 'em pay, but getting back to his situation . . . his method allowed his kids to live. When Justin and Nick cried in duet, he knew that he couldn't stop it.

Alls he did was make sure that they were comfortable and gave their bottles to them. No alcohol like I hear sometimes hear about by some sorry-ass parents. He then put pillows in their crib to make the bottles accessible to them. Then he left the room and closed the door. Then he would go back downstairs and lay the stereo wide open down in the basement. Not to forget, but to get sane and relax. Then periodically, he would go back upstairs to check on the boys to make sure that the Wild Turkey did its thing. Just joking. If you ever do something like that, then you are the sorriest ass parent since Joan Crawford. But he would go back and forth up and down the stairs to see how they were doing until they went back to sleep. Beats the hell out of going off on someone that you helped make. If you can't do that, than take a vacuum cleaner, turn it on, then put it in the corner of the room and that will *séance* them to sleep, believe it or not. No one ever told that to Johnny back then so he had to figure it out for himself. But now his kids are doin' just fine. Beats the hell out of becoming a total complete asshole. This . . . you will ultimately pay for, and if you still do the unthinkable, then I would love to meet you because then you might have a problem that stands about the same size as you . . . me or anybody else, not a foot-and-a-half tall sparring partner. Leave the midget alone! It's not his or her's fault! *Did your parents do that to you?* Obviously not, 'cause your sorry-ass is still here.

Getting back to the young and restless. The family was coming together and everything was just great. Those were the days, but just like I say, ain't no time like now. Depends on what you did in the past to make things that way. Johnny had a perfect family just like we all got. Two cats in the yard . . . white picket fence. Basketball court in the driveway, two-point-three children, and a devoted wife. What more does any man want? A lot of money would help, but making do with everything but that seemed to work out just fine for the longest time. When he had a good week and everything was paid up, he would take his wife down to the Connecticut River where the Deerfield part of town was bordered by the river. Lots of good parties down by the banks of the river. They were close enough to walk there. The whole town was down there. The banks of the river were as nostalgic as any river that is close by to you. The Red River back in Louisiana was another real good place to shake and chill at when it was time to tune out and tune in with nature. Where they would go would be a remote, almost not seen by modern man, way out in the deep woods where the setting just spelled "old New England." This was a really good place to fish at but since his wife didn't fish, he would only take her out to the parties that they all had when down on the lazy river. They had pig roasts and countless keg parties at this place, with all the trimmings . . . beer, and wine. On one particular throwdown, Johnny, now being the self-proclaimed prophet of self-control, under any circumstance, got alittle loose one day and if it weren't for fate and fate alone . . . 'cause with his cohesive decision-making skill out of control, fate stepped in to help him out . . . he could of gottin' seriously hurt. Johnny the Prophet is a new adventure in his life and I hope it works out for him.

But one day they took both the boys down to the river for a day of festivity with a large turnout of friends and neighbors. One of Johnny's friends had made some very tasty wine in his basement. Johnny is not much of a wine drinker. He maybe drinks some red wine after some pasta, and was amazed by how good it tasted. It even had all the grape pulp in that to him was like eating food as the same time you're drinking your juice. In fact, he put up all the beer bottles for a while and worked the wine all afternoon long. After the party, everyone was headed down to Hartford for the annual Italian festival later that evening. They hustled up the boys and throwed them into the van and headed back to the house. Once the babysitter arrived, they got in the truck and headed south to Hartford for the southend party. I don't know about you, but a wine buzz is much different than any other kind of alcoholic buzz and I don't care if it's North Carolina kick-ass moonshine. He had no idea about the damage he had done to himself with this wine that tasted like grape juice. Once he got there, he really knew he wasn't drinking no beer hours before the party, but being invincible back then, he didn't care. First thing he did was to go to all the food vendors lined up on all the streets with the best damn Italian food in the world. This party closed up most of the south end for the festival in which the police made sure to block off whole entire blocks at a clip and no matter where you went, you couldn't help but smell the aroma of some real good kick-ass Italian food. From Brown Street all the way up Main Street. No amount of food could undo the damage that the wine had done to him. Not even real pastrami with all the fat just the way he likes it on Jewish rye with provolone, sautéed onions, garlic, mushrooms, and peppers with French's real mustard . . . the best in the world could help him now. Not even two of them.

After a few beers from all the street vendors he was walking in and out of reality. He was pretty damn hammered beyond comprehension, and according to his wife, he picked a fight with someone on the street and took a nice shot to the head while only armed with two draft beers he had in each hand. He went flying backwards and landed like a ton of shit on the street while all the beer went all over his face and hair. Alls he can recall of that night was going back to his van when it was time to leave and seeing nothing but two complete doubles of the truck, then driving home by the use of just one eye. Two eyes open? Then everything looked like a kaleidoscope and he couldn't tell what was going on. He couldn't and shouldn't have done that at all. If that don't press the panic button, well, then our DUI laws are just fine. He's not the only one out there. I don't need to get back into this again, we all know. That's why we can all read this book. How can we drive home the errors of our ways had we not tried them out first so that we can actually know what we're condemning? If you try that?, then you really know what you're condemning. But don't ever do anything like that! If you gotta work only one eye, then work yourself into a taxicab and don't listen to anything that Johnny has got to say.

The next morning he wakes up and notices his beer hairdo in the mirror and realizes that he can't move his jaw without a tremendous amount of pain. His wife walks up the stairs and walks into the bedroom to tell him that breakfast is ready. She also asks who he's talking to on the phone. "Dentist," he says. "I have a real nasty toothache, and I can't move my jaw and I can barely talk." She immediately hangs up the phone and tells him what happened last night. He was dumbfounded and real pissed at himself for allowing something like that to happen while dropping his guard and becoming anyone's game. This certainly wasn't habitual but if that's the case as with some of us, some vultures (people) will sense the weakness and work off of that, usually out of your wallet. He wasn't anywhere near that but that's how you start and somehow that crossed his mind. It did bring him back a few years earlier before marriage back in Tariffeville when he was at a party with his future wife. Seems like they went to a lot of parties. Someone had arrived with a bottle of nitrous oxide . . . laughing gas, and he just had to check that out. When he came to, he noticed that everyone was staring at him, and he hardly knew anyone there. That to him was an indication that somehow, he had made some kind of spectacle of himself. Even with the acid in the older days and with the crackrock in the days to come, he has never succumbed to an artificial substance in such a way, and he wasn't too happy about it. In such a wandering state, alls it takes is an instant of sheer stupidity to change your life forever by your own hand . . . or worse, someone else's. What Rusty had told him back a few years ago went on the back burner, but he always thought that he had the dope game by the thingys. Well, this time it was the other way around. But it was only for an instant, but that's all it takes. But just like anything else, some of these lessons have to be learned the hard way for anything to be actually learned at all. Just learn quickly and only once, but if it takes a few more times, don't worry . . . *what do you think this book is all about?*

It's about a lot of things, like trying to grow up as you gradually age day by day. It's also knowing that someday you'll be the old man of the family, and not the little runt anymore who used to sit at the kids' table during Thanksgiving. We're all going to be replaced by each passing generation. Johnny doesn't quite agree. To him, that has nothing to do with growing up at all. He tried it for a few weeks a long time ago but said it was too hard and gave up. He says it happens when it happens. But he also said something was happening when he moved into Babe's house with his young family. He realized that indeed, the newer generations are coming up. He used to play musical chairs on his birthday in that house; now he's the man of the house. Babe's house. He always thought that those were pretty big shoes to fill. Even with all that, being the man of the house gave Johnny a feeling of importance and maturity, ready or not, and that felt good to him. To sit in the same chair in which Babe smoked his pipe. These were good times back then. He had planned to stay there forever. Hometown and all that. He was going to look into, with Rusty's help, some way of obtaining a mortgage to buy the house from grandma. That's exactly what happened, only to his sister. Things don't always work out the way he plans things. Lisa lived up Interstate 91 a few towns north in a part of Enfield called Thompsonville where she and her husband rented an apartment. Lots of Thompsonville is rental and a lot of the inhabitants liked the same thing that Johnny liked, and he fit right in there. Johnny and his wife would drive up there occasionally to visit his sister. Also, Rusty would be up there quite often. Johnny's sister's husband Dee-Dee and Rusty were pretty tight and that's because Rusty knew real people and if he's gunna let someone marry his daughter, then he's gotta have something pretty good going for him. Lisa has since divorced, but remarried one of Rusty's good cop buddies from hometown. Johnny's known John real good since he was a little kid and Lisa did very well twice. John was probably the strongest person Johnny's ever met. He remembers a long time ago when John picked up a snowmobile out of the snow like it was a beer can. That's pretty damn strong! Both of his sisters are married and have normal, stable lives.

Johnny's youngest sister, Patty, married a really good guy whose name is also Pat. Pat and Pat, pretty cool. Not like what you're thinking if you're thinking about *Saturday Night Live*. Johnny's kinda the odd ball of the family, practically living in a stable as I pen this novel. But Johnny hopes he gets that lucky when his own daughter marries. She has since met someone at college whom she's now seeing. Daniel graduated college and took on one of the noblest but gotta-be-kiddin-me under-paid jobs anyone can undertake and now works for the betterment of society as a cop in Dekalb county right smack-dab in metro Atlanta just trying to help out. Since law enforcement came to an end with Rusty and Babe, it's kinda still in the family. That's not bad. But at Babes house, Johnny's next door neighbor, who's been a part of the family since the Thirties and Forties and who Johnny's known since he was knee high to a grasshopper, just didn't want any part of him anymore. This took him completely by surprise. When I say older established citizens didn't want any part of him, he didn't expect that. This situation made living at Babe's house practically unbearable. But one day while cruising around Thompsonville with his wife and Rusty, they came upon a huge house for sale. It was a two family house and everyone thought the same thing; rental help. Do it right, and your bank note is partially covered by rental profit. Line up all your ducks and take a chance. That's exactly what he did. After a few more altercations from next door, they made arrangements to see the real-estate agent involved and went to inspect the house. The rental unit was on the first floor, which was occupied, and the second and third floor were vacant. They inspected the rental unit which was all real good then moved on to the basement. This house was built in the early twenty-ith century and the basement showed it, with the old solid brick foundation that was built to last forever. Then they moved up to the second and third floor to check out where they would be living at.

Actually, Johnny never made it to the third floor. He took one look at the second floor and told Rusty and his wife to hurry up. "I'll be in the car. Make it quick." Bear in mind, this is the first house that he was shown on appointment, and he's always seen the real estate commercials on TV and it all looked so good. He was shown a friggen wreck that reminded him of one of his forts from yesteryear. Once back home, he mulled over the idea of rental help and back in the Eighty's with the double-digit interest rates just going up to who knew what, he decided to put the work belt on before it was too late. He took his wife and kids up to Thompsonville and his sister and Dee-Dee moved back into town. The old switcheroo . . . according to Herman. Learn anything?

Everything worked out perfect. Johnny had his first home with an apartment to boot, and Lisa was back in town. Hey Lisa! Didn't Elton John make a song that sounded something like that? Only joking. He's got two he can pick on. But he wouldn't do any of that; in fact, they both know that when the rain is coming down alittle harder than he likes, they occasionally call him up to tell him that's he's not the only one. His own kids cousins, aunts, and uncles also have to work for a living. This is what probably keeps a person alive longer. Johnny's sisters and both their husbands, along with the most of us, sometimes have to endure some trials' and tribuls' that we all probably think we don't deserve. But all of Johnny's kin folk, even through marriage are fine, respectable people, because he's seen none of them fail. And he could show them real easily how to the first time, just by walking through their houses once without even touching a thing. After that, the Johnny spores have set in, and life as you know it now gots a few gremlins in it. Sorry . . . can't helps where I go.

Now here comes a whole new environment, and things happened in Thompsonville. First, alittle history about the town. Thompsonville was once a carpet—producing part of the trade. Now, as most of us know, especially in the trade, almost all your carpet needs come from Dalton, Georgia. None of what I know of really comes from the north anymore. The carpet mill, Bigalow to be exact, closed up shop in Thompsonville back in 1971 and moved to Georgia, the same as Johnny. As a result,

Thompsonville, which relied heavily on carpet-making jobs, became economically distressed, which it still was when Johnny was living there. Most of that part of town became rental with all the mill houses still standing but now vacant. There are some homeowners, but for the most part, it remained rental. That's why he liked it there so much; people just like him. Thompsonville is a community within a community with everything you need is within walking distance. Not supermarkets, but homegrown markets, which are homier and makes you feel real local, no matter where you come from. It had its own fire department; local merchants including all the package stores, restaurants and a couple of real good bars . . . and lots of real good people. Perfect place to live if you lose your driver's license. Johnny has lost his for long stretches at a clip, but not here. He'll lose his when living in the middle of nowhere. But now he's a homeowner. Time to get down to business. With help from Rusty, George, plus a bunch of other friends, they remodeled the second and third floor, even installing a working bathroom on the third floor. Johnny knows how to use his hands quite well, but in the beginning when he first saw the house, he didn't care if both his dickbeaters worked magic 'cause he didn't want no part, but now he sees the end product in his head, and makes it so. He went through the entire place, even ripping out the tenant apartment bathroom right to the bone, floor joists and all, then rebuilt it, finishing it off with ceramic tile. That was only a drop in the bucket when he was finally done with the entire house. By the time he was done, he had even ripped out the old antique oil fired boiler in the basement and replaced that with two separate gas fired boilers, one for each unit in the house. He really didn't do all that by himself, he had some good help. This is around the time that he met Vaj. Johnny thought Vaj was pretty cool right from the get go. He's one of those people whose got more common sense than most, so much in fact . . . he could sell the leftovers. They both remain tight to this very day. Vaj had gone to school with Johnny's wife and was a lot of help with Johnny's family and damn near became blood.

Now he's got his first house and all that comes with it, including a mortgage. They are a way of life. You cannot afford to call anything a home without one. Their very core of existence lies in the real estate you occupy whether residential or commercial. An equilibrium exists with the occupant residing in the structure, and the mortgage lender allowing that according to terms. As we all know this agreement is based solely on credit and responsibility. A lot of money moves this way, so the agreement is written in stone with some leeway as far as the lendees ambition to own the premises. Imagine being able to lend out the paying price for a home for someone, *times* all your customers. Where to get start up money for something like that is beyond me, but what's keeping the wheels rolling? I do know that it's the interest paid upon principle, but I think that it's predominantly the structures themselves that run the show. Here's how I think it works. You get married, get responsible and look for a home. Unless you're a star, live within your means. Much easier to keep your castle that way. But now, no more renting. Once you obtain your mortgage, you live there all your life. Bear in mind, this is strictly ultra-hypothetical. Most of us buy and sell homes over life's course. This only strengthens this theory. *Now it's time to move to Jupiter, Florida for the twilight years. Time to sell the house.* It has increased in value after all these years, with some equities increasing tenfold or less depending on location. Very good news for the sellers . . . useless news for the mortgage company. They don't need that money, They made theirs on interest until the birth of the second mortgage because equity is not the vehicle to keep the wheels rolling. Equity belongs to the seller or homeowner. This old house, for the most part, is going to be sold again to its new occupants by use of a mortgage. More business for the lenders. Just one house in the course of thirty years could have had four or five mortgages, not including refinances, and that all equals up to mega-interest on mini-principle lended. That's a lot of money. As long as there are brick and mortar, stick and stone structures whether commercial or residential, there will be lenders. The price is high and also fair and no one really likes to admit that they don't really own their castle, because it really belongs to the bank. It's fair because you now own a piece of ground in your hometown. Alls you have to do is make it work. That became somewhat of a problem for Johnny and the way he did it was somewhat unusual. But to me, collecting all that monthly interest is like one of the best businesses to be in.

But now it's time to expand on the untapped the vast reservoir of matured money. All that equity going to inheritances, the sellers, and even charity looks mighty enticing. Enter the second mortgage. A mortgage itself can be at times somewhat constraining, who the hell wants two? People who want to expand in any way on their existing home who can't do some or all of the work involved. People who want to send their kids to college. People who want a get-away cottage out in the boonies or on the coast. People who want anything that working nine-to-five isn't going to get you. You can now piece out some or all of your equity to obtain these things. Nothing really wrong with any of that except that for most of us, we have now taken a chance. Not ever being afraid of chance, I can honestly say I've always known my odds. *Odds are, a second mortgage could be a monkey on the back.* Everybody's got something to hide 'cept for me and my monkey. Everything had better go like in rehearsal or chances are, your castle might be overrun by lender gladiators while you're writing bogus checks trying to fend them off. Better make them good or now you and your family will be playing catch up and might find yourself downsizing or on the street. I don't think that's the ulterior motive for the second mortgage but who knows? But maybe I know this. Maybe not just me either. By giving Joe Blow a mortgage just knowing that he won't be able to survive on thirty-five cents on the dollar 'cause the rest pays the mortgage just gave you basically a free house minus the corporate scam-jam-ram-up-the-masses'-asses stuff we never see but only feel because Joe Blow finally caved in after a few years. For lending you an amount that pales to the actual appraised value of your home, something went wrong and now you lost it and now some bank who don't even want it now owns it. Sure about that? You cough up land plus a dwelling no matter how slum or penthouse 'cause you can't afford to pay anymore. They don't make land anymore, especially land with an already built tee-pee on it that traditionally retains some liguidable value. Not just tee-pee's . . . what about an actual house? If I'm a bank CEO, that's good enough for me. I can make that work. That does have a corporate ring to it. Look what's goin' on right now in America with all these mortgage lenders in dire straits because they're too busy selling off a large portion of real estate notes to other companies without the homeowners approval and don't really know how it works, but now you must pay your house note to some other company and usually not for your agreed amount. Yeah, that does sound corporate. All of us working stiffs who play by the rules don't really have a choice if you want your own home and no one is twisting your arm to obtain money for equity. What about some of these scams I see on the news regarding the lending trade? We seem to live in a distrustful corporate environment who favor profit at any cost . . . even their integrity. Baby boomer generation? Possibly. Any one generation could pull this off, but they have lots of experience and it does seem to lie with them since now is now, not then . . . before or after. But the common man just seems to keep on takin' it on the chin when trying to get alittle bit better and not all of what I just mentioned is as rampant as lead to believe in the news . . . otherwise the capitalistic experience is now over. There is a *moral* threshold between profit and obscene. Obscenity is going to rear its pretty expensive head sometime soon . . . because now is pretty expensive. But now I hafta pay a bank to retrieve my own money, write my own checks, and I hafta to also pay overdraft charges even when I covered that five days prior! Fuck a bank!! Enron and WorldCom come to mind along with many other cesspool companies, even ones back in the past like the *savings and loan* rippp-off basterds back in the Eighties. Can't even trust a friggen bank anymore. Drug dealers have more scruples than some of these cocksucking-shitface-assholes! One of these corporate cockroaches recently just passed on . . . good. He screwed people who trusted him. He don't belong in no cemetery. Throw that piece of shit in the town dump where he belongs. Alittle harsh? Tell that to Joe Blow who now can't retire after thirty years!!

But now Johnny Rockets has jumped into the rat race complete with a mortgage and everythang. He has gone through the entire house and has moved in. As mentioned previously, he also inherited a tenant. Sounds pretty good. Income coming in. But you have to understand what a landlord does. A landlord is a mini mortgage company. You have a roof over your head for a monthly price. That sounds fair. Not to this piece of shit who came with the house. Some people can't pay the rent for various reasons. I'm very sorry but my own existence depends on your timely monthly rent, or you are going to have to move. This guy also came with a chip on his shoulder and felt oppressed by the big bad landlord or some kind of crap like that and felt that he could give alittle here and alittle there and the rent was always on the back burner. Up north, the landlord really has no rights. Down here in the South, you don't pay?, then here comes the sheriff with all the landlord's people and all your shit gets thrown out on the front yard right by the street. Kinda cruel, but reality. But anyhow, justice was served and out went the garbage. After that, everything was working according to plan and all the bills were getting paid every month with a good bit left over. Plus he was laying carpet on the side. He had a pretty good handle on everything back then; good income, nice home, good neighborhood, a family, and a new town.

The new town was the part he liked the most. This is the first in a series of moving all around he would soon experience. Nomadic to say the least. The bike was on the road and now going back to the shop to get an electric start installed on it. Things were looking good. He does run into some people from his hometown who live right up the street and gets in click with the tenents in the four-family house directly across the street. Go over there, stay up all night, never sleep, then do it all over again the next night. Johnny and his wife fit right in there. The two would be at some apartment or house in Thompsonville partying like there was no tomorrow and all of a sudden a full blown party would materialized and would take a few days to go away. Thompsonville was like that. Johnny ran a few down in his basement. Johnny met someone from Somers, a town just down the road a piece from Enfield and both of these guys got real tight. Someone else who can take a look around just once and just only once and know exactly what's goin'on. Johnny and Joe would be in all kinds of towns up in Massachusetts, especially in Springfield where Joe knew a lot of people. Johnny had no idea that soon Springfield would be his next home sometime way off in the distant future. They would also be out in towns in the middle of nowhere that Johnny never even heard of. One of Joe's buddies would show up at one of these country homes with a bunch of dope, either the snort it type, or-any-way-you-wanted-to-docto r-yourself-type. He would call up his wife and explain what's goin' on and why he can't make it home. She'd get pissed 'cause she wasn't there and would get pretty irritated at Johnny to say the least and would just tell him to just not get in trouble cause there's gunna be more trouble than you can handle when you get your ass home. Wasn't really all that smooth all the time when he called to say he was screwing up again but at least he called. They both liked to party and Thompsonville was party central back in the Eighties. Couldn't comment on it now. It's been some time, but I'm sure it still clicks like it used to. Once they nailed down the babysitters, they would go all over the place being young and crazy. *Bonnie and Clyde.* Johnny's wife's family had moved up to Old Orchard Beach up in Maine and some up in a small town just northwest of Boston called Ayer. They would drive up there and he loved all the new hangouts whenever they ventured up to either destination. They'd take the boys up to Old Orchard every summer from a couple of paid weeks from the postal service and always had a place to stay up there 'cause his wife's ma lived up there and had a real nice place right on the beach with a huge vacant apartment above. Every now and then they'd get some cottages out in the woods for a change of scenery plus a place for Vaj, Joe, and whoever else was hanging around. Huge bonfire and all the lobster you can eat. One after another. Didn't cost that much in Maine for obvious reasons. Plus all the dope which, of course, they all liked. Cocaine was now the drug of choice. If you wanted to smoke it, you had to cook it up yourself which they did. It would be a few more years later when crackrock was available to every man, woman, and child who wanted it. Johnny and his wife checked it out and they liked it.

If there ever was a loose night, one of these nights would be some of the loosest. Alittle while back, I was ranting and raving about succumbing to drugs and addiction, but I can say one thing about crack. It was about one of the closest choices of poison that he's done that almost had both of its hands around Johnny's neck. They both knew the seriousness of the consequences of screwing up with this substance and kept the recreational use of this stuff recreational. However, on the weekends all hell would break loose and after the boys were set with a babysitter, they would tear up any part of town they were in, and since they lived right on the Connecticut-Massachusetts line, who knows where'd they would wind up at. But once it was all over, she'd be back on the homefront tending to the boys while Johnny was either in the basement or across the street.

One day across the street, the strangest thing happened. Got the living snot beat out of him. In fact, he got the white beat off of him in the process. Pretty stupid story behind it too. While he was having the electric start put on his bike, he went and bought a 357 Python that was illegal. He didn't care. He wanted a big handgun. So he bought one. His buddy who got it for him gave Johnny two weeks to pay for it. Soon he realized that he couldn't afford the work being done on the bike and what it cost for the 357. One or the other. So he uses the gun for payment on the bike. Now I've seen some real stupid things in my life but this was just asking for a problem. While playing cards across the street on the second floor one night in walks in his buddy who he got the gun from. They were pretty good friends so he don't feel threatened. Only one week had gone by and he tells Johnny that he needs the gun back or the money. While they're talking about it, Johnny's buddy walks out to the deck outside and Johnny follows him. It was nighttime and once on the deck, he can't find his buddy. He was just right there . . . right where you don't want an enemy to be. Johnny finds out a half a second too late that what he didn't want to see had hid behind the door immediately when he walked out and grabbed Johnny by the back and threw him right through the railings onto the gravel driveway below. This guy was at least a hundred pounds heavier than Johnny and he went through those railings like they weren't even there. Takes a lot to do that. After landing flat on his back on the driveway and really stunned, the other guy came down and beat Johnny unconscious while beating his face into oblivion. Beatllejuice looked better than that. Didn't lose any teeth though. Got lucky there. He had to go to the hospital with a busted up head like you would not believe and here's something else. While all this happened, Johnny couldn't wear a shirt because he had a case of the shingles and any contact on his skin by anything really made the pain unbearable, and when he came to his senses in the hospital, he told all the doctors and nurses around him. Man! . . . they all immediately go wash up and then come back and write *shingles* in big letters all over his bed and other areas near him. Those shingles have actually left scars on him.

But after that happened, he took some time off from the postal service and took the family up to Old Orchard for a while to heal. While sittin' on the porch drinking a beer, he sees the mail carrier walking his route. He also sees someone else walking behind him alittle ways back. Johnny says to the mailman, "Who's that?" "That's my supervisor." He knows what this is. It's a mandatory postal-route count done by management to determine the time involved plus how many stops the letter carrier has, then divide that by amount of time required at each stop, square that by Pi cubed and come up with the correct amount of time it should take that mail carrier to do his route. Apparently, the mailman isn't smart enough to do that all by himself. He introduced himself to both postal employees and comments on the fine job the supervisor is doing. But he's up at Old Orchard beach and he doesn't need any more problems with the post office, so he parts ways and goes to the beach. His postal career becomes *iffy* for lack of a better word. That's another horror story. There's one thing about the coast of Maine. No matter what mood you're in, you'll be in a good mood just by gazing at the seven seas from the pier at Old Orchard. Spectacular! There's even a nightclub at the very end of the pier about thirty feet or so above the waves which sounds pretty cool when they come crashing in, one after another. In the nightclub the decking on the pier is gapped, so while you're enjoying yourself with the band and the brews, you can look down into the ocean and get that Captain Nemo feeling that you can only get at the shore. A real good time. Old Orchard is a tourist coastal town that swells up to four or five times its local population during the summertime. And the food! If you like lobster, this is it. All kinds of restaurants and lobster pens around if you want to boil them yourself. Johnny and the family would cook out during the evening with lobster and oysters, shrimp and fish all over the table. After dinner, all of them; Johnny and his wife, his sister-in-laws, brother-in-laws, and Sal would go all apeshit up and down the strip. Every tourist town has a strip. Old Orchard's got a good one. He's never really ventured into interior Maine, which I'm pretty sure has parts that to this very day hasn't been seen by anyone yet.

But by now he's pretty much all healed up and back to Connecticut they go. Now, his wife is pregnant with their third child on the way. One thing, Johnny doesn't like to talk about is straight-up sex about one's spouse, especially his own. Nowadays, all that shit is the talk of the town, especially on T.V. That is sacred, private, and considered rude when aired out to strangers with inquisitive minds. But he will say this, he considers his spouse at her most sexiest and most beautiful when eight or nine months pregnant. Something about your woman when pregnant that gives one a good warm feeling. Johnny considered that the peek of her beauty. "What about the baby? . . . idiot! Didn't think of that, now did you?" He did and that made it all the better. He likes big families. He's young, with his wife a lot younger, and now she's pregnant with baby number three. While at the hospital for birth, Johnny is pulled aside by her doctor and asked a very unusual question. Johnny immediately sensed a major problem. Her doctor asks him, "Have you ever taken hallucinogenic drugs like LSD or anything like that?" Johnny asks, "What's wrong? Doc," knowing that his wife has no idea of this. The doctor explains and gives Johnny the job of going into her room to tell her they are not going home with a newborn baby. His wife freaks out a little, like trying to get up to leave while still in the process of induced labor. He had to reach way down to assure her everything will be okay. To this day, he was the only one who has seen the baby after birth. She was dead, with a perfectly developed body from the neck down. From the neck up, all hell broke loose. If you knew that your baby to be had no chance like that, would you choose to abort? Would it matter what month? What if your baby had some kind of chance, but would live in a fog all of its life? Is that our call? Lots of questions. Millions of answers. Only in the twilight zone can any distinction of what we should and shouldn't do exist because in some cases, some seems to rub one of the Ten Commandments the wrong way and another case could be viewed as a mercy killing. Erica is buried on September 25, 1985, with a little pink headstone. There's something that can't be explained when you see a casket about a foot and a half long. To this very day, his now ex-wife has never been back to that cemetery and I cannot blame her. The mother/child bond was violated in the utmost sense of the word. But life goes on, and stuff like that, you must pack it away somewhere and move on. *Dead Flowers.*

Johnny is now very disillusioned with the postal service and finds it extremely difficult to make the four a.m. cut. Also, he sees a class of folks who fill the middle management positions to the point that there's about ten employees or less per supervisor. Lots of chiefs. All's he wanted was to get back to the airport where he started from. But by this time, about six or seven years has passed and he realized it wasn't going to happen. He sealed his fate by being the best he could be on the clock and who wants to trade their starting quarterback? He was that good on the clock. It was all downhill from here on in. He started bucking up on the system and more often than not, he would be suspended without pay for a week or two. That suited him fine, because him and Joe would go out for all that time laying carpet and make a killing. They got sent all over Connecticut on different jobs and one day wound up at BC's. BC's wasn't the job location, but instead a bar with the comic strip *BC* as the theme of the bar. This place was way past Meridan or Middletown and they got so lost that day that they probably couldn't find BC's to this day. They called the carpet shop to say the location on the job doesn't exist on Earth or anywhere else close by. You have a tendency to get lost every now and then in this trade. A little less than pleased, they went to BC's for lunch and left in time for the six at night closing time at the carpet shop. That's about an hour maybe half or so ride. "Good work boys," the shop owner states as he sees the roll of carpet still in the van. "Anytime," one shouts back. They had a very high completion rate but these boys liked to live it up on the job.

One time after a job, they both headed up to the Mass Pike to the south shore of Boston to go check out Dino. They went up the previous year and had a pretty good time. Johnny and Joe jumped into Boston Bay, got on a small sailboat, didn't know how to steer it, and rammed it into another parked boat by accident. Jumped off and swam like hell. Dino, by this time, was also a lobsterman. He had about four or five traps. Doin' pretty good. Anyway, they head up to the Mass Pike at around two or three in the afternoon, and when they hit Framingham, which is up the road a little more than an hour or so, something happens to Joe's car. Turns out to be the thermostat on the Dodge slant—six that has since vanished. Couldn't kill that motor no matter what you did to it. Here's proof. First of all, Joe was like Vaj, a pretty good auto mechanic. His father owned and operated a body shop in town and Joe worked at one out in Somers where he lived. Put a hand tool in his hand and the job gets done. Problem was . . . no tools. Not even a set of toenail clippers. They're not worried though, 'cause there's stores all around Framingham once they got off the Pike. They went into a bar instead and when they got out, it was early evening and not a damn store in sight open that could help them. Not much they could've done about that since that's as far as the Dodge Duster went. Shouldn't have gone in the bar, though. This car is overheating so bad they were lucky if they could hit five miles an hour. Two hours from home. They drive around Framingham around the Pike as long as the car lets them. No auto shops anywhere near the problem, and after overheating on the highway, will barely move, and dies every half mile or so, just totaling the entire night. Desperation sets in and they try to see if they sell tools at the local supermarket. Think it was a Big-Y. They walk out with nothing but plums and bananas 'cause they know all you can buy in there are basic tools. Joe is like McGiver, but nothing worked. After wasting two hours in Framingham looking for help, they head south down the Pike. It's taking around one hour to go from exit to exit. They got over a case of Bud in the back and some dope and chugged along. A cell phone would have helped but back then, they were scarce. It's now around midnight and they've only gone halfway, and now the engine is making noises, so they stop. Cars are whizzing by them as they lift the hood. They notice that the radiator cap is jus as they left it, loose, so as to lessen the water pressure. They have already stopped and put water in it about twenty times and that's what they set out to do again. Johnny looks back at the car to see who pulls up. That's what he thought. He says to himself, "Why would anyone back up to us?" He saw what he thought were tail lights. As he walks back to the front of the car, he turns again to still see the light, but sees no car. Joe looks down at the wet roadside only to see it bright orange. Johnny looks down and the road looks like it's on fire. The engine block is so bright orange you could almost see the crankshaft. It is reflecting itself off the wet roadside and I'm sure passing cars thought they had a car fire. There was enough light to see the entire undercarriage of the car. Throw a side of beef on it and it would have burnt to a sizzle of smoke in a second. Hottest motor they ever saw. "Touch it." "No you touch it." They close the hood and it's back on the road. If it lets go, oh well. By now, they are wondering about the police and decide to take Interstate 84 off the pike to Connecticut. They're alittle drunk like a couple of fools and they come up to either a toll booth or a weight station with Connecticut state police all over the place. Wrong time to need water. Not being allowed to get water there, they're walking in the nearby woods and find a stream. All of this being done in plain sight of the police. They fill it up and leave at five m.p.h, the fastest they could go with these cops just not believing what these idiots are doing. Johnny and Joe wave and off they go. Police probably thought *at five m.p.h, what could they possible do wrong?* They get to a truck stop and wake up some trucker and ask for help. The trucker wants some dope in return. Thanks, but no thanks. They came this far and they still had most of their dope. It kept them up all night long. The police are called by a truck-stop employee 'cause they are both drunk like what beer do and hassling people for help. After explaining the entire night, Joe tells one of the cops the trucker they asked for help pulled a gun on them. After rousing the trucker and getting his story they walk back to Johnny and Joe. "Looked like a gun." "I thought it was a gun too." "Didn't you?" "Yeah." "Shut-up!" the cops say. One of the cops looking under the hood walks to the back of the car and immediately bursts into laughter. "Come here." he says to his comrades. They come back to Johnny and Joe and asks if they drank all those. There were so many empty Bud cans in the back, they even covered the back seat. They said it took a couple of days. There's still a half case of beer left and one of the cops suggests dumping the rest into the radiator. Joe says, and this is quote unquote, "What are you fucking crazy?" These cops were pretty good guys, and when they laughed at that, they both knew everything was going to be okay. The cops left as also with both of them. I don't know why that trucker didn't run them over. They got home at six a.m. next morning from when they left. The thermostat was fixed and the old Dodge kept on running after being lit up like meteorite all night long. The slant six was a workhorse. That was a messed up night. By now, he is once again more of a family man. Amanda, his only daughter is born on November 30, 1986 and he is relieved to see her come out normal. Well, not really. This time he wasn't there. After seeing what he saw previously, he skipped out and told his wife to call him when it was all over. He went to the bar. Kinda pissed off his wife, but when he returned, he showed up in her room with a few of his buddies and some smuggled-in beer. She couldn't believe it. Besides, he watched both his sons being born and believe me, that's not really a lot of fun. When did expectant fathers decide to enter the maternity double doors? Who let them? Ever see an afterbirth? Real pretty.

At the post office, things are status quo. Nothing good and nothing bad. A whole lot of nothing. He doesn't like the shift, the yes men, and most of all, the fact that knowing this is it . . . as far as you go . . . forever. You gotta do something in life but in doing so, *like what you're doing.* That just wasn't the case here. He now rolls in late more often than not. Beginning of the end. When you are late for your shift in the postal service, it is documented on an official government form. Forms for being late. He now tells his supervisor, a really good yes man, stuff like he had eleven flat tires on his car when he came in late. Takes a good while to fix that. File it. Another time, whatever he was thinking, he said while on the way to work, he saw a light in the sky and the next thing he knows, its eight o'clock in the morning and then he's wandering about in the woods running away from baby alien mutants, but their hair was perfect, trying to take over Earth. He said it took most of the morning to save the planet.

But I like this one. Bear in mind, by this time, he was living in Springfield, Massachusetts, right on the Connecticut border. He said as he was going down the highway, he saw the sign that said Welcome to Vermont and realized right then and there that he went the wrong way. As you can plainly see, he really didn't give a shit anymore. If he did, then he didn't care about the wiping. Someone else does that for him . . . too gross. But it pays like shee'aaat. But he keeps it all together and waits about five more years to get fired.

Back in Thompsonville, things also happen. Here's where sometimes, more not than often, stupidity and sheer luck can combine somehow to save ones ass. He always did his own work on his own vehicles until they became too computerized and much harder to work on. He was fixing the muffler on his car. He's got the right rear tire off and the car is sitting on a bumper jack. No jack stands or anything else. Never do anything as stupid as that . . . lookin' for a place to breed. Before getting under it, he gets stoned for a while with his buddies at the house next to the driveway. While underneath the car, he sees it move, dismisses it as just being stoned, realizes again that it is moving and rolls out from underneath it just as it slammed the ground, even knocking his face in the dirt on the way out. All of this happened in less than a half a second. Luckiest yahoo I know. His friends come running out of the house and Johnny Rehab is just standing there smiling. He once again beats the Grim Reaper. Woulda been squished like an 'animal house zit' and would have probably survived it. I don't know why I'm getting into some of his misfortune, but just like everyone else, I just get a kick out of it, especially this evil little tale. This will make any man shiver and have a drink or two. Now bear in mind, he had never kissed then told. Maybe when he was younger, but just like everybody else, *he grew up*.

I briefly just discussed what I think about this matter because of the importance of what violating moral matters of traditional norms of society and subjects is doing to this country. Some things you just don't talk about whether sexual or anything else. From the media to the barroom I still can't believe some of the shit I hear. But anyhow, Johnny's wife was very attractive and some people would ask him about sexual relations and other sacred things between them both. I believe this subject to be a private matter, and to broadcast that kind of information all over the barroom or ballgame is very rude to your better half. But what about after a bottle of Jim Beam? You often hear about some famous celebrity or athlete who marries, then divorces and writes a tell-all book including their sex life. That's not low class, that's *no class*. Enough 1800s morality and value ridden lessons that all of us already know, but it could happen. But anyways what he did to himself by accident is much different from most accidents or as a matter of fact, it is the only time I've ever heard of it happening to anybody.

On a wild night, on alittle coke binge with his wife, they head upstairs to the bedroom in the wee hours of the morning. When she bent over while changing into nothing, he decided to keep her bent over. One thing led to another and while playing around on the bed, something went wrong. Some how, he knocked her off the bed and he went down with her while grappling as one. This caused the magic wand to bend downwards until it snapped. No more magic. That's right . . . harder than Chinese algebra and bent completely down until something gives. Off to the emergency room. If this didn't happen I would skip this 'cause after all, what two normal men and women do to each other should stay with each other. But this isn't normal. Well, now it's off to the dick doctor. Every nurse had to see once he got to the hospital. Just sitten'there with a busted up thingy with his pants off and nothing he could do about it. Not that he don't like to walk all around his own place like a pig with his drawers in the drawer with his girl all around, but this was downright scary and you could tell by the expressions on all the nurse's faces. He had to take couple of weeks off from work because of the damage. When I say damage, that be no joke. With reassurance from the doctor that he's seen this type of thing before, the doc said everything would be all right. Johnny freaked out and only thought about the worst. He was scared to death and couldn't sleep until it got better. You should have seen what he did to himself to make the swelling, *capital S*, go away when it happened. The doctor explained to him why that wouldn't work. Gotta try though, when something like that happens.

He had to wear sweatpants for the time it took it to heal. While sitting at the bar one night, one of their friends asked Johnny why he was wearing pajamas on a Friday night. He explains that all of his sweatpants are in the laundry and why he has to wear them. She laughs her ass off and asks

Johnny if she could see it. You should have seen her face. "What are you going to do if that stays like that?," she says. "Start screwin' elephants," he says. He looked like a Penosaurus without the saurus and he was scared to death. Anyways, that gets back to his wife and now he's not allowed to go out unless she is there. She wasn't too happy. But that's all the sex talk you're going to hear from me, unless it happens again or some other bizarre escapade pops up. But there was one little episode with a blow-up doll, 'cause his wife just had to see. Seems there was a plastic seam welded together inside one of the G-spots that was welded wrong. He got stuck. If only he had a male blow-up doll . . . I could be wrong there . . . this would have never happened. He defends himself by asking, "What? Am I the only one?" Next to your wife? Yeah, you are the only one, thee only one. Even *Jerry Springer* would have a tough time with that. Why don't you just chop it off or let someone else take care of it for you. Okay, he says. Think about me when you open up and look in this box.

During the summer, he was always bringing the family to his mother-in-law's house right on the coast at Old Orchard Beach in Maine. While driving back from Old Orchard one Labor Day, he gets into traffic from the Maine Parkway all the way down Interstate 495, west of Boston. He realizes he should have left a day later and is parked on the Maine Parkway. He stops, gets some beer, and rides the emergency lane all the way to Worchester, where he finally gets stopped. He has no patience. He explains to the cop that if he didn't have a couple of beers, he would kill somebody. He hates traffic. The cop tells Johnny that he smells like a brewery and to come clean. As they are sitting the front seat of the police car, they both look out through the windshield while Johnny is telling the truth about the only two beers he drank. They see all three of Johnny's kids looking out the back windshield of the station wagon crying because their father is in a police car. Johnny says to the cop "Look, I'm not going to kill my family over a few beers. I know who's in my car and that's why I drive all the better." From Maine to Massachuseets? All the way down in the emergency lane? Okay . . . but he was serious and the cop knew it. They are both aware of a town a few years earlier that was sued by the family of people killed in an auto wreck involving a person who was let go in a traffic stop by an officer just prior to the accident. Instead of instant incarceration, he was given a summons to the courthouse in Worchester with lesser charges, with the stipulation that while talking man to man, part ways as man to man and take care of your family. Johnny looked him in the eye and they shook hands and off he went.

I mentioned something like this earlier and a lot could be said of the "What if?" consequences involved with something like this. Any cases, not just traffic summons, have their own merits. These could be looked at individually, one at a time, or could fall under the term *zero-tolerance.* I call it zero intelligence. I do understand that enough is enough. If some of us screw up, well, then everyone is going to pay. We only have ourselves to blame. The some of us who screw up actually amounts to millions and millions of people. Therein lies the problem. But why lump every case, be it mountains or molehills into the same punishment? Hell, I'm not going to steal twenty-five dollars: I'm going for twenty-five thousand dollars. Punishment's the same. It all leads to the devaluation of intelligence and dumbing of America because now you only have to hit the trap-door button. No longer do you have to view all the factors, variables, merits (good or bad), as well as the information leading to the case before you hit the trap-door button. But like I said, with all the misfits out there, enough is enough, and zero-tolerance was created. Now it's abused. Zero-tolerance can be best defined as how justice was administered scores of years ago by mostly totalitarian governments to its inhabitants. *One size fits all.* I'm sorry, but that's not true. Old school: Judge each case solely on its merits and not how much money the county can make is what's true. *Mostly totalitarian governments* should have raised an eyebrow or maybe the hair on the back of your neck. Merits of the case? What merits? If we choose to demote the different merits of different cases involving the same offense committed to nothing but trivial remarks, we, soon as time goes on, will be looked at the same way Germany was looked at in 1940. And that's no good! America has within its judicial and legislative arm of our government some people who when they speak, I listen. That's because it's so ridiculous, abstract, and mostly dangerous, that I have to wonder *how that person got to where he got.* Who you know? I don't know. It has come to my attention about some intrusion upon our lives, either by the police or worse . . . our lawmakers. Some of this goes back . . . not too far, just back to the beginning of the dumbing of America, to the beginning of political correctness. Some of what I see seems to stretch our 4th amendment like an elastic band. Like back around the early Nineties, when some law-making woman in Massachusetts tried to introduce a most unconstitutional law requiring the police on any traffic stop, not just DUI, to take a blood test from all those stopped. Got anything questionable in your veins? Then you are now incarcerated. Don't worry; the police will only do that only if they think there's something wrong. Problem with America is some people believe that. Could have a cold or flu drug in you or maybe you were working in a paint booth with all that lacquer in the air, or worse, you smoked a bone some days before. Yeah, I'm still stoned and so are all seven of my brain cells. Maybe by now that's all you think I got left; if so, then I was born with six more than you got. Nobody wins here, except the system. You want blood from me? Get it the old-fashioned way, beat it out of me.

How much you wanna bet that some totalitarian, Big Brother bullshit like that don't cross the minds of politicians and other people who make up *think-tank* America. Should the police be able to obtain blood from you during a DUI check? Sure, but only after an accident! Otherwise, put the blackjake on me. That's the only way anyone will ever get blood from me . . . that is of course, you're a doctor or better yet, a big ol' nurse. Sure, I'm gunna lose, but I don't care. Screw your police state. I know some cops who also think that the push is much harder than the shove nowadays. That's what Nazi Germany was, a police state. Whatever happened to them? When push comes to shove, a person of liberty, life, and happiness will *NOT* stand for anything like that! What other kinda person stands for something like that? Pop quiz! The terms been mentioned previously, hint . . . four-legged peeple who bear wool. That's right! Sheeple-peeple! Some lawmakers mean well, however natural environments need no law. But not to one lawmaker who wants to administer a school no-bullying amendment to our already existing assault laws. Sorry ma'am, but growing up only requires waking up, taking a look around, and sitting where you best sit best. That's only natural. We all take a little shit . . . some more than others, but to regulate childhood by the use of laws, to me, is as soccer mom as soccer mom gets. Come on now!! Get real. We really don't need no more < fucking > laws. We already got enough that were all screwing up. I just can't keep up anymore. However, as we all know, even back in the day, alls you want to do to a bully is either make him go away, which don't work, or wish the worst on him, which also don't work. That's a problem, especially when you are in the juvenile cocoon of childhood trying to make your mark amoungst your peirs. That's another problem. More laws suck so what I think is to leave everything the way it is; just like it was. But that don't mean that if my boy is ridiculed repeatedly and the teachers at all of our public schools can't intervine at some point . . . they'll most likely get fired, then I will. Either professionally (go talk to school principle), or un-professionally (go talk to bully). Don't care about bully's father. Problem being?, he might not care about me. How does single ma do all this? This I don't know. She don't need no help with no beauracrazy; it's transparent . . . not really there. What she needs to do is to call bully's father or ma and explain what's goin' on. See what happens with adulterizes kids!? Pretty goddamn hard to be two parents in one especially with a problem like that and that's probably one of the best reasons. A friend of mine from jumpin' Jackson county told me that back when he was in grade school back around the early Fifty's and he got disciplined real hard in grammer school, his dad got real pissed and Bobby didn't want to go home when school was over. That's 'cause when Bobby got home from school, he got slapped again by his dad for getting slapped by the teacher in the first place. Do that now and you might get in trouble because some punk-ass teacher told your kids to call the police as soon as that happens. Society doesn't work against us? No, it only works for more government intrusion which could soon see spanking as a felony. None of this is gunna help out the kid gettin' picked on all the time. Cross-hair creek is located in Jackson county. Soon someday waking up in the morning on your stomach might be against the law. Insurance reason or something like that. Do you realize that cigarette lighters could become illegal someday? What do they do? Light up any kind of smoke you wanna light up, that's what. Once tobacco becomes illegal, in a logical society where everything else smokable is already illegal, why would anybody really need one?, except to break the law. Fight back hard when that happens!! Sumtimes I really like to torch stoopid shit all around me with mine and I really do know how to spell . . . but not according to the editor of this mess. Serial killings were once legal, check your history. We were doin' pretty good back when one person's word was law. Hopefully, law doesn't repeat itself like history does. What's next? No smoking in our own homes? Someone had the audacity to try that somewhere in Maryland. Maybe you don't particularly care for smoking but you must agree that my home is my home and no one has the right to tell me what to do under my own roof; that is of course, I'm living like John List or John Wayne Gacey or anything else totally whacked. But anyways, come to my house and try to stop me. Bring your lunch and toothbrush. I got the Marlboros.

This little story about the police in Indianapolis scares the shit out of me. This has civil cases pending, one of which will have far reaching implications upon society no matter which way it goes. Roadblocks. Not your ordinary road block. Let me see your driver's license, registration, insurance and oh yeah! "Been drinking?" No worse than that. Drug dogs are now part of the procedure and guess what? Lots of arrests, arrests that wouldn't have happened had there been no dogs. Good or bad? *Prevention or intrusion?* That is the sole basis of a civil suit filed by someone who was caught with a couple of suitcases full of Columbian spinach. Police had nothing to do with it, the dogs found it in the trunk. A lot of junk in the trunk. As mentioned previously, our roadways are merely the veins and arteries that traverse America, bringing it everything it needs . . . sometimes illegal. Our bodies have within it, an immune system that unleashes enzymes, hemogoblins, antibody-dudes, corpussles and other assorted weapons, when threatened by something foreign or alien to ourselves. I'm pretty sure I touched upon that analogy a little earlier on and I'm pretty sure I'll bang that drum again as I ramble on. But we all know that lots of bad and illegal stuff is transported by our roadways. The police know that too. Prevention or intrusion? The 4th amendment clarifies all that, that is before some people stopped caring about anything but law enforcement at any cost. No one wants carnage or unnecessary delays on any trip, plane, train, or automobile. No one wants drugs to overpower America's integrity or tarnish its image. The debate goes that on the police's side of the lawsuit, they say "How can we do our job if we can't use all avenues at our disposal? Especially our finely trained police dog used for this very occasion." On my side, I say, the police can use any time, any dog for any occasion to accomplish whatever they are trying to accomplish with proper suspicion of whatever crime (probably dope), by means of any visual abnormalities . . . slurring, being hammered, real edgy, or any criminal problem . . . a stolen car, police chase, etc., in which the phrase "What if?" doesn't even come into play. To subject all the people to a no-chance-in-hell of winning over a dope dog to catch just a few, just smells of East German checkpoint Charley back in 1965. Of course, aggressive intrusion will quell any problem, be it anything. How aggressive are some people willing to concede? That's a scary question with scary answers. I don't know about you, but I'm all about the 4th Amendment and I don't believe any institution, especially judicial, has the right to judge me based solely on first impression with absolutely no recollection of who I am or what you think I might be, and subject me to *what if* intrusion eating up my time in the pursuit of liberty and happiness. Expect another fight and a few dead dogs. Seizure, that's also part of the 4th Amendment. I've seen people's stuff get seized over low-volume but still dope busts that cost people stuff that wasn't even involved in the hit. Lots of cars. We got some tough ass laws, but you know, lack of responsibility brought all this on. Some police seem to thrive on it and it's never going away, unless you listen to me. *Don't do the crime if you can't do the time, don't do it!!*

There was once a crime in Connecticut that should have had seizure written all over it. But it was a happy ending. It was only a super rich woman judge who lived in this mansion whose son got caught selling weight out of this mansion. She was also very implemental in getting seizure-of-assets-and-belongings law into Connecticut back in the Eighties. Remember the Eighties? Draconian and medieval laws passed to kill the problem. Didn't do anything about the problem, but killed a lot of people's dreams even for just having just their toes dipped in the drug pool. Someone's doin' life somewhere in Michigan for one gram of cocaine. Two grams gets you a bullet in the temple. It should, the sheeple-peeple would say. About the same time, some rich and famous car designer gets tripped up with hundreds of pounds of cocaine. Alls he got were his thingies rubbed by the judge and walked. How does that happen? But for some reason, she didn't have to relinquish her home or wheels. Why do you think it panned out like that? But anyways, a happy ending. But I hear and see about a lot of questionable laws being considered by people who I have nothing but questions about. Unconstitutional rulings seems to be en vogue nowadays. That's another reason about my presence in this novel. Over my dead, rotted, but still pretty body. Even some lesser laws out there like no smoking on earth, ring of a socialistic overtone because of its parallel similarities with *everything equal* from labor and pay to no bond, no break, no bail, no bull, and no shit!! What'd I do? Get in the cell asshole! What'd I do? How come after work on the way home, I can't enjoy a beer or two even when I'm sittin' in the back seat? Is it because the driver has absolutely no moral competence about road safety even when he's as sober as a judge? Enough questions without answers, or at least some answers that I don't like.

Well, by now, you've heard the term sheeple here and there used to describe how herd mentality is out of control and is about to stampede. But let me elaborate as to what I refer to as sheeple. A fine herd. Very well trained. Sheeple look just like me and you and walk on two legs, not four as hinted a little while back. And they don't bear wool, only women's clothing . . . even the men. The only difference between us and them is what's floating around in the head. No, I'm not talking about dope, this is much worse . . . *reality.* Wish it were dope. That way, their thinking could be easily dismissed as impairment. But that's not the case. That's what's got me a little scared. They seem to be on top of their game. The easiest way is the best. It's the only way, some say. Yeah, that's all good and all that but there are some things worth taking a second look at. Stand up for something. Sheeple are content with letting the other person handle the situation even if it means relinquishing some of our hard fought liberties a little here, a little there, but as long as all the bad guys are all locked up and out of my gated subdivision. A friend of mine was just released from prison. Robbery I believe, and one of the conditions of parole was that he had to give up his 4th amendment. That means the man can just bust in your castle anytime and run around in there like bulls in a china shop. This kind of stuff makes sheeple smile. It makes me sick. Bring me back to my cell because I refuse to live like that. Expect another . . . no wait a minute, I'm sick of fighting. I haven't won one yet!! Sheeple can't envision the future 'cause they forgot the past and they all *live in a lullaby.* Horizons are clouded by personal safety or just plain safety in general. Never can be too safe. Acceptance of unconstitutional laws means nothing to them since they, if at all, break any of them. Nothing really wrong with that. They favor zero-tolerance over Perry Mason. They allow the redefinition and rewriting of America. There's a problem right there. They are herded like sheep into a safe and secure environment and everything's going to be okay 'cause someone just passed another law. You know, to make us safer. They have no regard for our founding fathers' vision of freedom for all. They try to rewrite that vision with much vigor. They are timid and weak. They are leaders and followers alike. It's the leaders who scare me. Very rarely is America right. They even view terrorists through diplomacy. A sensitive war against terrorists? What does that mean? Get rid of your M-60 and pick up that super soaker, 'cause if its war you want, how about some of this? They think we need another book of laws three feet thick. That would make me feel safer. How about you? Why do we still have lawmakers? How many more laws can they write? That's a dangerous question right there. Most of them are comfortable in life, so don't rock the boat even if it means getting out of the way of a tidal wave. This kind of thinking is what America is not about, even all the way back to the beginning. But I do believe that political correctness was born within them, 'cause after all, they're only watching out for us. Sorry Bill, I really didn't mean to twist those words so hard. All of this brings me back to zero-intelligence. If this keeps up, pretty soon all of our lawyers are going to get lax and dull because they're still gunna get paid but for doing only half the work 'cause that's all that's required now. What we don't want are dumb lawyers.

Zero tolerance. Zero means *nothing*. Tolerance means to *withstand*. So now we will *withstand nothing*. That's a workable theory but with lots of problems. It's easily abused 'cause it makes everybody's job a lot easier. You don't have to think, just press the button or pull the lever. Next! For instance, some time ago in Marietta, Georgia, a female grammar school student was suspended for bringing a chain to school. Rightfully so, 'cause a chain is a weapon and we all know the carnage caused by students bringing weapons in school. Zero-tolerance says any chain can be a weapon. Now here's where shear stupidity rears its funny looking head. I would hope that the principal was smoking the swag or something like that when she ruled on this little girl's chain, but she wasn't. She was on top of her game that day, too. That's the scary part. What this chain was, was a little three-inch keychain with a little yellow plastic Tweety Bird attached to it. A keychain!! Put your hands up! Nobody move, nobody gets hurt! Head for the hills, she's got a three-inch long Tweety Bird keychain!! When you look for weapons, question what a weapon could actually be. A three inch keychain would have never crossed my mind. This little girl got suspended because of political correctless with its zero-common sense policy. How about that? The principal in her mind was doing the right thing but still erred in judgment. I believe she underwent brain surgery to see if she actually had one. They found nothing but cob webs. After national attention, the little girl was allowed to return to school. Some other schools look at nail clippers as weapons. What happened to our country? **Who comes up with this garbage?**

There's another problem in America. It's underage drinking. We all know its hazards with the younger folk and it won't be tolerated. We combat this by ID'ing people who look questionable to make sure alcohol isn't getting into the wrong hands. Questionable is the keyword here. Here's zero-tolerance gone wild and there's nothing pretty about it. This also takes place in Georgia and I like the state of Georgia. But since I live here, I can only comment on what I see around me. Georgia is only one state and I can only cringe that Georgia represents only a drop or two in the bucket of all this ideological diarrhea. There's still the thirteen original colonies out there and everything is the same no matter where you go. But anyhow, to make sure no alcohol gets to underage people, in Alpharetta and now in other towns, bar merchants and package store owners must ID everyone. Not because that you might look questionable, but the law says they must. People with grey hair or no hair, so old hair is growing out of their ears. People who look like they died several years ago, but are kept alive by oxygen. People with walkers or those electric things they advertise on TV. Almost to the point where they dig up old nineteenth-century graves to make sure they were old enough to die. People who anyone with half a brain can realize that these people were old enough before I was born seems to have baffled the local politicians in these towns. The merchants are only doing what they are told to by the law. When I see someone walk into a bar looking like the crypt master on *Tales From the Crypt* and still get carded, I want to see the local official's office who implemented that order and see just what kind of diplomas he has pinned on his walls. Sounds like *pin the tail on the honkey* to me. What's going on here? Common sense is taking a nosedive in this country, almost to the point of flameout. The sheeple just stand there, all befuddled and discombobulated like turnips trying to figure out whose involved in the human race.

What about our airport screeners? Good work!! I should leave them alone and take a look at their supervisory functions at the upper level.

Can't offend a certain few even though they look the part, so let's offend everyone, even the president as he's boarding his flight. Even Aunt Bea on the *Andy Griffith show.* She looks like a questionable character. Too mom and apple pie. I have nothing against any God-fearing Muslim, but since the similarities between them and Osama far outweigh the differences, common sense tells you to take a second look. That's all. Not all Muslims are terrorists . . . you know the rest. Racial profiling? No, more like common sense considering the consequences. I know that this is a serious problem, but I can't help but believe that while the First Lady is getting stripped searched, Ali Baba just throws a towel over his AK and walks on by. We need to teach common sense at the local level nowadays. That would be in the public schools. Common sense can't be taught, but can only come naturally, so that's only a joke. While back in college at Psychodelick State, everyone at Johnny's old frat, *Kappa Tappa Kegga*, even drunker than shit . . . the old frat buddies had sense enough to know you can't reach ten without counting to nine first. At Tappa Kegga, we don't have no exotic, secretive rituals to let the world know that we made our mark upon society at such a painful cost. Some hazings that I occasionally hear about sometimes makes me wonder what's more important: My social status or my dignity. Put that paddle on my ass just once and we'll be tappin' a kegga on top of yours. Mine'z got diaper-rash stuff hangin' off it and it hurts allready.

What is iz: and what isn't izn't. I hope this izn't but it iz. Saying "Merry Christmas" is now offensive. Some judge up in NYC is finding out the hard way that that just isn't so. Some schools in our country were questioning Thanksgiving, even to the point the holiday wasn't going to be recognized out of respect for the native American I believe. I can only imagine what America was like before the white man colonized the new world along with the whole Cherokee nation. An era now erased. At least the native American is not forgotten by the use of Indian names we use for most of American towns, streets, rivers, and folklore all over America. Can't call it an Easter egg hunt anymore! Someone couldn't take it anymore, it being a Christian holiday and all, and since eggs are oval shaped, it was now called the oval egg hunt to the secular. Those are the three oldest, strongest, meaningfull, and most traditional holidays in America's history, and now they're under fire!! Are we going to allow that?

All of this is incomprehensible to me because I was brought up with these joyous occasions and I really don't see what some people are trying to accomplish by shooting them down. But like I always say, over my dead, a little more rotted and not-so-much-pretty-anymore body. Making me fight over something that shouldn't be fought for in the first place, gives me incentive to fight dirty. Shut the <very very bad word; this ain't no joke> up and nobody gets hurt. Some Americans can only take so much. Way too much and way too selfish!! **I don't fuck with your beliefs, don't fuck with mine!!**

Well, now that everyone is all offended, it's time to get back to Johnny Danger. Can't tell who he is anymore. Turn around, he's gone. Look left and right . . . he's right and left. Not on purpose. That's just the way things work out. By now, he's having a rough time at the post office, especially the four a.m. cut. He drives his van, gets off work at noon, lays a lot of carpet by himself, goes home, parties like it's 1999, and then does it all over again. We all do . . . it's what keeps us going and going . . . the work part not the party part. You can party if you want, but first you must work. Its about this time, cocaine is still the drug of choice. It comes to a head when someone showed Johnny how to cook your blow into rock. He learns the stupidest things sometimes. Johnny and his wife do this quite often, so often it goes on for over a decade. They were weekend warriors and left the weekdays for their future dreams. That means there is no future if alls you're gunna do is stay fucked up. But they still liked to put the kids up with a babysitter on weekends and go crazy with each other. Believe it or not, this may sound crazy, but the dope made it better. Maybe the sex or maybe not, but they had a good time even when out on the town. When she got a job at Denny's working the graveyard shift, he would drop her off at eleven thirty at night and then it was off to the crack house. But I'll get to that later when he really started doing some real stupid stuff. Stupid enough to make him shake his head nowadays when he thinks about it. Lucky he survived all this crap, 'cause that's what it is. Some people don't. I can rattle off a list of people I once knew who are six feet underground, some for decades because of it. What a useless way to go.

But now the kids are young and they don't know, so they took advantage of that. All of this really made the four a.m. cut extremely difficult. It's around 1988 and he decides he needs a major move. So without telling his wife, he comes home and informs her that they bought another house just across the state line up in Springfield, Massachusetts. She couldn't believe it and was shocked when they both went up to see it. This was his second time seeing it. It had a full basement, as many houses up north do, but one half of it was converted to an in-law apartment, complete with a full kitchen and bathroom. He was lucky. She loved it. What if she didn't? Besides, at that time both Justin and Nick were giving them hell. Amanda was just a toddler so she wasn't a problem. They had absolutely no control over the boys and often sat around trying to come up with a solution to a problem that was only getting worse. Like I said before, the kids didn't know, and they kept it that way for over a decade before they cooled down and put their parental integrity where they always kept it, up front and in charge. That meant change and there wasn't any decision involved here. You do the right thing and that's that. Kids are impressionable, and always keep that in the back of your mind while you're spinning up a blunt in front of your toddlers. But aside from all that, they had a problem. Their sons would wake up in the middle of the night go downstairs, wreck the place, escape outside and raise more hell with anything around, even kittens.

The first time when Johnny and his wife went downstairs when they woke up, they froze from what they saw. Johnny had a carpet job that day but had to postpone it. They had opened up the refrigerator and unloaded most of its contents on the kitchen floor, except the eggs. Those wound up thrown all over the apartment. The yolk had dried and the only way to remove it was to dig into the drywall. All of Johnny's trophies from the past were destroyed as with other small items. They got into all the spices, coffee, and flour, and because of that, the entire apartment had a white coating on everything in it. There was so much flour in the air, the toilet water looked like milk. A real mess. This caught the attention of the neighbors when Johnny lost his mind and screamed out words that haven't been invented yet. They found the boys way down the street, in their pajamas, playing withtheir friends. They were spanked so hard and Johnny didn't care who watched. After they cleaned up the mess, Johnny installed a deadbolt way up on top of the door. Problem solved. Not really. About a week later, it all happened again. Place was wrecked but they couldn't get out, so Justin opened up the back kitchen window and stepped out onto the first story roof extending out of the back of the house covering the back first story bedroom. Somehow, he falls off and lands just right without getting hurt at all. But the neighbors see that and run to help, and Johnny and his wife were still sleeping and that didn't look good. Family authorities were called and when they learned of what these kids were like, they were sympathetic towards Johnny and his wife.

This would not last. One day while working at the post office, Johnny gets a call from his frantic wife around eight in the morning. It happened again but this time, they managed to unlock the bolt way up on the top of the door and were gone. It was pouring rain out at that time. Johnny immediately punched out and left without saying a thing, gets in his AMC Gremlin and headed north on Interstate 91 passing out cars in the emergency lane and all the way over on the median when cars in the left lane weren't going fast enough. When he gets home, the police are there. The boys got out, and while walking around in the rain in their pajamas, threw some kittens down a sewer, who were later rescued. They wound up a half mile away playing at the pond. That's when the police are called and the boys are now at the police station. Johnny and his wife are grilled by the family police and the regular police. He doesn't take this shit and screams back, "Look at this place!! Locks everywhere, padlocks on the windows, nothing breakable available. Look at the goddamn lock on top of the door!! And nothing works!! We can't stop them!! No one tries like us and nothing works! They're fucking demons. "What would you do??" and at this point is told to shut up. His wife tells him "You have demons in your semens" without anyone hearing. Made him smile for an instant. One of the cops there is from his hometown. He knows Johnny. His father was a famous weatherman on WTIC AM, a radio station in Hartford for many decades. He had wit, sometimes saying things like this on the air: *If the rain keeps up, it won't come down.* That's good. Got character. Johnny's daughter is going to college and is working with meteorology, which soon into the future will be on more folks minds than some of us would like to think. No scientific survey needed. Just look back on the impact of mechanized man and take a look all around now and hopefully the earth is big enough to digest all that shit. Johnny just reported that on the news that they said that tomorrow's gunna be partly mostly followed by some somewhat scattered slightly maybe. If that ain't a party day, then I don't know what is. But anyways, they all go back to the police station to get the boys. They get there and Johnny's cop buddy talks to the boys like a Dutch uncle and explains that their parents might get in trouble. Do you want that? They both are shaking their heads, babbling stuff that's making people turn their heads so the boys can't see them laughing. They can now see it's not the parents' fault.

Some of our family police all over the country should be able to do the same, but alls they do is persacute the sane along with the insane to maintain that zero-intelligence will always be viewed as zero-tolerance. Come to my house and try to tell me how to run my family and see what happens to your stupid, zero-intelligent self for getting involved in something that you—know-absolutely-nothing-about-ass that I'll split in five ways and drink the fifth if I'm caught!! You'll think about it before doin' it again . . . no matter whose on your side and and I don't care about no jail!! You wanna snoop around in my 'fridge to see what's up 'cause some dumb-ass school teacher thinks a pricker thorn rip on my kids face from being out in the woods all day long was by my own hand? Then watch your ass, *'cause you might wind up in it!!* And that my friends . . . be no joke. Respect the ***family circle!,*** 'cause I really do and so don't all the rest of the people out there who are being lumped in the insane category by an insane bureaucratic part of government that has absolutely no resources for any sanity at all!! There's no money with insane people so let's tap into the vast and deep open pockets of the sane. But the other policemen, who remained at the station with the boys for about four hours, want them out. They had no choice but to not let their eyes off of them for an instant. Opening up drawers, running down the halls, writing stuff on official papers, and other things like that. "The parents are here? Good. Get them out." Things do eventually calm down because they know a good hard spanking is right around the corner. And itworked.

But a move out of Thompsonville to Springfield helped for a while and now, it was time for a change. He took the risk of keeping the two-family house and now rented out both apartments and now everything was running on *all eight*. They moved to the Forest Park section of Springfield right on the East Longmeadow line. They all reside there for seven years. Just like the two-family house, he goes through the whole place. First to go was the nineteen-fifties style bathroom with the pink tile with black trim.

It was an old-fashioned mud-job and what a mess that was! He thought about ripping out the old cast iron tub and replacing that with a walk in ceramic tub enclosure complete with a seat around mouth high. He decided against that because there was a lot else to do, plus what good is a sturdy ceramic seat that high anyways. However the bathroom came out great with brand new twelve by twelve tiles updating the bath to modern times. He even put ceramic tile on the ceiling, running the grout lines diagonaly. Point-to-point, as its referred to in the trade. All the floors were re-done and Vaj helped Johnny rip out the oil-fired boiler and replace it with a natural gas one. There seemed to be a problem with the oil around these times as with real time.

In December of 1990, it got super cold, the coldest December I can remember. Wasn't much snow though. Where the oil tank once sat in the basement, now sat a huge wood stove. Johnny cut a vent out of the floor directly above the stove and ran an inverted cone made out of sheet metal from a couple of feet above the stove to the vent to funnel up all the heat rising from the stove. Once, they had that stove so hot, it turned bright orange, including the stovepipe, and when you turned off the light, you could see the flames flickering around inside it. It looked like a reactor just before meltdown. Even with the temperature outside at around five or ten degrees, they had to open up the doors. Reminded him of working out in a netted tobacco field in August.

But with each passing day in December 1990, oil prices shot through the roof. Almost tripled in price. All in less than a month. The colder it got the broker you went. Poorly insulated houses required a second mortgage each month so you wouldn't freeze to death. Gouging is really nothing new. Neither is loan-sharking. Gouging; an American way for some of the privileged . . . living hell for those who aren't. Gouging or taking advantage of the crisis; six or one half dozen, all the same to me. I consider it a gross perversion of the greatest way to conduct daily business, capitalism. You get your best competition with capitalism. Gouging destroys competition, reducing it to Third World desecration of human needs. Not HDTVs or anything like that, but just basic needs like food, power, and water . . . stuff like that. That's what makes it Third World. Back in December of 1990 up north, lots of people had to choose between food or heat. There's lots of talk and speculation regarding energy prices, from gasoline to heating oil right now in real time. One question: How come diesel now costs more than gasoline? On one side there's a record profit for all oil companies, compared to what we pay for a gallon of gas for them to post record profits. This is not the result of Katrina's damage to oil refineries. That was a factor because back in May of 2004 gas jumped to over two dollars a gallon, resulting in their first record profit for the first fiscal quarter of 2004. This is a year and a half before Katrina. On the other side, the side of our very existence, supply and demand dictates the price of all commodities. That includes oil. Every company has the right to any profits made, no matter how obscene, because our structure demands competition to bring out the best. Competition is *thee* number-one reason why the price of fuel is skyrocketing and who's better at it than U.S. oil companies, some of which have been around before oil was discovered in the Middle East. As developing huge countries like China and India are going mobile as far as the roads will let them, so goes up the demand and as we all know the more the demand with a non-conforming supply, up goes the price. We are being done in by our own system. What to do about it? Since oil profits don't belong to us, then it's up to us to reach back in the bag and grab another chunk of good ol' American ingenuity and find a sensible way out. But because as with most highly competitive businessphere, it sometimes interferes with progress. This could have begun some thirty years ago when I was sitten' in those day long gas lines some of us recall. Riding a motorcycle was the only way to go.

But I just want to know. Why is gasoline called gas when it's really a liquid? Caught that one night potatoin' while watching *The Works* on the History channel. Pretty smart dude! But anyhow, how do monopolies compete? For instance, when natural gas was deregulated in metro-Atlanta back in the late Nineties, you'd think gas prices would go down. Now, I'm no commodity expert, but that's what's supposed to happen. That's what I thought. No, they quadrupled. Remember how bad it got out in California some time ago with rolling blackouts and obscene natural gas prices? Remember all the sheeple out west saying to their fellow, less fortunate Californians to just pay it? Compassion for your fellow man. You pay it dickhead . . . they just started a war, and won!! Joe six-pack don't stand a chance anymore. Before natural gas deregulation, Johnny's gas bill during the summer months was somewhere around ten dollars a month.

No heating, just hot water!! After deregulation, it jumped to fifty to sixty dollars for the same amount of gas during the same months. Pissed him off so much, he screwed every new gas company that came into existence back then by moving from one to another with outstanding debt. When they came after him, he told them there was absolutely nothing they could do to make him pay. Shoulda heard him on the phone. Getting the price of fuel shoved up your ass is bad enough. What about water? Even though hurricane Andrew happened a while back, some citizens were charging ten dollars for a gallon of water. Even in solitary, if your fellow man needs water, you give it to him. Charge him later. You don't charge anyone for water in a time of dire need. That is unless of course, you are a bottom-line-bloodsucking-asshole-feeder. Imagine on the battlefield your company gets shot up a little. What do ya do? Charge your wounded squad-leader for a drink of water?? Back when war was fought on honor, you even gave it to your wounded enemy. You charge no one!! After 9/11, some gas stations, just like after Katrina, were charging five to six dollars for a gallon of gas for no apparent reason whatsoever. Katrina gouging just goes to show just how easy it is to pervert capitalism and bring it to its lowest form of existence . . . loan-sharking to a lot of Americans and some of its immigrants, past and present, who own many or most of the gas stations and most of the Ghandimarts. That would be the immigrant part. I do have an admiration for anyone who can run and maintain a gold mine like Anymart-gas-n-dash for having what it takes to stick their necks out on a dog-eat-dog *survival of the smartest-go-for-broke* competitive society no matter where anyone came from or looks like and make it work. Capitalism was meant as *a dollars day work for a dollars day wages*, maybe some days better than that but to take the vagueness in which capitalism exists 'cause of its private sector . . . that's us, and to distort it the same way some scumbag warlord in the worst part of town is a disgrace to what our system is really all about. Don't mean to piss off the present, but I don't live in the past, so I can only comment on what I see around me. You don't even have to break the law in doing so! What more do you want? Set up shop and when the shit hits the fan? . . . stick it the world, or at least everyone around you. Don't worry, they'll soon forget, as Americans always do. Katrina's basis for gouging was the supply factor that drastically dropped because of refinery damage. Demand wasn't going to change. That wasn't so after 9-11. But some prices of gas became obscene immediately after 9-11. I can only take so much. I'd pay the price but fill up a bunch of empty beer bottles with little gas soaked rags hanging out of them instead. Let me re-think that. I'm a little older now but maybe in my distant past, like a month or two ago, something like that could have happened. As I've aged, I've also matured. Amazing what a month can do. But anyways, gouging can infect anybody. Another for instance. I've got a buddy down here in Georgia whose ma lives on the Georgia coast near Savannah at a place called Tybee Island. It's a swanky place often attracting lots of celebrities. Some real estate agent got wind of a famous actress who wanted to buy some property there. So of course, up goes the price. A rich and famous actress. If I were the real estate agent, I would play by the rules, and then she'd move in. Just like planned. Then, "Can I borrow a cup of milk?" I made a pie today. Here, I brought you some. That's a beautiful piece of furniture. Where'd you get that? I can fix that. You don't have to call no one. I forgot to charge my phone last night, can I use yours?" to finally those three little words women just love to hear . . . . Gimme some sugar, babydoll. Okay, it takes four words to get that what you want, but if you try some time . . . . Don't listen to that! No, I wouldn't do any of that. Playing coy and keeping my mouth shut except for the quest of brown sugar or any sugar at all seems to work for me so far. I betcha that those are the three little words women really love to hear. Just won't say so. But anyhow, gouging, no matter in what form is a desecration to people who should base their purpose for goodwill and fairness toward everyone, not just their wallet. So don't do it anymore. OK, now that the problem's solved, its time to get back to another problem, our subject, Johnny Walker Black. If yer gunna be a problem, be the best at it according to Johnny the walking-talking problem who'll never go away.

Now he owns two houses and the rental profits are making life a pleasant experience. He doesn't know it yet, but these will be his only good years and they don't last. But now is now, the hell with tomorrow, and they made the best of that philosophy. They get to know the area with help from Joe and other people he knew back in Thompsonville. He hooks up with carpet stores in the area. His wife loved the house and she has her own plans for the interior, so they painted it. Looked real good with new floors. The driveway is big enough for a basketball court with both baselines and a all —around three point land. A big court. It's on a quiet street with great schools and scenery was very pleasant with all the trees and all. That's why it's called Forest Park, huge trees everywhere. He works at the postal job everyday, and lands a job with an outfit out of West Springfield that does a lot of commercial work. The owner of the carpet shop also owns a titty bar in the same town and was well known and Johnny liked the people he met. He fit right in but had to hold back a little when everyone there was talking about his wife the same way we all talk about other women when the moon's out. He just told them, "There's only one and you ain't it."

He really likes living in Springfield because everything once again, is new. He goes to places almost daily where he would only see maybe once or twice a year previously. Plus traveling all over New England . . . you can drop him off anywhere, anytime, bound and gagged, and he'll be home before you for dinner. He likes branching out. But he also has the same passion for the homefront. When they move, the kids are five, four and three respectively, so the work is far from over. Undivided attention to the house and family is what keeps the oil between the gears, and as long as the oil is there, everything should just be fine, or so he thought. But before all that, they really like their new home and friends. George would come up and all of them would go out either in town or head up to Brattleboro, or maybe New Hampshire, or just Chicopee or Holyoke . . . some neighboring towns where lots of shit happened. The price of dope hit rock bottom and what used to cost, costs nothing now. Plus Springfield was really easy, but a harrowing place to buy already made crackrock. Johnny did some really stupid things while messin' around with on this crap. Not to sit here and bullhorn the negative aspects of Johnny . . . he has a good heart and a kind mind, but there's nothing positive about any of this. Getting bricks thrown through the back windshield, but still got the rock, getting shot at, ganged at, and other tales that make me wonder what's more important. All that was secondary, as strange as that sounds. His priority was his family and if that meant sleeping only two hours, then that's what he did. He would rather eat spiders than fail as a father and husband. He lives in both worlds . . . living a lie to his kids, but like I said, they never knew. Having children probably saved him because being a father made him aware of the utter responsibility of rearing children one would be proud of. That's a vague statement since what makes one proud doesn't do anything for someone else. America at its best, according to some.

What used to make people joyous and jovial now pisses some people off. What once was solid is now poised to sit in quicksand. America is always going to change because we are allowed to change by means of our constitution. Just think about what you about what you want to change. Everyone's opinion count? Yes, they do, no matter what is being discussed and as long as it remains within the realms of the Ten Commandments. Whether you like it or not, we all live within the realm of the Ten Commandments, public or private. Anybody kill anyone lately? Steal anything? Shoplift the Bible lately? Does the big bad government make me believe that? Excuse me . . . our forefathers' government. I believe in change for the better and as previously mentioned, it is imminent. Some opinions profess fast-forward or unnatural change. Do those count? Unfortunately, yes. What to do then? Very simple. "We the people" vote on anything that has the word ***change*** written on it. Only obstacle would be lifetime federal judges and appellants who seem to think *the masses are too stupid to vote* and could interfere with their own agenda. So on nation changing or moral matters, they have all the answers(?). Just the fact that they are lifetime judges, parallels with lifetime dictators to me, as previously mentioned. To me, they research very well every word of all of our governmental documents, from document to document, to fight another document that's in question for whatever reason. Some of what they say or represent are no means natural but artificial for lack of a better word. Natural means vitamins and minerals, but alls I see, more often than not, is lots of dumb (angel) dust and idiot (idiot) pills . . . comes in air now.

But back home at the new ponderosa. Johnny had the only lot on this street with woods behind him. He liked that and set up party headquarters, being one with nature. Nothing wrong with that 'cause without nature, what do you have? As time goes by in Springfield, he gets in tune with the local settings and knows where he's going anywhere in the area and now for the first time, he's got friends all over the place. He can go almost anywhere in New England and find some place to go. Not some bar or restaurant, but someone's place to chill or shake. But he occupies most of his time by working with the kids. He becomes a small-fry baseball coach for the Elks club and works his team like he's on it. This is when he discovers Nick is ambidextrous and both him and Justin got what it takes. He loves that. Nick, as he grows, becomes very proficient in basketball also. Good enough to win cigarettes in jail, one-on-one, but that's another story. Johnny used to shave his head up until 1993, every May. During baseball season. One day at practice, the team didn't even know he was standing amongst all of them. "Where's the coach?" he heard over and over again. "I'm right here!" "You got no hair! Sorry, we didn't recognize ya. Thought you were some bald-headed duck fart coming to help the coach." As a matter of fact, he did have two assistants, whose sons were also on the team. Pete and Pete (no kidding). All three got real close after practices and now Johnny knows what parts of town are pretty cool. These guys were about the most fun on the sidelines 'cause all of them ran the team like they had a hundred on it and were really good baseball coaches. Johnny liked that. They ran the team during practice. Then at night time, Johnny was learning all the places in town not to go to. But it was fun at the time. That's what you did to get your buzz. Johnny and his wife became pretty good weekend warriors, smoking crack rock till early morning, then going back out and staying up all next day. On Monday, nothing happened, all that was is exactly that, and now back to the grind, back to reality where good things happen. Not much good in reality when you can't even spell the word. I'm gunna go way back a couple of sentences and talk about senseless, stupid, and dangerous risks Johnny took to mess with dope. You can get it both ways . . . the bad guys or the police. Either way, it won't be good. You'll wish you were somewhere else real quick. But he didn't care. A good family man but still needs a little more work. He did some things to get crack rock that most other people would say "To hell with that." He once while riding around Springfield was stopped in rocktown and the police aren't stupid. Pete number one was in someone's house getting some dope while Pete number two and Johnny were sitting Johnny's car. The police came up on the parked car and eye contact was made. It's over right there. Pete number one saw this and left on foot, with all the rock. Johnny looked at Pete number two and they both knew. Pete and Johnny were geeked like a couple of fools and that really plays on Johnny's stuttering. Couldn't say the word shit, even if he had a mouthfull. When he gets pulled out of the car by the police, he can barely say his name. "How long have you had a crack problem, Mr. Warts?" the officer said over and over again. He appears simple and stupid but in reality, he's sharper than most tools in the shed, but he's so geeked, he can barely talk. What a fucking curse!! First impressions count. Easy for most . . . hell for Johnny. But the cop is relentless and now has Johnny barefoot and is trying to make him say something sensible. He struggled with his speech and for some reason the cops cut them loose. Good guys. That was strange. Johnny with his flowing speech looked at Pete again and said, "Screw it, let's get out of here." He said that with no problem. They got lucky. Pete number one got real lucky that day, depending on how you look at it.

While on the subject of stupidity, he went back to the same place sometime later, and once again, he has to talk to police . . . about four in the morning. He's not to cool with me going through all this crap, but says it happened, so hopefully someone reading this will know what not to do. This time he was driving around in a stationwagon with a bunch of carpet samples visible through the back windshield. Everyone he knows are holed up in other apartments and can't get to them, so he cruises the hood. His wife is working the graveyard shift at Dennys, so alls he has is time. He spots some dude and once he's in the car, he tells Johnny he needs to pick up someone else. Johnny wants some dope but he's not too cool with all the company, with him being *odd man out.* Could get ugly, but didn't. While making a pretty good deal according to Johnny, the person in the front seat says "Cops." Johnny turns his head and sees "To Serve and Protect" on the fender of the sqad car that had pulled right up next to him. Already having the deal done with rock in Johnny's front pocket, he instructs both people in the car that he's a carpet layer, they are his helpers and they are having a dispute over pay. "Play it off, that's all we got," he says to them. When the police see that Johnny is the only white boy and in the drivers seat, they yank him out. Both dudes in the car are screaming money this and money that and the cop says to Johnny "What the hell they talking about?" Before Johnny said a word, they both go off on getting ripped off 'cause the works too hard, not enough money, gettin' fucked by the white man, and on and on. They both deserved Oscars. Absolutely brilliant performance. They got Johnny with his hands against the back windshield with his legs spread getting ready to be searched and eventually arrested for crackrock. Johnny says to the pat-down cop, "Look at all my carpet samples, they ain't lying!!" All this while misfiring on almost all the words thus making the pat down cop laugh a little. Geeking and talking is like a 1966 GTO all smashed up. Your mind is on all Pontiac V-8, but your mouth got hit by a telephone pole. The cop had already gone into the empty pocket in Johnny's shorts, and before he found the rock in the next pocket, the other cop chastised the pat-down cop for laughing at Johnny's speech impediment. He apparently was the boss 'cause for some reason, *guardian angel* most likely, the cops suddenly were gone. No going into the other pocket, no police anywhere in sight. He got on his knees and prayed and said that he wouldn't do it ever again. That much was true, but not at that time. But that was downright scary. He told his newfound buddies to hit the road and he went immediately home with still lots of time to spare. That's real lucky and the years taken off your life from an actual confrontation with the police aren't worth it. That's my general consensus. Not Johnny. He doesn't cherish it, but likes to speak his mind in front of the judge when he gets arrested. We all know that's the only time you can speak to a judge.

In his middle age years, he has since lowered his vision of judges, with no disrespect at all, and instead of talking to the *Wizard of Oz*, he now realizes he's talking to the dude behind curtain. That's now the only way he can now approach a judge. No lawyer knows like him. I guess you gotta be there. Myself, I'll take a lawyer. He says he's past all that. That's some dangerous philosophy if you ask me. He's got a case coming up soon and he chooses to represent himself. That didn't work out at all. That's in the future from now and soon I'll get to that. But aside all this dope daze, let me get him back on sacred ground. Plus he told me just now, "No more dope shit or whatever. Gimme a break. This is starting to sound like fiction."

Anyway, back at the post office, he's completely disillusioned with the same *lifer* attitude he had back in the Air Force. He doesn't like that at all. He wants something different. He's got family responsibility and now he wants to rock the boat. What's wrong with that? You only have one life to live. Strap a bomb to it, or better yet, do something you like to do, like weigh the pros and cons of such a major move. Losing postal benefits with a wife and three toddlers is major. He was ready but had no choice but to be ready when it all came to a head because of his mouth. But before all that, while in Springfield, living pretty good with his rental profits, he explores the stock market. He remembers *Black Friday* back in October 1997. He also starts to mess with patents. To him, patents are Black-Friday proof. Just use your head, logically and with common sense. Take a look all around. See what's not there. Sounds simple but not really. Just don't get discouraged and don't listen to negative bullshit. Stay the course and never, but only if you have to, go to some invention company you see on TV. Nothing against them, but what about the profits? Johnny's got something but the fish is still in the lake. It's seen the lure. But remember, "Don't count your chipmunks until they all hatch." Don't mess with chipmunks anyway 'cause in Gainesville, Georgia, one of the major chicken processing plants in the country, all's you see are semi-tractor trailers carrying live chickens going to the slaughter for me and you. The only thing that tastes like chicken is chicken. Turtles or frog legs do not taste like chicken. Sometimes I hear different. But the guy who carried fifty-thousand chipmunks on his semi must not had a sprint cell phone. We do chickens, not chipmunks!! *What's da matta' fo' you?* All that static. Could happen. I wanna talk to the driver chipmunks gots no wings and they taste nothing like chickinbeaks!!

One thing about technology he knew about back then in the early Nineties was a company called Nextel. Anyone can claim the past, but he knew. On NASDAQ, it was around ten or fourteen dollars a share and they had potential for walkie-talkie capabilities which when Johnny was a kid, he knew that was free airtime. Everyone had a walkie-talkie . . . right? We used to have nice ones, thought we were GI Joe. He had some money from postal retirement to mess with. He does retire as we will soon discover. He does his homework with cellular airwaves that he knows will soon reach Pluto and sees a booming market in wireless communications, especially two-way. He chooses to get in on the ground floor. Joe tells him not to. Cost him five thousand dollars for *one share.* Only five-hundred shares were being sold for dominance of the airways in Alaska with a company from California called Rip-off Communications. Actually, the real company's name did sound pretty close to that. They promised two-way communications the same as Nextel nowadays. He saw the future. He didn't see the basterds behind it. Anyone can do as they choose, but if you choose to be a limited partner in any venture, you must remember, a large majority of your profits will be based on hope and hope alone. Hope is a good thing but don't put your money on it 'cause you'll hope you'll never do that again. He checked and checked and it all looked good 'cause after all, it was the future. He got the check that was cashed from them in the mail from his bank and then he checked his decision and decided not to second guess it and live with that decision. Well guess what? Ten years later he still has hope. That's all he got. That ain't bad. He pays his cell phone bill every month, mostly late . . . but by now, you would think he wouldn't have to worry about something like that anymore. Never count your chipmunks before they get sent back to the wild. Not to disillusion most about corporate partnership, just do a better job of seeing who you are dealing with than Johnny, and remember corporate mingling can be beneficial to your wealth. Problem is at real time is that you have to be a combination James Bond and Sherlock Holmes just to see who's real and who's not. You have to be something of a gambler who knows the house odds with lots of confidence mixed with a lot of dreams. Money for nothing. If you can sleep at night, that's okay, just remember, someday you will have to meet your maker and I'm sure that's gunna come up on screen. Just bullshit Him . . . worked down here.

But back to baseball. Being a coach and watching the game in action, he got the bug again. He soon got wind of a baseball league forming in the Springfield, Chicopee, and Ludlow area that was comparable somewhat to the Tri-county leagues down in Connecticut. They were pretty good, making the papers and all. Fastball, nothing less. No softball. No pulse. He became a player-coach with all the responsibilities of obtaining a sponsor to fund the team and year. He, along with his assistant coach, Rolando, went to Teddy Bear pools, naturally a swimming pool store in Chicopee, and his team became the *Forest Park Bears*. Naturally, he was the catcher. He loved the butterflies in the stomach when facing some weirdo fast-ass pitch . . . battin'. As a matter of fact, the Bears had the fastest pitcher in the league, and Johnny had to get his skills back real quick. He liked that. Like riding a bike for him. Even got his glove ripped off by the bat twice during preseason. He had to remember how close to squat behind the batter. First time . . . he couldn't make a fist for some days. But the Bears had Forest Park main ballfield with a stadium-like seats for its patrons with all kinds of concession stands. Forest Park is a real park in the Forest Park section of Springfield. It has trails, picnic areas, petting zoos, real zoos with all kinds of wildlife, family-oriented fun, and now, its own police force. That's good 'cause it wasn't always that way. Johnny can remember going there years before he envisioned living there way back when he was in high school. Him and his buddies would hitchhike up there from Connecticut to buy dope 'cause that's where you got it. Anything. Johnny and one his buddies went up there one time to get some blow. This musta been in the early to mid Seventies. Back then, things get a little cloudy, but they got the blow, but also bought some really good acid at the same time. Hitchhiking on the way back, they got picked up by some old farmer and most likely his grandson. They were driving an old 1960 black Falcon. Johnny and his buddy got in the back, tripping like hopping from earth to the moon and back. The grandson looked back and knew something was up. Seemed to get a kick out if it. They're going down the road and the old man driving says all his crops are fucked up. "Look at this" he says. They had some produce up in the front seat to be examined by someone, and then he holds up a strawberry the size of a baseball, cucumbers that looked like logs, and potatoes the size of footballs. Both these assholes in the back seat see that and they laugh like they just saw all *the Three Stooges* episodes at the same time and can't stop. Cannot stop at all. The grandson really gets a kick out of it now and the old man says, "Boys, its really not that funny" but he's talking to an empty brainstem. No one's home. I could go on with this story 'cause it got pretty weird, but back to baseball.

Forest Park is the best home field in the league come to find out. It had shade and character. Shade being more important. Plus all the dope is gone at this point. This is about twenty years since then. Even the neighboring areas are spruced up, which is good for everyone. Dope was gone from Forest Park but you would think that dope and baseball don't mix. Not steroids like we hear about all the time, but *dope* dope, *why do you think they call it dope?,* kinda dope. One night, Johnny and some of his team were smokin' cwack-wok in his basement all night before the game at noon on Sunday. No problem, well just stop and go to bed to get ready for the game. Yeah, they stopped, but that's 'cause the game was only about an hour away. Johnny's geeked like some Martian, not really too human at this point and he's the starting catcher. Well, the game was an away game. It was the complete opposite of the Forest Park field, being completely in the sun with absolutely no shade whatsoever. He calls that his worst day ever playing baseball going the entire distance behind the plate. There were two backup catchers but he was bent on self-punishment mixed with baseball to help him forget the previous night. A good fastball made him forget, but it only lasted a second or two. He told me that he was vibrating in his catcher's suit. He was surprised the batter and the ump couldn't hear any static electricity emanating from his electrified presences. He hit two out in left field and prayed that they got caught which they did 'cause he wouldn't have even made it to first base. Woulda been like running the mile. Not even with all the money in the world that professional catchers make in the big leagues, would any of them drop a couple of hundred bucks to do something as mindless as that. I'm sorry Johnny boy, but when I hear about something as stupid like that, the dope shit ain't gunna go away for awhile. This book is a cleansing and you need to come clean. How'd those fastballs feel?, when that's the last place on earth you wanted to be. Aside from that, he only made it halfway through the season, not because of dope, but because he miscued on a breaking ball, probably 'cause of dope, and instead of the ball hitting the center of the mitt, it caught only his thumb and bent it completely backwards, thus knocking it out of the socket. Took six months for it to get back to normal. He tried to catch the last game but after taking only four pitches, he went to DH and only batted. That was the first season and he couldn't wait for the second. Little did he know, he wouldn't be around. Life will go on and instead of riding the wave, he's caught up in it almost drowning. Soon other things start to happen.

Around this time he catches his second DUI, thus really screwing things up. This happened in Connecticut. He sold a carpet job and got a down payment for the carpet. The customer and Johnny had a few beers together before Johnny left. Johnny drank about four of five which he can handle. Only thing was that these weren't ordinary beers. I'm not going to announce which brewery shot him down, but if you're not used to something new, then watch your ass! He wasn't ready for that and left when he realized how powerful these beers were. And he should have known better with weather conditions the way they were and beer conditions the way he found. Two absolute wrongs, but that all shot over his head. On the way home during the snowstorm, he wrecked his car. Police showed up and asked what happened. "Someone cut you off? Was another vehicle involved? Anyone else present?" No, no and no. Alls we see is that you are intoxicated and you just drove through the break in the guardrails and destroyed your car. "That's exactly what happened officer," he replies. He had trouble walking from the beer and off to the police station he went. *Watch what you drink, and watch what you do drinking.* This comes back to haunt him because he refuses all sobriety tests. I don't know why. That was pretty cut and dry. Its not that he likes trouble, its that if he only knew the immediate future, he would definitely reroute his trip. Wouldn't we all? Things happen, but yeah this is his fault. Should have made another decision. A lot of his demise around these times regarding his driving privileges occurred in rapid succession, including the incident in Worchester. These came to be darker times as it seemed that nothing was on track with lots of things going wrong and the word *failure* loomed out in the distance. Seemed like he couldn't even hit the ground pissing. That was toward the end of his stay in Springfield, but in the beginning, like I said, it was very exciting and vibrant. He was new and everything was different now. He did, however, have a problem with his next door neighbor, just like years before, and actually questioned if it was in fact himself who is always the problem. He quickly realized it wasn't his fault and that this older couple next door wanted peace and quiet and that don't come easy with three young children and all their friends right next door. One thing after another and finally Johnny had enough and cussed them both out enough to make a nun blush. Don't like little kids? Good. I don't like grumpy-az-death old fucks. Hope all your grandkids all come out pinka' *than pinko shee'at.* Whatzz zat?? So howabout that!, dickhead ol' grump? I'll make sure that I'll be there to be the first one to piss on your last dead estate. Man! . . . sounds like I need some kind of attitude adjustment! But by now, he's been with the postal service for over a decade. With all the stupid excuses for coming in late he's stated, this one with anybody else would register a high on the weird scale but raised nary an eyebrow with the post office. And it really happened.

One morning, on time, he's getting ready for work. He goes in the basement to check on a floor he laid the previous day. That's when he gets attacked by two birds. That's what he thought they were. While attacking him, that's when he realizes that they are bats, not birds. He kills them both with a broom. In doing so, he has now made himself late.

No problem. He'll just scoop 'em up in a shoebox and bring them to work for proof. When he gets to work, he says, "Look, this is why I'm late" and states what's in the box. When he takes off the top, everybody comes to take a look. That's when one of the bats that he thought he killed but only stunned, gets up and flies all over the place scaring the shit out of everyone, especially the women. To this day, they all think he did that on purpose and it didn't help in the cause. He felt like Typhoid Mary that day. Typhoid Mary was quarantined a hundred plus years ago for the safety of the local population. Typhoid Mary nowadays now has a right to movement regardless of social interaction culminating in infection of everyone she meets. Have we gotten better or worse? Do individual rights take precedence to mainstream society? But anyhow, other days made up for that. Like the annual Shad Derby Fair held every May I earlier mentioned. The post office was right in the center of town. He should have taken his lunch break in the break room. Sorted one tray of mail after lunch. That's twenty minutes a letter. Probably still sorted all wrong. Quality takes time especially when your half-twisted. He's got the postal routine down to a science and knows what buttons to push and levers to pull. He's been there so long, he's like a piece of furniture. But by the early Nineties, because of his professional but cavalier attitude toward his superiors in the postal service, he had done himself some serious damage. Only one or two supervisors talked to Johnny if anything at all. But Johnny would talk to them in a professional-but-demeaning manor which caught the attention of most of the employees in the building. He had all kinds of friends at work. In fact, I could go on and bring back days when he lived at Babe's house. All his mail carrier buddies would park their Jeeps in the back, out of sight from the road, and now its time to relax before returning to the post office after the route's done. Became a daily affair. Johnny would even invite some of his supervisors. Come one, come all, you don't know what you are missing. But aside from all that, he should have kept his mouth shut. After all, they are just doing their job.

One thing that didn't help was that there were a lot of supervisors. Couldn't make all of 'em happy. By now, he has a stack of dossiers against him like he was on the FBI Top Ten list. He can't help but remember all the energy his supervisors expended in their pursuit to hurt Johnny rather than to help him. One thing he didn't like in his own building were the catwalks up in the ceiling with the one-way window in which to look over all the employees. More often than not, he just look up and wonder if anyone was up there, not care, and just flip 'em off. I don't think that was a good idea. I know I wouldn't do that with a wife and kids to look after. Big Brother or not, that's your damn job. He just didn't see it that way. He didn't even care for his own union. Didn't care for the union president and stewards. He saw no loyalty. He remembers a staunch union president for the mail carriers toward the end of this career come to work the next day a full-fledged, bonafide upper management supervisor. Democrat to republican overnight! Even got a Buck Rogers super-decoder spy ring. Your pension is based on your annual income at the end, so I really can't say that I wouldn't have done the same. Next day you are now looking at, not standing with all that you once were. As long as everyone remained friends, but that just seemed to be so difficult for some. Johnny could care less about friends and would tell this new supervisor how nice he looked in his new suit and commented on how he made the perfect *yes* man. Yeah, Johnny could care less about his job also.

As time rolls on, things start to get cloudy in the northeast's economy. Early Nineties. Tough times loomed in the closet. He was glad he was employed by the postal service, but after realizing he wasn't going to get what he wants . . . a return to the airport, he lowered his expectations to the point where he had a recession-proof job and lost it right in the middle of it. The heyday of the Eighties took a sharp left turn in the northeast in the early Nineties.

I can't recall in economic history when all the portfolios hit the fan and all the interest rates . . . ***fell to rock bottom.*** Lots of people with double digit mortgages who couldn't refinance for whatever reason got hurt. Lots of companies either folded or moved south. New homes being built were tacked with hundreds of business cards for different trades or a bunch for the same trade. Competition was fierce. Foreclosures filled the newspapers. Unemployment was on everyone's mind. So were all the monthly bills. Couldn't pick a better time to get fired. Johnny did some refinancing before a lot of this happened, and because of that, he did make things a little easier. Refinancing your home is one of the most beneficial things you can do for your castle. He's lucky he did that and that was awhile before the northeast economy went to hell in a handbasket. He refinanced his duplex in Enfield, lowered his monthly payment and walked away with seventeen thousand. He used that for a roof on the duplex and for payment on the house in Springfield when he bought it. Mortgage companies are good companies with which to have parts of your portfolio involved, with even if being just a limited partner. Nowadays, they get a little more than just a slap on the wrist. What's good for me is also good for you, the man says. Refinance companies and mortgagee companies. One is the other, the other the same as the first. Brothers in arms. No difference. When you already have a mortgage and you want to refinance to secure a better interest rate and payment, why do they make it so tough? But to choose not to move at all but use the system to lower your burden on an existing mortgage and get five pounds of shit thrown at you 'cause your great-grandfather was late on a squatter payment don't mesh too well with me regarding mortgages. I might stumble at eleven-hundred bucks a month; give me a shot at eight-hundred!! Community banks would probably do just that, not those mega— glomerate nationwide banks who only look at numbers. People look like E.T. to them. Seems like that if your tighty-whiteyz have a hint of brown on them . . . you lose. Keep that stupid-ass high payment 'cause they just told you that you're not capable of making a lower one. It'll probably cost you a few hundred dollars just to find that out. Mortgage and refinance is the only way anyone has any chance for a part of the American dream. But when refinancing, don't even think of anything evil, they'll know and guess what? You'll stay at ten percent 'cause your not smart enough to pay only five percent. Only stupid people pay low, the rest of us know better. But anyhow, while during these unstable economic times and still with the postal service, he sees a lot of his friends and others toughing it out, with little or no success. Around this time is when the shit hits the one-way windows at the post-op office.

One day, he blew a gasket. He's not really tight with the postal clerks' union steward 'cause he couldn't care less about his union. Politics. Nothing more, but a lot less. He got into a loud confrontation with his steward, threatening him with lots of physical fitness and a good boxing workout right then and there. Plus he called him a little runt or something that sounded like that. That was a mistake. Not only threatening another employee, he did throw a bundle of newspapers with everything he had at his head, and his language constituted sexual harassment. How about that?

Sexual harassment for loud obscenities pertaining to woman parts. I got no problem with that. If you're going to mouth off on the job, cuss like a sailor if you can't help it, but leave the lewd no class sexual or even racial derogatories at home . . . unless you work in a two-man submarine with just you and yourself. No one wants to hear your filth. Johnny knew right then and there, he screwed up. He knows he was the asshole of the bunch and he couldn't care less what he says and who he says it to. Nothing personally derogatory, but more as put-you-in-your-place using only intellect. It was that easy. Like one of his supervisors. He was once a mail carrier who couldn't do his route in the prescribed amount of time thus costing the postal service lots of overtime money, especially after eight, not forty. So they made him a supervisor. Where I come from, you can't do your job?, out you go, not up. But he did make some very disparaging remarks regarding a female employee with whom he worked with. You know, the way men talk about women when it's a full moon. I'm sure all dolled up and off the work floor, she would catch Johnny's eye like any other woman, but he was talking with little regard for class regarding the conversation. This all but sealed the coffin on the sexual-harassment charge. He knows that was uncalled for, but the postal caste system somehow brings out the worst in some people. He was well liked in the office, but mostly by the mail carriers. Not many postal clerks really cared for Johnny except a few or would have anything to do with him. "How's the kids? How's the wife? Any diseases yet?" and so on. The mail carriers would always, along with Johnny split up duties for organizing the next house party. They came to his rescue during firing proceedings, but a little too late. Hit the brakes before you go off the cliff, not in midair. That's the only time they work. He does receive postal representation on the house since he is a defendant and they don't want it to look like Johnny was railroaded. Not even the Supreme Court can help and it would probably go nine-zero.

Now this is the second government job that's flushed him down the toilet. *Second.* How many people would even acknowledge that? He's been twice removed from being removed twice. Violence on the work floor and sexual harassment. Good work . . . kids are only toddlers. He can only work for himself now. No company is going to hire a nutjob . . . background checks and stuff like that. It will follow you around like be B.O. for quite some time, more likely longer than that. Thank God he knows a trade and good enough at it to get paid for it. It's been six years since Rusty passed on and falling down now hurts a little bit more. It's now time to straighten up, tighten up, persevere, and carry on. Wish I could say that's what happened. Nope. It's time to get it on with that freaky old lady who's always on the sidelines . . . the elegant crackwok' Katy. This was a hurricane binge. The thought of blowing thirteen years in the postal service and current economic conditions the way they were are all too real to dismiss just as . . . we'll make it. His wife was kind of oblivious to the severity of the situation believing that his flooring skills would pull them through. She remembers the Eighties. The Nineties hasn't quite sunken in yet. Remember . . . she was a rare breed, a stay-at-home mom, so she really wasn't aware of life outside the house. Johnny always brought everything home. For a while there, he had it made. Ten years with a nineteen-fifties type household. He didn't want to alarm her and said everything was going to be all right. This was about the eleventh or twelf year they've been married and now she's been working as a waitress at some local bar and restaurant for a couple of years. That did help out. She did what she could. His sister Patty was staying downstairs in the in-law apartment with Johnny's niece Emily. That's when his wife was working the late late shift at Denny's. That's also when the stupid stuff out on town happened. He had all night. After paying twelve-hundred a month for his mortgage for six years, he now fell behind four months. Double-digit rates are good for you, but **Johnny was on the wrong end**. He now tells his wife there is no work out there. If there is, it's hiding. No flooring. No nothing. He now collects unemployment. All four weekly checks fall a hundred short of the monthly note. A lot of bad shit. So what? Just put the glass dick down and take it like a man. You started it. By now his wife is waitressing at a local Italian restaurant and finds solace with some waiter with whom she works with. She's disillusioned with Johnny. He should've seen the writing on wall right then and there. A while back in Texas, I heard you can shoot 'em for that. See how fate saved Johnny. Had he not gotten the shit kick out of him, he would've bought another gun on the front. That's one hell of a law, kinda like Muslim law. Not much crime over there except genocide, brainwashing, and hell of a lot of cases of a spontaneous-human-combustion. Very sensitive. War that is. And,oh yeah . . . fooling half the stupid world that by shaking hands will make it all go way.

He had asked for and received all of his retirement money . . . roughly seventeen stacks. That seems to be his lucky number. It is here he gets tripped up by cell-phone-investment-trickery, but he also makes some other investments. But before that, he now has the mortgage company up his ass. He's behind a hell of a lot of money and there is no comeback. Because of being late on a payment on his rental property, he could not refinance his own house. Thich really pissed him off. Foreclosures filled the newspapers and now he was really scared. Finally, he called them up and told him to take that last check he sent them for twelve-hundred and frame it as that was the last one they were going to get. Buying a house in the Eighties was unlike anything you see now. Twelve beans a month for Gilligan's hut? That's how it was. That's how our economic system works, or at least worked for me and Johnny. It wasn't bad timing at all . . . if you wanted a home. He coughed up a lot. Especially closing costs. The closing on their first house was around twelve grand. Second house . . . over twenty stacks. That included five or ten percent the price of the home. Economics is a combination of luck and decisions and you must do your homework. It's like being in school . . . always learning. The more you know, the smarter you get and the easier things get. It's competition, usually against your own decisions. Is it door number one? Door number two? Or the donkey behind door number three? Did you do enough homework or legwork? If not, you'll pay. How many times does it take for you to learn? Very costly. Smarten up! That's economics. So ain't the donkey behind door number three. Sometimes there's nothing but donkeys no matter what door you open up.

Throughout America's existence, there have been troubling times known as recessions, a terrible depression, market corrections . . . and on a personal level; nothing going the way its 'sposed to be: *i.e*; house fire with no insurance, health problems, gettin' locked up too long, life running amuck, and other really strange things. I hope another depression never happens again, they seem to be rare, but I'm not too sure about another recession. Screwed up commodity markets, the Dow Jones up on Wall street, and messed up futures markets have major consequence on our economy. I don't even know what the hell future markets are. Pretty sure it's got something to do with my future. But there's something else that I mentioned earlier. The structures we all live in which nowadays, dictates much of our economy. Johnny moved down south because of a nasty real estate crash that was caused by something. I think I know what it was, 'cause the same symptoms are popping up down here around metro Atlanta. *Overbuilding.* Can't really blame the home builders, iz what they do. However, you really can blame them. First and foremost, where's all these people supposed to come from to fill these new homes? I see some sub-divisions around here where construction has come to a complete halt 'cause lots of these new homes have been sitting vacant, for sometimes up to a year. The builder and the financer are getting their asses handed to them 'cause of no demand and the builder involved sometimes has to default on construction loans and still has to pay the property taxes on all these unsold homes until they're sold. Talk about cuttin' your own throat! This also effects the financer 'cause the builder can't come through on his part unless he goes into his own pocket. **That's not gunna happen.** So, now the lender, on whom we all rely to forge ahead in our quest for the American dream, is now in trouble and by taking such a financial hit, might go out of business or now doesn't have the available resources to fully accommodate everybody it wants to accomodate, to keep profits up so that they don't go out of business. Too much overhead, then out you go.

I think I'm gunna write another novel and call it The Great American Nightmare. My trade comes and goes, with not too much coming but a lot going. Where? I don't know. All's Johnny's made in 2007 according to the only 1099 he got from the one of the only real jobs that year was twelve-hundred twenty five dollars and fifty-cent plus the few jobs he got off his cell phone. By the time the rent was paid, the next rent was due. That lasted all year. I honestly didn't believe that anyone could live off of that without losing any weight. I'm sitten' here in my crib during the winter freezing my balls off because I can't afford no < didn't have no > heat. But that's my problem. I'm keeping warm by guzzling ice cold beer. I also got a broken shoulder, but again, that's my problem. Kinda look like Quazimodo. Wouldn't have it any other way. Took me 'bout fifty years to do it, but I finally succeeded in destroying the entire left side of my upper body. 'Bout friggen' time!! But when new construction is flat on the markets, that trickles down like a tidal wave into the existing structures. With so many homes to choose from, that creates a buyers market, and now those homes also fall flat with some sellers reducing the selling price . . . sometimes dramatically. That makes people tight with their money and that's one of the reasons it's so cold in here. When one of your most major investments and the entity that makes the mortgage industry go round, your roof, is in peril . . . we all suffer.

He's also having trouble with his rental property also. That's the first to go. He simply could not rent out both apartments. The whole town and region became rental or closed up. He just couldn't compete anymore. All the heart and soul he put into that house just evaporated with every month of no rental income. He simply cut it loose and walked away. Not without consequence, however. They came after him just as he arrived in Georgia. The recession depreciated that house so bad, even if he got top dollar for it according to real time at the time, he couldn't come near the price for which he bought it for. He told them, "I got fucked. So did you. Have a nice day," and never looked back. There was major consequence to pay for that. He just didn't care. He told them to eat what he ate. You can't get blood from a dinged-up lendee, and he made sure of that. His mortgage company for his own home hears his profanity-laden pleas for help and directed him to the regional HUD office located in Boston. With HUD's help, he lops off a thousand off his note, and now only pays two-hundred per month. He loosens the noose around his neck a little and now realizes alls he's got to make it now is his own two hands, and what knowledge he's got, especially construction. But with the good slap in the face about reality, sometimes he'd loosen it up alittle too much and wind up somewhere in town where you're really gunna get nothing accomplished by doing that. *Government help can be hazardous to your health.* But he still tried like hell to save his sinking ship. One week he pulled an ad in the Springfield Sunday newspaper. He still has copies. It's a full sized pullout flyer proclaiming his trade and credentials regarding his new venture, bathroom remodeling. He's done some bathroom work before and got pretty good at it. He sent out several thousands of these ads, and alls he got back was one call. Those are not good times. He also invested in three fairly new cars he got from a car dealer he knew crosstown. He got all three for really good prices, and here's how he can make up for lost time. But before he put them in the papers, one rolled down the backyard hill into a parked tree and got demolished.

Down to two just like that. Even when priced lower than the same cars in the classified, he got no calls. A decision was made. Time to get the hell out of the northeast. That's when the seed to seek shelter elsewhere was planted, but not before other things just popped up right before his very face. He didn't want to leave before experiencing just one more motorcycle wreck. They yanked his driver's license when he wrecked his car during the snowstorm I mentioned earlier. Of course, this comes back to haunt him just like everybody else. After they pulled his license, he drove around on a little 1969 Honda 90 he bought for fifty bucks. It kinda looked like a moped so the police would usually leave him alone while on the road. It was actually considered a motorcycle and required a motorcycle driver's license but the police paid him no mind and he drove that thing all over the place. This happened early in 1993. While on the way to the store, a parked van blocked the stop sign at a four way intersection that he had no idea about. The intersecting road he was coming up on had the right of way and Johnny was supposed to stop and let the traffic go by, then proceed. He approached as usual, wide open. The little Honda would top out at around 50 m.p.h. Just as he got to the intersection, out of nowhere there's this car five feet in front of him crossing the four way. He had no reaction time whatsoever. He was still on the throttle when he centerpunched the drivers side rear quarter panel so hard that he totaled the car along with the bike. A little Honda 90 demolishes a car. Says something about all those look-alike-tin-can-cars I see all over the place. He leaves the bike, flips through the air and lands flat on his back forty or so feet away. He wasn't wearing a helmet, no shirt and was barefoot. He bounced to his feet and all the people who ran out of their homes after hearing the loud wreck expected to see bodies. They were all screaming trying to help but couldn't find Johnny. He shouts, "Over here," and they all come running over to where he was at. They all shout, "You should be dead! You should be dead," over and over again. The rear of the car was halfway sliced in half with the bike embedded in it. If he had gottin' there one second earlier, he would have met Mr. Grill along with both headlights and *nothing else would have really mattered after that.* He had a bruise on his back that went from his shoulders to his lower back. It took him ten minutes just to get up and change the channel on the TV for weeks after that. Don't mess with overtime money. That would really piss his guardian angel off. That's one of the richest angels up there thanks to Johnny. According to Johnny, his angel told him, "Go ahead. Do what you want. I got your back . . . gettin' pretty old, though . . . Why don'tcha' smartin' the fuck up?" Carelessness seems to go on forever. That's got to be some damn good luck even though he gets punted around like a football when he screws up.

But as he's healing up, he's making ends meet with HUD's help and by collecting unemployment. Now HUD now tells him he can no longer obtain help from them anymore. Time to tread water. Sink or swim. *Being a white able-bodied male can be hazardous to your future. That is, if you base your future on government help.* That really wasn't Johnny's thing and he would have never heard of HUD if it hadn't been for his mortgage company. Yeah, he became a burden to society for a while, while the taxpayers were footin' his bill for a while. He didn't know he could and really didn't have any choice. Bad decisions cause all this? That . . . plus some miscued timing and alittle rain. He wouldn't take welfare. Rusty would have crawled up out of his grave and beat him senseless. He only took their Massachusetts Department of Welfare card, because it was just as good as a driver's license 'cause practically everyone was on welfare around where he lived at. You'd see more of those gettin' whipped out for ID than a drivers' license. He also got sixty dollars worth of food stamps when he got his ID 'cause he had to. He went and traded those for some chronic. The government helps out all of its citizens, even the ones who can take care of themselves. He shoulda went and took welfare 'cause now the unemployment office informs himhe can no longer collect unemployment anymore. Apparently after an appeal by the postal service, the unemployment office cuts him off. This is during the same month HUD told him to go pound sand. His disciplinary problems at the post office came back and bit him in the ass. He explains his situation and that he has three toddlers to look after. He also tells them that he's about the one of the only ones not using his checks for free dope like everyone else was. Family came first, anything left went in the pipe. They respond by telling Johnny that not only is he cut off, he also has to pay back what they already gave him. That came to around nine thousand dollars. He replies that he has nine thousand handrolled bullets and he'd be more than happy to oblige if they wanted those instead. He tells them to kiss his ass, spits on the carpet, and leaves the building.

It's also about this time his wife tells him he's gotta go. I guess she's had enough, wasn't gettin enough, or who the hell knows? But now he's got absolutely nothing, not even a woman. By now Vaj was staying in the in-law apartment. His brother Tom was by now living in Atlanta. Johnny and Vaj pack up Vaj's van with all kinds of tools, some dope for fools, and a lot of beer then it's off to the Deep South. Some call it the Dirty South. Just like anywhere, that depends on where you are.

PART THREE

THE BEGINNING OF THE END

It's November 1994 and it's off to the South. He doesn't like leaving the kids behind but with all opportunity all but washed up, he had no choice but to leave. But what a ride. Sorta reminded him of moving around back in the military. They ride nonstop, stopping for only beer, food, and rest-room stops. To ride the country, broker than shit, without knowing your future is kinda like riding in a spaceship. You don't know what's gunna happen next and that was appealing to them. They feel like they're going somewhere when they cross the Mason-Dixon Line. They are southerners now. Yeah, I can hear all the laughter from the Deep South. A Yankee becoming a southerner? What does a southerner become when they move up north? The same as Johnny movin' down South; either lost or a nomad. Or as in his case; a southern-frei'd Yankee. But Johnny always liked the southern, defiant, in-your-face-Yankee attitude he's always heard about. Plus something about losing the Civil War but sticking the middle finger up when looking north appealed to him and made him smile. Yeah, he's gunna love it down there. As I write this, he's been there for alittle over a decade. Even if he wanted to go back to the northeast, legal matters in both Connecticut and Massachusetts would make that highly improbable. If yer gunna get locked up, do it for a valid reason, not because the man says so. If it will, however make your life better, consider it. Sometimes things get worse before they get better. But he'll have none of that. *Some of us possess that come-and-get-me attitude that seems to always burn us all.* But anyhow, they are cruising Interstate 85 going towards Georgia and that's one long-ass haul. They pass Earnhardt road with the big green sign on the highway and now they know that they are in NASCAR country. Or at least where it started from. They finally get to Atlanta and don't have a clue as to where to go. Alls they got is Tom's phone number. Once they hooked up with Tom, they had a place to crash for awhile and relax after that hell ride. Johnny brought his crazy ass dog with him 'cause he's got to have his best buddy with him for sanity. When everything turns into shit, it's time to talk to your dog to find out what to do next to get rid of some of the smell and make it all bearable. Once settled down in Tom's apartment, Tom says, "Lets go to Buckhead." Johnny says, "What's a Buckhead?" Boy, did he find out. Both him and Vaj were flat broke and Tom said it's on him. Buckhead is like the lower east side Manhattan with money being thrown all over the place with good times at every upscale bar and restaurant . . .

just as long as you're packing a wallet with lots of cash and plastic. Johnny screwed up his plastic back up north trying to keep the wolves away from the front door and he's got no cash. Buckhead gots no use for him, but Tom takes care of business and Johnny really likes Buckhead. But after all that, it's time to get down to business. Construction is red hot in Atlanta and off to the carpet stores they go. They were both shocked by the wages, some even to this day. As in most trades, we are paid by the *square this, cubic that, or linear those.* In the *floor-whore* trade, depending on what type of floor, we get paid by the square yard or by the square foot. The more square whatevers, the more we make. The bigger the job, the better you do. But the wages made them both wonder if they made the right move. One day they pulled a job, the only job from this place, from a carpet shop, and by calculating by the size of the roll of carpet, how much they would make that day. Little did they know that just because it was an apartment they were doing, it only paid half of what it should have paid; 'bout a buck and a half a square yard. Johnny was incensed and told the forklift driver to get it off his truck or he was gunna take it out somewhere and sell it, certainly not install it. The carpet shop owner told Johnny never to come back. He replied that if he did, it wouldn't be to *pull a job.* Apparently because of the short life span of carpeting in rental units, one should only charge half price for installation. As all carpetlayers know, a floor is a floor is a floor, and the physical labor required always remains the same. A buck and a half a yard is real bad. Johnny got that when he first got in the trade back in 1980. All carpetlayers should listen to Johnny.

But here's where *cut-throat economiks* comes into play. Almost all immigrant carpetlayers, legal or not in Georgia will work for that and that's dead wrong. The land of opportunity for some becomes the land of concessions for others. Never concede! But how? A 64,000 dollar if I don't say so myself. Everybody will go for the lowest bid, provided that the quality is still there. That's only natural. That is the capitalistic way. That's good for all the movers and shakers out there, but for those of us who work a trade, that's as bad as it gets when my competitive rates are slashed in half by cut-throat economics. That is of course a good thing, if all the prices for everything we all buy and need suddenly drop which is **never going to happen**. No, everything just keeps on going up. This makes it a bad thing. By looking at how some of these people in Washington view my situation and others like me and look at illegals . . . not legals . . . they're full fledged Americans . . . but illegals who drive *MY* wages down as *potential votes* and screws the working man in doing so, is only going to turn America into a dog-eat-dog land like ***you have never seen before.*** When people stop working together, which this will cause, dogs tend to run in packs and someone is gunna get hurt. If that someone is someone who thinks that I'm too expensive . . . and this might sound cold, then I don't really care what happens to them. I gotta live too!!! Hope to hell a very well-honed, skilled, quality grade tradesman is always recognized for his worth to modern society. We build everything everybody lives and works in, 'cause without us, some skilled quality might be hard to come by. Just remember, the shock of paying alittle more money wears off a lot sooner than the shock of poor quality . . . which never wears off. But all that really don't solve the problem but I feel a lot better. But they both find work all over the place and go out and do it.

One day they pull a job for some remodeler which turns out to be a godsend. They've been in Atlanta for around three weeks and really need a place to call their own. Well, they found it. This remodeler, whose name is Vic has a large house in the Drew Valley section of Atlanta and needs some roommates to lessen the load. They each have their own room. Not bad, since at one time Johnny was once a landlord. If you got to start all over, at least have a room to live in. Johnny and Vaj are laying carpet everyday but alls Johnny's got on his mind is his family back up north. It's real tough to leave your kids behind. He gets over it 'cause he has to get over it if he's going to do work that is visual which also has to be acceptable. After some time, Vaj splits his time between the remodeler and Johnny. Vaj knows how to do anything so when Johnny hooked up with a commercial carpet crew, that gave Vaj a shot at doing some remodeling. Johnny's new crew did some extremely large jobs, including the Fox theater in downtown Atlanta. To think that it almost got demolished back in the Seventies would have been a sin. Some of the money from Lynard Skynard's 'One More from the Road' album went to saving that landmark. They did Target stores and major hotels, including all the guest rooms and corridors. This was kinda new to Johnny. He did homes, not football fields. But he learned real quick 'cause he already had the skills. But he did learn a lot of different procedures and methods to accomplish his trade. Moving to Atlanta really honed his skills. *In fact, he's one of the worst in the biz nowadays.* He stays with Vaj for about three months or so and moves in with his new friends, but not before him and Vaj make a few journeys up north in Vaj's van. Johnny's just got to see his kids every now and then to let them know that he didn't abandon them. Nick kinda took it hard and that tore Johnny up. Plus he straightens things out with his wife and she is now considering a move down south. He was also flying up north every month to see them for about six months. It wasn't expensive at all. That's when Valujet was around before the crash in the everglades. He was laying carpet, around nine-hundred square yards at some old train station in Gainesville that got converted to some arts and crafts center, which is now called the Smithgall Arts center when it came over the radio about the plane crash in May of 96. He had just previously flown several thousand miles with that airline. But aside from flying, he and Vaj do that hell ride quite a few times in Vaj's van up north. Back and forth. Not without incident, of course. What's an east-coast trip without gettin' arrested on the way? Got alittle boring so lets check out some blue light specials! On one ride, they get as far as South Carolina. I guess a black van just looks conspicuous. Vaj don't speed, he don't even lie and wasn't speeding but they get stopped anyway. There really was no *what if* or any other reason to stop or search the van which is what happened. It coulda been described by someone previously by a witness to the police as a vehicle near a crime scene. That's a good *what if,* but there was no mention of that. All the paperwork was correct and Vaj was sober as a judge. Not longhaired Johnny, which the police probably didn't like. The police said that people with long hair run drugs up and down Interstate 85. They really didn't say it like that. But anyhow, no shit! Shit happens on all major freeways, so you just stop anyone you feel like stopping? But it was a black van. Everyone runs dope in black vans. But during the search, they find two huge bails of chronic, each one containing eight joints. Pretty big haul. The police haul them in, take all their money, and cut them loose. Around seven-hundred bucks. Wonder what would happen if they were broke? Probably doin' around one to five . . . joints that is, not years. One to five years means you really screwed up, one to five joints means you're probably gunna waste four of them. Sorry about that unusable information. This is the first comic book I ever wrote. Eight joints is eight joints the sheeple would say. Those kinda people who smoke sawed-off Lucky Strikes are thugs. There was no judge or prosecutor involved during the whole entire incident. A complete 4th Amendment rape, rob, and plunder! Hate to be Robin Plunder. After staying up north for a couple of weeks they decide to head back south. During the winter of 95 they get as far as Lords Valley in Pennsylvania when the motor lets go. Right in the middle of a blizzard. They had picked up a friend so there were three of them. Vaj had one of his fifty-gallon aquariums in the van with the smallest amount of water in it so his fish could also make the trip. They turned into ice. They froze to death the same as Johnny and his buddies were about to do. They would crank up the motor every half hour for heat and let it run for five minutes or so. The motor had a tremendous lower end knock that made it sound like a jackhammer when running. A decision was made to go back to Connecticut because no one knew where they were and it was so blistering cold, Johnny's canoliz were only about the size of BBs. That's pretty damn cold! It was so cold it was impossible to sleep no matter how tired and beat up they were and Johnny was wearing only shorts. Anyhow, they limp along around five or ten m.p.h all day long virtually going nowhere but make it to Sandy Hook, Connecticut, when the motor completely shuts down. A connecting rod blew a hole right through the engine block. End of the line. They found a bar and got so fucked up, their buddy they picked up was laid out on the bar, out cold. The bar owner didn't care after hearing about their ordeal. They got towed back, got Johnny's van and made the trip back to Atlanta. Cold, snowy weather is cool as long as you're in control, not the other way around.

Right about now is when his HUD program is about to dry up. They gave him some time to get straight and realign back with his original mortgage company. While he was staying in Atlanta, HUD was picking up the tab for his family back up north. Realigning back with his mortgage company was all but impossible. I guess because he had small children HUD cut him alittle slack. His family has now decided to move to Atlanta. He has already been down south for close to a year. The mortgage company tells him about other programs that one must jump through hoops and walk on water to obtain once you get cut loose from HUD. He sees the writing on the wall but he thinks he can pull a rabbit out of the hat. His wife has just at that time received the first of a few inheritances she will receive. It was several thousands of dollars. His Springfield home has now become rental and to save it would eat up quite a bit of it. Bear in mind, at this time everything was either rental or closed. I remember all the vacancies, both residential and commercial. There was one store that's been around since World War II that closed up shop. Many people survived all this but many, like Johnny, got their asses handed to them on a paper plate. This home also depreciated dramatically and the monthly mortgage wasn't worth the effort. While in Atlanta, he decides to rent it to a woman lawyer. All lawyers should be women. It's womenzz work anyway, only for the fact, *who wants ta cross a woman?* Shouldn't have rented it at all. Being way down South, there's nothing he can do when all of his monthly rental checks are short because this is wrong, that is broke, or any other bullshit she can muster up. This happens every month. That was once his castle, rebuilt by him to the T and there was nothing wrong with the house. It is now that he realizes that there is no hope for that house, blows off HUD, and just keeps her bullshit monthly rent checks for himself and it's just a matter of time before she gets thrown out to get the house ready for auction. In a small way, he gets the last laugh. Lawyer bitch! Pay the friggen price or don't move in!

But now his whole family is with him and they settle in Doraville, which is part of metro Atlanta just outside the beltway, Interstate 285, northeast of downtown. It is also that Jonathan Livingston Woodpecker thinks about his wife and the affair she had. He sees her in a different light now. Sorta like a black light: still there but the color looks different. But as for the kids, he lives with it, but any man loses a little part of himself when stuff like this happens, never to be gotten back ever. Real men think like this, lesser men can think whatever they want. Not Johnny. He wanted to shoot holes in either him or her or both and probably would have, had the kids been alittle older and didn't need his help anymore. It's all downhill from here but the slide is a long process which takes many years. He's already been married for fifteen years which ain't bad. But now a new start. He is dependent on other people for work since he's got no license . . . mostly Vaj, and his Chevy van was sold for a bigger Chevy van that had an unknown interior engine problem which wasn't detected upon purchase. Trying to get alittle bit better came back and bit him in the ass. He decides to work alone and keep all the money. This works out for a while. He financed a 1990 Ford 150 pick up truck, ignores the law and drives to his own jobs. He knows that it's against the law but the money was right. No driver's license. Four million cars in Atlanta. Surely, they'll never catch him. Well, things don't quite work that way. But I just mentioned that he ignored the law and drove anyways. Once you lose your license, you really aren't worth too much to anyone because not only do you become dependent, but anyone gets sick and tired of holding your hand. That's something to think about but it's too late for Johnny. He gets stopped year after year for some of the lamest reasons, but any reason on the road is a good enough reason. A lot of people in Atlanta drive like tomorrow is not going to happen which pisses him off. NASCAR bump drafting on the interstates. Blinker signals don't mean shit to some people. To hell with the church van next to me in the right lane, if I cut it off to get nowhere, they might wipe out but I'll get to my destination fifteen seconds earlier than I was supposed to. Hope they're okay. He drives amongst all this crap and loses his temper twice behind the wheel. Both times involved wanting to make a lane change by using his blinkers. You'd think that someone would oblige and be courteous by allowing him to proceed on. Not in some of Atlanta. That makes you an asshole if you are courteous behind the wheel. After realizing he's going to miss his turn, even with the blinker signal on for nearly a quarter of a mile, he just cuts the van over with no regard for anyone, just trying to hit someone. In one case, he sent one car into a jersey barrier and in another, he sent someone else over the median on a major main drag in town. Alls they saw was Johnny's middle finger as he waved to them on his way to wherever he was going. Now we all know that's wrong. He got away with that. But he gets stopped for the simplest of things. Like coming to a California stop while dropping off his daughter at school grounds like everyone else was doing, but they got him. Two million people driving around on drive-out tags in metro like he was, but his musta had bright neon lights on it or something else to catch the police's eye 'cause they got him. Quite a few of the other cars around him were driving around the same way, but they got him. He even had a roll of carpet on the truck. Both times it's off to jail. This is the second time of the beginning of the end of his pursuit of liberty and happiness. This is all very expensive, with all the judges talking to him like he had just molested his truck, not drive it. "Alls I'm trying to do is support my family" he tells the court. They musta thought *Charley'zz fam-oly* 'cause he got fined like some inside-trader. This is the first of two of his driving problems and he is humbled for a while. They did not like his prior driving record at all. The second time he got caught, he was fined sixteen hundred duckets. This really hurt. That's a whole bucket of duckets! When you make your own bed, you must sleep in it.

He's doin' pretty good with the trade now and a large portion of his money is going to the probation office every month to keep him out of jail. Little does he know, this ain't going away anytime soon. He now knows everyone in the trade and can work just about anywhere he wants. It's good to know how to use your hands along with your head to make things work. He does it all; carpets, linoleum, hardwoods, ceramic, and other tiles, and can put down whatever any customer can design, either in their head or on paper. Think about something abstract, tell Johnny, come back two weeks later, and it's done. Alittle expensive though. Quality hurts. *Hit a bottle of Jack wrong* and puke all over the floor. That's also floorcovering according to Johnny. Pay him. Not too much demand for that though. One job that he talks about is the state capitol in downtown Atlanta with its huge gold dome for the roof. He was there for an entire summer on that job. The Georgia state capital is an immense area with all the hallways and lobbies done in eight by eight marble tiles laid next to each other with no grout. They are one inch thick and are laid only in sand and haven't moved at all since they were laid back during the Civil War. Now that's talent! This is on all four floors with all the great stairs throughout the place done in solid marble. Pretty nice work. While working nights laying some real nice patterned carpet in the state senate chamber, they all sat at the big podium where all the senate hot shots all sit, and after their break when they went back to work, the podium looked like a junkie's poker game. Dope, empties, ashes and cigarette butts . . . some in the ashtray littered the whole damn desk. *Wonder if that's ever happened since?* They did pass a few laws while working in there like making power-walking illegal, lowering the drinking age to twelve, gettin' rid of all the sick and elderly, and everyone in America has to give Johnny one Confederate dollar. However, they haven't been properly enforced. But the bottom line, the job got done. But somehow, Johnny went broke once again.

Johnny's working the state capitol in Georgia and passing some pretty absurd laws but let's get serious about politics if that's possible without letting the child in you take over. Remember, politics are for adults, Trix are for kids, dix are for chicks, and so on. I recall the 2000 election between Bush and Gore. At the time, I thought it was between Mush and Mushier. I couldn't care less who won. But there was one episode at the democratic national convention in Chicago that made me think alittle. That's when the Boy Scouts were introduced during one night at the convention. They got booed. Why's that? Most likely 'cause the Boy Scouts had the right givin' to them, by the Supreme Court to keep gay scout leaders out of their realm. Not to say some gay scout leader is going to make some sick move, but who knows? It went five-fo.'

Apparently, four Supreme Court judges either don't have kids or *don't have a clue* whatsoever. Thank God or Allah or anyone else for that decision. That has some bearing on the human purpose to keep the reason for living alive. Gay men have all the same reason, *but not with my son in the middle of the woods.* Argument for the four who got confused could be that there are more perverted straight people out there than gays. That's strength in numbers if you wanna call it that. There are far more heteros than homos out there. The fact that lots of people are pissed over the Supreme Court's decision about this tells me that ***if the democrats want to remain a respectable party, they had better leave the artificial change alone and get back to nature.*** Five minutes is five minutes *no matter what anyone says.* Ten dollars is also ten dollars but who cares about money when my son is led into the woods by a ????? 'cause the government says it's okay. Whose government? ***Not mine, that's who!*** Like I said before, I know a few gay people who I'll stand up for, but I like the odds a lot better if Hank Hill or Homer Simpson led my boy into the woods rather than take a chance. I probably won't have any gay friends left anymore by the time this book is completed. That's not okay 'cause the gay people that I know are mostly professional people with professional opinions about the norms of society and pretty much know that most parents who have sons in Boy Scouts would be dead against letting their young sons be lead into the woods by someone most, if not all, parents would not want their kids to be like. I really don't mean to offend a certain segment of society but if I did? *Good.* Wipe yo' tearz and turn the page 'cause I don't think I'm finished yet. The 2004 election just goes to show that not too many people are turned on by the attack upon ourselves (mostly democrats) *on the edge* who seem to think the past two hundred plus years has been nothing but a waste of time and we should now legalize damn near anything, leaving damn near nothing sacred . . . I got a real big problem with that.

I think *weave* done pretty damn good so far considering our human inferiorities with compassion towards our fellow man. Yeah, we ain't perfect . . . nobody is. Our history shows us that. At least the U.S. has compassion and if need be, we'll help others get back up on their feet. *Why doesn't our media try to portray that with the same vigor that Al-Jazzarra portrays us as demonic?* A really good question, Wizzbang. Our communist media, damn near all of em' . . . including Communist Nitwit News, not what it once was. Now they take sides. Good night, David. Good night, Chet. Those days are long gone. One question though . . . how come they don't take our side? They aid and abet the enemy with the same vigor as the Islamic news media does also. Does 9-11 mean anything anymore? Oh, that's right, it's George Bush's war and no one else's. He was the first to call in air strikes against New York and the Pentagon. *Only idiots believe that!* They try to come up with proof for the absurd. Like the fake documents proclaiming him unfit for duty. Putting up false news knowingly, cost some *dumb-ass* famous reporter his job. Good!! George Bush or not, no one has the right to attack someone with bullshit, unless of course, they're scared of something. ***Newsweek*** back around 2005, with their article loaded with ***pure bullshee'at***, sent the U.S. back to *square one* while putting my brothers and sisters out in the battle zone in harms way! They are so lucky that this isn't 1942. They would have been charged with aiding and abetting the enemy and I would have made sure that I'm in the front row if I could . . . to watch 'em hang till death. Not good enough. If allowed to, I'd like to do the honors myself just to get that ear to ear smile I'm noted for just before sentencing. I *REALLY* don't like traitors!!! What the hell happened to all the newspapers lately? They all seem to bat left handed nowadays. I thought that the democrats were all about the little guy trying to make it big? How can they afford almost all the newspapers in most of the country with little money? I really can't comment on a national level on who's true blue in America, and who's not because all through our history, the democrats have always been about the little guy. What's wrong with that? Me too. But in doing so, sometimes the heart overrides the mind and too much attention is paid to the perpetrator and not enough to the victim. The victim now being much of old school America and many of its doctrines. Leave the apple pie Boy Scouts alone and stop drawing mustaches on Norman Rockwell's art!! Even the media in which I do see some sense really shouldn't take sides the way they do. That's not journalism, unless you write for the tabloids or *High Times.* The media is supposed to be unbiased, but those days are definitely in our past, certainly not in the present. Traitor TV is all around us. If I want opinions, I'll read *Sports Illustrated.* If I want facts, I'll read *the Sporting News.* Pretty hard to find something like *the Sporting News* on cable traitor TV. I still get some facts but it comes with alittle bullshit like shouting matches, somewhat partisan, and portraying themselves as judge, jury, and executioner. Some high profile cases on TV based solely on circumstantial evidence have already been tried on cable TV. Yeah, it looks like your call, but leave that up to the judge and jury . . . not your *female* emotions.

One case involved the unseen slaying of a wife and fetus and it looked fishy right from the beginning. All for another woman. Unobtainable women can sometimes warp a fellow's mind. Warped is a fitting term for what politics is doing to America right now in real time. The chasm between the parties is light years apart, affecting many decisions, some major, that make a majority of the masses ask questions while scratching their heads. What I would do if an issue was that important is I would put it up for the masses to vote on. Believe it or not, we're not stupid. The state and federal judges, all the way up to the Supreme Court, would act as guides with encyclopedia knowledge and legal finesse to question a decision or two. Some very important decisions with staggering social ramifications toward our future should be sent to the people . . . *We the People. Remember us?* to look at, along with judicial institutions to be used as professional guidelines, all the way up to the Supreme Court if need be, to be just and fair. But who will administer law and order if that happens? The title *judge* defines what he does. Can the people do the same? I want my fate determined by twelve jurors or three judges, not the lynch mob masses. But that's not what I'm talking about. I'm talking about social and moral decisions, not law and order. If the masses can vote on that with respect to decency like we've always known, then the judicial leg of government should respect majority rules, not all this behind-the-doors crap I see going on in real time. Decency is getting railroaded out of existence because some federal judges think that five minutes is really five years. Some rely on rehabilitation alittle too much while forgetting about the crime committed. With something like I just mentioned, then can something the majority represents be hammered between the two. The federal judges out in the Ninth District seem to think God is a four-letter word in our national documents and our forefathers musta been out of their minds, so they take it upon themselves to right that wrong, making the general public walk around scratching their heads wondering what's goin' on here. Five people can have that kinda power? Here's my résumé. I want in. Even the president must be kinda envious of that job. All five look at you and say, "Squat and blow some mud now." You say, "Mud? you mean like mud like out in the garden? It's raining out. I'm not goin' out there! Please tell me it's about the garden, I'll getcha all you want." "Oh!, c'mon now!! You're kidding!! . . . . right?" That's a lot of f&c#ing power.

They're not elected, but placed there by each different administration in power which I think is dead wrong. May as well be a lifetime dictator. I don't think that the 9th district came from the Reagan administration. More like the *Ren and Stimpy* administration. But as far as myself, I take a look at the different moods of the country during certain times and vote for what's right, no matter what the party. Even the Keg party. I'm all for the little man trying to make it big, but the peoples' party has metamorphisized into damn nearly the same stuff I saw on college campuses back in the day. ***I don't want that steering the Enterprise!*** But when the going got tough, usually with wars, both parties have stepped up to the plate throughout our history. We are back on the plate and I would blame the nemesis like no other, much much more than pounding the president into the ground like a thumbtack. Do any of you loudmouths out there know something the rest of us don't? Like exactly not who, but what's responsible for 9-11, or the whereabouts of WMDs which we knew existed at some point in time. Or maybe you know the Middle East like I know Main street and we're just barking up the wrong tree. If you know something then say it 'cause alls I know is we got attacked and no longer will two oceans protect us from all the vile ideology scattered all over the planet. Some protester at the republican national convention in New York City in 2004 was carrying a sign proclaiming a *stupid* slogan saying < war breeds terrorism >. Either she was afraid to fight back, or she forgot how we got to be a free people. She was probably born during peacetime and doesn't really realize how fragile freedom really is. What she should have wrote was *terrorism breeds war* because when my future is in danger of blowing up in my face, it's now war whether you like that or not. If some of our national or international leaders had their way, we could be wondering if some hell-bent-on-whatever terrorist who does what he does, does so knowing that some of these leaders believe that *he also has rights.* He does have rights, like the right to try and stop the bleeding. Nevil Chamberlain never went down in history. He did, but it's not good. He went down as a wimp. What a way to be immortalized! But Winston Churchill did. Do you think there's any difference between Adolph and Osama? Osama and Saddam? Saddam and Cap'n Crunch? Cap'n Crunch and Colonel Klink? Hmm . . . somehow we got back to Adolph. I don't think that Adolph was as wimpy as the aforementioned, but he went down in history as far worse.

Okay, a little history, or at least what I know. Since America's inception, we have had all kinds of political parties. Somewhere around the beginning, we had democrats, federalists, and some others that I just can't put a name on. Many have come and gone. Many had no focus except for only one particular theme and that one only, and that's no good. There was even a group or party that was known as the Whigs. Remember them? They wore snow-white wigs. I think they all did. They should do that nowadays. No one would want to be a politician anymore. Nowadays, that goes against that *individual* look that we're all looking for. Republicans didn't show up until the mid-nineteenth century. I believe the Industrial Revolution had a lot to do with their rise into politics. Since then, the republicans seem to now be the employers with much of the democrats being the employees. Conservatism and liberalism weren't just confined to one party as widely believed today, but crossed over from party to party throughout our history. Check out who the evil party was back in Vietnam. Also, do you think this is the first time Christmas has been under attack? It even became outlawed for a while. The couldn't-hurt-but-only-help Freemasons enjoyed their role in early America; then were treated like the plague in the nineteenth century for a while, and for over a hundred years to now, operate in every community only to help people. *2 B 1* ask *1.*

So you see, what's happening now is nothing new. How many of you loudmouths knew that? There's one thing about the Freemasons that I always thought was intriguing. They are thought of as the decedents of *The Nights Templar.* If that's true, then that, to me, would be about the only thing that history has not repeated. It has always remained that way since the day of their inception. So have their advisories, our modern day nemesis in which why we're at war at the present. Not too much has changed. America was built by politics and has become both right and left for a good reason. One made sense at the time and the other didn't, and vise versa. It's called checks and balances to keep Uncle Sam always standing tall. It has worked this way with partisan politics working together until we hit the 1960s. That's when all those *social programs* we have today were introduced to us under the Democrats under LBJ. In doing so, they portrayed these millions of Americans as victims of society and they should be compensated for that. Not socialism as it might sound, since only that sector of America was receiving money for nothing. The rest were competing for it. I believe this to be the birth of the haves and the have-nots as we know it today. African-Americans were the primary beneficiaries of the program since it was a democratic effort, not a republican effort that helped with the Civil Rights movement. It was a noble gesture since a lot of blacks were living in poverty and were denied work 'cause of race. But it's not just blacks fueling the Democratic Party simply because of numbers in the population. There's a lot more whites than blacks which tells me that there's a hell of a lot more workers than owners in America. So how does the hated Republican Party exist? Being smart helped a lot. So did being needed. Democrats are now making money hand over fist but I still believe that it's the republicans who employ us more. America runs on taxes and employment generates taxes. One thing that is mind boggling is our national tax system, expenditures and, of course . . . our national debt. One dollar is taxed numerous times, just with the same person who owns it. From the feds all the way down to the sales tax. We have the brown taxed out of us. Why get rich, showing ambition, only to have 'bout fifty percent of it taxed. That is if you play by the rules and most of us can't afford that. But to be penalized hard for being successful just don't make any sense. *Ax the rich, feed the poor, till there are no rich no more.*

A long time ago in the northeast, they try to impose a fifteen percent tax on top of all small businesses. They called it a small-business tax and was good at making small businesses smaller. It didn't fly. I called it a *small-business buffet tax . . . all the people's portfolios you can eat.* Enough already!! Why don't they just impose mass burials like Saddam did? We even have a death tax! *You can't even die unless you can afford to!!* Saddam didn't care about that, you still gunna die. Get yo' mama to pay for it or she goes too! What about our probate and estate taxes? Those taxes and most of the others can take whatever don't belong to them. Those taxes are also there only to keep us all working, same as our legal system. Keep the working man a working man. Someone actually has to work. Can't have too many well off people. Who's gunna do my gardening? What about my new floors? I'll do your new floors 'cause after all, it's got to be done by someone and there is no substitute for hard work. But it still sucks. That's only because after I install them, I now want the same floor in my crib. Alls I gots is 1970's orange shag carpet. I dropped a sandwich in it in 1982 and still can'ts find it.

Localities, states, and the feds all need taxes to keep America running on all eight. We must expend money to accomplish that and between all three levels of government, that's a lot of money. Remember Johnny's fourth law he passed in the Atlanta statehouse? That's one dollar from every American going to one person. Our tax system runs the same but with hundreds and thousands going to Washington. If every dollar was accounted for, we would have the perfect country with no pressure from within. Maybe a war or two might come down the beaten war path, man is just not gunna learn from now into eternity, but for that to happen, it would have to happen with hopefully (favorable results) for the better or why waste the blood, sweat, and tears? Just like all the wars we've fought in the past and I realize that the present is real, almost surreal for all of the Coalition troops and most of the planet but the fact that it's real . . . it means that all of us must try to find a way out but with favorable results. Tryin' not to let the mind keep on wandering off somewhere, but not just April the 15th, but coupled with property taxes, sales taxes, gas taxes from hell, sin taxes on all of our vices, and even taxes on basic commodities and services; i.e. water bill, phone bill, etc., in which I don't agree with . . . generates an exorbitant amount of money that is supposed to be going to the correct municipalities to make our lives better. How come I got left out? My shit don't change. But anyway, that should be enough money to make all things work. There are government bonds that generate money for the government and also enhance your portfolio. What I'm trying to say is, with all that money, "Where does it all go?" How come no one knows? Makes one wonder. From local public works, police forces, fire—fighting, road building to social security, welfare, federal money to states, and *defense defense defense,* all of these costs the most. Taxes covers all that. But all's I hear is about the shortages and this massive debt we have. I do understand that America was in the black in the Nineties and ten years later, we're in the red. Mismanagement or misguided? That's something that's gunna take some time to decipher, so we'll do that some other time. I don't like it either. Costing me around thirty grand for whatever and that's only me. Multiply that by the whole population and if that's the way it's going to be, then what's the sense of working if what I make in one year is just my part of the tab. What about my rent? We all hear about stupid, exorbitant prices the government pays for twenty dollar items and that's all true. I've heard that too many times for it not to be. Hard to keep the checkbook balanced with less-than-honorable people working on both sides of the fence; the unscrupulous government person or agency and the high price vendor who has a contract. Together, between them both, we're all gettin' raped. *Government people should not become bankers.* Sometimes I hear that money, lots of money was just lost. That's pure bullshit. No one loses that kind of money except at the casino for a year straight just screwing up hard every night with my money. Someone needs to check out some offshore bank accounts versus the job that the bank account shows. How much you wanna bet most offshore accounts involves . . . yer not gunna believe this . . . lawyers. The government needs an internal monetary police to clean things up. They got a few. Good fucking work. You're supposed to fix the problem, not make it worse. Who is the monetary police? ATF?, FBI?, ESP?, you or me?, rich and powerful lobbyists?, Republicans?, Democrats?, Idiots? How about a red-blooded all-star cast of trusted CPAs? Believe it or not, they're not that hard to find. The Salvation Army would be a good place to look first. Can't trust them? Then trust no one! Anyone that knows a penny saved is a penny earned. Problem is, pennies don't mean crap in the world of dollars. Means alot with the price of gas!! Last I knew, a dollar contained a hundred pennies. That's how you start; rub two cents together. Does Sezzpoo' Jo'nezz need ta' go ta' Washington? Nope, I'm going to Vegas, the odds are a lot better. I can make money there, not lose it as *strange as that sounds.*

When Johnny was working for the postal service, on the first of every month would come all the government checks, mostly welfare checks or Section 8 for picking up most of the tenent's monthly rent. Those were local or state, everything else was federal. Some of Johnny's tenants back in Enfield relied on Section 8 and that was guaranteed rent. Most cases of section 8 are single moms who now have to be two parents in one and that is a difficult job. Johnny brought up three great kids and it took two to make that work! Only the Social Security checks were *actually paid for* to have those checks go out every month. And you know how skinny a government check is, same as your tax refund.You can fit a lot of them in one two-and-a-half foot tray of mail to be sorted out. One tray of government checks could equal the amount of people in a small town. At Johnny's post office, they got five to six trays of checks every month. Combine that with every town, village, and hamlet in America. That's a whole lotta money for nothing getting kicked out every thirty days. This is tax money being used to accomplish this. Now I do realize that out of three-hundred million of us, there's gunna be fame and fortune, and the rest of us. Some of us are gunna experience hard times, rough shelter, bad medicine, no school lunches, and other bad shit and since the government collects all these taxes, they should kick out some kind of free assistance for people who really need someone to lean on. But what I just mentioned is so immense that eventually it is going to . . . if not collapse . . . severely hinder our government simply for the fact it goes against the capitalistic creed that for every dollar earned, it cost twenty-five cents. This simply isn't the case. Even though I walk in and out of the gates of poverty and that-a-be-um-no-jokem' I'm sorry to say, but I'm still, and always will be a capitalist no matter what comes down the pike. Need to get alittle bit better and some of my own demise was my fault and some not but anyways, this is money for nothing. It works yearly with taxes collected to make the wheels spin. Or fall off if a lot of people don't start carrying their own weight. Carry your own < heavy > weight. Pretty damn hard to do that when after you pay your monthly bills, you're flat broke. That makes the luxury part of life alittle boring after the neccessity part has been paid for month after month. To all you higher-up capitalistic pigs out there who forgot what *an honest days work for an honest days pay* means, it means this. Keep on pounding up our wallets your overpriced goods and services from fifty-thousand dollar pick-up trucks to three-dollar stocks that cost sixty bucks and your endless source of revenue (working middle-class America) is soon gunna dry up. We just can't afford it anymore. Guess what that's gunna lead to? Don't know? ***Howabout socialism!*** Smartin' the *<buck up>* and come back down to earth before it's too late!!! Last part of that last sentence just as might said it all.

But America wouldn't work if it were just for that though. That really doesn't chew up, along with Medicaid and Medicare, as much of the national gross revenue as you might think. I get this from cable TV news so if I'm incorrect, it's still right. People have always complained about pork bellies in Washington and I always wondered, "What does that mean?" What's a stupid pork belly doin'in Washington causin' all kinds of gases anyways? It took a while but I now understand and I really don't see too much wrong when a representative from different states and districts use federal money to better their local environments. Used appropriately, of course. I guess the problem is that there's too many hands in the cookie jar just screwing everything right up. And what I believe happens to the national gross revenue is that once counted, it gets nickeled and dimed to death. That screws up anyone's checkbook. Grants for sciences that go to universities are good for the advancement of all sciences, since science can help better explain ourselves to ourselves. I don't want to get back into that, but I can clearly see that government money goes all over the place. Everyone has a right to a piece of that pie, but some grants going to some people who call themselves artists but really ain't make me raise my head to take a second look. Freedom of expression is our God-given right, but let me get this straight. I can roll around in donkey shit naked and then roll around on the stretched canvas and call that art? No shit!! I still don't understand all that 1980s Mapplethorpe art purification, since most of America didn't understand what art was at that time. Mapplethorpe showed us and now we know fine art is. Who gives out these grants? ALCU? We have national debt like no one's business and these factors that contribute to this like the uncontrolled DC bulldozer no matter who or what's in power have all played into our federal checkbook. War certainly doesn't help, either. All wars cost lots of loot and whether you are for or against the Iraq war, I don't see it getting any better soon until the dust settles. This is going to take years to settle, but as the old saying goes, it will happen sooner or later. The sooner the better, and better days are comin. Nothing's gunna settle until all Americans settle into a common ground cohesion regardless of opinions and beliefs about where this country is going. History shows me that all empires fall. First they divide. But when led (only from some kinda leadership communication-breakdown) by Frankenstien, empires fall from grace *straight into space.* Bill Clinton, no war and thus a *workable* budget as he showed. George Bush doesn't have that opportunity 'cause of the war that he didn't start, only look blindly and fight back. Call that anyway you see fit. I call it a *Brave New World* no matter what part of the world *confuses bravery with tyranny.* I would have done the same thing. He just happened to be in office when the Manhattan skyline was altered forever and must deal with it. He is just one of those presidents on his watch where shit happens like Fort Sumter, *the Luistitania*, Pearl Harbor, Bay of Pigs, and maybe even the Tonkin Gulf. Some of us even question whether or not 9-11 should be included in those messes just mentioned. Some of us should just really keep things to ourselves.

But anyhow, who's gunna pay off this huge national deficit? When you stay up for three days, sometimes concentrating on one subject don't even last a minute. But it's a good minute. I could help. Give me a list of government payees who shouldn't get paid for basically doing or servicing nothing and they won't get paid. That's a good start. But they charge hard 'cause after all, nobody in the governmental, bureaucratic infrastructure really knows who's paying them. I hate to say this, but you have got to be a real idiot to pay somebody for forty hours when he never even showed up. Think about being a taxpayer the next time your property taxes goes up a hundred percent next year. Fed or local? Who cares? It's still tax money that could have been properly managed. Give welfare to the locals. Washington has done a terrible job. Restructure it to make it so. Don't ask me how? I don't even know what I'm talking about. How come all though the ages with deficits here and deficits there, I never really felt it? One reason would be that I really don't exist. I'm sure there's other reasons but as mentioned, I'm not really too sure what's going on here, so instead of talking in circles, let me get to something I know. Two words that don't go together are *competence* and *incompetence.* They might almost sound alike, but both could be used to describe our modern day society. One harder than the other. One goes hand-in-hand with indifference. I just wanna know, as previously mentioned, how come some of the competent are overrun by the other? Maybe it's me, but all my buddies who work with what they were born with are nothing but competent. And how did some of us, some a lot more than I care to comprehend, gets so goddamn loose? In the information highway era in which we live in now, never before have I seen so much miscommunication in my life. Misfiring all over the place from national security to "Why does it take sixteen minutes to get ahold of the human when calling some major corporation?" Or any minor corporation. Makes me wonder if anyone gives a crap anymore. I'm sure we all do, but sometimes the easiest way is not always best. Sometimes you gotta sweat. And too many people going after the easy hit without counting to nine first. Screw the easy hit . . . yer gunna get caught, and there's no easy hit that taught most people anything *'cept stretching the odds until it's too late.*

Even though most people by now can see that all my diplomas were mail-order I would like to continue this political essay on what it's supposed to be like when you're either a Democrat or a Republican or a mixture of both. Let me start out with the Republicans. Them first 'cause I flipped a coin just like in a football game. They are the champions of the business community, from small to mega-corporate. They advocate self-reliance above all. Not that no one else does, but they incorporate it as one of their pillars for survival. America was built on self-reliance. They live like Johnny, "If I can, then they can." They practice what I would call *advanced capitalism* and do not believe in money for nothing. What's wrong with getting rich? We all strive for that goal. Not to cast them as kill the poor, but more as *you get what you give.* You wanna eat the rich? Then do it for what some have become; self-centered-I'm-me-and-you-ain't-snotnosed-little-bitch-fucks, but not for achieving the American dream. Some of the poorest people I know are the hardest working people I know. Their dreams are real. They know that this is it, there is no easy hit and that to survive, they've got to grind out one day after another. They know how to count; at least to ten. To make life easier, some depend on all these money-for-nothing social programs . . . not all of them, but the ones who have no other choice. We need to take care of our people and I believe that, quite more than you think, Republicans also believe this. They also believe that much of this aid should be more localized as I do also. Washington just has a rough time seeing past the horizon. Johnny is one of these people whose life seems to have turned brown. He could also use a little help, maybe see a doctor for a physical or anything he don't have to pay for. A rich bitch. That would be perfect. A rich bitch with a fine ass. Now that's better. Dream on idiot. She'd divorce ya, then take your last can of Spaghetti-O's. You couldn't win a boxing match even if you were the only one in the ring. How does one hook up with a rich actress? While I ponder on that . . . do you think the locals and states would raise taxes to take on funding of nationwide social reform? I can only believe that by abolishing the federal income tax system as we know it, rearrange it so what I just proposed is feasible, could that be accomplished. Funneling money down from the feds is nothing short of disastrous. A little mismanagement I believe. I have no idea where republicans stand on that, as also the same goes with the democrats. They both seemed to screw up a lot of money.

There's a movement out there called *the Fair Tax* and I think that it needs a second look. Sounds pretty fair to me. You wanna know what needs a second look besides the Fair Tax? Howabout this? Since the Fair Tax is nothing but common sense, that means that the DC monster is the reaction to the action . . . reaction meaning nothing. So if that's the way it's gunna be? . . . ***then let's force it in.*** Anyone out there with any *moxie* left at all needs to do this . . . and who cares if you get caught. But run like hell! Stop paying taxes on April 15th . . . all of us, including all the small businesses who will be the first to get < sick of this fucking word > when a democrat gets back in the oval office. That could happen . . . alls we are to them are walking talking dollar signs. Shut the corrupt system down and start all over the way it was back when we ran down the Boston *Tea Party.* Something really important needs a second look no wait a minute!, lets do a sixty million dollar study to see which end of the earthworm is the head and which end is the feet. There are no feet. Gunna cost you sixty mil to find that out. As you can plainly see, I don't know a fucking thing about politics. That makes me an expert, neither do most politicians. But I do know that I'm not above the law, so maybe I'm a little smarter. America is all about money. I don't see how taxing the shit out of the rich is going to help. Alls that does is penalize success. And I don't see that by taxing the shit out of the rest of us is going to help either. Alls that does is penalize.

Getting back to principle over power in Washington, with all the morality, integrity, and other closely related words that they shouldn't really need a dictionary to understand in DC would help. Nah, how about another fifty-one percent pay hike. I really don't like to bash the headquarters of our country, but it's just that year after year, episode after episode, alls I see are more questions and less answers involving internal and international problems. Usually, it's either not enough was sufficient to quell a problem or, enough is enough!! If you can't fix it, then give it to someone who will. *Not enough?* But who's above Washington? Stupid amounts of tax money should be able to fix anything, but it don't. But let's see how the working man's party would handle this. As mentioned, democrats came up way before the republicans. Workers existed before owners, at least in America. Or at least outnumbered them one hundred to one. We now have some kind of equilibrium between both parties, but before that, workers had no choice but to take it or leave it 'cause if they left it, someone's right behind you to take it, no matter how small it is. Beats nothing, especially if you had a family. Before democracy went worldwide, many workers in other countries, led by people who worked for all their lives, resorted to *socialistic ideas* to make things fair and level for everyone. But we all know how that works since some workers give a hundred percent and others don't. Nothing fair and level if I'm totin' two and you only totin' one. Pay us both for what were worth. Obviously, I get more. Not according to socialism. That's why it don't work . . . or at least in America. But there are people out there who can only tote one while I'm totin' two who are trying just as hard as I am. Who's better? The student who gets all A's while not even trying, or the C student who's trying like hell but that's the best he got? Capitalism knows how to distinguish between the both so that everything is trying to work out. Capitalism brings out the best of both worlds. It also sets up an equilibrium between private enterprise and government by simple supply and demand. If there is no fair equilibrium between government and free-enterprise, then it's either *oppression* or *civil war.* One good thing that makes democrats true blue Americans was that they were the first to figure that out. Old-school democrats know how to roll up their sleeves. In fact, they were the first. New school democrats got me a little on edge. Socialism forgets individuality. *Some* ***American unions*** *could be explained as such.* Some of us get paid for slackin' while others get paid for actually doing their job. If he can't, let 'im sit down and I'll hitch his wagon to mine and still get the job done. Pay me more. We can't. The union for-bids that. But I'll take his overtime . . . I *make it back* on my own.

Getting fired from the postal service wasn't really all that bad, I get paid for what I do or don't do nowadays. Nothing is guaranteed, especially a paycheck while trying to *figure out the American dream on your own.* I believe that I'm entitled to some things like solid ground, freedom of movement, pain, air, clothes, a corner bar, and to tell you what I think of it all, but I don't think I'm entitled to a living. I don't think anyone owes me anything . . . *even a chance.* I always thought that, that stuff was earned, the same as respect. Chances are, you'll get a chance. Somehow that does happen and that's when you make it right, or screw it all up. If you want it, it's out there. Prepare. College, vocational school. Hone down a trade. Be aware and on the ball all help. Keep in mind that these days, not too much is fair anymore. Society now works against us rather than with us as in the all too-recent-past. We are all entitled but *you get what you give.* If you don't give anything, then you really don't give a damn about much and it's not my job to hold your hand. Some democrats think otherwise and it was all for a good and noble reason. *For our fellow man.* Back then, even now, to make ends meet takes up a good portion of my day and that just sucks. It was their way to extend a helping hand and the timing was precise. It has gotten immensely obese since then. Remember, no one owes you anything. If you don't want it, then that could only mean you don't need it. I'm not as so cold as to throw the weak overboard, but to heal the weak, then throw 'em overboard. Fly or die. Rock bottom hurts, so fly like hell. Democrats, while recognizing compassion also recognize competition, especially within themselves nowadays. No, *some* of them are not socialist by no means, but how else do you make social programs for the downtrodden work? It was a necessary evil needed to accomplish that. Sometimes you got to look to the devil, but as mentioned most of America competes for it. The welfare queen is dead? I just wish that the ultra-democrats who gave up on competition would look at historical America and smile at it, and not sneer at it as I see much too often nowadays. They were also part of that history. What about our heir's history? What are they gunna think about their fucked-up world that they live in now 'cause for whatever reason, we chose the wrong people for politics no matter what the party to clean our mess up by *phantasm* votes from *wish-it-were-real-land* to deal with present-time reality. *Lenny and Squiggy* votes will turn the American government into the same kinda government that was elected into Spain just after the Madrid bombings that claimed the credibility of Spain. Being taken seriously now comes at a cost like "Who's on first?" I don't know? I don't know's on second. No he's not! I don't know what Who's doin' when What's in charge of a government trying to steal second. As one can clearly see, what little I do know . . . I do know.

Anyway, Johnny is working all over the place. He's now accustomed to large commercial flooring jobs. His first few years working in Georgia were spent on the road doing huge jobs. He was hired help and got paid for what he'd done. One job that he'll always remember was a heavy patterned carpet they laid down at some country club down in Albany, Georgia. That's way down yonder ways, almost to Florida. He's been to Florida for his first time in 2001 and really liked it down there. He's done a lot of walking because of his annual driving problems but got a ride to this job in Albany. He don't care about rides. He's walked to Florida a few times even did the worm on the way 'cause Florida rocks and got there once in two months. Not really, 'cause if he can't twist a throttle, even illegal, he's not going unless last resort air out the thumb. But anyway, it wasn't the job or ride to it that got his attention. It was all the woods and forests all around there. Huge trees over a hundred feet tall, all in order or rows. Rows and rows of forest and if you look across the woods even at a forty-five degree angle, even that was on the money. I can only guess on who planted all these trees. If you gotta guess, then we need a little more history taught in school. Like you wouldn't believe! With all the dense forests he has seen before, he's never seen nothing like a gardened forest before.

Back at his place in Doraville, he's got his rented house all set up and his family likes the south. In fact, his kids are southerners now. He's flown back up to the northeast with his oldest son and a friend and retrieved an old 1971 Camaro and hauled all that all the way back to Georgia. He put that in his garage at his house he rented. Lucky to rent, I should say. They do credit checks on anything that walks, crawls, or slithers in the South. Even to deposit good amounts of money at a bank. Naturally, the landlord checks them out and tells Johnny he's a risk. Johnny says he knows, explains a little, but offers to pay six months in advance and shows the landlord a portion of one of his wife's inheritances on paper. The landlord is impressed and a good financial timing save the day. They had that house for five years. Having a house with a lawn made him feel whole again, even though it wasn't his. He brought down with him from Massachusetts the family dog, Cocoa. His wife picks up two more pups and now they also have three black german shepherds in the family. Johnny is a dog person, the more the merrier, He likes giraffes too, but can't get any shelter when inquiring about large fields with no power lines to keep them. Got a short kid and concerned about high school basketball? Feed him giraffe meat. Better than growth hormones. He'll be able to dunk the ball with his lips while standing flat-footed on the court. Sorry about the dumb-ass joke but he'll settle for dogs. He's got his Ford-150 pickup with a sliding back window and the dogs are in and out while going down the road. He named the two pups Otis and Pups and they got big. On one particular day while going down the road, Pups gets his paws on the steering wheel and the truck looks like it's going out of control. Cops everywhere but they don't do anything but wait until he's going down the road in the immediate future doing virtually nothing that would attract any attention. No umbrella is gunna stop this. Had he only obeyed the law, none of this would have ever happened. But since his family was carbon-based and relied on food and nutrients to sustain normal life, he felt obliged to drive regardless of his menace-to-society status to see that nobody lost any weight in the household and that all the bills were paid. Sounds like he needs one in the back of the head to me.

By now, he's gotten his first of six arrests for driving without a license. One thing that he still calls really good luck, is during the course of three or so years was all the trips to cracktown around four in the morning He was never caught doing that 'cept once. He even drove through a roadblock, but the police were checking only the traffic going the other way. Racial profiling being what it is and with him being the only white boy in the truck, he would've had a problem. But he did step in something on Thanksgiving night back in 1997 about three a.m. He drove up to the apartment with an acquaintance who knew the people who had the rock and sat in the truck waiting. While waiting, here come the police and they see a white boy in a truck in rocktown at three in the morning. Naturally they stop cause they ain't stupid and ask "Which apartment you waitin' on? Tell us and you be doing yourself a favor." Johnny knows he can't do that and now they know he has no license either. He explained that he didn't drive there, but he did, and he's having a dispute over money. Worked in Springfield but not here. They accused him of driving and he got arrested. While in court, the arresting officers explained to the judge that they really didn't see him drive and that the keys were in the glovebox. Johnny pleaded not guilty, but the judge didn't hear that and Johnny got whacked again. Sucks being Johnny. Even with parts missing, he can't escape the courthouse without something not going his way. It's supposed to be *unequivocally beyond a shadow of a doubt.*

But all this is nothing new, 'cause he's getting stopped once every year for some pretty petty infractions, but with an infraction being an infraction, it doesn't make any difference. He is, however stopped for an infraction that the cop who walked up on the infraction just couldn't believe. The cop asked him if he cared about anyone else on the road beside himself. This was downtown Atlanta on Peachtree street and he wasn't driving. And his buddy who was driving Johnny's pick-up that day got fined pretty hard. This happened when he was laying carpet at the state capitol. They had then Governor Zell Miller was out of his office for a while, while they revamped his office. Johnny was told to speed it up, the Governor wants out of the hall. What took so long was that Johnny's budding political career began in that office and if Zell Miller wanted it back, then he needed to enforce Johnny's four laws passed by him few months before. Didn't happen. But anyways, on this pickup truck was around six-hundred square yards of carpet rolled up in the bed, on the roof, all over the windshield, and on the hood. That's enough carpet to do five or six medium size houses. Johnny was hanging out the window telling his buddy when to turn and where things were. When writing the traffic summons for excessive dumbpidity, the officer couldn't even tell what make or model the truck was. He looked on the registration. When he left, they just continued on.

His first few years in Atlanta was another new era in his life and Johnny liked new experiences. There was construction everywhere and even with the not-so-hot wages like up north, he was making money and the family was thriving. Kids were doing well in school. Amanda got sent to Huntsville space camp for a week, and went to prestigious Fernbank College in Atlanta for a summer in where you had to prove your worth before being accepted. Johnny's wife was now laying floors with Johnny and that worked out pretty good. From waitress to carpetlayer. If you're going to learn something, learn it good and she did. Sometimes during the summer they would bring a small charcoal grill on the job and when the coals were ready, it was time to eat. In the wintertime, we would switch to small microwaves. It costs a lots of time to go out for lunch with Atlanta metro traffic choking the traffic down to a crawl. At least an hour. That's okay if you work by the hour, but as a subcontractor, it's *blow and go.* Sooner the better. On to bigger and better. But once home from work, they would tend to the kids who are now just hitting teenage super-human years. Remember how bullets used to bounce off of us? Thought that it really was an endless summer. They couldn't tend to them all at once though.

One day, Justin was screaming down the hill leading right into the driveway of their house on his bicycle and hit a bump he didn't see. He lost control and hit a car parked in the driveway while wide open on the bike. The bike crunched into itself and Justin hit the rear windshield like an RPG and almost broke his neck. Instead, he bounced off the rear windshield so hard, he screwed up some of his front teeth. They got that fixed after he got out of the hospital. Johnny was tickled-pink when he realized his oldest son was going to follow in his dad's footsteps. He blew his arm apart just like Johnny did and now this. He had the same kind of smile on his face as Evil Knievel *God bless his soul*, did when he realized his son was going to continue to jump bikes over things like eighty or so aircraft carriers and stuff like that. When Justin came running out of his room one day right after he sliced two pounds out of his hand with an X-Acto knife, Johnny had a heart-to-heart talk with Justin and said that this crazy fad has got to stop. Johnny was hung over like a Christmas drunk 'cause of a pre-ve-us party and had to go to the hospital. He was in no shape that morning, but Justin would have been scarred for life.

Johnny's second arrest for driving without a license occurred in Doraville and part of his punishment was to work off a certain amount of hours with the public works department. He liked that and got to know a lot about the town's infrastructure and sometimes felt privileged to be mingling with the mayor and others who ruled the roost. Alls he was doing was bullshit work in the town hall and told the mayor that they needed a new floor in the lobby. The mayor asked him if he did that kind of work and Johnny replied, "On my time, not on downtime. I make more money on my time." It got done but Johnny didn't do it. By now he's working in all the high-rises in downtown Atlanta and gets to know the area a little better. He likes to hang out around Virginia Highlands and the Little Five Points area of Atlanta. Little Five Points is like a much smaller version of Greenwich Village. Pretty cool. There used to be a bar where Johnny and all his buddies used to hang out at for years. It was called Nine Lives Saloon and Johnny was good friends with the owner. The bar was right in the center of Little Five Points and had rock—n-roll bands playing all the time. Johnny and Dave, the owner, hung out at the bar and Johnny wound up doing some work at Dave's house. They've never mixed business time with personal time and that's how you run a business. Johnny's shit always got mixed up but Dave just dealt with it. Not every Tom, Dick, and drop shot hung out after hours. You keep your customers honest, otherwise all your customers have tabs. Alcohol tabs suck, 'cause you got nothing to show for it.

But anyways, now his dogs are getting arrested. Pups and Otis are Johnny's dogs, plain and simple, crazy as hell. He put a fence around the whole hilly backyard. If they both weren't climbing the chainlink part of the fence like rock climbers . . . you actually had to see this, then they both were jumping over it at the hilly part like gazelles, not even touching it. He had a rough time with them, going to court all the time telling the judge how they are good dogs but a little rambunctious. Judge says fine, just pay the fine and we'll see ya next time. Johnny drives around in his pickup without a license, just blending in with traffic. It got pretty rough trying to blend in when you're going down the road not knowing that your dumb-ass dog is standing on the roof while the others are going berserk back in the bed. Pups was just plain nuts, but he couldn't help it because his brain was pumped with massive doses of doggy testosterone because he had the biggest set of doggy-nuts on him and girls blushed and gasped when they saw this four-legged freak of nature. Not that any of this trivial matter matters, but this dog kinda looked like a billy-goat from the south side if he were moving north and everywhere Pups was with Johnny, Johnny would always remind people that a pet is a reflection of his owner. Pups always wondered while everyone was laughing all the time. He would retaliate and bite the hell out of Johnny, chasing him all over the yard while nipping Johnny's ass real good. Tore his wallet and back pocket clean off one time. Johnny went the extra mile for his dogs. It cost a fortune to feed them. They ate very well. Some of the things people do to animals *should be done to them.* Nothing more, nothing less. If I get to 'em before the police, that's exactly what will happen. Pick on someone as smart as you and see what happens! Sometimes the fact that humans can think and animals can't, makes me wonder sometimes . . . who's smarter? Certainly not the poacher *I would love to get a hold of.* When it comes to proper treatment of domestic and wild animals, sometimes the human-race-ain't-nuthin'-but-a-big-disgrace. **All species** make the world spin a lot easier. Some species of animals already know *what we're all about* and are retaliating in defense the best they can, but they will need the help of people like me and you . . . 'cause those species just don't know how to shoot back, but I do. And so don't the rest of you 'cause soon . . . ***that's what it's gunna take.***

By now it's around 2000 and according to Johnny, that's the year the world ended. No, he's not one of these mystical oracles of the new millennium phrofets' of death and destruction running into a cave at the stroke of midnight December 31, 1999, but it's around these times that not only is he not running on all eight, but he don't even have a motor to run with. Some more bad stuff, but this happens all too frequently to most of us, so many of you will understand this. First, his wife has had enough and he's got to go once again. See, I told ya you'd understand. Nowhere to go except over to Tom's place. Tom had just moved to Little Five Points and Johnny, Tom, and Dave tore it up around there for a while. Tom played in a rock-n-roll band and the clientele at his apartment were pretty cool in Johnny's book. It's also around this time that makes him think about drugs a little different than how he used to. All these years . . . then the very first bad experience. He thought that would never happen, just like a flashback would never happen. He heard about it, but it never happened. Well, this is life in the *last* lane.

One night early in the morning after the bar closed, himself and some friends were holed all up in some apartment and Johnny did alittle bit too much cocaine. He told me that he did a shitload. To anyone who don't know what that means . . . it means a shitload. You don't know how lucky you are to not know that. He realized that something wasn't right and goes off to a bedroom and lies on the bed on his back with the light on. It's now that he realizes that he has never ever felt like this before and felt like he was going to explode. He's super-scared 'cause he now realizes that he's on the brink of ODing and he actually thought that this was it. He took one toke over the line right after the other one. He's lying there just freaking out and terrified. There's a land line home phone right there and he's considering calling 911 for immediate help. Then he picked up the phone, then thinks about it. Do you really want to put yourself in the system, one in which you'll never get out of? He's torn between his situation and his situation once he punches in 911. With a tough decision to make, he decides to ride it out and he tells me, *"You want scared? Screw yourself up on too much dope, that's scared!!"* Know thyself, just do a better job than that, no matter what you think you might be. That night changed his perception on our dope forever and he lives by that to this day. Know thyself. Sometimes in learning so, it's trial and error. That's the very scary part of messing around with dope. You think you know, but sometimes you really don't. A thousand times and its all good. Then there's a thousand and one . . . the next time, and to *know thyself* takes all you got, and that's just downright scary.

But he's staying down in Little Five Points and Tom is now working with Johnny. Tom did remodeling and framing so it really wasn't that hard to figure out the flooring trade enough to not only to drive for Johnny, but to bust out the job also. By now, it's around May of 2000 and he's now got a big one-ton 1991 heavy duty Ford van along with his Ford pick-up. He can definitely get to the job with no problem. He can, if he had to, now hire two drivers. Early in the week while they are driving around in the pickup, the transmission blowed slap-up, leaking tranny fluid all over the parking lot like a friggen river. Still not a major problem, he's got a big van. Later during the same week, the transmission on the van also blows. Blowed up two trannys in the same week. That only happens in NASCAR, not everyday work vehicles! Now he's got no way to get there. Still, not a problem. Everything is going to be just fine. He lands a huge ceramic job, enough to cover both the repairs, pay everyone and still wind up in the black. On one real rough day before the job, he contracted some really bad food poisoning from a popular fast food franchise that specializes in fried spidermeat that layed him out for three weeks where he spent in hell. That caused him to lose the job. When you work for yourself, and if you ain't there? See ya later, we'll find someone else. That's exactly what happened. Now, it's hardcore reality. Now it's not just the willingness to work hard, but now there's absolutely no way to carry the product to the jobthat weighs more than your grandmother which grinds everything to a screeching halt. While everyone else is having fun bobbing for apples, his head is in the toilet and those ain't no apples. Actually, brown apples do exist, but if you find them in the shitter, sober up, then go to a waste-treatment plant and get them at wholesale cost. He doesn't know anyone who could help him out and never wanted to alarm anyone in his family up north that not too much was working out. And this is the beginning of the way the new millennium is going to be for a long time but he still thinks he can overcome the odds.

As things spin out of control, he still drives. What little work he does, he still needed to get there. But it's like trying to bail out a boat with a spoon and reality sets in again. To have an understanding of what must be done, the will to do it, and knowing what can happen if you fail, then fail because of failure all around you is as degrading as it gets. So maybe you caused some of that failure, but it's still all around you. Not too much of this had anything to do with decisions, good or bad. This was a lot of downpour piss-ass luck. Not everything is really working the way it's supposed to work and he was so broke, he even had to re-route a short road trip a few times because of tolls. Even fate takes a back seat. This is tearing him apart because now he has become that four-letter word that he despises so much; *dependent*. Because of legalities, he's not supposed to drive but he did. But because of all this mechanical failure, he can't drive at all . . . legal or not. He felt lowered a couple of notches and moved back in with the family after slumming around Atlanta for a while. People now call him up and now he's got lots of work and because of being dependent for wheels, he now has to split everything fifty-fifty with a friend who has a truck. Work that he could do by himself, he now has to split in half. Some people enjoy stories like this, the same way some people like to watch other people fail, then fall. Living off *misery enjoys company* deludes the united we stand divided we fall atmosphere in which Americans are famous for. Why get off on someone else's misfortune? What would cause something like that? The rat race? Mine is bigger than yours? I don't know. I don't wanna know. If I see someone whose life has never left the beach, then the more power to them. That coulda been me, but it wasn't. Next time. Got to work a little harder, get a little better. Best thing I can do is to just keep myself alive and congratulate my co-worker who just got the promotion and everyone should stop talking about his wife behind his back. Hell, if it weren't for her, you probably would have gotten it over him. She's just doing her job. You know the saying, behind every man there outta be a woman . . . or something that looks like a woman. Better half and all that . . . hmm; maybe not.

But by now, going fifty-fifty while working his ass off wasn't working at all. Some of the jobs were just too brutal . . . moving all the furniture, relaying the carpet, and then moving everything back just didn't pay enough for a fifty-fifty split. But now he's got his pickup truck back with a rebuilt transmission. He's off on his own again. In less than one month upon getting the truck back, the motor blows all apart at the seams. Got one month out of it. Not bad. Back to the fifty-fifty split. This becomes unbearable and now he's super-pissed. Not a damned thing he did worked. It's not like he didn't try. He wishes the truck were alive so he could let it know who he was. It is now he decides to retire. Not really retire, but he threw in the towel. He don't need no stinkin' pension, annuities, or social security. That's for wimps. He doesn't do anything for a month or so and gave up. Why work your frigging ass off when you can sit home doing nothing and get the same results? That sure didn't work. Life was still going on and if you decide to retire, go through the proper channels. Planning and getting ahead works. Problem was, he was trying to do all that. He sure ain't stupid but that was a stupid move. In the situation he was in, the only way he could retire would be by high-risk, high-yield 'ski mask and shotgun' funds found usually in prison or on Wall Street. Call your broker. In this day and age, he probably can get you the shotgun. Ski mask is up to you. Prison retirement blows, so he didn't do any of that but if I were to say he didn't think about it, I'd be lying to you. He thought about some things not too many of us would even consider. I told him to keep all that to himself.

But now, he's got to go again. He and his wife were just not seeing eye-to-eye. He can't go back to Tom's 'cause Tom's girl moved in. But now a savior arrives. The first commercial carpet crew he worked with has moved up north a couple of counties and asks Johnny if he wants back in. They were doing the carpet in the Atlanta Falcons' brand-new football training complex located way out of Atlanta up by Gainesville in a small town called Flowery Branch. He got to meet the whole team. He was a little shocked when he saw the size of some of the players who looked like they hadn't even had their first shave yet. But he can drive by the complex and tell other people that he had a hand in some of the construction of the complex and he likes that. He's still paying the rent back in Doraville so his kids still have a roof. They are all still in school and now he knows divorce is imminent. The amount work he has is with his old crew in between phases of the football complex, was most of the subdivisions being built northeast of Atlanta. He has by now gotten his pick-up back with a new motor and now it's time to fix the big Ford van. He still does a few jobs in Atlanta when called upon by old contacts. As he traverses the parking lot at the Home Depot in Buckhead, someone backs out of their parking spot without looking first as he is just coming up on them. The car hits the front of his pickup and as he wheels on by, his truck is demolished on the entire passenger side. He wasn't in the wrong but he had to scoot away 'cause he's not legal. That truck just wasn't meant to be. It looked like a bowl of hammered something or other. He just put in a tranny and motor for a lot of money and he got nothing out of it. It still ran but it sure wasn't a pretty truck anymore. Maybe some long-dead lawyer was trying to tell him not to drive from beyond for his own good. That's what he thought. Hell, why don't some divine intervention come down and break all his bones? . . . 'cept for his left forarm ones . . . those had enough. That will stop anyone from driving. Anyways, the truck is now staying parked in his family's place in Doraville and now he's staying up in Gainesville at one of his buddy's house down in the basement. He remembers how it used to be and wonders if this is the way life is supposed to be. Not everything one does is going to work and he knows that he is only a drop in the bucket of lots of people who are going through the same thing or something equally depressing or dark. Simply deal with it . . . but that's startin' to get old now . . . sorta kinda like Fumunda.

When he lived in Atlanta, he used to think of it as a northern city in a southern state. Almost everyone he met when he got there was from some northern state or from out west. Seemed to be a lot of people like him; transplants from somewhere else. Some for opportunity, others to lick their wounds. The northeast early Nineties recession kicked a lot of folk's asses. Atlanta, to him, was a *family tree is still a sapling kinda town.* Roots only went down a couple of inches. Of course, that's not entirely true. There are lots of parts of established Atlanta that go way back into the town. But alls he met was Michigan, Pennsylvania, Connecticut, etc. people wherever he went. And that was usually at some club or restaurant patio. He used to hang at the bar and restaurant back in Doraville where his wife once worked at. He became a regular there. And that was the only bar he hung at that was comprised of mostly people from the south. He learned a little southern heritage in there. Sometimes, he'd hear a yankee this or yankee that, but for the most part it was mostly in jest but every now and then he'd have to speak his mind about his northern heritage. But that's Atlanta. Now he's up in Gainesville which is about roughly forty-five or so minutes northeast of Atlanta by freeway where the foothills of the Appalachian mountains began. As I write this, he's been up there for five years and instead of Gainesville, it is now referred to as Gaines-Vegas . . . the other white meat. That's according to him and a few others. What happens in Gaines- Vegas stays in Gaines-Vegas . . . for a minute or so, then spreads like geniticized kudzu. Lots of inner-country towns seem to be like that. Keeps you on your toes. Beats bein' caught flatfooted! But anyways, that's a stupid little joke 'cause therezz only one Vegas. One thing that I find remarkable about Gainesville is the actual age of that town. By recent archeological excavations done by Johnny, he somehow proved that Gainesville is older than Atlantis . . . the oldest town on the planet . . . older than space-invaders and pac-man. But, even though he's only sixty miles out of Atlanta, he seen a noticeable difference between where he's at now, and from when he was staying in Atlanta. Aside from the fact that most, not all, of his new friends are from Gainesville and got grandparents and other kin-folk living there The social atmosphere was different there. This was appealing to him. Towns folks, just like back home. But these are southerners. That's a major difference and these people know that just like anyone else, we're here for the long haul, and if an easy hit comes down the pike, good, but why waste good time chasing it? Do that when the work is done. A little bit more real than some people back in Atlanta. People know what they have to do here and Johnny fit right in. And yeah, a little Yankee this or that and here is where he really learned about the 'Southern Heritage.'

First of all, America went through a fierce Civil War in and no one ever forgot that down here. Not because of racist reasons but for good old-fashioned Southern Heritage, and after that war, good 'ol Southern Hospitality. And who else came out pretty good after losing a war? The Japanese? They worked a defeat like nobody's business. The South is a close second. They both mean business. The Japanese are all about economic stability within itself and especially globally. The South . . . to rise from defeat years ago, to rise to pure Southern pride that ironically will use that pride to most likely try and save the nation they once tried to change so long ago is what I like about Dixie. Southern rock? . . . not anything like it used to be but the South will always roll. How come Southern rock don't roll like it used to? Bring back the 'Dixie Dregs and Wet Willy'. Dig 'em up if you hafta, just get 'em back up on the stage again. NRBQ could have made it down here. They could've made it anywhere . . . I believe they did. Johnny learned more about Jefferson Davis, Robert E. Lee, and Stonewall Jackson here than he could have anywhere else. One thing that must be understood is the amount of hatred demonstrated toward each other one hundred-and-forty years ago during the war. Each had even set up concentration camps. Some might not agree, especially with current events the way they are in the Middle East, but I can't recall any other war . . . other than the Civil War, in which where *sheer dominant nothing-but-hatred-and-nothing-else* was demonstrated towards each other. Islamic fundamentalists don't hate us. They hate everything for which we stand for. Alls we got to do is convert to a cult-like mindset and everybody is friends. There was no option like that back then. The only conversion you got came immediately after you got hit with a 50 caliber musket ball into a crumpled heap. The heritage of the South is evident everywhere, with streets named after confederate heroes, statues, and the *Stars and Bars* flying in a lot of people's homes in yards. Morals and family values . . .

two heated topics nowadays (for whatever reason), take precedent over anything else in Dixie, whether black or white, latino or asian. There were no blue states in the South. A once-democratic stronghold has had enough. Guns don't kill people, bullets do. Punish the trigger finger, not the gun manufacturer . . . and other things. Like there's nothing wrong **whatsoever** about the Salvation Army and dresses belong on women and women only! At least around here. I never really saw any of that being a major topic down here. Not even with the *Stars and Bars* . . . the Southern flag. That became a sore topic down here with some states. That represented the old, dirty South to a lot of blacks and I can understand that. **But that's history, water over the fall.** No matter what it once represented, alls it represents to most people now is that southerners are proud to be southerners, even lots of black folks. Look at the first CD by 'Li'l John and the Eastside Boyz' when they first made it. Looks like the *Stars and Bars* to me. It's even on one of their posters. I don't know where they stand on this but what I don't like is what it means to certain people who are nothing but racists. It was, during the war, a battle flag against northern intervention . . . the Feds over States, and the core of northern aggression was of course, states rights then slavery. I hear different things sometimes and you'll hear different opinions about it down here in the land of Dixie. That's also another pleasant word . . . Dixie. Dixie sounds like a romantic landscape. It conjures up the Southern Cross on a moonlit evening. What happened in the South all the way back is just that . . . history. **And I'm aware that some of it is recent**. That doesn't mean it isn't happening now, or is never gunna happen again anywhere in America and to piss on a part of America's history 'cause we don't like it and try to erase it . . . is similar to censorship and I never really cared for that. But just like anything else, that too for whatever reason, is also debatable. It shouldn't be just like lots of other old-school subjects, but for some reason, it is. Change? Or loose change? The perversion of the First Amendment makes me wonder, *how free is free?* This *anything goes atmosphere* in which we live in now is somewhat troubling and the First Amendment police . . . the ACLU, should really start to **think twice, and speak once.** They should start to realize that morality is not a four-letter word. George Washington really didn't mean that anarchy in the form of decaying moral and traditional values was supposed to be embraced by the First Amendment the same way the First Amendment has allowed us to become what we are by use of morality, compassion, comradeship, and sympathy.

Another topic that could be closely related south of the Mason- Dixon Line, and by some could be construed as its beginning, would be racism. We all know racism isn't just confined to the South. Johnny views racism the same as most decent folks view it. He don't judge a book by its cover. That's hard for a lot of people, black or white. He lives by proof. *Lemme see **what you are** . . . no matter what color you are.* Then I'll be the judge of that. Racism exists everywhere. Everywhere, you will find people of different colors and origins living and working together in the same region or country trying to better themselves by competing for jobs, housing, entertainment, etc . . . while at the same time interjecting different culture into all these things. Some people like change, some don't. There will always be conflict and things like understanding and acceptance are tools against racism. Not to compromise, but a *meeting in the middle* . . . sorta speak. No one is to give up what he or she be, but maybe to give a little more when talking to someone who don't look like you. I can tell you where you won't find racism . . . in young children, almost all elderly, and most of all . . . on the battlefield. When on patrol during the Vietnam years, our enemy was fully aware of all the *internal strife*, especially racism during those years in America. When we were on patrol in the jungles, our enemy would pick off black GIs first just trying to bring racism from stateside to the jungles of Vietnam. It didn't work. It just fueled more hatred for the enemy. If you don't live by united we stand in the battlefield, you're just plain in trouble and it makes dodging bullets just a little bit harder. There's another place where people co-exist very well with each other and this is regional so only if you're there, you'll know what I'm talking about. It's a part of Atlanta in which I've mentioned already. Little Five Points is where festivities are everywhere even all over the streets. Make a trip there if at all possible so you can see how people are people no matter what anyone is or looks like. Nuthin' like hanging out on the corner of Morelands and Euclid.

But back in Gaines-Vegas. He's staying in his buddy's basement, and after a few months, it's time for his own place. He got in Gainesville around May of 2000 and by August he purchased his own house where he brings his dogs. He purchased his own house with pretty much nothing.

He needed five grand to put down on it. This he borrowed from his now estranged wife. This was no conventional mortgage at all, but a purchase with an option to buy. You simply put down the upfront money, and paid your rent for two years. Ten percent of the rent went towards the principle for those two years. Then in August of 2002, you get to purchase a mortgage right at two years. One month after moving in, work slowed up and since he was last hired, when it got slow, he was the first to go. He's got a nine-hundred and forty five dollar payment each month and now he's a little stressed. Plus by August 2002, things aren't quite the way they once were and Johnny should just leave real-estate alone. His pickup is also at his new house but since it looks likes it lost in the demolition derby, he rides his big Ford van that cost him eighteen-hundred bucks to fix the transmission. He starts to hang out at Applebee's a lot and begins his new stakeout in a new bar to come to just relax in. It's around now he gets into his last fling with crackrock and to this day, don't really fuck with it anymore. One of his carpetlaying buddies got an apartment in town where Johnny hangs out at. This was all too convenient 'cause alls they had to do was make a call to a certain taxi company, ask for a certain driver, then in fifteen minutes they had whatever amount of crack they wanted. Once while sitting outside the apartment drinking beer, here comes the cabbie on legitimate fare. Johnny and Tony had just dropped a huge marinated steak on the grill and the plan was to enjoy a real nice steak with some beer. Johnny whistles. The cabbie stops. Then they decide to rock-it-up, and inside the apartment they go. After twenty minutes or so of having a freight train blow through the brain, the steak needs to be turned. "You turn it." "No, you turn it." "I don't want to, you do it." "I don't want to either, you do it." Needless to say, it never got turned and several hours later, it looked like one of those charcoal briquettes which cooked it. After that little episode, it was time to smarten up and Johnny hung up his crack pipe for good. From here on in, there's not too much more dope shit to talk about all the way to the end of this novel. Maybe alittle heroin on his pasta and pesto, but that's about it.

It's lonely at his new house. If it weren't for his three dogs, he probably would have gone nuts. The house is relatively new and has an attached two-car garage, where he likes to hang out. Problem was, it was located on the outskirts of town in a place called Candler, Georgia. But without a driver's license to get around with, he became kind of a hermit with nothing much to do. It's around this time, with all the time in the world that he really starts to mess around with patents. A long time ago back in Atlanta, they were laying carpet at some patent lawyer's office and he noticed a book in a bookcase called *Patent it Yourself* which he stole. It was this book that showed him how to make an idea work. To this day things look promising. His first patent, which is a utility patent, same as the telephone, was issued to him in August of 2003. It is a hammer with a unique grip that enables the user to grasp the hammer with a secure but less-clenched fisted grip. Therefore the user expends less energy to perform the same task for as long as he wants . . . comfortably. He has no takers on this one. Some companies don't like ideas not conceived within their own walls. If he had a hammer, he'd hammer *da-Da-da-da* on their foreheads. His second patent is probably the most low-tech idea ever thought of. And he has a taker for this one. It's a cigarrate holder just like Greta Garbo back in the day . . . only this one has a clip. Not really. Alls it is, is four canvas straps sewn caddycorner on the inside of a set of kneepads to contain a small scrap of carpet with the pile side facing towards the user's knee for additional comfort. The carpet scraps are replaceable. This is a plus. You can insert anything soft into them, not just carpet scraps. As I pen this, he still waiting on the patent office for the final issuance so he can sell it. As you can see, depending on who and what you are, priorities take precedence no matter how much dope you do or did. *Put that in your pipe and hit it!* Everyone who does dope is stupid? Sez who? Some are smarter than you think but just don't know it. All these people who work for these companies with which he's trying to forge an alliance with need to get off the kapooter and on the floor, knees first, if they want to think of stuff like Johnny does. You need to actually work with or without something to know what you need. Screw a 'pooter; it can't lay carpet like Johnny does. He even has his prototypes of these kneepads made by the company who was interested in them. He tried to make them himself, but before they were finished, Pups ate them. Not the whole kneepads, just straps he had sewn in. Pups was watching the whole time and I guess Pups just didn't like comfortable kneepads.

About this time, he was now driving a little Ford ranger that he bought for six-hundred dollars from his ex-wife. He still had the big Ford van.

The title to his real pretty pickup was pawned for five-hundred bucks. He lost that five weeks later. It was demolished anyway. He couldn't drive his big van 'cause about six months after he got it back from the tranny shop, it blew up again. The very same part, the whole thing. He got six months out of eighteen-hundred shillings. Pretty damn good. In between the explosions of his vehicles he bought an old Chevy van that in human years, was close to a hundred that had no heat and no passenger window. In the winter of 2001 to 2002, he drove around wearing his great uncle's old WWII flight bomber coat. This is old school, before goose down and other stuff, and he drove around looking like Kenny on *South Park*. He wore the scarf for pizzazz. While driving around during the winter before he went to jail, he was somewhere up in north Georgia freezing his goon-yones off, when it also blew up. That proved to him that there are in fact motor-vehicle-gods that one must always keep happy to make sure all this don't happen to you. Human sacrifices were next on his list 'cause everything else has been done twice and nothing worked. He drove around a lot and would drive up to Applebee's quite a few times a week in the little Ford ranger.

One night while sitting down, and getting the feel of the place while sitting at the bar with a draft, in walks up a college student and sits next to Johnny. Since there are so many colleges in Georgia, college students are more often than not, waitressing, delivering pizzas, working construction, or anything to make extra money in a lot of places everyone goes to. A pretty educated state. The HOPE scholarship sure helps. I'm pretty lucky, most of the people I know are a mixture of both colleges, tuition and the kind I was made to go to. You get to learn a lot from friends like that. As a matter of fact, when he got to Atlanta, he was amazed to see how much a college sports town Atlanta was. He never saw that up north. Cars driving around all over the place with banners like, Georgia, Georgia Tech, LSU, Vols, Auburn, etc. was all you saw. Pretty cool. Same as the SEC. The whole southeast is college sports orientated from what I see . . . any conference. But the SEC is the baddest college football division of them all. Not only do they not like other college divisions, they don't even like other teams in their own division. They even eat their dead. Beat that!! Big East basketball is an easy tie. But anyways, this kid was from the University of Georgia 'cause up in Gainesville ninety-nine percent of college students go there. We had already removed Saddam's statue from the square in Baghdad and were into Iraq for a few months. They were watching the cable news at the bar and Iraq was the main topic, as it is now. Naturally, they both begin to comment on it. They also go back to the Gulf War in 1991. The first thing that got Johnny's ear was my professor said this and my professor said that when talking about current events on TV. From the jist of the conversation, America's ulterior motive by freeing Kuwait back in 1991 was to freeze or alter current oil prices. Maybe Saddam would jack up the price a hundred percent after securing Kuwait's oil fields, so what's wrong with that anyways. Other political and military discussions followed, cause this kid was letting Johnny know that he was paying attention in class.

Johnny was actually the one who straightened this kid out by undoing everything he was taught. He gets nothing; the professor took it all. He almost needed a pendulum. We all too often hear of lullabies like this and I got to wonder why. That professor practically pissed on everything the U.S. was doing! We got a major problem right in the very heart of America. I thought we all wanted to be safe? Never can be too safe and all that other stuff. Remember? The poor souls suffering under tyranny from the Death Star in Guantanmo Bay. My heart pumps piss for them, it really does. It urinates a river. I'm gunna get something off my chest. As the world turns might sound like some daytime TV show to a lot, it really means how many more turns are gunna be left if this thing goes unchecked. We have a situation like none before. We also have rights. We have the right to be in thesituation we are in now. I think we got attacked or something like that. Islamic fanatics piloted those planes. And yes, they didn't come from Iraq and I don't care if they came from Mars, they still came from the messed-up Middle East. We are not dealing with just violent small factions anymore. Now we are dealing with entire governments who've been conceived from these small factions. And no, it didn't start in 2000 when George Bush first took office! It started decades before that so get off your jack-ass and mount up the way you're supposed to when this country is in peril from bound and determined enemies like damn near none before! The blame-game is getting pretty old and is now stagnant. Blame this!!! Don't ever blame a scapegoat (only for fighting back) from the past when this passes (presidents always do every four years) 'cause when it happens again and the only clue you got is to blame everything wrong but the very scary real reason . . . even pissing on past presidents, then you haven't learned a goddamn thing from your history classes!! Screw history class! Let's go straight to detention! We have enemies locked up in Guantánamo Bay who spit at suicide and despise every American from the frailest infant to the feebleist senior who are now rendered harmless. How many times do you want to cut the head of the Hydra? This should be enough said on this matter but because of < everybody's opinion counts > nowadays, we are laying seeds of uncertainty for the future that our heirs and great heirs are going to have to clean up. What are they gunna think of us? Certainly not the way we think of ancient Greece, that's for sure. I believe that the Geneva Convention can work. Problem being; the other side needs to too. If not? Well, I'm sorry, see ya on the bottom of the pit. We haven't been faced with this problem since WWII, Korea, and Vietnam . . . . man!, we've had a lot of wars. Don't blame war itself, *blame the reason.* If you were a caught-red-handed bad guy, don't let the fall kill you. Sorry, you shouldn't have done that. That was all the way from Nuremburg to the company walking patrol capturing Germans in American uniforms. We all know Islamic suicide bombers are just a chain of desperate people fighting while knowing they really have no other conventional ways to carry on their carnage. By chain, I mean they weren't really the first. I would talk about guerrilla warfare but I consider that and spontaneous-human-explosion two different subjects. Viet Cong employed suicide tactics to advance battalions. Kamikazes wreaked havoc in the pacific destroying over a thousand ships. Americans died on those ships . . . 'case anyone cared. And the Germans had the Brandenburger's during WWII. That's equivalent to the WWII German terrorist employing tactics we see used daily in the Middle East. Desperate people fight in desperate ways. Whether or not you got nothing to lose or just having a bad day, I don't know what goes through a suicide bomber's mind except other body parts, and I don't know about you, but I consider that extremely *needs someone's attention* social behavior. We now have an enemy who for reasons nobody wants to hear about who will do absolutely anything to advance their cause while at the same time destroy anything whatsoever to destroy ours. Flying jets into American buildings also falls in that order. No one likes a dirty fighter, dirty cop, dirty ass . . . or anything else that's covered with puss. Especially a dirty fighter, dirty like *never* seen before. No one likes to be hit below the belt. Don't hit a man with glasses on. **This means *nothing* to these people!!**

This is a pretty good way to explain exactly what we're facing. A friend of Johnny's back in the postal service served in Vietnam. He fought for the liberation of Hue. If anybody knows anything about Hue, then you know what I'm talking about. It was war just like in all the old John Wayne movies. Well, anyways, he told Johnny about a local Vietnamese barber who shaved you so close, it took three days to feel stubble. He did this by using a straight razor and stretching the skin in all different directions and shaving in the same manner. He shaved many American G.I.s. One night during a sapper attack . . . war talk for suicide attack, his unit fought tooth and nail to repel them. This is after the enemy broke through the perimeter, employing suicide tactics to accomplish that. They fought all night and the next morning when his unit went out to count bodies, guess whose punk-ass body they found amongst the enemy? That's right, the barber. Friendly by day, *charley* by night. He once held a straight razor to many American throats. This is what we're faced with nowadays . . . only times ten.

Well, what if some of these poor souls in Guantánamo bay aren't barbers? What if they're innocent? Not likely. Well then, if they are presumed guilty, how come they're not given due process? *Because that's only for Americans or foreign people caught committing a crime in the U.S. that represents any kind or type of crime committed as defined within the parameters of all enforced laws.* From jaywalking to murder in the most henious form. Excluded would be war atrocities, and in this day and age, whether committed or not. Guilty by association works. Just thinking about it warrants severe retribution. I have no down home feelings for these people whatsoever, I care not for cultists at all, and I wonder why other Americans do. These are sheeple I'm talking about for cryin' out loud!! They sympathize with the enemy. I don't. No one does!! When words are absolutely useless, that puts me at a crossroads and I gotta figure out something and something quick! People who will not be told no to, who are now really armed to the grill and who've had these same sentiments for scores of decades . . . haven't even begun yet. Wait and see. Sheeple are afraid of retribution. They know that you should head for the basement during stormy weather . . . even during a light drizzle with bright skies. They seem to always be scared. Some of our elected officials could be described as such. Stalin had a good term for them. *Useful idiots.* I'd rather get screwed in the ass than go down in history like that. ***Tough decision.*** I'd deal with the first with a shotgun, no ski mask. The second, there's nothing I can do. I'm going down in history as a *schmuck*. Your words and actions follow you for life. I don't think some politicians really know that . . . most notably the democratic senator from Illinois who compared Guantánamo Bay to Russian gulags and American guards as thugs. Iz zat so? "What should we do for these people locked up in Guantánamo Bay?" According to the senator, and with some kinda respect, war criminals who fought back hard against us while trying to protect Al Qaeda who orchestrated 9/11 who got caught while fighting back, should now enjoy American due process the same as if my dog bit your kid and now I'm getting sued? Of course you're getting sued. We were held for all these years with no official charges in Guantánamo Bay. This is a problem that's not going to go away anytime soon because some Americans are conveniently forgetting our past so they can dominate our present only to finally screw up our future. Nuremburg could wind up being censored in future history books. That's screwing up right there. It was wrong to hang those people who killed six million of their countrymen who happened to be the wrong religion. Nowadays . . . same game. Only the religion has changed . . . alittle bit. So, what did we do wrong at Nuremburg? A lot, according to some Americans since the war atrocities committed by Al Qaeda and Taliban which are parallel and close to what the Nazis did. But they shouldn't be punished like the Nazis 'cause we're nothing but a bunch of thugs who got lots of tortured souls locked up in a gulag. All's they did was participate in the modification of the New York skyline. My heart pumps whatever it's got at the moment for them. It really does. It really does for people who side with these tortured souls.

You know what I want, we really really want. I want people to stand back and take a look at what *kind of monster* we are really facing. The more civilians dead, the better. Look at the history of empires . . . nowadays a superpower, and look at what they did with their armies. They smited the crap out of any country for just being there and conquered with ruthless methods of warfare. The USA fought also, but that was to save the world years ago, not to conquer it like the Soviet Union was trying to do in the not-too-distant past. We've done nothing wrong. Nothing to justify 9/11. Some Americans are really, really pissing me off 'cause they think otherwise. It's almost as if they're saying we asked for it. **Watch where you tread.** And it's squarely set in the political arena. I can also look at it like this and we all know how many ways this could be looked at. I see it as a hornets' nest in the wrong place. It needs to be removed cause those things hurt real bad. Problem is, it's as big as a city and will live to die fighting for religious dominance. I didn't know that hornets had found religion but I really don't get out that much anymore. The only way to exterminate the nest would naturally be by total utter destruction by whatever means available. But that's completely out of the question 'cause amongst all these hornets are also billions and billions of good hornets. The only good hornets that I can think of are referred to as the Georgia Tech Yellow Jackets. Nothing like watching the *Bullfrogs* play the *Bumblebees* in the fall down here in the South. On this part of the earth, if you are deemed wrong for whatever reason, you now have stepped into a hornets' nest. You won't win no matter who or what you are! From the neck down you'll be just fine. The nest is growing and are now navigating to new battlefields. Some real stupid people in Washington either don't see it or blame fighting back for it. Even going to the point of coming up with nothing but pure fantasy on how to deal with it or ignore it completely and blame absolutely unobtainable reliable intelligence as flawed . . . even made up. That there is neck and neck with treason, and to second-guess a decision to go to war in which many of them said yes to when all of this happened like a bunch of armchair assholes is a *disgusting show* of American policy. Going down in history as a whole **gaggle of schmucks** all at once. These are the ones who should be wearing those white wigs so everyone knows who is being played the fool. When you get educated enough to make a difference, open up your eyes. I hate to see all that education go to waste. Shameful. Dogs lick it up. That's why they're man's best friend.

Some people, most notably the senator, should look at what America has, as opposed to what it has to lose, when every inhabitant of the planet is entitled to American due process no matter how heinous a *Biblical changing catastrophe* they would like to impose on us. When I say "Brave New World", I really don't say that as a joke. Do you know that there would be no word whatsoever on this subject had not the communist American? media; looking under every rock, nook, and cranny to see what we . . . our own people, were doing wrong to get the big scoop and hadn't sent it over the airwaves, even to Mars, for everyone to see how fucking evil and wicked we really are. Lucky this ain't 1941 or times like back then! ***You'd be on the carpet for treason!!*** Let me give you a hint or a good swift kick in the ass, you're supposed to work with us. Yeah, we make mistakes, but nothing like you make the military out to be more often than not. Whose fucking side you on anyways? *Just because you despise the other party gives you no right to commit blatant treason!* And you need to pay for that. *I don't care how many years it takes.* Policing and soldiering for one's country are the noblest of jobs one can have. Sometimes policing and soldiering for one's country requires decisions made in less than a half a second . . . another half would have been too late. For some ***armchair asshole*** on the air to dissect events while safe within their walls, and throw out all the questions like he's the *gifted wizard* who knows all about combat and inner-city alleys are the same people who should realize that they really don't know anything . . . like hardcore reality, it's very ugly and should really shut the < suits this discussion just fine > up. More like the *skittesh joker*. But they don't. The media; it's not your father's media. Now, all the Guantánamo Bay *Newsweek* reported atrocities, that even if it did happen as they reported it, has sent the U.S. back in a few notches. What scares me is that some of this news article has been questioned and why would a major weekly magazine print questionable matter? Especially what they were printing. Any moron would know it might start a squabble . . . like lighting a fuse . . . like the ones attached to suicide bombers. What do some people think?

Other people say if there is torture and inhumane conditions in Guantánamo Bay that is a crime. I can say yes or no on that. I want my prisoners, excuse me . . . prisoners of the side I'm on, I don't have any prisoners, to know that I will show them the same that was shown to me when my character was in doubt when I got caught. I think that by letting the inmates live as normal a Muslim life as they can without being persecuted is beneficial toward some kind of jailer/captor relationship, but if someone needs to tell me something, but won't, and if I think it's worth it . . . I might not get medieval, but I'll get my way. After all, they are wrong, not me. What their fate may be? I'm not sure. Are they doing life? What will they do if we cut them all loose with a real bad spanking? These are more questions without answers. Some people have to be second guessed. If they explode all the time, then maybe second guessing isn't going to work anymore.

Too bad they don't like time like the present instead. They seem to live in the past. What's the problem they have with us? First and foremost would be our cultural differences from A to Z. We barely hold anything sacred anymore. Everything they say or do is sacred. Religion is life in the Middle East. The dollar bill has replaced the Cross and religion is evil in the U.S. Not byme, it's what I hear and especially see and feel sometimes. There's a red flag right there. I'm not talking about what some Islamic people think of our religious denominations in the Middle East, it's what some of us think of ourselves. Not really ourselves, but other people amoungst ourselves who believe in dreams.

We value interest on borrowed money. That is a sin to them. I like that. I think it's a sin too. Especially those double digit nineteen-eighties interest mortgage rates. Johnny's still wiping the blood from his nose. That, I believe would be fromthe Crusades. To make the long jouney from Europe to the Middle East, many Templer Knights would have to get money *on the front* to get to the Middle East. This was the very first banking system . . . interest on borrowed monies as we now know it at the present. This was originated to accomplish the Crusades. Muslim culture, even the moderates have never forgotten that. Myself, I'm really not that interested on interest on any money . . . unless I'm on the right end this time. I'd make a good, but fair capitalistic pig 'cause I know what it's like to borrow . . . I'd rather steal because of my pride. But they have taken their ancestors' methods of applying work and use them to this day. We have discarded all that and now press buttons to make things work. Osama Bin Ladin once called Americans creatures of comfort. Good or bad? That also goes both ways. Bad, 'cause if all the fast foods closed down, America would starve to death. Good 'cause what's wrong with a little more time on your own time? I hope I don't get sued by McDonald's. Especially after eating McWhoppers along with a bowl of blow-fly soup but I just don't want another McProblem. Most of them come from McMyself. There is no substitute for hard work. For most people living in the McMiddle

East as their ancestors did centuries ago, that's hard work. Americans are different. Americans work hard. That's how you make it here. It doesn't have to be hard, just effective, and what's wrong with that? Off on a tangent here, but about the only thing we have in common is that we're all humans. To make things better in the future, that's probably alls we got to work with. And you know how humans treat humans! It's about time it gets to something better than that. War gets results, no matter how much carnage. As mentioned before, to avoid that, *all sides* need to participate in dialogue. If only fifty percent of both participants want to participate, then that's called war. Here's what I think is about the simplest way to describe conflict. To solve a problem, ante up what you got, what you don't got, what you want, why someone else can't have it, and why do they got that?, and why that pisses me off so much. Those are very generic questions, but when applied to this very subject, every one must be answered, otherwise it's a war or some other kind of problem. But this seems to be a religious crusade, once again.

With all the questions religion raises, and the fact that the world has shrunken to the size of a beach ball, this could be a major bloodbath. That things get worse before they get better couldn't be more truer. I'm not in fantazoid-land, I see things the way they are and we all watch the news. A bright spot in the day, just like watching *The Simpsons.* Red Sox got beat. That's worse news. Yankees won. Back to bad news. Iran and North Korea got nukes. Now that's really gunna piss off our futuristic heirs. Who cares about sports at a time like this . . . 'cept me. That news should have been taken care of already and now because of very unconventional warfare by any means, the future now has a polluted planet from hell and dogs now resemble centipedes and my futuristic son's son' son now gots antlers . . . on his ass. This is my world. This is also your world. Most of the world is scared stupid of North Korea and Iran. A little unstable and now playing with M-80's. An old biker saying, FTW . . . I'll do it myself. If you can't depend on the world, what other choice do you have? It's rough being a superpower nowadays. Technology rolls on with every new day and irrational and unstable governments also have access to the same technology. The bomb ain't going away. Now, it's being disguised as electrical power for the populations of these so-called underpowered countries. Maybe they are, but sitting on top of *energy squared times two* and to not utilize it to its full potential just don't make any sense to me. But the same catastrophic fear that gripped America in the 1950's and 1960's and is more real today since now we know what side is willing to use them first. No more *mutual assured destruction.* During the SAC years, that was refered to as *MAD* which is exactly what it means as opposed to the way you might decipher it. Suppose that did happen. We took a first strike, most likely a city, from an enemy who blends in then gets out. No one to shoot at. Now, what do we do? First of all, no one would take responsibility, putting the United States in a blinded shoot-from-the-hip position. Why you pickin' on me? ***I didn't do it*** will be the headlines. But that position doesn't last too long. Guilt by association which is good enough for me dictates international policy regarding revenge. Second of all, they care not for our civilians. Look back at what three or four Palestinians almost pulled off in New York City back in 1997. Without details, it would have been bad. I believe a New York City cop lost his life during that. Civilian deaths in the most heinous ways is now fair game. But the Geneva Convention?! Do two wrongs make a right? In this case, I believe so and I believe I can explain. These people who despise us, do so in a very carefully, secretive, and orchestrated manner as to not get caught. You see, if you are afraid of getting caught, it can't be for anything good. Being from the Middle East, these terrorists blend right in to their own society, which is our biggest and most complex problem. Someone also in middle-eastern society must know at least one, possibly two of these terrorists and where they hang out at. I also believe that this is rampant. Find some of those most rampant places and those now become targets. Let's see if the Trident works if we lose a major city from terrorists. Hopefully that never happens. If the Trident is never used, then something right is being done. But I do not see any diplomatic relations really working at the present. We do care for your civilians . . . we really do, but since your inactivity for taking action for whatever reason, just cost many American lives for nothing and we feel that you need to feel what it feels like too, and when you're done with that one . . . we got more. *No one in their sane mind* would ever want anything like that to happen. Even a drunken mind would wake up and say no.

But this takes a hundred percent perticipation, ***not fifty percent.*** Any attack on an American city with cataclysmic results is going to result in revenge with the same cataclysmic results thus killing many innocent people on both sides. Talk about getting caught in the crossfire! Wait until America or anywhere else has got to call a real mean bluff . . . 'cause it's gunna happen. The world could step in any time. Right about now would be perfect. If the world don't get it right this time, then its gunna be *a long hard slog.* At least many generations into the future, they will know that America tried along with our allies who fight by our side from other countries 'cause the *Mothership Enterprise* is the only one we got. Still that only represents a micro-fraction of the worlds population. This is everybody's ship, *Enterprise* or whatever else. We need much more commitment than that to see that someone's warped sense of religion doesn't mess with the Earth's rotation, make it cough or sick in any way, blow parts of it away or do anything that could affect future generations from the same thing that happened to the Medievals . . . reverse evolution. Since the parts of it that could get blowed-apart would most likely be in the USA, maybe that's America's problem and not anybody elses. No one seems to care except me and other guerillas so I believe I should comment on that. Maybe starting from the beginning would help. Johnny Bravo ain't goin' anywhere, really ain't goin' anywhere when I get back to him.

Years ago, the United States earned respect from many oppressed parts of the world. We did that by pooling our industrial and military might together to rid the world of governments who shoot-first-then-deal-with-the-problem later . . . the two largest problems, of course WW1 and WWII. The amount of blood, sweat, and tears America expended on these world wars got the respect of much of the world for making it better. Seems like those days are over. Granted, we are only a few generations apart from those who fought but everyone wonders what went wrong. Is it our fault? Can in only the span of a few generations we completely turn everything upside down? If we practice business overseas the same way we sometimes practice it over here without getting caught, I could see where that could happen. Plus there are other variables in which we have no control over. For instance, some American companies operate in countries where human rights abuse is common. Somehow, it becomes their fault because they got the money to do something about it, should tell existing government that they'll leave if not fixed, they should leave anyway, or anything to spread blame where it don't belong. They are there for business purposes only. Yeah, something can be said like, "Why does stuff like that happen around here?" I know I would say something but nevertheless mega-companies and even the U S government really has no say on how another country treats its inhabitants, that is of course, some heavy atrocities are occurring. It's always good to help out those who can't help themselves. Since the United Nations *picks and chooses* which world event it participates in, usually mild passive ones . . . that leaves the dirty work to someone else. Dirty work that unfortunately really needs to be done. And no one really wants to mash the red button but it really needs alittle more attention than the United Nations are willing to give. Parts of Europe, North Africa, and most notably, the United Nations, just sits there and watches 'em all get slaughtered. *Can't help out might get hurt.* When other nations close by the genocidal chaos just don't do too much or anything at all, that shows you the power of the modern-day outlaw. No more Colt 45s, Winchester's, fast horses, and Nine Lives Saloon. Now outlaws are strategically equipped about the same as the government troops. They can do what any other army can, wreaking havoc like no one's business. If you're not armed, that makes you an easier target. I think a lot of countries should maybe look to the grass roots level of all people to see what maybe they think. Genocide should be the top priority for the United Nations. There's no question about it. No one can say or do anything in the defense of the people being slaughtered, unless they are prepared to do so. Do you think that peoples all over the world hearts bleed when they see the genocide on TV in Dafar? Think anyone's gunna do anything about it? If so, why has it not happened by now? National boundaries mean nothing anymore when this kind of disgusting crap is going on daily, and the United Nations should either realize this or get the < nitwits united > out of the united nation business and get into something alittle more tamer. A friggin' rat has got bigger ballz than that!

I just think that with the entire world's population, some kind of entity with force like the U S would help out these completely helpless people so that they don't keep on dying because they see a different, but still sane God as their advisories do, but in a different way. Much of our world is run like this and until certain regions of the planet are free of that kind of severe oppression, life will go on as usual and most likely, the U.S. will be dragged into it. In some cases, the U S didn't react. Other cases the U S is overreacting. Damned if you do and all that. It's tough being Uncle

Sam nowadays. I do know that back in the Vietnam era, the only countries that had a problem with us were all communist run countries. That was solely political. It had nothing to do with cultures, values beliefs like at the present. America went through an economically disastrous 1970s and some countries took advantage of that, but that was for financial reasons. The dollar wasn't worth shit over in Europe the same as now. How come that always happens? But now, we seem to have turned half the world against us. It's probably more like half the world's governments against us. I really don't see the average person on the street with much animosity towards America or the average American, but in some parts of the world where the government comes first no matter what, there are these problems. I think I have come up with a pretty good analogy on how all this came about but I haven't quite figured it all out yet so I'll just sit on that until later.

Do you think that much of the food and aid that gets sent to Third World countries actually makes it to the people on the street? Warlords and government officials rape it first, then chuck the carcass over to the people. What's good is that not all countries are run like that and everything does what it's supposed to do, but the people who are really in need seem to not live in those countries. Theirs are operated by warlords and governments who take care of government first, the people second. Same as probation officers. Not 'cause they want to, 'cause they have to . . . if you believe that. The Middle East *Free News* will continue to criticize us with the fervor of Joseph Goebbels. Not too much good we say or do gets down on the street to the people. Between that and our own *disgusting media*, that's a problem. It's 1993 and the famine in Somalia is overwhelming just as past famines in Biafra and Ethiopia. Haven't heard too much about Biafra anymore. Wonder if it still exists? We saw all the heart wrenching pictures all over TV and something had to be done. The United Nations set up aid for these starving people. United Nation troops started taking hits and started dying while trying to help these people. Much aid wasn't getting to where it was supposed to go. The United States then steps in. Al Qaeda knew that was going to happen and while working with the warlords, takes up position. Like clockwork, the US helps out the needy, and everyone knew we'd be there eventually. You would think these warlords would get much more support from the people by working with them rather than by use of force. Power don't corrupt? *It even makes some people stupid.* We all know what happened and if me had anything to do about it, then that part of Mogadishu would still be smoldering to this very day! As a matter of fact, you would be able to see the fire from outer space. To parade around a dead body of your enemy means that the world is going backwards which parallels all the Roman technology that was lost for 'bout five hundred years during the Dark Ages. Those people went backwards and paid for it for a long time. Did you know that the republicans wanted immediate pullout right then and there with no regards but then President Bill Clinton refused that? Don't send the military into a mess, then pullout while the mess still remains. Just make sure the mess is worth it. You can take that anyway you want to.

Ten years before that, while trying to help the good guys in Beirut, some psycho drives a rolling psycho-bomb into the Marines barracks, killing two-hundred and sixty of them. I heard a story about the Marine sentry guard who try to stop the truck, but he only had blanks in his magazine. I hope to hell that's not true. I wanna meet the son of a bitch who sent my son to the jungle armed with only blanks. Where's your son? He's running my company while I practice politics on the side. It's almost like chess. I can move you anywhere I want. This is *soooooo* cool. I'm even ten thousand miles away. I even have a drink. America now must take a serious look at the rest of the world and realize the rest of the world doesn't seem too concerned if America stumbles and falls. There's a lot of wrong in the world, so how come America is so wrong when it is surrounded by wrong? I don't think America is wrong at all, I just wanted to throw out all avenues that led to all of this. The only thing America is guilty of is being freer than free and maybe some people or governments don't particularly care for that. That's too bad 'cause it don't bother me at all 'cause I'm doin' what I want . . . as we speak. How about you?, my Third World brother. I'm on your side.

A lot has changed since WWII. Countries are gone. Countries were born. American governments have changed also to either democrat or republican like we're supposed to, while some other historic countries governments have changed entirely into another form of governance. I don't see that happening *any time soon* in the U S. What would make an old-time country with roots in the early part of the first millennium, scrap their government and try something else? Especially nowadays.

You'd think they'd have that down by now. Forgetting history? I'm not sure. Repeating it? It does seem to be in pattern for that to happen. What a lot of countries are doing, and quite poorly, is weighing what they got to gain versus what they got to lose. You're not going to gain anything by excluding the future in the framework of your system, whatever that may be. *Live for today, the hell with tomorrow* is for kids, not countries. The U S does a real good job of incorporating its future into its doctrines no matter what party is in office. That's why I really don't hold America guilty of the worldly wrongdoings at the present like a lot of people do, even our own. When everything changes weekly and you don't, what makes you so wrong? Changing parties during elections does create change in America. That's what we chose in the beginning, so we swung from left to right or vice a versa, but we're still swinging from one of the fairest and most humanitarian documents ever written . . . our Constitution. In some countries, you could be swinging from the end of a rope just for believing that. Nowadays, that makes us wrong. I just don't see anything I like swinging from a rope with my hands tied behind my lips.

To make the world a better place, why don't all the countries just become democratic? I just wanna know what's wrong with calling your own shots? If they wanna play dirty and let the government run the people instead of the other way around like it's supposed to be, that' fine. *Just keep your mess out of my backyard.* Dirty players like Japan and Germany are doing quite well after all these years. They've been clean and sober for a long long time. *Schnops and Saki mixed; something was bound to happen.* When someone plays dirty like flying airliners into buildings, American or not, there shouldn't be any question about it than blaming just one man on the present situation when these sentiments have been reverberating for decades throughout both parties administrations. We are despised all over the Middle East, mostly for cultural differences and our sane and rational support of Israel, but whose ever fault it is, Muslim fundamentalism hates us. Wake up!! Blame us if you must, but wake up. 9/11 is all I had to see. What's your problem?

Once everyone is playing properly, that might also ease up immigration to the U S as previously mentioned. Sounds pretty good. I wouldn't get too carried away, that's Star Trek generations away. Get to get my job back. South America now practices democracy in much of the hemisphere.

It's not standing as tall as it should be considering the amount of time democracy was introduced. Reason being, it just seems that the voting population who got the most votes just doesn't have as much munitions as the party who lost. We have sore losers in America . . . however, they don't take up arms and cause anarchy in the streets. This might sound abstract, but I believe that could change considering the almost even-split in partisan politics. Fifty percent of America's population who's pissed off for the same reason the world hates us is not a good thing. Sooner or later, *the volcano's gunna erupt.* History has showed that if a problem can't be solved, then it's usually war or some kind of major civil disobedience. It's the fastest result getter. The problem in America is that some people are forgetting about the future. Live for the thrill!! What a rush!!! That's for teens, not adults. The poople's party is wearing blinders and I don't understand why. Democracy is scattered all over the world, giving all those people a fair say in their country's doctrine. But a lot of democracies are weak. The power-mongers have bigger guns. Seems that people who espouse democracy are maybe a little more refined, a little more cultured, and maybe a little more meeker, than the gun toting loser. Democracy has always been fought over, so maybe they need to get a little more firmer and maybe get a little more help. We didn't go into Iraq to shore up no democracy. There was none. We went in there because we were scared. Scared of what could happen next. When TWA flight 800 went down in the Atlantic back in 1996, the first thought on everyone's mind was *terrorism.* Same as the federal building bombing back in Oklahoma City. We've been scared for a long time. I don't believe Saddam and Osama were in cahoots against America at all. But this is the murky Middle East. Who knows? That makes one scared. And back a few years ago, who knew what was going on inside Iraq. Alls most people knew was that there was nothing but hatred aimed at the U S from all over the Middle East, including Iraq and it was now time to take away weapons of mass destruction from whoever had them. We knew who had them once. I can hear the chorus, all in harmony; "There were no WMDs! He lied!" With all that money from exported oil leaving Iraq and the *sheer hatred* also being exported to anything western . . . especially America, alls I know is that if I were Capt'n Crunch, I would use a lot of that money to get my hands on anything that would make a statement such as 9-11. Weapons of mass destruction makes a pretty good statement if you ask me.

A long time before that, Saddam tried to go nuclear, but the Israeli Air Force took care of that. But our intelligence lied to us. George Bush disregarded data saying there were no weapons of mass distraction. The intelligence was flawed, and so on. First of all, if anyone thinks the president sent U S troops in harms' way by way of deception, knowing that lives will be lost, then you are flirting with a notion that borders the treasonous. That's a complete vote of no confidence or in more detailed terms, an ultra radical way to look an elected official who was allowed to wage war by following the proper procedure . . . Congress. **A landslide Congress.** No one should ever accuse a person whose prime executive order to run this country is to *defend and protect.* Maybe the prez' is not all that to some of you, but that's his job and that is the bottom line, just like it's always been. The United Nations surprised the hell out of me by voting no on the *liberation of Iraq* for the *good of mankind.* But if I were involved in security, I would probably check you out, whether you like it or not. But my rights say you can't do that. The Patriot Act says I can. I don't like the Patriot Act too much myself, but it's a necessary evil . . . you know . . . looking to the devil to make things alittle bit better. We do have an alternative. We can close all borders, check all travel, fingerprint all citizens, and order ten at night curfews. Terrorists would have a tough time dealing with all that. I'll take the Patriot Act myself. What I don't like about it is that too many people with their crossed up P's would have access to it. What I like about it is we don't live in a closed society, so it is a precaution with a few hurdles for terrorists to jump before they set up shop in America. ***Just Don't Tread On Me.*** I did nothing and I can envision arrests that have nothing to do with terrorism by use of this act. That's not good. You know what power does to some people. The Patriot Act falls under the new Homeland Security department set up to keep America on its toes. The concept is noble and good. However, it is run from Washington. Unless it has already set up a failsafe method of instant communication right down to the locals, and got serious with borders and ports, which is easier said than done but I don't see too much progress, then I cannot help but think that it is just another bungling bunch of birdbrain, bureaucratic bullshit artists who were helping put the word *inadequate* in capital letters. I know that's a tough nut to crack but some of the shell still remains after all these years. But we do have a color-coded terrorist thermometer to work with. This is another department that needs to be more localized. Wonder how much that would cost? Somehow, I envision billions.

We also need intelligence. Whether or not anyone wants to admit it; without real-time proffessional intelligence, the *gunna happen* future that one forsees might only be as far as ones' nose. I'm absolutely amazed that some people watching the sunset while standing on the shores of Malibu beach can't even see it. Nose, and all that. Sometimes . . . it makes no sense. The sunset is alot bigger. But because we are not Muslim, no one's going to get inside *underground* Muslim life simply for the fact we don't look Muslim. You had WWII intelligence. This is intelligence 101; computerized and no more snagging codes from the airwaves anymore. You have to be there. You pretty much have to learn a different culture. This is very time-consuming. But because we live in an open society, they can figure us out in less than a week. We are at a huge disadvantage. What I don't understand is that many of our own people seem to think that the CIA, NSA, or any other part of government can just press a button, turn on a computer or snap your fingers and everything you want to know about the Middle East is automatically right there in front of you. The Middle East isn't as far away as Mars, but given our disadvantage . . . it just as well may be. It will be many years before we have viable intelligence in the Middle East and that will only be accomplished by winning over some hearts and minds. Right now, alls we have is a foothold. What good is a foothold when it is the only one you know that is not going to blow up in your face? Makes one think twice about taking the next step. We need much more than that. "He lied!! There were no WMD's!" No, I don't think he lied. I think he knew the same as you and me or maybe not quite that much as some of us are saying and maybe the intelligence was flawed because we are at such a disadvantage in Middle Eastern terror intelligence, but to give Iraq three months to come clean the way we did, just gave them three months to move, dismantle, or hide them somewhere else. ***Even if they never existed, this scenario was real.*** The element of surprise would probably have yielded much better results, but that would have made us look entirely imperialistic. So what? That's what should've been done. No one else plays by the rules. Why should we?

Because we, amongst the rest of the world as a world leader in the past defeated our previous adversaries who were wrong and who also operated in the same manner. Some people remember the Blitzkrieg. The stigma would have been overwhelming. What's more overwhelming is how our newly found unconventional nemesis has conventionaly dismantled all the rules of engagement (Geneva Convention) by our newly found, and nasty unconventional enemies. But that only applies to them. We have J.A.G. rules we must adhere to. *Sometimes we bend the law. Other times you only need to break them.* In the future, people will always know we played by the rules. However, in the past we have employed strike first tactics to accomplish missions that were deemed detrimental for America and most importantly, other people affected by the whole mess.

In 1983, some totalitarian coup or something like that happened in Grenada in which the regime now in charge was ultra-pro-communist and wanted to militarize itself, even building a large airstrip. They never got that far. Grenada is an island situated in the Atlantic just somewhere near Bermuda I believe, and it's not too far away from the east coast. Also, a lot of American medical college students went to school on that island and they were now in peril. With chaos in the capital, the U S military solved that problem under then President Ronald Reagan's keen insight on national security and everyone on the island got to be free again. We also saw how a criminal country was poisoning everyone around it, and Scarface-wannabe Manuel Noriega is now doing hard time. All of that was *for the good of mankind* and if you need to use the big guns to accomplish that, then the choice is simple . . . accomplish that. The phrase for the good of mankind is exactly what the Coalition is trying to do right now in real time. But since that's another man's nightmare, it looks like *logic and sensibility* should be enough to do what really needs to be done. What really needs to be done is a real nightmare! All throughout mankinds' history *using the big guns* in one cultures dominance over another usually resulted in imperialistic ideology with genocidal results. It was for total dominance of the succumbing culture with almost Gestapo-like tactics employed to make that so. There were some scattered exceptions throughout mankind's history that used their dominance to enhance for the-good-of-mankind to the succumbed culture. The Muslim warrior and leader Saladin was one. I think current situation is another. *It's ironic that they both worked the Middle East.*

Convert or die!! My Holy Book tells me that what I'm doing is not wrong! How you gunna beat that? You can always convert. Even if it was entirely one-hundred and eighty backwards and these extremists became Santa Claus and Humpty-Dumpty, that still constitutes a rather *odd sense of behavior.* Borders the cultish. Some previous cults in our past were based on religion and very quickly resorted to violence when questioned or cornered. These are fellow American citizens who exhibit some kinda profile that closely resembles one of those who are willing to live for . . . or willing to die for Allah. No, I don't think your local brain-drain cult down the road is going postal any time soon. Some cult leaders seem to rise to the challenge of entering one's mind and move in without coercion, force, violence or anything else that makes little Miss Suzy Stepford's transformation seem other than willing. However, you know how we despise cults for their undermining the human entity inside that body. Making them do what I believe is some kind of abstraction, refraction, and detraction what normal behavior regarding many aspects of life should be like including religion thus giving *that* someone or some institution, be it anything, total dominance of any individual. That's where the problem lies. We will hurt, maim, and kill anyone who don't believe in Allah. We have a problem. Well, maybe in a few generations things will smooth out, especially third generation reform in Iran, and we can all just get along. With religion as deep as it is in the Middle East along with the hateful madrasses operating everywhere, we'll need the help of many God fearing, Allah loving, moderate and sane Muslims to keep the earth spinning without everyone spinning off of it. When terrorists killed children, as in Russia, and no Muslim condemns that or expresses any outrage for that inhuman atrocity, then alls I can say, iz we have a long way to go.

So this is George Bush's war. Well . . . got some bad news. It's also going to be the same, if not worse, for the long line of presidents after him. Not because he was the first president to deal with a lethal invisible enemy . . . but because we now have a lethal invisible enemy. It was only a question of time before the Crusades once again rose from 900 AD bent on mercy for no one 'cept Muslims. I'd be alittle concerned about that if I were you. I believe the Crusades lasted for centuries. Given our modern capacities, it won't last that long, but long enough to affect many generations into the future. But I wouldn't mash the panic button, because the Muslim faith has many good people amongst its own who also despise the current situation. Johnny used to lay carpet with two Muslims back in Atlanta. One was from Palestine and the other was a Jordanian. Maybe he got fooled but he doesn't think so. Alls they cared about was doing a real good job and if one of their jobs were in question, they got just as pissed as Johnny would. Omar was just as crazy as Johnny and they both liked to have a good time when the job was over. Rafik was a little more laid back and thought those two were a little nuts. If one had a problem, Johnny would stop by to correct it; likewise they would do the same for Johnny. Whatever it takes to make the customer unhappy . . . like breaking antiques when moving furniture.

Some *questionable* Americans seem to think the U S started this whole mess. As time goes on, you'll see that alls we did was crack the lid to peep inside 'cause we did get attacked and the lid blew off right in our face, unleashing all that's in Pandora's Box. Afghanistan was where the problem originated. I knew the Taliban were nothing but problems when in March of 2001, they blew up immensely large thirteen-hundred year old solid rock statues of Buddha located within Afghanistan's borders. *It's not Islam so kill it.* When Mount Rushmore is blowed to pieces 'cause someone didn't agree with one of the four's agenda or doctrine, that would be pretty much what I expect from a government that forgot history or just never learned it, such as the Taliban. Actually, they never left history. What a concept . . . never left!

It was a matter of time before they made the news again. No one would be able to comprehend what they had a hand in on the next calamity . . . 9-11. I heard some noise prior about 9-11 . . . all the warnings that it was coming, but it was left to vagueness and still no one would conceive the plan they had. Even though there was no good intelligence, just knowing about plans to blow up multiple airliners over the Pacific years before and the World Trade Center bombing in 1993, too many government officials couldn't imagine and visualize the evil amongst these people. Pretty hard to visualize anything when your head is two feet up your ass. I do, however, give these officials a little credence since I would have expected the hijacking to occur prior to entering American airspace, not the way they did it. Afghanistan ain't going away any time soon because fighting in such terrain is just about the same scenario *tunnel rats* had to deal with in Vietnam. Pretty damn scary! I would rather walk point than do that. Actually, I'd rather sit home and play with my little green plastic army dudes like I had when I was a kid and just pretend. This is not a joking matter and I'm very sorry about that last comment. We are at war that we did not start with an entity that espouses only their ideology and only their religion. This entity does not represent all, but a part of their culture and mark these words down . . . Afghanistan is ground-zero for a conflict that will dictate all of the planet's future . . . for the time being. As we all know, this cancer can spread anywhere around the world . . . especially the Middle East. But anyways, we opened up the lid and began to deal with Afghanistan with absolutely no viable intelligence. I want to put some emphasis on intelligence 'cause I'm amazed at some of our own people who think we can just snap our fingers or say a few magic words and *allakazam*, now we know where Bin Laden and the Holy Grail is. *Some of these people have extensive education!* One thing about Afghanistan is all the underground caverns and tunnels under its landscape. A lot of these are huge and have been around since before Christ. Our intelligence has every one of them mapped and located. Only Ralph Cramden would believe that. Did you know that when Bob Hope toured Vietnam every Christmas, the VC enjoyed the show just the same as our GIs? Alls they did was crawl out of their termite-sized tunnels located all around Ton Son Nhut Air Force Base located in Saigon where Bob Hope performed, and got in the arena and just sat right next to G.I. Joe passing around popcorn just like anyone else. They could have killed him if they wanted to kill him. It probably would have been gone underground. Just like Bien Diem Puh. Never saw it coming. That happened in Vietnam in 1954. An enemy with resolve . . . just like now.

In Turkey, to this day, there is a cave that could contain twenty-five something thousand people. I wanna see it! Wonder what they got underground in Afghanistan? It's ironic that Afghanistan is in the news for what it is now because many many moons prior, the only thing we knew about Afghanistan was that all the best dope came from there. Didn't even know were it was on the map. Alls I knew was that it was somewhere in the Solar System. After our *liberation* of Afghanistan, what happened next?

Well, the first thing I recall . . . America was scared. This was Pearl Harbor all over again but worse; civilians are now fair game. With all due respect to Pearl Harbor survivors, who would expect a massive attack on civilians? What's next? The last question was on everyone's mind. The media quickly showed us. *Do you realize that the media immensely helped the president make his decision to go to war with Saddam Hussein with all their* ***What ifs?*** Then they flipped from heads-to-fails just like the **scum-bag-traitor-bitches** they've become!! What's the difference between our advisaries and the media? Our advisaries don't reley on instinct. But they said Saddam could biologically, chemically, atomically, or almost anything wreak havoc of biblical proportions upon us and we needed to know that. Then came all the anthrax. This brought the two parties together for a while and then showed the American way: United we stand. Being deathly scared of all that, we had to know who had such weapons and disarm them one way or another. I won't go over it again. We know what happened. Because Saddam's empire closely resembled that of Manuel Noriega, with the only difference his being a much more severe national threat even though it is much farther away, I really don't see any problem with a problem since removed. From the first Bush administration to the Clinton years, Saddam was nothing but a thorn in America's and the rest of the free world's side and if there was anything that needed changing, Iraq was it. And besides all that, I only recall minimal opposition to Iraq during the three months we allowed them to clean house before we entered Iraq. Damn near all of Congress and America was with the president on that, and as we've seen, the enemy learned what happened during the Gulf War and adjusted according to their handicaps and that has turned many Americans into *fair-weather* fans. America has never ever before been about something like that! Change? Passive change? Loose change? Whatever you want to change into, just remember; your heirs will either look up or dig you up about the current situation. Just because you'll be dead and gone by then means nothing 'cause it's still up to you because you were once here. If it gets real bad in the future because present day leaders can't or won't lead us out of temptation? . . . then our future heirs need to dig up what's left of thier sorry asses and throw it the local landfill and use the old grave plot to grow dope on. No difference. Just exchange one dope for another.

But it was for oil! I know it was! It's got to be, that's all we got left. Given the much larger picture we must face, the only oil that matters is the oil contained in the motors of our military machines. That's the same as what is being taught in political science-fiction in some schools. We invaded like the Huns for oil. Here's something they ought to teach in all the sci-fi political studies going on in all the classes in all these colleges. First of all, all that oil does matter. It is the life-blood of all modernized existence. Even the oils in the fish you eat matter. Along time ago, even that was warred over. What does a valuable commodity do to all those involved? By that, I mean from the suppliers all the way to the end users. It makes them somehow cooperate with each other so that the circle is not broken so that no one goes without. In the past several decades, the U S and other oil-consuming western countries have been using the Middle Eastern oil fields as a watering hole and paying the going rate and everyone was happy on both sides. This is before volatile politics and extreme religion took over. As one can plainly see, this is and was a very translucent Middle East. It's pretty hard gettin' down on the streets being your *indivisual self*, especially not coming up Muslim. Only on the streets will anyone really know. No western country including the U S has ever been down on Main Street anywhere near the Middle East. Maybe in the past when extremism wasn't so blatant. This would be construed as a fact. We've only been to peace accords, summits, negotiations, treaties . . . *round two* . . . peace accords, summits, negotiations, treaties to now wars, resentment, extremism, beheadings and now isolationism with much of the people on the streets in the Middle East. This has gotta be someone's fault. In quite a few sci-fi classes it's taught that it's the U S's fault for a host of various reasons. Here's something that lots of schools don't really touch on that much. If they do?, and I don't think that all schools are run by commies . . . West Point is pretty cool, then it seems to only make page eleventy two of *Who gives a shit* magazine. To keep the commodity circle unbroken, staying on good terms on both ends of the chain is usually the best medicine. In the Fifties, America was close to Iran by way of the Shah because of Iranian oil reserves. The Shah never got down to the street level throughout his reign with the common Iranian population and in 1979 an Islamic revolt led by the Ayatolla Komeni led to the end of the Shah's existence in Iran. He spent the rest of his life in *Exile on Main Street*. We all know what happened after that revolt. At the same time, the U S is on the other side of the tracks with Iraq which is run by the Ba'ath party which was modeled after and behaved just like the German Nazi party. So now we have very scary friends over there. Then in 1980 the Soviet Union invaded Afghanistan. Lots of action during the times. With the Cold War still in full swing, and now with major oil reserves now in Soviet peril, it was time for the U S to back Afghanistan and whatever resistance they could muster up to repel the Russian invaders. The United States armed the resistance (Mahajedeen) to the gills, gives them the ways and means to defeat the Soviets after a decade of control. One major Arab fighter and leader was Osama Bin Ladin who later rejected his Saudi government for allowing the U S to occupy Saudi soil while defeating Saddam Hussein in the Gulf War. He had an army of his own fighters left over from Afghanistan and offered the Saudi government his army to defeat Saddam. He was rejected and despised his country for allowing non-Muslims to fight for Muslims on Muslim land and you know the rest of the story. Also in 1980, Iraq invaded Iran resulting in a bloody eight year massacre that killed over a million people. Now the U S looks to the devil and backs Iraq for revenge on the Iranian hostage crises and now arms Saddam to the teeth with arms and logistics. No wonder we gotta problem over there! We've armed damn near every man, woman, and child with automatic weapons!! Other Middle Eastern countries take up sides with this conflict in which resulted in the Lebanese hostages in which a few Americans were held for years at a clip back in the Eighties. Sounds like a real perilous place on the world to live in back then and nothing's changed. So if anyone can 'cipher all that, put then and now all in order to get a handle on the situation, say something 'cause the elected officials we have seem to be having a rough time. Uncle Sam don't even know which way to point his finger anymore in the Middle East with all the political and religious climate changes happening somewhat weekly.

But anyhow, the U.S. wasn't prepared for the major social upheaval immediately after Saddam was on the run. Look at what these crazy mobs are doin! Stealing and wrecking everything right here in front of my entire platoon! It's like we're invisible! I believe that there tells a story. When we liberated other nations in our past, I can't recall any succumbing nation carrying on like that, or not to that extent. Most defeated nations knew they were wrong, or going about some doctrine in the wrong way. Most of its defeated inhabitants felt humbled, rather than joyous and chaotic. You become joyous and chaotic when a burden has been lifted off your back. Getting killed or castrated 'cause Qusay like your girlfriend is rough living. Makes one wonder, there couldn't have been too many pretty girlfriends walking around. Mine would have the Halloween witch glued-on-the-face warts . . . the real kind, not the Johnny kind. A big one with long black hairs on the nose. Qusay would take one look then kill her right in front of me for being too ugly. A catch-22 situation. I don't want to live like that. Obviously, neither did most Iraqis. There's a movie out there that condemns the Bush administration's handling of the war. I'll go along with that. Too timid. However, this movie goes on to state that Iraq was never able to recover from all the post invasion looting and violence it said led to the insurgency and sectarian violence. Maybe that's true, but what we're the coalition troops supposed to do? These people were oppressed for decades and wanted payback and I believe that if we acted on them, we would have fueled what we see now happening happen right from the get go. And what's up with the term post-invasion? Could be a post anything but looking at it from a completely different perception, it could be perceived as an invasion. So wasn't Normandy and Okinawa. I do believe, though, that the administration aired in judgment by declaring victory and all combat over. I viewed that day as just the beginning of a huge problem. In 1991, the Iraqi army saw what superior firepower can do, and by *retaining* history, they don't want to make that mistake again. The insurgency fight in the only way they can; guerrilla warfare and being urban is equally just as terrorizing as being in the jungle for the fact you can't see your enemy. What disturbs me is the inability from Vietnam to now to reduce casualties from booby-traps. Suicide car bombs are much different because they drive around looking for you. Working a convoy in Baghdad seems like tricky business. Any unrecognizable vehicle less than fifty yards away from the convoy gets a good warning shot or gets wasted when that don't work. Given what these robots put in these cars, fifty yards probably would be too late. Terrorists do make the innocents drive into the kill zone to make us look stupid, but since the world would know the convoy doctrine, the world should be able to figure that out. Some countries haven't even figured out what they could win versus what they could lose. Some more catch-22.

Being the oil-rich area of the world, there is one thing about oil in which I really don't understand. I do realize one thing about gas prices; a little more than a year from May of 2004, they were the same . . . spiked. I read one day in the *Wall Street Journal* about the three major factors that make a commodity go up that drastic weren't really in play. That's what I hear, myself I don't have a clue. I think our own traders are taking full advantage of the grim outlook on what it's gunna cost for a barrel of crude oil in the not-too-distant future. I'm all for capitalism, but sometimes what can be done legally is a perverse way to conduct anything. Gouging, the American way. Think about all the people up north who rely on heating oil to survive, not just to get by, but to actually survive, are going to go through. Wall Street is making a ton-of-money-a-second off all our energy needs. I don't want to come off as some commie or socialistic-progressive-wak-job activist but America is pricing itself into an economic nightmare for the not-to-distant future. Energy is a commodity. Anything we need to sustain normal life is a commodity. Commodities are the foundation of the stock market and free market strategies. Futures and commodities. You guess how much one can cost three months from now. They might go up or might go down. That's American investing. No shit! Sherlock, get to the point. Because you sound like a commie. Well, let me try to set ya straight then. My paycheck is losing ground to the cost of living. Bits and pieces over a relatively short period of time. In 2002, my basic cable bill was twelve dollars and ninety-five cents a month. Now (2004) it's almost fifty bucks. Anyone's paycheck jump four-hundred percent like that? I didn't think so. It's only one bill that I had to pay. That's not bad. But my home and transportation rely on energy to keep me chuggin'. That's two more bills I gotta pay. You can call me anything you want, but in no way, shape, or form is my paycheck going to compete with that and now to keep the family and shelter safe, it is now going to take seventy cents on the dollar. The other thirty cents gets my beer, smokes, money for the kids, and stuff like that. You'd better have a lot of discipline to make seventy cents work. Or, you can get a raise. With what we are paying for what it cost now for one gallon of gasoline, I can buy a cheeseburger while oil execs made eight billion in one quarter of the fiscal year. All this is legal for it is the foundation of our economy. Is the working man being forced to give big corporate the rope so they can hang us with it? It's beginning to look that way. Pay or lose. I got a problem with that. The sky's the limit on how much anyone or any company can make. That's why we are the land of chance. You can do it over here better than anywhere else. But we are being done in by a nemesis we slew in the past, but now with the dollar bill large and in charge, it is economically fashionable and chic. *The game of Monopoly.* Mom-and-pop don't stand a chance. Screw your fifty cable bill. I'll just go somewhere else. You can't. It's the only game in town. Take it or leave it. You got no choice. Deregulation don't work. Look at natural gas deregulation in Atlanta. It became a feeding frenzy. Suck us dry. Things like this are perversions of capitalism, plain and simple. The haves have all the leeway, the have-nots have none and they're not even getting a chance. What happened to the land of chance? Lordy Lordy . . . I'd better shut up. I am starting to sound like a commie!! Just as electricity needs only one line to travel through, cable and all, so goes the same with gas and oil so it's pretty much impossible to have a business-like competitiveness in commodities such as those. I just hope someone doesn't figure out how to make us pay for air and water: staples of life. Because they will. I know that we all pay for water but hopefully not by the mouthful.

But oil was discovered in the Middle East somewhere around the Thirties or Forties. That's quite sometime ago. American and British oil companies immediately set up shop over there and we all know about American ingenuity that got the most out of the ground per day. This is been going on for about seventy years. Makes one wonder, how much freaking oil is down there? Or anywhere else on the planet. We gotta be extracting it much faster than it's being produced. We've been using oil for centuries. While we didn't know what crude oil was, it was whale oil. That also was flammable. The whales payed dearly for our heat and light a long time ago. Now we use crude not just for gasoline, but also for engine oil, hydraulic fluid, gearbox oil, three-in-one oil, WD-40 and many other petroleum products not even thought to be associated with oil; carpet padding, believe it or not. With all the oil wells working, I just wonder when it's all gone, are there going to be huge wide open caverns deep underground where the oil once was? What if the earth above the void weighs too much? Man, that would sure screw my day up. That's pretty much a wrap on what else I can make up on our current situation 'cept this. By trying to talk to some of these fanatical people who live by all this oil, to figure them out or tell them how to behave like us and they could also have a wonderful life like us, is a mistake. They'll shoot your wonderful lives full of wonderful holes, even lopping off your dome and I want everyone to know that when election time comes rollin' around again. But vote with your mind, not your heart. Vote for me, I'll set ya free!

Johnny's still in white-meat Vegas waitin' on me. By now, he got into some double-trouble. First he gets stopped behind the wheel again. This is the fifth time. Second, his dogs get arrested again. The animal control officer where he lives at don't play. When he got stopped, he was still driving his Ford 150 pickup 'cause he had to since it was the only vehicle he had that still worked. The big Ford van that blew up got rebuilt again, this time for a thousand trinkets, but around six months later, it also blew all apart again. He spent two thousand bucks for a boat anchor. Twenty-eight hundred bucks for the motor and the tranny on the pickup too. This is how the year 2000 started out . . . motor vehicle hell. That van is still blowed-up to this day. Can't say he didn't try. He went to court for getting stopped again and just seemed to not care too much anymore. He don't see the wizard, just the person behind the curtain, and when asked a question regarding the ten days he was about to do, his response was noted by the stenographer. His sentence; do ten days, a thousand dollar fine, two years probation, and if he goes anywhere near a car, he can be gang-tackled by the police and they can't get in any kind of trouble. Can't even get on a skateboard. When he does finally become legal, he is to have training wheels attached to whatever he is driving. When someone is about to be willingly incarcerated, that means that's the best you can do. In Johnny's case he was asked, "Mr. Warts, has anybody tried to coerce you, intimidate or threaten you in any way, shape, or form and is this decision entirely on your own?" by the state prosecutor who was a woman. "No ma'am, this decision is entirely my own." "Are you under the influence of alcohol, any narcotic, or any kind of drug?" His response was, "Not today, ma'am," in which he noticed the prosecutor trying to hold back a quick smile. A hard-ass judge could have intervened and it probably won't be good. His lawyer was pretty good. He got stopped in December of 2000 and didn't do his ten days until January of 2002.

It's also at this time his estranged wife is receiving much of a pretty good-sized inheritance. She's had enough of Johnny and after twenty years and she wants a divorce. She has also since moved from Doraville down to Little Five Points into an apartment. She lived there with Nick and one night it was fortunate that he was there. Amanda and Justin were also staying in Atlanta with Vaj at a huge house Vaj's buddy bought and northern Atlanta. Amanda eventually moved down with her mother. But someone Johnny knows also moved in, and his ex-wife now has a boyfriend. Pretty good timing. He gets the loot, Johnny gets the boot. They enjoyed quite a bit of money he heard from his kids. She did let him borrow five grand to get his house. At least he's got a roof. He's having problems like this, and everything he puts on the road blows up. Thee ol' proverb still carries on . . . *if it's gots tits or wheels on it . . . it's gunna give you problems.*

While during the course of the year it took to work with his court case, his dogs were now wanted also and on the run. One of his dogs, Pups as a matter of fact, chased down and scared the hell out of some kid riding his bicycle in front of Johnny's house. All's this did was get worse, then worser, and now he starts to think about the rough times he had backed up north. Stuff like that can't happen again . . . could it? This all may sound trivial and petty to some people 'cause it really is; but without a guaranteed paycheck for the simple fact that he just can't get there and almost a thousand dollar rent, several hundred dollars a month for fines for him and the dogs, living like solitary hermit, and no one really knew him around town really lets someone know what reality is and how sometimes it's not really all that. Some would say to unload the dogs with all their bad luggage. But he wouldn't do that for a couple reasons. The county is getting its money regardless, dogs or no dogs and who in their right mind would unload three beautiful black German Shepard dogs? Plus, they were all he had. More often than not, he would spend the better part of a week there, week after week and all four of them had a routine down. When the dogs wanted something no matter what Johnny was doing, they're going to get it, or Johnny was. Johnny made the mistake of making dinner for himself first one night, then feed the herd. Pups would have none of that. While he's making dinner one night on the counter, Pups jumps right up on the counter, barking in Johnny's face nonstop just like a drill sergeant.

Johnny just grabs his snout with one hand and blows a whole bunch of air in his nose. Pups lips looked like Homer Simpson when he's burping, and when he lets go, Pups goes into a sneezing fit. Pretty funny to watch. He had some pretty crazy dogs. Shoulda' seen Otis when he first touched the electrified fence with his nose. Woulda' won the men's pole vault world record. He bit Johnny in the ass too. Even though he was down but not gone, he still had fun being by himself.

He now drives only when he has to go out and make some money. No more being on the road all the time. He only went to work and Applebees occasionally. He wishes he could have fixed all that before he moved down South. With the situation the way it was up there, coupled with his own situation personally and with the law made that impossible. In Connecticut, he refused all urine tests for probation and blew it off entirely. He stopped going. He feels the same way I do about that. My body, inside and out, belongs to me and me only! If you want some, you had better be real good looking! He had a court case up in Massachusetts. He only had enough money for either that or his family. He chose his family. The system can steal someone else's loot this time. Connecticut tells Massachusetts to pull his license. This they do in 1994 and it's been like that ever since. But anyways, he now rides one of his kid's bicycles around, and from where he now lives, it's like a Tour de France workout anywhere he goes. There were some days when in need of something . . . the hell with it, he'd do without. He always wanted to ride a bicycle from Gainesville to Atlanta but he never had the right kind of bike. No whiskey this time. Instead of drugs and alcohol, how about milk and vitamins? Now it's bacon-n-eggs instead of a bowl of Lortabs-n-Jack instead of milk for breakfast. He only uses milk to saturate a bowl of Soggy Squishies 'cause you don't need teeth to eat those. He screwed some of his up. He even had to pull one himself. But now he's starting to do that . . . about age forty-five or so. What took so long? He does drive to Atlanta almost every weekend to see his kids back where they're both staying over at Vaj and Vics place. It was a big house and they each had their own rooms. Amanda painted her's electric green, even the ceiling. Johnny had a nice three-bedroom, two-bathroom new house for his kids to move into but none of them wanted to leave Atlanta. They would come up and hang out for a week or two but that was about it. Nick's reason was because there wasn't enough strip malls, only woods and fields. Johnny felt obliged to help out for Justin and Amanda's room and board, but after slaying his monthly demons armed with only pocket change, there wasn't much left he could do. In 2000 and 2001, he made nearly what he made back in 1973 picking tobacco. Somehow he pulled it off every month but he was in way over his head. Up north it was the recession. Down South? To this very day, he still can't figure it out. Now, he's working at various flooring shops in Gainesville. He gets back with his old carpet crew for a while and some of the rapids go away for a while. Then he works somewhere else. Then somewhere else after that. For some reason, he never found a home at a carpet shop. People he taught from scratch are leaving him in the dust and he's watching people who were toddlers when he started laying floors make more in one week than he makes in two months. So what does he do? He finds alittle peace while walking around the woods stoned like a scatterbrain with all of his dogs. If you're going to be a hermit, live the hermit life. If you live in the sticks, you may as well be amongst the sticks. He once seen a stickbug out in the woods. Then he got scared. What if he came up on a logbug?

Walking around in the backwoods of Georgia . . . pretty cool. Can't have that Atlanta or in any metro county where new constructions' financial windfalls are coveted. Don't plan a subdivision with trees and other natural settings to emphasize what once was. Just plow the whole fucking ninety acres right down to the bedrock. You know it costs less. Everything is about the dollar bill. In the environmentally damaged not-too-distant-future, it will be the dollar bill that's guilty of that. Did you know that uncontrolled terrorism and environmental genocide are neck and neck in importance? No one knows which one is gunna do us in first. And no one knows, or wants to know what to do about it. What a strange planet in which we all crawl upon. I just got distracted for a minute on a subject closely related to environmental Russian roulette. Me and Johnny are sittin' here watching *Live 8* on TV and Elton John just came on. We never got to see Elton John back in the day. *Saturday Night's Alright for Fighting* is in the top-five of the coolest rock 'n roll songs. *Louie Louie* takes the top honors. If there ever were a *who gives a crap? . . . screw everything twice* song, this is it. Elton John is a rock legend, there's only one, and I got to make it to a live show sometime. I just can't afford a ticket anymore. The Rolling Stones played at Madison Square Garden and it only costed twelve fifty. So what it was 1975! Johnny did some work at where he lives at in Buckhead in a while back. Elton John lives pretty good in Atlanta. Yeah, I like the concept behind *Live 8*. Starvation in the world is a blight on mankind's presence on this planet. Can't do everything to help everybody, but if everyone gave a dollar or gave a shit, what a difference that would make. This ain't like missing lunch or anything like that. People in the free world need to live like some people in the Third World for a week or two. I betcha things would change after that! I do like the concept, but as in *Live Aid* twenty years prior, I feel that lots of warlords and Bozo-the-Clown governments that dot the earth will greatly appreciate this effort by a truly humanitarian people. You want the food to get there? Then you must bring it there yourself. Keeping yourself alive while doing this is the only hurdle in your path.

But our environment all around us, not just Africa, is eroding; and believe it or not, faster than you think. We should realize that once all species have evolved into the end, the human race won't even make it halfway. Too many of them and not enough of us, and we should leave the kitchen the way we found it. I heard somewhere that the human brain, though superior, will not be able to defeat eighty billion inferior brains. Who came up with that? Who cares what the kitchen looks like ninety million years from now? How about ninety years from now? I don't know. I'll be gone by then. That response that I hear all the time, just don't cut it. What's worse; living in the past or living for the weekend. That's an easy one. It's living for the future. The weekends I'm talking about exist in episodes of *Star Trek* for our future heirs to party in. An equilibrium between the animal kingdom and the plant kingdom is about to become tilted. Can it be fixed? You simply put the lime in the coconut and just hope you did the right thing because in reality, it don't look good at all. This equilibrium replaces this, replenishes that, turns this into that, keeps the continents oiled, makes the wind blow, makes the snow drop, and so on and does so in a passive way. That means if one side weighs more than the other, nature has built into itself a failsafe procedure or method to correct itself even while we sleep. Just by looking around, then applying what I see about the future; from what I can tell is, pretty soon the equilibrium is going to shift. That's equally as catastrophic as messing around with the Earth's tilt. Although that is impossible so far, man has cut too many of these down, spilt too much of this over in there, pulled out too many of those, dug too many of those and now in doing so, has aged the natural biospherical balance into that of an elderly man. Maybe not yet, but that's what I see sooner or later. From what I see, it's hard to walk and get in and out of cars. You go blind, can't hear and so on. From what I hear it's hard to piss, can't wipe your own ass, and bungaing is virtually impossible and so on. Welcome to the twenty-first century. If it's going to take a whole lifetime to get old?, then we don't wanna wait, we'll just make our own natural environment old and noxious all around us. Hell!!, we're only eighteen. This ought to be good. No, it won't be good, and to be eighteen and live somewhere in the future amongst all the man-made garbage that's accumulated throughout the centuries from our disposable lifestyles throughout the generations is a travesty to the testament of what we could have showed them. It's disposable. Just use it, then chuck it. When did Pampers first come out? Just throw them out. Wonder where they all are? They're not in the house no more, but they and all the other plastic articles and containers that we just throw away do not just disappear when you can't see the tail lights on the garbage truck anymore. It's not the consumers' fault at all. Everything we buy is virtually made of plastic. Damn near everything. Sea turtles die from it because it doesn't digest. Don't eat plastic stupid turtle!! They don't know!! *Howabout stop loading the bottom of the ocean with all of our bullshit.* Okay. What do I do with it then? I knew I'd find a problem as I continued on. That's a very tough one to answer. Burn it all and we won't be able to breathe.

Eliminating and controlling the use of plastic is ***a real good start.*** You would think that a paper milk container like there used to be would cost less than a plastic one. Because paper milk containers went the way of the backyard wrench, it's obvious that's not true. When you pop the hood a modern day car and the engine looks like something out of a sci-fi movie? . . . then the backyard wrench had better look like one of those sci-fi freaks just like Marco to even know what friggen tool to pull out first. Gotta be a nuclear-quasar mechanicanoid nowadays. But profit over our environment is going to make the earth begin towobble someday, and by then, it's probably too late. But we are not evil. We don't want this at all. We all need electricity and heat. That comes from coal and coal is dirty when burned. Comes from nukes also, and that is an entirely different chapter. You can make nuclear weapons from the spent fuel from the reactor. We have to guard that obviously, but I can't right yet 'cause we're going out to go get a pizza, watch the game, and work a few beers. I'll be there at eight o'clock sharp tomorrow morning. Make sure nothing happens. I think the whole entire world needs to step up a little bit more on the nuclear threat. Because of the huge need for electricity, we now have made the atmosphere more of a greenhouse. This is a fact, not fiction. And there's no need for any political spin on this subject. Just look around. From the birth of the first furnace to the very first car, this was bound to happen. This time span is only about a hundred and fifty years. That's an awful short time in relation to time and I do value science. Science says that if we stop all omissions right this very moment, it would still take Mother Earth a couple of hundred years to clear itself out. I'm not too sure about that. The earth will always clean itself up, but now man is not allowing that to happen. We have interjected our presence into how it's going to be, like it or not, and now it's time to interject our presence of how the future should be. What to do about global warming? The only thing you can do, Expect it, and expect it to change a few things. Daytona could be a couple of feet underwater in only six or seven generations from now. That just downright blows. This is no joke and if we got a give up a few things, I think I can help with a little exposé on transportation. You do know that to fix the problem, we're all going to have to kick in a little . . . the whole entire world. What about cars? That's a good start and just as I don't beleive in a 100 mile-per-gallon carburetor; not one that would work sitting on top of a 350 anyway, I do believe what I saw on the History Channel one night. If there's anything being shelved, this would be it. It's what we need; something other than the internal combustion engine. *Harleys are excluded.* I hear about fuel cells, hydrogen cars, hybrids, kryptonite, solar-powered, and other sources out there but this I believe car was electric . . . maybe. As you can see, if it takes more than a half an hour to watch on TV, I start getting a little lost. But this was interesting. The Army, private corporations, and universities came up with a promising motor for the future. You won't be giving up anything at all. In fact, you'll be gaining something. They put one in an M1 Abrams seventy ton tank and it blew the doors off existing diesel motors they use. It was in the tank and it was very quiet. You always knew when an armored division was coming across your countryside. Not with these tanks. Imagine an armored division with the element of his surprise? Not only that, a little British sports car equipped with one of these motors beat a 400 horse-power Dodge Viper in the quarter-mile. How they are powered or how far they go, if they charge themselves, I don't know. Next time I report on something, I'll pay a little more attention. I should be on cable news. Mr. Jones, where do you stand on that? What? Stand on what? Sorry, whadjyasay? We can get off of Mideast oil dependency. The question is, will we let ourselves? Remember, all that oil still in the earth is still for sale. Are sales going to take precedence over need or change? I don't think so. Oil companies are rich and also know that this can't go on forever. They have the capital to change and adapt to a changing world to keep themselves pretty much where they were when gas was thirty-five cents a gallon. I remember that. When it got to forty cent, I got pissed.

Johnny is now down to two dogs. He did have a problem containing his dogs but after turning his house into a dog fortress after the county animal control got hold of him 'cause of Pups, he followed all the county ordinances. Now a dinosaur couldn't even get out of his house. But before all that, Otis got loose and one of his neighbors shot and killed him right in Johnny's backyard. Once he can afford to be in trouble, he says he's gunna take care of that. Out of nowhere. Hopefully, he re-thinks that. After the county animal control got through with him, it cost around fifteen-hundred. That was based only on two dogs. His dogs were deemed potentially dangerous, as demonstrated by Pups, and animal control now gave Johnny list of things to do to make the fortress. They even went as far as telling him what rooms they are allowed in the house to be in. Johnny told them to lick Pup's balls and if it's war you want . . . you know I'm gunna lose, but you'll never forget me . . . it's war you got. Altogether, there were seven ordinances that he had to meet, which he did. Believe it or not, this comes back to haunt him. Not good enough for a farm animal. All is good. Both sides are happy with each others' understanding until a few months down the road, well into 2002. While fighting off animal control throughout most of 2001 and while in court for county ordinance violations, he sees that no one in that courtroom wasn't walking out without some kind of slap, so he wants a trial by jury some other day. This also comes back to haunt him. Shouldn't have done that. Early in 2002, he did his time in lockup in the next county down the road and he's now starting to pay for his sins. He was kind of glad to be locked up 'cause he just got through 2001 which he calls one of his worse years ever. Not one thing went right and if alls he can afford for some time off, and this may sound weird, is county lockup . . . so be it. A little problem with breakfast though. Two hard-boiled eggs, papier-mâché oatmeal; about a half cup, and two pieces of bread at five in the morning. Don't get caught swapping food at this county lockup.

He's now free and has now settled into a local carpet shop and things start to smooth out for a while. But that don't last too long. He got in a car wreck that he caused. Things are now looking good for a change, and in May of 2002, he rear-ended a car in front of him because he hit the clutch instead of the brake which makes the vehicle speed up a little bit. He came up on a stop light and screwed up. The truck was a little red Mazda pickup that belonged to his neighbor. All his vehicles were blown up or gone and now he was down to his little Ford Ranger he got from his ex-wife and his neighbor's little truck. The Ranger was also broke or in the shop. The truck cost only six-hundred bucks but after being in the shop four separate times, add fourteen-hundred more to that. I know that's chump change to all you movers and shakers out there, but not here. He couldn't even afford his rent. But anyways, this happened as he approached a line of cars parked at a major intersection at a red light. Here comes Johnny and everything that had smoothed out now, in a very instant, wadded back up into a ball of confusion for him to live in. All because he couldn't figure out the brake from the clutch. He jumps out of the truck to make sure the woman he rear-ended was okay. Even though it was a hard hit, there was nothing wrong with both vehicles, which was good. She gets out of her car crying and screaming, "My new car!! My new car!!" over and over again. A brand-new car! He assures her that the car is okay and explains his situation and tells her he's got to go. She screams, "You ain't going nowhere!" and is asking anyone in traffic around the accident for a cell phone. He doesn't want to leave her all distraught and is asking people around him for a cell phone, knowing once he gets one, she's going to hang him with it. He doesn't wait around. "Exit, stage left. Gotta go" and he does so after staying there for almost ten minutes. Now we've all seen the high-speed pursuits on TV and everyone says, including myself,

"Why don't he stop? He's gunna kill someone." We see on TV people running lights, going the wrong way on the road, driving over lawns, and other driving skills not taught in driving school. Johnny would watch that and say, "How can anyone drive like that?" After it happened to him, he said it's very easy. Once you're scared to death of going back to jail and losing everything again, you do what you need to do to get away. He blew through a stoplight while laying on the horn, passed cars where only an idiot would, and drove up on the sidewalk to pass parked cars; all while seeing the blue lights behind him. Had he left thirty seconds earlier, he would've made it. He ran for almost a couple of miles before he gave up. It wasn't really a high-speed chase, but it was as fast as a little four-cylinder Mazda would go . . . fast enough. Once he left the scene of the accident, he immediately saw the police lights and he decided for once in his life to actually make the officer earn his money that day and he floored the truck right through a stoplight and give it all it had.

Once he stopped after realizing he didn't have a chance, he immediately got out of the truck while the arresting officer is telling him to get back in the truck over the loudspeaker on the police car. He refuses, telling the officer that he's got him, and there's no sense in getting back in the truck. "Come on and do your job. I'm not going to interfere anymore. I don't have a driver's license. They even told me I can't even be on a skateboard." The officer gets out of his car and because Johnny was upfront with him, he tells Johnny something you wouldn't expect from some cops who look like once they step out of their squad car and you watch him approaching your car in the side view mirror, you start administering Last Rites to yourself. He tells Johnny that what he did constitutes a felony, but since Johnny was clean and up front, he's going to forget about the little game of cat-and-mouse and disregarded the chase. You see, cops are human too, and sometimes when you speak to one man to man, you get treated like a man. What a break!! Amongst all this stuff, he got lucky. But he still got arrested. This is when his buddy had to sell all his dope to get Johnny out around one o'clock in the morning. Next day, he goes down to the next county to see his probation officer and the rest is bad history. He's now locked up and once he gets dressed-in and is in his pod, he tells his cellmates how he got there. They tell him, "You wanted to come here! Why did you tell your PO about the accident? Whadja think he'd do? He wants to advance, this helps him." At Johnny's age, he should've already known that. His PO assured him everything was going to be okay. Plus, he thought that if he didn't tell the PO about the previous day and he found out on his own, things could have been much worse. He was wrong, a hundred and eighty days is a hundred and eighty days no matter how you get there. The little fuck lied to Johnny.

By reading all this, is anyone learning who and who not to trust? In case you're wondering what a *pod* is, it's another name for a cellblock. It's been modernized and we now live in pods for that special jailer-captor feeling. Makes one warm all over. It is now he does forty-five days even though that's a real short stretch. But this is no glory story. This is jail. Someone puts you in a small room; feeds you shit, locks the door, then walks away. Not much glory in that. This county corrections institution is a huge complex. It holds something like fifteen-hundred people. It was built for a state or federal prison, but for some reason it became a county lockup. I have heard that for each occupied bunk, either the state or the feds pay X amount of dollars per night to the county for every occupied bunk in there. Any empty bunks? Yeah, there's a few every now and then, but when overcrowded to the gills, some people even sleep on the floor in things called *boats.* It's easy to get in there. Hard to get out of there. Now, that depends on the individual. It could be hard to get in there, but for Johnny, it's the other way around. All's he's got to do is close his eyes, click his heels three times, and repeat over and over again, "There's no place like jail. There's no place like jail." His first day there, he screwed up by drawing attention to himself. In the processing department there are five or six large holding tanks that are packed with new recruits. Smelled like feet and ass in there. Processing and getting dressed-in takes all day and after ten hours or so, he's alittle pissed. People who came in after he did were getting dressed in before him and he wanted a bunk real bad. One of the guards on duty that day was a dyke. How some people perceive gay women is the same as reading a book just by looking at the pretty pink cover, but she was fit and trim and she shore didn't like men. After ten hours in the tank, you get to know some of the people in there and comments were being made about this guard. Here she comes again. She unlocks the door, walks in and calls another name and now Johnny's super pissed and opens his mouth. He turns to someone and says, "She's probably got a dick bigger than mine. She needs one up her ass." That was it. He was now out of the holding tank. He is immediately removed by the guards and he's wondering what they're going to do to him. Alls they did was throw him in a smaller holding tank with no heat or excessive air conditioning and made him wait another day before getting dressed-in. That's it!! Wonder what they would do if he really plowed her from behind? Well, first and foremost, she wouldn't be a dyke anymore. Don't want to know anything after that. Someone's gunna snap!

All of this passes and now he's in A-pod in a three-man cell . . . actually a two-man cell with a boat where he now resides. There is an upstairs in the pod and the thirty minute breaks during the day are staggered so that while the downstairs is out in the courtyard, upstairs is locked down and vice versa. Anyone can use any of the phones lined up on the wall and you can only call collect and not to a cell phone. Only a landline phone. The call is completed after and only after the person on the other end says, "Yes, I'll accept the charges." During his first day in A-pod he was on the phone all day; telling people where he's at, what to do, where his truck was at, and where the keys were, someone to take care of the dogs, and there's no bond so just put some money in my inmate account so I can make store. You can buy stuff, including extra food each week which is deducted from the account. To make it work, money is deposited weekly by a loyal friend or family member whose name you seem to forget upon getting released. If you don't make store, you'll starve and that's no joke. Some people say, "So what? They're inmates." I'll get to that later. But the first day on the phone cost pretty close to what his monthly home phone bill was. For only one day. I hear that there was a class-action lawsuit filed on behalf of all the Florida inmates against the phone company in that state for the stupid, ridiculous, and disgusting collect phone rates people were being charged. And as high as the law allows. It's bad enough being locked up. To talk to someone on the outside for five minutes is going to cost at least five dollars. I would assume that the state is making money on these phone calls. I would also assume that lawsuit doesn't stand a chance in hell. Why don't you just kick me in the thingys? Hell, I'm already down! Good people do screw up every now and then. They are really reminded of that just trying to get a call out. On the second day he rested. All affairs are taken care of and now it's time to relax and enjoy himself.

His first cellmates are gone within two weeks. One got released in the other went to prison work camp or PWC. Johnny now occupies the lower bunk and life was wonderful. His bunk isn't even warm yet and now he's got another cellmate. He was a nineteen year old black kid from Decatur, Georgia who went by "Lil' Bit" back in Decatur. He was a transfer from another pod and had already done eight months in there. They became pretty good friends 'cause Johnny likes common sense and that's all this kid was. He showed Johnny all the tricks of the trade like how to light a cigarette by using the wall switch in your cell and disposing of the smoke 'cause if you get caught smoking in your cell, you go to solitary. What you don't do is blow it into the air vent. There are smoke detectors right behind them. They just turned their toilets into chimneys, and that's what they did. Don't let your do-dads get caught on the bottom of these toilets while you courtesy flush for your cellmates 'cause with this warp speed pychco flush, they'll get ripped off so fast, by the time you look down, they'll be a mile away. Johnny had always heard about it while working construction but never got to see one, but this little stainless steel water-tight beauty was nothing but the infamous Dumpsucker 5000!! Right down to China!!! This book also has its origins in a dumpsucker in cell 116A and Lil' bit and Johnny's future cellmate all had a hand on what they thought about each page that was going through Johnny's head. Then he started to write it all down which is considered the first writing of this novel. When we hooked up after he got out, he gave all this to me along with a very offbeat short story that I really shouldn't print and probably won't and this is the fifth time around on this novel. Offbeat short story. Some times in jail, your mind wanders. I probably shouldn't but there's alot of stuff I shouldn't do. I consider some of these ideas previously shown to light earlier in the novel somewhat controversial to some, but it's my turn to air out my First Amendment 'cause if I can't, then I'll use my Second to my opinion, and I consider this short story only as a joke . . . but a funny one. Can't we joke around anymore? He had lots of time on his hands.

After he read his fourth book in there, he decided to write one. Inspiration comes from the strangest places. Being in jail reminded him of being in boot camp. Regimented living. In boot camp; one screws up, then everyone pays; in jail, you're on your own. Shouldn't have done that. See ya later. Some of the comradeship was also the same as in boot camp and I can also speak for Johnny but some of the most real and some of the best people I've met were locked up behind bars. Most, over some dumb shit, ain't that some shit. This ain't prison. There are no segregated factions within the walls. Maybe somewhat, but not what you see on TV about real hard time. Most people in jail, black, white, or Latino got along with each other and alls you can do is talk in there. You can think anything you want about the word *inmate*, but sometimes the best comes out of a humbled man. Family people just like me and you who are now paying the penance for legitimate reasons and others for reasons that made me think I was in some third-world jail. The system really isn't all that once you hear some of these stories that you can draw your own conclusions to. It really is all that and if you ain't respecting the law, even county ordinances . . . beware. Your life could be so rearranged, you'll be blowing your nose while you think you're wiping the tears from your eyes 'cause forced rearrangement hurts just alittle too much. Ya seem to lose a lot. What's fair for one is not fair for the other? How come we both did the same crime?, he got off and I got fucked. When someone goes to jail, it's usually for a good reason. Even for little bullshit crimes like shoplifting or peepin' tommin.' You do them enough times, what else they gunna do? Obviously probation and fines didn't help, so howabout alittle lesson? But America locks up more of its citizens than any other country in the world, from the meanest dictatorship, to a fairytale monarchy. I believe I may have found one way in which this is accomplished. It goes maybe like this.

The police are called to a scene, be it criminal, or anything. Unfortunately, you are on the scene and for some reason when you meet the officers, something don't feel right. Bear in mind, maybe you're guilty on some misdemeanor at the scene, or one of your friends ran over the curb by accident and got stuck in a flower bed like a fool, and the police wanna know why. After some time, DUI has been ruled out but the officers realize they are nowhere near their quota. Well, if it's not DUI, something else made them go off the road. Let's try again. Quotas are a concept that tells the whole story right there in a nutshell. What if everybody turned into an angel or an apostle for a week or so? Who is gunna get arrested during that time? Simple. Either the angel or the apostle, that's who. The county is going to make its money come hell or high water. Everybody knows that some people screw up and when that happens, you must pay the fine or do yo time. That's the law and that's the deterrent to not screw up. That's a good thing. Seems like a whole bunch of county fiscal planning incorporates *screwing* up into its agenda. Many, many moons ago, someone in some local government office or some local government outhouse realized that the *might be sheeple* public has an enormous accumulation of money at their disposal that could really add the county fiscal portfolio. Enter the quota. Even without quotas, people will always screw up. But to tell your police force that you will get X amount of certain citations monthly, usually DUIs even if there really wasn't that many DUIs committed, means some people will be getting stopped for really doing nothing wrong. Like driving around at four in the morning with ten people in the car with the windows down and the tunes wide open. During quota season, everyone is fair game, especially idiots like that and I think that's excessive towards the public. I know cops who feel the same way. X amount of revenue for each citation will be generated or that cop who really doesn't see any *what if* factor and waves as he passes you by, might be standing on the carpet explaining that he is a public servant, not the tax man. He might have a problem. On the flip side, some other officers get somewhat aroused by the notion of quotas. I banged that drum alittle earlier like a lunatic so you know what I think about all that. But we do have a choice. Question authority, but your property taxes go up, or some more local sin taxes are imposed. I think a dollar a cigarette is fair. Either way, the judge is getting paid today. Anyhow, they walk back to the stuck car and start asking questions that have pretty much nothing to do with the situation, or put up scenarios that are surprising to the occupants of the stuck vehicle and usually pisses off one or both occupants of the car. Your emotions could get the better of you, but this here is bad timing. "We want to know what happened and we're gunna do some background checks all the way back to your chromosomes. We wanna search the vehicle and we also think we know what DUI is. Please get out of the car and put your tits behind your back. Quota is being made. I've seen DUIs for only two beers and with a breath test of as the same as looking at two beers for five seconds. Makes me cross-eyed. Driving into a flower bed is a hypothetical situation that I made up. Could be sober as a judge, or maybe two beers did the car in. We still don't know. That's why we got what we got. You can draw your own conclusions. Officer's discretion is what it's called. Officer {kill 'em all,

I'll sort 'em out later} got some kinda problem with the public and maybe should be behind some desk or walking a beat somewhere in the town of Bedrock. Fred and Barney are some bad muthafuckas and so ain't both those prehistoric bitches! Stuff like this, and I really really hate to put it this way; but it's so close to as what could be coined as domestic terrorism . . . only without the fireworks . . . sometimes. "Didn't do anything? Well, I guess I did." License and registration please.

Johnny remembers one inmate who was doing one year in A-pod for attempting to steal a car. But while trying to unlock the car with a coat hanger, he got caught. Stealing cars is not good. Johnny knows. He boosted two. But this is really not about stealing a car. The inmate was one of the two housemen in the pod. Housemen helped run the pod, mostly for helping out during chowtime. They are out of their cells more than anyone else throughout the day. This guy was a carpenter by trade. One day, his wife took her car to one of the huge malls in that part of Georgia. He had a job that day and realized one of the tools he needed was in the back seat of her car. She had been gone for about an hour or so. She had no cell phone so he couldn't call her so he drove to the mall and found her car. And he didn't touch the car, but instead went to the major department store where he knew she was at. He then went to the front desk and had her paged over the loudspeaker with no success. She had come and gone and went to another store. After that, he went back to the car and could see his skillsaw that he needed. He decided to get into the car without hurting a thing like some of us know how to do and be on his way. Here comes the police. They see someone trying to unlock a car with a coat hanger, so they stop. That really don't look too good. "What are ya doin'?" the police says. He explains everything that just happened. Cops say okay. Then they ask who the woman is that the license plate is registered under, seeing that he has no breasts. He explains that it is his mother-in-law's and is registered that way for insurance reasons. He shows the police all the paperwork that he told Johnny was all legit, and still everything is still okay. "Sorry about that. Have a nice day" and off the police go. While around dinner time at home sometime later with his family, all of a sudden here comes every cop in the county and once again, they got their man. He was charged with a charge that's one step down from grand theft auto, which ain't no good. His own wife's car! They went as far as asking his mother-in-law in court if she would like to press charges. She says, "What's wrong with you? That's my son-in-law! Of course I'm not going to press charges!" Not good enough for hangman's court. One year, get him outta here. Next! Zero—tolerance gone stupid. Anything kinda wrong with that picture? If not, well let me make up another one. Johnny had to go to solitary confinement for six days and met some black queer while out on one of the two twenty minute breaks they got each day. He found out that he was in there for arson. Just like Johnny, his own place, and he lost almost everything. For some reason, the police tell him that if you don't take the hit on this, we will tell your parents about this gay website you have, with some of this stuff starring yourself. He told Johnny that his parents would die if they saw that. So he did what he had to do to keep everything status quo. He got stuck-in-the-muck and wound up in a one-man cell in solitary. Why would some police act like this? I don't know. But I do know that if you balk at the scary-ass, ridiculous offers the police give you for whatever reason; you won't snitch or won't even consider doing half of some stupid amount of time they offer like they're also the judge, it's going to be a long time before you get bail, never mind make bail. X amount of dollars per day. Even jail is all about money. Money that's not yet earned, but now gone. So now you got to play the legal charade with a public defender and fight your way out. This takes huge amounts of time and money so either way you lose. Johnny's seen a lot of people in the there where if the same crime was committed up north, it might have been handled with a stiff fine and maybe some probation. That could mean maybe they're doing it wrong up north. Maybe, but I don't think so. I think that . . . that part of Georgia is real tough on crime, even made-up crime.

But aside from that, he's getting pretty used to jail and it's like a social event going on the courtyard during one of the two forty-five minute breaks each day. A lot of people in there knew about this book in there. Plus all the really good art coming out of people, even poetry, from people who look like they couldn't even spell the word. Artwork that takes about the same amount of time and talent it takes to learn how to play a musical instrument. Talking all day about family and morals. During this time, his youngest son was up in Maine getting in his own trouble resulting in lockup. This gets back to Johnny and his buddies in jail. All help to try to help to help out a kid. This impressed him and the only way to know someone is to talk to someone and that's how it is in jail. He gets to know another inmate during chow and during the breaks. He read some of what Johnny wrote and in turn, let Johnny read some of his poetry. This inmate had a health problem which turned out to be hepatitis C . . . the bad one. He had a problem with one of his cellmates and when he came back fromthe hospital, he moved into cell 116 with Johnny and Lil' Bit. He needed the bottom bunk so Johnny moved back into the boat. This inmate's name is Dave from Buford, Georgia. At the time he was about thirty years old and he had a pretty rough life. Prison tattoos all over the place and real good Salvador Dali poetry. He told Johnny and Lil' Bit about his condition, not the jail. They don't have to. They can put a *full-blown AIDS* person with you without telling you. I think that's dead wrong and wonder why it's like that. Not all inmates are evil like our *head-for-hills! . . . scared of their own shadow* certain segments of society would like to portray. Dave was a junkie and used only a needle. He told Johnny stories that would make *America's most Wanted* involving girls who like to kill that he had no control of and it was real. These girls are all done. They are so far into jail, even their unborn children will be in their fifties when they get out also. Both his cellmates had nothing to do with this book. All's they did was tell Johnny to do it. Tell a story, someone should. Sounds like you been around. They like Johnny's loose style and told him what he was writing down made sense and to take it for all it was worth. They both proofread everything he wrote, then gave it a thumbs up or thumbs down. Then Johnny continued on after that. There was more common sense in that cell than half of Washington. One thing about jail is how a lot of people find religion and change overnight into something they are not entirely or entirely not at all. Someone walked up to Johnny wanted to lay down some palms and scriptures on him. Johnny responded how Israel is mentioned throughout the Bible from Genesis all the way through all four Gospels so how come Israel is only fifty-four years old? He got no response. Then he mentioned something like, he who finds God at the eleventh hour is already dead at ten-thirty and that was the end of that. I got no problem with religion in jail, but I do consider the source. Johnny was given permission to print a poem or two from Dave. This is how life is for some of us. Here's a couple:

I'm lying here in silence *I'll try to clear my mind*
I try to find some peace but peace is hard to find
I pray for God to help me *break free from all these chains*
To chase away these demons that caused me all this pain
I fall upon my knees *cry out to the Lord for help*
Take me from this torture and save me from this hell
Oh God can you hear me? *Please give me a sign*
I'm growing oh so weak I'm running out of time
I feel my soul is lost *never to be found*
I've run out of energy as I lie upon the ground
My destiny's uncertain *I'm feeling oh so cold*
Please God hear my prayer for I fear I've lost my soul

I believe that there is a scream for help, but there is none and alls you can do is *expect no help* and work with that. Maybe this one will help.

As I sit here in jail alone on my bed
My only way out *is through the visions in my head*
Things that used to make me happy now they make me sad
The things I used to have *are now things that I once had*
When I think of ones I love all I feel is pain
What used to make me smile *now makes the tears fall like rain*
I should be more optimistic that's what people say
But if things were turned around *I think they'd see a different way*
So don't psychoanalyze me and try to look inside my brain
'Cause you will never understand *you'll just drive yourself insane*

Sometimes, alls we have left are words, so choose them carefully and arrange them so that your message is heard loud and clear. Here's some clear words Johnny wrote to his then wife some years ago seeing as how we're on poetry. This is called 15 times 3.

I love you by numbers *multiples of three*
15 times love square root of me
One for your radiance *two for your charm*
Three for my word I could do no harm

all of my heart belongs to you . . .
ahh what the hell *the other ten percent too*
divide the question I'm hopin' to see how much do you love me?

15 times 3

Sometimes, alls we have left are words. Sometimes, words aren't enough. Well, enough of that. I think I'm gunna puke fifteen times. Just joking. That was kinda pretty good. I'm sittin' here takin a look at this very short story and I think I'm gunna take a real tasteless, but tasteful stab at this. This could be considered offensive but we both assure this was written strictly for comical reasons only and do not mean to offend anyone. Besides, if we can't laugh at ourselves, what can we laugh at? This also went through a lot of the pod with mixed reviews. This would be a pretty good bedtime story for the tiny tots. It's not quite as good as the 'Hooker and the Pimp' like ma used to read to me back in the day, but my kids liked it. But here goes.

"A Fractured Love Story"

By Johnny Warts

As we were about to conclude our beautifully planned candlelight dinner in our posh SoHo apartment, we consumed the last morsels of filet mignon arm-in-arm and washed it down with a wonderfully selected chardonnay wine. As we gazed into each other's eyes, the air of romance quickly fluctuated into a passionate lust only felt like bytwo lovers in love. I stood up with a love lost stupor and picked my lover up in my arms and proceeded to the bedroom. As I approached the double French doors, I kicked them open with a quick thrust with exploding pleasure. As I put my lover down, we caressed and groped each other until we were both naked. I laid my lover down on the satin sheets with eyes transfixed upon each other and when I was about to penetrate and consummate my love that's when I looked down and said, "Hey, move your ballz. I can't see where I'm goin'." The end. Thank you.

I don't know, Johnny boy. That's pretty offbeat all right. Pretty wild shit.

We need to leave this one out.

Come on . . . if we can't laugh at ourselves and all dat. Lay it down. Whad'day do to you in jail?

Someone showed me how to insert a slap-on in me . . . . Hey! What kinda question iz zat!? It just came to me one day and my cellmates were askin' whaa'tz so damn funny. They the one'z who passed it 'round the courtyard. Print it, blowhole! I was just jokin' 'round so why I can't have sumpthin' stupid to laff at . . . just like everyba'dy else do?

I'm gunna ask ya again. Tell me all about jail . . . weirdo!

Fug-U!! How'bout if I sho' you where it go and I don't need no damn jail! Yer pizzin' me 'ride da fug off!! Slap-onz . . . 'day not just fo' hoboz no mo.'

I'm gunna pretend I didn't hear dat. What a *ozone* thought! Yer cell-dude teach ya that? How come you no think of normal shit like every-body else do? You gunna pizz' someone off!

No I'm not! You da one wid da pen. Hey, I read a book in there that had 400 pagez in fo' days.

Big deal. Was it as good as a fractured luv' story?

Ever hear of *Dirk Pitt?*

Dirk what?

Baddezzt muthafucka on da planet. He gets all kinds of chicks that straggle from the herd. And he likes love stories.

Stupid ass ones like 'dis one? You no think it's gunna piss off parts of Atlantis that Johnny hazent yet diz'covered?

Who cares!! We put in a disclaimer in the beginning. **We are not accountable for our words or actions!** . . . remember?? *Only in America twilight zone.*

Yeah! Of course, that's gunna make it all good. I don't know 'bout this one. I thought we had to choose our words and all other stupid shit carefully, and all that good stuff.

I did. Haff 'deez words don't even exist! What'd ya think?

I think you had alittle too much early '70's. Okay, it stay. Anything else?

No, that should do it. I don't want to deviate from our *zone* any more than we hafta. You ain't no fun nowayz. Maybe alittle stretch in A-Pod in a dumpsucka' 5-stacker would do ya some real good. Enough of that crazy stuff 'cause even while paying for the trouble he caused, he still gets in trouble. One day while the bottom pod is locked down, three inmates' names are called over the intercom. One of them was Johnny. They all reported to the front desk to see what's up. A senior guard was there to inform all three of them that they were going to be made into trustees. That's great! You get to leave your pod and do groundwork and other maintenance, like running floor cleaning machines down the long corridors. You get more freedom and the food is a whole lot better. Johnny was thrilled. One catch though. You had to have your head shaved. Johnny's got hair halfway down his back and he freaks. He says, "That's a negative. Bring me back to my cell." Wrong answer. This guard gets super friggen pissed and crawls up one side of Johnny and down the other just like a drill sergeant. "Pack it up!! Get all your shit out of your cell. You're coming with me." He goes back to cell 116A for the last time and its off to J-pod. J-pod is solitary confinement, real jail. To this day, he's never seen Lil' Bit or Dave since. J-pod is made up of one-man cells with a tray gate on the door that the guard opens up when it's time to eat, then opens it up again to take back the empty trays. You don't make store in J-pod. The dinner is at four o'clock p.m and you don't eat again until five o'clock a.m. in the morning. For Johnny, that's a long stretch without eating. He couldn't wait to get the hell out of there. On his second day there, he is called to the front desk to be informed that he picked up another charge; obstruction of justice. They're talking about more time and Johnny says, "I didn't mean to piss anyone off. You're still not cutting my hair." Alls they did then was determine how many days in confinement he was going to do and after his sixth day, they took him to K-Pod. After J-Pod, you never go back to your original pod. This was good anyways 'cause his buddy Tony was in for a long stretch and maybe they would drop Johnny in the same pod. That didn't happen. A long stretch to one is something else to someone else. This isn't no prison time. After a year or so in jail, then it's off to prison. We try to not let that happen. A little county downtime here and there, 'cause after all, some of us step in shit more often than we should, but I'll take shit over quicksand any day 'cept weekends.

He made a last-ditch effort to save his house by calling the carpet shop where he worked at to collect and borrowed money to cover the July 2002 payment. His boss helped him out and he felt a little relieved. It's been two years and now it's time to buy a house by the agreement. The real estate agent had his own mortgage people and alls he had to do was just to be there. That turned out to be a problem. Also, he was due to be in court up in Gainesville on a date when he still locked up in the present county. He found that out and freaked out. They can hold you for a few days in the holding tank while the other county can take its sweet time to come and transfer you. Holding tanks smell like crusty ol' sharts and that would have sucked. But it never came up on the radar and he didn't say anything stupid like, "Oh, by the way" starting to use his head. As a matter of fact, when he was back home after he got out, he was hanging out with his buddy Tracy who got him out the first time and cared for the dogs, there was a benchwarrant for him at his own county. As they were messing around Johnny's house, Johnny spots a police car going real slow up and down his road. He goes out to see what's up, but he knows. The cop says, "Are you Johnny Warts?" 'Yeah." "I have a warrant for your arrest." "I know." "You know?" "Yes sir. I missed an important court date." "How come?" "'Cause I just got out of lockup today." "No kidding!" "Yeah." "Got proof?" "Yeah, I got a letter of incarceration from Gwinnett county." "Go get it." "Okay." "I'll tell you what I'm going to do. I'm going to leave and you gotta leave too." "How come?" "'Cause after my shift, the next shift will be out here and you might have a problem." "Good enough for me officer. Thanks a lot." He meets lots of good cops up in Hall county, real good cops. I'm sure there are Robocop's in that county but he doesn't know any. The police either like Johnny or they hate him. There's no in the middle. Sorta like AC/DC. Either the song is really really good, or it blows. Anyways, now he is free.

He is now back home but his power has been cut off. His little Ford truck is back in the yard along with the blowed up big Ford van. His house was broken into while he was in jail and he got cleaned out pretty hard. Both Pups and Coco were in the house during the break-in and who in their right mind would break in a house with two German shepards? Tracy felt bad about it, even calling the police to report it, but if it's going to happen, it's going to happen, especially after a pattern of house observing. Only one other person knew the dogs. It was someone who worked with him a while back and Johnny didn't know his whereabouts. But when this happened, some windows were left open and Pups escaped. Coco was too old and couldn't jump the window so she was still there. He never saw Pups again. He actually cried. He cared more for Pups than all of his stolen shit. He went out to try and find him. He then goes to the local Humane Society to see if maybe he got locked up again. It was next door in the same building as the animal control headquarters. He walked right into it a hornets nest. The animal control chief asks how the dog got loose. One of his conditions to keep the dogs was to never let them escape. He explains it happened during a break in while he was locked up. The head dogcatcher didn't care and he told Johnny that he broke the law. "You're now in trouble." He's only been free for two days! Since now he knows that Johnny was incarcerated, he says, "Well, the guy who's watching the dogs is guilty." "Guilty of what? It was a friggen break-in!" If Johnny was a good ol' boy, none of this would've happened. This was pure yankee hater, pure and simple. Anyway, he walks out with the dog that looked like Pups. Even though it wasn't the same dog, animal control even wanted to classify this dog is also potentially dangerous. Johnny asked, "Why?" "We don't think you're too capable of handling dogs." To satisfy them, they came through his house one more time, this time turning it into Al Capone's vault. Now, he's got animal control up his ass one more time. The personnel at the Humane Society next door, especially the director, had compassion towards Johnny, telling him there's nothing he can do until animal control says it's okay. They did become friends. You got one guy who devotes his work towards animals. You got another who's concerned deeply about his dogs. Of course they became friends. Anyway, these fucking pricks at animal control make this shit stick about Pup's disappearance and it's off to court once again. It was either Johnny or Tracy and he told Tracy, "I got this in the bag. I got proof where I was, where you were, and what if lightning struck my house and the dogs got out, is that our fault? Of course not. I can't lose. I'll take care of this." It wasn't quite as simple as that.

Well, now he's back to two dogs. About this time, Amanda wants to move in with her father and he is very pleased about that. She already had her room all done up in her style at Johnny's house and she wants to start her junior and senior year in Gainesville. But he needs to come up with quite a bit of money because he is in arrears on his house and if he can fix that, he can still purchase the house as agreed. Plus he needed to get his utilities back on. A few weeks before school, him and Tracy travel a little past Macon down to a town called Cordell, just off Interstate 75 in south Georgia to install a whole bunch of carpet at an old soldier's retirement and entertainment center. Actually, it's almost a community. These old soldiers must have been officers because these places were real nice. When he got out of jail, the shop he worked at didn't have enough work to keep everyone going. So they traveled down to Cordell and worked like they were getting paid a hundred bucks an hour. The more hours you work, the more you make 'cause the more square-yards that are laid in. They got the job done in pretty good time. Tracy had to drive back to Atlanta to get some boxes of VCT tile that also was getting installed. VCT are those twelve-by-twelve tiles you see on the floor at Wal-Mart, Kmart, Target, and any other commercial buildings. Strictly a commercial floor but every now and then, someone wants it in their home. He left Johnny behind by himself to carry on while he was gone. It's about three hours each way, so Tracy and his girlfriend were gone all day. While they were gone, Johnny laid in three complete apartments all by himself. When they got back, he was done with all the apartments and all done trying to walk around without looking funny. He almost had to be carried out on a stretcher. That day put it on him pretty damn good. At the bar that night he sticks to beer. One shot of anything would've knocked him off his bar stool. But it wasn't enough to save his house.

Amanda came up and stayed with her father and even started school up in Hall County for a while. Three days of school, then she had to go back to Atlanta because it just got too rough for her without any utilities. Cold showers are rough all the time. And Johnny lived like that for a couple of months when he finally realized that it was futile to come up with the money needed to retain the house. He stopped giving up all his good money to pay for bad money. He threw up his hands in defeat once again. This is when he loads up his big blowed-up Ford van with everything he can get in it. Everything else that won't fit gets left behind. He gets pretty lost right around these times and he's lucky his buddy let him keep the van out in the woods on his property. That was all the belongings he had.

One thing about that house that he won't forget is that it's where he lived at when 9-11 happened. Everyone knows where they were that day, just as everyone knew where they were when JFK was assassinated. Johnny was laying a hardwood floor in Alpharetta when it came over the radio. When the second plane hit, the looks he saw on everyone's faces around him is forever etched upon his mind. If there ever were a situation that needed to be resolved years ago, this be it. Being the second to know someone else's intentions, especially on a scale such as this should tell every American, regardless of political parties, maybe safety isn't such a bad thing after all. 'Cause now, no one is safe anymore. No ones safe anyways. Life is too fragile. Disease, accidents, murder and crime, natural disasters, brainwashing, suicide, and even UFO abductions . . . like what probably happened to Johnny, decimates our numbers daily. A lot of this is a natural. To board public transportation as in Spain and London and get half your ass blown to the moon is not natural.

Not too long ago, the Middle East was splintered . . . more tribal and the real power was further north in Turkey. This was somewhere around the last days of the Ottoman Empire which went under some time around in the early twenty-ith century. Some time ago way back when. From what I hear about the Ottomans was the culture and the compassion for other cultures and I wonder how after all these years, why that really has not taken root in much of the Middle East nowadays. This is about the time Lawrence of Arabia united all the Arabs together and defeated the Ottoman Empire. I have very limited knowledge on the Ottoman Empire and I'm not about to go down to the local library or learn how to mess with a kapooter to learn, but it sounds like a whole lot of oppressed people uniting under Lawrence to rid themselves of a problem. Not much has seemed to changed after that until the birth of Israel. One of the only things that unites some of the Mesopotamians and Persians together nowadays is their choice of isolation and their somewhat disdain view of anything western. Mesopotamians and the Persian culture were some of the first cultured civilizations on the planet. It is noble to remain true to your origins, but with such a headstart in existence you would think that it would have been different . . . with the Middle East . . . now with all the embodiments of the western world and everyone else living Third World. The Middle East has a lineage that goes back forty to fifty generations squared. I find that fascinating. But some of the Crusades has risen again and this creates fertile ground to twist religion in knots and create a in-the-name-of-my-religion robot. I'm going to strap a suicide psycho bomb to myself and walk into some restaurant in Baghdad and light it off, all for the Palestinians.

The Palestinians really have no borders or boundaries with which to call a nation a home. None that they like anyway. In essence, they seem to be living in limbo, but what they have now is so established the only way to pull up all the roots would be to have a full-blown war. It seems that, and that only is what damn near all of the Middle East wants. It just doesn't make any sense to not negotiate what's mine and what's yours because both Israel and Palestine ain't going anywhere anytime soon if ever at all, so work it out, not slug it out.

I saw on TV, on either *60 Minutes* or some cable news show that showed how kids are kids, past and present. Only these kids were from sectioned-off parts of Israel and Palestine the way those cities are. I don't recall the city. One kid was Israeli and the other Arab. When they learned of each other's interests, hobbies, sports, and everything else kids talk about, they became good friends. This also spread to both families. When they parted, they were both saddened by the fact that once they got older, they'll be on different sides of the minefields. The Palestinian kids don't seem to have a choice. They are taught to hate while still in the womb. If some able-bodied young Palestinian doesn't participate in extreme violence and is looked at by those who do and is questioned about it, that could make for a real bad day. By my Bible studies, I know that Palestine and Israel have never moved. They have always been in the same spot. Borders and boundaries might have changed throughout the ages but that's about it. If you look at the geographical features on a map, from the shores of the Mediterranean to the shores of the Dead Sea, you'll see a mountainous range between both shores that runs parallel to both shores. This creates a very thin strip of land with which to travel north to south or visa versa with various seaports along the way. This thin strip of flat land has been coveted by many civilizations throughout the centuries as we all know, especially now. This is called the Promised Land. It's something like twenty miles wide. This is where Jerusalem is located, with all the origins of Judaism, Christianity, and Islam religion. It's called *Canaan* in the Scriptures in the Bible. It's the birthplace of modern present-day religion. It is where two cultures are trying to occupy the same space. That's really not that hard to do. What about the Jews? They are a people living entirely surrounded by an Arab nation and who throughout almost all of twenty-ith century were unsympathetic to any Jew. Never in the history of peoples and cultures can any other group of people except the Jews lay claim to the title of the most persecuted and targeted peoples since Cain and Abel. From conquest by the Egyptians and the Babylonians in BC, to the Holocaust, Soviet second-class citizens, and now white knuckle bus rides, I can't think of anyone who can tell me about such a besieged people. Why is that? How did all this come about like this? Moses led them from Egypt and gave his followers the Ten Commandments and finally, they reached the Promised Land. They were in present-day Israel and Israel is mentioned throughout the Bible. Maybe I should go down to the local library to learn, but what I can't understand is the question Johnny asked his religious inmate buddy. How come Israel exists only from 1948 to now? Where did the other two millennia go? I know that the Palestines lived there during those times. After WWII the Jews were given back their Promised Land and for many years after the war, thousands migrated back to the Middle East. This immediately sparked Arab revolt and throughout the years till now, battle-ready is a way of life for many Jews. I remember the seven-day war in 1968 when Israel obtained the West Bank from Jordan and the Golan Heights from Syria. The U S backs up Israel because of a few reasons. Well, first and foremost, they are greatly outnumbered and the same thing that happened at Masada, would happen again. They are also a democracy with friendly views towards any free and sane nation. In Bible studies, we also learned how way back during the days of Jesus, the Promised Land has always been fought for by the Palestinians, Jews, Philistines, and others and this just doesn't compute that in real time nothing has been accomplished. We've had two thousand friggen years to work this out!! That was then. Now is now. Now is bad. What I see now are a group of people amongst a people who live in a super-isolated ideology that dictates its belief over anything else no matter how violent they have got to get to get their point across. They even use innocent civilians as shields and tell these people they will die if caught fleeing. Don't call that war by no means. That's terrorism, pure and simple. This is the complete opposite of global. Brainwashed Japanese civilians during WWII killed their own families and loved ones, rather than face what lies were told to them by the Japanese government of what the Americans would do to them once defeated. Wonder if they regret that? Brainwashing makes anyone do anything . . . even while thinking about it.

I don't know about the Koran, but in the Bible, Jesus was a Jew, and the Jews occupied Israel just as the Palestinians did, so I say, no one is going anywhere soon and given the fact that there is more than enough land to satisfy everyone involved, someone just don't want peace at all. Given that fact that it don't seem like Israel is going away, that makes some of their adversaries 'bout the same as early twenty-ith century gangstas. They remind me of criminals who employ some of the most brutal tactics used by anyone, especially on civilians. I see them on TV wearing masks or scarves to cover their faces. Could it be 'cause they don't want to get caught or be known? Some people call it Israeli occupation. That's fine, but I hope you're just talking about border disputes not their very presence. Because if that's the case, zen you're no better than Uncle Sam the terrorist and I've always said getting real with your environment helps you get sane with yourself. ***Call Uncle Sam a terrorist in front of me, then I'll show ya a domestick—terrorist!*** In this day and age in Israel, they might have to resort to building a wall to keep all the warfare out so regular everyday life remains that waywithout all the carnage because someone or some group believes differently and is occupying my land. We all see daily in the news how this situation is never gunna change with one side of the dilemma refusing to budge. *You are not Muslim. You must die.* Says who? I'll build a huge wall to keep your viciousness out of my town. That's only logical. Well, we know where logic stands with much of the world . . . sometimes not too tall. The idea of a wall seemed to have pissed off much of Europe. Probably more the governments more than the average Joe. Logically speaking, how come? 'Cause it isolates the Palestinians. That's not good, but when the Palestinians can figure out or wanna figure out the people behind the carnage and do something to prevent all these brutal bombings, maybe the wall can come down or not be built at all. I know that it takes two to tango but the Israelis do not fire rockets indiscriminately into civilian populations. No wall is gunna fix that problem! Right about now, it seems that they do not have any choice but to build a wall, but some of Europe says they do. As a matter of fact, some of Europe says it's wrong. This is the same Europe that just sat back and watched as the Serbs create the most genocide since Adolph Hitler. Your resume stinks right there. If the U S hadn't stepped in and calm the killing, it would still be going on. Some of Europe just doesn't see eye-to-eye with America and certain other planets.

Johnny's daughter just got back from Europe. She went to Paris, Amsterdam, and somewhere else with her aunt for ten days. I think the other city was Brussels. She was extremely impressed with the rich history everywhere she went, and how nice the people were no matter where she went, and how more efficient some things were as compared to our own . . . especially riding a train. I would love to do the Orient Express but I'm about seventy years too late. She had a good time with the people and that's always good down at the grass roots street level 'cause that's the only way one culture gets a feel for the other. It's no secret most Europeans would be democrats if they lived in America. Not that Republicans aren't health conscience. Amanda said she rarely saw obesity anywhere she went. They vote the same as us following the same democratic standards. Only thing is, sometimes they vote as socialists. That's the lesser of two of the for-the-people governments. In the past, socialistic reform usually led to fighting in the streets like the Bolsheviks. At least now it's voted on. Even though Adolph Hitler was a dictator, he came to power by the popular and majority vote in 1934. There's more voting going on in the world than some people believe. The problem is about what's getting voted in and what's getting left out. Rigged? Why would anyone vote for socialism? It keeps costs down. Capitalism is very expensive. Socialism versus capitalism could be construed as low risk, low yield versus high risk, high yield. That's a good way to look at it. Maybe personal competition is not so important in the workplace as it is in America. Alls I know is the better I am, the more I want. What I like about Europe is the fact that everything was done by the vote and the defeated party carries on the just as the defeated party carries on in the U S. Better luck next time. There was alittle problem in France when they voted in a pro-American president recently. Anarchy in the streets once a decision has been made probably won't go away anytime soon and that's one of the reasons no one really cared about the casualties at Kent State. Get off of the streets and try again, but bear in mind, mediocrity just stinks. Get the best minds, which costs money. *Socialism breeds no innovation or creativity, never mind imagination.* It takes one more step up to make that happen. Good things happen when you call your own shots. Much of the third world should look at Europe and the

U S to see what's supposed to happen once the vote is over. Nothing. Well, almost nothing, but a civilized nothing. No anarchy in the streets. No bloodbaths. Unless the results are blatently wrong. You see, the democratic experience is for civilized and cultured people no matter what gets the vote. What about a para-pschyo quintessential tranny-vestite? First of all, what the hell is that? Then I think the whole experience needs to be reviewed and tossed around for a while for second thoughts about the first. How could something like that happen? Don't worry Dorothy, that's not gunna happen and if it ever did, I would definitely make a trip to that country to see what makes it tick. Definitely a must-see. Bring the kids! Sounds like fun for the entire family!

But I don't know if it's the rich history or the cloudy future that's gunna hurt or help Europe. Like Nostradamus, Europe certainly must see all the clouds in the future by not fully incorporating it in their present. Some say that the U.S.A. is doing the same thing, but that's only some. The term *get the job done* means that sometime in the future, it will be over. This is supposed to make things better, not worse. They are much closer to the enemy than we are which makes them easier prey than us. Europe has sustained terrorists' attacks since the Seventies. Something has gotta give soon. Not that it can't happen here, but it's much more costlier. They have a huge influx of Muslims in all the different countries in Europe just as we do. From what I hear, they don't really assimilate too much into mainstream European society. You don't need to jump into the melting pot, but you need to make your presence not only good for yourself, but also for the community around you. That means that it really helps to know your neighbor no matter where he comes from while trying to figure out who's not going to blow the place all to pieces. Otherwise, if it continues on the way it is, or gets worse, get ready for racial profiling and worse. Just so ya know, at least what I know alittle too well is that racial, all the way to social and ideological profiling is alive and well right here in the good ol'U.S. of A. and its been that way for a few decades. But don't think it came out of thin air. We gave the American *establishment* a cold hard slap in the face some forty something years ago with something called *the Generation Gap* and much of established American institution hasn't forgotten that. Some to this very day. But don't take it personally if you think you're being profiled; you're just part of someone's filing cabinet of past priors of someone seen once or maybe a couple of times too many in too many places or whatever. And too many terrified people also out there who with some kind of sense do realize that as times they-are-a-changing to a very volatile global environment, it's time to look at where we might be ten or fifteen years from now.

America rounded up Japanese Americans for less than what we're facing now. That's also another part of America's history that no one likes to talk about, but it happened. But that was war mixed with alittle terrorism 'cause civilians were then off-limits. Not primary targets would be a better way of putting it. Major European and Japanesse cities were leveled . . . two with major impact, with huge civilian casualties but as everything all around us erodes away with every new casualty . . . war becomes hell. Anyone who questions anything regarding America's involvement during WWII really should keep that to themselves. Better yet, go to your local VFW and listen to what they got to say! But we don't live in those luxurious days anymore because now we are all targets . . . even those of us who think that Uncle Sam can't even tie his own shoes anymore. I got an idea. If anyone else thinks that they can better help out the grave situation in which we seem to be mired in than what we got now, like traveling to the Middle East like the Speaker of the House did to snivel and cry like Americans NEVER do, then do so 'cause alls I know that the target tattooed on your forehead is the same as mine even though what's in our heads is entirely different. She could have traveled to Gilligan's Island and got the same results. Just so ya know, people (rest of the world) laugh at sissies.

Are things always supposed to get worse before they get better? In July of 2006 it got really worse. First of all, with all the action going on in the world, to write about one aspect takes quite a few modifications as time rolls on. Writing sucks, but if done right, sticks to your ribs. Same as Napalm . . . sticks to my lips. In the Middle East, the phrase "Death to America" is as common as houseflies on shit. It's been that way for decades. With something like that festering halfway around the world, something is eventually going to happen. And it did. Israel now has two military fronts, Hamas in the Gaza strip which is old news, and now Hezbollah in southern Lebanon which is bad news. Things just seem to just get worse, but just with the term *religious dominance*, anyone should realize that anyways. Someone just said, we welcome WWIII. Me too dickhead, can't wait to meet ya in person. What's the problem? I don't want your head, why you gotta problem with mine? Got some bad news but I think you already knew this. WWIII could very well happen. Not like war in the movies, but more like 9-11, with civilians now takin' the hit. No more wars like in the land, sea, and air or like anything you thought, but now in your own backyard. I'm no guru but it's gunna happen. Matter of time. Much of the world is scared senseless about some realities. Somehow, terrorism does that to people. All jokes aside, it will happen and it will happen with absolutely no dialogue on behalf of one side of the situation. This is really nothing new. Only a fool would give up the play first, then pounce second. Adolph wasn't a fool, just a homicidal maniac.

A lot has to do with oil. OPEC could seriously shut us off to the extent that life has just shown its underside. Can we live as tough as our predecessors did? They had no idea about future inventions that would make all that go away. Without routine energy, many of us will either perish or become imprisoned by someone who knows how to live the hard life . . . for a price. Here's how helpless mankind is now or then with energy needs. We have untapped mega-sources of usable clean energy. We just don't know how to tap them. A bolt of lightning which happens around a hundred times a second all over the planet can power most anything just with one bolt. That's pretty hard to reign in, but what about solar, geothermal, and wind? I'm told that it's too hard and expensive to use. Anybody believe that? Then I got some new and improved snake-oil for ya. Just as the medievals lived way below the standards of living of their Roman ancestors centuries before them, wait until fossil fuels become as rare as gold . . . and modern suburbia, just a stone throw away, may as well be on the other side of the moon 'cause you won't be able to get there the way you're used to. But if we got cut off, lots of profit money would be lost but nevertheless, OPEC could rearrange our lives. We all can ask ourselves, "What would the Middle East be like had no oil existed under its terrain?" It would be just as poor as it was before someone struck oil there. They probably didn't realize it was there. Maybe they did. I don't know but it was extracted by westerners. How about that! Now they can afford any new and modern weapon to use against the very people who actually drilled for it. Strange how some things work.

Although some of the Middle East accepting the Jewish state, much of it doesn't. Most notably are Syria, Iran, Hezbollah, Al-Qaeda . . . you know, the radical ones who shoot first, then scoot behind women and children like the soldiers they think they are for protection. You killed them, not us. What's Israel supposed to do? They, just like our own troops in Iraq sometimes don't have any choice. No one I ever heard of before uses grammar schools, hospitals, churches, or anything else civilian to stage a battle. Not only do they not care for our civilians, they also care not for their own. That's why ultimately, they will lose. As time rolls on, even their own people will realize that this is terrorism, not war. No one likes an asshole. Wait a minute, let me get a little diplo and remain civilized so maybe I can help with intellect. Well, that only lasted four seconds. The other side needs to stop laughing when the word *diplomacy* is mentioned. Hezbollah, like all the rest Islamic radicals know their history like no ones business. They know how the Viet Cong went underground like the piss ants they still are and fought a high-tech army with low-tech evasion, right underneath the enemy. And it works. Ask the French about Bien Dien Puh. After that happened, the U S inherited Vietnam. When the Israelis left Lebanon in 2000, Hezbollah dug in real good. Just knowing that Hezbollah is backed up by Syria and Iran tells me that those two countries have really bad plans for Israel. It's too bad Iran is what it is today for in Iran are some of the prettiest women in the world along with pretty little dolls in Iceland. Saw that on TV alittle while back. Pretty good show. Got my attention. Nuclear Iran? Pretty scary concept. One of Iran's motto is *A World without America*. If anyone can picture the future of the Middle East, along with Iran's agenda, then one should see WWIII is going to happen. Iran probably won't shoot first, but most likely will dictate to the rest of the Middle East what to do, or else. Who's gunna participate when that happens? First and foremost would be all the bad guys who are afraid of getting shot at. Most anybody is afraid of getting shot at including me. Blows when you're not fast enough. Second and most important . . . I'm not too sure. The rest of the world? Maybe. I do know that we'll get no help from any of the other planets in our solar system,'cept our own, so its probably up to a responsible free world and this time when we save the world again, maybe this time we should own it. Enough of the blood, sweat, and tears!! Everyone is afraid of getting shot at, but not everyone runs into some grammar school in session when that happens.

Anyways, we all want peace in the Middle East, and also that includes many Muslims, some of whom I know. America is very diverse. We all live together around here. But what about over there? Iraq has now a taste of what it's like to think for themselves. That seed will sprout. How long will it take remains to be seen. But the seed has been planted. You see, when all peoples can think for themselves instead of being told how or what to think, good things could happen. There is a chance. Before Iraq, there was no chance whatsoever. Whatever you think of this war, more good than bad will come from this. Not so according to the democratic loser in the presidential race in 2004. He says that if he were elected, none of this would have mattered 'cause none of what happened since 9-11 would have happened. Now I for one do not think he is incompetent by no means, just limited peripheral vision, that's all. I'm pretty sure he would have done Afghanistan. Iraq is what's in question in which I believe he would have had no part in, even though I don't know how he voted in February of 2003. I open up a pretty good theory about Iraq in the summary of this novel of which I really can see happen or happened according to multi-dimensional points in time where we all think we might be at. By that I mean my dome isn't just for stylin' with baseball caps and Oakley's. It also needs to be able to see the future by looking at the present. People like him dot and criss-cross the country daily with opinions and views about how things are supposed to be. That's his and everyone else's God given right. But when him or anyone else disrespect the military on active duty with totally asinine, completely uncalled for remarks with regards to, that's where I draw the line. Even though my service was in peacetime, those are my brothers and sisters *out there,* and if I was active right now, I would never forget what he and others had said. Screw the Oakley's and baseball caps! Use your goddamn head next time before you spew!!

We have an enemy that cares less about compassion for their fellow man no matter what the circumstances are. What's so hard in seeing that? Even Mr. MaGoo can see that. We have in Congress some people who should be working elsewhere simply for the fact that they're scared, and now-time is no time to be scared. Same as night time ain't no time to be here in this here neighborhood. Says who? What if I want my shit that bad? What if I want my freedom just as bad? Then guess what? I want everyone to know that I couldn't care less about any kind of shit, just as long as my hood is free to do whatever it wants. That came out kinda wrong but sometimes freedom lets some of us think that anything goes no matter what the results may be. That's why we have law and order. Freedom don't mean all that. It's not supposed to. Mix freedom along with alittle morals and values combined with goodwill toward our fellow man, or stranger for that fact, and that is exactly what our radical Islamic fundamentalists is all up in an uproar about. No one should be free for whatever reason, and if you are, you are now fair game. Even their own people. I'm startin' to think that I'm one of the only ones whose got a problem with that. Probably a few more than that, but you should be able to see what I'm trying to say. If not, then burn the rest of this book just like Nazi Germany did along with anything else that you don't think makes sense. Myself, if I don't like something I'm reading, I just tear out those pages. Problem solved. My copy of *War and Peace* is down to twelveteen pages. Osama, Hamas, Hezbollah, and all others like them could make Adolph look like Colonel Klink and that there is no joke. That's pretty tough to distinguish 'cause that was then and this is now. Both problems were, and are genocide and as evil as it gets. Not too much has changed. The *Enterprise* has a major problem and with the passing of time . . . will only get worse. And that's not even our call! Democrat or republican, these religious fanatics couldn't care less. Both parties are both Western. Most of the world and even worse, parts of the U S don't get that. I'm a fifty year old ex-screw-up . . . every now and then, and I can see that before I see my nose. Get all the bottom-line-in-it-for-themselves-nothin'-but-lawyers out of Congress and let me and my posse . . . that's posse, get involved with what's going to happen to our only *Enterprise* in the no-too-distant future. We're real people with real problems but because we're not real lawyers, we just continue takin' what they're givin 'cause we're cryin' for a livin. Not to piss on Congress, but everyone else with some kind of authority seems to not get it either. Westerners have been hated for scores of decades in the Middle East, pretty much for personal reasons in that most of us get over with the passing of time. With the passing of time and personal grass roots level of living . . . personal reasons for anything will evaporate with the common touch. I'm talking about your local town hall saying a few things also. **That's where government starts.** It's about time someone with federal authority realized that. All of us real people seem to just have no say in matters like this or a lot of other issues that matter. But we're the ones getting' burned. Even the seventy-five percent majority of the people from New York who think that *illegal aliens* in that state shouldn't have the privilege to drive but because one man says they do, and because of that, they might. See! There's many reasons why *real people* should have alittle more than just a singular vote. A very incompetent world in which we all crawl around upon.

I do have an idea on another subject closely related, which could be viewed as rather abstract. Since the United Nations, with all its peacekeeper soldiers, can't put its peacekeeping agenda on the front burner to keep them honed, let someone else do it. The U N has within itself the power to do so. What they're missing is the balls to make that happen. Any soldier from any country who is soldiering for the U N to try to help has my total utmost respect, no matter what country, religion, national origin, or race. You're in it just like everyone else involved with soldiering or policing and you know what I think about that. But here's what these soldiers don't have; first class leadership and hardcore motivation. That's not their fault by no means. What they're missing is leadership and when you ain't got that, no military force will ever succeed. They don't have that get-the-job-done-lets-go-home mindset like the U S armed services and the rest of the armed services no matter what free country they serve in. The U N is nothing but a carbon-copy of bureaucratic politics made up of people who will never get shot at or never have to make their own bed. Most of the U N is composed of countries whose agenda is somewhat, if not allwhat questionable. But someone else does their beds for them. These are people *who I'll never take orders from.* I want to live. They can't make that so . . . way too many chiefs with ideas that do nothing but collide with each other. If you can't even get to first base after hitting a triple, what's your army supposed to do? They're on the bench, just watching. Let someone else work the U N peacekeepers so that they become a viable force, not just targets. Let the U S Rangers, the British Commandos, the French Foreign Legion, and other respectable military units work them so that they can make a difference, not a mess. The U N has within it no one who can make that happen, but other people do. I'm not afraid of working with strangers, been doin' it all my life. I'm still here. Plus it brings us all down to where we belong; the grass-roots level and thatz always a good thing. Work off the street. That's where it all begins. Let me run 'em through boot camp and we'll go where no man's gone before. Wait a sec. I already done did that. Let someone else do that. But I'll still go first. Whether or not I still got it, I'm pretty sure I do, I got no problem serving with them. They got balls enough to take orders from blithering idiots and that's no lie. Remember this: They went to Somalia in 1993 before we did and no one should ever take that for granted. Actually, that was a good call by the U N. Want a righteous world army? Call me. I'll come up with common sense rather than nonsense. Whys it always gotta be me? Hey, I just got divorced. Ain't got nuthin' better to do. Remember, idle hands are the devil's medicine and I've had enough of that. Let's kill someone. So much for idle hands. Letz heal someone instead. Also, so much for this tangent I ran into.

Let's take a look at the other side. The other side being people who run airliners into the ground, welcome WWIII, and got no problem blowing themselves to smithereens. These people want war at any cost and can't fight back in any other way because of their low-tech world in which they live in. Guerilla warfare with horrendous results has worked for many decades in our recent violent past and has worked all the way from its inception way back, back into time. Back around BC. But who would've thought that your own army is now expendable to accomplish your mission? Myself, if that's all I got to fight back with, and this may sound obtuse, I might consider it. It would be as a last resort. I want my enemy to feel pain, nothing less. If I gotta go in the process . . . well, it's been real, see ya on the other side. No one really knows what its like on the other side. I believe that you must pass the test of life throughout your trek through life, no matter how much misery you'll encounter along the way, to advance to God's paradise. Passing the test of life by blowing up and murdering scores of people isn't gunna get it in a sane man's world. Hope that what you believe in is the God's honest truth. If you ain't got hope, then don't press the button. I believe that sex is only a gift from God to make mans presence in flesh and blood bearable and worth preserving the future for. I'm pretty sure it doesn't mean all that in the after life. But now, Israel is now once again at war with now, a more visible enemy. There's more of Israel's enemies underground than there are ants. They are going to have to resurrect the tunnel rat. That's a hell of a way to fight. Johnny knew someone else who worked in the postal service who served in Vietnam as a tunnel rat. He heard some pretty wild stories. Over three quarters of a tunnel rat's body weight is all ballz. They also have to watch out for hundreds of missiles that are only going to get bigger and better as time ticks on. Underground and from the air. And they also have to face one of the biggest problem of them all. Some of Europe, along with many others, even some Americans, have turned their backs on them. Much easier to do that, rather than to stand up and fight back, even phililosophically. Wambly pambly world. I can understand parts of Europe; look at what happened to the Jews during WWII? Not too many friends in Europe. I wonder why that is? What the hell did the Jews do wrong? Jesus was a Jew, and now Jews take more heat than anybody else in the world. Johnny's *Muslim* carpet-laying buddies didn't have no problem with no Jew. The Promised Land has spawned three major religions in the very same location Israel now occupies. If we all can't just get along while coming to terms with all that, then in the future, you ain't seen nothin' yet. Fanatical Muslims will come to terms with nothing. They are only going to make every Muslim an enemy. This is what they want, so now we have to walk on eggshells to figure out who's who. You need to fight fire with fire, 'cause a new head grows upon the hydra just after you chopped the other one off so let's get the body. I hate to demonize our situation, but that's just the way it is at the present. One last thing about Europe that to me would be appeasing if I were a criminal is the girl scout punishment that is meted-out to people who should hang. What the Serbs did constitutes a Nuremburg trial, not the World Court that does nothing as opposed to the crime committed. Didn't the U S come to the aid of Muslim Croatians who were the underdog during that mess? What do we get? F T W!!

Anyways, Johnny's hanging by a thread just like a spider. No, he don't think he's Spiderman. That's 'cause . . . what if he found a Spiderwoman? Then run as fast as your eight legs will let you go 'cause that's gotta be the most ugliest, hideous looking womanthang ever found under a rock. He takes everything day-by-day 'cause he's got no plans and can't make any plans. He needs paychecks for that and those aren't too common around these times. He had his TV without cable and alls he got is one channel to watch. Then one day it turned Mexican so alls he did was watch real pretty Mexican girls and wondered if they were talking to him. He had just got cable just before he went to jail the first time and he recalls all the war protestors on TV when we just went into Iraq. At a time when everyone was wondering how safe are we really? Along with a huge majority wanting action taken to ensure we're safe, I always thought that these people musta' known something the rest of us didn't. *War is not the answer.* Well then, visionary . . . what is? Alls it's done in the past was get rid of slavery, fascism, oppression, communism, crime, *socialism* and gave birth to mother freedom. I really don't mean to make fun of anyone so please tell me about some other recourse so that we can avoid war. Diplomacy, you say? Please feel free to make that work while they are about to cut that growth off your neck. The ones you wanna get to don't care about me or you . . . only them. Actually these people really didn't know anything and are some of the most *useful idiots* I ever saw on TV. Protesting anything is anyone's right, but just after 9-11 and anthrax? What are you thinking? I say find the source. Then kill it. No protest involved. Were the Iraqi war protesters protesting the decision of the act of war, or were they protesting a republican who initiated that decision? Were the Vietnamese war protesters at the democratic national convention back in 1968 protesting the war?, or a democrat in power who left the presidency because of the war but passed the baton to another democrat who chose to *stay the course?* We all know that, that democrat was defeated by Nixon who also stayed the course. Wars waged by the U S to diffuse internal chaos in other countries such as Vietnam and Iraq have always led to protests. Democrat or republican, some of these people who protested these wars have absolutely no peripheral vision regarding how things could have been had these wars had not been waged at all. Vietnam: the domino effect which was very real back in those days and could of happened and Iraq, a major exporter of Middle Eastern American hatred and all that goes with it which also could of happened. Wooda cooda. Pretty lame reasons for anything but what was at stake takes precedence over shooda any day of the week, especially while hangin' out in my hooda. Whadaya think? Pretty gooda? Not really. None of this discussion is any gooda. Cooda wooda. I should have dida, but I didn't. Can't take them days back, wish I cooda.

Which leads me to a lot of our patriotic Vietnam protestors who took some of their frustrations out on returning GI's. Do me a favor. Go into your bathroom and look yourself in the mirror. Then reach way down in your gut and yours lungs and spit a nice gooey, slimy hunk of snot right back at that mug staring right back at you in the mirror. That's what I think of you. That's what Nixon thought of you too. About as patriotic as Osama. *They still need to pay for that!*

Charge or debit? It shouldn't be that easy.

Okay, back to Mexican girls. He lives amongst a huge influx of Mexicans who make up much of North Georgia's population nowadays. He has decided he wants a real pretty Mexican girl but so far, no takers. He has come close but one was just out of high school and another was involved with Mexican gangs and he wanted no part of that. The fact that someone in high school liked him made him feel ten years younger and set his mind back another twenty-five. That made him almost the same as her and he really wanted to pour the coals to her but her being about the same age as Amanda finally got to him and he smartened up. He was older than her parents. Still no takers, though.

Around this time, he's driving down to Atlanta every weekend to see Justin and Amanda who were staying with Vaj. Nick was staying with his ma and her boyfriend down in Little Five Points. On one particular night in Atlanta, Justin and Amanda decided to go see their Mom and Nick. Johnny, Vaj, Vic, plus some others stayed at the house and had a barbeque along with beer and other assorted goodies to pass the night away. After the feast and when the night was over, Johnny went and laid out on the couch. About three in the morning, in come Justin and Amanda. They wake Johnny up and tell him Nick is in jail. "What happened?" "He beat up Mom's boyfriend real bad." Johnny thought that was real good and asked for the details. Amanda said, "Boy, Nick can fight!" His ma's boyfriend had put his hands on her in front of Nick and alls he did was protect his ma. He put her boyfriend up for three weeks. He even had a fractured noggin. He beat the crap out of him and opened up a can of high-octane-whoop-ass which made Johnny proud. Johnny don't care about her boyfriend. Amanda could go down there and light 'im up also and he'd give her the keys to the Caddy. Now that's pretty damn crude dude: live and let live . . . asswipe. But because of all the police and ambulance at the scene, they were held up for awhile and they finally got back around three o'clock. Since it was on a weekend, he spent the weekend in jail and Nick got to see the judge on Monday morning. Nick looks like Johnny and some of the dockets before Nick's appearance who seen the judge who got their judgment and released, walked by Johnny and asked, "Is Nick your son?" "Yeah. Why?" "'Cause that crazy-cracker took all our cigarettes." "How'd he do that?" "One-on-one basketball." "No shit. Pretty good." Anyhow here comes Nick and the judge says, "First-degree assault. This is pretty serious son. What happened?" Nick is explaining everything and when he got to the part about protecting his ma, the judge stops him right there. "You mean to tell me you were protecting your ma?" "Yes sir." "Why did you do what you did?" "'Cause he pushed her real hard, your Honor." "That's all I got to hear. Case dismissed. Next!" Johnny saved a lot of money that day, no bail and no fine. That's always good. He was a black judge and what Johnny already knew in jail about family values with a lot of his black inmate buddies turned out to be just that . . . truth. You take care of family, no matter what.

Johnny would never go back to his ex-wife, but he doesn't want to see her hurt. He's pissed, but not cruel. You hear about people getting married, then getting divorced and then getting married to each other again. Why? Get another car. The last one blew up and got wrecked. Why fix it? Get a brand new one. Do yourself one better and get a motorcycle. They come with girls. "Hey, you wanna hear about some off-beat religion? Then we'll go and get another car. This time I think I'll try brunette, South-Beach style. Soon as I get to South Beach . . . if that ever happens . . . can't even make it to the county line anymore. Anyway, Johnny and his crew go to Talladega in Alabama to go and do a flooring job. As they cross the Georgia-Alabama line, out come all the Alabama jokes. Johnny would say, "What's wrong with Alabama?" You got Talladega super speedway, Huntsville Space Center, Auburn Tigers football team, Bear Bryant from the University of Alabama where Joe Namath came from; with about the same amount of national titles at Alabama as the Yankees have World Series titles, and a religion that'll make ya take a second look. Alabama isn't the only state where this occurs, but that's where he has seen it. Actually, I don't know the denomination but I know I like mine much better. There is a sect of people that worship serpents. Live ones. For serpents, obviously they use big snakes. That must be symbolic of Eve with the apple. Throughout most of the sermon they are encouraged to handle and piss off these snakes. Pissed off snakes that consequently bite the shit out of anyone who touches them. There's one guy who's been bit over a hundred and fifty times and likes it!! I don't know about snakes, maybe tarantulas but definitely not snakes. Tarantulas crawling all over your face. Sundays will never be the same.

Well, now that church is over, its time to go home. Now at this time, Johnny hasn't got a home to go to. He put up no fuss with the landlord and he just moved out. Not too many landlords/lenders get that lucky. Usually some piece of shit is going to string you out for as long as possible without paying the rent. He couldn't pay no more, so he moved on. With his van holed up in the woods, his buddy Tracy gave him a place to stay. At this point in time, he's back to one dog. He's got Coco, the only one that came from Massachusetts. The other one he got at the Humane Society when he went to find Pups, upped and bolted away. Next door at the animal control, they had just relished in their joy that Johnny was all wrapped up in court again 'cause all the infractions in the past that he fixed were now unfixed in the courtroom. They are now telling the judge that Johnny hadn't done anything and completely ignored the ordinances. None of that was true. The judge didn't know that. That's double jeopardy! A court case comes up that gets combined with everything else in the past. This is when he's living in limbo; not really working, just existing and the court case gets lost in the shuffle. Not the legal shuffle . . . the Johnny shuffle. Like having three left feet. I'm not even sure what friggin' court case I'm talkin' about anymore! He's also beginning a new term of probation for the hit-and-run from the police episode. They gave him a break where he lived at. When the cop who told him to take off after he left on Johnny's first day out of lock-up, before he left, he gave Johnny a court date. "Don't screw this up. You had better be there." "I will." When he went to court, the judge asked why he didn't show up for his court date awhile back. "You do know that you have a benchwarrant and I can have you locked up indefinitely." "Yes, your Honor. I know. I was locked up in Gwinnett." "Got proof?" "Right here, sir." "Good enough for me. This case is now bound for Superior Court. Next!" His bench warrant was lifted and Superior Court gave him probation and a fine and all together, he has had to do eight years of probation in Georgia. You can run but you can't hide. This, however, would be the last time he's seen probation. It was Justin's and Nick's turns next. He passed the baton to his sons. What a father!! Amanda sits back and shakes her head. My whole family is screwed up except me.

As you can probably deduce by now, is Johnny's failure rate on everything he tried. That's not going to put the beans in the pot. Trying in America don't mean shit. You've got to make it. In a way, he made it. Its not gunna put the beans in the pot, but it is the most important job anyone can undertake. There is no margin of error. You cannot fail; if you do then you're not worth your weight in spit. That job is being a parent. Johnny and his ex did a very good job of bringing up three fine kids. A lot of what's out there in America they know about and a lot of what they know about isn't too impressive to themselves or Johnny. A lot is, and they know the difference. They don't call elders "hey" or "dude" but instead elders are referred to as Mister or Ma'am. They were taught right from wrong and wrong won't be tolerated. Yeah, the boys get into a little trouble but that's pretty easy to do nowadays. You don't even have to be wrong anymore. But they were, and there's none of that wasn't-my-fault bullshit going on.

I really can't rag on carnal behavior on prime time TV anymore. There's too many commercials on to see anything anymore. I'm not sure if it's me or not, but a lot of the commercials I see on TV, its either I'm not quite sure what they're all about?, or I'm not sure if I'm gettin my intelligence insulted. I can tell one from the other but I just didn't know that everybody who has their TV sets on in America owns some kind of profitable business with all kinds of profitable investments padding the portfolio. That's all you gotta do?, just turn on TV? Hell, I should have been CEO Jones back in the 70s!! Not really, there's one commercial about tradesmen like myself who build all these things for CEOs and other movers and shakers to move and shake in and alls we get is Angie's list. Alls she does is take the working man and show him at his worst. Anyone can be on their worst. Try it when you're welding and the melted slag is dropping down your upheld sleeve and you can't react 'cause the weld's not done yet. You only get one shot to do it right. Professional people could also be on their worst but Angie don't piss on any of them. Just the ones who work with their hands, not the rest of their bodies. But that's not what the commercial is all about. It's about making fun of people who work with their hands and I could be wrong here, but it seems to *corperate* blue collar America. What do you think of *corperate* white collar America?

Pretty touchy subject here, but it touched me wrong! Me, to be in a trade, I wouldn't be on that shit-list even if it mean't coughing up two-hundred thousand square feet of vomit at twenty duckets a bucket!

But America has changed. No more Frank Sinatra or Frank Zappa. Now we got/*had* Michael Jackson. Many people have many opinions about Michael Jackson and I will admit some of what I hear makes me take a second look, but there's one thing about him that I remember from way back when he was the frontman for the Jackson 5. Not once in my life have I seen such a pure, dominant talent for the lead player in any band since then till now. Mick Jagger was a close second but Michael Jackson was probably the best performer I ever saw and that was on TV. But he does raise a whole bunch of questions. I have an idea for a *perfect-for-the-times* sitcom for prime time. Remember *My Three Sons?* That was in 1968. Fast forward to 2005 and they still be livin' home. How about 'My Three Bums?' Three fat, balding, drunk mu#hafu%k#s just screwin' up Dad's and Uncle Charlie's inheritance real good. I'd like to see that. I'm not sure why. I got different views on Hollywood, even its awards. Some actors and actresses are very good at what they do but not as good as "the Torso" in the movie 'Thirteen Ghosts'. I didn't see no award going towards that performance. Didn't no one else watch that besides me? I think that Schwagmire is probably the best actor-dude right now in Hollywood even though he ain't real . . . sorta in swagnito!! Hollywood is against our policies in the Middle East but now I'm starting to see some TV shows about the U S military's presence *over there*. That would be because much of America knows what has to be done and wouldn't mind seeing a little armchair action. I think that's good. If Hollywood were smart, they would show how in the future, Iraq breaks out into Civil War 'cause that's going to happen. It will happen after the U S leaves major military operations to the patriotic Iraqi army once it's capable and reduces our presence to *supply* and *logistics*. The only thing that can't happen is a re-vietnamesvation like what happened in Vietnam. They were also ready, but the ARVN . . . the South Vietnamese Army failed miserably. It was a disaster. They even ate fine war dogs that the fucking army left behind. They didn't do that in WWII. Those dogs got citations. Not these dogs, they got eaten. Without those doggies, the Vietnam Memorial in DC would be at least one third larger than it is. These dogs were so effective, they became primary targets.

They should make a war-dog memorial along with the *asshole's* name who gave the order to leave them all behind.

Let's see. What else do his kids know about America? Well, Amanda knows a few things. She knows what's important, like the future, and she's getting prepared for it by going to college here in Georgia. She knows it don't come to you. You got to go to it. She knows, with help from her father, how society now works against us, rather than with us as in the past. Sometime she needs no help from anyone; she can see for herself some of the problems. She, along with her father, saw how some major clothing manufacturer decided how to market adulthood to pre-teen girls. Now I put the thong right up there with the telephone, electricity, and the wheel, but NOT ON A TEN YEAR OLD GIRL!! What's wrong with that picture? We got enough need-to-die pedophiles out there! You wanna' make it worse? Whose fucking stupid-ass idea was that anyways? But what I like about my country is when stupid shit like this makes the news; it gets shot down in a ball of flames. Lasts as long as a meteorite. What scares me is someday, maybe that's not going to happen. I just hope that in the future, when I'm long gone and forgotten, Americans and peoples all over the world will realize that right is right and wrong is wrong no matter what the neo-quasi-HDTV; new-definitions-on-life-with-no-morality-flameout-on-values *new-age-no-age* says. I don't want to mention the 2004 election again. Just so ya know, people really like morals and values.

While we all look at each other out on the deck, Johnny now resides in the Oakwood part of Gainesville with Tracy and Michelle, his girlfriend. He's done lots of work with Tracy besides that trip to Cordele and just sits around the apartment with Michelle all day long watching TV while Tracy's working his ass off. Tracy's up and out of the house before six in the morning. Johnny's getting up between ten and noon. The crew that Johnny used to work with doing the Falcon's complex and numerous subdivisions, Tracy still works with. Not Johnny. This is probably one of the first of his pitfalls of moving so far away from Atlanta without a driver's license. He drove all over, got caught and paid for it, and now, he's dependent and that got all screwed up. If he gets caught driving again, then there's a remote chance that he might face prison, so he don't drive. Go to prison for driving without hurtin' anyone? Anything wrong with that picture? Yeah, Johnny's the one bent over. But he's also the one who bent over the system by doin' what he did to make what happened to make it this way. It really don't take much nowadays to screw it all up, but if what he did in yesteryears was warranted for nowadays, then it would be all screwed up for his next three generations to drive before they're fifty and they would be looking for Johnny's grave about two in the morning to ask why . . . with shovels to ask why. Gets the living shit kicked out of him . . . even when he's dead! I told ya he gots real bad luck! He needs someone to hold his hand from now on.

He got into physical confrontation with the crew leader and got fired. He really can't wrestle anyone unless it's to kill, 'cause if anyone gets ahold of his left arm, he's in big trouble. Because of his old injury, his forearm doesn't rotate the way it's supposed to and it could be pretty easy to break. He can only box his way out. But on that day, the first thing that happened was the other guy grabbed Johnny's left arm the wrong way. This is the first time since 1972 that he felt like it was going to snap again at the same spot. The other guy could have ripped it off from his shoulder and beat him over the head with it if he wanted to. But because of that, Johnny's got to fend for himself with no license. So he sits around watching TV with Michelle all day, bored like a marooned pirate. So what's he do? He asks his buddy's girlfriend to go out with him. Don't let that vulture alone with your girl even for only one minute. Says he can't help it. Talk to Mike Tyson's girl like that and see what happens! He'll make you help it. She's real pretty and all that but not my type. Myself, I like my women battered. Not what you're thinkin' either. At the Waffle House you can get 'em battered, smothered, covered, then slobbered all over. What do you want, something that tastes good or something with good taste? No taste when you can't even keep away from your buddy's girl.

But aside from all that, one day he got a little unexpected excitement . . . which came pretty close to unexpected excretement. It's usually three strikes and yer out. How many times can you fuck with a moving train and still walk away? Like some kind of weird ritual, he almost gets mangled up with a train again and as usual, just walks away. While he's walking down the railroad tracks coming back from the convenience store with his newspaper and 40-ounce Budweiser in his hand and the sunflower seeds he also bought in his chest pocket, he just got lucky . . . didn't even know. These tracks lie in a ravine and run under a bridge on one of the main drags in town. There is only one track so a train could be heading right in front of you or right behind you as you walk the track. Occasionally, as he's walking, he looks back. He sees nothing, and thinks if one is coming, he'll hear it. He continues on and decides to eat some of those sunflower seeds in his chest pocket. With his back to the way he came, he puts the beer and newspaper down in the middle of the tracks. He gets out his sunflower seeds, rips open the pack, and dumps 'em in his mouth. As he tilts his head back to eat them, he turns his shoulder alittle when he raised his arm. By doing so, he slightly moved his field of vision a little to the right . . . thank God. Out of the corner of his eye, he sees an intense radiant bright light. He turns around and doesn't hear anything. Trains make noise, so for a second or two, he's baffled as to what this bright light is. As he's staring at it . . . now thinking UFOs, he finally realized that it was a train. Because of the ravine where he was at, the Doppler effect took full effect and threw the noise completely behind the approaching train. He never heard it. He panicked, grabbed his beer and paper and two to three seconds later after he jumped off the track, this long freight train just cruises on by. There wasn't even a whistle. He was too small to be seen by anyone in the engine. No one would have ever known what happened to him. Thank God for sunflower seeds.

But anyhow, he lived to make the New Year's Eve party of 2003, all by himself. Well, not really by himself. He was in downtown Atlanta with about a half a million other people trying to get into the same bar with a rock stage right next door to the Hard Rock Café. He's taking public transportation all over Atlanta, going here, going there, and decides to go see one of his buddy's band that was playing next to the Hard Rock Café that night. Well, he got confused about what doors went to what establishments. He wound up standing in line at the Hard Rock Café instead, and it is so packed with around a hundred people standing around that if two people leave the Hard Rock, only two other people get in. Sounds like they sold more oats than fits the bag. It wasn't really a line of people, but more like a mob standing all around the place. He was out there for over an hour. He first gets there and realizes he's the only one there with blue eyes. He looks around and alls he sees is dark hair, dark complexions, and brown eyes. He rubs his own eyes and begins to wonder what's goin' on. Not a blue eye in the house. His first reaction is, "Holy

Cow! I'm with a bunch of Muslims! How'd this happen?" He's hanging out and gets to know lots of the people around him and they're just as pissed as Johnny about the overflow and wait. Johnny and some of them were doin' what Muslims ain't supposed to be doin.' They're the ones who called him out. Whose wrong? . . . no one. But he cannot for the life of him, figure out where the door is for where he's supposed to be at. During the *pissed off* time, he's making friends outside while bewildered like a wino. Finally, he says this and this unquote, *Screw all this* and left. Sorry about the bad word, but the Hard Cock really pissed him off that night. He went to 9-Lives.

But aside from that, he's staying in a place where he can keep Coco. A mans got to have at least one dog. As I pen this, Johnny's got another one. This one's name is Goober, a sub-species of genus from the loose Goober clan. There can be only one. One night he thought he got scalped. Around three or four in the morning, Goober went and grabbed Johnny's hair while he was asleep and pulled him off the couch. He woke up and there's Goober just pullin' and a growlin' cause he can't pull Johnny across the floor. Goober is just a two month old puppy. A mentally deranged one. But at this time, Goober is in the future and Coco is in the present. Pretty hard having a dog and trying to find a place to stay. Especially when you're homeless.

Well, by now Johnny has overstayed his presence at Tracy's cause he's been there a little too long and now its time to move on. He's got no where to go, so he stays back down in Atlanta with Vaj, Vic, Justin, and Amanda who now has been renamed "Kid Rotten." That's short for rotten kid. Actually, Amanda is the only kid that he always caves into 'cause she's daddy's little girl even when she hits ninety years old. He'll still be around to make sure nothin rotten ever happens to her. So what!, he's a hundred and twenty five years old!, if that's what it takes. She ain't too cool with the new name but Johnny's the father so it's written in stone. Written in shit according to her. He's down there for a couple of weeks when he gets a call from another one of his carpet laying buddies back up north in Gainesville. He thinks Johnny is still up in Gainesville and when Johnny tells him what's up, his buddy whose name is also Johnny, offers him a room at his house. Having lost touch with most of Atlanta anyways, he takes the offer but he's got to get rid of Coco. Here's a dog that's been with the family for over ten years and because around these times Johnny Fukup can't put it together anymore, he decides to put her down at some veterinary clinic. Coco didn't know what was going on and he'll never forget the last time he looked at her. She was wagging her tail and Johnny thought about shooting himself when he walked out never to see her again. He really likes dogs, especially one he's had that long. It was done so he could carry on 'cause now he's completely dependent. Anyhow, he's staying with his buddy way out in the outskirts of Gainesville a little past the house he lost and its real country. When left home 'cause there wasn't enough work, stranded with no license, he would often look out the window at all the cattle out in the pastures and say to himself, "I'm no better than any of them."

A funny thing happened at this house to Johnny that wasn't so funny at the time. In fact, that's one of the scaredest he's even been since his ghostly experience decades before back at technical school back in the service. While sittin at the house by himself getting messed up on whiskey and spinach late at night around one in the morning, he hears a knock on the door. He checks it out but no one's there. So he goes back to his business at hand and cranks up some *New York Dolls* for a little spice for the buzz. He hears a knock again and again no one's there. Now he's concerned. Then he hears some knocks and bumps, one of which was coming from under the crawlspace. Now he's really concerned and starts to have flashbacks of the lower south latrine. He runs into his room, closes the door, and gets ready to light up a blunt to make it all go away. Just as he lights it, he hears a tremendous thud on the back deck which shook the whole house. He spits out the blunt and runs out of the house thinking that after all these years, they're back and they found him. He was scared senseless and runs down the hill to the next house over where his buddy Johnny's parents lived. He pounds on the door forever. "Answer the door. I'm not going away," he screams over and over. Johnny's ma answers the door and says "What the heck is going on?" He responds, "Something's wrong at Johnny's place and the house is moving." "What!" "I'm not going back up there!" "Don't let that crazy drug addict in here," he hears Johnny's father say in the background. "I'm not on drugs. The house got someone in there I can't see." His Ma says, "Listen, calm down a bit, rest for awhile, go back and if anything else happens, come back down." "Okay." Halfway up the hill, he sees the lights inside the house flicker on and off. He's thinking of Poltergeist and flies back down to Johnny's parents pounding on the door screaming, "Call Johnny, tell him not to come home, wherever he's at." His parents are eventually concerned and call Johnny to tell him that his roommate is here scared shitless and he says your house is haunted. After some other calls are made, it comes to find about five or six people were playing a joke on him. He goes back up and they're all laughing their asses off. The loud thud he heard on the back deck was an old weight bench someone tossed on it. All is good 'cause he'll take a joke over what happened back in the lower south latrine. Do you think he needs prescription drugs? He says, "Sure, where day at?" He prefers the new and improved Oxyncotin now with vitamin B! I don't think he does but our pharmaceutical drug companies think we all do.

Wanna see a drug problem? Watch TV commercials. Even got one to produce tears. Now I've seen many people with many problems. Lack of tears wasn't one of them. The only thing I've seen was too many tears. Way too many. Does everyone out there really have all these strange health problems? I'm startin' to get scared. There might be something wrong 'cause I take no pills to quell my imaginary problems. Apparently the prescription dope out there has saturated the market, so its time to invent new ones. Now don't get me wrong. Pharmaceuticals are beneficial to people who really need them, from antibiotics to cancer drugs. But they have side effects . . . like costing your kids' inheritances and maybe the shoreline cottage. Competition breeds the best, but at what cost? Twenty bucks a pill to make sure that both my feet aren't pointing a hundred and eighty degrees backwards when I wake up tomorrow morning is a lot. It's something that some of us can't prevent. Give it some time. That'll probably also pop up on TV soon. Do you find yourself stumbling about all the time? Well, sometimes . . . this could happen! No it can't!! Then there's the one about basic life according to some doctor on T.V. Hello, my name is *Dr. Splotch.* Is life getting the best of you? Are you going to hell in a handbasket? If so, then I got all these pills for you. Uppers, downers, all-a-rounders, in-betweeners, and lots of beaners. I'm not really too sure, but I'd rather get my shit off of the streets . . . . safer. All the best pharmaceuticals come from America and the cost involved to invent and produce them are staggering so it gets passed on to the consumer. Same way the oil execs pass on their costs to us. Remember, they have been posting record profits ever since it cost more for a gallon of gas than it does for a double cheeseburger. Wonder how pharmaceutical companies are doing? Wait till their stocks split, then get in. I'm not joking either. This to me is the doping of America, legally and ruthlessly. Plain and simple. They got drugs for ADD, which is nothing more than an invented calamity. It wasn't invented by any doctor or medical facility or even any pharmaceutical company by no means. It was invented by parents who deprive their children of attention either because of massive workload or for some other reason that leaves the kids out. Dope 'em up. That's the easy way out. Who in their right mind would do that? . . . unless absolutely necessary. If I was a little kid and only saw Mom and Dad after they picked me up from daycare, I might begin to wonder if I'm worth anything. Daycare is a necessity because Mom and Dad work too much to make ends meet or work too much to get what they want out of life. Some parents not only over-extend for their children but some do it for themselves, relegating little junior as nothing more than a small hurdle in the way. But the main fact remains: single ma has no choice; if for better or worse. If America wasn't so nomadic and hectic, instead of daycare there would be grandma and grandpa. C'mon, that's so 1950s. When you're in your fifties and little Junior doesn't bring over the grandkids except only on holidays, well, he's only doing what he was learned. Can't really blame him. That's all he knows. How about all these hard-on commercials? Give it a few years. That's what they'll be calling them. Erection just sounds too medical. If an erection lasts more than four hours, then call up all your ex-wives and girlfriends. Don't call no doctor, 'cause I don't need no doctor. I'm amazed that these commercials are allowed on TV and Mark Martin's stock car shouldn't say Viagra on it. Nothing against Mark Martin by no means . . . only the polluted atmosphere of which this creates. I never thought that at my age that having a sex-change operation would give me E.D. Wait a few more years, that kinda bullshit might be plastered on billboards all over the highways. We had a problem with a shortage of flu vaccine awhile back 'cause there's no money in making that anymore. How you gunna get ten bucks a whack for that? If 1918 happens again, there won't be no flu vaccine shortage, only a shortage of humans. That's strictly a corporate view, has nothing to do with my hard-on or lack of one. I don't know what's worse, the affliction someone is trying to wash away with prescription drugs, or the side effects. Lowering one's cholesterol is good for the body and soul and if it takes drugs, then it takes drugs. But remember, this little pill could cause migraines, raise boils on your forehead, turn your mouth upside down and shouldn't be taken by anyone other than females who are nursing or wish to become pregnant. This new drug invasion just mirrors our society. The easiest way is the best. Roll those sleeves back down. You might get dirt under your nails. Eat a pill. It makes the dirt go away . . . just like that!! If I got my way and got rid of all those hard-on commercials, except that woman on the Levitra commercial, I believe I would probably wind up going toe-to-toe with the ACLU cause pharmaceutical companies have a right to pervert our country. Putting them on late night TV would be good enough for me. First of all, their cause is right and just for the fact they believe in freedom. I do understand some of their crusade, I couldn't agree more. My question is. At what cost? How free is free? According to them, all Americans are still bound by *constitutional chains.* I don't see any chains on me, except of course when I'm incarcerated. That would be my fault, now wouldn't it, not some section of society's? Well, according to them, I'm wrong. It's the other way around. I'm supposed to be able to do and say anything I want with no regards for anyone or anything around me. We live in a free-and-open society where anything goes, even art that depicts the president as a killer and portrays him as a terrorist. I believe he was the one who flew Flight 77 into the Pentagon, then took office after he walked out of the rubble completely unscathed. I do understand some of the animosity directed toward him from the 2000 election in which everything regarding elections failed . . . especially common sense. Common sense didn't fail. *It wasn't allowed to blossom.* Where's the sense when people can't even figure it out for themselves? So, they call the Supreme Court. It was pretty simple. You count votes. Mechanically, not computery. No one can ever refute a mechanical problem. It's right there in front of your eyes. Not so with computers. Wait until we all see the widespread voter fraud that's gunna happen in the future because anyone can chop into a computer and change its mind, no matter what safeguards are in place. I believe this to be an ill-fated move. Wonder why they couldn't count the votes down in Florida back then? Think anybody was cheating? Someone had to cheat 'cause its very simple, you simply count votes. Not these votes, they got recounted so many times that finally they had to give it to the Supreme Court like a bunch of fools. The popular vote versus the electoral vote. Someone once told me how the electoral vote made more sense. How much more sense do you need when the majority of the masses are over-ruled? That happened in 2000 according to the seventeenth recount. But if the electoral vote makes more sense, then what doesn't is California's fifty-three electoral votes. That sets a precedent for our future because it has always been shown that most innovative and social adaptation to something new came from out west. All of that was good 'cause California was first, then the rest of us caught on and we all had a real good time. But that was before politics took over. Some of the notions of elected officials out west, one of which I discussed earlier which is real bad, should be shown only on Comedy Central or MTV 'cause that's as far as *that* goes in this book. *South Park* would work pretty good. The electoral vote in California needs to be chopped in half; one for me and one for you. I know that lots of people don't like the president and don't like the war, but to piss and shit all over him during one of America's trying times 'cause someone pissed in your cornflakes last election is something that America's never faced before, with some of the democratic party just intentionally hindering a war in which they don't believe. No one likes war, but don't put my brothers and sisters in uniform in harms way 'cause you think that you have all the answers and that they're being led astray by actually fighting something that should have been fought many years prior! I won't say I don't believe in it, but I will say I can't believe it. I can't believe all the intelligence leaks, media abuse which Congress seems to care nothing about . . . which puts American and Coalition Forces in harm's way . . . intentionally and the back-up it receives from from this Congress. Also, by a lot of our movie-starz. When they start makin' tawlkies? Now alls they make are kartoonz and we're supposed to take them seriously? What's being taken more seriously by most of the world is some of the garbage, no-mind-B-movies and T.V. shows (mostly movies) that have been leaving the Hollywood studios since the Eighties. Don't get me wrong some of them are very good, but others glorify some of the very same reasons that Heaven and Hell was created in the first place. What about some of the *loose-noodle* garbage that nothing but complete three-foot-two loudmouths put on the can't-see-me-ten-feet-tall internet? Most of these pigmies are the very same people who blame the conservative sector of America for fighting back *a demon-like-from-no-hell-before*, because of themselves emulating a *questionable* sector of modern society for many decades all over the world, that instead should have been viewed as maybe some kinda social ill or a-slightly-lower-standard . . . with maybe even expulsion from society for a while, not this mass media mindset of "might make a buck off of it mentality." If that's not western decadence?? Then I don't know what is!

Maybe it was a mistake to *"impose democracy"* on Iraq after the tragical mystery ride WMD's went *mysteriously mysterious* to try to make things look some kinda mysterious. I think that things will always get worse (in lots of cases) couldn't be more *nower than now*. To impose any kind of democracy could be an atrocity on any country. The "speak easy local yokel" vocal population who might be able to call their own shots might have something important to say. *Do you think this might spread?* I just cannot for the life of me see that as a bad thing especially from a place where lots of bad things came and still come from with psycho-ill intent mostly towards Westerners or modern western ideology . . . and believe this or not, is probably gunna haunt your heirs and great-heirs *way yonder ways* into the future when Marco's and *Fluff's* flyin' saucers start rollin' in for a night on the town, even if nothing had been done about no democracy nowhere! It's now or never! Don't mean to get pushy, it's just that I never thought I'd see another now like this never ever before . . . B.C or now!! If talkin' to a problem don't work? . . . then you tell me!! I really don't mean anything in reference to the last election but a total lack of respect, for any reason, some noteworthy, directed at an elected presidential candidate is nothing new and probably won't change. But this too will soon reach critical mass and cause major internal upheaval sooner or later that will do America no good. I don't know. Maybe it's time for a change like that? **This shit cannot go on forever.** By retaining and going back to my history, America has faced this before many times. How many more times before we just disintegrate into what we once were; hunters, gatherers and nomads? What will it take to keep ourselves unified? How many more World Trade Centers? You know, I never really cared for Congress. I believe I touched on that earlier. But this is probably the best reason. *This, to me, is treason* and nowhere in our history was that tolerated and if I had some say, **it wouldn't.**

FDR pissed off a lot of folks before WWII by interjecting a lot of government into people's daily lives because everyone was out of work and starving, so he started the New Deal and the TVA project that employed many people who needed help. But in no way, shape, or form was he depicted as a Big Brother Monster in art galleries, newspapers or billboards. The ACLU thinks otherwise. We're free so that means we can stretch and distort the First Amendment into whatever mood we happen to be in that day. Even if it means calling my female principle at school a skank 'cause she doled out a little discipline to me. That happened. ACLU said that's his right. I got rights too. Even got lefts and uppercuts. Enough has got to be enough!! If that principle were my ma, that ACLU lawyer sure wouldn't like me. My God! This writer is too violent some are saying. There are an awful lot of people out there who disagree with the ACLU. So far, everything regarding both sides has been passive, with everything being done civilly . . . sometimes without a handshake, but still being done the way civilized men behave. Alls I can say is keep on sticking thorns in the belly of traditional, historically based foundation America as we know it, and some ACLU lawyer out there might meet someone who makes this writer smell like blowed-smoke. Hope it don't happen but sane people can only take so much. The ACLU have taken cases in the past whose merits of the case were correct and rightfully so, they won. Problem is, that's far and few between. Every American has rights. However, when you screw them all up, the law steps in. If it's cut and dry, that should be it. The ACLU also doesn't see it that way. Somehow the reason you broke that law really wasn't your fault and the big bad man somehow has trampled all over your right to create havoc and terrify other people. With freedom comes rationality, morality, justice, compassion, sympathy, but most of all . . . sanity to differentiate between one over another. The ACLU believes that our judicial system is full of lunatics and they must step in to see that no one is trampled on. Civil liberties for all a free man, even the one who really likes little children of any gender, who's paid his penance to society and now has a guaranteed right to sit in the town park with all the little kids. Some town parks have stupid, asinine, and ridiculous rules like no running. I'd be more concerned about the "rehabilitated" psychopathic pervert rather than watching my little precious fall down 'cause he or she was running. What kind of braindead moron comes up with these stupid rules?

I don't see them going after the Nineth District lunatic fringe out in the Pacific western region. I'm sure the ACLU has got a lot of headquarters out in the Pacific western region, most notably is probably San Francisco. That's only a guess and I really shouldn't be writing down stuff I don't know, but that's an *edumacated* (with a yeuoo) guess. Well, let's see. The California voters voted down gay marriage but the mayor of San Francisco saw that the voters really didn't know what they were doing so he corrected that wrong and married them anyway. This sounds like ACLU land to me. A floating WWII vintage aircraft carrier wasn't allowed to dock there. Musta brought back bad memories of winning WWII. San Francisco, with the exceptions of the Giants, the 49ers, and the Hells Angels is a joke . . . an American embarrassment. I saw on TV a real along time ago and just again recently again on how the Hells Angels volunteered for duty in Vietnam for some of the sorriest missions that specially trained personnel do nowadays and were willing to train for that and got turned down. Sucks to know what your doin' and sayin' plus volennterrin' and get turned down as "boots on the ground" 'cause you got some kind of bad reputation. So don't street gangs but lemme see 'em do that!! Anyhows, *I left my heart in San Francisco* should be changed to I left my wristwatch in someone in San Francisco. As crude as that sounds, I gotta better idea, let's just leave it the way it was. But hey, what do I know? I do know this. They are still, and always will be, my people and I would do anything to help out anyone in San Francisco, just like anywhere else in the USA. I would probably get a thanks in return then a right cross to the head. After this little tirade, I would expect it. I'd expect more than one 'cause I can run my mouth just like the rest of ya'lls and I'm sorry if anyone is offended, but if yer gunna run yours, then I'll stutter mine like you wouldn't believe.

Three-hundred million of us ain't gunna agree on everything but I'm pretty sure all but about fifty would agree on this. Its where the ACLU stands on an exceptional group of outstanding American citizens to whom to me are *perfect fodder* for another Holocaust. These people certainly got the trait for that. They produce queers the same way madresses produce terrorists. Now, I for one do not believe for one instant that the ACLU or anyone else would stand up for this organization, but for years I've seen only on TV how this organization is well protected, so I will comment because by now I would have figured that they would have been disbanded or disfigured. It is an organization called NAMBLA. That means National Association of Man-Boy something or other. Guess what they do? Their motto is, "Sex after eight is too late." *Welcome to the twenty-first fucking century.* The ACLU says that because they are a national organization, it is their right under the First Amendment. Our forefathers never intended for the First Amendment to represent something like that. So, what do you think of them now?

They also say freedom fighters, i.e. terrorists or anyone associated with them also possess American-born rights. Say what? Just as Thomas Jefferson had enough of his federal judges and fired them all, serious thought should be given to something like this at a time in which God is mentioned numerously upon our documents of our inception and in no way separated itself from God, but only religion and key influential elements of our society who are standing too close to the forest and only see bark can dictate what the majority of folks don't want along with the ACLU lawyer's help. They could use some lawyers from real earth not rare earth, which would be middle earth . . . you know, with everything as you would expect in a Harry Potter movie, and what they stand for would be much easier to understand. If you want to turn America into Sodom and Gomorrah, then expect a real good fight. I hope I changed the other fifty's minds.

Freedom of the press is very important to them as it is to all of us. But a lot of us have something they don't have; national pride even if Uncle Sam has a black eye. Use our very system to hurt our system? Lacking common sense? Or just don't care? I don't know but I know this. I'm not gunna show everybody nude photos of my buddy's wife that I found up in the attic while getting out his fake Christmas tree while he's fixin' the eggnog. That would cause a lot of duress and cause a lot of commotion, do ya think? Some things, you simply must use your head first, unless you just don't care for whatever reason. Like those *stupid ass* photos at Abu Ghraib prison in Baghdad. Free press is free press no matter who gets scalped is their agenda. And with a vengeance! There's something deep down they don't like about law and order. Me too, but when wrong is wrong, why try to make a right out of it? Sometimes I wonder who Osama's lawyers are. Abu Ghraib. That was beautiful, showing the whole world the sordid, acrid underbelly of America. That was stupid. I wonder if these abused prisoners have made any calls to San Francisco. ACLU have already been to Guantanmo Bay. When I say America is going belly-up, I hope it's a dream and soon I wake up. We're doing it to ourselves, no outside help. ACLU people are still my people and you know the rest, another shot to the noggin. You're welcome.

Wonder where they or anyone else for that matter stand on New World Order? Remember that? Men in black suits, black helicopters, national ID cards, the revoking of the Second Amendment, and numerous governments and bankers covertly working together to enslave us all. Private militias were born from this. Wait a minute, oh my God!! That already happened!! How did I miss that? No, wait a minizzle. I still got my AK. Whew! Thought I was enslaved for a minute there. Who knows?, maybe a New World Order is what this world needs to contain the *no world order* that seems to be enslaving us all at the present. That-a-no-makum'-no-sense. New World Order is no world order. **I take no orders** from anyone who orders me with a new order about no order. Imagine that . . . a world without odor. One of the subjects that the ACLU is correct on, is someone's suggestion that all Americans must have a national ID card. They are against it, as I am also. Johnny would oblige by when asked for his, it would have a picture of one of those cavemen on the Geico Insurance commercial. He'd then smile, then blow a farmer snot for identification. Disgusting mu#ha$uc%a! They do go too far when they insist we don't need it when voting . . . or do they? We got some creepy muthafuckers out there is pros for the first, but I'm here to vote. Yeah, that's my street address, here's one of my utility bills for proof. What? That's not good enough? Sorry, but in this sorry-ass environment in which we live in, it's not. Why? I'm still not sure, but you know who's who and that's good enough for me.

The Second Amendment, America's favorite. The right to bear rifles, handguns, and cruise missiles. We're all entitled to them. Some people want to change all that. *Not going to happen!* It's written in our Bill of Rights . . . for reasons. Writing takes many modifications, especially when writing about stuff like this. On this very day, the Supreme Court is going to decide the future of the Second amendment. Now I'm certainly not above anyone, especially the Supreme Court, but I already decided on that. Come and try to take all my dart guns and see what happens!! People shoot people, not guns. This is pretty simple. Goes like this. People use guns to shoot people. Guns don't do anything unless people have them in their hands. ***Put the crime in capital letters if that's what it takes.*** What to do about the *something snapped* suicidal, sadocistic losers who indiscriminately kill anyone in their way while everyone's shopping at the mall or some school? . . . then kill themselves? Who knows? **How 'bout hanging their worthless, garbage bodies upside down on the public square for everyone to see what an *asshole* really looks like!!** I know that we're supposed to be above all that, but how much you wanna bet, no one wants to go down like that and would **think twice.** Too brutal? Then what do you got to do besides taking all my ammo away 'cause that's just not going to happen. Assault weapons should be sold to people who possess a class three-license, **no one else.** A class-two . . . almost, but not quite good enough. A class-one means anybody . . . only the basics though. Now I don't believe that once the government has all our guns, we will all soon be enslaved. Cheap labor, I guess. Some countries who work like this already, haven't succumbed to the temptation of enslaving us all . . . but some have. Most notably, some Third-World dictatorships. So let's not take any chances and pass the blue-dot so I can re-roll my bullets . . . three-thousand grain this time. Two-hundred and eighty doesn't penetrate inch-and-a-half kryptonite.

A bittersweet incident happened here in Georgia recently. In North Georgia, a stellar citizen carjacked some woman's car with her in it. She fought back, so he shot her dead and left the scene on foot and would have gotten away. Enter a more stellar citizen, much more who witnessed the whole thing and being right there, pulled his gun and blew this dickhead's face right through the back of his head with a real nice shot. I betcha he won't do it again. Next time buy a car asshole. Had he gone through the system, he would have gotten out two years later, only to do it again. And Johnny can't get a license after eleven years. Fuck the system, you weren't born rich or famous, idiot. How many times do I gotta tell you? Proponents of gun control would say, "Well, the carjacker had a gun." I would say, so didn't the Good Samaritan and leave it at that. Compare what sentences **child molesters are getting compared to eleven years.** Modern law needs to go back to Perry Mason and work with society for a change and get off all this I'm-on-TV-I-might-get-rich-bullshit and other fundamental judicial abortions for a lot of people to respect it more. Somehow, they get it when Johnny's hands and head are sticking out of the stockade, out on the public green. Okay, the cry has been sounded. We all must turn in our guns. Some would, some won't. Down here in the South, some people would oblige, but most will send you the bullets first. Hardcore constitution believers, the way its supposed to be. They don't get the blues, only sing them. *If guns are outlawed, only outlaws will have guns.* Read that word for word. **If you don't believe that, you'll believe anything.** Do you believe they put a boy on the moon? a boy on the moon? No, they put a man on the moon. Careful what you believe. No one is going to leave me defenseless!! Did you know that nine out of ten vicious criminals prefer unarmed victims walking alone at night? The other one likes likes a challenge . . . *believe that too!!*

Well, go to the fridge, grab a cold one 'cause it's time to toast Johnny. He's now gets four paychecks a month, equal to the same amount of weeks. *He has now stepped up to paycheck to paycheck.* Things are looking up. He still lies to bill collectors north and south and tells them he's still not quite working. His buddy Johnny, where he's staying at informs Johnny Rotten that he'll give him one more month rent-free but after that he has to go. He's got his girlfriend, kids, and grandkids staying and hanging there and he needed the room back for the growing family. Johnny understands. Too many Johnnies. There can only be one and Johnny wasn't it. Not that Johnny, the other one. While he was staying at Johnny's, he really wasn't working that much 'cause of past cases of spontaneous-vehicle-combustion happening all the time plus his legal matter with his privilege to drive. Privilege, not a right, and rightfully so since no one has the right to maim and disfigure you once they lose control of their car. In a way, it's an earned right 'cause it's one of the few for which you have to pass a test for. With certain conditions to be met for use of the Second Amendment and other laws which pertain to public safety, all others are given. He hears all these words, rolls them around inside his head for awhile, spits them all out on the table, then rearranges them all to say, fix your motorcycle. The poor bike just sits in the kitchen like a piece of broken furniture. Maybe to bring back the glory days, it's time to put the old bitch back on the road. If riding a Harley all day long doesn't help one sort out one's mind to the easiest it can think next to mathematical acid, the next best thing would probably be hitting the lottery. Nothing like the wind in your face, especially on the highway and the best part is you're never in a traffic jam. You can even use sidewalks like Johnny did, but face the risk of incarceration. From here on in, don't listen to me. He keeps his old horse in his kitchen in the trailer he now lives in to this very day and into the night. He repeats that process daily.

He's doing pretty good with work, just confining himself with linoleum and vinyl floors. He considers those the easiest. He's got people to drive him around from job to job and since he lives in the middle of Gainesville, he can walk to anywhere he wants to in little time. He walks to Applebee's Neighborhood Bar and Grill quite often and often walks back, except the one time when he decided to run. Felt good at the time. Twenty-four hours later, half paralyzed. He never thought about going to the hospital for temporary paralysis cause it could have mutated into a permanent paralysis once he saw how much it would have cost to quell a temporary problem. He doesn't have any insurance, none, not any kind except for on his van he uses for work. Last time he had health insurance was back in the postal service. While doin' pretty good back in Atlanta, he checked it out but because he had a family of five, it cost too much. Insurance for yourself is very obtainable. Just don't get married and have a lot of kids. About the same as rent. Our healthcare system is state of the art, the cutting edge of medicine and the best around. Just don't get sick. Not only is your health in question, so is your financial future. Especially if you don't have any insurance or government help. He has neither. If Doctor A and Doctor B all the way to Doctor Quack are practicing medicine and Doctor S, P, L, O, T, C and H have no problems with medical suits pending as they are with all the other doctors, how come they're all paying the same for malpractice insurance? Could it be zero-tolerance? Let's not take any chances, screw 'em all. What if Doctor Q never has any problems? What does he get? He gets satisfaction in knowing that he has contributed to the massive payouts insurance companies have to deal with 'cause someone's surgery was for someone else but because you had that someone else's name on your wristband instead of your own, you now have three legs, not two. It was just a small mistake, that's all. We're very sorry. We all make mistakes. Not in a < word that means yer' horny > hospital!!

So, you see the vicious circle, cut your throat insurance companies, stupid doctors and discombobulated medical personnel. And they're all at our disposal. When I say misfiring and miscommunication sprinkled hard with pure ugly incompetence, I didn't think back then that it would find itself alongside me while I was lying in a hospital bed. You go to a hospital and you're not sure if your doctor is competent or not while at the same time he's thinking about how many tonsillectomies and addadictomies he's gotta perform to make malpractice insurance coming up soon. No one's thinking about medicine, even basic procedure anymore. Too scared of the *not **when** I screw up but **if** I screw up* scenario that our corperate medical gurus have created.

Not all doctors screw up so why call in the lawyers on them too. Here's what we should do. Get rid of all the greed from over-expectant family members of someone not looking too good by some accident to some nasty disease. Get lawyer beauracracy out of the patient's room, that is of course, it's warranted. Medicine is like outer space, we barely know it. So how can some blow-job lawyer guarrentee something even a doctor isn't too sure about. Kill all the lawyers and make sure doctors are thinking about medicine again so this don't happen again. There's two kidneys. One's got cancer and they take out the good one? Even crazy ole' Klem Kadiddlehopper could figure that out. Not with hitman lawyer breathing down his neck! Incompetence brings the worst upon us. Problem is, we all gotta pay for someone else's mistake and that's just plain wrong. Given some time, I believe that I could figure out a viable solution to all this along with total revamping of our national tax system as we know and don't know it today . . . its five feet thick, but I would probably *come out of it* like Capt'n Blackjack Sparrow in the movie 'The Shining'. *A little bit better.* With the Fair Tax and mis-lawyer-management-free medicine, we're all alittle bit better. The day that big government controls every American citizen into its medical who's who and who's not list for medical care just gave me the right to show Big Brother how pissed little brother can really get for gettin'all up in li'l bro's face when he's playin' by the rules, *as stupid as some may be.* What happens between me and my doctor stays between me and my doctor!! If a lawyer wants to see, it would have to be for a damn good reason, not because he's entitled to see!

Oh yeah, what's up with the eleven dollars a piece asperin tablets that I hear about being charged by some hospitals? I'm already fucked once I'm admitted in your hospital don't < do me > me again!! I got an idea, make me better, not broke for the rest of my life!! Do you realize that if you got no insurance and you are on the downhill slide of life (over fifty or so) and you get real sick, then guess what? You might die a gruesome death. No money? . . . well . . . we'll see ya later. Take two these and hope it don't hurt that much. Nice < piss me off > system we got! And I don't think that nationalized healthcare is gunna work. Ever go to the emergency room and see it packed full of nothing but g.o.o.m.e.r's? That's exactly what will happen to the entire hospital building, every square foot, if healthcare becomes nationalized. It'll take you three years to get two stitches. But none of this tells me why there are no more doctor house calls. That's 'cause the assembly line lies at the office or hospital, not at your home anymore. Liability insurance on anything that could go wrong would, absolutely forbids it. You know what else can go wrong? Your health . . . if not checked, that's what. Health care would make much more sense if more attention was aimed at prevention rather than hoping that you caught it in time. A friend of mine with no health insurance and another friend who only has to pay the deductable on his, can't afford most anything preventive. That's because a colonostomy exam cost four thousand beans and a complete respiratory check-up cost about the same. You can thank a < lawyer > lawyer for that! With preventive measures used first, most potential problems would be nipped in the bud and drastically save the system lots of money. What!! . . . takezz a friggen' carpet-freak to figure dat out??

Wonder why we have so many stupid lawsuits? Someone at the window at McDonald's gives someone a coffee. That person drops it. Really bad place to drop your hot coffee. I'd rather get burnt in the face than that. McDonald's gets sued for what reason I still don't know. McProblem? Now if the person working the window actually took the coffee in the to-go cup and threw it at the person who got scalded, then I see lawsuit squared. That wasn't the case. I'm clumsy and somehow that wasn't my fault. You should have sent out five people to position my hands so that this wouldn't have happened. You erred, not me. I might screw-up every now and then. I just don't like to admit it. Especially when there's five mil riding on it.

The sick American way nowadays. Now we have the words “caution hot” on all of our coffees in styrofoam cups. No kidding!! I thought it was at minus eighty-five degrees. Thanks for telling me. Might have gotten hurt. The dumbing of America. You can thank your local insurance company for that for a couple of reasons that they'll probably agree with. When the word “caution or danger” is written on damn near anything you open up or whatever to get the product out, even on a carton of eggs . . . you do it wrong? . . . you might die; that tells me either one of two things. First, the insurance companies either thinks that most Americans have the IQ of a retarded gnat with no wings, or they're sick and fucking tired of paying out stupid amounts of money for something that really wasn't their fault. Look what Katrina and Rita are going to do to them.

Me and Johnny are gunna build both our homes on the Atlantic and Gulf coast. A stone throws away. If they're not constructed like the pyramid at Giza, then maybe no insurance. Could happen. Insurance is bittersweet. Insures us also to get *back on our feet*, even on a bright sunny day. Even when it was *my own fault.* Nothing like screwing up and laying there counting your settlement with the nice warm sun in your face. Take the pain, itz worth it. *You even caused it!* Just remember, *shit like this* was illegal way back in the early twenty-ith century . . . alot before and alittle after, and I think that we all should be responsible for our own actions . . . that's all. Lawyers who take on frivolous, stupid, and insane lawsuits need to be disbarred. What's a frivolous lawsuit? Call me, I'll tell ya. Call anybody else too. Everyone will tell ya also. Lawyers who practice clogging up the judicial system all the time by presenting all these questionable lawsuits should be disbarred for a certain amount of time when called to the carpet for less than professional behavior regarding the system. If done again? *Then barred for life.* See ya later peckerhead. Get a real job, one where you get what you make . . . professional or not, not what you swindle. What happens when I get called on the carpet by some plaintiff with a lawyer from inner hell who couldn't care less if his or hers client is somewhat flim-flam but as long as he's gettin' his. What if it's all legit? All hands above the table. What if I win either way? Then my astronomical legal bill which was caused by others needs to be paid by the others who initiated all this. That would be dickhead lawyer who thought that I'd fold like a house of cards in court but instead will file an appeal the very same day I won just to ensure the fact that I'll be working a legal bill for years to come. No bloodsucking bastard, get some Listerine lawyer has the right to push me around all over lawyerland unless he's willing to pay my legal bill if he loses the case! Likewise, if I see fit to sue someone who come across my path, hire hitman lawyer, then lose . . . *then that should be on me*. I just woke someone up and screwed him hard, probably thousands and the son-of-a-bee'atch is still wiping the sleep from his eyes!! Poor bastard, real poor bastard when the vultures finally leave!! No one has the right to *fleece me* by using the legal system . . . and I use that term loosely, unless he is willing to pay my legal bill if he loses. As one would probably see, most of these cases would be civil, with maybe a few criminal cases making it to the kangaroo courtroom where most of these cases are heard. Some of these hotshot lawyers need a reality check. While I'm paying off my "successful" lawyer tab, you be paying off yo' doctor bill at the same time . . . or dentist bill . . . either way, I'm flexable. You damn sho' won't do it to me again!! Screw a lawyer with *crossed up P's*, one of them meaning puke!! And I gotta clean it up according to our dinged-up system even when I'm deemed right!! *Suewage in the system.*

By now, Johnny's rolling along pretty good with work. One day while rolling down the road, they got stopped by the county police. Johnny was riding shotgun and wasn't wearing his seatbelt in his van. His buddy Scott was driving and one of Nick's friends whose name is Chad was working with Johnny for awhile. All three of them were questioned by this woman cop like in the interrogation room. She had all of their IDs which like I said before is proper protocol 'cause we're all a bunch of fuck-ups or something like that. She don't even crack a smile when she asked Johnny his last name and he said Rehab while looking at her cross-eyed. Next thing you see are four more police cars pulling up. Johnny says, "One of us is going to jail." Now all three of them are out of the van and the police know everything about them, even their sperm count. Is that a little out of hand? Are we all really that bad? Or, if you fit the profile of a potential public menace . . . you know one of those long-haired-hippy-punk-pinko-fags or a black Charlie . . . do you get specialized attention? Sheeplez-peeplez say, "Damn right." Anyone could say that with good reason. Just don't let anyone with long hair who looks like Johnny in your house. But anyway, another $64,000 question whiz kid. Bang-a-gong, 'cause something's wrong when they get stopped and almost got stripped-searched over a seat belt by over ten cops. Cops musta thought they were part of the Chicken-Dumpling gang. Words of wisdom. Keep your shit right on the road. Keep your shit at the house while driving right down the road. That's right . . . keep on listening to me. What'd I say before? They now know that Chad's got some problems, Scott used to be a Corrections Officer, and Johnny is the man they want. Cops everywhere. Over a seat belt. Remember one thing. Stops over seatbelts have resulted in arrests of a lot of bad people. To me, that's bittersweet. That's not the case here. This woman wasn't cuttin' anyone loose without a cavity search. Relentless. Cops gotta be that way, but when everyone is frisked and patted down plus surrounded by half the police force, lighten up ya frustrated bitch. Remember when I said his animal court case got lost in the shuffle? Well, they found it that very day and what a bad day it turned out to be. It was his own fault. He knew all about it but trying to live under a roof took precedence and everything else got lost in the shuffle. Plus, it's over dogs that really did no one no harm and he sorta blew it off. He had no idea what a mistake he made. They inform him that he has a bench warrant because he missed a court date regarding city ordinances. He's sick of bench warrants! He goes to jail by this woman cop who tells him that it's really over nothing and you'll be out the same night 'cause its really a miniscule charge and if you tell the correction officers the same you told me, you'll be all right.

Well, six days later, he's wondering if they crossed him up in their computer with some murderer or rapist cause now it's been a week locked up. This county jail is not the same as the other lockup. Here, you're allowed to swap food and he was in P block, an open dormitory, so you are with all the inmates all of the time. That made things a little bit better 'cause this is the south, not the cutthroat open dormitories like up north. Being in there for only a week doesn't qualify you for making store. He didn't starve though; some of his buddies helped him out, throughout the week. On his last day there during breakfast, he was served his tray that couldn't even feed an infant. He saw that and took it and threw the entire tray, baby food and all right in the garbage can. "I don't need you assholes to starve me! I'll do it myself!!" He went off and how he got out that same day is astonishing to himself and others around him. He was working at a carpet shop right next door to the jail and walked over there after he was released and ate up all the bagels in there that day. Animal control gave him another court date and the status quo was just that. They did not like Johnny one bit. But now is now and the court date is in the near future. This is where he decides to defend himself.

Some counties throughout the country need money to keep the bureaucracy booming, especially the one he lived in. I should get to that a little later but throughout America's recent past, some counties really had no choice. Not just counties but most of all states. Welfare, Medicaid, and other federal and state programs aren't enough to break the bank. Now we got deadbeat dads. Not a couple of hundred or thousand, but so many thousands that sent single moms running to the local and state governments for help. Something had to be done. Go to any jail and you'll be amazed on how many inmates are there for lack of child support. You don't pay for your kid? Don't get caught by us the authorities say. This also goes both ways, with nothing but bad things happening to both moms and dads. It's very easy to be a deadbeat dad nowadays 'cause it's very hard to pay two rents every month. Imagine paying your ex's boyfriend's rent every month. Johnny couldn't and refused to. You are going to go to jail anyways, why not take a piece of your ex's boyfriend's ass with you? It'll keep ya warm for awhile till it gets rigor mortis. After that, toss it. First of all, the states said enough is enough. All these thousands of desperate single moms need money and we don't got it. Plus that's not the state's job. That belongs to the family involved. All of them. Time for Dad to pitch in and rightfully so. You don't support your kid or kids? What kind of father are you? The old saying, "Anyone can father a child, but it takes a man to be a father all the way to graduation" rings loud and clear. Here's where that gets all muddled up. What if ma won't let you? I've seen custody battles that resembled parts of Iraq. Ma says you're a piece of bad work. You're not allowed to see my kids. My kids? What happened to our kids? Here's what happened. Some fathers care and some don't. *The state don't* ***have the time*** *to differentiate between the two.* This has nothing to do with zero-tolerance. This all began way before that. Child support is the most catch-22 situation there ever was. No one really knows who wants what or who cares for that matter. I got an idea. You people who no longer see eye-to-eye need to get down on your knees and look into the eyes of your child and see what he or she sees and work off that. Put the knives and pistols down and pick up your kid and assure him or her that both Mom and Dad are both there for you, one way or the other. Mom needs to realize that Dad can in no way pay two rents and the states need to lighten up on Dad. Being in jail for lack of child support equals being in jail 'cause you're poor. Overcrowded? With a little bit of leeway towards dad's paycheck, maybe a two-man cell will become a two-man cell again. Some fathers don't even try. Lock those pieces of garbage up till their beards look like ZZ Top. But the ones who do try, but can't, have some of the longest beards I ever saw. And that's not right.

Ever see a pretty divorce? Same as seeing a pretty suewage backup. Nothing pretty, no matter where you look. Here's where being a man is a major setback, no matter how long your shit is. I've seen people catch their wife red-handed, file divorce, then she gets everything. Some judges need everything at their disposal to see that something like that just don't happen at all. Some judges also need everything homeowner Harry can throw at him including a Muhammad Ali rope-a-dope twelve rounder for saying its okay for ma to fuck the New York Giants. When Dad is messin' with the cheerleaders, he also has the same smell as a nasty backup. What's good for one, is good for the other has no business here. One is just as bad as the other. But if you're going to run that route, Dad may as well smile at some cheerleaders, 'cause he's gunna get screwed regardless and may as well do it with a kiss. Ma could go through the entire secondary defense, get caught, then scream, "He made me do it! I don't know why I did it." Judge says, "I feel your pain honey. That son-of-a-bitch over there drove her to this and now its time to pay." This is from a friend of mine who in my mind got the *worst fucking* I've ever seen in court. If this ever happened to Johnny, this book would be nonexistent or extinct before its time 'cause he would have committed a double-murder right there on the spot. Including the judge. Three times lucky. He says that would never happen, but I'm not too sure about that. He says he would just walk away. Okay.

Crimes of passion are much harder for a *jury* to try 'cause it's spontaneous, spur of the moment, you open the door and "Oh my God!" Getting real pissed is only natural. I feel more sorry for the woman who opens the door and sees a cheerleader. What can she do? She might even get beat up, for christssakes! Some of the shit women take makes me glad I'm a man. But we're the ones who will administer justice in our own way sothat someone will always know that they really screwed-up every time they look in the mirror 'cause they beat the crap out of a woman. Or worse, a kid. Everyone should think like this. Most of our problems would be solved right there on the spot. No stupid judicial intervention that seems to care more about the perp the same way normal America cares more about the victim. Amanda has nothing to worry about. Justin, Nicholas, and Johnny. Johnny told me about someone in jail who did just that and killed his girl and her boyfriend or whatever when he entered the house and caught them. Johnny asked him if he always walked around the house carrying a rifle. He said to Johnny, "I knew." Jury's not gunna like that. The word jury used to command the law of the land, justice and redemption. Now some of it has also been relegated to underbelly, paid for in full justice and all of America, right and left, look at some justice the same way we look at flying elephants. How can that happen? Give me a mil, I'll make an elephant fly too if that's what it takes. Some high profile criminal cases from all the way back to Manson to O.J. have brought twice the sentence on half the evidence to ordinary folks 'cause alls they had was a public defender. Not that public defenders don't know anything. They're good lawyers just like the prosecution, but when the county needs to meet its monthly needs, indigent folks go down first no matter who defends them. *Empty bunks pay nothing!* Perry Mason would help but no one even knows who he was anyways. Makes no difference. He's no longer with us, but he was good . . . TV lawyer that is. I'm not too sure in real life. I probably wouldn't use him. Something needs to be looked at regarding jury gross incompetence and something else needs to happen to them when they puke up justice instead of administering justice. You want respect? your Honor! Then earn it!! When money makes Lady Liberty take off her blindfold to see how much, then you're no better than Al Capone. I wonder if the Patriots are gunna win three out of four years. That's my AFC team. For some reason, I like the Giants too. Ladies men. But anyways, a judge is only the man behind the curtain until guilty is guilty, and *not guilty walks out the door.* Not the other way around. I'm not talking about no misdemeanor or anything like that, 'cause the more I miss, the meaner I get. The meaner I get, the more I miss. The more I miss . . . Moral of the story . . . don't get mean and never miss.

But now Johnny lives right in downtown Gainesville. Lead guitars and movie stars. Not really but he's not surrounded by cattle anymore. He gets to know a lot of people involved in different trades just by hanging around Applebee's and other places. Some people really don't take him that seriously because he looks like he couldn't care less who you are, probably 'cause of having that *you gotta problem with me?* attitude most of his life. Sometimes he gets on a job and the customer really doesn't know what they got in their house until the job is done. Then they say, really good work and they're good friends at this point. Don't say anything; let your talent speak for you. This is an important notice to homeowners who pay for service work be it flooring, framing, or anything else. If all the contractor's hand tools are all brand new, you could be inviting disaster into your dreams. All of Johnny's hand tools are held together with duct tape and spit 'cause they've been used to their max, but he don't care. They're still good to him. Plus he can't afford new ones. Some contractors just re-upped on some new tools, so it's easy to get fooled, but always listen to Angie 'cause we're all a bunch of fuck-ups.

Carpet tools are strange items. It's the only sector of flooring in which many different hand tools that do only one thing are needed to accomplish the job. In fact, if you opened a carpet toolbox, you wouldn't recognize most of the tools that you're looking at. What the hell does that do? When Johnny was learning the trade with Dino way back, someone stole Dino's toolbox. They were in Hartford and after looking down a few alleys, they found the box and tools strewn all over the place. Apparently, the thief opened the box and didn't recognize anything, got pissed, and threw away the toolbox. He got them all back. When Johnny was learning the trade, it took him many minutes to figure out how to change a razor blade in a certain tool. Now he can do it with his eyebrows. In fact, he's the only carpetlayer I know who can cut in a room with either his left hand or his right hand. But he don't care. What he knows is not going to make him rich. Even though he could do the Empire State building in a week, he never gets the chance to get the money makers anymore and he now draws an attitude. He says he would rather be a runningback than a carpetlayer 'cause the money's a lot better and the work is a hell of lot easier. He works for many stores, many builders and for some reason, some cases his own, he only gets enough to get by after paying his help. He lost one store 'cause there was a dispute between himself and some dickhead builder over electricity. He needs electricity to make hot seams that bind one carpet to another. The builder calls up the store and says Johnny got rude and loud about it. That's not how you build your reputation, especially when working a new store and nothing like that ever happened. The store took the builder's word over Johnny's like he's some <really bad word> liar and he didn't even know what was goin' on! He always said, "You don't believe me? Hope I never see ya drowning. I'll just watch and yawn. Hurry up! You're starting to scare all the kids who are watching." Do unto others. And do it good. Thank God this stuff don't happen all the time. I don't care how good you are, you ain't gunna be working. Maybe night work, wearing a ski mask. And that's no good. Rule of thumb in the flooring trade; be anyone you want on the work floor, except Johnny. Even if you only got one tenth the experience, you'll do much better if your name's not Johnny Warts, even though he's one of the *best in the biz.*

He spends more time trying to figure this out than laying down floors. This is now taking years, same as all the rest of us so he really doesn't feel out of place. Just out of synch. No more MoJo. Never say that! Once that's gone, you could be mistaken for a man-made woman-dude! But anyways, he's learning more and more southern heritage with each passing day. He learns stuff like how war can sometimes be good. Like WWII. It unified America, not just by Pearl Harbor, but by something much different. WWII began eighty years after the end of the Civil War. The South still tasted bitter defeat from just a few generations after the Civil War all the way to the beginning of WWII. To beat the Axis powers, America pulled together with the Blue and Grey fighting together to win this one. Did you know that in Vicksburg; a very bloody Civil War battlescene, that the Fourth of July wasn't even celebrated 'cause it was a northern thing. Not so after VJ day when we defeated Japan with superior technology. WWII unified us. That doesn't seem so in fighting *no honor* terrorists nowadays. If some of America joined in on this fight, maybeAmerica wouldn't be the bad guy. How do you get to be a bad guy anyways fighting for something that is right? Take five to figure that out. And I don't mean years!

Maybe we're a bit too technical nowadays. Technology rules the world. Maybe so, but this is what I think about technology. It is good and bad. You can't beat technology. It can outrun your life. It can tell someone where you are. It can de-privatize your life even putting it online without your permission. It can also make life much easier and it can read your daily agenda faster than anything around. But there's one thing it can't read. *It can't read my mind.* That's why I'll prevail over any computer. To be left alone nowadays is somewhat difficult, but I know what it's doing. It has no idea what I'm doing. That just makes me a little smarter. Smart enough to see how hard it actually is to outrun technology. People who don't want to work steal identities faster than I can say my name. Actually, they're really not stealing my identity; they're really stealing my money. As said earlier, I got more respect for the street thug with ill intent just knowing that when he gets caught, he's all done for a while than some kapooter geek just ripping me off while safe behind his feminine walls. A little smarter isn't going to work here. Concealing ones identity should be as simple as just putting on a Halloween mask, but it ain't. Smartening up with technology is going to take some diligent work and devotion. Why would anyone want to outrun technology? is a pretty good question. Problem with the law? Bills? Or just a problem with privacy? I don't need all my personal shit plastered all over someone's kapooter screen especially on government pooters' (don't tread <*nationalize*> on me) and perhaps someday, I can do something about that. Believe me, if I can, I will.

Problem with the law. Johnny just can't seem to outrun that. He's finally put a handle on all that dope in the past. Now he's gotta work on our judicial system. They seem to like him or really not like him. It depends on your perspective on this matter. Some people are magnets for trouble whether you want it or not. He went to court again in December of 2004 for all his dogs that he hasn't seen in over a year and a half. His benchwarrant says he's got seven charges. Seven separate infractions that happened years earlier in which he has taken care of. If he hadn't, animal control would have eaten him alive with all the vengeance they had demonstrated towards him. Plus he had to, if he wanted to keep his dogs. That's still double jeopardy! To make a long drawn out story short, the county fined him four-hundred dollars regardless of the six days he's already served. His kids didn't have a Christmas in 04. The county needed to pay for a new courthouse and six days paid nothing. He decided to represent himself armed with time served in case he lost and thought he could pull this off. If you're gunna represent yourself, be prepared to lose.

Even mentioning that he gave Justin his blessing to the prosecutor when Justin decided to join the Army didn't sway anyone in the courthouse. Your son don't owe us, you do. In March of 2004, Justin shipped out for boot camp at Fort Sill, Oklahoma. Johnny saved all the letters he received from Justin while he was in boot camp. Johnny did mention in a letter back to Justin how Iraq will soon splinter into civil war or continuous guerilla war until the government and population of Iraq realizes that enough is enough and stands up for themselves. Fear of severe retaliation is enough to make most just sit right back down. Johnny, being pretty upfront about reality, realized that the absolute worst could happen and wrestled with that while Justin was going through boot camp. Johnny's ma wasn't too happy at all when he told her about Justin's decision. Some of our "famous elite" question the U S for trying to figure out why the Middle East spurns anything western, especially America. This means fighting back. I question why some people can't see the future by looking at the present. If you like what you see at the present, you know big bad America pushing the rest of the world around, then you would have fit in like a *jig-saw puzzle* back during the American Civil War with all that hatred being spewed all over the place. Alittle history lesson. All that passed. I believe it took a war to make that so. But the Civil War was national. This is global, but the theory remains the same. To all you utopians out there, I'm one your side but that's just never going to happen. Too much diversity in everything on this big 'ol planet that tells me that.

But Justin is writing to Johnny about his concerns about Iraq. Johnny responds by saying if you do go, just like Vietnam, don't touch anything. If it looks fishy, it probably is. If it don't look fishy, it also probably is. If you're walking point or first in the house, keep the eyes on the back of your head wide open and open fire first. They know you're coming. They wouldn't be there in the first place if they were the good guys. Leave the females alone, alls they are, are human shields. That's all he could offer but he lay awake at night just wondering. In 2006, Johnny's cousin up north whose name is also Johnny shipped out to Iraq with the Connecticut National Guard for a three hour tour. Alittle bit longer than that, and he served his country for his countrymen and for the betterment of all the world and that folks, is as noble as it gets. John McCain says no combat vet will ever have to stand in line for anything once back in the states. I second that motion. Some banks and mortgagers who take away the homes of people while on duty oversees should all be drafted for sniper practice at Fort Benning . . . *if you catch my drift on this matter.* That's not nice. All of America's wars were to save the world. Iraq is a war to change the world. For the better. Some could and would call that artificial change. Some say we should have more precise proof for the rest of the world. We do; 9-11. But we really need to fully understand the motive of the pissed off persecuted 900 AD souls who refuse to enter the twenty-first century so we can see with an open and worldly view of the earth's future along with the military who are dying to make that so. I call it natural change since with the way things are now, something's gotta give and it needs to happen now. That was pretty cold about insinuating about others who might not really like the military's worldly and sane views and not really standing behind them while they die. They even protest the American war dead at funerals here at home in the most disgusting, despicable ways. They couldn't care less for our Armed Services dying trying to help the world. I know most Americans are behind our military and I apologize for that but I do have a question. The fact that it's not all Americans means some of all of us are not really Americans. Might think so but your long dead grandparents would have been appalled at you for what you did to their generation's grown *morals and values* . . . but back to the question. Whoa!! That was a little rough, but true!

What's the difference between a terrorist and a freedom fighter? Some stupid Americans see a big difference. A freedom fighter fights to expulse an unwanted presence from its borders. Vietcong could be construed as freedom fighters, although the circumstances are slightly different. I don't believe I have to define a terrorist although the circumstances between them and freedom fighters are slightly the same. Wonder what the British thought of the revolutionary American soldiers fighting behind trees? Probably what we think of Iraqi insurgents planting booby traps all over Iraq. So some Americans believe we are now invading marauders. Others think the President lied through his teeth for war for the hell of it. The price of oil wasn't high enough. The only people jacking up the price of a barrel of crude are up on Wall Street. Yeah, I know he's an oil man and never really had to work, until now. And I'm also aware that the Vice-President is the major player with Halliburton, but think about what you are insinuating? Walking over dead soldiers for more loot? I don't think that even *the Riddler or the Joker* would have thought about something as despicable as that. It sure looks like I might be looking through a fogged up windshield, but I don't think so. Maybe I'm stupid, got fooled, but I got alittle more trust in civilized mankind than that. Something like that would make Jack the Ripper look like little Cindy Loo-Who. Wonder what would have happened if Americans said that about FDR? But no doubt about it, what we are doing in Iraq is forced changed, but in this case, not artificial. First of all, there is no difference between Vietcong and Iraqi insurgents. Vietcong fought for the right to tell South Vietnam that you will not change. You will do what you're told. The same as Iraqi insurgents. These people want to keep the Middle East or at least Iraq in the Stone Age. The planet is evolving and getting smaller every day. Either we all come to terms with that or war will remain for generations to come. The Middle East has been at war ever since the birth of Israel. Before I was born, and I remember J F K's assassination. That's because everyone is considered Zionist infields, whatever that means?. To me it means I believe what I want. No one tells me anything unless I want to listen! Convert or die. No ones gunna convert. But they might die if they don't. That's one of the problems. To be Christian and live in Iraq is like a mouse living in a cage full of snakes. It shouldn't be that way. I don't know the Middle East like you know Main Street, but I think I'm somewhere near the mark on that. Iraq wasn't Club Med before February 2003 and it's not Club Med at the present. But things get worser before they get better. But it needs the chance to get worser first as strange as that sounds. That's one of the reasons why were there. To force a change, most likely a change for the better. Forced change has always been very controversial, but with much of the Middle East festering to critical mass, past and especially present, maybe the future will show some desirable results from these wars we are now waging. Before these wars, there was no maybe. 9-11 could be a blessing in disguise and I'm extremely sorry for that last statement but that's just the way I see it. It seems to me that the Iraqi people are happy for a change to be allowed to make a change for the better. Under Saddam, most of the population seemed doomed to a life of a second class citizen. What sane leader of a county allows his two thug sons to carry on the way they did? That kinda crap don't fly anywhere else. Iraqi athletes don't get tortured anymore 'cause they got beat. That's no reason to wage war, but it's one of the results. They made some city street gangs we have over here look like boy scouts. Over here, it's illegal. Over there, it was condoned. Not just his two thug sons, but almost all the Ba'ath Party. You don't think most of the Iraqi people don't appreciate what's going on in their country in real time? Only common sense tells anyone that they do. All except freedom fighters. And American *commie media* who in my mind could use a couple of *real good* slaps in the face. And that's the difference between freedom fighters and terrorists. Freedom fighters fight for freedom. Terrorists fight for anarchy. In this case, there is no difference. Freedom fighters in this scenario can't even spell the word freedom. What should happen to people who protest or protested in the past in the most despicable and disgusting ways, dead Iraq war vets at their funeral? This question should be typed in capital letters. So shouldn't the answer. *But in BLOOD!!*

But when Justin only had one more week of basics left he was medically discharged because of scoliosis which is hereditary. He got that from his ma who by now is being treated for it. The Army docs told Justin that because of it, one of his legs is a little shorter than the other and they can't help him. Johnny wrote back to Justin after finding out all this that that's not your leg idiot, that's supposed to be a little shorter. Disregard that. But anyhow, Justin and his high school sweetheart, Candy, made Johnny a grandfather. Ethan was born August 4th, 2005. He's got a grandson. Nothing like carrying on the family name. Warts. But anyhow, I wouldn't compare Iraq to Vietnam. I would compare it more to Tet. A lot of similarities. Tet was only a small part of Vietnam, even though it was large. Like Iraq, it was guerilla warfare. Vietnam and Iraq have many similarities. Both enemies employed hit first and hard, then run like hell. During the American Revolutionary War, the colonists employed the very same tactics, most notably by using real long muskets for distant accuracy. Instead of lining up like toy soldiers just getting mowed down, they now had the luxury of sitting in the woods and picking off the enemy with the convenience of natural camo. The sniper was born. Conventional warfare wouldn't even recognize the sniper until around WWI. In the beginning, the sniper was considered dirty fighting. That's because he was smarter. Born and bread in America. Nowadays, they are an integral part of the military. That's a job I could do, only if I were good enough. You'd be amazed on how many people ain't. Actually, the sniper really showed his worth during Vietnam. VC did not like LRRPs, tunnel rats, recondo (all services), and they did not like snipers. Who does? Unless he's on my side. There was a price on all their heads. Wonder how many VC now live in the U S nowadays? Another damn good question whiz—kid! Pack a bong! Something really wrong when VC have oceanfront property on American property. Huh! Stay away from bongs, even the word itself sounds weird. Instead, send them all to this address. The Capitol, Washington DC. Got politics? Not anymore. We're all friends now . . . for a couple of hours or so. Don't do any of that either. I don't need ta talk to the F B I or Inspector Gadget again. Back to Tet.

Tet was a military disaster to the VC. But all their effort during that defeat was a major victory to their side. They didn't defeat the American presence in Vietnam by no means. Alls they did was defeat the hearts and minds of the American public. That was huge. They choreographed a guerilla effort that hit all through Vietnam in every major city during the same night, even hitting the U S Embassy in Saigon, which was supposed to be impenetrable at the time. American civilians at the embassy had to be shown by the military how to use a firearm to defend themselves.

Before Tet, all that was covered by an armed military presence. But because of this, the American public was appalled that some backwoods, jungle-living enemy had the capacity to do all this, even though they were defeated. To this very day, Tet is probably one of the main reasons why Americans cringe at the concept of guerilla warfare. Cringe or crunk, guerilla warfare is now the choice of all the persecuted. Guerilla warfare has been around centuries before BC. It's the only way David can beat Goliath, to this very day. *Iraq. 1991. Wide-open. Wiped out.* If it takes more than one time to learn a lesson like that, that means they all got wiped out and no one was left to tell the future what not to do. That didn't happen. Now they know. David is now learning all his schooling at your local Madrassa right down the road off to the left on Main Street. Not too much math though, only trajectory. Strange. Not to people like me. Strange to a stranged mind. Uncle Warts wants you. No strangers, though. People are strange when you're a stranger; people are strangers when they put me in danger. A danger of not realizing what letting people who if said no to, just blow up two complete blocks along with themselves sometimes which to me is socially unacceptable behavior no matter what your fucking cause is. People don't believe me either!! I wanna kill 'em or at least watch 'em drown. I can't do that 'cause all my earthly gots need to be gotten here on earth and there should be no spontaneous eruption 'cause I couldn't get it here. This is not going to help in the cause of peace and goodwill towards man. *Blind faith* decision making with catastrophic results toward your fellow man is not what our Good Lord is seeking. No faith is really blind especially the faith that led Jesus to the cross . . . voluntarily. Was Clapton ahead of his time? Of course, that's a Christian view. The Great "Mali Wali's" views are a little different. He's already condemned Johnny's earthly presence to a presence of *earthly hell.* Don't even have to die anymore. It comes to you now. Helping out your fellow man seems to make more sense to me. Who knows? It's obvious to me that the Muslim faith is a religion much more aware of its followers than most. Hassidic Jews practice their faith with the same zeal and dedication as all true Muslims. And they are true enemies to each other. The Jews being on the defensive while the Muslims on the offensive . . . depending on who you think wants what. I just don't understand the concept of receiving earthly pleasures once you're gone to the afterlife, no matter what you did to get there. I don't know about you, but my earthly presence has been nothing but bits and pieces of hell mixed with lots of good times. But mostly, it's been hell. But that was done on purpose 'cause it was more fun at the time. That's called temptation. It comes from hell. Why in God's name do I want that once I'm gone? If that's the case, then I'm not going. But I'll tell you where I am going. I am going to die. Old proverb; *death is certain, life is not.* It's tattooed on a friend of mine's upper arm. It's scary, that is if you are afraid to die. I know that I'm not really too cool with that. I'm not done screwing everything all up yet! I like misery 'cause I'm pretty used to it. Pain and misery . . . man!, I need a different plan! Surely it can't get no worser than this. Only one way to find out, but count me out. But when I do go, I wanna go the natural way; killer bees. Just like real men don't wear parachutes . . . the same here. Real men don't run from killer bees. Some people who commit suicide certainly aren't afraid of bees or death. Even back in the day . . . during high school, some friends of mine decided to make that one particular day their last. Just so you know, everyone will soon forget about you except your family. Even friends carry on and you are lost and forgotten. But family never forgets, with each day worse than the previous. *Just so you know.*

Palestinian culture hangs pictures of suicide killers all over town the same way we hang up pictures of athletes and music stars. Culture clash? Just a little. Can't we all just get along? Dead and gone. Cut and dry. Not according to organized religion. We are taught to do at least one good deed a day and be the best you can be just in case it's not so cut-and-dry when were dead and gone. What happens after death? No one really knows no matter what any religion says. Alls I can say is once you are on death's threshold and there's nothing earthly you can do about it, think about it as entering a new mysterious, never-to-be-seen-by-flesh-and-blood new realm that makes all the pain and suffering go away forever. That is of course, you've passed the test of life, otherwise the pain is only beginning. Dante's Inferno is schooling for the mean and wicked, but a little too late. I know nothing of how that school grades its pupils. Nor do I want to. Little tiny earth means nothing in all the cosmos. Maybe it does once we can see it from different perspective once were six feet under. All you atheists: Please stop laughing. Count all the stars and once you get up to a couple of kabillion, then try to figure out why you can't count the rest. Maybe once you're gone, you don't need to count anything. Counting stars might become as important and counting nothing. Natural or supernatural? The unseen but there? I don't know. Back to talking in circles.

But I do know one property that is natural, unseen and real. Totally invisible but affects our lives and all the cosmos since the beginning of time. And it has a by-product. This would be magnetism. Magnetism is the belief in the unseen because science proves it exists. I don't need no scientist to tell me that, just a compass. I don't want to get into the science of electro-magnetic psycho-fields like the ones found in black holes, but more to look at the unseen concept! Just because one cannot see something with their own two eyes doesn't mean your life isn't affected in some manner by something that might mystify someone, if even only for an instant, such as visions, dreams, deja-vu, or just plain karma. We're even affected by the natural energy expelled from magnetism. We all know that it's electricity. No magnets, no juice. That's universal. An unseen force gives us the capabilities to make life much easier. Magnetism also does that. Bad karma could be explained on the sports minded level. Look what the Red Sox do to their fans. They give them heart attacks and stupid high blood pressure during playoffs for decades. Before they win, they put themselves five and a half feet down before coming back. The 2004 World Series is about as classic of an example even though it's recent. Came back again in 2007 for more-for-the-taking World Series rings. This was good, but not quite as rough as the lose-before-you-win 2004 World Series that probably didn't help out our already screwed-up healthcare system in the north back in dem days. Bad karma? Probably not, more like typical Red Sox bad folklore. It's that old. Bucky Dent puts the last nail in the coffin back in 1977 with the only home run he ever hit. At least the only one I remember. Typical Sox, but they're still the best no matter what karma.

While watching the Discovery Channel one night about the earth's magnetic field, they mentioned something that sounded pretty disturbing. Sounded like the Philadelphia experiment. Not the *USS Eldridge*, but the whole damn planet. No one escapes. Seems that everything in the universe runs in cycles, even magnetism. Somehow north becomes south and south becomes north. Even our own earth, and they say, I don't know how, that it's due. In fact, overdue. Reverse polarity. And that's supposed to be natural? Wonder what's going to happen when that happens? The whole planet becomes poltergeist and we're all floating all over the place. I could dig that, just as long as once it's over, I'm not embedded in some rock cliff with my ass sticking out or something like that. There are lots of natural hazards in which we can't stop but only cope with. Floods, earthquakes, bad weather, volcanoes, the Teletubbies, and other bad things. Not that the Teletubbies are a bad thing, just a keep-your-kids-sucking-thei r-thumbs-till-they're-a-twelve-thing. Yeah, they are a bad thing. Johnny wants Ethan to be watching WWE Raw when he's two. *Die Hard* by three. Guess where the most volatile part of the planet is considering natural disasters? It's from sea to shining sea. America is a powder keg. Not North America, only America. It's been specialized for your convenience. How do you like Columbus now? Only in America exists tornados, the San Andres Fault . . . when that lets go even the moon is going to shake, the worlds worst volcano, a possible underwater landslide hundreds of miles off the east coast resulting in super tsunami, and hurricanes. *Katrina* was the first republican, racist hurricane I ever saw. Didn't know they've gone partisan.

What a mess it caused, even the carnage and destruction. It brought the absolute best and worst out of everyone involved.

First of all, I never knew that New Orleans was surrounded by walls of water. Talk about an accident waiting to happen. Second of all, the outpouring of aid and help from the whole planet goes to show me that the world is a good place and there is hope. But who's to blame? Lots of that going around. I blame the hurricane. Aid was sorely slow to get there. Evacuation was somewhat not taken that seriously. Lots of people thought we've survived Betsy and Camille, we'll survive this also. I saw on TV, the size of this hurricane. It took up almost all of the Gulf of Mexico. I would have gotten my young, punk,crazy white ass the hell out of there. Lots of buses sat idle. A whole lot of them. The argument was there were no drivers. Years ago, Johnny was walking down the street in his hometown during a fierce snowstorm. Here comes a city bus making its way back to Hartford 'cause the north part of his hometown was the end of the bus route and it always turned around at the same spot. This time the woman driving it got it stuck in a snow bank real good. As he came up on it, he saw she wasn't going to get it out. He knocked on the bus door and asked the woman driver permission to get it out. He got in the driver's seat and rocked it back and forth, just hitting the transmission just right, and backed it out to the street. He put it in drive and parked it. She gave him a ride all the way into town. He says anybody can drive a bus, just as long as you know the meaning of wide blind turns. I betcha next time a hurricane occupies most of the airspace above the Gulf, you're gunna suddenly see lots of bus drivers. I believe that all of those buses that seen Betsy then Camille four years apart from each other, metaphorically speaking, most of these buses probably don't exist anymore, said to themselves, "We rode out the last ones. We'll ride out this one." Many, many people were there to ride this one out. People expected excitement, not the monster they received. There were lots of monsters that day and night. Now, in the past, looters have been shot and killed and rightfully so. Best way is in the forehead! A looter here, a looter there but that's about it. That's 'cause many hurricanes, with the exception of Andrew, didn't result with the complete annihilation of a major U S city along with the total devastation two-hundred miles along the Gulf Coast. Even Andrew pales to Katrina. Katrina had an oblong eye that was parallel to the coast resulting in a much wider hurricane. New Orleans first got hit with a Category 5 storm surge, then another surge came from broken levees all over the place. Now we have a city that's completely lawless. Not completely. I do recall seeing that big black cop, a real big man with a shotgun on TV pointing it at people with stolen items. Everyone he pointed it at dropped their items. Did you notice how he witnessed a crime, pointed his gun resulting in un-stolen items but not arrest the person but move on to the next? That's because he was overwhelmed and seriously outmanned. The problem with shooting looters in New Orleans is that it could have resulted in genocide. I thought it was scenes of Baghdad. Police were even being shot at along with EMTs. Don't call me no racist, what happened in Baghdad right after Saddam's fall was also bullshit, and they weren't black. Third World if I'm not mistaken.

Lots of rescuers refused or were ordered not to venture into the flooded like you wouldn't believe streets and parishes, for fear of being a moving target. Hopefully there won't be another city that will experience complete annihilation like New Orleans, resulting in wild-west chaos, but if there ever is, the closest government agency to the chaos needs to gear up, then mount up and quell the problem . . . no matter what they have to do to make that so. Needs to be one of the first things done. The closest government, locals or maybe your county has an army base near it or every cop for miles around, hour's away, need to be back on mandatory duty. Not *mandatory* mandatory, but we got lots of problems. We could use your help. What happened to the police force in New Orleans was as close as you get to the wrath of God, completely immobilizing them. They had to worry about their own families, lost all their transportation, even the precinct headquarters, and had to deal with a mob rules environment. A smart general would retreat. Some became the very same public they were trying to stop. You know what I think of that. Farm animals do not belong on the force. The fact that mob rules made what had to be done all that more difficult is very distressing in modern society. The right to assemble doesn't give anyone, regardless of race, national origin, and all that shit, the right to disassemble by no means. Civil disobedience with extreme violence almost to the death should be met with the same force, to make sure almost to the death doesn't happen. Even a greater force. And don't no one call me no damn racist!! I used to chill at many a crackhouse in many a town for close to twenty years and I've seen the hopelessness, poverty, having to do things most people wouldn't want to do to survive, but really not having too many other choices, so they have to, and other acts of survival hard life. Some people got nothing to lose; some other people just don't give a damn. It's the ones that don't give a shit that screw it up for all the rest. Everybody knows that and I'm pretty sure a lot of the people stuck in New Orleans days after musta' thought no one gave a crap about them. I know I would have. I think that every major natural disaster like the December 2004 tsunami, Katrina, hardcore earthquakes, and the such is a slap in the face from God. That's a hard hit. It will take awhile to get up. But four days? The geographical location of New Orleans isn't in the middle of nowhere like where some natural disasters occur making logistics all that more difficult. New Orleans even has freeways going to it. You can even drive there.

The federal government just to make things happen, needs to go through forty-seven different chains of command just to get started no matter who or what the president is. But this was stupid slow. Things like Katrina don't happen too often. FEMA and our homeland security department are a sector of fuzzy and fuzzier. I just don't understand why they can't come off the starting blocks like sprinters. That's all. Don't call the feds. That's all I meant. Fighter pilots are the only people in government who know how to scramble. That's piss poor. That tells me that there are way too many chiefs and guess what? . . . they're all managers!! That's Federal Government 101: too many chiefs, not enough fighter pilots. Local and state governments could use some fighter pilots also, even if alls you got are Sopwif Camels. So, how come the locals and state weren't there first? They're closer. Sure, all the chaos is justified by the magnitude of the disaster, but after a couple of days get in there. If personal safety is at stake, use your National Guard, but get law and order to the people who want it and need it. That could cause some national uproar, especially with some people, but right is right and *mob rules* is wrong. People who don't give a shit really don't matter anymore and the ones who care come first. For any nation to remain a nation, especially one with might, it is incidents like this that show me that some people don't care about any nation, and when that nation is in serious peril, these people become merely speed bumps on the road to help. You go a little slower, but you still run them over. We're all in it for the common goal. If your goals interfere with that, then you are no better than some Iraqi insurgent. And you know how most of us feel about that. Those who don't can simply convert any time you want to . . . to make the world go away.

Who sang "Make the World Go Away?" Whoever it was, was light years ahead of their time, but I'm pretty sure there was no social strife in that song, only personal strife. That could be Johnny's theme song! He says thanks but no thanks, he's already got one picked out for his eulogy. While he's laying there staring at the ceiling of the chapel, you'll be paying your last respects listening to "Super Fly" 'cause Freddy's dead. Ran a 90 mil blast, went straight to his head. *Super Fly* gots his own idea about his last day in Oz, and there will be no funeral parlor rituals except only the party afterwards. He says he didn't spend his entire life on earth only to become some stone, rock, or creepy building in a cemetery once he's done all he could, can't do no more. So look to the sky, it's time to die. These are his last wishes and if one can't be done, the other must. First he wants to be contained in a shoebox, not a coffin. The funeral will still proceed for people to stand in line and pray to the shoebox. In this shoebox will be Johnny's shrunken head just as you've seen in the movies, with the mouth and eyes sewn closed with jungle twine and his ears shaped like points . . . just like Spocks. His hair will look like Zombo's . . . a character in one of the episodes of the Munsters. It's just his way of saying, "It's been real," on his way out. After the funeral, Justin or Nick can hang him off the rear view mirror for guidance or good luck. Put a smoke in his mouth for conversation. "How come your shrunken head is smoking, mine don't?" If that can't be done, then this should be done to emphasize what once was. Flush the toilet and dump in his ashes and also dump in his last beer and salute a fallen soldier who couldn't beat anything in life but himself. Myself, I prefer a more traditional way out on my last day on Oz. I wanna be shoved about twenty feet up a whale's ass feet-first along with all of my dogs, of course, so that on my way out to my second term I can honestly say . . . this time it wasn't my fault. But anyways, he's still alive so disregard all that crap. What was that all about? Scary. Let me put this thing out. I'll save it for later. A friend of Johnny's wants his ashes put in a douche so he can take one last ride. I like that. Me too. Maybe therezz sumthin' wrong with me, but ahh don't think so . . . I thoughtz.

But contrary to the belief, Katrina was neither democrat nor republican. *It looked like a natural disaster to me.* When did politics become cool? I thought no one could stand all those congressional crooks. Even stopped voting. Crook A or Crook B? No crook 'cause I'm staying home and snuff out my vote. That's not good. Everyone's go something to say. Say it. But the partisan on damn near anything has got my attention. What's next? Partisan aliens? Marco Alien is pissed 'cause the Big Dipper's gone republican? This partisan spin on damn near everything is only a symptom of a society of which one half of it refuses compromise, even in the face of hardcore reality for a reason which still remains cloudy and fuzzy. What kind of stupid shit we gunna hear next?, when something else happens? New Orleans needs to be rebuilt, only better. Same as what should have happened with the World Trade Center. That means fail-safe levees 'cause New Orleans will someday have to withstand another hurricane, then another. And so on. When the levee breaks, Mama you got to run. That's already happened. Next time it shouldn't break. The Dutch can reclaim parts of the ocean with superstructures that rival the ancient wonders of the world. How come we can't? How much will it cost to achieve that? Because living in a free country isn't free at all. In fact, very expensive. We've practically priced ourselves out of constructing wonders of the world to rival our ancients 'cause I can't imagine what it would cost to reproduce the great pyramids at Giza. Money couldn't be printed fast enough to pay for that. I'd like to see it done anyway, the same way the Egyptians did it, just to see if it can be done by modern man. Don't call me! I'm fishin' somewhere.

But down around the Big Easy, containment of water has been a problem as with this story I saw on the History Channel. A little while back, there was another problem with another lake somewhere near New Orleans. I caught this on TV and was absolutely amazed at what I saw. This lake just disappeared right before your very eyes. Actually it splilt into an enormous salt mine located directly beneath it. I don't need salt bad enough to crawl around underneath some lake looking for it. I'll just use heroin. Looks the same. Anyhow, while drilling for oil in this lake only four-hundred yards away from this massively enormous salt mine, a fourteen inch drill bit found the ceiling of this salt mine. This mine was so huge; it took two days for the lake to fill it. As a result, this fourteen inch hole expanded into a huge cavernous gaping hole that turned this lake into a giant whirlpool, even sucking down boats and barges half the size of a football field. A terrestrial black hole. When the salt mine was completely filled, equilibrium was established, resulting in many barges popping back to the surface, many of them capsized. This lake was reduced to a puddle and was the only time the tributary that ran out of it to the gulf reversed itself. The gulf replenished the lake with spectacular waterfalls, filling up a now extremely deep lake. Imagine being the person operating the drill that day? Whoopsy daisy! Sorry 'bout that. Sounds like a distant cousin to the Warts clan.

Anyhow, America has gotten its first taste of total natural disaster resulting in the loss of a major port city. Now we know what not to do. If it happens again, not the natural disaster itself, but the mindless chaos that followed it, then the days of learning from history are over and the U S is forever relegated to an empire that will soon find itself extinguished. Stupidity is not a trait found in leadership. But as I said before, the help that followed was soon under siege. Even in the safety of the superdome, crime was rampant. So what is one to do? One of our constitutional amendments says no military action will be aimed at American citizens. What kind of army is that? "Point the gun the other way, fool! We're on your side, remember?" Is that really true anymore? I was disgusted by the episode involving the branch divisions in Waco, Texas back in 1993. No one likes cults, especially ones that advocate child molestation but I don't believe that military intervention was the answer. There was no viable force visible enough to justify that. What they should have done still remains an issue of trying to get the job done without calling in the military. That's still a question with no answer. But not in New Orleans. In the future, when total chaos rules the streets and the police aren't the answer anymore, then it's time for the National Guard to take matters in their own hands. This also pertains to massive civil disobedience anywhere in the U S, when the lid can't be put back on the can. What happened in New Orleans reminded me of the Bolshevik revolution and I wasn't even born yet. But I know alittle. The ones who care need to take care of those who don't. It's a safety issue. I thought we all wanted to be safe, that's all. Motorcycles are the answer. If anybody in the Wild West parts of any town wants instant respect, then ride a motorcycle. You can cover more turf on a bike. Plus you look better. That would be a fly way of finding a solution to the pollution. But aside from that, when something goes wrong in America, people who can't accept blame look for scapegoats to exonerate themselves 'cause after all, how could this be my fault?

This really isn't anything new. Admiral Kimmel was blamed for Pearl Harbor. He was in charge of Pearl Harbor at the time. After eight or so federal inquiries, it comes to find out that the Japanese were really at fault. Congress has never really changed from then all the way to now. Blame the stinkin' perpetrator, not the victim!!! Anyone remember in the movie *Jaws* when captain Quint was explaining the demise of the *USS Indianapolis?* At the very end of WWII, that ship dropped off its atomic cargo at Guam then proceeded to rendezvous with a large task force. It got torpedoed on the way and sunk. Four days and many sharks, later, what was left of the survivors were finally rescued. WWII ended August 5th, 1945. This happened only six days prior. The captain of the ship somehow was blamed for losing his ship. The Navy didn't want to fess up to the fact that four days is a ridiculous amount of time to launch a search and rescue, and during some inquiry, instead of blaming the Japanese, they blamed the captain. He finally couldn't take it anymore, and in the Sixties, he killed himself. The phrase *question authority* isn't there for rebellious reasons only, its also there because of cases like this. Authority does not mean smarter. Sometimes it means you got no right no matter how right you are. Katrina is over. Get off the blame game and fix the Mardis Gras. Johnny lays floors. He would love to help. This is kinda strange, but he told me he's never been laid by a floor, but he sure has been fucked by a few. That's 'cause he did it her way. Well, I hope we learned something from all that.

Johnny learned that most hurricanes' paths go right through the Bermuda Triangle. Somehow that's all he learned. He wants to learn what happens when you witness a fierce hurricane when you are right smack dab in the middle of the Bermuda Triangle. Go right ahead. Tell me what you found out if you make it back. He's a crazy homosapien . . . the worse kind. Anyhow, things have taken a turn for the worse. Johnny's paycheck-to-paycheck existence existence has all but dried up. One carpet store that kept on ripping him off. Another that thinks he ain't nothing but a low-life liar. Ain't no life like low life.Another one that he had to replace a huge linoleum job he did 'cause it failed. The conditions weren't right but he did it anyway. That was his fault. It was the only job he had on the books that week and he knew he should have flagged it but didn't. It was too wet out and he shoulda known better but with all the completely unsuitable substrates he was told to lay linoleum on, he thought that it might work out. When you leave the job with your fingers crossed, you really don't have a leg to stand on when it blows up sometime soon in the future and in your face. Up north, some of the substrates that are legal in the south have been illegal since the Eighties. From now on, it's his way or find someone else to be the fall guy. Another Ford van that he bought. A 1991 model. Guess what blew up? He now has a real nasty attitude and wants revenge. He now wants people under his feet. He wants blood flowing down the streets three feet deep. But he keeps his cool. He wants no more trouble. He's pretty damn good in the biz but can't get off the starting blocks. He's got a problem.

Now he's got another problem. Nick was arrested and this was serious. He knows how to juggle problems. You can't ignore them. They'll just get bigger. In front of any other judge, this could have been bad. If Justin wound up going to Iraq, Johnny would then have both sons to worry about. When Johnny got divorced and moved up to Gainesville, Nick decided to quit school in the tenth grade. He's now at the present, pretty adept to a little street life. Anyways, while driving without a license, he gets stopped. Looks like this is a curse that's never going to go away. It's even hereditary. Anyway, the police go through the entire car. If you're not legal on the road, I can't see where that wouldn't be constituted. That's the only way, unless you're wanted. I'm pretty good with the Fourth and if shoved in a corner, will plead the Fifth. Anyone who pleads the Fifth got something to hide. Or takin' the hit. That's loyalty. That's pretty rare. I'd better get a *twelve-pack of PBRs* when I get out. But anyhow, the car got stripped searched and they found more than an ounce but less than ten tons of pscho-Popeye spinach. Not really pschyco, It just didn't do the same to Popeye as it did with Olive Oil, especially the goons. And with other people who smoke it rather than eat it. The goons look like they invented it. Johnny's not too happy about this. No parent would be. Some parents would say, "What did I do wrong?" Some parents couldn't care less. Some have no clue, but not here.

To a lot of parents out there who are wondering the same thing, I think it goes like this, trying to show your kids right. Tell 'em why it's wrong. If that's a problem, spanking at age sixteen ain't gunna work. If that's not a problem, you still probably did nothing wrong. I'm not gunna blame society, even though that's debatable, but rather blame an old Sixties saying that's always gunna be with us. Goes like this, "Do your own thing." It was cool for alittle while. Kids are impressionable, especially Generation X, Ys and Zs. Especially when they become old enough and start spending more time with their friends which is inevitable. I think we brought this upon ourselves with our hectic daily schedules. Johnny don't buy that. Neither do I. If your schedule excludes the kid or kids, something needs to be rearranged. Tell that to single ma who doesn't have a choice. Johnny might not buy it, but I see asocial problem that's been around for a few generations. But you're still a parent. Nick knows the same as Johnny when Johnny was at that age. If not, more. Johnny certainly wasn't stupid in his early twenties, just careless. But careful enough to not get stupid, but sometimes that's gunna happen. Drop your guard for one second and you might have a problem. Keep your guard up for ten years before that, then drop it? Then guess what? No one cares about the ten years, only the one second. Johnny and his wife brought up Justin, Nick, and Amanda the way you're supposed to be brought up, knowing right from wrong and if wrong is what you want, at least keep your heart and mind on the people around you, especially your mind. And there is a difference between bad people and bad decisions. Nick made some bad decisions and Johnny could never turn his back on his son who seems to be a reincarnation of something he once was, and sometimes still is when he gets bored. Other baby boomers do just the opposite. That's why they called it flower power. How much power is in a flower? We all know by now. Not much. But a whole bunch in a Venus flytrap. Johnny had some of those. Pretty damn wild the way they eat. Now thatzz what I call real flowa' powa'!

But like most parents nowadays, we all can't be with our kids all the time, especially when they're in their late teens. Soccer mom's can, though. But those ain't no kids, they're more like prisoners. Alls you have to do is instill upon your soon-to-be adolescent offspring is that life is good, but not fair. Keep your heart in the right place so that when your mind wanders, your heart is big enough to pump whatever into your mind enough sanity to differentiate what you're about to do and why it's wrong, along with the consequences. That's all we got as parents, especially nowadays. That's definitely nothing new but these times in which we live in work against us more than ever. Capitalize the words *sacred morals and values* and why those words made us what we are at the present. But parents have to actually be there to make that happen. We all know how hard that is. Johnny knew Nick was his own carbon copy and worked with that. He knew what to do because of that and told Nick the consequences of legalities or worse, dropping your guard and letting' someone else do your thinking once that happens. I'll take the police over that any day. At least I'll know why I'm in handcuffs. But since at the time Johnny lived kinda like in the dark, along with geographics that required not gettin' in trouble while driving around to close the geographical gaps, sometimes it was too dark for his kids to find him. But anyhow, what Nick gets caught with is enough for a good stretch behind bars. What these cops do is what a lot of cops do to make the arrest of someone look bigger. Can't blame them for that. First, they scare the shit out of him with the threat of ten years and they said they'd make it stick. They got a real good way of scaring the hell out of you, especially when you get caught with dope. Second, they want him to roll over on some Mexican dope dealer. There's a lot of Mexicans in this part of Atlanta. Third, they tell Nick not to tell his parents. In return they write Nick up an infraction for less than one ounce of chronic. That's way less serious. Nick takes the deal, then tells Johnny. Johnny is incensed. He knew family would get involved, and they did. Nick plays it out to see just what they had in mind and who they had in mind. This goes on for a few months 'cause the people the police target know Nick pretty good even where he lives.

At that time he was staying with his Ma down in Little Five Points with her boyfriend and Amanda. The way it was set up was pretty foolproof, and they probably wouldn't suspect that Nick was the leak. Nick wasn't going to take that chance. After a couple of months went by, Nick was still very concerned about the bear trap he stepped in and all the time the police mentioned. Nick was not going to snitch and he and Johnny talked about it repeatedly. Johnny was not happy with the fact that the police had no regard for the safety of most of Johnny's family down in Little Five Points. Actually both the police and Nick were between a rock and a hard place. Most of the targets Nick knew and said no to the police, made him realize that they didn't care about his family and told him to do it anyways. Johnny could not confront the police because Nick would have been instantly incarcerated. He was pissed and told Nick to take his chance in court. *Thirteen and a half.* Twelve jurors . . . one judge . . . half a chance. Nick had already made up his mind when he took the deal in the first place to not take the deal. Nick and Johnny wanted to see how the police worked. They were both disappointed. Maybe they wanted something less than dangerous, but that was not the case. That's wishful thinking, but sometimes wishes come true. When court day comes up, the court has Nick up on a charge of less than on ounce of spinach. Plus no driver's license. When the prosecutor reads the charges to the judge, the two arresting officers who were also there intervened and told the judge what really happened and nothing more. This pissed Johnny off so bad, he turned to the police and said, "Tell him the rest. You forgot something." They failed to mention the deal they made to Nick. They only mentioned the quarter pound of pot and nothing else. The judge wasn't too happy about the lie that was written on Nick's docket the prosecutor gave him. The prosecutor didn't know. You know that the judge recognized Johnny! I've seen you before in here. Johnny responds that he laid the carpet. He really didn't. Johnny then tells the judge the whole story. He tells the judge that he was the one who puts the brakes on the whole police deal. He points out that these two officers had no regard for the safety of his family while pointing to his ex-wife, who was also there. And he was pissed at those cops. The judge is visibly not comfortable with the fact that all this came from Johnny and not the police. Nick was re-arrested right there, made bond, went to court again and got probation. A happy ending. Could be happier. It couldn't have happened at all. The police were just as pissed at Johnny as he was at them. He was dropped off at the courthouse by his buddies who then went to a titty bar about a half a mile away. After everything was over in court, he's walking to the club to meet his buddies. The road to the club is on a main drag in metro Atlanta and while he's walking down the sidewalk, the police are trailing behind them in their cruiser on their loudspeaker telling Johnny all kinds of things like "Stay off the dirt. Get on the sidewalk" and other things he was trying to ignore. They scared him real good. He really pissed them off. Like I said before, they were only doing their job the way it's done sometimes, but this was too scary and dangerous. All and all, most of our police force are good people, real good people to take the risk of public guardian and some of the things people do make me wish sometimes they had the power to be the judge, jury, and executioner right there on the spot. Wishful thinking.

By now, all that has passed and things are good and bad. It was the best. It was the worst. It was the best of the worse. He makes money solely from whatever calls he gets off the cell phone. Just from people who know a friend of a friend, family member and occasionally a builder or two. He was considering going back into plumbing for a friend of his in town who owns a plumbing shop. He gets by though. He also does work for someone who does large commercial flooring jobs all over the southeast. Road trips are a *gas, gas, gas*. Charlotte, Daytona, and Wilmington were good times, but a lot of ball bustin' work as well. He thought Cape Fear was just the name of a movie, not an actual town. But he's also waiting for his patent for his kneepads to come through so he can finalize the deal he made with the company that's interested in them. That ought to be something. This is what he needs. This is what anyone needs. But in the meantime, he knows what he is. He's a good father with virtually no resources to help any of his kids if anything goes wrong. He also knows that for every passing day, the uncertainty remains the same. He'zz a real mix-upped man, livin' in a ga'bage can . . . izn't he a bit like ya'll and meeee. ***When will all this end?*** He is no different than you or me. Well, maybe a little different. He's lucky he's not carrying a big house note like in the past. He'd fold in a couple months but he sacrifices a lot just to make ends meet and they do meet.

He now has found out that his favorite holiday, Halloween, is now also under attack. Some school has renamed it the harvest party. I've been to harvest parties after tobacco harvest and they are nothing like Halloween at all. Johnny was at a tobacco harvest party when he was sixteen. His buddy is going down the road in his van and Johnny goes to flag him down. After two bottles of Boone's Farm, he flags him down but for some reason, he walks in the road. Well, he looked like a thirty yard field goal. The van stops, Johnny lands and gets up like nothing happened. After ten minutes, it never even happened. But anything but Halloween!! What did Halloween do to piss someone off? We get to dress up like witches and goblins. What's wrong with that? It's nothing but fun and games for cryin'out loud! And besides that, it's not even an American founded holiday. Halloween, like Christmas, has its origins through religion and Halloween is even older. Check out a documentary like I did on the History Channel. Stuff you had no idea about right there on your TV set. Between that and the Spice Channel, sometimes couch potatoin' ain't all that bad. Halloween is great but I guess its too much fun, probably. Can't have that anymore. Might live longer. What about the Great Pumpkin?

Well, let's whip out the 'ol crystal ball and see what the future has in store for us. Pretty ballsy statement, I'd say. These are my quatrains. Nothin like the originals, but I'm gunna try. This is according to Lump-Lump MaGoo, one of the strangest of the MaGoo brothers. *Lumpy* likes to lay low nowadays but has a pretty good insight on lots of things. *Change will no longer be natural.* Putting a square peg in a round hole seems pretty much impossible, but it's gunna happen. Vocal minorities know very well how to redefine our existence and for some mysterious reason, they gunna make it work. The police will be allowed to assassinate speeders. Just kidding. On the economic home front, people will continue to fuel Wall Street and many fortunes will be made. But for a whole lotta other people, the word work will be with them many years after an imaginary retirement. I see the gap widening. Anyone can see the gap widening. Competition for jobs will spiral as the supply catches up with the demand. One reason will be larger populations. Another reason is there will be more demand for cheaper labor overseas than in the U S. We haven't priced ourselves out of the market by no means; we just finally discovered an untapped human resource that will work for much less. There's no end in sight on this and this will get much more serious. Dollar loyalty will dominate national loyalty. Americans will go through a sort of Renaissance to deal with this dilemma. One good way to cope with and actually win the battle is for the emergence of many more Mom and Pop shops to cover what big business left behind. Americans aren't gunna fall down over this. This could actually work in our favor. If a town doesn't have a Wal-Mart or Home Depot in it nowadays, it's considered a village, hamlet, or just a gathering place. Look at all the items for sale in those stores. They have many vendors and contracts many of which are in the U.S. Mom and Pop would have a hard time competing with the real cheap labor. Retail Mom and Pops really can't compete although a lot do but with a specialized service or methods. The Mom and Pops that I'm talking about will come mostly from the manufacturing and service industries, both trade and professional. Small business will become booming business. The word *pension* is getting bits and pieces chipped off it daily and no one wants to work forever so I don't really see it any other way. Job outsourcing isn't going to choke us . . . it's going to make us better. But it will get worser before it gets better.

On the science front, things will happen that will make many question why they're happening. Playing around with the design of the human blueprint will question the conscience of many a mind except the ones blazing these God-like trails. Genes and chromosomes will be altered to make super humans. Steroids will become obsolete. This will all be done to make us better. No defects. Good or bad? Don't make no difference 'cause it's gunna happen. If it can be done, it will. The human race will go where no ones been before. It takes God's natural selection method and turns it into hand picked selection. I don't mind pissing off other people, but I'd rather piss off a Great White shark than piss off the Man. Science will soon have the ability to mimic in a God-like way what many people believe should remain God-like. Stem cell research uses parts of dead humans who were never given the chance of life to heal those who were. That's super catch-22. Other sciences in the future won't question such a moral dilemma as medicine will. Space shuttle needs to be scrapped and serious thought needs to come up with something that doesn't have fifteen million moving parts in it. Bending the crap out of gravity works, but I guess we'll just have to wait on that. Plus, you could easily overshoot your destination and wind up in San Francisco by accident. Actually, San Fran is a pretty town according to Nick. He's been there on jobs in the past. It just seems alittle extra-terrestrial to me.

On the subject of global warming, our climate is going to turn itself inside out. Hurricanes feed off warm water at least a hundred and fifty feet deep. That's pretty damn deep and some say global warming is the reason for such a warm depth. The ocean's pretty deep to call a hundred and fifty feet deep. Most likely, it's natural but then again, it's very easy to conceive all the smoke and ash released into the atmosphere since the firing of the very first furnace to your automobile sittin' out in your driveway. Can the earth continue to cleanse itself at such a rapid pace, or can it soon overload with such a workload? For most of the Soviet Union's existence, they put the P in Pollution with capital letters. They existed during the heyday of the industrial revolution and cared less where all the waste material went for some seventy plus years. Plus China cares less right now about the same damn thing! I'm sure that's all added up to the job Mother Nature is trying to do to cleanse herself. This is like the dog chasing its tail. Not only does all life in the animal kingdom, including Johnny, produce carbon dioxide as waste, so do man-made engines and mechanical engineered existence. That's a big word for other motors. Natural equilibrium gives the plant kingdom carbon dioxide as the fuel and oxygen as the waste so no ones run out of anything. The more plant kingdom, the more carbon dioxide that gets consumed. So what do we do? We chop down all the fucking trees we can see and turn the tropical rain forests all over the planet into parking lots, complete with strip malls! Lots of exotic hardwood floors nowadays are made from these trees. Turn these floors down. Don't use 'em. That's almost sacrilegious. Like ripping out your lungs. Instead use a number two red oak, two and a quarter inch width with a natural stain. There's no wood floor that looks like that. All kinds of colors. Prettiest floor I ever saw. Also, the prettiest floor I've ever laid.

The equilibrium is slowly being tilted with more humans and declining vegetation. That could lead to famine, disease, or natural disasters or better yet . . . all three at the same time. The earth constantly changes, from the ice age to continental drift. Alls I'm saying is that we are throwing some artificial into nature. Those two mix like oil and water. By removing all the oil in the earth, or more than we should be, which I believe is the grease between the gears (continental plates) which float upon all this oil, could maybe sometime in the future cause some of these continental plates to seize and buckle up. Sorta like running a V-8 with no oil in it. I also think that if something like that happened, it would cause massive 20 point fives on the Richter scale that would pretty much wipe out all those on the surface. Stay in your basement when that happens. That's right, keep on listening. Something like this, though, would make that psycho volcano under Yellowstone look like a pimple on King Kong's ass. This might also mess with the earth's degree of rotation. Something also like that could be construed as the grand finale of 'The Book of Revelations" when all hell is released upon the earth when Armageddon is coming around the bend.

Anyways, I think I found a girl who wants to go out with me. She's been riding a dead horse for along time and she's always werin' a black, twelf century grim-reaper get-up like some kinda runway supermodel scarecrow and I've never been so scared of a woman so far in my entire life!! That's 'cause she always dissappears when she turns sideways!! Scares the living shit out of me!! And I was married once. The hell with a chicken leg!! Need to stop . . . don't want some part in making the word *leg* politically incorrect. But what about "legggggzzz?" Dems da ones ahh like. The best part is when you finally makes it down to the feet.

Well, let's stop thinking about chicken legs or how to keep on keepin' on, but no one I know knows a supermodel, but imagine being in an airliner during that? Hey pilot, you may as well fly this thing to the moon. Cosmic rays will heat up and cook all the cheese on the moon and it will explode. Whether or not we have seriously harmed the planet or have done nothing at all will only be told by the passing of time, but I see real long hot summers, shore lines getting closer to the beach front bungalow, crazy weather, and then an ice age. Something that was going to happen anyways. We just sped it up.

Something else is also going to speed up. That would be American resentment *south of the border* due to clamping down on border control. Everyone knows that, especially the White House. This will need serious attention and will require a damned-if-you-do-damned-if-you-don't approach. Warfare. Considering our present, that's not too hard to figure out. First of all, one side will even it up, one way or the other. As we degress into the future, technology in the wrong mindset will make a superpower buckle at the knees. Don't think that a super-duper-can't-be-sunk aircraft carrier is invulnerable to whatever lurks twenty thousand fathoms under the hull, 'cause someday, it might become front page news. If they can get nuclear, then what else can they do? And also keep in the back of your mind that the brutal (death means nothing) suicide charge that has been employed by many a empire: past (Japan) and especially present (Iran; the Iran-Iraq war in the Eighties) could happen at any time. On your toes and on top of your game couldn't be any more realistic than really, really now, especially in real time. We are waging a war(s) that these people wanted in the first place back when all these new found "political experts" on *fantasy island* . . . mostly with our coddled whorno stars in Pornowood who had mommy scraping their little baby diaperholes as toddlers 'cause some of them were only two or three at the time, same as some of these toddlers now: some now even in their 20's or 30's, maybe 40's? as I spew right now . . . while all the rest of us watched all of this *fanatical theocracy* born before a time when a gallon of gas was only thirty cents a gallon unfold into the eventually un-equalibreumlated, no-remorse and somewhat ugly world which plagues us at the present. Say that three times!! Now-time is no-time for the Cub scouts to be steerin' the Enterprise through these make or break times that are-a-comin' like a bullet ***like they were adults*** or sumthin' like that. If I were Ahab-the-Arab, I'd vote for Osama too . . . makes Ahab's job a whole lot easier. Time for a change we can believe in. *Or you can make pretend in a make-believe world.* Little green plastic army dudes. That sho' don't work for me.

Running out of beer has ignited major wars in the past. Guess what side I'll be on? The one that's stunk and droned. War has also been fought over mistakes. Remember the U.S.S. Maine!!! *NEVER forget the U.S.S. Cole!!!* And never forget Pat Tillman!! That's something that don't go away. But war is kinda weird. Like during some battle during WWI when Christmas came around. Both sides of the *no man's land* trench-warfare stalemate decided to stop all acts of warfare and celebrate the holiday together, which they did. They even had a soccer game together. Not saying that something like that couldn't happen again but if it did, that would show some kinda human spirit. Don't hold your breath. Christmas means nothing to some of the western-haters out there. First of all, two nuclear countries, Iran and North Korea, are run by very unstable people. The president of Iran was voted in for socialistic reasons to make the have-nots somewhat equal to the rest. At least he was voted in . . . which was a major mistake. The leader of North Korea is the closest to an escaped mental patient that I can think of. I used to party with people like that. In no way, shape, or form could they run a country into the ground like that. My party people know very well how to "drive while blind." They, along with just about anyone else, can always think correctly. No nuclear exchange in the Middle East 'cause now Iran has the technology? Well, I thought that the cheese on the moon was edible. Two wrongs ain't gunna make anything right. Not this time. Iran isn't too much farther from the Taliban even though they both are different. Wipe out Israel. Problem is, not everyone in Iran feels that way. That's not really a problem but some Iranians have no say. Some Iranians, some more than you would believe even like our "evil as sin" president, believe that or not!

Where does China fit in on world situations? Seems like nowhere. The biggest most massive populated country in the universe. Now a huge consumer of commodities under free market rules and now capitalism has a firm strong grip in China. Oil and water. How does communism allow its psychological enemy to get such a foothold? I think piles of dollar bills has something to do with it. Communism and communism alone, isn't gunna get it. We saw that with the Soviets and all of the Iron Curtain. There's no money in mediocrity. Will China become democratic? That certainly would help out the planet. Taiwan would breathe a little easier. I'm not too sure about the allure Taiwan has on China, but it can't be capitalistic money being made over there. They're much bigger and just by utilizing only one third of their population; they could be the economic giant of the future. Whether or not they go through a governmental change doesn't matter. China will rival the U S in economic might in the not too far away future. Only thing that would prevent that would be a government crackdown like Tieneman Square. At the present, I don't see any imperialist countries, maybe internally, but no countries taking what's not theirs. Not yet. Militarily, if China wanted to charge, there's not much one can do except to duke it out and expect no help from anyone until it's over. China still has ninety-eight percent of their military. Now whaddya' do? As scary as that sounds, that's just highly unlikely. But still, the $64,000 question that hasn't been answered since 1953. What's gunna happen when North Korea erupts again? Will Chosun (major battle during the Korean War that most Americans would rather forget about) happen again? Ask modern day China. Are they any worse than olden day China? Who the hell knows? Anyday China should be able to see all the poison coming from modern day North Korea. But that would be another Middle East battlezone now in the Far East. But China wants to rule on the economic front. They work with American companies. Maybe we're just giving them the rope. You know how it works. Money rules. Everything else comes in a distant second.

But aside from China, as previously mentioned throughout this novel, most wars will be fought on the religious front. Only exception that comes to mind would be North Korea. Pretty good work. Keep virtually the entire population on the throes of starvation. How many folks can you feed versus how many bombs you can make? Must cost less to make bombs. By allowing rogue nations to process and make the bomb, there's really not much that you can do. Only good option is negotiations which works really good . . . on other planets, even the lost planet earth . . . or air strikes. Columbia University? That's a terrible thought but they got no basketball or football . . . only brainwashed students. I mean faculty. No, I think it's the students. Actually, I can't tell them apart at that *communist garbage college.* Now that's a rude and highly most unwarranted statement that anyone can make when the passion of power far overrides the power of principle, which borders hatred. This is how some far left media mouthpieces operate everyday. I only speak what I hear, that's all. You hafta be able to talk to people, not psycho-prophesize-dictate to them. Sucks when you're on the other side . . . don't it? But when a rouge nation moves or sells a nuke, that should give the world *carte blanche* to do whatever it takes to see that that don't happen. The key word here is world. That's spelled WERLD with a double-u. May as well be. We all live on a lost planet now. Anything involving nuclear psycho nations needs the world's attention. Not just the way it is in Iraq. To try to change the world for the better and no one's interested. In the future, Iraq will turn out to be a good thing in the history books and will make those who participated in it look good enough to remain the great nations they are. I believe that what the Coalition is doing will catch on after many episodes of carnage filled days of deja-vu. It's all because war breeds terrorism.

But as we know by now, the art of war has changed dramatically. No longer is it being painted by a Picasso but has been reduced to a child finger painting on the wall. It is a mess. All wars are a mess. Your goal is to win hearts and minds, nothing less. Shooting little girls in the back 'cause they weren't wearing their Muslim face veils doesn't win anything. But here's the double edged sword. These are the same people who give to all local charities, including building public buildings needed for the local population. Hezbollah and Hamas both do good for their localities. But it's what they really stand for, any sane person should be able to see. They'll win hearts and minds, *even if they have to cut them out.* War has been reduced to nothing but hiding behind women and children while fighting like sissies. But in the history of warfare, even guerilla warfare, which extends centuries before BC, there's not too many, if any at all that I can recall that advocates fighting out of major civilian gatherings. Those are institutions such as schools, hospitals, shopping malls, or anywhere civilians can be used as shields. I've been doin' some research on that since the last time I brought that up. Still nuthin.' I don't believe even Hitler would have condoned that. But we all know that he did. These fanatical views on religion have made these people the most dangerous people in the world. Evil? That all depends on how you view it, from either your ideological and or religious beliefs and biased or unbiased perceptions you have accumulated throughout your trek in life. That seems that that's what it's been reduced to on both sides of the oceans. Never have I seen so much radical change in so little time in the name of something that's supposed to be good and beneficial toward mankind. All in the name of religion. All religions. This is going to cause war. Problem is anyone can start a war with nothing but a ragtag army using civilians as shields and proper firepower. How do you defeat that? First of all, you're not. You can only quell the problem. The problem will never be solved until the slogan that's written on license plates on cars in New Hampshire echoes in the minds of all those who truly want it: ***Live free or die.*** How's that for Northern heritage!! Nothing says it any better. Being scared isn't gunna get it. If that offends anyone out there; keep that to yourself. But you need to stop mashin' the button 'cause everything is offensive to you. Anyone else out there also.

Battalions, companies, and platoons will soon have to become invisible to match the enemy in their own game. This is something that's never been done on a world-war scale. Nevertheless, it must be done. And as most of us know, nothing's impossible. But there will be many trials and tribulations in doing so. Iraq is the first. Iran is probably going to be the second. Not to give away the game plan, but Iran has declared war on Israel. Not formerly, but you just wait and see! Something about the Middle East that doesn't mesh too well with the rest of the world. The real $64,000 question is: Why? This cannot be found in the twilight zone although it should because it is. This can be explained by two words: the Crusades. A disaster past and especially the present. To try to make an entire religion succumb to your beliefs via medieval warfare was about the stupidest thing that's ever been done in history by either side. Ghengas Khan and Attila the Hun conquered for real estate, not to pound their beliefs into someone's head. But since Islam was founded in Jerusalem along with both Judaism and Christianity and was also conquered by the Muslims, the European heads of Christianity wanted it back. Jesus walked in Jerusalem six-hundred tears prior. But you'll never make me believe anything no matter how many times you try to pound in my head. That's what happened a thousand years ago and we are paying the price at the present. The mother of all grudges. We know by history that Islam was also born in Jerusalem as just mentioned and was conquered by the Muslims during its inception as also just mentioned. This sparked the Crusades. This, to me, was looked at by European Christians as a bastard religion. The same way Christians are looked at by some Muslims nowadays. This is no cycle. Even after two millenniums, I think it's still too new. Eons before that, we had mythology. We all do know how ruthless medieval Christianity was to the condemned especially during the Crusades; condemned meaning no belief in Jesus Christ, but by my religious history studies, never have I seen a religion, early days Catholic, nowadays, all Christians, evolve into a most humanitarian belief in the unseen with goodwill towards all. Not that others don't, just don't get caught stealing back in 1247, or in Saudi Arabia nowadays. Maybe it is a cycle.

To a sane mind, that would slowly heal over the ages. Look at the American Civil War. To a sane mind. A sane mind has many definitions even in an insane world. According to some people, insane has now become sane. And they stand by that!! The artificial shall prevail. The square peg will fit in the round hole. No it won't. Just my little 'ol individual self won't let it. But I'll need some help. People need to put down the remote, get off the couch and take a look at the cesspool ideology and philosophies being puked up all over the place. Democrats need to just give in to what the republicans want. Republicans need to just cave in to whatever the democrats want. By that I mean Awh shit! I just dropped my crystal ball. No more future, sorry. Like I really know. But what I want to know is what's gunna happen on December 21st in 2012? Man, for a writer who thinks he knows all that, he shore has a whole bunch of questions. Like this: If you believe in science mixed with some religion, what existed before when the Big Bang Theory happened? If it did happen as explained by science, then it is still expanding at a phenomenal warp speed. If so, what exists beyond our expanding universe? Will the Boston Celtics finally put it all together this year? If so, will it happen in the same year as the Sox and the Patriots and will it all end in 2012? Damn! I need to put this stuff up and save what's left for tomorrow morning and go to bed. Not before this though, how much longer will the middle class exist? If anything is moving out at warp speed, they, along with myself would be it. That's it! I'm putting everything up and I'll be down with the rest tomorrow. I should give the rest to my boss. That'll also make him ask a bunch of stupid questions and I might get a raise out of it. He might think that he'll never know, but sometimes "reality" is the scariest drug of them all. Actually, it's the best. Worst part, it's free! Be careful what you do with it. *Could make it all real.*

Well, ain't no time like the present anyways. Back to reality. Laughing, joking, drinking, smoking is all we ever do. Pretty much alls Johnny's got left. Maybe trying too hard is the same as not trying at all. As mentioned way back, not Rockefeller-rich, but something! Anything but this! Even welfare. No, he won't go there even though he would relish the lift. He maintains purely by word of mouth. And he does maintain. That's why it's real good to hone a trade and respect it. Its alls he's got. He's very lucky he respected it all through the years. Even a professional person should learn the halls of Home Depot's tool department just in case the portfolio blows all to hell and the stock margin is due. But he just wants to pursue his pursuit of life, liberty, happiness, and the bird watcher's elusive Holy Grail; the *double-breasted mattress thrasher* in overdrive to take the torque off the gears of life. He just can't get out of second gear. He just wants to blend in. He cares nothing for being famous . . . nothing against the famous, only the glass houses they live in. He says if you want a good picture of him . . . look at the picture of the planet earth. He's in there somewhere. If ya want a closer picture, look down any microscope and you'll see him dancin' with all the other organisms such as himself down at the club. Bump city, bump sha-bump sha-bump! Happy microbes. We could use a few of those now. The ones I read about in the news rag don't seem to be so happy. Seem to don't like us much. Natural intervention would be a very much appreciated and genuine way to cope with unhappy microbes, but the end result in matters like this would most likely come from science.

He's pretty adept at being a southerner now. He adapts to southern words and phrases, not only for their simplicity in meaning, no beating around the bush, but also for their simplicity that less words are needed to say something. That's real good for Johnny. Any help he can get. When someone asks him where he's going alls he says now is "Yonder ways," and points his finger. That eliminates an entire conversation and both parties know what's up. After being in the Deep South all these years, he does see something that's worth mentioning. Charlie Daniels sang "The South's gunna do it again.' I always said, "Do what?" *Now I know.* Now I certainly don't want to piss anyone off, but if there's gunna be any salvation for America, I see it coming from south of the Mason-Dixon Line. Or at least a huge share. True-blue Americans ring from sea to shining sea. Especially down here. Seems like I hear a lot of *southern belles* all the time out in the country. I think the South will rise again. Southern hospitality will step from the shadows of the past to what it wanted in the first place, to be reckoned as a segment of America whose vastness and folklore was to be taken seriously. It was done once by force and was humbled. But what hasn't changed, by what I see, is the breed of southerner from then to now. Cut from the same cloth, scores of generations later. Same stand up for something attitude. No one down here likes terrorists just as in all the U S A, but it just seems that no one down here refers to them as freedom fighters. A lot of common sense is pretty much what you hear down here in reference to anything past and present. I think old school is going to save America and that's pretty much alls I see down here. Anyone can save America. Don't think it makes a difference where you're from. Look how many times America's been saved. Look at our past wars. As previously mentioned, both parties made America what it is today and never judge an entire political party by the actions of a few. *Remember, it was a democrat who dropped the bomb.* By that action, over a half a million American servicemen and who knows how many Japanese lives were saved. Narrow-mindedness would say, "What about Hiroshima and Nagasaki?" Common sense says you gotta crack a few eggs to make an omelet. Hell of a way to put it, considering the future of the invention. The Japanese casuaties of both those cities would have paled in comparison to a full-scale invasion.

But go to any Waffle House. Omelets are all you see in Dixie. Now Johnny hasn't forgot his northern roots by no means. He's done pretty good considering all that's been said about him so far. He knows about decisions one must constantly make through the course of life. Radar Love or Muskrat Love? Gee, that's a tough one. He has now decided to join a lodge. Some people say that's for old people. He'll be fifty in just over a year. Not that fifty is old, but it's half a century. Ancient time is measured in centuries. Modern time is measured in weekends. Weekends at the lodge works for the time being. He has joined the *"Fraternal Order of Eagles."* **The Eagles** have been around before WWII and have had many an influence on society to this very day. From sponsoring many charities, to making Mother's Day a holiday in 1904, they are established to the same extent as the Elk's Club is presently. The present clubhouse is closer than Applebee's from his trailer. Too many bars within walking distance. Since he just works off his phone, he doesn't turn anything down. Even stuff he's really not too sure about. Stick with what you know. He doesn't have that luxury. That's how you learn sometimes: baptism by fire. He has in the past sanded and refinished new and old hardwood floors and when asked how much he charged for fifteen-hundred sqare feet of open space, he had to go back almost twenty years when he last did it and quickly add inflation to the rate to come up with a price. In all actuality, the rates then and now have remained the same, but everything I need to buy keeps on going up. But it's been awhile since he's sanded floors and being that's all there was, he rented a drum sander and off he went. You don't just go get a drum sander and an edger for the walls and go sand a floor. It had better be your own 'cause if it's for a customer, not only will you not get paid, you'll also get sued. But he's got flooring mojo in his blood and knew what to do along with the confidence just to do it and never gave it a second thought. He's just as good as anyone else in the trade nowadays. But like most other refinishers, he's a little leery of soft pine. One wrong move and you could sand yourself down to the apartment below.

New Year's Day has just passed. It is now 2006. Times runnin' out but as in his case, you only get better with time. Cheap ass wine. This is the part of life where you start thinking about the rest of your life. He's still waiting for the mid-life crisis. Time for concessions if need be to maintain. Maybe shelving the kingdom of kicks; wine, bikes, drugs, and chicks. Nah, that's about fifty years or so off. He's just gunna keep himself alive and in shape to fight off the inevitable, the second marriage. Who knows? He might get married again. People who get married should really think about what they are doing. How come everyone gets divorced? I gotta new two word phrase for trust . . . *prenuptial agreements.* Wait a sec . . . till debt do us part or till wealth do we really part. Something not quite right with that. Gimmi a nuther sec. That means I could write a tell-all book? Or do I just tell it on the seven o'clock news? Either way? I never thought that trust and all that shit could be bought with loot. I maybe lost but religion and all that goes with it, including trust should mean more than just a dollar sign. Only me, lost the moment again . . . sorry 'bout that, just stepped on it, now it's broke. Doggone it!!

This may come across as rather strange and maybe I shouldn't say this, but Johnny don't care but he thinks that someone on the presidents cabinet is rather attractive. And he's gay by no means. Call the F B I off. He means nothing by that. He's on our side. And you won't even know he's not there!! But anyhow, when you get to real midlife, you'll want to either get in shape or maintain the pear shape you already got. People want to live longer and all the commercials on TV depicting many various products to enhance midlife living shows me that. Many diets. Diets since the Sixties that came and went. Diet here, a diet there. Here a diet, there a diet, everywhere a diet diet. Looks to me diets require discipline and dedication. I got some good news. I just saved anyone who wants to diet from those two horrible words. Send ten dollars to Johnny and he'll send you a copy of the newest, hippest diet around. It's called the brain diet. You can eat brains if you want, but this diet is not about eating brains. This is different. It goes like this. Johnny says send him ten bucks anyways. But with this diet, losing, then gaining pounds will be a thing of the past. First of all, remove the brain. Throw away everything else. In the butcher trade, this is referred to as *the throwaway.* Then fashion some tent poles into legs. Use bendable hinges for the knees. You can adjust the height so you can be as tall as you want. Now carefully mash them into the bottom of your brain. See how the torso has been eliminated? Just like that. Now, take a broomhandle and stick it through the brain where ears once were. Make it even on both sides, and put a glove at the end of each side. These are your arms and hands. Be careful to make sure the left glove is on the left side and vice versa. Failure to do so could screw things up. Get a nice pair of sunrays for the eyes so you can see yourself in the mirror. Buff or what? Males are identified by a goatee, females by those huge red lips old ladies paint on their faces. Do all this and weight problems are a thing of the past. Ten dollars is a steal. That should help ya live longer. Hell, that even takes care of that aging problem that plagues us all. Two birds with one stone! But just like everything else, do so at your own risk and consult a doctor first, one in a sanitarium. Hopefully, something as innovative as that doesn't come to light sometime in the future.

By what I see at the present, I'm not so sure. As sure as the wind blows, change is imminent. But what are we going to give up to embrace any kind of change in the future? That's a real $64,000 question there, whiz-kid! When will the casual overtake the formal? Will that ever happen? When the word sacred no longer means anything, any civilization or culture will soon turn to dust. Check your local history book on that. Never let any school, government or not, rewrite or delete any kind of history in any way, shape, or form so as for others to adjust to their agenda. That only relegates history into repeating itself. Besides, that's censorship and just like wide open, "Shut up! You're giving up the play," even though they're on opposite ends of the spectrum, they both do America no good. When is drugs and the atmosphere associated with them finally going to overtake mainstream America? At the rate some of us are going, that's pretty hard to tell. If that ever happens, America is over . . . nothing but an empty shell. When the Saturday morning cartoons start showing the adventures of Heroin Boy and the Crackfart Kid for an hour, alls I can say at least I tried to prevent it. Heroin, it's not just for breakfast anymore. "Heroin Boy! Heroin Boy! Someone's robbin' the bank!" "Hold on a sec. Lemme power up." "Heroin Boy! Heroin Boy! Get up!! What are you doing? Do something! Where's Crackfart?" "Uhh . . . he's in the bathroom. Been in there all morning." "Oh my God! What kind of super zeros are you?" In Iran, they have children's cartoons depicting very young suicide bombers as if they were watching Scooby Doo or Charlie Brown. The absurd has happened over there. But I really can't see that happening here, but with all the loose change in the air and all the airheads talking and not listening, maybe soon, cartoons will soon carry some stupid message in the future. Myself, I like watching old re-runs of *Judge Junkie.*

I really doubt anything as abstract as that could ever take centerstage but I do see lots of "questionable innovation" trying to dig its way into modern culture. We all know how young America is in relation to past empires. To all those in high school; that's some real, phat, heavy time ago. Maybe we haven't settled into what we're supposed to be. I think that we have. So do most Americans. That's why I can't understand all the problems today. I got a problem. What if some of us haven't? What if America folds like a house of cards who knows when and who knows how because the common thread of common decency wasn't sewn throughout each succeeding upcoming generation to maintain that a civilized culture can always remain a civilized culture? Always is a key word here. Always somehow becomes this way, or that way, or no way but my way. Maybe America hasn't gotten that far (out) yet. Hopefully it hasn't, but back to my problem. But I just don't think it's important enough to clog up all the airwaves and cyberspace in the universe. I think that's a problem. I got an idea. Why don't you loudmouths out there *with nothing to say* shut up for a second and listen for a minute. I can't hear everything when it's all being said at once. It gets kinda confusing. An old WWII saying: loose lips sink ships. Don't mean too much anymore. Especially to the media covering Iraq to this very day. Something needs to give on that too. Change is imminent, but just as there's a lot of loose booty all over the place, the same goes for loose change.

Now at real time, any county, township, or any area that is incorporated can now determine its own destiny by casting off all the folks who don't fit in to its utopian Ritz-Carlton-Jetsons perception of real people and bring in all the glitz and golden just by taking. That means the town can now take my dump without my permission and turn it into condos. Real-estate agents aren't needed. In fact, they're non-existent when your property tax dollars just don't cut it. Tax on appraisal. What's wrong with that? A lot, according to the Supreme Court. The county's economic and social future depends on sound economics. That works into a sound future, if done right. That's what I think should be in question. It looks like some of a lot of us, as previously mentioned, aren't economically reliable enough for that peaches-and-cream future. Localities have been given the same rights as state and federal governments to take, not ask. Wonder if the builders' association had any input on this? They're the ones who wind up with your spread. I'm pretty sure there's no kickbacks, pretty toys . . . mechanical or anything else working their unconstitutional selves into play here. I also thought there was cheese on the moon. But what about the future of American municipalities? They need to be on sound ground also. Fiscal instability for whatever reason within many municipalities seems rampant. This is fiscal management gone way past wild . . . it's gone corrupt, both private and public. I call it skimming-off-the-top . . . **right down from the bottom up.** I also call it too many freebees . . . nothing in return. This has severely called out and questioned the credibility of capitalism . . . the only system that promotes progress. Call me crazy, but these people responsible for our capitalistic embarrassment need to be *shot* or at least *crippled.* They won't do it again. Then that way, the next batch of higher-up Wall Street *movers and shakers cookbook bakers* will quickly learn what not to do.

But anyways, this has resulted in many strange taxes in lots of localities. I once heard of a mountain-side home with a spectacular view out west somewhere. The county where this home was located wanted to charge the homeowners a "view tax." I thought that America's existence was founded by rebelling against excessive taxation. Taxed to death pretty much means *fight the death* . . . to the death! Why doesn't someone just start taxing air? But to me, this new ruling by the Supreme Court on eminent domain is very disturbing. By leaving out some of us with this newly spewed philosophy puts the word *corporate* in all areas that is deemed incorporated and now some people won't stand a chance. Some of our existence now has also been reduced to nothing more than a stinkin' commodity. Everything for which somebody worked for is now for sale. Eminent domain says that my five acre spread doesn't generate enough tax revenue for the county. I'm not smart enough to cough up that kind of jing-a-ling anymore. But someone else is. Alls I gotta do is move whether I like it or not. Once again, the God-almighty dollar bill, or lack of it, can control where I can live or can't live . . . . even when my five acre spread is paid off!! You wanna take my spread to pad your county portfolio? Then clean up the toxic waste dump I'll turn it into and expect a real good gunfight! Some Supreme Court judges should stand trial for stealing some people's piece of the American pie. You wanna build a road? Then there's nothing I can do about it. You wanna give my spread to some developer? Then there's a lot I can do about it . . . after I get out of prison. Loose change? *Don't tread on me.* Leave my shit alone unless you ask not take! Loose booty. Now there's a lot I could do about that. Like make it a little looser. That's always fun.

Fun in the buns even under the sun. Yeah, there's something wrong with me, *but I like it like it yes I do.*

If this little novel ever makes it, I'm sure some people would like to meet Jonathan Livingston Woodpecker either to shake his hand or break it. He might not be around though. He has a looming problem from the past that he's just waiting to catch up with him. No one can outrun this. The taxman cometh sooner or later. This has already happened once. Pay up or else. He has no choice except the or else. Its not that he doesn't want to pay. He just can't. He can't even give his kids and grandson what they need. No one wants the taxman breathing down your neck. He just can't avoid it. When he fantasizes retirement, he can't even do that without thinking about ten-hour days till the day he croaks. You've got to pay into social security to get anything out of it. He's where no one wants to be. When you work for yourself, instead of getting a W-2 from your employer in January, you get a 1099 form indicating what you brought home that year in gross earnings.

No tax, FICA, Social Security, or anything else is deducted. That's up to you. That's very easy to do, provided your social atmosphere is stable. You can usually tell you're stable when life settles into a routine day in and day out. Johnny don't even know what's going to happen tomorrow. His only routine is somehow he seems to pull all kinds of rabbits out of the hat when absolutely needed at that time. Sometimes he pulls out a cobra, but that happens to everyone. Needless to say, it's been several years since he's fessed up to the taxman and someday he's gunna look in the mailbox and see a pipe bomb shaped in a fess-up letter from the IRS inquiring where he's been since a few administrations ago. That will be a sad day in Mudville. He has tried to work a legal and legit business with a business license, little office, credit with supply houses, all kinds of work and a pretty good reputation. He called his business *Carpet Commandos* which was printed on his checks. But just like everything else, that was a failure too. His most recent business ventures: *Johnny's Fetus Recovery and Disposal Service* and *Johnny's Porno Euphourium and Child Care Service* were dismal failures and he almost got arrested. Because of what you just read and also by what he has done and said made that so. When you can't even hit the ground pissing, just the basics are going to take everything you got. But when the IRS comes, he might have to pay off his share behind bars. They want money and he can even spell the word. He'll go voluntarily, without the use of tasers. Those things kill people and the people who use those things get away with it. Free murder. Be alert. We need more lerts. I heard that somewhere before. But as always, he's still alive and well and he'll cross that bridge when he gets there. As usual, no bridge Where's that confounded bridge? That would probably be because of his attitude. You must answer to yourself. But maybe that might be a little difficult as explained by this short story written by his Uncle Jimmy, Rusty's older brother. Although the circumstances and setting are slightly different, this could almost describe Johnny to the T. This is very uncanny because this was written around 1980. Maybe Uncle Jimmy knew something way back, back into time. Caveman, cavewoman, *troglodytes*. But anyhow, it goes like this:

"Till Birth Do Us Part"

It was on a mid-June early evening in 1970 at the Deerfield Hills County Club where relatives and friends had gathered in the dining hall to honor John and Joanne on their 35th wedding anniversary. Their children had spent that afternoon decorating the hall. All their arrangements were now in place. After John and Joanne had received congratulations from all, everyone was seated for dinner. Dancing followed and Joanne table-hopped, thanking family and friends. John was dancing the evening away with many partners. The party ended with Joanne happy but tired while John had energy to spare wishing the night could continue on.

A few years pass and John and Joanne's younger daughter graduates from college. Her circle of friends, family and neighbors attend a backyard buffet at home. Swimming, games and talk of future expectations are enjoyed by the younger crowd. John joins in to the surprise of many.

As time goes by, John reaches sixty-five years of age and retires from his company. A banquet is held in his honor with company officials, co-workers, family and friends attending. Accolades, toasts and some roasting about John's younger appearances-nearer fifty years of age-are laughingly made questioning if John is really ready for retirement. John claims he is "fit as a fiddle" but it is now leisure time with Joanne and family. She beams proudly . . . a gracious lady of sixty-three years.

St. Paul's Church is the scene of John's daughter's wedding to her boyhood sweetheart. John walks down the aisle and gives her away in marriage. He now has regressed in age with hair no longer grey, smooth skin and no wrinkles. At the reception he partakes in antics with people half his age. Comments are heard among the guests about John's appearance and behavior. Joanne and his children John has seen medical specialists and they concur he has an unusual genetic condition never before encountered that seems irreversible.

The couple's young grandson completes high school and a subdued get-together of family and grandson's friends is held. John's regression is now more pronounced as he plays football with his grandson and high school friends. Joanne now handles John more like a son than a husband.

The family returns from the Christening of John and Joanne's new granddaughter. As her mother changes the baby girl's clothing Joanne does the same for John—now a baby himself.

Death notice appears for John at birth. His obituary mentions wife, children and grandchildren. His condition has become well-known. At the same time that day, a son is born in the same hospital. Peering from his hospital crib this newborn bubbling baby boy has a coy smile on his face and also a slight wink of one eye.

The End?

That's pretty cool. Earlier I asked, "Did he grow up too early? Or has he not grown up at all?" I'm sure that's pretty obvious by now. But he just don't care anymore. He don't care if he doesn't work for a stretch here and there 'cause he knows there ain't no easy hit coming down the pike . . . he's not gunna make it, so a little time off is no problem anymore. If you can't see any change or help all the way to the horizons, then there's no sense in bustin' your stones while spinning your wheels. When you do see some help or favorable change, then it's time to downshift and let the rubber grab the road. Alls we have is hope. He does also. He won't give, up even in the face of hardcore reality. But he knows time is of the essence. Timing itself don't mean shit no more to him. Seconds ticking away means no more to him than anything else now. He thought that with all the hard work and diligence, his late forties would have been anything but this. He's not afraid of dying. He's afraid of dying trying. How much longer this gunna take? He doesn't want to play the lottery. When he does, he don't even get one number. I guess you gotta have people like him around to show everyone else no matter what, it could always be worse and how to work off that. I have previously mentioned his past life including his marriage but I believe I failed to mention his X's name. I only know her by what he tells me and what he tells me is that her name was *Bugs*. That's a pretty good nickname and something like that is pretty much what I would expect from him. Wonder if it says that on her birth certificate? It don't. It says Anita but now her last name is something different.

I just read a pretty good piece in the editorials in the *USA Today*. Killer sports section. Anyways, it comments on the decline of religion over in Europe. A major decline in religion, and the consequences or results thereof. It goes on to say how an almost secular continent is condemning itself to a future of demographic suicide. I don't know what that means either so let me quote alittle bit form this article. Because of abortion, birth control, and the total acceptance of gay marriage, Europe is not repopulating itself to sustain *out with the old in with the new*. There's not enough babies being born over in Europe to replenish the old. Their "anything goes" lifestyle is going to turn Europe into a giant old folk's home by the year 2050. Our ultra-secular or even just plain secular think-tanks right here in the U S want to take us down this path of self-destruction by turning the word *sacred* into a four-letter word. *We cannot let anyone accomplish that, no matter what happens in doing so.* No violence though. I don't want to see another Civil War. Maybe a vote or two. That always works . . . so far. Johnny's got a grandson and wants the kitchen just the way he left it so Ethan doesn't have to clean up someone else's shit. That is the goal. Some people who occupy these think tanks that second guess past events and think they can help in future events that demotes religion are really thinking from a septic-tank 'cause without **faith, hope** and **charity**, there is no direction except straight down. Neanderthals lived like that, but they were illiterate. What's your reason? I know you most likely have valid reasons for your stance and I'm sure you think they're all valid, but carefully look at what you want to change and the effect it would have on a people who are religious and even those who aren't who really don't want to fast forward America into a morally lawless society. You can twist your philosophy and even back it up with our documents of our inception but you're way too late. Something like this should have been brought up five years or so after our inception. Nowadays, we are entrenched in our ways and the Cross on public property really doesn't bother anyone, except you. To those of you out there who want to remove any cross anywhere in the country. *Someday, someone is gunna find a Cross in the middle of nowhere with your name on it.* of But you are still an American and as always, I'm on your side . . . right after I baptize you . . . on the public square, next to the federal building in between the courthouse. Let's work together and not alienate each other for the common cause . . . our future. In that case, I'd better change the subject. ***Expect no help from me.***

As a matter of fact, I think it's about time to wrap this entire essay up. I'm out of issues. If I forgot something, then it's probably not that important or controversial 'cause as ya'll can tell by now, I'm a controversial dude. Hey dude! *Whatzzz* my controversy? Good name for a book. As I roll outta' here and since this book is about Johnny, what's a story without a little Johnny joke. Yeah, I know he already is a joke, but this is when he was younger, a younger joke. Goes like this. Little Johnny is in class in the first grade learning his ABC's with the rest of the class. Little Johnny also has a real foul mouth for such a youngster. The teacher says, "Class, we're gunna start with the letter A all the way to Z and I'm gunna call on each of you and you will say a word that starts with that letter and then use it in a sentence. Okay, who wants to start?" Everyone raises their hand including little Johnny. She scopes out the class and sees that he's got his hand raised along with everyone else. Well, I'm not going to call on him. Who knows what he's going to say. "Jane, you go first." Jane responds, "Apples. I just love apples." Very good, as the rest of the class claps at her success. All of a sudden, little Johnny blurts out, "Ain't that some shit." "Young man. I'll have none of that kinda talk in my class. Understand me?" "Yes, ma'am." "Okay, class who wants to do letter B?" They all raise their hand, including little Johnny but she doesn't pick him. "Okay Billy it's your turn." "Baseball, I like to play baseball." Once again the class erupts with clapping and cheering. Once again, little Johnny blurts out, "Ain't that some shit." This time some other students laugh. Little Johnny, what did I tell you? I'll not have that kind of language in my class!! Do you understand?" "Yes, ma'am." "Okay, the next letter is C. Who wants to do that one?" Everyone raises their hand including little Johnny but she picks Elmo. Go ahead Elmo. "Caterpillar, I just love eating caterpillars outside during recess." "Very good Elmo. That was a big word. Nice work. By the way . . . something not quite right with you. And wipe that crap off your chin." Once again, the class erupts in jubilation and once again, little Johnny blurts out, "Ain't that some shit." Everyone laughs and the teacher has had enough. "Okay, young man. Maybe a little time by yourself in the hallway will help. Get up and go stand in the hall until I let you back in." "Yes, ma'am." He's out in the hall and she goes through some more letters, then excuses herself to see how he's doing by himself. He's standing there facing the wall like he was told to do. "Well, little Johnny, have you learned anything?" "Yes, ma'am. I learned a poem." A poem, she says to herself. How could a little terror like this learn a poem? "Can I hear it?" "Sure ma'am. As I was standing in the hall, I saw a cockroach climb up the wall." "Very good, would you like to recite that to the class?" "Sure, ma'am." She then says, "Recite it without the cock 'cause that's a bad word." "Okay, ma'am." He goes back into the class and recites this. "As I was standing in the hall, I saw a roach climb up the wall . . . without a cock. Ain't that some shit." That's my boy for good or bad.

Okay, this, the brain diet, stupid cartoon heroes. I'm definitely out of ammo. Shrunken heads and other useless garble. I've got to go before I come up with something worth writing and I'm all wrote out. How do people write ten or so books? Writing just one sucks! Imagination helps and mine's impaired so this is it. It's time to fade away into some barstool somewhere 'cause a day without alcohol is like a day without sunshine. What's up George? Been awhile!! But not before this. Life goes on no matter what happens. Good or bad. Deal with what you're dealt with. Just as Johnny, you ain't got no choice, so live life to the fullest no matter how good or bleak it is and be happy even in the face of adversity 'cause happiness, even artificial always helps. He knows all this but still there's that hardcore reality peering through his window just letting him know once he steps outside the door, he's on his own. He's not going to end it all; he just wants it all to end. He cares about everything but now, he couldn't care less. But he will never stop trying but would rather die trying. He ain't scared . . . *just human-like you and maybe me.* The end of the ride! Capiechio

PART FOUR:

THE END (SUMMARY)

Well, that's my expose on my perception of life in general or in the jungle for that matter. To make some kinda sense of certain aspects of how life should be, one must now become a contrary thinker. Used to be the other way around. Back into time, before the *dumbing* and *wussy-f#*ation* of our land, common sense even flowed in all the water we drank. Seems like solution pollution has turned water into Kool-Aid. My message was to enlighten, but if I've also embalmed a few, that was also the message. You need to wake up. First and foremost, I don't speak in tongues or speak with nothing to say, and will tell you how I think it is, **but sometimes you gotta look on both sides of the fence.** And I don't mean to shout, but **too many people refuse to do that.** And that's what this novel is all about. And I also don't mean to offend, but some people leave themselves wide open for it and just seem to beg for it. Ain't too proud to beg. And also, just so most of us are on the same page, I really didn't mean to come down so hard on the gay community in the context in which I used to express my views. But since most *tangents*, no matter what . . . personal or worldly views, religion, fashion, behavior, culture, or anything else that could be seen differently by a few will always be viewed as only a tangent to most. And that brings on the jokes. Sorry, I'm not the one who made them up. Even though any loving parent can raise a kid, I cannot see too much good come out of gay marriages. But I live by a double-standard. It might be wrong but I'm me and no one else is so that's something I just gotta live with. I really don't care if two women who live together raise up a kid. It's when two men who live together who want to raise a child that I'm dead against! Why that is? I don't know, but as you read all this, you've seen that there's a lot I don't know. But this is not about what I know . . . it's about what I think. I do however do not see any problem with any estate, power of attorney action, or anything else in which pertains to anybody else. *They're people too*, but I just can't see how any *adopted* children involved in any gay matters would view *their* environment *inside* and *outside* of the house? Other than that, I'm down with it . . . especially the women-dudes. "Let me be there in the morning', let me be there in the night." I know that's **course** and I also know that goes against the grain of lots of folks' thinking including lots of our social guardians . . . our morally anemic *family?* judges. To me that's alarming. But people are poople so get used to it. Get used to alotta things.

There's only one thing that I hope no one will forget, only if time slowed down a little . . . is how it used to be. Not that things are worse now . . . things are just different. Everything's way too serious nowadays. Can't even be a kid anymore without constant adult interaction from the womb to the tomb anymore. That flows in both directions. Overprotective parents and parental hefty goal setters for three-foot-two inch junior to reach yet, to numerous internet pedophile predators who need to be *poached-without-the-egg* and other socially unacceptable adult interactions with children. Real bad behavior that deserves no second chance. South Carolina has had enough. Legislation wants death for pre-adolescents sex that's forced upon them. Me too. Georgia introduced legislation also. You'll like this. Registered sex offenders must vacate their premises, whether owned or not, if they live within a thousand feet of a public or private school. I told ya you'd like this, but there's more. This piece of legislation defines all but about twenty Georgians as sexually offensive. It's on the right track, but needs to go back in the pot for a few hours more. Getting caught taking a piss in the middle of the night behind a tree could put you in the sexual predator catagory according to *the dumbing of America.* Say What??? Yer better off killing me if that happens because I don't think that's right. Let's see . . . becoming a sexual pre-vert ***OVER NOTHING*** according to *beauracrazy* or pulling out the jugular vein of beauracacy. What's the difference? You're going to jail either way . . . may as well make a mess of the process of beauracrazy. *Commen Sence* really needs to make a comeback or I hope I see jugular veins all over the place . . . even between my teeth. But in the old days, it wasn't met with legislation. Usually, it was kept quiet 'cause the age old $64,000 question that still hasn't been answered to this day, "How could something like this happen?" persists to this very day. Our town, county, or even state might be deemed as evil as it gets, so hush! Zip yo' lip. Back in the day, once it got public, the public went postal. This was in no way, shape or form to be tolerated, no matter who said what, 'cause that's what you are supposed to do to make sure something as disgusting as that doesn't happen again. Now, you get in trouble for that and the perpetrator can even smile and sneer at you while he's standing trial for screwing your ten year old daughter. Ain't no time like the present. That didn't happen back in my day. Even the police saw to that. Nothin' like the old King Arthur days when society used to work with us.

But as mentioned previously, most people aren't that demented, so what else has changed? I'm certainly not an expert by no means but I think America has become a little bit **OVERPROTECTIVE**. Some even scared Helter-Skelter. Mercy mercy me, tunes ain't what they used to be. Ketchy little tune. The previous topic shows just how a sheeple mentality could swing the pendulum from left to right or vice versa with no time or room for rationality to rear its ugly head. I think that there's more than twenty sexually offensive Georgians out there. I can flip-flop along with the best of them. My excuse is that I really don't know what I'm talking about. I think hideous crimes have a way of doing that to a cultured society. That's also not how it used to be. Used to be case-by-case, not all cases lumped into a nice easy-to-carry package. We want to protect but in doing so, we also strangle the sane with insane implications and procedure. I probably need some documentation to back this up. Let's see . . . now we got zero-intelligence and public parks with signs that say no running. Kids have to wear helmets on bicycles, can't play dodgeball in school 'cause it offends geeks, and liability insurance that views Jell-O as potentially dangerous as hell. There's a shortage of baseball catchers 'cause ma would rather watch Junior chase a soccer ball and other anemic can-never-be-too-safe norms of modern present day society. It may sound it, but I really have nothing against the game of soccer. It's a game where if you're not in shape, real good shape, you'll have a rough ass-time out on the field. You've gotta have the same amount of stamina as a long distance runner and if anyone's ever done that, you know how tough that is. It's just that with all the sports I've played, I was always allowed to use my hands. That's what a ball is for. You catch it. Sometimes even a fastball in the noggin. Made me what I am today . . . master of beanballzz.

But anyways, soon we'll all have to dress up like NASCAR drivers just to go get a gallon of milk. Helmet and all. Just keep it under 25 mph. Common sense is soon going to have to be taught in grammar schools, if that's ever possible. Even school's not quite like it used to be. Learning anything seems like it's now on the back burner. What you're learning and why now rides shotgun in the classroom. Back then we all knew why. We all wanted good jobs and going to school made it that much easier. Now why you're learning something means that somehow, it is politically correct 'cause it meets all the requirements for the pussification of America. Some schools teach very young children by use of a gay agenda, and other schools now teach ten year olds about sex and why they should try it instead of playing 'cops and robbers' or building forts. My kid gets immediately pulled from those schools and the person responsible for that gets to really hear why that's a bad idea! **It's my job** to school my kid in those matters, not some stupid-ass board of education idiot who wants to pervert my kid! Why don't you teach history, math, science, social studies, geography, English, and gym class like you're supposed to? Young kids don't even know whatzz goin' on anymore 'cause of our politically correct grossly inept *off the chain* curriculum that is being shoved down their throats. I got somethin' for your throat!! Who knows? *A fractured love story* might become required reading . . . in the fourth grade!!

We learned about the Holocaust during social studies. How many schools still teach that? How many teachers even know what that was? How many teachers who always knew about the Holocaust and ones that teach it and continue to teach it will soon be banned to teach that? Political correctless, you know. It was so bad, let's bury it in the sands of time and hopefully everyone will just forget it. That's how we live nowadays and that there is simply the beginning of the end. What we don't like, we simply impose a ban. A ban on this or a ban on that 'cause a ban quickly snuffs out all the bad things in society and everything now is just going to be fine. Some of what's being banned just goes hand-in-hand with utter nonsense like what I heard awhile back about bringing physically and mentally handicapped people into public restaurants because it upset some prima-donnas who didn't like the mess they made while someone else was trying to feed them. We need a ban on the word *ban*. I don't even use Banroll-on anymore because of the word. I use Raid. It seems to work on anything. Kills anything, even potatoes and onions you got growing under there.

But where's the sense of ragging on present time where we all reside now? If anyone's ever lived in the past era I've described throughout this book, then you'd know how much more efficient and competent many daily procedures were conducted as opposed to the *smoke-and-mirror-new-age-sorority* I see now all around me now. Argument could be that technology was embryonic back in my day and it was a simpler and less hectic time.

After all, without technology, where would we be? I'm not sure, but the Egyptians built mathematically and astronomically precise forty-kabillion ton pyramids with nothing but rocks and soft metal hand tools. *Top that when you're not sure.* Johnny says no problem. While he's tinkerin' away, that was thousands of years before BC-AD and all societies and cultures since with lots of well-known exceptions, have always known how to utilize whatever they had to work with to get the best results. Any exception most likely didn't utilize its military properly. Either too timid or too brutal. But I think their technology included ideology and philosophy which helped make them timeless. Technology enabled one to get better then the previous. Technology, if used correctly, is supposed to make life more efficient and competent, not the other way around. Technology finally got to us and for the most part, I don't think we're utilizing it to its utmost. Lots of fumbles, strikeouts, and called-back plays 'cause someone's just not paying attention. Technology requires attention. Just 'cause the plane flies itself once the pilot presses the button and kicks back and reads the paper, doesn't mean something couldn't happen or go wrong with the autopilot that requires a split-second decision, so you fly not die. We have become way too complacent with a computerized society and it shows. The computer check-out at K-Mart goes down and now no one can count change? C'mon! That's real bad. There's all the world to gain and beyond with computer science but don't take away my basic simple mind skills in doing so, that's all. Take Johnny's. He's having a bargain-basement sale. Ten cents each. Pretty soon, technology is going to read your mind. Maybe yours, but never mine. And there's nothing that's been done in the past with embryonic technology that couldn't be done now. Wait a sec; they put a man on the moon using only slide rules. We are hooked like dope on computers. After many generations come and go well into the future when we've completely lost all our simple and basic mind skills to a Pentium II . . . don't say I didn't say so. Take calculators out of schools. That's a start. *Make them think for themselves just like we had to.*

On an even darker side, when technology has come of age, with physics and more detailed physics . . . such as switching polarities on sub-atomic particles of which when becomes reality, I hope the good guys come up with that first. Otherwise, it's over. Someone just got home in the condo upstairs and wants to talk about something different. But the choice is yours. Convert to Islam or anything else against your will or convert into your own basic atoms. That could soon be easier done than said without your consent. I know I talk about a lot of far-out and abstract things, but what I've just described is about the simplest way to describe anti-matter. Anti-matter is simply an electron with a positive pull instead of a negative one, or a proton with a negative pull, just like Johnny. It's not some gas or cloud you might see in some sci-fi flick or some force with force fields all around it. All of the mass in our known universe has the polarities which we know to be as they are. Electrons are charged negatively and protons are charged positively. Pop quiz. What charge does Johnny Neutron have?

While we strain over that, astronomers, physicists, and mathematicians have theorized by the structure and motion of the universe, that not all matter was distributed evenly, as I tried to portray earlier, and also some of it may be charged in a way by which we've never seen before. Let's say that it is also veryrare, sorta' like gold on earth or common sense in Washington. Man, I need to lighten up on DC. I've already had the feds come down on me once and push me around for awhile a long time ago. I don't ever want that to happen again! They hurt my feelings. I also hurt theirs, but I still lost. But anyway, an example would be that for every positively charged electron in the universe, there's 10,000 cubed to the eleventh power squared to the bone normal ones out there. There's not much anti-matter in space simply for the fact that when two oppositely charged electrons or protons for that matter come in contact with each other, because of their magnetic attraction towards each other, they do so with such a force that all the mass of the particles has been expended into nothing but pure energy. A hydrogen bomb expends around in the single digits percentile. The rest is useless blowed-up mass. What do ya' think so far? I told ya' I had a PhD in snot-rocket science. With a controlled matter-anti-matter explosion, all the matter within the explosion would cease to exist. Scientists have recently created controlled matter-anti matter explosions in huge powerful super electrical behemoths called Accelerators. This machine is almost one or two miles big! However, they cannot create an environment suitable for anti-matter to exist in, so it annihilates itself in millionths of a second. *Better know what the hell they're doin'!* Sorry about the science class but imagine a bomb that could cripple a city the size of Gotham only being the size of a quarter! That's no joke. This involves sectors of the universe that soon can be mimicked by man. Einstein was the first to figure it all out and that was a long time ago. Imagine what's goin on now! Given time, that will probably become a reality way off in the future when we've come to our senses. What if some of us don't?

Enough techno jibber jab. Givin' me sophomore fifth-period flashbacks. That was after skipping fourth period and taking all four lunches. Could wind up down in Virginia Beach doin' that. Could wind up anywhere not knowin' what's goin' on. There's a lot goin' on right now anywhere in the world you look at. Not knowin' what's goin' on nowadays could be this short of catastrophic. Also, knowin' what's goin' on and remaining inert for whatever reason is equally catastrophic. Please don't put any political spin on this. Look at it for what it is; two entirely different cultures with one bent on dominance and even worse, revenge. Revenge, for the other existing. If anyone thinks for an instant that the Western world is evil for whatever reason . . . probably freedom of anything in which I got a problem with, then you only got half the message. You took the first part for a touchdown, but the second part that goes, "but what you can do for your country" and I might add to that, "and the rest of the world" is just another annoying chore that someone else has got to do. What's gunna really piss off our future is that nowadays, that phrase now has reverse-polarity. *Ask not what I can do for my country, but what my country can do for me.* If that's the way anyone thinks, then you need to get someone else to hold your hand because I refuse to do it . . . and ***no fucking government*** will ever make me!! That's my decision and mine only!!! I hope I'm wrong but if not, stop thinking, let me do it. Hell, I just gave ya'll a real good diet for nuthin.'

Whatever future is coming is a product of present and past. That doesn't make any sense nor does it have to. Anything could happen no matter what variables are involved. That's why I say, the free west is not responsible for our current situation as also neither is the United States for trying to make it civilized. Any civilization can remain as Stone Age as it wishes to forever into the future, just don't force others who oppose, even your own. Every person can make his or hers own choices in life and still remain true to their own religious denomination. But as we all know, that's not good enough for some. The word *change* is erased from some people's context. Or it has two meanings. You change but we won't. I see problems all over the place with that. Make me. Problem is that it's not a taunt to them, but a promise for them to keep. Anyone else see a problem with that? We have left the precarious Cold War era and entered a much more clandestine and lethal era of ideological and religious unrest. Jesus freaks . . . Muhammad speaks. Louder than ever. Some people say the U S Government was the first to hear him. The U S Government orchestrated 9-11. George Bush musta got into a bad one with the first lady. Given the precise timing of all the logistics and planning to make 9-11 happen, the conceivement of such an act must have happened way back into the Clinton years. It takes time in honing the insane. Clinton . . . a democrat. Bush . . . a republican. *Certain Muslims could care less either way.* Infidels come in all shapes, sizes, colors, national origins, deep space origins and political ideologies. Democrat or republican . . . they are all the same, *non-believers.* I don't understand any debate with that. People want peace and that's very understandable but as mentioned previously, *all sides* must want to play. We all know that it's up to rationale that's not yet recognized at this point in time. Extreme religion dictates that an infidel is someone who doesn't believe in true religion as only found in the Koran.

You would be amazed at some of the similarities between the Bible and the Koran, such as Abraham and his sons, the Great Flood in Genesis, and parts of Jesus Christ's life. Then again you'd also be amazed at the differences. Here's *whare* things start to fly apart. As I had also previously mentioned regarding our differences and similarities between our cultures . . . some of the more religious values of the Muslim world, I failed to mention. That's because I'm no Jesuit priest just like I said before. Talking about religion gets me into fistfights . . . keep on gettin' my shit knocked all over the place. But here's where the chasm lies. I take no credit for this area of discussion because I watched it on TV. But it is real, just the same as all of our predecessors' ideas and philosophies were real to them back in their time. But as far as religious differences go, much is the same with Judaism and Christianity and Islam except that Jesus wasn't the Son of God, but much of what Jesus did in flesh and blood is the same as we believe. There was no immaculate "reception" unless you look back to the fall of 1972. Jesus was not crucified as in the Bible, but lifted to heaven by God when He passed on. There is no resurrection after death, no stone rolled away from the tomb's entrance, no Easter, and no Passover or anything else except that when His time was up, God simply lifted Him up into Heaven. While we include Baptism as one of the Sacraments of Christian religion, Muslims do not. The Islamic faith dictates that every Muslim is responsible only for their own sins and no ones else's that's born into them. There is no *original sin* as from the story of Adam and Eve. Religiously speaking, those are some mighty big differences in opinion. Other religious denominations share lots of noticeable differences such as reincarnation. This is believed with the Hindu faith and then the Buddhist faith which has been in Asia since the ancients. They believe in nothing but peace. What the hell is wrong with them? There are five major religions scattered all over the planet. Most are cultured and civilized towards each other, 'cept one. And the one I'm talking about is getting a bad name by the actions of a few of their own kind. If that's true then the show I just recently watched called *Obsession, the Islamic Threat* or something like that must be showing these vengeful, hateful Islamic religious leaders in sparsely populated areas of the entire Middle East because they are only the few. Maybe it's me, but that's not the impression I got. Just as our own media spews far-left rhetoric with the fervor of Joseph Goebbels, so goes the same in the Middle East, with many mullahs all over the Middle East who make Joseph Goebbels sound like a mute proclaiming that all infidels must die no matter what and that the entire planet will be forced to become Islamic. I got the impression this is rampant throughout the Middle East. Because we believe what we believe and not the Koran, we therefore have been reduced to infidels . . . sorta like cockroaches. And for that, we all must die. Anyone see a problem with this? Me neither, so let's move on.

Our bodies are our temple. We take care of them . . . even show them off because we like what we look like on the beach, in the groove or on the move. Vanity? No . . . more like pride in our temples. That's what carries us from the womb to the tomb . . . our own selves. We like to be in shape to make the tomb just alittle bit farther away. It just seems to me that to some of the Muslim culture, the temple of life is nothing but an obstacle that just stumbles along year after year to get somewhere that western culture just can't comprehend. With Sharia muslim beliefs, the human body isn't even recognized for its value. Sharia women have to wear tents as clothing to keep the temple a hidden asset. If our own selves is that repulsive or forbidden to a certain few who view no temple, then that means *death means more than life* to them and that's why our enemy is much more scarier then any we have ever faced before. Our children are our future. Children over there speak of marching to their death for Islam and that Jews are descendent from apes and pigs at the age of four. How you gunna beat that? *The Island of Dr. Mourneau* was only a movie! Picture the earth haulin' ass through space. Now picture an asteroid ten times the size of the sun headed right for it. For a pretty good hypothetical description, picture this asteroid as the militant fanatical Muslim world whose mind you can't change except with weapons. Quick!! We gotta' do something!! Someone's gotta go out there and talk to it!! Say what?? Yeah! Someone's got to go out there and talk some sense into it. Here, once again for the last time, is what we face. Actually, this would be the first time it was explained like this. This is a first for all of us. I would liken that with which we are dealing to the same problem the entire human race and the earth itself was dealing with in the super cool sci-fi movie called *Starship Troopers*. For those who haven't seen it, it's about a futuristic war between two planets, one being earth. On the other planet are these immensely large, ugly, and grotesque insects about the size of eight-legged giraffes that possess the same intelligence as some people presently on earth. They can think real good. However, just as in our current situation, there's absolutely no dialogue with these herds of insects because the earth has not been conquered yet. I see our real problem as worse because it is amongst ourselves, the same species. This has got to be someone's fault.

Time to blame someone. We could check out the problem itself but I prefer to look at some other variables being mentioned *all over the place* so that we all can see for ourselves if I'm right or not. Or even close, someone tell me when I stray off. Call me. I'm always home. The number is *fi-fi-fi—fo-fo-fo—fi-fi-fo-fo-two.* To further refine this little expose', I'll start with real time just as I'm penning this. Iraq, Afghanistan and the Bush Administration shake-up and the new congress. All of these opens up many possibilities for many different results. First of all, America has had enough of the stalemate, the civil war in which anyone could have seen coming, and out went the old, in with the new congress. So also went the Secretary of Defense for waging a war with no viable procedure for unconditional surrender or any ways or means for obvious victory. Sure, Iraqis can vote and work free-enterprise and reap its rewards. Women even enjoy more freedom, kinda. I wanna see what would happen in America or any western society if women were treated as they are in most of the Middle East. Women enjoying the same rights as men is construed as western decadence according to Muslim law and beliefs. And that's just moderate Muslim law, never mind the super strict fundamentalists who make their women wear circus tents from head to toe. If they don't, cockroaches are treated better than that! That is a major difference in both of our existing present societies. According to 900 A.D. Islamic fundamentalism, women had about the same rights as cattle and sheep. That was eleven hundred years ago. Old school ain't going away. *Baghdad, we have a problem.* What good is all that during a ferocious civil war involving barbarians? What good is all that also during an illegal, immoral and personal war? Lots of questions, no real good answers. Well, maybe, but I got my own two cents to play with. 'Cause that's all I got. Amazin' what two cents gets today. Absolutely nuthin! Don't even have to go to school to count to that. That's not bad. But only for the few. Now, that's real bad. Here's how bad.

The world is changing faster than anyone wants to think . . . physically, mentally, and most disturbing of all . . . spiritually, and is spinning faster than some people can stand and is now showing some symptoms of dizziness in some people who seem to think that's normal. They'd rather *switch than fight.* Some of these people have some power. That's gunna become a four letter word soon. So what happens soon after 9-11? Afghanistan, which most of the world expected, then Iraq which also most of the world expected . . . sooner than later. Here's where things start to fly apart again. I don't know about you, but I expected it. Actually, I thought that something mighta happened back in the Nineties. I'm kinda surprised that nothing happened. We'll catch up with each other in a few more pages from now to let that congressional leak out to the public. This time I'll print it, not the Traitor Times. Just wanna keep it all bleeding and flowing, maybe in the wrong direction. What's wrong with runnin' down the wrong road every now and then? Might find a good-ass party or a party that means no good. Might also find something that you really need to know. Not that I know . . . I'm just lookin' for a house party. I remember Saddam's patriotic middle finger pointed at the U S throughout the entire Nineties. I mentioned how deathly scared the U.S.A was immediately after 9-11, the anthrax, the WMDs, which now is a four-letter word, and the fact that Saddam Hussein was not only a thorn in America's side for about a decade under the Clinton administration, but his regime represented all that was wrong in the Middle East. No one can refute that. Do so, then let me think your tank 'cause it's on empty. No brains. I hate to go over this again and again, but **NO ONE'S LISTENING!!** Throughout the Nineties, the American public and unfortunately most of Washington DC, refused to see the problem with the Middle East 'cause it was once again in remission and the Nineties roared, even if only on plastic. The Middle East was tamed in 1991, we forgot about the 1993 WTC bombing, the two American embassy bombings back in 1998 on the same day in two African countries was too far away to mess with my buzz, and we cared less how much Saddam toyed with the general consensus of the rest of the world, even other Arab countries. That's because we thought that two oceans in between could isolate us. So much for that. Now we know. At least some of us. Most of us at best, which ain't bad. There seems to be a problem with American resentment throughout much of the world. Is that our fault? As previously mentioned, if some American corporations abroad practice business the same way it's practiced here, then I can see a problem. People are *NOT* commodities no matter where on this planet!

Many Americans seem to think that by going global, that there is the problem. Going global is nothing new. Colonization was practiced hundreds of years ago. America was born by it. Going global isn't the reason, maybe it's part of it, but there's something else. I think that it's very basic going back to neanderthal and before. When we were kids, we used to play King of the Hill. Very simple. All of us would try to climb a steep grade dirt pile or hill all at once. The first person to get to the top became the target and everyone else tried to dethrone him by tossing him off and then that person became the target and so on. America right now in the eyes of certain parts of the world is the king of the hill and that now makes us the target by these certain parts of the world. Especially the Middle East, parts of Europe, and some of South America. Politics has some bearing, but not much. It could be a democrat or republican on top, but whoever's on top is still the target. The WTC bombing in 1993 was on a democrat's watch. The way I see it, the U.S.A is despised by these parts of the planet because of one of the rungs on the ladder of simple human nature. Envy. That's something that has never changed.

All through the history of empires, other peoples have always coveted that position. That doesn't make them any lesser, just curious. A lot of this has led to conflict,either by war, civil disputes, or some other internal dissemination. I wanna hear Johnny say that last word three times in a row without throwing up. To anyone out there who questions our system of capitalism. Colonization spread capitalism all over the world with all the spice and grain routes by centuries old sailors coming and going out of Europe. These people already knew how to advance as rapidly as possible by using the best system of advancement . . . **capitalism**. Anymore stupid questions?

But after 9-11, things changed whether you like that or not. Some college professor not only teaches that the Bush administration orchestrated 9-11 and all other combat in Iraq, but that after he crashed both planes into both buildings and walked out unscathed, those poor souls didn't jump from the twin towers, he pushed them out! That college professor should be doing a little regrouping while thinking about that *behind bars.* Fuck your First Amendment. The First Amendment needs to be watered, weeded, fertilized, and cared for . . . not neglected to a dead weed that some people seem to not care about as long as its still grass. Who cares if it's brown and dead? I do. That's why I'm here and I say what I do. Jones can hear. But aside from that, now the dems have to clean up the mess the president got us into. What the hell was he thinking? Fighting an enemy while blind? If anyone of you loudmouths out on Main Street think you got 20-20 vision, then please tell the next president 'cause this human conflict isn't going away anytime soon. Some of these people in power are the same people who completely dissed the military, leaked everything except how to break into Fort Knox, and tossed a wrench into everything the coalition was trying to accomplish. The anti-future *New York Times* for printing all this needs to stand trial for treason, then close up shop. Censorship? No, more like national and *international* security. About as traitorous as the problem. As professional as Zap comix but not as serious. I'd like to see their prison time set in eighteenth century France! They, along with many other *fringed-out* democrats actually seem to **hate** America's folklore and past history for whatever reason. What they fail to understand is that America is nothing but an experiment that has never been done before in the entire history of all mankind . . . we are a land of mixed breeds that have figured out to make that work so that we all, no matter what, have some kind of chance to excel . . . 'cept Johnny. Yeah, that creates problems, but so far the results have far overpowered the problems, one of them even being brutal slavery in the South which will always will be a part of our history. Learn from the past . . . *never second quess it?* . . . it already happened! Our second quessers have already screwed up some of my recent past. Peppermint Patty was origanily a tomboy when Charlie Brown was first introduced to TV as we all know. Now she has been changed into a diesel dyke. Nice work . . . < what the f#%k > America . . . 'least she'zz a diezal.

Some *question-mark myster-re-us democrats* blame the Bush administration for being the most secretive administration ever. *The last few sentences should explain that!* When American soldiers' lives are on the line 'cause of traitorous leaks like that, you *really really* need to keep your **fucking mouth** shut! Because of all this, I'll vote for a Nazi before I ever vote for a traitorous American no matter what party. But as we all know, these patriotic, *playing with fire* government secrets being made public have come from some ***congressional democrats.*** Along with some snide remarks regarding the military. An old Marine saying: *Never ever before, have so few, been so foul, to so many.* Semper Fi! This saying could be the new motto for ***treasonous democrats.*** That's as foul as it gets. But not all democrats. The ones I'm talking about know who they are. I believe that they will go down in history as nothing but **complete assholes** for interfering during a war, whether or not them or you agree with the war. Wanting to pull out is one thing but intentionally interfering while making the warfare alittle more risky for the troops is another. But I won't pass judgment on an entire party by the actions of some, not a few . . . 'cause there's a few too many. Plus, who the hell am I? Who gives a rat's ass what I think? . . . I do. Democrats however, are not only to blame. We've got some pretty low-on-the-food-chain republicans out there who have placed themselves above the law. Others who don't even know what the law is, but most importantly, the super deficit America is now mired in. As said in the novel, wars cost money, but this makes me think money grows like dope out in the woods which pays good. And also, like I said before, I don't know how deficits and surpluses really work, therefore that makes me highly qualified for that job. Back to the situation at hand. Iraq happened for reason I pulled out of thin air explained much earlier in the novel. I will state this though: I questioned that move to one of myselves and firmly believed something else was going to happen soon after 9-11. Goes like this. When in a boxing match, you stun with your left jab (9-11), then come back immediately with the big right hand (nothing happened, gave us some time wonder what's gunna happen next). Even though quite a bit of time was between Afghanistan and Iraq, that gives anyone who hates the U S with that much determination lots of time to come up with the big right hand.

It's obvious that we had no choice but to go to Afghanistan. Iraq is what's in question. Just suppose we never went into Iraq. First and foremost, the Ba'ath party had deep resentment from the Gulf War. They got the sand beat off of them. Don't think for one minute that Saddam wouldn't start pointing that patriotic middle finger towards Afghanistan to covertly pay back and get even. And also don't think that he wouldn't think about exporting some of those mysterious, magical WMDs to Afghanistan for a big right hand. Or even a light love tap. War was waged the way it was to see that something like that was impossible . . . because it was impossible. And it also staged another vent of fanatical Islamic (key word; fanatical) extreme aggression that has been, whether or not some of you wanna hear this, contained to the point that their stay in Iraq will soon be overstayed. But as we all know, most of this novel is all about the future, whatever anybody thinks about that. I think alot about it. **Grand-kids and all that**. What about the future of Iraq? What if the Coalition hadn't stopped Saddam? Who knows? How will the new Iraqi government resist the mindless carnage that can never be seen, until way too late, but only felt only for the fact people with absolutely no honor whatsoever can roam all over the place in broad daylight, but yet remain unseen. No honor means telling *by terrifying* other people to not act the fug up or they might get smacked the fug up. We all know what that is? Some poor souls really know! One of the worse decriptions for any wanna-be government ever conceived by twisted man. Makes living in the freak world look like living in an insane world. Tyranny!!, which seems to never go away. Some people seem to get used to that 'cause they got no choice no matter where on this planet. I'm pretty damn sure that's not their call to get shot in the head for getting caught smiling at someone across the street. The future of Iraq remains to be seen, but Iraqi's now have the ball in their hands which now gives them a chance to move forward without the tyrant and that's also good for the rest of the world. The C.E.O of tyranny told me it only hurts for a minute, walk off the rest . . . for the rest of your life. NOBODY likes tyranny!!!

Saddam had power and hatred pointed toward the U S. But mostly power. What does that say? It says that power can make some people sick. Even some of our own. What if Saddam did give a very bad weapon that targets civilians to someone like Osama? "Well, that never happened," the nearsighted ones would say. The stormy global atmosphere soon after the shock of 9-11 was evident of "A Brave New World" which said that *anything could happen* when something like 9-11 had already happened. I don't like it either, but if you're gunna take care of business, then take care of business or just don't do anything at all. That was not an option. Hans Blix was led around Iraq like a dog on a chain and he believed it. He convinced the world there were no WMDs. It was simply a game of hide and seek. We sought and sought and couldn't find any WMDs. Someone knows where they are or what happened to them or if they even existed, but it's not the Coalition. And they'll stay hidden or whatever by whatever entity that has them or not to make the Bush administration look foolish. I know that's what I would do. It seems to be able to split a superpower at the seams. The people who hate us so are not stupid. Never underestimate anyone, no matter what you might think. But let's go the other way. Suppose nothing existed in the realm of WMDs. He lied. Many died. I don't like that either. This is very touchy. 'Cause many have died or gotten hurt, many severely. Booby- traps are the way inferior forces say hello to another. That's something that has not changed since day one and to me, that's unacceptable, and probably not going to change. Do unto others, and do it good.

Suppose there weren't any WMDs? First of all, we all know that there wasn't anything nuclear. There are two reasons to believe that. First would be what the Israeli Air Force did to Saddam's nuclear ambitions long ago. Second would be the U.S.A.s satellite surveillance which found nothing in Iraq since Israel destroyed Saddam's nuclear facilities in 1981. But we all know what Saddam did to his own people back in the Eighties with chemical weapons. Some Kurdish towns and villages were exterminated, wiped clean off the map. Saddam stood trial for that and ultimately paid for that with his life and considering what he did, what's wrong with an eye for an eye? That was the Eighties. What about the Nineties and beyond? What about biological weapons? Much has been said about flawed intelligence and since none have been found, maybe that's true. Three months is three months. I could move a mountain in three months if I absolutely had to, to save my convictions or worse. But only a small mountain though. But how small is small? How big or small are biological or chemical weapons? A biological weapon is a big as a germ. A chemical weapon is as big as a molecule. Just a bushel of each would constitute a tremendous weapon of super-mass destruction. How big would the facility be needed to produce that? That would be what needs to be found to establish that there are in fact, such weapons in existence. So far none of that has been found. Three months is three is three months whether or not anyone can or wants to comprehend that. In Saddam's Ba'ath party, there was a top official called Chemical Ali. Wonder what that means? General Colin Powell went in front of the United Nations to argue the fact that before the Iraqi war, that there was in fact WMDs with the intelligence that the Bush administration had obtained. Flawed or half backed? Could be either. Since the Middle East's reliable reliability on reliable intelligence could be viewed as anyone one of us knowing how ants make honey, then I say someone needs to speak up 'cause lots of us and other peoples of importance like the *rest of the world* just don't know. If you know sumthin,' then let the next target know so that half the country don't piss and shit on him just like the last one who got *9-11nd* in the ass. There's a billion bucks on the moon. Go and get it! It's that hard!! That's just a drunkin theory, I don't know. But I know this.

The only intelligence obtainable in the cloudy Middle East is only going to be got by a friend of a friend of a friend, because to obtain something of such importance for world posturing is only going to come from people who don't look and maybe not trust anybody western, who comes from the culture that they and only they know. We all know what Russian roulette is. This is worse. This could be based only on just trust and hope. No problem with that, but I'll never bet my life on those two fantasies, because sometimes that's all they are. *Trust* and *hope* mean nothing to some people who could sell you anything while smiling through their teeth. And it's probably gunna remain that way for some time to come which is one of the messages that I'm trying to convey. How come our media never said that? . . . theirs did! This mess was written between the years of 2002 (down time) to 2005, 2006 with a few amendments thrown in along the way after 2006 while trying to find an imaginary publisher until now which would be real time which seems to have become tough times. Even Katrina was an amendment. I was done by then. Went back to trying to survive the next day as the moon sets and the next moon falls the following night. Iraq, Iran, Syria, Israel, Palestine, North Korea, Afghanistan, Mars and bedbugs plague us all at the present as I whine in my time. What about your time? Both the same if you readin' this right now. It was supposed to be about democracy which has been around for around two thousand years till now. *Amendment numero thirty.* Russia couldn't cope with democracy with its now democratic free nations who split from the crumbling Soviet Union such as the ones like Georgia whom like some of the others, was looking at NATO for membership. Time to drop the *certain curtain* of something that never really went away. Russia knows what happened to it during the disastrous years when the popular vote meant nothing to the general population 'cause they really had no say in anything important 'cause alls they were was the general oppressed population. Try that in the United States and see what happens!! But during the years when Reagan challenged Gorbachev, till now in real time, Russia was intoduced to democracy with a goodwill-towards-mankind mindset that made all the world breath easier which was good. Putin should get in step and let the people run the government which I thought had happened, not his fear of second class citizenship on this planet! Crazy world when "for the common man" don't even make sense. Mess with my Georgia like that and see what happens!!! LIVE FREE OR DIE!!!

But anyways, Iraq has been as long as WWII. Pretty hard to target your enemy when they hit and run behind civilians. Iraq and Afghanistan will define how to fight an unconventional but lethal war. If it were conventional, B-52's would have bombed Iraq the same way B-17's bombed Europe in WWII. Problem solved. Not that easy anymore. It will get defined but to parade around in convoys like moving targets plus engaging in urban warfare is all anyone's got right now. To fight a guerilla, you must become a guerilla. Problem being, first you look like a guerilla. Blond hair and blue eyes or being black isn't gunna work. We must define, and then define some more till no one knows who anyone is anymore. There is no more effective way then that. That's a big challenge to tackle. I don't think the president erred in judgment of what he did. He erred in judgment by not knowing what to expect. Cockroaches run and hide, then come out at night while you're sleeping. What the new democratic Congress will do is predictable, but effective? That remains to be seen at this point. It's 2006 and we just had Thanksgiving. As usual, by myself with a hundred ounce mutant-turkey . . . tastes like crap, even the blue meat. But a friend of mine stopped by with a Thanksgiving plate for me 'cause Kelly knows I still got no game anymore. What the hell's goin' on? ***Whad-ahh-do wrong?*** Anyhow, war breeds terrorism doesn't work for this writer and I put the blame squarely where it belongs: America haters going back several decades who publicly say they will occupy the White House soon. *I got no problem with a Muslim in the White House, as long as it's done by election . . . not genocide* . . . if that's possible. If not? . . . see ya next *fixed-election!* One last note. These people are very touchy. They blame all of their problems on westernization and focus more on coalition countries and mark my words, America is *numero uno* target. Just as Tet in 1968 when every major city in Vietnam was attacked by Viet Cong in a remarkable guerilla effort, who's to say that can't happen here. But I'm not talking about guerrilla warfare . . . if you know what I mean. Don't say it couldn't happen. Alls these people gots is time. It's already been about a thousand years since the Crusades. We all need to look at our watches and wonder how much more time or better yet do something about it. *I believe that the Bush administration already knew that.*

But I know something too. CONTAIN THE FU%K@NG BORDERS!! Legal is legal, but when I screw up, I pay for it! When I'm legal, I still pay for it! Pretty much blows being me. But when myself or anyone else is not legal, including immigration issues, then what's wrong with enforcing the law? What kind of questionable thinking is going on with some politicians, especially in this day and age? Just so all you Inspector Gadget's way out there in federol-demerol land (national security) know, the enforcement of the borders of this country is not just about illegal Hispanics. It's also about whatever else that can pass unchecked into our midst. Latinos work! Whatever else? . . . who knows?

Check every container coming into our ports. Check their underwear. Every last one of them. Probably too late by now anyways. Costs too much anyways. That would slow America down to a crawl . . . the underwear part, and we all know time is money. Ultimately, we are going to hang ourselves with our profit over damn near anything attitude until we realize that some trials and tribulations take precedence over the bottom line. Excuse me, that was just the commie in me coming out. Like I said, the word *game* went lame on me. It's a good idea but I see politics slamming the brakes on that. The world's a *cesspool* and no one seems to care. People refuse to concede but instead cop attitudes for any reason, rational or not and make it stick. Johnny's not the only floor-whore out there with an attitude. I'm also in the trade, only without the attitude. As time rolls on and things just don't plan out in rehearsal, try something else and lose the attitude. The attitude now in America is to defeat the principle in the name of power no matter what the consequences may be. That just flat-out sucks. And at this point will probably never change until the word *change* isn't going to contineau to go at warp speed forever . . . out of control, headed for something that might not have been really thought out in its entirely in the nuts-and-bolts American way of the way things are really supposed to go. That could mean anything to everybody, but it only means one thing to me. It means I need another beer. But the only way I see it, *forced change* has now become natural change to many liberals who oddly seem to have forgetten what *natural* means to which could become another American Civil War. How do I know? When alls I hear during any election be it local, state, or federal is shitslinging . . . way past mud, and the merits of any candidate can't be read 'cause they're caked in crap, then I see a fight brewin.' Am-too-am-not-R2-I know I am but what are you? Shut the < what up > up and do your frigging job for a change. Let me straighten one thing out before I go. No one has to shut nuthin' the < party up > up if they don't want to. Always do what you want no matter what me or anyone else says or thinks. That's what Americans are famous for!! I want it to be clear that I don't even care what I say or think. Livin' in limbo does that to a person. But anyhow, that kind of behavior is not politically correct. There, problem solved. How come no one, even TV commercials, can project themselves by their own merits anymore? We've had cut- throat TV commercials for at least two decades. McDonald's beat McWhopper in a taste test according to nine out of ten obese people. Nine out of ten McLittle lawyers will catch the ambulance to explain how McDonald's will pay for one of your Seven Deadly Sins. Wasn't your fault. Of course not. It was mine. But anyhow, what makes some commercials even more irritating are their frontal attacks on their competition instead of focusing on what makes them better. But hey! Modern times rock and roll. Get used to a lotta' things and make sure you adapt to your new environment the best you can.

I hope that by taking the time to read this novel, someone out there can see that this writer hasn't lost hope but realizes that hope is going to take a little longer than once expected. One just realizes that some of the not too distant future is going to take a little more guts and all that goes with it to see that a cultured civilization can remain a cultured civilization. Other than that, *The Munsters* just came on again, and it's time to put this flashback to bed. No more ideas, visions, or delusions to talk about. Plus brass-knuckle season opens up for raindeer tomorrow and I gots to get ready. The end, again. Thank you, again.

Sayonara,

Sincerely,

Cesspool Jones

P.S. I'm the luckiest man on the face of the earth. Lou Gerig (1939)
Johnny Warts (1957—when I've had enough)

I want eight crapshooters for my pallbearers, let 'em all be dressed down in black. I want nine men going to the graveyard, but only eight mens coming back. I want a gang of gamblers gathered around my coffin side, with a crooked card printed on my hearse. Don't say that crapshooters will never grieve over me, my life's been a doggone curse.

. . . . Blind Willie McTell_________ "Dying Crapshooter's Blues" circa 1955

With a special thanks to: family and friends of mine mentioned in the novel who are no longer with us . . . also Anthony Allen, David O'Bryant, prison bars and grills, Ethan, the Ames family, King Tut, Scott Johnson, Rock Lobster, Bobby Patton, Oscar and Felix, Lloyd Fagan, Marilyn Monroe, all my cousins, the Fonz, all me enemyz' fo' makin' me what I be today, Batwoman, cellmates, Fat Albert, Frank Ledford, Gilligan, Witt, Tracy Staddon, Rasputin, Tim Martin, Joe-Joe Carrol, shit-stain politicians, Jo Jo Gunne, Blind Willie McTell, Joe Ashline, Ron Campbell, Marco's cuz' Fluff, Grote and Weigal hotdogs, HOPE scholarship (R.I.P), Mills Ruby, Saddam Hussain's ghost, Don King, Bugs Bunny, Poochy Meyers, 23 Irene street, George Dudack, Vaj, Girly-Girl(the prettiest doggy you ever saw), Aldor Therian, Loni Epps(R.I.P), Paula Wallace, *dead* poachers, Cousin It, the First Lady, Particle Man, the Last Dance, Casey Jones, Doc Dre, debt molesters, Rory, to the entire crew that demo-d the MLK building in Atlanta prior to implosion on Valentine's Day 2010, Bill Worley, Chelsie West, Kkaniptchyon Fitzz, F.O.E 4452, Boom-Boom, Lumpy, Bunny Andrusko(R.I.P), Rick Share, Stinky and the Beerfarts, Little Lucy, Kassim Reed (fo' lettin' me be myself), Lil' Boosie, Dickey Smalls, Rat-Fink, Cool Hand Luke, Patrick Allen, Doc Holliday, Greg Malloy, Peter Griffin, Bonnie and Clyde, Jimmy Martochio, all the MaGoo brothers . . . 'cludin' Mudflap, Uncle Jimmy, Frank Burns, Auntie (R.I.P), the Humane Society, Bigfoot, Ronnie Pierce, Dale Earnhardt (jr.), Tony Antill, DJ, The UnDouchables, Dino Brooks, Benny Hill, X-crackheads, Pisspot Pete, Playboy center-dudes . . . who's who anymore?, Joe Namath, Mayhem, Leon Marable, Johnny Dude and the Dudettes, The Who, J F K, Dirty, Scotty Smith, Jack Ruby, the Czar, Warren Ledford, Flash Gordon, The Why, John Sheheen, Kate Brundage, Glenn Beck, Napoleon Solo, all my cousin's families, Johnny Appleseed, me in-laws (Eisenbachs), Sal, Danny DeMotus, me out-laws, Marie, Millie Breed, Elmo Dipthong, John Witkins (R.I.P), 751 Kennedy Road, Matt

West, Particle Dog, Jim West, V-man, 2081 Skelton Road, Muhammad Ali, Mike Pugliese, Jimmy Crawford, Dr. Derek Pendarvis, the Fugowie Indian tribe, Skillet, Brian Linde (R.I.P), purdy girlz, Helen Back, Nick Riccio, The Rolling Stones, the Prez, A.S.P.C.A, Wise potato chips, Vic Younkins, Paul Bunyon, Gabby Gifford, Shaq, Daniel Dennerline, Mother Fletcher, Candy Campbell, Jack Black and the Heart Attack, all me species, Kelly Wiley, Marteen and Sergio (tile-setters), Sargent Shultz, Jose and Johnny (tile-setters), John P., little Igor, Yosemite Sam, Purple Hearts, Jack Everatt, Applebee's, Ronnie Turpin, Chef-boy-ar-dee, John Wayne, Rick Schramm, Svengoolie, Johnny Mayhab, Bill Sheik, Chester Cheeto, flat-line leaders (the why), Jeff Baughy, Billy-the-Kid, Jeff Ashline, Lurch, Mark Montieth, Superfly, Johnny Finklestein, Billy Jack, Glenn and Bruce Ford, Bobby Senk, Jackie Coogan, The Pope, Randell Lingerfelt, 007, Lucille Ball, Hughy, Mike Hart, PBR, Kim Wak-Job, Brandon Giles, Uncle Tom's Ghetto, Kid Rotten, David Eldrege, Frank Lombardo, Agent 99, Bill Bracken, MSLSD News, the Booger Man, My Guardian Angel, the Bird Lady (Tybee Is.),VFW Post 8452, Jim Tom, Tim Tebow, M L K, Billy Wheaton(R.I.P), Bela Lugosi, John Sordyl, Matt Helms, Thing, Dick Cheney, Jimmy'Bahama'Coyle, Joey Coffee, coach Roach, Mr. Jiggy Fly, Jackie Robinson, aunt Dotty, shrimp-n-grits, Rin-Tin-Tin, party Poopers, Cheeta, Syd Barrett, Brain Salad Surgery, Flipper (Winter), Ira Land, Reagan-n-Thatcher, Pete Newell, King Daddy Polecats, Helene Apanovich, D.C. smells, shotgun shells, Nashville Pussy, all the Sandamena's, Guts, Vambo Marble Eye, the 1%er's, the 99%er's, the in-be-tweeners, congressman Wiener . . . and to all others not mentioned throughout this ride.

www.ingramcontent.com/pod-product-compliance
Lightning Source LLC
Chambersburg PA
CBHW060849120626
46553CB00001B/20

9798893305029